Index to Biographies
of
Contemporary Composers

Volume II

by

STORM BULL

The Scarecrow Press, Inc.
Metuchen, N. J.   1974

Library of Congress Cataloging in Publication Data   (Revised)

Bull, Storm.
    Index to biographies of contemporary composers.

    1. Music--Biobibliography--Indexes. I. Title.
ML105.B9   016.78'092'2   64-11781
ISBN 0-8108-0734-3 (v. 2)

A NOTE ABOUT THIS WORK
AND ITS PREDECESSOR

The first Index to Biographies of Contemporary Composers was published by Scarecrow Press in 1964. In that volume, the criteria for inclusion of a composer were if his or her works were listed in one of the reference sources indexed and if he or she was then (1964) alive or was born in 1900 or later or died in 1950 or later. In all, 69 reference books were indexed and more than 5800 individual composers were listed.

In the present work, Volume II of the Index..., the criteria for inclusion of a composer are quite similar: they are all either still alive (1973) or were born in 1900 or later (regardless of death date) or died in 1950 or later (regardless of birth date). In Volume II, over 8000 composers are listed; about 4000 of these appeared first in Volume I but are included in the present work because of additional information derived from new sources indexed. About 4000 of the entries--one half--in this Volume II are new names that did not appear in Volume I. A small number of composers have been included even though there is no reference work to which the reader can be directed.

The present work indexes 108 reference works, almost all of which were published after the appearance of Volume I (in 1964). Somewhat under half of the material that was indexed is in English, the balance of the material that was indexed is in eighteen other languages.

At the very end of the present work is a brief section of "Corrigenda for Volume I"; inconsequential slips in alphabetization are omitted from this list of corrections.

iii

INSTRUCTIONS FOR USE

The sequence in which information is given in each entry is as follows:

First column: name (a name preceded by an asterisk (*) indicates that additional information related to this name can be found in Volume I); second column: country with which the composer is identified; third column: year of birth; fourth column: country of birth if it is different from that with which the composer is identified; also date of death if known.

These data are followed on the next line by an alphabetical list of abbreviations of the sources in which information concerning the composer may be found, and this is followed by variations in spelling of the composer's name, pseudonyms, etc. When dates given in various sources vary from those listed on the first line they are listed after the variant names and the sources in which these variant dates are found are cited.

The Abbreviations list of the 108 sources used begins on page vii.

Surnames, whether hyphenated or not, are alphabetized as though continuous in spelling, e. g. :

LOPEZ de VILLALOBOS, Rui
LOPEZ DOMINGUEZ, José
LOPEZ VELARDE, Ramón
LOPEZ y FUENTES, Gregorio

Mc has been alphabetized as though Mac; ä and ö are alphabetized as a and o despite the German procedure of alphabetizing these letters as ae and oe; ø, æ and å have been alphabetized as o, ae and a despite the fact that these letters are the last three letters in some of the Scandinavian alphabets; č, š and ł are alphabetized as c, s and l despite the custom of the Czechs, the Poles, and others of treating certain letters with accents or diacritics as separate alphabetical entries; sz is alphabetized as two separate letters instead of following the Hungarian custom of treating sz as a separate alphabetical entry.

Transliteration from the Cyrillic alphabet has been letter by letter excepting those names for which a different spelling has already become established. Entries with names for which Russian or Bulgarian sources have been listed also cite the Cyrillic spelling so that the additional dangers of double transliteration can be avoided.

ABBREVIATIONS

AA73   Pan Pipes of Sigma Alpha Iota. Vol. 65, no. 2
(January 1973), p. 38-80. "The Composer Amer-
Allegro." Comp. by Marguerite Kelly Kyle.
Lists 207 U.S. composers, 1972 premieres, per-
formances, publications and other news. Pub-
lished quarterly through George Banta Co., Inc.
Menasha, Wisconsin.

ACM   Anthologie des Compositeurs de Musique d'Alsace.
Ed. by René Muller. Strasbourg: Fédération des
Sociétés Catholiques de Chant et de Musique d'Alsace,
1970; 189 p.
Biographical information, general list of works,
bibliography, address. French text.

ACU   Who Is Who in ACUM. Compiled and edited by
Menashe Ravina and Shlomo Skolsky. ACUM Ltd.,
Société d'Auteurs, Compositeurs et Editeurs de
Musique en Israel, 1965; 95 p.
Biographical information, education, pseudonyms
and activity in the cultural life of Israel. Lists
main works, prizes awarded. English text.

ACUad   _____. Addenda and corrigenda to ACU above;
1966; 11 p.

AMM   Glennon, James. Australian Music & Musicians.
Adelaide: Rigby Ltd., 1968; 291 p.
Biographical information. English text.

ASUC   American Society of University Composers. The
Society, c/o Department of Music, Dodge Hall,
Columbia University, New York, N.Y. 10027.
Lists members of the above society as they appear in published proceedings of annual confer-
ences, 1966, 1967, 1968 or 1969. University
affiliation listed.

AS66   The ASCAP Biographical Dictionary of Composers, Authors and Publishers. Comp. & ed. by The Lynn Farnol Group, Inc. New York: American Society of Composers, Authors and Publishers, 1966; 845 p. Presents "highlights in the careers of the Society's members." Lists of selected works.

BB65   Baker, Theodore. Baker's Biographical Dictionary of Musicians. 1965 supplement to 5th ed. rev. & enl. by Nicolas Slonimsky. New York: G. Schirmer, 1965; 143 p.
Includes information and entries supplementary to the 5th ed. of 1958. English text.

BB71   _____. 1971 Supplement. 1971; 262 p.
Includes information and entries supplementary to the 5th ed. of 1958 and the 1965 supplement (BB65 above). English text.

BB71ad   _____. Addenda and corrigenda to BB71 above; May 1972.

BCI   Schafer, Murray. British Composers in Interview. London: Faber and Faber, 1963; 187 p.
Biographical information not found in other sources is a byproduct of these interviews.

BCL   Avant-Garde. BMI Canada Limited, 41 Valleybrook Drive, Don Mills, Ontario. 112 p. Copyright 1968.

BMK   Yontziklopedya na Bulgarskaya Muzikalnakultura [Encyclopedia of Bulgarian Musicianship]. Edited by Petko Stainov (Pedaktzionna Kolegia); Benelin Krustev; Raina Katzarova (Sekretari); Agapia Balareva; and Rozalia Biks. Sofia: Izdatelstvo na Bulgarskaya Akademia na Kannokityo, 1967; 466 p.
Biographical information, many pictures, holographs and comprehensive lists of compositions. Articles are extremely detailed and complete. Information is focused on Bulgarian musical life. Bulgarian text.

BS70   Biographical Sketches of Winners of 1970 BMI Awards to Student Composers. New York: Broadcast Music, Inc., 1971; 8 p. (mimeo.).
Short biographical sketches of 17 student composers who shared in the 19th annual BMI Awards to Student Composers ($10,150).

BS72   Biographical Sketches ... 1972.... 1973; 6 p.
         (mimeo.).
              Short biographical sketches of 12 student compo-
              sers who shared in the 21st annual BMI Awards
              to Student Composers ($15,000).

CA   Composers of the Americas/Compositores de
         America. Washington, D.C.: Organization of
         American States. Vol. 1- . 1955- . Spanish
         and English text.
              CA8 vol. 8 (1962)   CA13 vol. 13 (1967)
              CA9 vol. 9 (1963)   CA14 vol. 14 (1968)
              CA10 vol. 10 (1964)   CA15 vol. 15 (1969)
              CA11 vol. 11 (1965)   CA16 vol. 16 (1970)
              CA12 vol. 12 (1966)   CA17 vol. 17 (1971)
              Biographical information, catalogue of works
              giving date of composition, title, instrumentation,
              duration of performance, publisher, photograph
              of the composer, some facsimiles of holographs.
              Volumes vary in length from about 140 to 200
              pages.

CAP   Composer. Ed.: David H. Cope. Composers'
         Autograph Publications, 1908 Perry Avenue, Re-
         dondo Beach, Cal. 90278. 1969 Catalog, 29 p.
              Includes biographical information. English text.

CBC   Music in Belgium; Contemporary Belgian Composers.
         Published in cooperation with CeBeDeM (Centre
         Belge de Documentation Musicale). Brussels: A.
         Manteau, 1964; 158 p.
              Biographies, teachers, discussion of musical
              style, abbreviated list of works. English text.

CCM   "Catalogue of Chamber Music" (1966). Available
         on loan from the library of the Canadian Music
         Centre, Toronto; 288 p.
              Biographical information, addresses, titles, in-
              strumentation, movements, degree of difficulty,
              duration, recordings, descriptive notes mostly
              by the composer, availability of score and parts.
              English and French text.
CCM71   "List of Canadian Chamber Music" (1971). Supple-
         mentary to CCM above. Canadian Music Centre,
         Toronto; 18 p. (mimeo.).

CCZ   Gardavsky, Čeněk, ed. Contemporary Czechoslovakian

Composers.   Transl. from Czech by Josef Hanc.
Prague: Panton, 1965; 562 p.
    Biographical information, listing of compositions
    by categories, i. e., Chamber Music, etc.   Sep-
    arate discography of contemporary music, pub-
    lishers, etc.   English text.   Presumably avail-
    able in different languages.

CHC   Czigány, Gyula, ed.   Contemporary Hungarian Com-
         posers.   Budapest: Editio Musica, 1970; 156 p.
             Listed are 73 composers.   Biographical informa-
             tion, photographic portraits and extensive lists of
             compositions with dates of completion.   Publishers
             listed.   Discography.

CIS   Monographs.   Published by Ceskoslovenské Hudebni
         Informacni Stredisko [Czechoslovak Music Informa-
         tion Center].   Malá Strana, Besedni 3, Prague 1.
             Biographical information, creative development
             list of works, publishers, discography, illustrated.
             Russian, English, French or German text (pam-
             phlet form).

CME   Lang, Paul Henry and Nathan Broder, eds.   Con-
         temporary Music in Europe: A Comprehensive Sur-
         vey.   New York: G. Schirmer, 1965; 308 p.
             Originally published in 50th Anniversary issue of
             The Musical Quarterly (January 1965).   Informa-
             tion ranges from mere mention of name to bio-
             graphical information in considerable detail.
             Also discussions of philosophical concepts as well
             as idioms.

CMF   Le Courrier Musical de France.   Raymond Lyon,
(+ vol.) ed.   Paris: Association pour la Diffusion de la
         Pensée Française, 1963- .
             Quarterly periodical with section devoted to bio-
             graphical information.   Chronological listing of
             important events in the composer's life.   Informa-
             tion updated at irregular intervals.   Biographies
             are several pages in length and the pages are
             perforated for removal.   French text.

CNO   Contemporary Norwegian Orchestral and Chamber
         Music.   Comp. by the Society of Norwegian Com-
         posers (Norsk Komponistforening) Oslo 1.   1970;
         386 p.

          Picture and short biographical résumé.   List
          of composer's main orchestral and chamber works.
          Instrumentation, title, length in minutes and name
          of publisher.   English text.

COF   Karila, Tauna, ed.   Composers of Finland.   Hel-
          sinki: Suomen Säveltäjät, 1961; 102 p.
          Professional biographies and abbreviated lists
          of works.   English text.

COO   Eckstein, Pavel.   Czechoslovak Opera.   Prague:
          Theatre Institute, 1964; 115 p.
          Includes a listing of contemporary Czech operas
          performed since 1945.   Lists birth date and
          where applicable, date of death of each composer.
          English text.

CVM   Canadian Vocal Music.   Toronto: Canadian Music
          Centre, 1967; 64 p.
CVMa   _____.   Addendum to CVM above; 1971; 17 p.

DAS   Directory of American Scholars.   5th ed. Vol. I:
          History.   Managing ed. :   Dorothy Hancock.   New
          York: Jacques Cattell Press/Bowker Co. , 1969;
          573 p.
          Biographical information related to scholarly
          activities: composers are included when also
          active as musicologists.   English text.

DDM   Dictionnaire de la Musique.   2 vols.   Ed. by Marc
          Honegger.   Paris: Bordas, 1970; 1200 p.
          Biographical information including schools and
          teachers, abbreviated lists of works sometimes
          quite inclusive, date of composition, publisher's
          bibliography, short description of musical idiom.
          Titles originally in English, Dutch, German,
          Italian and Spanish are printed in the original
          language.   Titles in other languages are trans-
          lated into French.   French text.

DMF   Dictionnaire des Musiciens Français.   Paris: Edi-
          tions Seghers, 1961; 379 p.
          Biographical information, list of principle works,
          some pictures.   French text.

DMM   Dibelius, Ulrich.   Moderne Musik 1945-1965.
          Munich: R. Piper & Co. , 1966; 392 p.

        Dates of composition, description of composi-
tional style or idiom, musical examples, pictures.
Separate chronological listing of important events
1945-1965.   German text.

DMTsp Dansk Musiktidsskrift.   Special issue in English.
Copenhagen: Unge Tonekunstnerselskab, 1971; p.
109-136.
Includes biographical section on Danish composers.
English text.

DN70   Directory of New Music.   Los Angeles: Crystal
Record Co. , 1970; 59 p.
Annual directory of all works that have been
listed in Composium during the preceding year.
Composium is a quarterly index of contemporary
compositions of recent works by living composers.
Directory of New Music includes a paragraph
biography of each composer, name of composition,
instrumentation duration, publisher, price.

DN72   _____ .   1972; 64 p.

DNS   Music from Denmark, Norway and Sweden: The
Young Generations.   Edited by Wilhelm Hansen.
Copenhagen: ca1967; 27 p.
Biographical material, photograph of each compo-
ser.   List of compositions published by Wilhelm
Hansen.   English text.

EL:1   Hellenic Week of Contemporary Music.   First Hellenic Week of Contemporary Music, Athens, April 14-
21, 1966; 86 p.
Hellenic Association for Contemporary Music of
the International Society for Contemporary Music.
In collaboration with the Studio for New Music
(co-directors, G. Becker and J. G. Papaionnou)
of the Athens Music Institute (director, K. Shulz).
Extremely inclusive publications of annual pro-
grams.   Included in each program: biographical
information, lists of works, program notes, pictures, other pertinent information.   Complete
text in Greek and English.

EL:2   _____ .   2nd ... Week..., Athens, March 29-
April 5, 1967; 57 p.

EL:3   _____ .   3rd ... Week..., Athens, December 15-
22, 1968; 84 p.

EL:4   _____ .   4th ... Week..., Athens, September 19-
26, 1971; 76 p.

EMS   Entziklopedichesky Muzükalnüi Slovar [Encyclopedic
          Dictionary of Musicians]. Edited by B. S. Shein-
          press and I. M. Yampolsky. Moscow: Izdatelstvo
          "Sovetskaya Entziklopediya," 1966; 632 p.
          Biographical information, abbreviated list of
          works, some pictures. Russian text.

EVM   Encyclopedie van de Muziek. Edited by L. M. G.
          Arnitzenius, H. H. Badings; J. B. Broeksz; Flor
          Peeters; E. W. Schallenberg; and Jos. Smits van
          Waesberghe. Amsterdam: Elsevier. Vol. 1,
          A-H, 1956; 717 p.; vol. 2, I-Z, 1957; 718 p.
          Short biographies including names of teachers,
          category of compositions, i. e., chamber music,
          vocal, orchestral, etc. Some biographies longer
          and more detailed. Dutch text.

FBC   Mariz, Vasco. Figuras da Musica Brasileira Con-
          temporanea. 2nd ed. updated & expanded. São
          Paulo: Universidade de Brasilia, 1970; 209 p.
          Mostly four- to 10-page biographies, separate
          complete lists of works including date of compo-
          sition, title, instrumentation, duration, publisher,
          comments. Portuguese text.

FST   Föreningen Svenska Tonsättare (FST 1969). Stock-
          holm: Föreningen Svenska Tonsättare, 1969; 16 p.
          Membership lists. Active membership list in-
          cludes: address, telephone number, date and
          place of birth, year in which member joined FST,
          dates and offices held in FST. List of active
          members who have died: list includes place and
          date of birth, death date, date of joining FST,
          dates and offices held. Swedish text.

HCM   Kovacević, Kresimir. The History of Croation
          Music of the Twentieth Century. Zagreb: Udru-
          zenje Kompozitora Hrvatske, 1967; 111 p.
          Organization is by musical types rather than in-
          dividual composers. Textual emphasis is on
          overall musical-historical development. Index
          gives dates for those composers who have a
          larger number of works mentioned in the text.
          Pictures of some composers. English text.

HET   Heterofonia. Bimonthly periodical. Vol. 1- .
(+ is-   Mexico City, 1968- .
sue no.) Includes a page of biographical information with

pictures of Mexican composers under the age of
45. Spanish text. Summaries in English.

IMD   Katalog der Abteilung Noten. Darmstadt: Das
           Institut, 1966; 293 p. (Informationszentrum für
           zeitgenössische Musik).
           List of published "contemporary" music, giving
           publisher and date, general instrumentation;
           grouped under alphabetical listing of composers.
IMD2   . Noten-Katalog Nachdrag [Supplement],
           1967. Darmstadt: Das Institut, 1967; 52 p. (In-
           formationszentrum für zeitgenössische Musik).

KEY   Catalogue of Canadian Keyboard Music (1971).
           Available on loan from the Library of the Canadian
           Music Centre, Toronto; 91 p.
           "This catalogue of Canadian keyboard music is
           intended principally for the serious or professional
           player and encompasses Canadian music suitable
           for recital, broadcast and such use." Listings
           by piano and harpsichord and also listing for
           organ. Evaluation of degree of difficulty, per-
           formance time, movements, publisher, recordings,
           year composed. English and French text.

KKO   Kuka Kukin On [Who's Who in Finland]. Keuruu,
           Finland: Kustannusosakeyhtiö Otavan kirjapaino,
           1966; 1201 p.
           For those unable to read Finnish there is a sec-
           tion "English Equivalents of Some Common Signs,
           Words, and Abbreviations Used in This Book."
           Biographical information, compositions by cate-
           gories, hobbies. Finnish text.

KMJ   Kompozitori i Muzicki Pisci Jugoslavije [Yugoslav
           Composers and Music Writers]. Edited by Milena
           Milosavijevic-Pesic. Editor in Chief: Zija Kucu-
           kalic. Belgrade: Savez Kompozitora Jugoslavije,
           1968; 663 p.
           Biographical information including awards, decora-
           tions, quasi-complete lists of compositions by
           categories, address and picture. Serbo-Croation
           and English text.

KSV   Katalog över Svensk Vokalmusik [Catalog of Swedish
           Vocal Music]. Compiled by Per Olof Lundahl.
           Stockholm: Stims Informationscentral för Svensk

Musik, 1968; 160 p.
A selection of solo songs (together with a few
duets and trios) chiefly by 20th-century Swedish
composers. Dates of birth and death, some
pictures, vocal range of each song, author of
text, languages in which available, publisher,
date of composition.

LCI A Catalogue of Representative Works by Resident
Living Composers of Illinois. Carbondale: Southern
Illinois University, 1960; 28 p.

LMD La Musica. Parte seconda dizionario [part 2 dic-
tionary]. Ed. by Guido M. Gatti. Turin: Unione
Tipografico-Editrice Torinese. Vol. 1 (A-K) 1968;
1165 p.; vol. 2 (L-Z) 1971; 1581 p.
Biographical information with many quasi-complete lists of compositions. Italian text.

MCO Catalogue of Orchestral Music at the Canadian
Music Centre. Toronto: The Centre, 1963; 154 p.
Includes orchestra, band, concertos, operas and
vocal-orchestral. Includes biographical information, address, approximate duration of works
listed, movements within works listed, degree of
difficulty, instrumentation, listing of first per-
formances and recordings, recordings other than
commercial which are available at Music Centre,
descriptive notes by composers, copyright, avail-
ability of score and parts. English and French
text.

MCO68 List of Canadian Orchestral Music. Supplement to
MCO above. Toronto: Canadian Music Centre,
1968; 30 p. (mimeo.).
No biographical information

MCO71 List of Canadian Orchestral Music Accepted into the
Library of the Canadian Music Centre, June 1968 to
July 1971. Supplement to MCO and to MCO68, both
above. Toronto: Canadian Music Centre, 1971;
15 p. (mimeo.).
No biographical information.

MEH Malá Encyklopédia Hudby. Compiled by Marián
Jurik; Editor-in-Chief: Ladislav Mokry. Bratislava,
Czech.: Obzor, 1969; 642 p.
Some photographic portraits, biographical informa-
tion, abbreviated list of works. Supplement section

lists biographical bibliography and includes some
contemporary composers.   Czechoslovak text.

MGG   Die Musik in Geschichte und Gegenwart.   Edited by
        Friedrich Blume.   Kassel: Bärenreiter-Verlag.
        Vol.   11   (RASC-SCHN) 1963, 1926 p. ; vol.   12
        (SCHO-SYM) 1965, 1918 p. ; vol.   13 (SYR-VOLK)
        1966, 1955 p. ; vol.   14 (VOLL-Z) 1968, 1543 p.
        Biographical information, comments on style,
        lists of works, bibliographies, pictures of some
        composers, some facsimiles of holographs.
        German text.

MJM   Soltes, Aavraham.   Off the Willows; The Rebirth
        of Modern Jewish Music.   New York: Bloch Pub.
        Co. , 1970; 311 p.
        Includes biographical information.   English text.

MLA   Hudson, L. Dale.   Index to Music Necrology.
(+ vol. Annually in June issue of Music Library Association
& no.) Notes.   Music Library Association, 104 West Huron,
        Room 329, Ann Arbor, Mich. 48108.
        Magazines and newspapers are indexed for obitu-
        aries and death notices.   Bibliography.

MMX   Grial, Hugo de.   Musicos Mexicanos.   Colección
        Moderna.   Mexico City: Editorial Diana, 1965,
        1969; 275 p.
        Includes biographical information.   Spanish text.

MM59   Gradenwitz, Peter.   Music and Musicians in Israel:
        A Comprehensive Guide to Modern Israeli Music.
        Tel Aviv: Israeli Music Publications Ltd. , 1959;
        226 p.   1951 ed. rev. & enl.
        Includes appendix with lists of publishers of Israeli
        music and an alphabetical list and catalogue of the
        works of Israeli composers.   English text.

MNG   Musik der Neuen Generation.   Catalog.   Vienna:
        Universal Edition, 1968; 85 p.
        Composers listed alphabetically with short bio-
        graphical paragraphs in German, English and
        French, list of works published by Universal
        Edition.   Some replications of individual pages
        from scores.   Chronological listing of composers
        by year of birth.

MNP   Music News from Prague.   Edited by Pavel Eck-
(+ yr. stein to August 1971, and Ivan Jirko from Septem-
& no.) ber 1971.   Indexed: 1964, no. 1 through 1973, no.
        3.
        "The Bulletin is published at irregular intervals
        as required."   Presently nine or ten issues an-
        nually.   Occasional articles about contemporary
        Czechoslovakian composers, interviews, mention
        of performances, quotations from reviews, men-
        tion of publication, pictures.   Separate editions
        in Russian, French, German, English.

MSC   Cvetko, Dragotin.   Musique Slovene.   Zalozaba
        Obzorja Maribor, 1967; 336 p.
        Lists of works and discussion of idiom.   French
        text.

MZW   Häusler, Josef.   Musik im 20. Jahrhundert, von
        Schönberg zu Penderecki.   Bremen: Carl Schüne-
        mann, 1969; 442 p.
        Includes two- to 12-page sections devoted to each
        of 56 20th-century composers: first paragraph
        contains biographical information, remainder of
        entry deals with aesthetic and philosophical rela-
        tionships, distinguishing technical features and a
        selected list of principle works.   German text.

NED   Monnikendam, Marius.   Nederlandse Componisten
        van Heden en Verleden.   Amsterdam: A. J. G.
        Strengholt, 1968; 280 p.
        Some biographical information, some compositions
        listed for each composer, composers grouped by
        idiom or musical philosophy and also as disciples
        of previous generations of Dutch composers.
        More than half of the book is devoted to "contem-
        porary" composers.   Dutch text.

NLC   Catalogue of Canadian Choral Music (1966).   Avail-
        able for perusal from the library of the Canadian
        Music Centre, Toronto; 192 p.
        Listing of choral music according to usage--
        mixed voices, female voices, male voices; list-
        ing according to composer, subheadings by form,
        motets, etc., degree of difficulty, duration if in
        excess of five minutes, and type of accompani-
        ment.   English text.
NLCa   _____.   Addendum to NLC above; 1970; 15 p.

OCM   Scholes, Percy A. The Oxford Companion to Music.
        10th ed. rev. & reset. Ed. by John Owen Ward.
        London: Oxford University Press, 1970; 1189 p.
        Exceptionally short biographies.

PAP   Anadromi. 50 Ekdiloeis. 30 October 1962--22
        February 1971. Dieithinsi Günther Becker Yannis
        G. Papaioannou. Athens: Germaniko Institouto
        Goethe Athinon Ergastiri Sighronis Mousikis; 67 p.
        Index of 50 recitals of contemporary music per-
        formed in Athens between October 30, 1962 and
        February 22, 1971. Alphabetical lists of compo-
        sers including year of birth, and in some in-
        stances death, country of origin, works performed
        cross indexed to specific programs. Other group-
        ings and cross-indexing. Greek text.

PCM   Eagon, Angelo. Catalog of Published Concert
        Music by American Composers. Metuchen, N. J. :
        Scarecrow Press, 1969; 348 p.
PC71   _____. Catalog of Published Concert Music by
        American Composers. Supplement to the Second
        Edition. Metuchen, N. J. : Scarecrow Press, 1971;
        150 p.

PKW   Almanach Polskich Kompozytorów Współczesnych
        Hanuszewska. Ed. by Mieczysława and Schäffer.
        Cracow: Bogusław Polskie Wydawnictwo Muzyczne,
        1966; 164 p. (Copyright assigned to Sesac, Inc.,
        New York.)
            Biographies of 161 contemporary Polish composers.
            First copyrighted in 1956. Updated in 1964. Ex-
            tensive lists of compositions. Many photographs.
            Polish text.

PPU   Prominent Personalities in the USSR. Edited by
        E. L. Crowley; A. I. Lebed; and H. E. Shulz. Com-
        piled by The Institute for the Study of the USSR,
        Munich, Germany. Metuchen, N. J. : Scarecrow
        Press, 1968; 792 p.
            A directory containing 6015 biographies of promi-
            nent persons in the Soviet Union.

PPU   Portraits of Prominent USSR Personalities. Edited
(+ yr. by E. L. Crowley; A. I. Lebed; and H. E. Schulz.
& vol.) Compiled by The Institute for the Study of the USSR,
        Munich, Germany. Metuchen, N. J. : Scarecrow

Press, 1968- (issued quarterly).
Complete biographical articles in length as well
as additional data concerning previous biographies.
Picture, bibliography, address. Quarterly and
annual indexes.

QLA   Catalog of String Quartets of Latin America. Ester-
hazy String Quartet of University of Missouri--
Columbia. Edited by E. Gratovich; R. M. Allen; U.
Dannemann; and C. B. Spotts. Department of Music,
University of Missouri, Columbia, ca1971; 16 p.
A listing of string quartets by mostly contem-
porary composers of Latin America. Some in-
formation about composers and quartets.

QQF   Who's Who in France, 1971-1972. 10th ed. Edited
by Jacques Lafitte. Paris: 1971; 1593 p.
Biographical information, education, career, works,
decorations, hobbies, address. French text.

RCL   Cosma, Viorel. Muzicieni Romani, Compozitori si
Muzicologi. Bucharest: Editura Muzicala, A
Uniunii Compozitorilor; 1970; 473 p.
Biographical information, quasi-complete lists of
compositions, bibliography. Rumanian text.

REM   Enciclopedia della Musica. Editor-in-chief: Claudio
Sartori. Milan: G. Ricordi. Vol. 1 1963, 884 p. ;
Vol. 2 1964, 596 p. ; Vol. 3 1964, 574 p. ; Vol. 4
1964, 628 p.
Lists professional schools attended and years of
attendance. Some biographical data, selected
list of compositions. Italian text.

SCD   Krebs, Stanley D. Soviet Composers and the Development of Soviet Music. New York: W. W. Norton, 1970; 364 p.
Chapters dealing with historical aspects of Soviet
music as well as numerous chapters about individual composers. English text.

SCHW   Schweizer Musiker-Lexikon / Dictionnaire des
Musiciens Suisses. Zurich: Atlantis Verlag, 1964;
417 p.
Biographical information, lists of works quasi-
complete, date of composition, publisher, bibliography. Some of the text is in French and

                some is in German.
SCHWn   Addendum to SCHW above, 1964; 4 p.
SCHWs   Schweizer Musiker-Lexikon / Dictionnaire des
        Musiciens Suisses. Supplement. Zurich: Atlantis
        Verlag, 1965; 15 p.

SIM   Nyare Svenska Orkesterverk. [Contemporary
        Swedish Orchestra Works]. Stockholm: Föreningen
        Svenska Tonsättare, 1964; 133 p.
                Orchestral works listed by composer, instrumen-
        tation, publisher and additional information.
        Swedish, German, French and English explanation.
SIMa   Svensk Instrumental-Musik. Supplement. Stock-
        holm: Föreningen Svenska Tonsättare, 1964; 40 p.
        Swedish and English explanation.

SML   Seeger, Horst. Musiklexikon. 2 vols. : A-K,
        528 p. ; L-Z, 563 p. Leipzig: Veb Deutscher
        Verlag für Musik, 1966.
                Short biography, short description of idiom; se-
        lected list of works with dates of composition.
        Biographies of East German composers generally
        in greater depth. German text.

SMT   Connor, Herbert. Samtal med Tonsättare. Stock-
        holm: Natur och kultur, 1971; 223 p.
                Thirteen Swedish composers interviewed between
        April 6 and November 19, 1970. In addition
        there are two "pretend" interviews with Gösta
        Nystroem and Karl-Birger Blomdahl. Also in-
        cluded: short biographies, lists of compositions,
        lists of articles, bibliography concerning com-
        poser, discography pictures. Swedish text.

SOW   Swedish Orchestral Works. Stockholm: Föreningen
        Svenska Tonsättares Internationella Musikbyrå, 1968;
        47 p.
                Selected chronological listing of each composer's
        orchestral works, date of composition, duration,
        instrumentation, publisher, date of composer's
        birth. Also some pictures of composers and bio-
        graphical paragraphs. English text.

STI   Swedish Music Information Center. Stockholm:
        Föreningen Svenska Tonsättares Internationella
        Musikbyrå, various dates.
                Mimeographed biographies of Swedish composers

including lists of their works. Available in
various languages.

STS   Svensk Ton på Skiva och Band. Stockholm: STIMs
Informationcentral för Svensk Musik, 1970; 32 p.
Listing of Swedish music available on record and
tape.

SWE   Contemporary Swedish Music. Edited by C. M.
Cnattingius. Translated by Claude Stephenson.
Swedish Institute, 1966; 40 p.
Quoted from preface, "Its main purpose is to
try to give a survey of the main development
and to suggest the principle phases in the development of the individual composers"--43 are
listed. English text.

TCM   Cohn, Arthur. Twentieth-Century Music in Western
Europe. Philadelphia: J. B. Lippincott, 1965;
510 p.
Composers listed alphabetically, description of
idiom, musical examples. English text.

TFB   Thirty-Four Biographies of Canadian Composers.
Montreal: Prepared and dist. by the International
Service of the Canadian Broadcasting Corporation,
ca1964; 112 p.

TJU   Gösta, Percy. Svenska Tonsättare i det Tjugonde
Seklet. Stockholm: Musikrevy [Swedish music
periodical], no. 5 (1967) p. 220-242.
Biographical information, lists of works. Swedish
text.

TSC   Carlson, Effie B. Twelve Tone and Serial Composers. Metuchen, N. J.: Scarecrow Press, 1970;
233 p.
Includes biographies of 80 dodecaphonic composers. Also selected biographical material.
English text.

UEP   Habenstock-Ramati, Roman [composer]. Pamphlet.
Vienna: Universal Edition, ca1969; 17 p.
List of published works, picture, biographical
information, reproduction of single pages from
various works. German text.

VNM   Zillig, Winfried. Variationen über neue Musik.
        Munich: List Verlag, 1964; 169 p.
        Information relating to idiom.   German text.

VTM   Wallner, Bo. Vår Tids Musik i Norden.   Stock-
        holm: Nordiska Musikförlaget, 1968; 435 p.
        Discussion of and descriptions of the musical
        idioms and performances of the music of con-
        temporary Scandinavian (Denmark, Finland, Ice-
        land, Norway, and Sweden) composers.   Ninety
        pages of bibliography, discography and index.
        Swedish text.

WAN   Schwann Record and Tape Guide.   April 1973 Issue.
        Boston: W. Schwann, Inc., 1973.
        Selected list of records and tapes available in
        U.S.A.   Lists name and year of birth of com-
        posers whose works are available.   Only composers
        ers who were not listed in other sources were
        indexed for this volume.

WHI   Who's Who of Indian Musicians.   New Delhi: Sangeet
        Natak Akademi, 1968; 90 p.
        Biographical information, teachers, principle
        performing instruments, recordings, concert or
        lecture tours, publications, address.   English
        text.
WHIad   _____.   Addendum to WHI above; 10 p.

WI69   Who's Who in Music and Musicians' International
        Directory.   5th ed.   Editorial director: W.J. Pot-
        terton.   New York: Hafner Pub. Co., 1969; 432 p.
        Biographical information, partial list of works,
        addresses and telephone numbers.   English text.

WSA   Who's Who of Southern Africa including Mauritius,
        1969.   Managing editor: P.J. Gibson.   Johannes-
        burg: Combinede Publishers, Ltd., 1969; 1355 p.
        Biographical information, picture, address.
        English text.

WTM   Ewen, David.   The World of Twentieth-Century
        Music.   Englewood Cliffs, N.J.:   Prentice-Hall,
        1968; 989 p.
        Information ranges from slightly more than a
        mention to detailed biographical information in
        addition to listening and superficial analyses of
        compositions.   English text.

WWG   Who's Who in Germany. 3rd ed., 2 vols. Edited
        by H. G. Khemann, and S. S. Taylor. Montreal:
        Intercontinental Book & Pub. Co., 1964. Vol. 1,
        1076 p. Vol. 2, 879 p.
             Biographical information, short list of composi-
             tions, hobbies, membership, address. English
             text.

WWI   Who's Who in Israel. 13 biannual ed. Tel Aviv:
        Brofmann-Cohen, 1968; 566 p.
             Biographical information, categories of compo-
             sitions mentioned, address. English text.

WWS   Who's Who in Switzerland, 1970-1971. Geneva:
        Nagel Publishers, 1970; 732 p.
             A biographical dictionary containing about 4000
             biographies of prominent people in and from
             Switzerland (including the principality of Liech-
             tenstein). Biographical information, hobbies,
             clubs, reasonably complete list of compositions,
             address. English text.

X64   The Music Index. Annual cumulation. Editor-in-
        chief: Florence Kretzschmar. Detroit: Informa-
        tion Coordinators, Inc., 1949- . Annual Cumula-
        tion 1964 (vol. 16), c1968; 902 p.
             "A subject-author guide to current music peri-
             odical literature." The number of periodicals
             indexed varies from year to year. The approxi-
             mate number would be 270 periodicals in 19
             languages. Inclusion could vary from articles
             written by or about the composer and/or his
             music to merely being mentioned in an article.
X65   _____. Annual Cumulation 1965 (vol. 17),
        c1970; 864 p.
X66   _____. Annual Cumulation 1966 (vol. 18),
        c1971; 980 p.
X67   _____. Annual Cumulation 1967 (vol. 19),
        c1971; 1126 p.
X68   _____. Annual Cumulation 1968 (vol. 20),
        c1972; 1566 p.

ZE   Slovenska Hudba/Slovak Music. Edited by Ernest
(+ yr. Zavarsky and Marcella Mesarosova. Published
& no.) three times a year. Bratislava: Music Information
        Centre of the Slovak Music Foundation, 1969-1972.
             Articles concerning the composer or a specific

composition, statements regarding idiom, pictures, contemporary works recently published,
lists of newly finished compositions by Slovak
composers.

ZSZ   Földes, Imre. Harmincasok Beszélgetések Magyar
        Zeneszerzökkel. Budapest: Zeneműkiado, 1969;
        231 p.
        A series of interviews and conversations with
        Hungarian composers in their thirties at the time
        of the interviews (1966-1967). The interviews
        are mostly 20 pages or longer and cover a wide
        range of aesthetic topics related to music. A
        separate section includes biographical information
        and lists places and dates of performances through-
        out the world. Portraits (photographs). Hun-
        garian text.

INDEX

*AALTOILA, Heikki   Finland   1905
   COF, KKO

*AALTONEN, Irkki Verner   Finland   1910
   COF, KKO, MEH, VTM

AAV, Evald   Estonia   1900   1939
   BB71

*AAVIK, Juhan   USSR   1884   Estonia
   BB71, LMD

*ABBADO, Marcello   Italy   1926
   BB71, IMD

ABBASOV, Ashraf Dzhelalogly USSR   1920
   PPU

ABBATE, Gennaro Maria   Italy   1874   1954
   LMD

*ABBIATI, France   Italy   1898
   IMD

*ABBOTT, Kenneth John Dearle Great Britain 1919
   WI69

ABELIOVICH, Lev Moiseevich USSR   1911
   EM, X67
   EMS: АБЕЛИОВИЧ

*ABENDROTH, Walter   Germany   1896
   EVM, IMD, LMD, REM, SML, WWG, X64, X66, X67, X68

*ABRAHAM, Paul   Hungary   1892 1960
   BB65, BB71, EMS, EVM, LMD, MEH, SML
   EMS: АБРАХАМ

ABRAHAMSEN, Hans   Denmark
   DMTsp

*ABRAMSKY, Alexander
  Savvatievich   USSR   1898
    BB65, BB71, EMS, EVM, IMD, X68
    EMS: АБРАМСКИЙ

*ABRANYI, Emil Ifjabb   Hungary   1882
    EMS, EVM, LMD
    EMS: АБРАНЬИ

ABRAVANEL, Claude Israel   Switzerland   1924
    ACU, X67

ABREU, José Antonio   Venezuela   1939
    CA14

ABRIL, Antón Garcia
    See GARCIA ABRIL, Antón

*ABSIL, Jean   Belgium   1893
    BB65, CBC, CME, DDM, EMS, EVM, IMD, IMD2, LMD,
    MEH, OCM, REM, WI69, X65, X66
    EMS: АБСИЛЬ

ACKER, Dieter   Rumania   1940
    MNP66/4, X66, X67

ADAM, Frédéric   France   1904   Germany
    ACM

ADAM, Fritz   Germany   1904
    IMD

*ADAM, Jenö   Hungary   1896
    EVM, LMD, SML, X65, X67

ADAMCIAK, Milan   Czechoslovakia
    ZE70/3

ADAMIS, Michael   Greece   1929
    EL:1, EL:2, EL:3, EL:4, PAP

*ADAMS, Ernest Harry   USA   1886 1959
    AS66

ADAMS, George   USA
    PCM

ADAMS, Henryk   Poland   1880
    REM

ADAMS, John   USA   1947
    BS70

*ADAMUS, Henryk   Poland   1880
    EVM, LMD

*ADASKIN, Murray   Canada   1906
    CA8, CCM, CCM71, CVM, CVMa, IMD, KEY, MCO, MCO68,
    MCO71, TFB, X65, X68

*ADDINSELL, Richard   Great Britain   1904
    EVM, MEH, OCM, REM, SML, X64

*ADDISON, John   Great Britain   1920
    OCM, PCM, WI69

*ADENEY, Marcus   Canada   1900
    X68

*ADLER, Israel   France and   1925   Germany
    X66, X67, X68   Israel

*ADLER, Samuel H.   USA   1928   Germany
    AA73, ASUC, AS66, PCM, PC71, X64, X65, X66, X67, X68

*ADMON, Jedidiah   Israel   1894
    BB65, WWI
    BB65: ADMON-GOROCHOV

ADMONI, Iogann Grigorievich   USSR   1906
    EMS, PPU69/2
    EMS: АДМОНИ

ADOLPH, Heinz   Germany   1915
    WI69

ADOLPHUS, Milton   1913
    WAN

*ADORNO, Theodor Wiesengrund Germany   1903   1969
    BB65, CME, DDM, EMS, EVM, IMD, LMD, REM, SML, X64,
    X65, X66, X67, X68
    EMS: АДОРНО

AEBY, Georges   Switzerland   1902   1953
    SCHW

AEDONITZKY, Pavel Kuzbmich   USSR   1922
    EMS
    EMS: АЕДОНИЦКИЙ

*AESCHBACHER, Niklaus   Switzerland   1917
    BB65, IMD, LMD, SCHW

*AESCHBACHER, Walter   Switzerland   1901
    LMD, SCHW

*AFANASEV, Leonid Vik-
  torovich   USSR   1921
  EMS, PPU69/2, X65, X66, X68
  EMS: АФАНАСЬЕВ

AFFERNI, Ugo   Italy   1871
  LMD

AGABABOV, Sergei Artemie-
  vich   USSR   1926 1959
  EMS, X64, X68
  EMS: АГАБАБОВ

AGAY, Denes   USA   1911 Hungary
  AS66, BB65

*AGERSNAP, Harald   Denmark   1899
  IMD

*AGOSTI, Guido   Italy   1901
  EVM, IMD, LMD, REM, WI69

*AGOSTINI, Mezio   Italy   1875 1950
  EVM

AGRAFIOTIS, Dimitris   Greece   1932
  EL:2

AGUILAR-AHUMADA, Miguel Chile   1931
  AC14

AGUIRRE, Manuel   Peru   1863 1951
  CA13

AHARON, Shashoua Ezra   Israel   1903 Iraq
  ACU

AHARONI, Shalom   Israel   1893 Russia
  ACU

AHARONOWITZ, Dan   Israel   1909 Poland
  WWI

AHLBERG, Gunnar   Sweden   circa 1940
  X68

*AHLBERG, Tor   Sweden   1913
  SIMa, X64

AHLBOM, Pär   Sweden   1932
  FST, VTM

AHLSTROM, David   USA
  ASUC

AHMEDOV, Bely   USSR   1918
  EMS
  EMS: АХМЕДОВ

AHMEDOV, Mithat Mamed-
  Gasan Ogli   USSR   1914
  EMS
  EMS: АХМЕДОВ

AHMETOV, Husain Faizullovich USSR   1913
  EMS
  EMS: АХМЕТОВ

AHNELL, Emil G.   USA
  CAP

*AHRENDT, Karl Frederick USA   1904
  WI69, X64, X65, X66, X67

*AHRENS, Joseph Johannes
  Clemens   Germany   1904
  EVM, IMD, LMD, REM, SML, X66, X68

*AIM, Vŏjtĕch Borivoj   Czechoslovakia 1886
  CCZ, MEH

AITKEN, Hugh   USA   1924
  AS66, BB65, PC71, PCM, X65, X66, X68

AITKEN, Robert   Canada
  MCO71, X68

AIVAZYAN, Artemy Sergiviech USSR   1902
  EMS
  EMS: АЙВАЗЯН

AKBAROV, Ikram Ilkhamovich USSR   1921
  EMS, PPU, PPU69/2, X67
  EMS: АКБАРОВ

AKHMETOV, Khusain Faizul-
  lovich   USSR   1913
  EMS, PPU69/2
  EMS: АХМЕТОВ

*AKSES, Necil Kâzim   Turkey   1908
  IMD, LMD, REM, X65

AKSIUK, Sergei Vasilievich USSR   1901
  EMS, X64, X65, X68
  EMS: АКСЮК

*AKUTAGAWA, Yasushi   Japan   1925
     EMS, LMD, X68
     EMS: АКУТАГАВА

ALADOV, Nikolai Ilyich   USSR   1890
     EMS, X66
     EMS: АЛАДОВ

*ALAIN, Jehan   France   1918
     CMF-11, DDM, LMD, MEH, REM, X65, X68

ALAIN, Olivier   France   1918
     DDM

ALAN, Robert
     See: WILLIAMS, Alan Robert

ALBANESE, Guido   Italy   1893
     REM

*d'ALBERT, François (Ferenc)   France   1918   Hungary
     X66

*ALBERT, Karel   Belgium   1901
     LMD, REM, WI-69

*ALBERT, Rudolf   Germany   1918
     X64

*ALBERTI, Solon   USA   1889
     AS66, X65, X66, X67

ALBIN, Anatol   Rumania   1903
     RCL

ALBIN, Roger   France   1920
     ACM

*ALBRECHT, Alexandre   Czechoslovakia   1885   1958
     CCZ, EVM, MEH, X65, ZE70/1   Rumania

*ALBRECHT, Georg von   Germany   1891   Russia
     EVM

*ALBRECHT, Max Richard   Germany   1890
     EVM, LMD, REM

ALBRIGHT, William   USA   1944
     DN72

ALBU, Sandu   Rumania   1897
     RCL

ALCALAY, Lucia   1928
    IMD, X68

*ALDERIGHI, Dante   Italy   1898
    EVM, IMD, LMD, REM

ALEKSANDROV, Anatoli Nikoleavich
    See: ALEXANDROV

*ALEKSANDROV, Boris
    Aleksandrovich   USSR   1905
    EMS, EVM, MEH, PPU, REM, X65, X68
    EVM, MEH, PPU and REM: ALE<u>X</u>ANDROV
    EMS: АЛЕКСАНДРОВ

ALEKSANDROV, Ya.   USSR
    PPU69/4

*ALEKSANDROV, Yuri
    Mikhailovich   USSR   1914
    EMS, IMD, PPU69/2, X64
    IMD: ALE<u>X</u>ANDRO<u>W</u>
    EMS: АЛЕКСАНДРОВ

ALEMSHAH, Kourkene M.   USSR   1907   1947
    BB65, BB71   Armenia

ALESKEROV, Suleiman Eiub Ogli USSR   1924
    EMS
    EMS: АЛЕСКЕРОВ

*ALESSANDRESCU, Alfred   Rumania   1893   1959
    BB65, BB71, CME, EMS, EVM, LMD, MEH, RCL, REM, SML
    CME and MEH: ALL<u>E</u>SANDRESCU
    EMS: АЛЕССАНДРЕСКУ

*d'ALESSANDRO, Raffaele   Switzerland   1911   1959
    BB65, DDM, EVM, IMD, LMD, SCHW

ALEXAEV, M.   USSR

*ALEXANDER, Arthur   Great Britain 1891   New Zealand
    X68

*ALEXANDER, Heinz-Haim
    (Chaim)   Israel   1915
    ACU, MM59

*ALEXANDER, Josef   USA   1910
    AS66, PCM, PC71, X66

ALEXANDER, Joseph   USA   1910

ALEXANDER, Leni   Chile   1924
    LMD

ALEXANDRESCU, Ioan   Rumania   1912
    RCL

*ALEXANDROV, Anatole
    Nikolayavich   USSR   1888
    BB65, BB71, EMS, EVM, IMD, LMD, MEH, PPU69/2,
    PPU71/4, REM, SML, X65, X67, X68
    LMD: ALEKSANDROV
    EMS: АЛЕКСАНДРОВ

ALEXANDROV, Boris Alexandorvich
    See: ALEKSANDROV

ALEXSANDRESCU, Romeo   Rumania   1902
    RCL, X66

*ALFANO, Franco   Italy   1876   1954
    BB71, DDM, EMS, EVM, IMD, MEH, LMD, REM,
    SML, X64, X65, X67, X68
    EMS: АЛЬФАНО

*ALFVÉN, Hugo Emil   Sweden   1872   1960
    BB65, BB71, DDM, EMS, EVM, FST, IMD, IMD2, KSV, LMD,
    MEH, REM, SML, SIM, SIMa, STS, TJU, VTM, WTM, X67
    EMS: АЛЬВЕН

*ALGAZI, Léon   France   1890   1971
    DMF   Rumania

ALI AKBAR KHAN   India   1922
    WHI

ALIVERDIVEKOV, Nazim   USSR   1926
    X68

*ALIX, René   France   1907   1966
    DDM, DMF

ALLAN, Lewis   USA
    AS66, X65
    Formerly: MEEROPOL, Abel

ALLANBROOK, Douglas   USA   1921
    PC71, X68

ALLAUDIN KHAN (ALAM)   India   1862
    WHI

*ALLEGRA, Salvatore   Italy   1898
    LMD

ALTER, Martha   USA   1904
   DAS

ALTHÉN, K. Ragnar   Sweden   1883   1961
   FST

*ALTMANN, Hans   Germany   1904
   EVM, X65, X67

ALVAREZ JIMENEZ, Mario   Mexico   1898
   MMX

ÁLVAREZ SOLAR-QUINTES,
   Nicolás   Spain   1893   1967
   DDM

*ALVES deSOUSA, Berta   Portugal   1916
   LMD

ALVIN, Frantisek   Czechoslovakia   1898
   CCZ

*ALWYN, William   Great Britain   1905
   BB65, BB71, LMD, REM, WI69, X64, X65, X67

AMBESI, Alberto Cesare   Italy   1931
   REM

*AMBROS, Valdimír   Czechoslovakia   1891   1956
   CCZ, IMD

AMBROSI, Alearco   1931
   IMD

*AMBROSIUS, Hermann   Germany   1897
   EVM, IMD, LMD, X67

*AMELLER, André-Charles
   Gabriel   France   1912
   BB65, BB71, WI69, X68

AMENÁBAR, Juan   Chile   1922
   CA17

*AMENGUAL-ASTABURUAGA,
   René   Chile   1911   1954
   IMD, LMD, REM, X65

*AMFITEATROV, Daniele   USA   1901   Russia
   AS66, EVM, LMD, REM

AMIR, Itshak   Israel   1915   Greece
   ACU

*ALLEN, Creighton   USA   1900
   AS66

ALLEN, Gilbert   USA   1918

ALLEN, Harold   Australia   1917
   WI69

*ALLEN, Paul Hastings   USA   1883   1952
   LMD, REM

ALLEN, Robert E.   USA   1920
   AS66

ALLENDE BLIN, Juan   1928
   WAN

ALLENDE SARON, Adolfo   Chile   1890   1967
   LMD, X67

*ALLENDE SARON, Pedro
   Humberto   Chile   1885   1959
   BB65, BB71, DDM, EMS, EVM, LMD, REM
   EMS: АЛЬЕНДЕ

ALLESANDRESCU, Alfred
   See: ALESSANDRESCU, Alfred

ALLGÉN, Claude L.   Sweden   1920
   KSV, SIMa

ALLISON, Howard K., II   USA
   CAP

ALMEIDA, Francisco Antonio de Portugal
   CME, X66

*ALNAR, Hasan Ferid   Turkey   1906
   EVM, IMD, LMD, REM, X65, X66

*ALONSO LOPEZ, Francisco   Spain   1887
   EVM

ALOTIN (Rywerant), Yardena Israel   1930
   ACU, MM59, X67

*ALPAERTS, Florent   Belgium   1876   1954
   CBC, CME, DDM, EVM, LMD, REM

ALSINA, Carlos Roqué   Argentina   1941
   IMD2, X66, X67, X68

AMIRAN (Pougatchov), Emanuel   Poland   1909
  ACU, IMD2, WWI

AMIRKHANIAN, Charles   USA   1945
  BB71

*AMIROV, Fikret Mechadi
  Dzhamil Ogly   USSR   1922
  BB65, BB71, CME, DDM, EMS, EVM, LMD, REM, PPU69/2,
  SCD, SML, X64, X65, X67, X68
  EMS: АМИРОВ

*AMMANN, Benno   Switzerland   1904
  IMD, IMD2, LMD, REM, SCHW, WWS

AMODEI, Roberto   Italy   1880
  REM

AMRAN, David Werner   USA   1930
  BB65, BB71, PCM, X65, X66, X67, X68

AMY, Gilbert   France   1936
  BB65, BB71, CME, CMF36, CMF39, DDM, EL:3, IMD, IMD2,
  LMD, MEH, QQF, REM, TSC, X64, X65, X66, X67, X68

ANCELIN, Pierre   France   1934
  DDM

*ANČERL, Karel   Czechoslovakia 1908   1973
  BB71, EVM, REM, SML, WI-69, X67, X68

ANDELKOVIĆ, Radoslav   Yugoslavia   1923
  KMJ

*ANDERBERG, Carl-Olof   Sweden   1914
  CME, IMD, IMD2, KSV, MLA29-4, REM, SIM,
  SIMa, SOW, SWE, TJU, VTM, X67

*ANDERS, Erich   Germany   1883   1958
  EVM, IMD

*ANDERSEN, Arthur Olaf   USA   1880   1958
  AS66, EVM

*ANDERSEN, Karl August   Norway   1903   1970
  BB71, CNO, VTM

*ANDERSEN-WINGAR, Alfred   Norway   1869   1952
  EVM

ANDERSON, Garland   1933
  WAN

ANDERSON, Laurel Everette   USA   1896
   DAS

ANDERSON, Ruth   USA
   ASUC

ANDERSON, Thomas
   Jefferson, Jr.   USA   1928
   WAN

*ANDERSON, William Henry   Canada   1882 1955
   CVM, NLC, NLCa   England

ANDRAE, Volkmar
   See: ANDREAE, Volkmar

ANDRAŠOVAN, Tibor   Czechoslovakia 1917
   CCZ, COO, MEH, MNP68/8, X65, X66,
   X67, ZE70/2-71/2/3-72/1/2

ANDRE, Edouard   France   1930
   ACM

*ANDRÉ, Franz   Belgium   1893
   LMD, REM

*ANDREAE, Volkmar   Switzerland   1879 1962
   BB65, BB71, EVM, IMD, LMD, MEH, REM, SCHW

ANDREESCU-SKELETTY, Mihail Rumania   1882 1965
   RCL

ANDRES, Walter
   See: ANDRESS, Walter

*ANDRESS, Walter   Austria   1904
   WI-69, X64

*ANDREWS, Herbert Kennedy Ireland   1904 1965
   X65, X66, X67

ANDREZEJEWSKI, Marek
   See: MARKOWSKI, Andrzej

ANDRIASHVILI, Akaky
   Kirillovich   USSR   1904
   EMS
   EMS: АНДРИАШВИЛИ

ANDRIASYAN, Iosif Arshakovich USSR   1933
   X68

ANDRIĆ, Josip   Yugoslavia   1894   1967
     KMJ, HCM, X68

ANDRIĆ, Stojan   Yugoslavia   1912
     KMJ

*ANDRICU, Mihail Jon   Rumania   1894
     BB65, BB71, CME, EMS, EVM, IMD, LMD, MEH,
     RCL, REM, X65, X68
     EMS: АНДРИКУ

*ANDRIESSEN, Henricus
     (Hendrik) Franciscus   Netherlands   1892
     CME, DDM, EVM, IMD, LMD, NED, REM,
     X65, X66, X67, X68

*ANDRIESSEN, Jurriaan   Netherlands   1925
     BB65, BB71, DDM, EVM, IMD, IMD2, LMD, NED,
     REM, X64, X65, X66
     NED: 1935

ANDRIESSEN, Louis   Netherlands   1939
     CME, IMD2, LMD, NED, X64, X65, X66, X67, X68

*ANDRIESSEN, Willem
     Christiaan Nicolaas   Netherlands   1887   1964
     BB65, BB71, DDM, EVM, LMD, REM, X65

ANDRIX, George   USA
     CAP, X68

*ANGENOT, Laurent   Belgium   1873
     EVM

*ANGERER, Paul   Austria   1927
     EVM, IMD, IMD2, LMD, MEH, MNG, REM, WI-69,
     X65, X68

*ANHALT, Istvan   Canada   1919   Hungary
     ASUC, BB71, BCL, CA8, CCM, CVM, KEY,   1969
     LMD, MCO, MCO68 NLCa, TFB, X67, X68

ANJOU, Emil   Sweden   1876   1963
     KSV, SIMa

ANNOVAZZI, Napoleone   Italy   1907
     LMD

*ANROOY, Peter van   Netherlands   1879   1954
     BB65, BB71, EVM, IMD, LMD, REM

*ANSERMET, Ernest   Switzerland   1883   1969
   BB65, BB71, DDM, EMS, EVM, LMD, REM, SCHW,
   SML, WI-69, X64, X65, X66, X67, X68
   EMS: АНСЕРМЕ

ANSON, George   USA
   AA73, X66, X67, X68

*ANSON, Hugo Vernon   Great Britain   1894   1958
   EVM, LMD

*ANTHEIL, George   USA   1900   1959
   AS66, BB65, BB71, DDM, EMS, EVM, IMD, LMD, MEH,
   PC71, PCM, REM, SML, WTM, X64, X68
   EMS: АНТЕЙЛ

*ANTILL, John Henry   Australia   1904
   AMM, EVM, REM, SML, XI69

*ANTONINI, Alfredo   USA   1901   Italy
   AS66, CA15, X64, X67

ANTONIOU, Theodor   Greece   1935
   BB65, BB71, CME, EL:1, EL:2, EL:3, EL:4, IMD,
   LMD, MEH, PAP, X65, X66, X67, X68

ANTUNES, Jorge   Brazil   1942
   CA16

ANZAGHI, Luigi Oreste   Italy   1903
   LMD, REM, X64

APERGHIS, George   Greece   1945
   EL:1, EL:2, EL:4, PAP
   EL:2: 1940

*AP IVOR, Denis   Great Britain   1916   Ireland
   DDM, EVM, IMD, LMD, OCM, REM, SML, WI69, X67, X68

APONTE-LEDÉE, Rafael   Puerto Rico   1938
   CA17

*APOSTEL, Hans Erich   Austria   1901   1972
   CME, DDM, EMS, EVM, IMD, IMD2, LMD,   Germany
   MEH, MLA29/4, REM, SML, TSC, WI69,
   X65, X66, X67, X68
   EMS: АПОСТЕЛЬ

APOTHÉLOZ, Jean   Switzerland   1900   1965
   DDM, FCS, LMD, MLA23/4, REM, SCHW, X66

APPIA, Theodore   Switzerland   1887   Belgium
   SCHW

*APPLEBAUM, Louis   USA   1918   Canada
   BB65, BB71, CA10, CCM, CCM71, CVMa, LMD,
   MCO68, MCO71, NLC, NLCa, TFB, X68

APPLETON, Jon   USA
   ASUC

*APREA, Tito   Italy   1904
   LMD

*ARAKISHVILI, Dmitri
   Ignatievitch   USSR   1873   1953
   EMS, EVM, LMD, MEH, REM
   LMD: ARAKISVILI
   EMS: АРАКИШВИЛИ

*ARÁMBARRI y GÁRATE, Jesús Spain   1902
   DDM, EVM, LMD, REM

ARANOV, Shiko Benyaminovich   USSR   1905   1969
   PPU
   Formerly: ARANOVICH

ARAPOV, Boris Alexandrovich   USSR   1905
   BB65, BB71, EMS, PPU, PPU69-2, X64, X65, X68
   EMS: АРАПОВ

*ARATÓ, Istvan   Hungary   1910   Serbia
   EVM, REM

*ARAÚJO, Gina de   Brazil   1890
   REM

*ARBATSKY, Yury   USA   1911   1963
   BB71, DDM, EVM, LMD, REM, X64   Russia

ARBENZ, Wilhelm   Switzerland   1899
   SCHW

*ARCHER, Violet Balestreri   Canada   1913
   AA73, BB65, BB71, CA9, CCM, CCM71, CVM, KEY,
   LMD, MCO, MCO68, MCO71, NLC, NLCa, TFB,
   X65, X66, X67, X68

ARCHIBALD, Bruce   USA
   ASUC, X66, X68

*ARDÉVOL, José   Cuba   1911   Spain
   DDM, EMS, EVM, IMD, LMD, QLA, REM, X64, X66, X67
   EMS: АРДЕВОЛЬ

*AREL, Bülent   Turkey   1919
   BB71, IMD, X65, X68

*ARETZ de RAMON y RIVERA,
  Isabel   Venezuela   1909   Argentina
    CA17, X65, X66, X67, X68

*ARETZ-THIELE, Isabelle   Argentina   1909
    EVM

ARGENTO, Dominick   USA   1927
    AA73, AS66, DM72, PC71, PCM, X64, X65, X66, X67

*ARGENTO, Pietro   Italy   1909
    LMD, X64

ARISTAKÉSSIAN, E.   USSR
    X68

*ARIZAGA, Rodolfo   Argentina   1926
    BB65, BB71, LMD, REM, X64, X65

ARKAN, Y. Muzaffer   1923
    IDM

*ARLEN, Albert   Great Britain   1905   Australia
    AMM

*ARMA, Paul   France   1905 Hungary
    DDM, EVM, IMD2, LMD, REM, WI69, X67, X68
    Formerly: WEISSHAUS, Imre

ARMBRUSTER, René   Switzerland   1931
    SCHW

*ARMSTRONG, Thomas Henry
  Wait   Great Britain   1898
    X64, X66, X68

ARNATT, Ronald K.   USA   England
    X67, X68

*ARNELL, Richard Anthony
  Sayer   Great Britain   1917
    ASUC, BB71, DDM, IMD, LMD, REM, SML, WI69,
    X65, X66, X68

*ARNESTAD-BJAERKE, Finn
  Oluf   Norway   1915
    CNO, VTM

*ARNIĆ, Blaž   Yugoslavia   1901
    EMS, EVM, KMJ, LMD, MSC, REM, X67
    EMS: АРНИЧ

ARNOLD, Hubert   USA   1945
    DM72

*ARNOLD, Malcolm Henry   Great Britain   1921
    BB65, BB71, BCI, DDM, IMD, LMD, REM, SML,
    TCM, X64, X65, X66, X67, X68

ARNOLD, Pierre   France   1909
    ACM

*AROKHATY, Bela   Hungary   1890
    EVM

*ARONOWICZ, Dan   Israel   1909   Poland
    ACU
    ACU: ARONOWITCZ

AROUTIOUNIAN, A.
    See: ARUTUNIAN, A.

*ARRIEU, Claude   France   1903
    BB65, BB71, CMF35, CMF39, DDM, DMF, EVM,
    LMD, QQF, REM, WI69

ARRIGO, Girolamo   Italy   1930
    BB71, IMD, IMD2, LMD, X64, X65, X66, X68

ARTAMONOV, Aleksei Pavlovich USSR   1905
    EMS, PPU69-2, X68
    EMS: АРТАМОНОВ

ARTEMIEV, E. N.   USSR   Estonia
    X67, X68

*ARUNDELL, Dennis Drew   Great Britain   1898
    EVM, WI69, X65, X66, X67, X68
    Formerly: ARUNDEL

ARUTUNAN, Alexander Grigorievic
    See: ARUTUNIAN

*ARUTUNIAN, Alexander
  Grigorevich   USSR   1920
    DDM, EMS, EVM, MEH, LMD, REM, PPU, PPU69-2, X67, X68
    DDM: AROUTIOUNIAN   EVM: ARUTJUNJAN
    LMD: ARUTJUNIAN
    EMS: АРУТЮНЯН

ARVINTE, Constantin   Rumania   1926
    RCL

*ASCHAFFENBURG, Walter   USA   1927   Germany
   ASUC, PC71, PCM, X65, X68

*ASCHENBRENNER, Johannes   1903
   IMD

ASCONE, Vincente   Uruguay   1897
   CA16, EMS, IMD
   EMS: ACKOHE

ASHFORD, Theodore   USA
   X68

ASHFORTH, Alden   USA   1933
   ASUC

ASHLEY, Robert   USA   1930
   BB71, EL:2, IMD2, X64, X67, X68

*ASHPOLE, Alfred   Great Britain   1892
   WI69

*ASHRAFI, Muhtar Ashrafovich   USSR   1912
   EMS, EVM, SML, X65
   EVM: ASJRAFI   REM: AŠRAFI SML: ASCHRAFI EMS: АШРАФИ

ASHTON, John H.   USA   1938
   CAP

*ASKEW, Norman   Great Britain   1901   1966
   X67

*ASMAIPARASHVILLI, Shalva
   Ilich   USSR   1901
   EVM, REM
   EVM: 1902   REM: 1903

*ASPLÖF, Herman   Sweden   1881
   SIMa

ASRIEL, Andre   Germany   1922   Austria
   SML, X68

*ASSALY, Edmund Phillip   Canada   1920
   CCM, KEY

ASUAR PUIGGROS, Jose
   Vincente   Chile   1933
   REM, X64, X68

ATANACKOVIĆ, Slobodan   Yugoslavia   1937
   KMJ

ATANASOV, Nikola   Bulgaria   1886
  BMK, X67
  BMK: ATAHACOB

ATEHORTÚA, Blas Emilio   Colombia

*ATHERTON, Percy Lee   USA   1871
  EVM

ATHERTON, Robert   Great Britain   1910
  WI69

*ATKINS, Ivor Algernon   Great Britain   1869   1953
  EMV, LMD

*ATTERBERG, Kurt Magnus   Sweden   1887
  BB71, DDM, EVM, FST, IMD, LMD, MEH, REM, SIM,
  SIMa, SML, SMT, SOW, STS, TJU, VTM, WI69, WTM,
  X66, X67, X68

AUBAIN, Jean   France   1928
  BB65, BB71

AUBANEL, Georges   1896
  IMD

*AUBERT, Louis François
  Marie   France   1877   1968
  BB71, CMF21, DDM, DMF, EMS, IMD, LMD, MLA25/4,
  REM, X68
  EMS: ОБЕР

*AUBIN, Tony Louis Alexandre France   1907
  CMF24, CMF39, DDM, DMF, IMD, LMD, MEH, QQF,
  REM, WI69, X68

*AUCLERT, Pierre   France   1905
  DDM

AUENMÜLLER, Hans   Germany   1926
  SML, X68

AULA GUILLÉN, Luis   Spain   1876
  EVM

*AURIC, Georges   France   1899
  BB65, BB71, CME, CMF4-39, DDM, DMF4, DMF20, EMS, EVM,
  IMD, LMD, MEH, QQF, REM, SML, VNM, WTM, X64, X67, X68
  EMS: ОРИК

AUST, Alois   Czechoslovakia 1899   1961
  CCZ

*AUSTIN, Frederic   Great Britain 1872 1952
 EVM, LMD, X68

AUSTIN, Larry D.   USA   1930
 BB71, IMD2, PCM, X64, X66, X67, X68

AVARMAA, Ovid   Canada 1920 Estonia
 CCM, CCM71

AVDORI (Ladendorf), Chanan Israel 1902 1965
 ACU   Germany

*AVIDOM, Menahem   Israel 1908 Poland
 ACU, CME, DDM, EVM, IMD, IMD2, LMD, MEH, MM59,
 REM, X67, X68
 ACU: MENACHEM
 Formerly: MAHLER-KALKSTEIN, M.

AVILA JORGE, Gonzalez Mexico 1925
 HET/11/12

*AVISON, John Henry   Canada 1915
 X67

AVNI, Zvi   Israel 1927 Germany
 ACU, IMD2, WWI, X67

AVRAMOVSKI, Risto   Yugoslavia 1943
 KMJ

*AVSHALOMOFF, Aaron USA   1894 1965
 BB65, BB71, IMD, LMD, REM   Russia

*AVSHALOMOFF, Jacob USA   1919 China
 LMD, PCM, PC71, WI69, X65, X66

*AXMAN, Emil   Czechoslovakia 1887 1949
 BB71, CCZ, CME, X67

*AYALA PÉREZ, Daniel Mexico 1908
 EVM, IMD, LMD, MMX, REM

AYUSHAYEV, Dandar
 Dampilovich   USSR 1910
  EMS, PPU71-1
  EMS: АЮШЕЕВ

AZERBAEV, Kenen   USSR 1884
 EMS
 EMS: АЗЕРБАЕВ

*AZKUÉ, Resurrección María de Spain 1864 1951
 EVM, LMD, REM

*AZMAIPARASHVILI, Shalva Ilich USSR 1903
 BB65, BB71, EMS
 EMS: АЗМАЙПАРАШВИЛИ

*AZNAVOUR, Charles France 1924
 CMF65-10, X64, X65, X67

*BAAREN, Kees Cornelius
 Leendert van Netherlands 1906 1970
 BB65, BB71, CME, DDM, EVM, IMD, IMD2, MLA27,
 NED, REM, X64, X65, X66, X67, X68

*BABADZHANIAN, Arno
 Arutyunovich USSR 1921
 BB71, DDM, EMS, IMD, MEH, PPU, PPU68/2-69/2-71/4,
 X67, X68
 MEH: BABADŽAŇAN
 EMS: БАБАДЖАНЯН

BABAYEV, Andrej Avanesovic USSR 1923 1964
 EMS, MEH, X65
 MEH: BABAJEV
 EMS: БАБАЕВ

BABAYEV, Sabir USSR 1920
 EMS, PPU69/2, X67, X68
 EMS: БАБАЕВ

*BABBITT, Milton Byron USA 1916
 AA73, ASUC, BB71, CA12, EVM, IMD, IMD2, MEH, OCM,
 PCM, REM, TSC, WI69, X64, X65, X66, X67, X68

BABER, Joseph 1937
 WAN

BABIČ, Konstantin Yugoslavia 1927
 BB65, BB71, KMJ, X67

*BABIN, Victor USA 1908 1972
 AS66, BB71ad, EVM, MLA29/4, REM, WI69,
 X64, X65, X66, X68

BABUŠEK, František Czechoslovakia 1905 1954
 CCZ, HEM, X64, ZE69/1

*BACARISSE, Salvador Spain 1898 1963
 BB65, DDM, EVM

*BACEWICZ, Grazyna Poland 1913 1969
 BB65, BB71, CME, DDM, EMS, EVM, IMD, LMD, MEH,
 MLA26/4, PKW, REM, SML, X64, X65, X66, X67
 EMS: БАЦЕВИЧ REM: BACEVIČIUS

BACEWICZ, Kestutis-Anastas   Poland   1904
  LMD

BACEWICZ, Vincas   Poland   1875 1952
  LMD   Lithuania

BACEWICZ, Vytautas   Poland   1905
  LMD, REM
  REM: BACEVIČIUS

BACHMAN, Tibor   USA
  ASUC

*BACHMANN, Alberto Abraham   Switzerland   1875 1963
  BB65, LMD, REM, X66, X67, X68

BÁCHOREK, Milan   Czechoslovakia
  MNP69/4

*BACK, Knut   Sweden   1868 1953
  EVM, LMD

*BÄCK, Sven-Erik   Sweden   1919
  BB65, BB71, CME, DDM, DNS, FST, IMD, IMD2, KSV, LMD,
  MEH, REM, SIM, SIMa, SMT, SOW, STS, SWE, TJU, VTM,
  X65, X66, X68

*BACKER-GRØNDAHL, Fridtjof   Norway   1885 1959
  EVM, LMD

*BACKER-LUNDE, Johan   Norway   1874 1958
  CNO, EVM, VTM

*BACON, Ernst   USA   1898
  AA73, AS66, BB71, EVM, IMD, LMD, PCM, PC71, REM,
  X64, X65, X66, X67, X68

BADALBEILI, Afrasiab Badal
  Ogli   USSR   1907
  EMS, X67
  EMS: БАДАЛЕЙЛИ

*BADEN, Conrad   Norway   1908
  CNO, VTM

BADGER, Harold   Australia   1930
  AMM

*BADINGS, (Henk) Hendrik
  Herman   Netherlands   1907 Java
  BB65, BB71, CME, DDM, EVM, IMD, LMD, MEH,
  NED, REM, SML, WI69, X64, X65, X67, X68

*BADURA-SKODA, Paul   Austria   1927
    EVM, SML, WI69, X64, X65, X66, X67, X68

BAERVOETS, Raymond   Belgium   1932
    EL:1

*BAEYENS, August Louis   Belgium   1895   1966
    CBC, EVM, IMD, LMD, REM, SML, X66

BAGADYROV, Vsevolod
  Alaverdievich   USSR   1878   1954
    EMS
    EMS: БАГАДУРОВ

BAGDASARIAN, Eduard
  Ivanovich   USSR   1922
    EMS
    EMS: БАГДАСАРЯН

BAGIŇSKÝ, Milan   Czechoslovakia
    MNP69/4

BAGRINOVSKY, Mihail
  Mihailovich   USSR   1885   1966
    EMS, X65, X66
    EMS: БАГРИНОВСКИЙ

*BAILEY, Parker   USA   1902
    LMD, PCM

*BAINES, Francis Athelstane   Great Britain   1917
    EVM, WI69

*BAINTON, Edgar Leslie   Australia   1880   1956
    AMM, BB65, BB71, DDM, EVM,   England
    LMD, REM, SML

*BAIRD, Tadeusz   Poland   1928
    CME, DDM, EL:1, EMS, IMD, IMD2, LMD, PAP, PKW,
    REM, SML, WI69, X64, X65, X66, X67, X68
    EMS: БЕРД

*BAJŠANSKI, Milan   Yugoslavia   1903
    KMJ

*BAKALA, Břetislav   Czechoslovakia   1897   1958
    BB65, BB71, CCZ, LMD, MEH, REM

BAKALOV, Leonid Ovanesovich   USSR   1908
    EMS
    EMS: БАКАЛОВ

*BAKER, Don   Canada   1903
   X68

BALADA, Leonardo   USA   1933   Spain
   WAN

*BALANCHIVADZE, Andrey
   Melitonovich   USSR   1905
   BB65, BB71, DDM, EMS, EVM, LMD, PPU, PPU68/3-69/2,
   REM, SCD, X66
   EVM: BALANTSJEVADZE   LMD: BALANCIVADSE
   REM: BALANCIVADSE
   EMS: БАЛАНЧИВА́ДЗЕ

BALANDA, Leonardo   Spain
   X67

*BALASANYAN, Sergei
   Artemevich   USSR   1902   Armenia
   EMS, LMD, MEH, PPU, PPU69/2, REM, SML,
   X64, X65, X68
   EMS: БАЛАСАНЯН

BALATKA, Antonin   Czechoslovakia 1895 1958
   CCZ, MEH

*BALAZS, Frederic E.   USA   1920   Hungary
   AA73, X64, X67, X68

BALCAR, Milan   Czechoslovakia 1886 1954
   CCZ

BALDI, Lamberto   Uruguay   1896 Italy
   REM, X66

*BALES, Gerald Albert   Canada   1919
   CA15, MCO, MCO68, NLC, X66

BALES, Richard   USA   1915
   AA73, AS66, BB71, PCM, PC71, X64, X65, X66, X67, X68

BALISSAT, Jean   Switzerland   1936
   SCHW, WWS, X66

BALKASHIN, Yuri Anatolievich USSR   1923   1960
   EMS
   EMS: БАЛКА́ШИН

*BALL, Eric Walter Johr.   Great Britain 1903
   WI69

*BALLANTINE, Edward   USA   1886 1971
   BB71, EVM, LMD

BALLATA, Zeqirja   Yugoslavia   1943
    KMJ

BALLIF, Claude André F.   France   1924
    DDM, IMD, LMD, MEH, PAP, X66

*BALLOU, Esther Williamson   USA   1915
    AA73, BB65, BB71, CA9, LMD, X64, X65, X66, X67, X68

*BALMER, Luc   Switzerland   1898 Monaco
    EVM, LMD, REM, SCHW, WWS, X67

*BALOGH, Ernö   USA   1897 Hungary
    AS66, X64, X65, X68

BALSIS, Edvardas Kosto   USSR   1919
    DDM, EMS, PPU, PPU69/2-70/2, SCD
    EMS: БАЛЬСЙС

*BAL y GAY, Jesús   Spain   1905
    IMD, LMD, REM

*BAMBOSCHEK, Giuseppe   USA   1890 1969
    AS66, BB71   Italy

BANAITIS, Kazimieras-Victoras   USA   1896 Lithuania

BANCQUART, Alain   France   1934
    DDM

BANCROFT, H. Hugh   Canada
    KEY, NLC

*BANDÁRA-HOFLAND, Linda   Indonesia   1881
    IMD

*BANDUR, Jovan   Yugoslavia   1899 1956
    EMS, EVM, IMD, KMJ, LMD, REM, X67
    EMS: БÁНДУР

*BANFIELD, Raffaello de   Italy   1922 Great Britain
    LMD, REM, WI69, X64, X65, X67

BANG, Elling   Norway   1887 1969
    CNO

*BANGERT, Emilius   Denmark   1883
    EVM

*BANKS, Don   Great Britain   1923 Australia
    AMM, BB65, BB71, DDM, IMD, LMD, WI69,
    X65, X66, X67, X68
    Formerly: DONALD, Oscar

*BAQUEIRO FOSTER, Jerónimo   Mexico   1898
   EVM, MMX

BÄR, Lothar   Germany   1901
   EVM

*BARAB, Seymour   USA   1921
   AS66, BB65, PCM, PC71, X66

BAR-AM, Benjamin   Israel   1923   Germany
   ACU

BARAMISHVILI, Olga Ivanovna   USSR   1907 1956
   EMS
   EMS: БАРАМИШВИЛИ

*BARANOVIĆ, Krešimir   Yugoslavia   1894
   BB71, DDM, EMS, EVM, HCM, IMD, KMJ,
   LMD, MEH, REM, SML, X67
   EMS: БАРАНОВИЧ

*BARATI, George   USA   1913 Hungary
   AA73, BB71, PCM, PC71, X64, X65, X66, X67, X68

*BARBACCI, Rodolfo   Peru   1911 Argentina
   EVM, REM, X64

*BARBAUD, Pierre   France   1911 Algiers
   X66

BARBE, Helmut   1927
   IMD2, X65, X66

*BARBER, Samuel   USA   1910
   AS66, BB65, BB71, DDM, DN70, EMS, EVM, IMD, LMD, MEH,
   PAP, PCM, PC71, REM, SML, WTM, X64, X65, X66, X67, X68
   EMS: БАРБЕР

BARBERIS, Mansi   Rumania   1899
   RCL

*BARBIER, René Auguste-
  Ernest   Belgium   1890
   CBC, EVM, LMD, REM

BARBIERI, Mario   Italy   1888
   LMD, REM

*BARBIROLLI, John   Great Britain 1899 1970
   BB71, EMS, EVM, LMD, MEH, REM, SML, WI69,
   X64, X65, X66, X67, X68
   EMS: БАРБИРОЛЛИ

BARBLAN-OPIENSKA, Lydia   Switzerland   1890
    SCHW, X65

*BARBOUR, James Murray   USA   1897
    DAS, EVM, LMD, X65, X66, X68

BARBU, Filaret   Rumania   1903
    EMS, RCL
    EMS: БАРБУ

BÂRCĂ, Mihail   Rumania   1888
    RCL

BARCE, Ramón   Spain
    CME, DDM, TSC, X65, X67, X68

*BARDI, Benno   Great Britain   1890   Germany
    IMD, LMC, REM, WWG
    Pseudonym of POSWIANSKY, B.

*BARDOS, Lajos   Hungary   1899
    CHC, CME, LMD, X64, X66, X68

*BARDWELL, William   Great Britain   1915
    X67

BARESEL, Alfred   1893
    IDM

BARGAI, Armand Avraham   Israel   1916   Rumania
    ACUad

BARGIL, Dov
    See: BERGEL, Bernd

BARIĆ, Srdan   Yugoslavia   1927
    KMJ

*BARILLI, Bruno   Italy   1880   1952
    EVM, LMD, REM

*BARISON, Cesare Augusto   Italy   1887
    REM

BARK, Jan   Sweden   1934
    BB71, CME, DNS, FST, IDM, IMD2, SIM, SIMa, SOW,
    STI, STS, SWE, VTM, X64, X65, X67, X68

*BARKER, Alfred   Great Britain   1895
    EVM

BARKER, Philip Stanley   Great Britain   1913
    WI69

*BARKHOUDARIAN, Sergei
   Vasilievich   USSR   1887   Armenia
     EMS
     EMS: БАРХУДАРЯН

BARKIN, Elaine   USA
     ASUC

BARLOW, David Frederick
   Rothwell   Great Britain   1927
     WI69, X68

*BARLOW, Fred   France   1881   1951
     ACM, BB65, BB71, DDM, DMF,   USA
     EVM, LMD

*BARLOW, Samuel L. M.   USA   1892
     EVM, LMD, REM, WI69

*BARLOW, Wayne   USA   1912
     AS66, BB71, EVM, LMD, PCM, REM, X65, X67, X68

BARNARD, Guy   France   1907
     CMF65/10

BARNEA, Aviassaph   Israel   1903   1957
     ACU
     Also see: BERNSTEIN, Aviasaf

*BARNES, Anna   Great Britain   1937
     WI69

*BARNES, Edward Shippen USA   1887
     AS66, EVM

BARNES, Milton   Canada   1931
     CCM, CCM71, CVM, KEY, MCO68, MCO71, NLCa, X68

*BARNETT, Alice   USA   1886
     AS66

*BARNETT, David   USA   1907
     EVM, PCM, X66

*BAROLOZZI, Bruno   Italy   1911
     BB65, REM, X64

*BARON, Maurice   USA   1889   1964
     AS66, BB65   France

BARONIJAN, Vartkes   Yugoslavia   1933
     KMJ, X68

BARONNET, Jean   1929

*BARRAINE, Jaqueline Elsa   France   1910
   DDM, DMF, EVM, LMD, REM, SML, WI69

*BARRAQUÉ, Jean   France   1928   1973
   BB65, BB71, CME, DDM, IMD2, LMD, TSC,
   X65, X66, X67, X68

*BARRAUD, Henry   France   1900
   BB65, BB71, CME, CMF3, CMF20, CMF39, DDM, DMF3,
   DMF20, EMS, EVM, IDM, LMD, MEH, QQF, REM, WI69,
   X64, X65, X66
   EMS: БАРРО

*BARRELL, Bernard Clements   Great Britain   1919
   WI69

BARRELL, Joyce Salisbury   Great Britain   1917
   WI69

*BARRIOS, Ángel   Spain   1882   1964
   BB71, EVM, REM

BARROW, Robert G.   USA
   CAP

*BARROWS, John Jr.   USA   1913
   EVM, PCM, REM

BARRUS, Charles La Mar   USA   1935
   CAP, DN70, X68

BARRYMORE, Lionel   USA   1878   1954
   AS66

BARSAM, Itzhak   Israel   1922   Austria
   ACU

BAR-SHIRAH, Shlomo
   (Baikaisky)   Israel   1915
   ACU

BARSUKOV, Sergei   USSR
   X65

BÁRTA, Jiří   Czechoslovakia
   MNP69/4

*BARTA, Lubor   Czechoslovakia   1928   1972
   CCZ, IMD, IMD2, MNP64/3, MNP65/6-67/2-68/7, MNP70/1-
   72/4, SML, X64, X65, X67, X68

BARTEL, Hans-Christian   1932
   IMD2, X65, X68

*BARTH, Hans Christian   USA   1897   1956
   AS66, BB65, BB71, LMD, REM, X68   Germany

*BARTLEY, Ewart Andrew   Canada   1909
   NLC

BARTOLOZZI, Bruno   Italy   1911
   BB71, IMD, LMD, X65, X66, X68
   X65: BARTELOZZI

BARTOLUCCI, Domenico   Italy   1917
   DDM, LMD, REM

*BARTOŠ, František   Czechoslovakia   1905   1973
   CCZ, EVM, IMD, IMD2, X65, X67

*BARTOŠ, Jan Zdeněk   Czechoslovakia   1908
   CCZ, EVM, IMD, LMD, MEH, REM, SML, X64, X67, X68

*BARTOŠ, Josef   Czechoslovakia   1902
   BB71, CCZ
   BB71 - death 1952

BARTOVSKÝ, Josef   Czechoslovakia   1884
   CCZ, COO, X65

BARTZER, Richard   Rumania   1927
   RCL

*BARVÍK, Miroslav   Czechoslovakia   1919
   CCZ, EMS, EVM, IMD, LMD, MEH, REM, X65
   EMS: БАРВИК

*BARVINSKY, Vasil   USSR   1888   1963
   EMS, IMD
   EMS: БАРВІНСКИЙ

BAR-ZIMRA, Simon   Israel   1909   Estonia
   ACU

BASARAB, Mircea   Rumania   1921
   RCL, X65, X68

BASNER, Veniamin Yefimovich   USSR   1925
   EMS, PPU, PPU69/2, X65
   EMS: БАСНЕР

BASNEY, Eldon   USA
   CAP

*BASSETT, Leslie   USA   1923
    AA73, ASUC, BB71, PCM, PC71, WTM, X64, X65, X66,
    X67, X68

BASSOT, Nanine   1901
    IMD

*BASTIDE, Paul   France   1879
    DMF, EVM

*BATE, Stanley Richard   Great Britain 1911 1959
    BB65, BB71, EVM, IMD, LMD, REM, X66
    EVM: 1912   IMD: 1913

BATSTONE, Philip Norman   USA   1933
    X66

BATTS, Harry Vincent William Great Britain 1887
    WI69

*BAUBET GONY, Pierre   France   1934
    X67

*BAUDO, Serge   France   1927
    BB71, CMF29, EVM, QQF, X64, X68

*BAUDRIER, Yves Marie   France   1906
    DDM, DMF, EVM, LMD, MEH, QQF, REM

BAUER, Anton   Austria   1893
    IMD, X68

*BAUER, Marion Eugenie   USA   1887 1955
    DDM, EVM, IMD, LMD, PCM, REM
    DDM: 1897

BAUER, Raymond   USA
    AA73, X66

BAUM, Alfred   Switzerland   1904
    LMD, SCHW

BAUMAN, Jon   USA   1939
    DN72

*BAUMANN, Herbert Karl
  Wilhem   Germany   1925
    IMD, WI69, WWG

*BAUMANN, Max   Germany   1917
    X64, X66, X68

BAUMANN, Paul　　　　　　Switzerland　　1903
　　SCHW

BAUMGARTNER, Jean-Paul　　France　　　　1932
　　ACM, DDM

*BAUR, Jürg　　　　　　　　Germany　　　1918
　　IMD, IMD2, LMD, REM, TSC, X64, X65, X66, X67, X68

BAUSZNERN, Dietrich von　　Germany　　　1928
　　LMD, X68

*BAUTISTA, Julian　　　　　Argentina　　1901　1961
　　BB71, DDM, EVM, LMD, QLA, REM, X64　　　　Spain
　　QLA: 1960

*BÅVEUDDE, Sven　　　　　　Sweden　　　　1896
　　SIM

BAVICCHI, John　　　　　　USA　　　　　1922
　　AS66, PCM, PC71

*BAX, Arnold Edward Trevor　Great Britain　1883　1953
　　DDM, EMS, EVM, IMD, LMD, MEH, REM, SML, WTM,
　　X65, X66, X67, X68
　　EMS: БАКС

BAXTER, Timothy　　　　　Great Britain
　　WI69, X64, X68

BAYLE, François　　　　　France　　　　1932
　　CME, X68

*BAYLEY, Robert Charlton　Canada　　　　1913
　　NLC, NLCa

BAYLOR, H. Murray　　　　USA　　　　　1913
　　CAP, DN70

BAZAN, Oscar　　　　　　USA
　　X68

BAŽANT, Jaromír　　　　　Czechoslovakia　1926
　　CCZ

BAZAVAN, Gheorghe　　　　Rumania　　　1916
　　RCL

*BAZELAIRE, Paul　　　　　France　　　　1886　1958
　　BB65, BB71, DDM, DMF, EVM, LMD, REM

BAZELON, Irwin　　　　　USA　　　　　1922
　　AS66, BB65, BB71, LMD, PCM, X65, X66, X68

BAZIRE, Jacques   France   1928
 QQF

BÁZLIK, Igor   Czechoslovakia 1940
 MEH, X68, ZE69/3

BÁZLIK, Miroslav   Czechoslovakia 1931
 CCZ, IMD, IMD2, MEH, MNP67/4, X65, X66, X67, X68,
 ZE71/1/2-72/1

*BEACH, John Parsons USA   1877 1953
 EVM, LMD, REM

BEADELL, Robert M. USA   1925
 AA73, PCM, X64, X65, X66, X67, X68

BEAKS, Brian Harold James Great Britain 1920
 WI69

BEALL, John   USA
 CAP

BEASLEY, Rule   USA
 ASUC

*BEAUCAMP, Albert Maurice France   1921 1967
 MLA24/4, X67
 MLA24/4 - BEAUCHAMP

BEAUMONT, Adrian Great Britain 1937
 WI69, X67

BECAUD, Gilbert   France   1927
 BB65, LMD, X64, X65, X66, X67, X68

BECERRA-SCHMIDT, Gustavo Chile   1925
 BB65, BB71, CA8, DDM, INT43, LMD, QLA, REM,
 X64, X65, X66, X68

*BECK, Conrad   Switzerland 1901
 BB65, BB71, CME, DDM, EMS, EVM, IMD, LMD, MEH,
 REM, SCHW, SML, WI69, WWS, X64, X65, X66, X67
 EMS: BEK

BECK, John Ness   USA   1930
 AA73, BB71, PC71

*BECK, Reinhold Immanuel Germany 1881
 EVM

*BECK, Thomas Ludvigsen Norway   1899 1963
 BB71, CNO, EVM, VTM

BECKER, Günther   Germany   1924
  EL:1, EL:2, EL:3, EL:4, IMD, IMD2, PAP,
  X65, X66, X67, X68

*BECKER, Heinz   Germany   1910
  X64, X65, X66, X67, X68

*BECKER, John J.   USA   1886   1961
  BB65, EVM, LCI, PCM, REM

*BECKERATH, Alfred
  Wilhelm von   Germany   1901
  ACM, IMD, LMD, REM

*BECKETT, Wheeler   USA   1898
  AS66, BB65, BB71, LMD

BECKLER, Stanworth R.   USA   1923
  CAP, PCM

*BECKWITH, John   Canada   1927
  BB65, BB71, CA8, CCM, CCM71, CVM, CVMa, KEY, LMD,
  MCO, MCO68, NLC, NLCa, TFB, X64, X66, X67, X68

*BECLARD d'HARCOURT,
  Marguerite   France   1884   1964
  DDM, DMF

BEDFORD, David   Great Britain 1937
  BB65, BB71, IMD2, LMD, MNG, X65, X66, X67, X68

*BEDNÁŘ, Antonín   Czechoslovakia 1896
  EVM

BEDŘICH, Jan   Czechoslovakia 1932
  CCZ

*BEECHAM, Thomas   Great Britain 1879   1961
  BB71, DDM, EVM, SML, X64, X65, X66, X67, X68

*BEECHER, Carl Milton   USA   1883   1968
  BB71

BEECROFT, Norma   Canada   1934
  CA17, CCM, CCM71, CVMa, IMD, MCO, MCO68, MCO71,
  MNG, NLC, NLCa

BEEKHUIS, Hanna   Netherlands   1889
  EVM

BEESON, Jack Hamilton   USA   1921
  AA73, ASUC, AS66, BB65, BB71, LMD, PCM, PC71, X65, X67

BEEZ, Joachim   Germany   1936
   MNP66/4, X68

BEGLARIAN, Grant   USA   1927   USSR
   ASUC, BB71, CA14, PC71, X65, X67, X68

BEGO-ŠIMUNIĆ, Andelka   Yugoslavia   1941
   KMJ

BÉGUELIN, Albert   Switzerland   1888   1963
   SCHW

BEHR, Stefan   Poland   1919
   PKW, X68

*BEHREND, Fritz   Germany   1889
   EVM, IMD, IMD2, LMD, REM

*BEHREND, Jeanne   USA   1911
   X64, X65, X67

*BEHREND, Siegfried   Germany   1933
   IMD, X67

BEHRENS, Jack   USA   1935
   AS66, BB71, CVM, MCO68, NLC, X68

BEHRMAN, David   USA   1937
   EL:2, X65, X67

*BEILSCHMIDT, Curt   Germany   1886
   EVM

BEKHTEREV, Nikolai
  Aleksandrov   Bulgaria   1896
   BMK
   BMK: БЕХТЕРЕВ

BEKKU, Sadao   Japan   1922
   BB71

BELAMARIĆ, Miro   Yugoslavia   1935
   KMJ

BELAUBRE, Louis Noël   France   1932
   DDM

*BELL, Leslie Richard   Canada   1906
   CVM, NLC

*BELLA, Rudolf   Switzerland   1890   Austria
   REM, SCHW

BELLEZZA, Vincenzo   Italy   1888   1964
  BB71, LMD, REM, X64

BELLIARD, Maxime   France   1888
  DMF

BELLINI, Edoardo   Italy   1873
  REM

BELLOW, Alexander   USA   1912   Russia
  AS66, X68

BELOIU, Nicolae   Rumania   1927
  RCL

BELORUSETS, Igor
  Mikhailovich   USSR   1910
  EMS, X65, X66
  EMS: БЕЛОРУСЕЦ

BELTRAMI, Antonio   Italy   1916
  LMD, REM

*BÉLY, Vikter Aronovich   USSR   1904
  EMS, LMD, PPU, PPU69/2, REM, X64
  EMS: БЕЛЫЙ

BELZA, Igor Fedorovich   USSR   1904   Poland
  EMS, LMD, PPU, REM, SML, X64, X65, X67
  SML: BELSA; also spelled BOELZA   Formerly: Doroshuk
  EMS: БЭЛЗА

BENA, Augustin   Rumania   1880   1962
  RCL, X65

BENARI, Asher   Israel   1911
  ACU
  Formerly: LOWISOHN, Asher

BENARY, Peter   1931
  IMD2, X65, X66, X67, X68

*BENATZKY, Ralph   USA and   1887   1957
  BB65, BB71, LMD,   Switzerland   Austria
  MEH, REM
  REM: 1884

BENAVENTE, Manuel Jose   Argentina   1903   Bolivia
  REM

*BENBOW, Charles Edwin   Great Britain   1904   1967

BENBOW, George   Canada
  KEY

BENDER, Jan   Germany   1909
  DN72

BENDING, Arthur   Great Britain   1923
  WI69

BENES, Juraj   Czechoslovakia
  ZE69/2-70/1/2/3-71/1/3-72/1

*BENGTSSON, Gustav Adolf
  Tiburtius   Sweden   1886 1965
  EVM, FST, LMD, SIM, SIMa

BENGUEREL, Xavier   Spain   1931
  CME, HET-I-4, IMD, IMD2, X65, X67, X68

*BEN-HAIM, Paul Shaul   Israel   1897   Germany
  ACU, BB71, CME, DDM, EMS, EVM, IMD, LMD, MEH,
  MM59, REM, WTM, WWI, X64, X65, X67, X68
  EVM: BEN CHAJIM
  EMS: БЕН-ХА́ИМ

BENHAMOU, Maurice Piere   France   1936
  X67

BENJAMIN, Arthur L.   Great Britain   1893 1960
  AMM, BB65, BB71, BCI, EMS, EVM, IMD,   Australia
  LMD, MEH, REM, SML, X64, X65, X68
  EMS: БЕ́НДЖАМИН

BENJAMIN, William E.   USA   1944 Canada
  BB71

BENKAMOU, Maurice   Netherlands   1936
  X68

*BENKER, Heinz   Germany   1921
  X68

*BENNER, Paul   Switzerland   1877 1953
  EVM, LMD, SCHW

*BENNETT, Richard Rodney   Great Britain   1936
  BB65, BB71, CME, DDM, IMD, IMD2, LMD, MEH, MNG,
  TSC, WI69, X64, X65, X66, X67, X68

*BENNETT, Robert Russell   USA   1894
  AS66, BB65, BB71, DDM, EVM, LMD, OCM, PCM, PC71,
  REM, WI69, X64, X66, X67, X68

*BENOIT, Francine Germaine
  van Gool   Portugal   1894   France
  LMD, X67

*BENSON, Warren   USA   1924
  AA73, AS66, PCM, PC71, X65, X66, X68

BENSON, William Eric   USA   1948
  BS70

*BENTINELLI, Bruno   Italy   1913
  BB71

BENTOIU, Pascal   Rumania   1927
  EMS, MEH, RCL, SML, X64, X66, X67, X68
  EMS: БЕНТОЙ

*BENTZON, Jørgen Liebenberg Denmark   1897   1951
  DMTsp, IMD, IMD2, LMD, REM, VTM

*BENTZON, Niels Viggo   Denmark   1919
  BB71, CME, DDM, DMTsp, DNS, EVM, IMD, LMD, MEH,
  REM, VTM, X64, X65, X66

BENVENUTI, Arrigo   Italy   1925
  BB71, IMD, REM, X65, X67

BEN-YAACOV, Gabriel
  See: JACOBSON, Gabriel

BEN-YOHANAN, Asher   Israel   1929   Yugoslavia
  ACU, MM59

BERBERIAN, Cathy   Great Britain
  X66, X67, X68

BERCERRA, Gustavo   Chile
  X68

*BERCKMANN, Evelyn   USA   1900
  EVM

BERDOVIĆ, Vladimir   Yugoslavia   1906
  HCM, KMJ, X65, X66

*BEREZOWSKY, Nicolai   USA   1900   1953
  AS66, EVM, IMD, PCM, REM   Russia
  Also spelled: BEREZOVSKY; BEREZOUSKI

*BERG, Carl Nathaneal   Sweden   1879   1957
  BB65, BB71, EMS, EVM, FST, IMD, KSV, REM, SIM, SIMa,
  SML, VTM
  EMS: БЕРГ

*BERG, Gottfrid   Sweden   1889   1970
    FST, KSV, SIM, SIMa, STS

*BERG, Gunnar   Denmark   1909   Switzerland
    CME, DMTsp, IMD, IMD2, VTM, X64, X65

*BERG, Josef   Czechoslovakia 1927   1971
    BB65, BB71, CCZ, CME, IMD2, MEH, MNP64-5/6,
    MNP71/6, X67, X68

*BERG, Nathanael
    See: BERG, Carl Nathaneal

BERGAMO, Petar   Yugoslavia   1930
    BB65, BB71, CME, KMJ, MEH, X65, X67

BERGE, Sigurd   Norway   1929
    CNO, VTM

BERGEL, Bernd   Israel   1909   Poland
    ACU, MM59
    Formerly: BARGIL, Dov

*BERGER, Arthur Victor   USA   1912
    ASUC, BB65, BB71, EVM, IMD, LMD, OCM, PCM, REM,
    X64, X65, X66

*BERGER, Jean   USA   1909   Germany
    AA73, AS66, BB65, BB71, LMD, X64, X65, X66, X67, X68

BERGER, Roman   Czechoslovakia 1930   Poland
    MEH, MNP67/6, MNP68/1, X64, X65, X66, X67, X68,
    ZE69/3-70/1/2-71/1/2/3

*BERGER, Theodor   Austria   1905
    BB71, CME, DDM, EMS, EVM, IMD, LMD, MEH, REM,
    WI69, X65
    EMS: БЕРГЕР

BERGER, Wilhelm Georg   Rumania   1929
    LMD, MEH, RCL, SML, X64, X65, X66, X68

*BERGESE, Hans   Germany   1910
    IMD, X65, X67

*BERGH, Arthur   USA   1882   1962
    AS66, BB65, BB71, EVM, LMD, REM

*BERGH, Sverre   Norway   1915
    CNO

*BERGHORN, Alfred Maria   Germany   1911
    IMD

BERGHOUT, Johannes Cornelius Netherlands 1869
   EVM

*BERGMAN, Erik Valdemar Finland 1911
   BB65, BB71, CME, COF, EVM, KKO, LMD, MEH, REM,
   VTM, X64, X65, X66

BERGMANN, Robert France 1907
   ACM

*BERGMANN, Walter George Great Britain 1902 Germany
   WI69, X65, X66, X67

*BERGSMA, William Laurence USA 1921
   AA73, ASUC, AS66, BB65, BB71, EVM, IMD, LMD, PCM,
   PC71, REM, X64, X66, X67, X68

*BERIO, Angelo Luciano Italy 1925
   BB65, BB71, CME, DDM, DMM, DN72, EL:3, IMD, IMD2,
   LMD, MEH, MNG, MZW, OCM, PAP, REM, SML, TSC,
   VNM, WI69, X64, X65, X66, X67, X68

*BERKELEY, Lennox Randal
  Francis Great Britain 1903
   BB71, CME, DDM, EVM, IMD, LMD, MEH, REM, SML,
   WI69, X64, X65, X66, X67, X68

BERKOVEC, Jiři Czechoslovakia 1922
   CCZ, COO, MEH, X65, X68

BERKOWITZ, Ralph USA 1910
   BB65

*BERLINSKI, Herman USA 1910 Germany
   AS66, BB65, BB71, LMD, PCM, PC71, X64, X67, X68

BERLINSKI, Pavel Mikhailovich USSR 1900
   EMS
   EMS: БЕРЛИ́НСКИЙ

BERLINSKY, V. USSR
   PPU69/4

*BERMÚDEZ-SILVA, Jesús Columbia 1884
   CA8, EVM, LMD, REM, X65

*BERNAL JIMÉNEZ, Miguel Mexico 1910 1956
   EVM, HET17, IMD, LMD, MMX, QLA, REM

BERNAOLA, Carmelo Alonso Spain 1929
   CME, DDM, X64, X65, X68

*BERNARD, Anthony Great Britain 1891 1963

BERNARD, Filip   Yugoslavia   1896
    KMJ

*BERNARD, Robert   France   1900   1971
    BB71, DDM, DMF, EVM, LMD, MLA28,   Switzerland
    QQF, REM, SCHW

BERNARD, William Ditchburn   Great Britain   1904
    WI69

*BERNARDI, Gian Giuseppe   Italy   1865
    EVM

BERNAT, Robert   USA   1931
    BB71, X68

*BERNERS, Gerald Hugh
  Tyrwhitt-Wilson   Great Britain   1883   1950
    BB71, DDM, EVM, LMD, MGG, X64

*BERNIER, René   Belgium   1905
    CBC, DDM, EVM, LMD, REM

*BERNSTEIN, Aviasaf   Israel   1903   1957
    MM59   Lithuania
    Also see: BARNEA, Aviassaph

*BERNSTEIN, Leonard   USA   1918
    AS66, BB65, BB71, CME, DDM, EMS, EVM, IMD, LMD, MEH,
    PCM, REM, SML, WTM, WWI, X64, X65, X66, X67, X68
    EMS: БЕРНСТАЙН

BERRY, Wallace T.   USA   1928
    AA73, ASUC, PC71, X65, X66, X67, X68

BERTELIN, Albert   France   1872   1951
    DDM, DMF

*BERTEN, Walter Michael   Germany   1902   1956
    EVM, LMD, REM, WWG

*BERTHELOT, Rene Camille
  Henri   France   1903
    QQF, X67

BERTHET, François   France   1873   1956
    DMF

*BERTHIER, Paul   France   1884   1953
    DDM, DMF
    DMF: 1885

BERTHOMIEU, Marc   1906
    IMD

BERTINI, Gary   Israel   1927 Rumania
 ACU, MM59, WI69, WWI, X65, X66, X67, X68

BERTOLA, Giulio   Italy   1921
 REM

BERTOMEU, Agustin   Spain
 X67

BERTONCINI, Mario   Italy   1932
 IMD, X64

*BERTOUILLE, Gérard   Belgium 1898
 CBC, EVM, IMD, LMD

*BESCH, Otto   Germany 1885 1966
 EVM, LMD, MLA23/4, X66

BESSELAAR, Jan Hermanus Netherlands 1874 1952
 EVM

*BESSEM, Saar   Netherlands 1907
 EVM, NED

*BESSIÉRE, Serge   France   1913
 QQF

BESTOR, Charles   USA
 AA73, X64, X65, X66, X67, X68

*BETT, Sydney George   Canada   1896 England
 NLC

BETTARINI, Luciano   Italy   1914
 LMD, REM

*BETTINELLI, Bruno   Italy   1913
 BB65, BB71, EVM, IMD, LMD, REM, X64, X66

*BETTS, Lorne M.   Canada   1918
 BB71, CA8, CCM, CVM, KEY, LMD, MCO, MCO68, MCO71,
 NLC, NLCa, X68

BEVAN, Gwilym J.   Canada
 KEY

*BEVERSDORF, Thomas   USA   1924
 AA73, BB65, BB71, LMD, PCM, X65, X66

*BEYDTS, Louis Antoine
 Hector Désiré   France   1895 1953
 BB65, BB71, DDM, DMF, IMD, LMD, REM

*BEYER, Frank Michael   Germany   1928
 PAP, X66, X68

BEYER, Howard   USA   1929
 PCM

*BEYERLE, Bernward   Germany   1900
 WWG, X68

*BEZANSON, Philip   USA   1916
 AA73, ASUC, PCM, X64, X65, X66, X67, X68

*BEZECNY, Emil   Czechoslovakia 1868
 EVM

BHATIA, Vanraj   India   1927
 WHIad

BHATT, Balwantrai Gulabrai
 (Bhavrang)   India   1921
 WHI

*BIALAS, Günter   Germany   1907
 CME, DDM, EVM, IMD, IMD2, LMD, MEH, PAP, REM, SML,
 X64, X65, X66, X67, X68

*BIALOSKY, Marshall   USA   1923
 ASUC, CAP, PCM, PC71
 PC71: BIALOWSKY

*BIANCHI, Charles   Great Britain 1901
 WI69

*BIANCHI, Gabriele   Italy   1901
 LMD, REM

*BIANCHI, Renzo   Italy   1887 1972
 LMD, REM

*BIANCHINI, Guido   Italy   1885
 LMD, REM

BIBALO, Antonio   Norway   1922 Trieste
 BB71, CNO, DNS, LMD, X65, X67, X68

BIEBL, Franz   1906
 IMD

BIEHLE, Herbert Johannes
 Richard   Germany   1901
 LMD, X64

BIEL, Michael von   Germany   1937
    IMD, IMD2, LMD, X64, X66, X67, X68

BIELAWA, Herbert Walter   1930
    X68

BIELLA, Giuseppe   Italy   1906   1967
    LMD, REM, X67, X68

BIELYI, Viktor Aronovich   USSR   1904
    MEH, REM

BIENERT, Olaf   Germany   circa 1911   1967
    X67

*BIERSACK, Anton   Germany   1907
    IMD

BIGGS, John   USA   1932
    DN72

*BIGOT, Eugène Victor   France   1888   1965
    DDM, EVM, LMD, MLA22/4, REM, X65, X66

*BIJL, Theo van der   Netherlands   1886
    EVM

*BIJVANCK, Henk   Netherlands   1909
    EVM, NED

BILIK, Jerry H.   USA
    ASUC, X67, X68

BILLÉ, Isaia   Italy   1874   1961
    LMD, REM

BILLINGS, Leopoldo   Venezuela

BILOTTI, Anton   USA   1906   1963
    AS66

BIMBERG, Siegfried   Germany   1927
    SML, X66, X67, X68

*BIMBONI, Alberto   USA   1882   1960
    AS66, BB65, BB71, LMD   Italy

*BINDER, Abraham Wolfe   USA   1895   1966
    AS66, BB71, EVM, LMD, MJM, MLA23/4, PCM, REM,
    X64, X65, X66, X67, X68

*BINENBAUM, Janco   Bulgaria   1880   1956
    BB65, BB71, LMD, REM

*BINET, Jean   Switzerland 1893 1960
 BB65, BB71, DDM, EVM, IMD, IMD2, LMD, MEH, REM,
 SCHW, SML

*BINGE, Ronald   Great Britain 1910
 WI69

*BINGHAM, Seth   USA   1882 1972
 AS66, LMD, MLA29/4, PCM, PC71, X64, X65, X67, X68

*BINKAU, Guido   Austria 1900 1969
 MLA26/4, REM, X65, X66, X67

*BINKERD, Gordon W. USA   1916
 AA73, BB65, BB71, CA16, DN72, LCI, LMD, PCM, PC71,
 X64, X65, X66, X68

BINNERT, Alfred   France 1886
 ACM

BIRIOTTI, León   Uruguay 1929
 BB71, CA13

*BIRIUKOV, Yury Sergeyvich USSR   1908
 EMS, EVM, MEH
 EVM: BIRJOEKOW
 EMS: БИРЮКОВ

*BIRKETT, Gwenhilda Mary Great Britain 1892
 WI69

BIRTALAN, Jozsef   Rumania 1927
 RCL

*BIRTWISTLE, Harrison Paul Great Britain 1934
 BB65, BB71, CME, IMD, IMD2, LMD, MEH, MNG, REM,
 WI69, X64, X65, X66, X67, X68

*BISCHOFF, Bernhard Germany 1881
 X68

*BISQUERTT PRADO, Prospero Chile   1881
 EVM, LMD, REM

*BISSELL, Keith Warren Canada   1912
 CCM, CCM71, CVM, CVMa, KEY, MCO, MCO68, MCO71,
 NLC, NLCa, X67, X68

BISVAS, Anil   India   1914
 EMS
 EMS: БИСВА́С

BITOV, Boris Leonidovich   USSR   1904
   EMS
   EMS: БИ́ТОВ

*BITSCH, Marcel   France   1921
   X68

*BITSCH, Viggo   Denmark   1890   1964
   X64

*BITTER, John   USA   1909
   EVM

*BIZONY, Celia   Great Britain   1904
   WI69

BIZZELLI, Annibale   Italy   1900   1967
   LMD, REM

BJARNASON, Fridrik   Iceland   1880   1962
   VTM

*BJELINSKI, Bruno   Yugoslavia   1909
   BB65, BB71, DDM, EMS, HCM, IMD, KMJ, LMD, REM,
   X66, X67
   EMS: БЬЕ́ЛИНСКИ

*BJERRE, Jens   Denmark   1903
   IMD, VTM

*BJÖRKANDER, Nils Frank
  Fredrik   Sweden   1893
   EVM, FST, IMD, LMD, REM, SIM, SIMa, STS, TJU, X67

BJÖRLIN, Ulf   Sweden   1933
   FST

BJÖRNSSON, Arni   Iceland   1905
   VTM

*BLACHER, Boris   Germany   1903   China
   BB71, CME, DDM, DMM, EMS, EVM, IMD, IMD2, LMD, MEH,
   MZW, PAP, REM, SML, TSC, VNM, WTM, X64, X65, X66,
   X67, X68
   EMS: БЛА́ХЕР

*BLACHFORD, Frank Edward   Canada   1879   1957
   CCM, MCO68

*BLACKBURN, Maurice   Canada   1914
   CVM, IMD, LMD, MCO, TFB

*BLACKWOOD, Easley   USA   1933
 BB65, BB71, IMD, LCI, LMD, PCM, WTM,
 X64, X65, X66, X67, X68

BLAGOI, Dmitri Dmitrievich USSR   1930
 EMS, X64, X66, X68
 EMS: БЛАГÓЙ

BLAHA, Ivo   Czechoslovakia 1937
 MNP67/1-72/4

*BLÄHA-MIKEŠ, Záboj Czechoslovakia 1887 1957
 BB65, BB71, EVM, LMD

BLAHNIK, Roman   Czechoslovakia 1897 1964
 CCZ

BLAKE, David Leonard Great Britain 1936
 WI69, X64, X66, X67, X68

*BLANC, Giuseppe   Italy   1886 1969
 BB71, LMD, MLA26/4, REM

BLANCAFORT, Alberto Spain circa 1938
 CME, X65

*BLANCAFORT de ROSSELLÒ,
 Manuel   Spain   1897
 DDM, EVM, LMD, REM

BLANCHARD, Roger   1919
 IMD

*BLANCO, Juan   Cuba   1920
 WI69, X66

*BLANCO RECIO, José Ramón Spain   1886
 EVM

BLANK, Allan   USA   1925
 ASUC, PC71, X65, X66, X67, X68

*BLANTER, Matvei Isaakovich USSR   1903
 EMS, MEH, PPU, SML
 EMS: БЛАНТЕР

BLATNY, Josef   Czechoslovakia 1891
 CCZ

BLATNÝ, Pavel   Czechoslovakia 1931
 CCZ, IMD2, MNP67/1-69/4-69/7-72/1, X65, X68

BLATTER, Alfred W.   USA
  ASUC

BLAUTH, Breno   Brazil   1931
  FBC

*BLAŽEK, Zdeněk   Czechoslovakia 1905
  BB65, BB71, CCZ, CME, EVM, IMD2, LMD, MEH, MNP72/9,
  REM, SML, X65

*BLECH, Leo   Germany   1871 1958
  BB65, BB71, DDM, IMD, LMD, MEH, REM

*BLEDSOE, Jules   USA   1898 1943
  BB65, BB71

*BLESSINGER, Karl   Germany   1888
  EVM, LMD

*BLEYELE, Karl   Germany   1880 1969
  BB71, EVM, IMD, LMD, REM
  LMD: BLEYLE   REM: BLEYLE

BLIESENER, Ada M.   USA
  ASUC

BLIN, René   France   1881
  EVM

*BLISS, Arthur   Great Britain 1891
  BB65, BB71, DDM, EMS, EVM, IMD, LMD, MEH, REM, SML,
  TCM, WI69, WTM, X64, X65, X66, X67, X68
  EMS: БЛИСС

*BLITZSTEIN, Marc   USA   1905 1964
  AS66, BB65, BB71, DDM, EMS, EVM, IMD, LMD, MEH, PCM,
  PC71, REM, SML, WTM, X64, X65, X66, X67, X68
  EMS: БЛИЦСТАЙН

*BLOCH, André   France   1873 1960
  BB65, BB71, DMF, LMD, REM

BLOCH, Augustyn   Poland   1929
  CME, MEH, PKW, X66, X67, X68

*BLOCH, Ernest   USA   1880 1959
  AS66, BB65, BB71, CA9, DDM, EMS, EVM, Switzerland
  IMD, LMD, MEH, MJM, PAP, REM, SCHW,
  SML, WTM, X64, X65, X66, X67, X68
  EMS: БЛОХ

BLOCH, Waldemar   1906
  IMD2, X68

*BLOHM, Sven   Sweden   1907   1956
  FST, KSV, SIM, SIMa

BLOK, Vladimir Michajlovich   USSR   1932
  EMS, MEH, X67, X68
  EMS: БЛОК

BLOMBERG, Erik   Sweden   1922
  FST, SOW

*BLOMDAHL, Karl-Birger   Sweden   1916   1968
  BB65, BB71, CME, DDM, DNS, EMS, FST, IMD, IMD2, KSV,
  LMD, MEH, MLA25/4, OCM, REM, SIM, SIMa, SML, SMT,
  SOW, STS, SWE, TJU, VTM, WTM, X64, X65, X66, X67, X68
  EMS: БЛУМДАЛЬ

*BLOMFIELD-HOLT, Patricia   Canada   1910
  CCM, CVM, CVMa, MCO68

BLÖNDAL, Magnus   Iceland   1925
  VTM

BLOOD, Denis Jeffrey   Ireland
  WI69

*BLUM, Robert   Switzerland   1900
  BB71, CME, DDM, EVM, IMD, IMD2, LMD, REM, SCHW,
  WWS, X64, X65, X66, X67, X68

*BLUME-STEINER, Paul   Germany   1897
  WWG

BLUMENFELD, Harold   USA
  AA73, X66, X68

*BLUMER, Theodor   Germany   1881   1964
  BB65, BB71, IMD, LMD, SML, X64, X65
  LMD, REM and SML: 1882

BLYTON, Carey   Great Britain   1932
  WI69, X64, X67, X68

BOATWRIGHT, Howard   USA   1918
  AS66, PCM, PC71, X64, X65, X66, X68

BOBCHEVSKI, Venedikt Petrov   Bulgaria   1895   1957
  BMK
  BMK: БОБЧЕВСКИ

BOBESCU, Constantin   Rumania   1899
  RCL

BOBOC, Nicolae RCL	Rumania	1920	
BOCCHINO, Alceu FBC	Brazil	1918	
*BOCHMANN, Werner EVM, WI69	Germany	1900	
BÖCKMAN, Alfred SML, X65, X68	Germany	1905	
BODA, John BB65, BB71, PCM, PC71, X64	USA	1922	
*BODART, Eugen IMD, LMD, REM	Germany	1905	
BODIN, Lars-Gunnar BB71, STS, VTM, X66, X68	Sweden	1935	
BODIN, Svante FST	Sweden	1942	
*BODKY, Erwin BB65, BB71	USA	1896	1958 Germany
BOEDASJKIN, N. P. See: BUDASHKIN, N. P.			
*BOEDIJN, Gerard EVM	Netherlands	1893	
BOEHE, Ernst EVM	Germany	1880	
BOEHM, Yohanan ACU, MM59	Israel	1914	Germany
BOEHMER, Alan CAP	USA		
BOEHMER, Konrad IMD2, X66, X67, X68	Germany	1941	
BOELZA, Igor Fedorovich See: BELZA, I. F.			
*BOER, Willem de EVM, SCHW, X68	Switzerland	1885	1962 Netherlands

BOERINGER, James   USA   1930
   PC71, X65, X66, X67

*BOERO, Felipe   Argentina   1884   1958
   BB65, BB71, CA15, LMD

BOGARDO, Florin   Rumania   1942
   RCL

*BOGATYREV, Anatoly
   Vaselievitch   USSR   1913
   EMS, EVM, LMD, PPU, PPU69/2, REM
   EVM: 1919
   EMS: БОГАТЫРЁВ

BOGDANOV, Feodor
   Feodorovich   USSR   1903
   EMS
   EMS: БОГДÁНОВ

BOGDANOV, Palladi Andrievich   USSR   1881
   EMS
   EMS: БОГДÁНОВ

BOGDANOV-BEREZOVSKY,
   Valerian Mihailovich   USSR   1903   1971
   BB65, BB71, BB71ad, EMS, LMD, PPU, PPU69/2,
   X64, X65, X66, X67, X68
   EMS: БОГДÁНОВ-БЕРЕЗОВСКИЙ

*BOGDANOV-KOČKO, Petre   Yugoslavia   1913
   X67

BOGLIUNI, Mario   Yugoslavia   1935
   KMJ

BOGO, Bruno   Italy   1917
   LMD, REM

BOGOSAVLJEVIĆ, Romulus   Yugoslavia   1922
   KMJ

BOGOSLOVSKY, Nikita
   Vladimirovich   USSR   1913
   EMS, PPU
   EMS: БОГОСЛÓВСКИЙ

BOGUSŁAWSKI, Edward   Poland   1940
   X68

BOHAČ, Josef   Czechoslovakia 1929
   CCZ, IMD2, MEH, MNP67/7, MNP72/4, X65, X68

*BØHLING-PETERSEN, Børge   Denmark   1911   1969

BÖHM, Karl   Austria   1894   1965
REM, X64, X66, X67, X68

BÖHMER, Helmut   Germany   1921   1972
MLA29/4, SML

BOHRNSTEDT, Wayne R.   USA
AA73, X66, X67

BOIKO, Rostislav Grigorievich   USSR   1931
EMS
EMS: БОЙКО

BOIS, Rod du   Netherlands   1934
BB65, BB71, IMD2, LMD, NED, PAP, X65, X67, X68
PAP: DU BOIS, Rob

*BOISGALLAIS, Jacques   France   1927
DDM

BOISTELLE, Paul   France   1936
ACM

*BOIVIN, Maurice F.   Canada   1918
CVM, KEY, MCO, NLC

BOKES, Vladimir   Czechoslovakia
X68, ZE70/1, ZE70/3, ZE71/1, ZE71/2, ZE71/3

BOLAÑOS, Cesar   Peru   1931
CA17

BOLCOM, William Elden   USA   1938
BB65, BB71, DN72, PC71, X65, X67, X68

*BOLDEMANN, Laci   Sweden   1921   1969
FST, KSV, LMD, SIM, SIMa, SOW, STS,   Finland
SWE, TJU, VTM, X65, X67, X68

BOLDYREV, Igor Georgievich   USSR   1912
EMS, X65
EMS: БОЛДЫРЕВ

BOLIN, Nicolai P.   USA   1908   Russia
AS66

BOLLE, James D.   USA
ASUC

BOLLER, Carlo   Switzerland   1896   1952
SCHW

*BOMBARDELLI, Silvije   Yugoslavia   1916
     BB65, BB71, HCM, IMD, KMJ, X67, X68

*BONAVIA, Ferruccio   Great Britain   1877   1950
     LMD, REM   Italy

BONDE, Allen   USA
     ASUC

*BONDEVILLE, Emmanuel
     Pierre Georges   France   1898
     CME, CMF3, CMF20, CMF39, DDM, DMF, EMS, EVM,
     LMD, QQF, REM, X64
     EMS: БОНДЕВИ́ЛЬ

*BONDON, Jacques   France   1927
     BB65, BB71, DDM, IMD, LMD, QQF, X68

BONDS, Margaret   USA   1913
     AS66, PCM

BONELLI, Ettore   Italy   1900
     LMD, REM

BONET, Narcis   Spain
     X68

*BONFILS, Jean-Baptiste   France   1921
     X64, X65

*BONGARTZ, Heinz   Germany   1894
     EVM, MEH, SML, X64, X66, X67, X68

BONHOMME, Andrée   Netherlands   1905
     NED

*BONITZ, Eberhard   Germany   1921
     IMD

*BONNAL, Joseph Ermend   France   1880
     X68

BONNARD, Giulio   Italy   1885
     LMD

*BONNÉN, Helge   Denmark   1896
     VTM

*BONNER, Eugene MacDonald   USA   1889
     EVM, LMD, REM

*BONNET, Joseph Elie
  Georges Marie   France   1884
  EVM, LMD

*BONSEL, Adriaan   Netherlands   1918
  EVM

BONSET, Jacques   Netherlands   1880
  EVM

BONTEMPELLI, Massimo   Italy   1878   1960
  IMD, LMD, REM

BOONE, Charles   USA   1939
  BB71, X66, X68

BOOREN, Jo van den   Netherlands   1935
  X67, X68

BOPP, Joseph   Switzerland   1908
  ACM, LMD, SCHW

*BORCHARD, Adolphe   France   1882   1967
  BB71

*BORCK, Edmund von   Germany   1906   1944
  MEH

BORDEWIJK-ROEPMAN,
  Johannaa   Netherlands   1892
  EVM, NED

BORETZ, Benjamin   USA
  ASUC

BORG, Kim   Finland   1919
  LMD, X65, X67, X68

*BORGOVAN, Ion   Rumania   1889   1970
  EVM, RCL

BORGULYA, András   Hungary   1931
  CHC, X67, X68

BORISHANSKY, Elliot   USA
  ASUC

BORISOV, Valentin Tikhonovich   USSR   1901
  EMS
  EMS: БОРИ́СОВ

*BOŘKOVEC, Pavel Czechoslovakia 1894 1972
  CCZ, CME, DDM, EVM, IMD, IMD2, LMD, MEH, MNP64/5/6,
  MNP65/5, MNP66/1, REM, SML, X64, X65, X66, X67

BORLENGHI, Enzo Italy 1908
  IMD, LMD

*BORNEFELD, Helmut Germany 1906
  EVM, IMD, LMD, REM, X64, X66, X67, X68

BORNSCHEIN, Eduard 1883
  IMD

BORNUM, Hans Sweden 1910
  SIM

*BOROWSKI, Felix USA 1872 1956
  AS66, EVM, LMD Great Britain

*BØRRESEN, Aksel Einar Håkon Denmark 1876 1954
  BB65, BB71, EVM, IMD, LMD, REM, VTM

*BORRIES, Fritz von Germany 1894
  EVM, WWG

*BORRIS, Siegfried Germany 1906
  CME, DDM, EVM, IMD, LMD, REM, SML, WWG,
  X64, X65, X66, X67, X68

*BORSARI, Amédée Pierre France 1905
  DDM

*BORTKIEWICZ, Sergei
  Eduardovitch Austria 1877 1952
  EMS, EVM, IMD, LMD, MEH, REM Russia
  EMS: БОРТКЕ́ВИЧ

BORTOLOTTI, Mauro Italy 1926
  IMD, LMD, REM, X65, X66
  IMD and X65: BORTOLOTTI, Mar<u>io</u>

BORTONE, Amerigo Italy 1914
  REM

*BORTZ, Alfred Germany 1882
  EVM, IMD

BÖRTZ, Daniel Sweden 1943
  FST

*BORUP-JØRGENSEN, Axel Denmark 1924
  CME, DMTsp, IMD, VTM, X65, X66

*BOSCOVICH, Alexander Uriah   Israel   1907   1964
    ACU, BB65, BB71, CME, DDM, EVM,   Hungary
    IMD2, LMD, MEH, MMI, MM59, REM,
    X64, X65, X66, X67, X68
    ACU and MM59: BOSKOVICH

BOSMANS, Arthur   Belgium   1908
    EVM, IMD

*BOSMANS, Henriëtte Hilda   Netherlands   1895   1952
    EVM, IMD, LMD, NED, X65

BOŠNJAKOVIĆ, Ljubomir   Yugoslavia   1891
    KMJ

BOSSELJON, Bernd   Belgium
    X67

BOSSEUR, Jean-Yves   France   1947
    BB71, X67, X68

*BOSSI, Constante Adolfo   Italy   1876   1953
    BB65, BB71, DDM, EVM, IMD, LMD, REM

*BOSSI, Renzo   Italy   1883   1965
    BB65, BB71, DDM, EVM, IMD, LMD, MLA22/4, REM,
    X65, X67

*BOSSLER, Kurt   Germany   1911
    X67, X68

BOSTELMANN, Otto   USA   1907   Germany
    BB65, BB71

BOTEZ, Dumitru D.   Rumania   1904
    RCL

BÖTTCHER, Georg   Germany   1889
    EVM

*BÖTTCHER, Lukas Josef   Germany   1878
    EVM

BOTTENBERG, Wolfgang   Canada   1930   Germany
    CCM, CCM71, CVM, CVMa, KEY, MCO68, MCO71, NLC,
    NLCa, X68

*BOTTI, Cardenio   Italy   1891
    LMD, REM

BOTTJE, Will Gey   USA   1925
    AA73, ASUC, LCI, PCM, X66, X67, X68

BOTTO VILLARINO, Carlos   Chile   1923
    CA14, X64

BOUCOURECHLIEV, Andre   France   1925   Bulgaria
    BB65, BB71, CMF31, CMF39, IMD, LMD, REM,
    X66, X67, X68

*BOUGHTON, Rutland   Great Britain   1878   1960
    BB65, BB71, EVM, LMD, X64, X66

*BOULANGER, Nadia Juliette   France   1887   1962
    CME, DDM, DMF, EVM, IMD, LMD, MEH, QQF, REM, SML,
    X64, X65, X66, X67, X68

*BOULEZ, Pierre   France   1925
    BB65, BB71, CME, CMF11, CMF20, CMF39, CMF65, DDM,
    DMF16, DMF20, DMM, EL:2, EMS, EVM, IMD, IMD2, LMD,
    MEH, MNG, MZW, OCM, PAP, QQF, REM, SML, TCM, TSC,
    VNM, WI69, WTM, X64, X66, X67, X68
    PAP: 1926
    EMS: БУЛЕ́З

BOULNOIS, Michel   France   1907
    DDM

BOURDEAUX, Lucien   France   1929
    DDM

BOURGEOIS, Derek David   Great Britain   1941
    WI69

*BOURGUIGNON, Francis de   Belgium   1890   1961
    BB65, BB71, EVM, IMD, LMD, REM

BOURKHANOV, M. M.
    See: BURKHANOV, M. M.

BOUTNIKOFF, Ivan   USA   1893   Russia
    AS66

BOUTRY, Roger   France   1932
    BB71, QQF

*BOVET, Joseph   Switzerland   1879   1951
    DDM, SCHW

BOWDER, Jerry L.   USA
    ASUC

*BOWEN, Edwin York   Great Britain   1884   1961
    BB65, BB71, EVM, IMD, LMD, REM

BOWERS-BROADBENT,
  Christopher Joseph   Great Britain   1945
  WI69

BOWIE, William   Germany   1925
  WI69

*BOWLES, Michael Andrew   New Zealand 1909 Ireland
  EVM, X68

*BOWLES, Paul Frederic   USA   1910
  AS66, EVM, IMD, LMD, PCM, PC71, REM

BOYADZHIEV, Petr Gregoriev Bulgaria   1883 1961
  BMK
  BMK: БОЯДЖИЕВ

*BOYDELL, Brian Patrick   Ireland   1917
  DDM, LMD, REM, X64

BOYKAN, Martin   USA   1931
  ASUC, BB71, X65, X68

BOZAY, Attila   Hungary   1939
  CHC, CME, MEH, X66, X67, X68, ZSZ

BOŽIČ, Darijan   Yugoslavia 1933
  KMJ, MSC, X66, X67, X68

*BOZZA, Eugene Joseph   France   1905
  DDM, DMF, EVM, IMD, LMD, MEH, QQF, REM, WI69,
  X64, X67

*BRAAL, Andries de   Netherlands 1909
  EVM, NED

*BRABANDER, Karel de   Belgium   1913
  EVM

BRABANT, Eric   France   1941
  ACM

*BRACESCO, Renzo   Peru   1888
  LMD

BRADIĆ, Zvonimir   Yugoslavia 1904
  KMJ

*BRAEIN, Edvard   Norway   1887 1957
  CNO

*BRAEIN, Edvard Fliflet   Norway   1924
   BB71, CME, CNO, VTM
   BB71: BRAEIN, Edvard

*BRAGA, Antonio   Italy   1929
   LMD, X64

*BRAGA SANTOS, José Manuel
  Joly   Portugal   1924
   DDM, EVM, IMD2, LMD, X64, X65, X67

BRAGGIOTTI, Mario   USA   1909 Italy
   AS66

BRĂILOIU, Constantin   Rumania   1893 1958
   BB65, BB71, CME, DDM, LMD, MEH, RCL, REM, SML,
   X64, X65, X66, X68

*BRANCO, Luis Freitas   Portugal   1890 1963
   CME

*BRAND, Max   USA   1896 Poland
   DDM, EVM, IMD, LMD, REM, X66

BRANDÃO, José Vieira   Brazil   1911
   CA16, FBC, IMD

BRANDELER, Henriette van den Netherlands   1884
   EVM, NED

*BRANDMAN, Israel   Israel   1901
   ACU, MM59

BRANDOLICA, Ljubomir   Yugoslavia   1932
   KMJ

*BRANDT, Fritz   Germany   1902
   EVM

BRÂNDUS, Nicolae   Rumania   1935
   RCL

*BRANSCOMBE, Gena   USA   1881 Canada
   AS66, EVM, LMD, PCM, REM, X64, X65, X66, X67, X68
   AS66: BRANSCOMBE, Gina

*BRANSON, David   Great Britain   1909
   EVM

*BRANT, Henry Dreyfus   USA   1913 Canada
   BB65, BB71, EVM, IMD, LMD, PCM, PC71, REM,
   X64, X65, X66

BRÂNZEU, Nicolae   Rumania   1907
RCL

*BRASSARD, François   Canada   1908
CCM, CVMa, KEY, MCO68, X68

BRASSENS, Georges   France   1921
WI69, X64, X65, X66, X67, X68

BRATU, Teodor   Rumania   1922
RCL, SML, X64, X65

BRAUEL, Henning   Germany   1940
BB71, X65, X68

BRAUN, Jehezkiel   Israel   1922   Germany
ACU, IMD2
IMD2: Yehezkiel

BRAUN, Peter (Pee) Michael   Germany   1936
IMD2, PAP, X66

*BRAUNFELS, Michael   Germany   1917
LMD

*BRAUNFELS, Walter   Germany   1882   1954
DDM, EVM, IMD, LMD, MEH, REM, SML

BRÄUTIGAM, Helmut   Germany   1914   1942
EVM

*BRAVNIČAR, Matija   Yugoslavia   1897
CME, DDM, EMS, IMD, KMJ, LMD, MEH, MSC, REM, SML,
X65, X66, X67, X68
EMS: БРА́ВНИЧАР

BREDEMEYER, Reiner   Germany   1929
SML, X67, X68

BREDICEANU, Mihai   Rumania   1920
RCL

*BREDICEANU, Tiberiu   Rumania   1877   1968
BB65, BB71, CME, EMS, EVM, LMD, MEH, RCL, SML, X65
EMS: БРЕДИЧА́НУ

BREHM, Alvin   USA   1925
BB71

*BREHME, Hans   Germany   1904   1957
BB65, BB71, IMD, LMD, REM

*BRENN, Franz   Switzerland   1907   1963
    LMD, SCHW, X64, X66, X67

BRENNER, Walter   USA   1906   Union of
    AS66   South Africa

*BRENTA, Gaston   Belgium   1902   1969
    BB71, CBC, DDM, EVM, LMD, MLA26/4, REM, WI69, X64, X66

BRERO, Giulio Cesare   Italy   1908
    LMD, REM

*BRESGEN, Cesar   Austria   1913   Italy
    DDM, EVM, IMD, IMD2, LMD, MEH, REM, SML, WI69, WWG,
    X64, X65, X66, X67, X68

BRESNIK, Martin   USA   1946
    BB71

BRET, Gustave   France   1875   1969
    BB71, DDM, DMF, EVM, LMD, MLA26/4, REM

*BRETAGNE, Pierre   France   1881
    DMF, EVM

*BRETEUIL, François de   France   1892
    EVM

BREUER, Karl Günther   1926
    IMD

BREUER, Mordechai   Israel   1918   Germany
    ACU

BREVIK, Tor   Norway   1932
    CNO, VTM

BREWER, George M.   Canada
    KEY

BREWER, Richard   1921
    WAN

BREWER, William Gordon   Great Britain   1901
    WI69

BREWSTER-JONES H.   Australia   1887
    AMM

*BRIAN, William Havergal   Great Britain   1876   1972
    BB65, BB71, CME, EVM, IMD, REM, X65, X66, X67, X68

BRICCETTI, Thomas   USA   1936
   PC71

BRICE, Jean Anne   Union of   1938
   WI69   South Africa

*BRICKEN, Carl Ernest   USA   1898
   EVM, LMD, REM, WI69

*BRIDGEWATER, Ernest Leslie Great Britain 1893
   EVM

BRIGHT, Clive John   Great Britain 1930
   WI69, X66

*BRIGHT, Dora Estella   Great Britain 1863   1952
   EVM
   EVM: 1864-1951

BRIGHT, Houston   USA   1916
   AS66, PCM, PC71, X64, X66, X68

BRIGHTON, Herbert   Great Britain 1902   1972
   MLA29/4

*BRINDLE, Reginald Smith Great Britain 1917
   WI69

BRINGS, Allen   USA
   ACUC

BRINK-POTHUIS, Annie van den Netherlands 1906   1956
   EVM

BRÎNZEU, Nicolae   Rumania   1907
   SML

BRISCOE, Gerald   Germany   1923
   WI69

*BRITAIN, Radie   USA   1903
   AA73, AS66, BB65, BB71, LMD, PCM, PC71, REM, WI69,
   X64, X65, X66, X67, X68
   AS66: 1904   WI69: 1906

*BRITTEN, Edward Benjamin Great Britain 1913
   BB65, BB71, BCI, DDM, EMS, EVM, IMD, IMD2, LMD, MEH,
   MZW, REM, SML, TCM, VNM, WI69, WTM, X64, X65, X66,
   X67, X68
   EMS: БРИ́ТТЕН

*BRKANOVIĆ, Ivan   Yugoslavia   1906
  BB65, BB71, EMS, HCM, IMD, KMJ, LMD, MEH, REM, SML,
  X64, X65, X67, X68
  EMS: БРОКА́НОВИЧ

BROCH, Hermann   Germany
  X68

BROCKINGTON, Howard   USA
  ASUC

*BROCKLESS, Brian   Great Britain   1926
  WI69, X68

*BROCKT, Johannes   Germany   1901
  WI69

*BROCKWAY, Howard   USA   1870 1951
  EVM, LMD, REM

*BROD, Max   Israel   1884 1969
  ACU, BB71, CME, DDM, EVM, LMD, MEH,   Czecho-
  MLA26/4, MM59, SML, X64, X67, X68   slovakia

BRODER, Teodor   Israel   1933 Poland
  ACU

*BRODERSEN, Vigo   Denmark   1879 1965
  EVM, X65

BRODY, Sarmad   USA   1941
  DN72

BROECKX, Jan P. K.   Belgium   1880 1965
  EVM, LMD, MLA23/4, X66, X67
  LMD, 1966

*BROEKMAN, David   USA   1902 1958
  BB65, BB71, LMD   Netherlands

BROESILOWSKI, Yevgeni G.
  See: BRUSILOVSKY, Y. G.

*BRØGGER, Reidar   Norway   1886 1956
  CNO

BROGUE, Roslyn   USA   1919
  BB65, BB71, LMD
  LMD: HENNING, Roslyn Brogue

*BROMAN, K. Natanael   Sweden   1887 1966
  BB71, EVM, FST, KSV, LMD, SIM, STS, X66

*BROMAN, Sten   Sweden   1902
   BB71, CME, EVM, IMD2, LMD, REM, SIM, SIMa, STS, TJU,
   VTM, X67, X68

BRONS, Carel T.   Netherlands   1931
   BB65, BB71, LMD, X67, X68

BROOKES, Oliver   Great Britain   1922
   WI69

*BROOKS, Ernest   USA   1903
   EVM

BROQUET, Louis Chanoine   Switzerland   1888   1954
   SCHW

*BROTT, Alexander   Canada   1915
   BB65, BB71, CCM, CCM71, CVM, EVM, IMD, KEY, LMD, MCO,
   MCO68, MCO71, NLC, NLCa, REM, TFB, X66, X67, X68

BROUSSARD, Fausto   Italy   1927
   LMD, REM

BROUTMAN, Emanuel   USA
   X67, X68

*BROWN, Allanson G. Y.   Canada   1902   England
   CCM, KEY, MCO, NLC

BROWN, Barclay   USA

*BROWN, Charles Louis
  Georges   France   1898
   DDM, QQF

BROWN, Christopher Roland Great Britain   1943
   WI69, X66, X68

BROWN, Earle   USA   1926
   AA73, BB65, BB71, CA12, EL:2, IMD, LMD, MEH, MNG,
   PAP, PCM, PC71, REM, TSC, X64, X65, X66, X67, X68

*BROWN, Frank Edwin   Great Britain   1908
   WI69

*BROWN, Gavin William   Great Britain   1925
   WI69

BROWN, Harold   1909
   IMD

*BROWN, James Clifford   Great Britain   1923
   WI69, X68

*BROWN, Keneth Arundel   Great Britain   1891
   WI69

BROWN, Lawrence   USA   1893   1972
   MLA29/4

BROWN, Newel Kay   USA   1932
   CAP, PC71, X68

BROWN, Raynor   USA   1912
   BB65, BB71, DN70, LMD, PCM, PC71, X66

*BROWN, Sebastian Hubert   Great Britain   1903
   WI69

BROWNE, Richmond   USA
   ASUC

*BROŽ, František   Czechoslovakia 1896   1962
   CCZ, EVM, IMD, LMD, REM

BROZEN, Michael   USA   1934
   X68

BRUBECK, David Warren   USA   1920
   BB71, EVM, LMD, PC71, X64, X65, X66, X67, X68

*BRUBECK, Howard   USA   1916
   BB65, BB71, LMD, X66

BRUČI, Rudolf   Yugoslavia   1917
   BB65, BB71, EMS, KMJ, LMD, MEH, X66, X67
   EMS: БРУ̃ЧИ

*BRÜCKNER-RÜGGEBERG,
   Wilhelm   Germany   1906
   X68

*BRÜGGEMANN, Kurt   Germany   1908
   LMD, REM, X68

BRUINSMA, Henry Allen   USA   1916
   DAS

BRUMBY, Colin James   Australia   1933
   AMM, WI69, X65, X66

*BRUN, François Julien   France   1909
   QQF, X67

*BRUN, Fritz   Switzerland 1878   1959
   BB65, BB71, EVM, IMD, LMD, REM, SCHWs

*BRÜN, Herbert   Israel   1918
    IMD, LMD, MEH, MM59, PAP, X66, X68

*BRUNETTI-PISANO, August   Austria   1870
    EVM

*BRUNI-TEDESCHI, Alberto   Italy   1915
    LMD, REM

BRÜNING, Eliseus   Netherlands   1892
    EVM

*BRUNNER, Adolf   Switzerland   1901
    CME, DDM, EVM, IMD, LMD, REM, SCHW, WWS,
    X65, X66, X67, X68

*BRUNNER, Hans   Switzerland   1898   1958
    SCHW

BRUNS, Viktor   Germany   1904
    IMD, MEH, SML

*BRUNSWICK, Mark   USA   1902   1971
    BB71, EVM, LMD, MLA28, PCM, REM, X64, X65, X66, X67

BRUSCHETTINI, Mario Augusto Italy   1896
    LMD, REM

BRUSH, Ruth Jackson   USA   1910
    AA73, AS66, X64, X66, X68

*BRUSILOVSKY, Yevgeni
    Grigorevich   USSR   1905
    EMS, EVM, LMD, MEH, PPU69/2, REM, SML, X65
    EVM: BROESILOWSKI
    EMS: БРУСИЛОВСКИЙ

*BRUSSELMANS, Michael   Belgium   1886   1960
    CBD, DDM, EVM, LMD, REM   France

*BRUST, Herbert   Germany   1900
    EVM

*BRUSTAD, Bjarne   Norway   1895
    BB71, CNO, DDM, EVM, LMD, REM, VTM
    EVM: BJARNE, Brustad

*BRUUN, Kai Aage   Denmark   1899
    VTM

BRUYNEL, Ton   Netherlands   1934
    NED, X68

BRUZDOWICZ, Joanna   Poland   circa 1932
   X68

*BRYAN, Charles Faulkner   USA   1911
   AS66

*BRYAN, Gordon   Great Britain 1895
   EVM

BRYANT, Allan   USA   1931
   X68

*BRYDSON, John Callis   Great Britain 1900
   X65

BUBÁK, Bohdan   Czechoslovakia
   MNP69/4

BUČAR, Danilo   Yugoslavia   1896
   KMJ

BUCCERI, Gianni   Italy   1873   1953
   EVM, LMD, REM

*BUCCHI, Valentino   Italy   1916
   EL:1, EVM, IMD, LMD, WI69

*BUCCI, Mark   USA   1924
   BB65, BB71, LMD, PCM, PC71, X66, X68

*BUCHAL, Hermann   Germany   1884 1961
   EVM, IMD

*BUCHAROFF, Simon   USA   1881 1955
   AS66, EVM, LMD, REM   Russia
   Formerly: BUCHHALTER

*BUCHT, Gunnar   Sweden   1927
   BB65, BB71, CME, FST, IMD2, KSV, LMD, MEH, SIM, SIMa,
   SOW, STS, SWE, TJU, VTM, X65, X66, X67, X68

*BÜCHTGER, Fritz   Germany   1903 Monaco
   DDM, EVM, IMD, IMD2, LMD, MEH, PAP, REM, WWG, X64,
   X65, X66, X67, X68
   REM, X64, X65 and X66: BUECHTGER

BUCK, Ole   Denmark circa 1943
   X68

BUCZYNSKI, Walter J.   Canada   1933
   CCM, CCM71, CVM, CVMa, KEY, MCO68, MCO71

*BUDASHKIN, Nikolay Pavlovich USSR   1910
    EMS, EVM, LMD, PPU, REM, SML
    EVM: BOEDASJKIN
    EMS: БУДА́ШКИН

BUDD, Harold   USA   1936
    BB71, PCM, X68

BUDER, Ernst Erich   Germany   1896
    WWG

BUDRIŪNAS, Antanas Mato   USSR   1902   Lithuania
    EMS
    EMS: БУДРЮ́НАС

*BUECHTGER, Fritz
    See: BÜCHTGER

*BUESST, Aylmer   Great Britain   1885   1970
    Australia

*BUESST, Victor   Great Britain   1885   Australia
    EVM

*BUFFIN de CHOSAL, Victor   Belgium   1867   1953

*BUGAMELLI, Mario   Italy   1905   Russia
    EVM, X67

BUGATCH, Samuel   USA   1898   Russia
    AS66

BUGEANU, Constantin   Rumania   1916
    RCL, X65

BUGHICI, Dumitru   Rumania   1921
    BB65, BB71, CME, RCL, X64, X65, X66, X68

BUHLER, Phillippe   USA   1919   Switzerland
    ACM

BUICLIU, Nicolae   Rumania   1906
    LMD, MEH, RCL, REM, SML

BUJARSKI, Zbigniew   Poland   1933
    PKW, X64, X66, X68

BUKIYA, Aleksandr Ionovich   USSR   1906
    EMS
    EMS: БУ́КИЯ

93

BUKORESHLIEV, Angel
  Atanasov   Bulgaria   1870 1950
  BMK, EMS, SML
  BMK: БУКОРЕШЛИЕВ   EMS: БУКОРЕШЛИЕВ
  EMS: 1951

BUKOWSKI, Ryszard   Poland   1916
  PKW, X67, X68

BULIS, Jiří   Czechoslovakia
  MNP69/4

BULL, Edvard Hagerup
  See: HAGERUP BULL, Edvard

BULL, Sverre Hagerup
  See: HAGERUP BULL, Sverre

*BULLING, Burchard   Germany   1881
  WWG

*BULLOCK, Ernest   Great Britain 1890
  EVM, X67

BULYICHEV, Yvacheslav
  Aleksandrovich   USSR   1872 1959
  EMS
  EMS: БУЛЫЧЕВ

*BUMCKE, Gustav   Germany   1876
  EVM

*BUNGE, Sas Ernest Alexander Netherlands 1924
  EVM, IMD, NED, X67

BUNGER, Richard   USA
  ASUC

BUNIN, Revol Samuilovich USSR   1924
  EMS, MEH, X66, X68
  EMS: БУНИН

*BUNIN, Vladimir Vasilievich USSR   1908 1970
  BB71, EMS, LMD, PPU
  EMS: БУНИН
  PPU: 1903

*BUNK, Gerard   Netherlands 1888
  EVM, X66

BURGE, David   USA   circa 1928
  ASUC, PC71, X66, X68

94

*BURGES, Peter Henry Great Britain 1908 1964
X64, X67

*BURGHAUSER, Jarmil Michael Czechoslovakia 1921
CCZ, IMD2, LMD, MEH, MNP64/3, MNP64/5, MNP64/6,
MNP67/2, MNP69/3, MNP71/3, REM, SML, WI69, X64,
X65, X66, X67, X68

BURGON, Geoffrey Great Britain 1941
WI69, X68

*BURIAN, Emil František Czechoslovakia 1904 1959
BB65, BB71, CCZ, CME, DDM, EVM, IMD, IMD2, LMD, MEH,
MNP64/4, MNP64/5, MNP64/6, REM, SML, X64, X65, X66,
X67, X68

BURIĆ, Marijan Yugoslavia 1913
HCM, IMD, KMJ

*BURKHANOV, Mutal
Muzainovich USSR 1916
DDM, PPU, PPU69/2
DDM: BOURKHANOV

*BURKHARD, Paul Switzerland 1911
EVM, IMD, LMD, MEH, REM, SCHW, SML, WWS, X66, X67

*BURKHARD, Willy Switzerland 1900 1955
BB71, DDM, EMS, EVM, IMD, LMD, MEH, PAP, REM, SCHW,
SML, X64, X65, X66, X68
EMS: БУРКХАРД

*BURKHART, Franz Austria 1902
X65

BURLAS, Ladislav Czechoslovakia 1927
CCZ, MEH, MNP67/1, X64, X65, X66, X67, X68, ZE69/2/3,
ZE70/1/2, ZE71/1/2

*BURLEIGH, Cecil USA 1885
AS66, EVM, LMD, PCM, REM, XI69

*BURLE MARX, Walter Brazil 1902
EVM, REM

BURN, John Paul Great Britain 1928
WI69, X65

BURNARD, David Alexander Australia 1900 1971
AMM

BURROWS, Ben (Benjamin) Great Britain 1891 1966
MLA23/4, X67

*BURSEY, Rosetta   Great Britain   1912
    WI69
    Formerly: CARTER, Rosetta

*BURT, Francis   Great Britain   1926
    BB65, BB71, IMD, LMD, MNG, REM, X64, X65, X68

BURT, George   USA
    ASUC

BURTON, Eldin   USA   1913
    AS66, PC71

BURTON, Stephen Douglas   USA   circa 1943
    X68

BURY, Edward   Poland   1916
    PKW

BUS, Ludwig   1914
    IMD

*BUSCH, Adolf Georg Wilhelm   Switzerland   1891   1952
    EVM, IMD, LMD, SML, X66, X67   Germany

BUSCH, Heinrich   Germany   1901   1929
    LMD

BUSCH, William   Great Britain   1901   1945
    EVM

*BUSH, Alan Dudley   Great Britain   1900
    BB65, BB71, BCI, DDM, EMS, EVM, LMD, MEH, REM, SML,
    WI69, X64, X65, X67, X68
    EMS: БУШ

*BUSH, Geoffry   Great Britain   1920
    EVM, LMD, REM, WI69, X64, X65, X67, X68

BUSHEL, Ben-Zion Orgad
    See: ORGAD, Ben Zion

*BÜSSER, Paul Henri   France   1872   1973
    BB71, EVM, LMD, QQF, REM, WI69, X68

*BUSSOTTI, Sylvano   Italy   1931
    BB65, BB71, CME, EL:3, IMD, IMD2, LMD, MEH, MNG, REM,
    TSC, WI69, X64, X65, X66, X67, X68

*BUSTINI, Alessandro   Italy   1876   1970
    BB71, IMD, LMD, REM

BUTAKOV, Aleksei   1907   1953
   IMD

BUTCHER, Vernon   Great Britain   1909
   WI69

BUTLER, Albert Henry   Great Britain   1904
   WI69

BUTLER, Lois   USA
   X65, X66

BUTLER, Montagu C.   Great Britain   1884
   WI69

*BUTT, James Baseden   Great Britain   1929
   WI69

BUTTERLEY, Nigel   Australia   1935
   AMM, X67

*BUTTERWORTH, Arthur
   Eckersley   Great Britain   1923
   IMD, WI69, X68

*BUTTERWORTH, David Neil   Great Britain   1934
   WI69, X67, X68

BUTTERWORTH, Ian
   Christopher   Great Britain   1940
   WI69

*BUTTING, Max   Germany   1888
   BB65, BB71, EMS, EVM, IMD, LMD, REM, SML, WWG,
   X64, X67, X68
   EMS: БУТТИНГ

BUXTON, Orr   Great Britain

BUYNISKI, Raymond John   USA   1939
   DN72

BUŽEK, Jan   Czechoslovakia
   MNP69/4

*BYE, Frederick Edward   Great Britain   1901
   WI69

BYFIELD, Jack Allen   Great Britain   1902
   WI69

CAAMAÑO, Roberto   Argentina   1923
   BB65, BB71, CA8, DDM, LMD, REM, X64, X66, X67

*CABA, Eduardo   Bolivia   1890   1953
   BB65, BB71, EVM, LMD, REM

CABALLERO FARFÁN,
   Policarpo   Peru   1901
   REM

CABENA, Barrie   Canada
   KEY, NLCa, X68

*CABLE, Howard Reid   Canada   1920
   NLC, PCM

*CABUS, Peter   Belgium   1923
   WI69

*CABY, Robert   France   1905
   DMF

CACIOPPO, George   USA   1927
   BB71, BCL, X64

*CAETANI, Roffredo   Italy   1871   1961
   EVM, LMD

*CAFFARELLI, Filippo   Italy   1891
   WI69

*CAGE, John   USA   1912
   AS66, BB65, BB71, CA8, CME, DDM, DMM, EL:2, EL:3,
   EL:4, EVM, IMD, IMD2, LMD, MEH, MZW, PAP, PCM,
   PC71, REM, SML, WI69, WTM, X64, X65, X66, X67, X68

*CAGGIANO, Girolamo   Italy   1896
   REM

*CAGGIANO, Roberto   Italy   1903
   LMD

CAGNACCI, Marcello   Italy   1897
   REM

*CAIRATI, Alfredo   Italy   1875
   REM

ČAJCOVSKIJ, B. A.
   See: TCHAIKOVSKY, B. A.

*CALABRINI, Pietro   Italy   1897
   REM

CALABRO, Louis   USA   1926
   AS66, DN72, PCM, PC71, X66

CALACE, Enzo IMD		1890	1961
CALBI, Otello LMD	Italy	1917	
CALCAÑO, José Antonio CA14	Venezuela	1900	
CALDWELL, Mary E. PCM, PC71	USA	1909	
CALKER, Darrell W. AS66	USA	1905	1964
CALLAWAY, Frank AMM	Australia	1919	New Zealand
*CALMEL, Roger DDM	France	1921	
CALONNE, Jacques IMD, X67	Belgium	1930	
*CALTABIANO, Sebastiano LMD, REM, WI69	Italy	1899	
CALUSIO, Ferruccio LMD, REM	Italy	1889	
CALVERT, Morley CCM, CCM71, X68	Canada	1928	
*CALVI, Gérard QQF, X65 Pseudonym of: KRETTLY, Grégoire	France	1922	
*CÁMARA, Juán Antonio IMD, REM	Cuba	1917	
CAMARGO GUARNIERI, Mozart DDM, REM	Brazil	1907	
CAMBISSA, Giorgio REM	Italy	1921	
CAMERON, Richard DN70, DN72	USA	1943	
CAMILLERI, Charles MCO, WI69, X67, X68	Canada	1931	Malta

CAMILUCCI, Guido   Italy   1912
  LMD, REM

CAMPBELL, Arthur   USA
  AA73

*CAMPBELL, Colin Macleod   Great Britain   1890   1953
  LMD, REM

*CAMPBELL-WATSON, Frank   USA   1898
  X64, X67

CAMPMANY, Montserrat   Spain   1901
  REM

CAMPO, Frank Philip   USA   1927
  DN72

CAMPOGALLIANI, Ettore   Italy   1903
  LMD, REM, X68

CAMPOS-PARSI, Hector   Puerto Rico   1922
  BB65, BB71, LMD, REM

*CAMPO y ZABELTA,
  Conrado del   Spain   1879   1953
  DDM, EVM, LMD, REM
  EVM: 1876-1953

CAMPS, Pompeyo   Argentina   1924
  BB71, X66

*CAMUSSI, Ezio   Italy   1887   1956
  BB71, LMD

*CANAL, Marguérite   France   1890
  DDM

CANBY, Edward Tatnall   USA   1912
  PCM, X64, X65, X66, X67, X68

CANINO, Bruno   Italy   1935
  LMD, X65, X68

CANNING, Thomas   USA   1911
  AA73, X66, X67, X68

*CANNON, Jack Philip   Great Britain   1929   France
  BB65, BB71, LMD, REM, WI69, X65, X66, X67

CANONICA, Pietro   Italy   1869   1959
  LMD, REM

*CANTELOUBE de MALARET,
  Marie-Joseph   France   1879   1957
    BB65, BB71, DMF, EMS, IMD, LMD, REM
    EMS: КАНТЕЛЎЬ да МАЛАРЕ́

CANTÓN, Edgardo   France   Argentina
  X67

*CANTRICK, Robert B.   USA   1917
  X65

*CAPDEVIELLE, Pierre   France   1906   1969
    BB71, DDM, DMF, DMF28, EVM, LMD, MEH, REM, X67

CAPE, Safford   USA   1906
  LMD, SML, X66

CAPOIANU, Dumitru   Rumania   1929
    EMS, RCL, X64, X65, X66, X68
    EMS: КАПОЯНУ

*CAPUANA, Franco   Italy   1894   1969
    BB71, LMD, REM, WI69, X68

*CARABELLA, Ezio   Italy   1891   1964
    EVM, IMD, LMD, X64

*CARBONARA, Gerard   USA   1886   1959
  AS66

CARDENAS, Flores Francisco   Mexico   1898
  MMX

*CARDEW, Cornelius   Great Britain   1936
    BB71, CME, IMD, IMD2, LMD, MNG, X64, X65, X66,
    X67, X68

CAREY, David   USA   1926
  AS66

*CAREY, Francis Clive Savill   Great Britain   1883   1968
    BB71, X67

*CARL, Robert   Germany   1902
  X68

*CARLID, Göte   Sweden   1920   1953
    CME, IMD2, SIM, SIMa, SWE, VTM

*CARLMAN, Gustaf   Sweden   1906
  SIMa

CARLOS, Walter J.   USA   1939
    X66, X68

*CARLSEN, Carsten   Norway   1892   1961
    CNO

*CARLSON, Bengt Ivar   Finland   1890   1953
    COF

*CARLSSON, Sune Gottfrid   Finland   1892
    KKO

*CARLSTEDT, Jan Axel   Sweden   1926
    BB71, CME, FST, IMD2, LMD, MEH, SIM, SIMa, SMT, SOW,
    SWE, TJU, VTM, X64, X67

*CARNEVALI, Vito   Italy   1888
    EVM, LMD, REM

*CARNEYRO, Claudio   Portugal   1895   1963
    BB65, BB71, CME, DDM, EVM, LMD, X65, X66

CARPENTER, Howard R.   USA
    X66

*CARPENTER, John Alden   USA   1876   1951
    AS66, DDM, EMS, EVM, LMD, MEH, PCM, REM, WTM, X68
    EMS: КА́РПЕНТЕР

*CARPI, Fiorenzo   Italy   1918
    EVM, LMD, REM

*CARPIO VALDÉS, Roberto   Peru   1900
    CA13, EVM, IMD, LMD

CARR, Albert Lee   USA   1929
    PCM

CARR, Arthur   USA   1908
    BB65, BB71, LMD, PC71

*CARR, Edwin James Nairn   New Zealand   1926
    WI69, X64

*CARR, Howard   Great Britain   1880
    EVM, LMD, REM

CARRA, Manuel   Spain
    CME, X65

CARRAZ, Pierre   Switzerland   1896   1964
    SCHW

CARREÑO, Inocente   Venezuela   1919
    CA14, BB71

*CARRILLO, Julián   Mexico   1875   1965
    BB71, DDM, EVM, LMD, MLA22/4, MMX, REM, X65, X67

*CARROLL, Walter   Great Britain   1869   1955
    BB65, BB71

*CARSE, Adam Ahn von   Great Britain   1878   1958
    BB65, BB71, DDM, EMS, EVM, LMD, REM, X65, X66, X67

CARSON, Philippe   France   1936

*CARSTE, Hans   Germany   1909   1971
    MLA28, WWG

*CARTAN, Jean Louis   France   1906   1932
    DDM, REM

*CARTER, Elliot Cook, Jr.   USA   1908
    BB65, BB71, CME, DDM, DN70, EMS, EVM, IMD, LMD, MEH,
    OCM, PAP, PCM, PC71, REM, WI69, WTM, X64, X65, X66,
    X67, X68
    EMS: КÁPTEP

*CARTER, Ernest Trow   USA   1866   1953
    EVM, LMD, REM

CARTER, Rosetta
    See: BURSEY, Rosetta

*CARVAJAL QUIROS, Armando   Chile   1893
    REM

CARVALHO, Dinora de   Brazil   1905
    IMD, LMD, REM

*CARVALHO, Eleazar de   Brazil   1915
    BB65, BB71, EVM, REM, X64, X65, X67
    EVM: 1912

*CARY, Tristram Ogilvie   Great Britain   1925
    WI69, X66, X67

*CASABONA, Francisco   Brazil   1894
    BB71

*CASADESUS, François Louis   France   1870   1954
    DMF, EVM, LMD, REM, SML
    EVM: 1870-1953

*CASADESUS, Marius Robert
  Max   France   1892   1972
    DDM, MLA29/4, QQF, REM, X68

*CASADESUS, Regina Patorni   France   1886
    LMD, REM

*CASADESUS, Robert Marcel   France   1899   1972
    BB71, CMF24, DDM, EMS, EVM, LMD, QQF, REM,
    X64, X65, X66, X67, X68
    EMS: КАЗАДЕЗЮС

CASAGRANDE, Alessandro   Italy   1922   1964
    LMD, REM, X64

*CASAL y CHAPÍ, Enrique   Spain   1909
    LMD, REM

CASALE, Guido Edmondo
  detto Primo   Italy   1904
    REM

CASALS, Enrique   Spain   1892
    REM

*CASALS, (Pau) Pablo   Spain   1876   1973
    AS66, BB65, BB71, DDM, EVM, LMD, QQF, REM, SML,
    X64, X65, X66, X67, X68

*CASANOVA, André   France   1919
    BB71, CME, CMF33, CMF39, DDM, EVM, LMD, REM,
    X65, X66

*CASANOVA VICUÑA, Juan   Chile   1893
    EVM, REM

CASANOVAS, José   Spain   1924
    CME

*CASAVOLA, Franco   Italy   1892   1955
    EVM, REM
    REM: 1891-1955

CASCARINO, Romeo   USA   1922
    AS66, IMD, PCM

CASE, James H.   USA   1932
    PCM, X64

CASE, John Carol   Great Britain   1923
    WI69

*CASHMORE, Donald Joseph   Great Britain   1926
    WI69, X64

CASINÈRE, Yves de la
    See: LA CASINIERE

CASS, Peter   Canada
    KEY

*CASSADÓ, Gaspar   Spain   1897   1966
    BB71, DDM, EMS, IMD, LMD, X65, X66, X67, X68
    EMS: КАСАДО

*CASSELS-BROWN, Alastair
    Kennedy   USA   1927   Great Britain
    WI69, X65

CASSUTO, Alvaro Leon   Portugal   1937
    CME, IMD, X64

*CASTAGNONE, Ricardo   Italy   1906
    EVM, LMD, REM

CASTALDO, Joseph F.   USA   1927
    AS66, BB71, EL:4, PCM, X67

*CASTAÑEDA, José   Guatemala   1898
    REM

CASTELLANOS, Evencio   Venezuela   1915
    CA14

CASTELLANOS-YUMAR, Gonzalo Venezuela   1926
    CA14

*CASTELNUOVO-TEDESCO,
    Mario   USA   1895   1968
    AS66, BB65, BB71, DDM, EMS, EVM, IMD,   Italy
    LMD, MEH, MJM, REM, SML, WTM, X64, X65, X66, X67, X68
    EMS: КАСТЕЛЬНУОВО-ТЕДЕСКО

*CASTÉRA d'AVEZAC, René de   France   1873   1955
    BB65, BB71, DDM, DMF, EVM, LMD, REM

*CASTÉRÈDE, Jacques   France   1926
    DDM, LMD, REM, X68

*CASTIGLIONI, Niccolò   Italy   1932
    BB65, BB71, CME, DDM, IMD, IMD2, LMD, MEH, PAP, REM,
    TSC, X64, X65, X66, X67, X68

CASTILLO, Manuel   Spain   1930
    CME, DDM, X65, X68

*CASTILLO, Ricardo   Guatemala   1894
  LMD, REM

*CASTRO, José Maria   Argentina   1892   1964
  BB65, BB71, CA11, EVM, LMD, REM, X64, X65

*CASTRO, Juan José   Argentina   1895   1968
  BB65, BB71, DDM, EMS, EVM, IMD, LMD, MEH, MLA25/4,
  REM, X65, X66, X67, X68
  EMS: КÁСТРО

*CASTRO, Sergio Federico de   Argentina   1922
  IMD, REM

*CASTRO, Washington   Argentina   1909
  LMD, REM, X64, X66, X67

*CATELINET, Philip Bramwell   France   1910
  IMD

CATTOLICA, Gilfredo   Italy   1882   1962
  LMD, REM

*CATTOZZO, Nino   Italy   1886   1961
  LMD, REM

*CATURLA, Alejandro García   Cuba   1906   1940
  REM, X65

*CAZDEN, Norman   USA   1914
  BB71, CA15, DAS, EVM, IMD, LMD, PCM, PC71, REM, X65,
  X67, X68

CECCONI, M.   France   circa 1940
  EL:3

CECE, Alfredo   Italy   1915
  REM

CECE, Antonio   Italy   1907   1971
  IMD, MLA28/4, REM

CEELY, Robert Paige   USA   1930
  BB71, X67

*CELIBIDACHE, Sergiu   Rumania   1912
  EVM, LMD, REM, X64, X65, X66, X67, X68

*CELIS, Frits Lode   Belgium   1929
  WI69

CELLA, Theodore   USA   1897   1960
  EVM

*CELLIER, Alexandre Eugène   France   1883   1968
    DDM, DMF, LMD, REM, X65

CENSI, Carlo   Italy   1881   1957
    LMD, REM

*CENTEMERI, Gian Luigi   Italy   1903
    LMD, REM

CERCÓS, José   Spain
    CME

*CEREMUGA, Josef   Czechoslovakia 1930
    BB65, BB71, CCZ, IMD2, LMD, MEH

ČEREPNIN
    See: TCHEREPNIN

*CERHA, Friedrich   Austria   1926
    BB65, BB71, CME, HET13, IMD, IMD2, LMD, MNG, X64,
    X65, X66, X68

*ČERNIK, Josef   Czechoslovakia 1880
    CCZ, X64, X67

ČERNIK, Vilem   Czechoslovakia 1909
    CCZ

CERVETTI, Sergio   Uruguay   1940
    CA17, QLA, X66

*CESANA, Otto   USA   1899   Italy
    AS66

CESI, Napoleone   Italy   1867   1961
    LMD, REM

CEZAR, Corneliu   Rumania   1937
    RCL, X65, X67

CFASMAN, Alexander
    Naumovic   USSR   1906
    MEH

CHAČATURIAN, A. L.
    See: KHATCHATURIAN, A. I.

CHADABE, Joel A.   USA
    ASUC, X68

*CHAGRIN, Francis   Great Britain 1905   1972
    EVM, WI69, X65, X66, X67, X68   Rumania

*CHAILLEY, Jacques   France   1910
   BB65, BB71, CMF16, CMF20, CMF39, DDM, DMF, EMS, EVM,
   IMD2, LMD, QQF, REM, WI69, X64, X65, X66, X67, X68
   EMS: ШАЙЕ

*CHAILLY, Luciano   Italy   1920
   BB65, BB71, DDM, EL:1, IMD, LMD, REM, X66, X67, X68

*CHAIX, Charles   Switzerland   1885   France
   DDM, EVM, LMD, REM, SCHW, WWS

*CHAJES, Julius   USA   1910   Poland
   AS66, BB71, DN70, X68

CHALABALA, Zdeněk   Czechoslovakia   1899   1962
   LMD, SML

*CHALLAN, Henri   France   1910
   DDM, EVM, REM
   EVM: 1907

CHALLAN, René   France   1910
   DDM

CHALLIS, Philip   Great Britain
   WI69

CHAMASS-KYROU, Mireille   France

*CHAMBERLAND, Albert   Canada   1886
   CCM

CHAMBERS, Joe   USA
   X67

CHAMBERS, Stephen   USA
   X67

*CHAMPAGNE, Claude   Canada   1891   1965
   BB71, CCM, CVM, DDM, EVM, KEY, LMD, MCO, MCO68,
   MCO71, MLA23/4, NLC, TFB, X68

CHANCE, John Barnes   USA   1932
   DN72

*CHANDLER, Mary   Great Britain   circa
   X67, X68   1915

*CHANLER, Theodore Ward   USA   1902   1961
   BB65, BB71, IMD, LMD, PCM, REM

*CHAPMAN, Joyce   Great Britain   1909
   WI69, X66

CHAPMAN, Roger E.   USA   1916
 ASUC, IMD, PCM

CHAPORINE, Juri A.
 See: SHAPORIN, Yuri A.

CHAPPLE, Brian   Great Britain
 X67, X68

CHAPUIS, Jacques   Switzerland 1926
 SCHW, X68

CHARKOVSKY, Willis USA   1918
 AS66, LCI

CHARLOFF, Aaron   Israel   1941 Canada
 WWI

CHARPENTIER, Gabriel Canada   1925
 CCM, EVM, NLC

*CHARPENTIER, Gustave France 1860 1956
 DDM, DMF, EMS, LMD, MEH, REM, SML, X66, X68
 EMS: ШАРПАНТЬЕ

CHARPENTIER, Jacques France   1933
 BB71, CMF30, CMF40, DDM, X68

*CHARPENTIER, Raymond France 1880 1960
 BB65, BB71, EVM, LMD, REM
 EVM: CHARPENTIER, Raynard

CHARPENTIER de CASTRO,
 Eduardo   Panama   1927
 CA17

*CHASINS, Abram   USA   1903
 AA73, AS66, BB65, BB71, EVM, LMD, REM, WI69, X64, X65,
 X66, X67, X68

CHÂTELAIN, Ami   Switzerland 1903
 SCHW, X65, X66, X67

CHATSCHATURJAN, A. I.
 See: KHATCHATURIAN, A. I.

CHAUN, František   Czechoslovakia 1921
 IMD2, MNP69/4, MNP70/1, MNP71/3, MNP72/6, X64

*CHAVARRI, Eduardo Lopez Spain   1871 1970
 BB71, EVM, LMD, REM
 LMD: CHAVARRI LOPEZ, Eduardo
 BB71: 1871 EVM, LMD and REM: 1875

*CHÁVEZ, Carlos   Mexico   1899
    AS66, BB65, BB71, DDM, EMS, IMD, LMD, MEH, MMX,
    REM, WTM, X64, X65, X66, X67, X68
    EMS: ЧÁБЕС

CHAYKOVSKY, B. A.
    See: TCHAIKOVSKY, B. A.

CHAYNES, Charles   France   1925
    CMF38, DDM, QQF, X68

CHEETHAM, John   USA   1939
    PCM

*CHEMIN-PETIT, Hans Helmut   Germany   1902
    DDM, EVM, IMD, LMD, REM, SML

CHENAUX, Antoine   Switzerland   1899
    SCHW

CHENNEVIERE, Daniel de
    See: RUDHYAR, Dane

*CHENOWETH, Wilbur Rossiter   USA   1899
    AS66, BB65, BB71, PCM, PC71, WI69

*CHERBULIEZ, Antoine-Elisée
    Adolphe   Switzerland   1888   1964
    BB65, DDM, LMD, REM, X64, X65, X66

CHERNEY, Brian   Canada
    CCM71, CVMa, KEY, MCO71

CHESHMEDZHIEV, Iosif
    Evtimov   Bulgaria   1890   1964
    BMK
    BMK: ЧЕШМЕДЖИЕВ

*CHESLOCK, Louis   USA   1899   Great Britain
    DAS, EVM, LMD, WI69

*CHEVREUILLE, Raymond Jean
    Fellcien   Belgium   1901
    CBC, CME, DDM, EVM, IMD, IMD2, LMD, REM, X66

CHIARAMELLO, Giancarlo   Italy   1939
    LMD, REM

CHIARI, Giuseppe   Italy   1926
    BB71, IMD2

CHIDESTER, Lawrence William   USA   1906
    DAS, WI69, X67

*CHIGI SARACINI, Guido   Italy   1880   1965
   MLA22/4, X67

CHIHARA, Paul Seiko   USA   1938
   BB71, PCM, PC71, X64, X68

CHILDS, Robert Barney   USA   1926
   AA73, ASUC, BB71, BCL, IMD2, PCM, PC71, X64, X65, X66,
   X67, X68

CHILF, Nicolae   Rumania   1905
   RCL

*CHIRESCU, Ioan D.   Rumania   1889
   EMS, EVM, LMD, MEH, RCL, REM, SML, X64, X65
   EMS: КИРÉСКУ

CHIRIAC, Mircea   Rumania   1919
   LMD, MEH, RCL, SML, X64, X66
   LMD: KIRIAC

CHIRICO, Andrea de
   See: SAVINIO, Alberto

CHISHKO, Oles Aleksandr
  Semenovich   USSR   1895
   EMS, PPU69/2, X65
   EMS: ЧИШКÓ

*CHISHOLM, Erik   Union of   1904   1965
   BB65, BB71, DDM, EVM,   South Africa   Scotland
   LMD, MLA22/4, REM, WI69, X65, X67

*CHLUBNA, Osvald   Czechoslovakia 1893   1971
   CCZ, CME, EVM, IMD, IMD2, MEH, MLA29/4, REM, X65,
   X68

CHOPIN, Henri   France   1922

CHORBAJIAN, John   USA   1936
   BB71

CHOSTAKOVITCH, D. D.
   See: SHOSTAKOVICH, D. D.

*CHOTEM, Neil   Canada   1921
   X68

*CHOU, Wen-chung   USA   1923   China
   ASUC, BB65, BB71, CA15, IMD, IMD2, PCM, PC71, X64,
   X65, X66, X67, X68

CHRENNIKOW, T. N.
See: KHRENNIKOV, T. N.

*CHRIST, Jakob   Germany   1895
X65

*CHRISTENSEN, Bernhard   Denmark   1906
IMD, VTM, X68

*CHRISTIANSEN, Christian   Denmark   1884 1955
VTM

*CHRISTIANSEN, Fredrik
Melius   USA   1871 1955
EVM, X64, X66   Norway

CHRISTIANSEN, Henning   Denmark   1932
VTM, X66, X67, X68

CHRISTIANSEN, Larry A.   USA   1941
ASUC, CAP, PCM, X68

*CHRISTOPHER, Cyril Stanley Great Britain 1897
EVM, WI69, X68

CHRISTOU, Yannis   Greece   1926 1970
BB65, BB71, CME, EL:1, EL:2, EL:4, LMD,   Egypt
MLA27/4, PAP, X65, X67
LMD: KHRISTU

CHRISTOV, Dimiter   Bulgaria   1933
BB65, BB71, X68

CHTOGARENKO, A. I.
See: SHTOGARENKO, A. Y.

CHUDACOFF, Edward M.   USA
ASUC

CHUGAEV, Aleksandr
Georgovich   USSR   1924
EMS, X65, X68
EMS: ЧУГАЕВ

*CHULAKI, Mikhail Ivanovich USSR   1908
EMS, PPU, PPU69/2, PPU69/3, X64, X66, X68
EMS: ЧУЛАКИ   Also see: TCHULAKI

*CHURKIN, Nikolay
Nikolayevich   USSR   1869 1965
X64, X65

CIAMAGA, Gustav   Canada
    ASUC

CICOGNA, Giovanni Ascanio   Italy   1883   1951
    REM

*CICOGNINI, Alessandro   Italy   1906
    LMD, REM

*CIGLIČ, Zvonimir   Yugoslavia   1921
    IMD, KMJ, X66, X67

*CIKKER, Ján   Czechoslovakia   1911
    BB65, BB71, CCZ, DDM, EMS, EVM, IMD, LMD, MEH,
    MNP65/5, MNP66/5, MNP67/1, MNP72/6, REM, SML, X64,
    X65, X66, X67, ZE69/1, ZE69/3, ZE70/1, ZE70/2, ZE70/3,
    ZE71/2, ZE71/3, ZE72/1
    EMS: ЦИККЕР

CIKOCKI, Jevgenij Karlovic   USSR   1893
    MEH

*CILÈA, Francesco   Italy   1866   1950
    BB65, BB71, DDM, EMS, EVM, IMD, LMD, REM, SML, X66,
    X67, X68
    EMS: ЧИЛЕА

CILENŠEK, Johann   Germany   1913
    EMS, IMD, MEH, SML, X64, X68
    EMS: ЦИЛЕНШЕК

CIMARA, Pietro   Italy   1887   1967
    LMD, X68

*CIORTEA, Tudor   Rumania   1903
    BB65, BB71, CME, IMD, LMD, RCL, REM, SML, X64, X65

*CIPRA, Milo   Yugoslavia   1906
    CME, HCM, IMD, KMJ, LMD, REM, X65, X66, X67, X68

*CIRY, Michel   France   1919
    DDM, EVM, IMD, QQF, REM

ČIŠKO, O. S.
    See: TCHISHKO, O. S.

*CITKOWITZ, Israel   USA   1909   Russia
    EVM, IMD, LMD, PCM, REM, X64

CITROEN, Henrik Jacobus   Netherlands   1905
    EVM

CIUCIURA, Leoncjusz   Poland   1931
   PKW, X66, X67, X68

*CIVIL, Alan   Great Britain   1929
   WI69

*CLAFLIN, Avery   USA   1898
   BB71, EMV, PCM

*CLAPP, Philip Greeley   USA   1888   1954
   EVM, LMD, REM

*CLARE, Derek John   Great Britain   1923
   WI69

*CLARK, Florence Durell   Canada   1891   USA
   KEY, X64

CLARK, Robert Keyes   1925
   WAN

*CLARKE, Douglas   Canada   1893   Great Britain
   EVM

CLARKE, F. R. C.   Canada
   KEY, NLC, NLCa

*CLARKE, Henry Leland   USA   1907
   ASUC, BB65, BB71, DAS, PCM, PC71, X64, X65, X66,
   X67, X68

*CLARKE, Rebecca   Great Britain   1886
   AS66, BB71, EVM, LMD, REM, X66

CLAUBERG, Claus   Germany   1890   1963
   SML

*CLAUSEN, Karl Søren   Denmark   1904
   VTM

CLAUSETTI, Pietro   Italy   1904   1963
   REM

CLAYTON, Herbert Kenneth   Germany   1920

*CLEEVE, Stewart Montagu   Great Britain   circa
   X66   1922

*CLEMENS, Johannes   Germany   1893
   LMD

*CLEMENTI, Aldo   Italy   1925
   BB65, BB71, CME, IMD, IMD2, LMD, REM, TSC, X64, X67

CLEMENTS, Peter J.   Canada
   CCM71, MCO68, NLCa, X68

*CLEVE, Halfdan   Norway   1879   1951
   BB71, CNO, EVM, LMD, REM, VTM

*CLIFFORD, Hubert John   Great Britain 1904   1959
   AMM, EVM, LMD, REM   Australia

*CLIFTON, Chamlers Dancey USA   1889   1966
   BB71, EVM, MLA23/4

*CLIQUET-PLEYEL, Henri   France   1894   1963
   DDM, EVM, LMD

*CLOÉREC, René   France   1911
   QQF

*CLOKEY, Joseph Waddell   USA   1890   1960
   BB65, BB71, PCM

CLOSTRE, Adrienne   France   1921
   DDM

CLOUGH, John L.   USA
   ASUC

*CLOUGH-LEIGHTER, Henry   USA   1874   1956
   BB65, BB71

CLOUTIER, Jean-Marie   Canada   1924
   CCM

CLUYTENS, André   Belgium   1905   1967
   BB71, CME, EMS, EVM, SML, VMB67/2, X65, X67, X68
   EMS: КЛЮИТЕНС

*CLUZEAU-MORTET, Luis   Uruguay   1889   1957
   BB71, CA14, IMD, REM

CMIRAL, Adolf   Czechoslovakia 1882   1963
   CCZ

*COATES, Albert   Great Britain 1882   1953
   BB65, BB71, EMS, LMD, REM   Russia
   EMS: КОУТС

*COATES, Erik   Great Britain 1886   1957
   BB65, BB71, EVM, LMD, X64

*COATES, Henry John   Great Britain 1880 1963
 X64

COBBING, Bob   Great Britain 1920

*COCHEREAU, Pierre Charles France   1924
 DDM, WI69, X66, X67

*COCHRANE, William Cecil
 Macvicar   Great Britain 1914
 WI69

*COCKSHOTT, Gerald Wilfred Great Britain 1915
 BB65, BB71, LMD, WI69, X65, X66

COCQ, Rosine de   Netherlands 1891
 EVM

*COELHO, Ruy   Portugal 1892
 CME, DDM, EVM, IMD, LMD, REM, X65
 EVM: 1891

*COEUROY, André   France   1891
 LMD, REM

COGAN, Robert David USA   1930
 ASUC, BB71, X65, X68

COGNI, Giulio   Italy   1908
 LMD, REM

*COHEN, David   USA   1927
 ASUC, AS66, PCM, PC71, X64, X65, X66, X68

COHEN, Mickey   USA   1952
 BS70

COHEN, Shimon   Israel   1937
 ACU

*COHEN, Sol B.   USA   1891
 AS66

COHEN-SOLAL, Robert France
 X68

*COHN, Arthur   USA   1910
 AA73, AS66, BB65, BB71, EVM, LMD, PCM, REM, X64,
 X66, X67, X68

COHN, Gregory P.   USA   1919
 AS66

COHN, James   USA   1928
    AS66, PCM

*COKE, Roger Sacheverell   Great Britain   1912   1972
    LMD, REM, WI69

COKER, Wilson   USA   1928
    ASUC, AS66, BB65, BB71, CA9, LMD, PCM, PC71

*COLACICCHI, Luigi   Italy   1900
    LMD, REM

COLAÇO OSORIO-SWAAB,
   Reine   Netherlands   1889
    EMV

COLDING JØRGENSEN, Henrik   Denmark
    X66
    X66: JØRGENSEN, Henrik Colding

*COLE, Hugo   Great Britain   1917
    IMD, WI69, X65, X66, X67, X68

*COLE, Rossetter Gleason   USA   1866   1952
    EVM

*COLE, Ulric   USA   1905
    AS66, EVM, LMD, PCM, REM

COLEMAN, Randolph   USA
    ASUC

*COLERIDGE-TAYLOR, Avril   England   1903
    LMD, WI69

COLGRASS, Michael Charles   USA   1932
    BB71, PC71, X65, X66, X67, X68

*ČOLIĆ, Dragutin   Yugoslavia   1907
    KMJ, X67

*COLIN, Georges Emile   Belgium   1921
    WI69

*COLLET, Henri   France   1885   1951
    DDM, EVM, LMD, REM

*COLLIN, André   Belgium   1898
    EVM

*COLLINGWOOD, Arthur   Canada   1880   1952
    EVM   Great Britain

*COLLINGWOOD, Lawrance
  Arthur   Great Britain   1887
  EVM, LMD, REM, X67

*COLLINS, Anthony Vincent
  Benedictus   Great Britain   1893   1963
  EVM, X64, X67

*COLLINS, Charles Frederick   Great Britain   1916
  WI69

*COLLINSON, Francis   Great Britain   circa
  WI69, X66, X67   1915

*COLLOT, Jean   Belgium   1907
  EVM

COLLUM, Herbert   Germany   1914
  EVM, X68

COMAN, Nicolae   Rumania   1936
  RCL

COMES, Liviu   Rumania   1918
  RCL, X65, X68

COMISEL, Florin   Rumania   1922
  RCL

*COMMETTE, Éduard   France   1883   1967
  DDM, X67, X68

COMPANY, Alvaro   Italy   1931
  LMD

COMPARETTI, Ermanno F.   USA   1909 Italy
  DAS

*CONE, Edward Toner   USA   1917
  ASUC, LMD, PCM, REM, WI69, X64, X65, X66, X67, X68

*CONFALONIERI, Giulio   Italy   1896 1972
  EVM, LMD, MLA29/4

CONNOLLY, Justin Riveagh   Great Britain   1933
  BB71, WI69, X66, X67, X68

*CONSTANT, Marius   France   1925 Rumania
  CMF8, CMF20, CMF39, DDM, EVM, IMD, LMD, QQF, REM,
  X65, X67, X68

*CONSTANTINESCO, Jean   Rumania   1908
  LMD, REM

CONSTANTINESCU, Constantin Rumania 1903
RCL

CONSTANTINESCU, Dan Rumania 1931
RCL, X65, X68

CONSTANTINESCU, Domnica Rumania 1930
RCL

CONSTANTINESCU, Paul Rumania 1909 1963
BB65, BB71, CME, DDM, EMS, EVM, IMD, LMD, MEH, RCL,
REM, SML, X64, X65, X67, X68
EMS: КОНСТАНТИНЕСКУ

CONSTANTINIDES, (Dinos)
Constantine Demetrios USA
AA73, X68

CONSTANTINIDIS, Yannis Greece

*CONTILLI, Gino Italy 1907
IMD, LMD, REM

*CONTRERAS, Salvador Mexico 1912
EVM, REM

CONUS, Sergey USA 1902 Russia
BB65, BB71

*COOK, Edgar Tom Great Britain 1880 1953
EVM

COOK, John Canada 1918 England
MCO, NLC

COOK, Richard G. USA
AA73

*COOKE, Arnold Atkinson Great Britain 1906
BB71, DDM, EVM, LMD, REM, WI69, X64, X66, X67, X68

COOLEY, Carlton USA 1898
PCM

COOPER, David S. USA 1922
PCM, X65, X67

*COOPER, Irvin Canada 1900 England
X64, X66, X68

COOPER, John Craig USA 1925
AS66

COOPER, Paul   USA   1929
   AA73, ASUC, X66, X67, X68

COOPER, Rose Marie   USA
   AA73

*COOPER, Walter Thomas
   Gaze   Great Britain   1895
   WI69

COPE, David H.   USA   1941
   CAP, DN70, DN72

*COPLAND, Aaron   USA   1900
   AA73, AS66, BB65, BB71, DDM, DN70, EMS, EVM, IMD,
   IMD2, LMD, MEH, PCM, PC71, REM, SML, TSC, WI69,
   WTM, X64, X65, X66, X67, X68
   EMS: КОПЛЕНД

*COPLEY, Ian Alfred   Great Britain   1926
   WI69, X64, X66, X68

*COPPOLA, Piero   Switzerland   1888   1971
   EVM, IMD, LMD, MM71, SCHW   Italy

*CORDERO, Roque   USA   1917   Panama
   AA73, BB65, BB71, CA8, DDM, LMD, QLA, X64, X65, X66,
   X68

CORDONE, Mario   Italy   1898
   LMD, REM

CORGHI, Azio   Italy   1937
   LMD

CORIA, Miguel Angel   Spain   circa 1937
   CME, X67

CORIGLIANO, John   USA   1938
   AS66, BB71, CA9, LMD, PCM, X65, X68

CORINA, John A.   USA
   AA73, X66

CORNEA-IONESCU, Alma Rumania   1900
   RCL

CORNEJO, José Maria   Mexico   1875
   MMX

*CORNELL, Klaus   Switzerland   1932
   Formerly: MEIER

CORNER, Philip   USA   1933
   BB71, IMD

*CORNIOT, René   France   1901
   QQF

*CORRÊA de OLIVEIRA,
   Fernando   Portugal   1921
   X64, X66

CORRÊA de OLIVEIRA, Willy   Brazil
   FBC, X68

*CORTES, Ramiro   USA   1933
   BB65, BB71, LMD, PCM, X64

*CORTESE, Luigi   Italy   1899
   DDM, EVM, IMD, LMD, REM, WI69

CORTI, Mario   Italy   1882 1957
   LMD

*CORTI COLLEONI, Mario
   Enrico   Italy   1914
   WI69

CORTOPASSI, Domenico   Italy   1877 1962
   LMD, REM

CORUM, Alfred   Great Britain 1890
   WI69

COSACCHI, Stephan   1903
   IMD

COSCIA, (Silvio) Sylvius C.   USA   1899 Italy
   AS66, X68

COSMA, Edgar   Hungary   1925
   WI69

*COSME, Luis   Brazil   1908
   FBC, IMD, LMD, REM

COSMO, Nicola   Italy   1918
   LMD, X67

*COSSART, Leland A.   Switzerland 1877 Madeira
   EVM

*COSSETTO, Emil   Yugoslavia 1918
   BB65, BB71, HCM, KMJ, LMD, X67

COSTA, Alessandro Italy 1857 1953
 DDM, LMD, REM

*COSTA, Luiz Portugal 1879 1960
 DDM, EVM, LMD

COSTA, Nicola Italy 1879 1963
 LMD

COSTARELLI, Nicola Italy 1911
 REM

COSTINESCU, Gheorghe Rumania 1934
 RCL, X64, X65, X66, X68

COSTY, René Belgium 1917
 EVM

*COTAPOS BAEZA, Acario Chile 1889 1969
 BB71, EVM, LMD, REM

COULTER, Fred USA
 ASUC

*COULTHARD, Adams Jean Canada 1908
 BB65, BB71, CCM, CCM71, CVM, CVMa, KEY, LMD, MCO,
 MCO68, MCO71, NLC, NLCa, TFB, X68

COUR, Niels Jørgen la Denmark 1944
 DMTsp, VTM, X68

COUSINS, M. Thomas USA 1914
 AS66

COUTTS, George Canada
 CVM, KEY, NLC

COWDEROY, Peter Sutherland Great Britain 1918
 WI69

*COWELL, Henry Dixon USA 1897 1965
 BB65, BB71, DDM, DN72, EMS, EVM, IMD, IMD2, LMD,
 MEH, MLA22/4, MZW, PCM, PC71, REM, WTM, X64,
 X65, X66, X67, X68
 EMS: КОУЭЛ

COWELL, John Rowland USA
 AA73, X67, X68

*COWLES, Cecil Marion USA 1898 1968
 BB71

*COWLES, Walter Ruel BB65, BB71	USA	1881	1959
*COX, David Vassall X67, X68	Great Britain	1916	
*COX, Harry EMV, REM	Belgium	1923	Netherlands
*COX, Noel Frederick WI69	Great Britain	1917	
COYNER, Lou DN72	USA	1931	
COZZELLA, Damiano FBC, X68	Brazil	1930	
CRĂCIUNESCU, Dumitru RCL	Rumania	1905	1967
CRANE, Robert PCM, X64, X68	USA	1919	
CRANMER, Damian St. George WI69	Great Britain	1943	
*CRANMER, Phillip WI69	Great Britain	1918	
*CRAWFORD, Robert Caldwell EVM, REM, WI69, X67	Great Britain	1925	1967 Scotland
*CRAWFORD, Robert M. AS66, BB65, BB71	USA	1899	1961 Canada
CRAWFORD, Thomas J. KEY	Canada		
*CRAWFORD-SEEGER, Ruth Porter EVM, IMD, PCM, REM	USA	1901	1953
*CREED, John Edward Hodgson WI69, X64	Great Britain	1904	
CRÉMIER, Jean Eddie QQF	France	1926	

*CRESTON, Paul   USA   1906
    AS66, BB65, BB71, DDM, EMS, EVM, IMD, LMD, MEH,
    PCM, PC71, REM, WI69, WTM, X64, X66, X67, X68
    Formerly: GUTTOVEGGIO, Joseph
    EMS: КРЕСТОН

CRISAN, Ion   Rumania   1913
    RCL

*CRIST, Bainbridge   USA   1883   1969
    AS66, BB71, EVM, LMD, PCM, PC71, REM, WI69, X64, X65,
    X66, X67

CROCKETT, Donald   USA   1951
    BS72

CROLEY, Randell   USA
    X68

*CRONER de VASCONCELOS,
    Jorge   Portugal   1910
    LMD

CROSS, Lowell Merlin   Canada   1938   USA
    BB71, BCL, X67, X68

CROSS, Ronald   USA   1929
    BB65, BB71, X66, X68

CROSSE, Gordon   Great Britain 1937
    OCM, WI69, X64, X65, X66, X67, X68

*CROSSLEY-HOLLAND, Peter
    Charles   Great Britain 1916
    LMD, WI69, X64, X67, X68

*CRUFT, Adrian Francis   Great Britain 1921
    MNP64/4, WI69, X64, X66, X67, X68

CRUMB, George Henry   USA   1929
    ASUC, BB71, CA15, DN72, EL:4, X65, X66, X67, X68

CRUMP, Peter Norman   Great Britain 1928
    WI69, X67

*CRUSIUS, Otto E.   Germany   1892
    EVM, LMD, WWG

*CRUZ, Ivo   Portugal   1901   Brazil
    CME, DDM, EVM, IMD, LMD, REM, X65

CRVČANIN, Milivoje   Yugoslavia 1892
 KMJ

CRZELLITZER, Franz   Israel   1905 Germany
 ACU

CSIKI, Boldiszár   Rumania 1937
 RCL

*CUCLIN, Dimitrie   Rumania 1885
 BB71, CME, EMS, EVM, LMD, MEH, RCL, REM, SML
 EMS: КУКЛИН

*CUCU, Georghe   Rumania 1882 1932
 EVM, RCL

CULLEN, David   Great Britain

CULLEN, Gavin Windsor USA   1946
 DN70

*CUMBERWORTH, Starling A. USA   1915
 BB65, BB71, LMD, PC71, X65, X66

*CUMMING, Richard   USA   1928 China
 AS66, PCM, PC71, X64, X65

*CUNDELL, Edric   Great Britain 1893 1961
 EVM, LMD, REM

CUNEO, Francesco Angelo Italy   1870 1956
 LMD

CUNNINGHAM, Arthur USA   1928
 AS66

CUNNINGHAM, Michael G. USA   1937
 AA73, CAP

CUPPETT, Charles Harold USA   1894 Chile
 AS66

CURCI, Alberto   Italy   1886 1973
 LMD, REM

CURRAN, Alvin   USA   1938
 IMD2, PCM, X68

*CURZON, Frederic Ernest Great Britain 1899 1973
 WI69, X67

*CUSENZA, Frank J.   USA   1899 Italy
 AS66

CUSTER, Arthur R.   USA   1923
    CA15, PC71, X67, X68

CUTEANU, Eugen   Rumania   1900   1968
    RCL, SML

CUVILLIER, Charles   France   1877   1955
    DMF, LMD

*CUYPERS, Hubert   Netherlands   1873
    LMD, REM

CVETKO, Ciril   Yugoslavia   1920
    KMJ

*CVETKO, Dragotin   Yugoslavia   1911
    DDM, EMS, KMJ, LMD, REM, X64, X65, X66, X67, X68
    EMS: ЦВЕТКО

CYR, Gordon   USA

*CZACZKES, Ludwig   Austria   1898
    X64, X66, X68

*CZERNIAWSKY, Cornelius   Poland   1888
    EVM

*CZERNIK, Willi   Germany   1901
    IMD

CZONKA, Paul   Austria   1905
    LMD, REM

CZOSNOWSKI, Sylwester   Poland   1908
    PKW

CZYZ, Henryk   Poland   1923
    MEH, PKW, WI69, X64, X65, X67, X68

*D'ABREU, Gerald Joseph   Great Britain   1916   India
    WI69, X64, X66

DABROWSKI, Florian   Poland   1913
    PKW, X64, X67

DACHWITZ, Kurt   Germany   1931
    SML, X67

DADÁK, Jaromír   Czechoslovakia
    MNP69/4, X68

DAGIROV, Nabi Sadykovich   USSR   1921
    PPU, X64

*DAHL, Ingolf   USA   1912 1970
 AS66, BB65, BB71, DN70, EVM, IMD, LMD,   Germany
 MLA27, PCM, REM, X64, X65, X66, X67, X68

*DAHMS, Walter   Italy   1887 Germany
 BB65, BB71, REM

DALBY, Martin   Great Britain 1942
 WI69, X65, X67, X68

*DALE, Kathleen Richards Great Britain 1895
 WI69, X68

DALE ROBERTS, Jeremy Great Britain 1934
 WI69

*DALEN, Hugo van   Netherlands 1888 1967
 X67

*D'ALESSANDRO, Raffaele Switzerland 1911 1959
 REM

DALLA LIBERA, Sandro Italy   1912
 LMD, X67, X68

DALLAM, Helen   USA
 AS66

*DALLAPICCOLA, Luigi Italy   1904
 BB71, CME, DDM, DMM, EMS, EVM, IMD, IMD2, LMD,
 MEH, MZW, PAP, SML, TCM, TSC, VNM, WI69, WTM,
 X65, X66, X67, X68
 EMS: ДАЛЛАПИЌКОЛА

DALLA VECCHIA, Wolfango Italy   1923
 LMD

*DALLEY-SCARLETT, Robert Australia 1890 1959
 AMM, BB65, BB71   Great Britain
 AMM: 1949

DALLIN, Leon   USA
 X66, X67, X68

DALLINGER, Fridolin   Austria
 X68

*DAMAIS, Émile   France   1906
 DDM, DMF, LMD, REM

*DAMASE, Jean-Michel France   1928
 BB65, BB71, CMF18, CMF39, DDM, DMF, EVM, LMD, QQF,
 REM, WI69, X64

DAMBOIS, Maurice   Belgium   1889   1969

*D'AMBROSI, Dante   Italy   1902   1965
  LMD, REM

D'AMBROSIO, Luigi   Italy   1885
  LMD

DAMDINSUREN, Beelgin   USSR   1918
  EMS
  EMS: ДАМДИСУРЭН

*DAMERINI, Adelmo   Italy   1880
  EVM, IMD, REM, X64, X65

D'AMICO, Fedele   Italy   1912
  LMD

*DAMM, Sixten E.   Sweden   1899
  FST, KSV, SIM, SIMa

*DAMROSCH, Walter Johannes   USA   1862   1950
  AS66, BB71, EMS, EVM, LMD, REM   Germany
  EMS: ДАМРОШ

*DAN, Ikuma   Japan   1924
  BB71, REM, X65

*DANBURG, Russell L.   USA   1909
  DN70

DANDARA, Liviu   Rumania   1933
  RCL

*DANDELOT, Georges   France   1895   1964
  DDM, DMF, EVM, LMD, QQF, REM, WI69, X64

*DANEAU, Suzanne   Belgium   1901
  EVM, LMD, REM

DANEV, Danilo   Yugoslavia   1915
  HCM

DANGA, Gheorghe   Rumania   1905-1959
  RCL

D'ANGELO, Nicholas Vincent   USA   1929
  DN72

*DANIEL-LESUR, Jean Yves   France   1908
  CMF7, CMF20, CMF39, DDM, LMD, QQF, REM, WI69

DANIELS, Arthur   USA
   ASUC

*DANIELS, Florence Nellie   Great Britain   1904
   WI69

*DANIELS, Mabel Wheeler   USA   1878 1971
   AS66, BB71, LMD, PCM, REM, X65, X66, X67

DANKER, Stephen   USA   1944
   PC71

*DANKEVICH, Konstantin
  Fiodorovich   USSR   1905
   BB65, BB71, EMS, LMD, MEH, PPU, REM, SML, X66
   EMS: ДАНЬКЕ́ВИЧ

*DANON, Oskar   Yugoslavia   1913
   EMS, EVM, KMJ, LMD, REM, X67
   EMS: ДАНОН

DA-OZ, Ram   Israel   1929   Germany
   ACU

DAPOGNY, James   USA
   ASUC

*DARKE, Harold Edwin   Great Britain   1888
   EVM, LMD, REM, X64, X66, X67, X68

*DARLOW, Denys   Great Britain   1921
   WI69, X64

*DARNTON, Philip Christian Great Britain   1905
   EVM, LMD, REM, WI69

DARVAS, Gabor   Hungary   1911
   CHC, IMD2, X68

DAUGHS, Eugene   USA
   CAP

*DAUS, Avraham   Israel   1902   Germany
   ACU, IMD, MM59, WWI

*DAUTREMER, Marcel   France   1906
   DDM, X64

*DAVELUY, Raymond   Canada   1926
   KEY, X67

*DAVENPORT GOERTZ,
  Gladys   Canada   1895   England
    CVM, NLC

DAVEY, Malcolm   Great Britain
    WI69

*DAVICO, Vincenzo   Italy   1889 1969
    BB71, DDM, EVM, IMD, LMD, MLA27,   Monaco
    REM, WI69

DAVID, Gyula   Hungary   1913
    BB65, BB71, CHC, CME, IMD, LMD, MEH, REM, SML, X68

*DAVID, Johann Nepomuk   Austria   1895
    BB65, BB71, CME, DDM, EL:1, EVM, IMD, IMD2, LMD,
    MEH, MZW, REM, SML, WWG, X64, X65, X66, X67, X68

*DAVID, José   France   1913
    BB71

*DAVID, Karl Heinrich   Switzerland   1884 1951
    EVM, IMD, LMD, REM, SCHW

*DAVID, Thomas Christian   Austria   1925
    IMD, IMD2, REM, X64, X65, X67

DAVID, Vincent   USA   1924
    AS66
    Formerly: DI BIASE, Edoardo J.

DAVIDOVSKY, Gregory
  Mihailovich   USSR   1866 1953
    EMS
    EMS: ДАВИДÓВСКИЙ

DAVIDOVSKY, Mario   Argentina   1934
    ASUC, BB65, BB71, REM, X64, X65, X66, X67, X68

DAVIDSON, Lyle   USA   1938
    PAP

DAVIES, Peter Maxwell   Great Britain 1934
    BB65, BB71, BCI, CME, DDM, IMD, IMD2, LMD, OCM, PAP,
    REM, X64, X65, X66, X67, X68
    DDM, LMD and REM: MAXWELL DAVIES, P.

DAVIES, Victor   Canada
    CCM71, CVMa, MCO71

DAVIS, Allan   USA   1922
    AS66

DAVIS, Jean Reynolds USA 1927
 AS66

*DAVIS, Katherine K. USA 1892
 AS66, PC71, X68

*DAVISON, Archibald Thompson USA 1883 1961
 BB65, BB71, X65

DAVY, Ruby Claudia Emily Australia 1883
 EVM

DAWES, Francis Edward
 (Frank) Great Britain 1910
 WI69, X64, X65, X68

*DAWSON, William Levi USA 1898
 PCM

DEAK, Czaba Sweden 1932 Hungary
 FST, SIMa, STS, SWE, VTM, X66, X68

DEAN, Mrs. B. H.
 See: HARKNESS, Rebekah West

DE ANGELIS, Arturo Italy 1879
 LMD

DE ANGELIS, Ruggero Italy 1896
 LMD

DE ANGELIS, Teofilo Italy 1866 1954
 LMD

DE ANGELIS-VALENTINI,
 Enrico Italy 1900
 LMD

DEBARO, Charlotte
 See: ROZMAN, Sarah

*DE BELLIS, Enzo Vincenzo Italy 1907
 LMD, REM, WI69

*DECADT, Jean Belgium 1914
 CBC

DEČI, Josip Yugoslavia 1904
 HCM

*DECKER, Franz-Paul Germany 1923
 X65

DE COLA, Felix　　　　　　USA　　　　　1910　Union of
　　AS66, X65, X67, X68　　　　　　　　　　　　South Africa

DE COURSEY, Ralph　　　　Canada　　　1918　USA
　　CCM

DECOUST, Michel　　　　　France　　　1936
　　BB71, X67

DECSÉNYI, János　　　　　Hungary　　　1927
　　CHC

DĚD, Jan　　　　　　　　Czechoslovakia
　　MNP69/4

*DEFAY, Jean Michel　　　France　　　1932
　　EVM, IMD, REM

DEFFNER, Clem　　　　　　USA　　　　　1914
　　LCI

*DEFOSSEZ, René　　　　　Belgium　　　1905
　　CBC, EVM, IMD, LMD, MEH, REM, WI69

*DEGEN, Helmuth　　　　　Germany　　　1911
　　DDM, EVM, IMD, LMD, MEH, REM, SML

DE GRANDIS, Renato　　　Italy　　　　1927
　　IMD, IMD2, LMD, X67
　　X67: GRANDIS, Renato de

*DEGUIDE, Richard　　　　Belgium　　　1909　1962
　　CBC, EVM

*DE HAAN, Stefan Johannes　Great Britain　1921　Germany
　　IMD, WI69

DEHNERT, Max　　　　　　Germany　　　1893
　　MEH, SML, X65, X68

*DEJONCKER, Theodore　　　Belgium　　　1894
　　EVM

DE JONG, Conrad　　　　　USA　　　　　1934
　　ASUC, BB71, PCM, PC71

*DE JONG, Marinus　　　　Belgium　　　1891　Netherlands
　　CBC, WI69

*DEKHTEREV, Vasili
　　Aleksandrovich　　　　USSR　　　　　1910
　　EMS, LMD, PPU, REM
　　EMS: ДЕХТЕРЁВ

DE KRUYF, Ton
  See: KRUYF, Ton de

*DELA, Maurice   Canada   1919
  BB65, BB71, CA11, CCM, CCM71, CVM, CVMa, KEY, LMD,
  MCO, MCO71, NLCa, TFB, X68

DELACHI, Paolo   Italy   1874 1957
  IMD, LMC, REM

*DELAGE, Maurice Charles   France   1879 1961
  BB65, BB71, DDM, DMF, LMD, REM, X65

*DELAMARTER, Eric   USA   1880 1953
  AS66, EVM, LMD, PCM, REM

DE LANEY, Charles   USA   1925
  AS66, X64, X67

*DELANEY, Robert Mills   USA   1903 1956
  EVM, IMD, LMD, PCM, PC71, REM

*DELANNOY, Marcel François
  Georges   France   1898 1962
  BB65, BB71, DDM, DMF, EMS, EVM, IMD, LMD, MEH, REM,
  SML, WI69
  EMS: ДЕЛАННУА

DELAPIERRE, André   Switzerland   1921
  SCHW

DE LAVA, Enrico   Italy   1867 1955
  LMD

DE LA VEGA, Aurelia
  See: VEGA y PALACIO, Aurelia de la

DEL CORONA, Rodolfo   Italy   1900
  LMD, REM

*DELDEN, Lex van   Netherlands 1919
  BB71, DDM, EVM, IMD, LMD, NED, REM, X64, X65, X66,
  X67, X68

DE LEEUW, Ton
  See: LEEUW, Ton de

*DELERUE, Georges   France   1925
  DDM, DMF28, DMF39, EVM, LMD, QQF, REM, X64, X65, X67

*DELGADILLO, Louis Abraham Nicaragua 1887 1955
  BB71, EVM, LMD, REM

D'ELIA, Antonio   Italy   1897   1958
    LMD

*DE LIMA y SINTIAGO, Emirto   Colombia   1893
    WI69

*DELLO JOIO, Norman Joseph   USA   1913
    AA73, ASUC, BB65, BB71, CA9, DDM, EVM, IMD, LMD,
    MEH, PCM, PC71, REM, WI69, WTM, X64, X65, X66,
    X67, X68
    DDM: JOIO, Norman dello

DELMAR, Dezso   USA   1891   Hungary
    AS66, BB65, BB71

DEL TREDICI, David   USA   1937
    BB71, PC71, X66, X68
    PC71: 1938

*DELVAUX, Albert   Belgium   1913
    CBC, WI69

*DELVINCOURT, Claude   France   1888   1954
    CME, CMF38, DDM, DMF, EMS, EVM, IMD, LMD, MEH,
    REM, SML, X68
    EMS: ДЕЛЬВЕНКУ́Р

DELYSSE, Jean
    See: ROESGEN-CHAMPION, Marguerite

DE MADINA, Francisco   USA   1907   Spain
    AS66

*DEMARQUEZ, Suzanne   France   1899   1965
    BB71, EVM, LMD, MLA22/4, X64, X65, X66

*DE MEESTER, Louis   Belgium   1904
    CBC

*DEMESSIEUX, Jeanne-Marie-
    Madeleine   France   1921   1968
    BB71, DDM, DMF, EVM, IMD, LMD, REM, WI69, X65, X67

DEMETAR, Ivan   Yugoslavia   1906
    KMJ

DEMIAN, Wilhelm Victor   Rumania   1910
    BB65, BB71, LMD, RCL, X68

DEMIERRE, François   Switzerland   1893
    SCHW

*DEMUTH, Norman Frank   Great Britain   1898   1968
    BB71, DDM, EVM, LMD, MLA25/4, REM, X64, X65, X67,
    X68

DENADAR, Dragoje   Yugoslavia   1930
    KMJ

DE NARDIS, Camillo   Italy   1857   1951
    LMD

*DENDRINO, Chenase   Rumania   1901
    BB65, BB71, RCL, X64

DE NINNO, Alfredo   Italy   1894
    LMD, REM

DENIS, Didier   France   1947
    BB71, X68

DENISOV, Edison Vasilievich   USSR   1929
    BB71, EMS, IMD2, LMD, MEH, PAP, X65, X66, X67, X68
    IMD2: DENNISSOW   PAP: DENISOV, Eddy
    EMS: ДЕНИСОВ

DENNINGTON, Arthur   Great Britain   1904
    WI69

DENNIS, Bryan   Great Britain
    X64, X65, X66, X67, X68

DENNIS, Robert   1933
    WAN

*DENT, Edward Joseph   Great Britain   1876   1957
    BB65, BB71, REM, X66, X68

DENTELLA, Pietro   Italy   1879
    LMD

DENYER, Frank   Great Britain   circa
    X68   1938

DENZA, Paolo   Italy   1894   1955
    LMD, REM

*DENZLER, Robert F.   Switzerland   1892   1972
    EVM, LMD, MLA29/4, REM, SCHW, WI69, WWS

DE PABLO, Luis
    See: PABLO, Luis de

*DEPRAZ, Raymond   France   1915
    EVM

DE PUE, Wallace Earl   USA   1932
    AA73, AS66, DN70, PCM, X65, X67, X68

*DÉRÉ, Jean   France   1886 1970
    BB71, EVM, LMD, REM

DERIVES, Jean
    See: Lacen, Jean Serge

*DE ROGATIS, Pascual   Argentina   1881 Italy
    LMD, REM

*DEROO, Maurits   Belgium   1903
    EVM

*DERVAUX, Pierre Jean Emile France   1917
    EVM, LMD, WI69, X68

*DE SABATA, Victor   Italy   1892 1967
    EMS, IMD, LMD, MEH, REM, SML
    See: de SABATA   MEH: double listing
    EMS: ДЕ САБАТА

DESARZENS, Victor   Switzerland   1908
    EVM, LMD

*DESCARRIES, Auguste   Canada   1896
    KEY

DESCH, Rudolf   1911
    IMD

*DESDERI, Ettore   Italy   1892
    DDM, EVM, IMD, LMD, REM, X64

*DESENCLOS, Alfred   France   1912 1971
    DDM, DMF, MLA28/4

*DESHEVOV, Vladimir
    Mihailovich   USSR   1889 1955
    BB65, BB71, EMS, EVM, LMD
    EVM: DESJEWOW   LMD: DEŠEVOV
    EMS: ДЕШЕВОВ

DES MARAIS, Paul E.   USA   1920
    AA73, ASUC, BB65, BB71, LMD, X64, X65

*DÉSORMIÈRE, Roger   France   1898 1963
    BB65, BB71, DDM, DMF, LMD, MEH, REM, SML, X64

DEŠPALJ, Pavle   Yugoslavia   1934
    BB65, BB71, CME, LMD
    CME: DESPALI

DESPIĆ, Dejan   Yugoslavia   1930
   KMJ

*DESPORTES, Yvonne Berthe
   Melitta   France   1907
   DDM, DMF, EVM, LMD, QQF, REM, X64

*DESSAU, Paul   Germany   1894
   BB65, BB71, CME, DDM, EMS, EVM, IMD, IMD2, LMD,
   MEH, REM, SML, X65, X66, X67, X68
   EMS: ДÉССАУ

DESSEL, Lode van   Netherlands 1909
   EVM

*DETHERIDGE, Joseph   Great Britain 1898
   WI69

DETONI, Dubravko   Yugoslavia   1937
   HCM, KMJ, X68

DEUTSCH, Marcel   France   1904
   ACM

*DEUTSCH, Peter   Germany   1901 1965
   X65

DEVATY, Antonin   Czechoslovakia 1903
   CCZ, MEH, MNP72/4, X67

*DEVČIĆ, Natko   Yugoslavia   1914
   BB65, CME, HCM, IMD, IMD2, KMJ, LMD, MEH, REM,
   SML, X65

DE VOCHT, Ledwijk   Belgium   1887
   LMD

DEVOTO, Daniel   Argentina   1916
   LMD, X65, X66, X67

DE VOTO, Mark   USA
   ASUC

*DE VREESE, Frédéric   Beligum   1929
   EVM, LMD, REM, X65, X66

*DEVREESE, Godefroid   Belgium   1893 1972
   EVM, LMD, REM

*DEVRIES, Ivan Daniel Marcel
   Louis   France   1909
   QQF

DEXTER, Colin   Great Britain

*DEYO, Felix   USA   1888   1959
    BB65

*DIAMOND, David Leo   USA   1915
    AS66, BB65, CA13, DDM, EVM, IMD, LMD, MEH, PCM,
    PC71, REM, SML, WTM, X64, X66, X67, X68

DIANDA, Hilda Fanny   Argentina   1925
    BB65, CA9, IMD2, LMD, QLA, X65, X66

*DIANOV, Anton Mihailovich   USSR   1882
    EVM

DI BIASE, Edoardo J.
    See: DAVID, Vincent

DI CAGNO, Pasquale   Italy   1888   1965
    LMD

*DICHLER, Josef   Austria   1912
    WI69, X64, X66

*DICK, Marcel   USA   1898   Hungary
    AS66, CAP, X64, X68

DICKINSON, Peter   Great Britain   1934
    BB65, LMD, WI69, TSC, X64, X65, X66, X67, X68
    TSC and WI69: 1935

*DI DONATO, Vincenzo   Italy   1887   1967
    LMD

DIECKMANN, Carl-Heinz   Germany   1923
    SML, X68

*DIEMENTE, Edward P.   USA   1923
    AA73, PCM, PC71, X64, X65, X67, X68

DIEMER, Emma Lou   USA   1927
    AS66, CAP, PCM, PC71, X65, X68

DIENER, Theodor   Switzerland   1908
    SCHW

*DIERCKS, John H.   USA   1927
    PCM, PC71, X66, X67, X68

DIETHELM, Caspar   Switzerland   1926
    SCHW, X67

*DIGGLE, Roland   Canada   1885   1954
    AS66   Great Britain
    AS66: 1887

*DIJK, Jan van   Netherlands   1918
    IMD, NED

DI JULIO, Max   USA   1919
    AS66

*DIKTONIUS, Elmer   Finland   1896
    VTM

*DILLON, Henri   France   1912   1954
    LMD, REM

DILLON, James Shaun Hamilton   Great Britain   1944
    WI69

DILLON, Robert M.   USA
    AA73, X66, X67

DI MAJO, Giulio   1933
    IMD

DI MARTINO, Aladino   Italy   1908
    LMD, REM

DIMITRIU, Florica   Rumania   1915
    RCL

DIMITROV, Asen Stadev   Bulgaria   1894   1960
    BMK
    BMK: ДИМИТРОВ

*DIMITROV, Georgi Petrov   Bulgaria   1904
    BMK, X66, X68
    BMK: ДИМИТРОВ

DIMOV, Bojidar   Austria   1935   Bulgaria
    BB65, IMD2, LMD, MNG, X67, X68

DINEV, Petr Konstantinov   Bulgaria   1889
    BMK
    BMK: ДИНЕВ

DINU, Stelian   Rumania   1912
    RCL

*DIONISI, Renato   Italy   1910
    LMD, REM, X67

DIRKSEN, Richard   USA   1921
   PCM

*DISTLER, Hugo   Germany   1908 1942
   DDM, EVM, IMD, MEH, MZW, PAP, REM, SML, X64, X66,
   X67, X68

*DITÉ, Louis   Austria   1891
   EVM

DITTRICH, Fred   Germany   1911
   SML, X66

DITTRICH, Paul-Heinz   Germany   1930
   SML

DJEMIL, Enyss   France   1917
   QQF, X68

DLOUHÝ, Milan   Czechoslovakia
   MNP69/4

DLUGOSZEWSKI, Lucia   1931
   WAN

*DOBIÁŠ, Vaclav   Czechoslovakia 1909
   CCZ, CME, DDM, EMS, IMD, IMD2, LMD, MEH, MNP65/5,
   REM, SML, X64, X65, X67
   EMS: ДОБИАШ

*DOBICI, Cesare   Italy   1873 1944
   REM

DOBOS, Kálmán   Hungary   1931
   CHC, X68

DOBOS, Viorel   Rumania   1917
   RCL

DOBRODINSKÝ, Bedrich   Czechoslovakia 1896
   CCZ, MEH, X66, X67

*DOBRONIĆ, Antun   Yugoslavia   1878 1955
   BB65, DDM, EMS, EVM, HCM, IMD, KMJ, LMD, REM, SML,
   X67
   EMS: ДОБРОНИЧ

*DOBROWEN, Issay
  Alexandrovitch   Norway   1893 1953
   BMK, EMS, EVM, IMD, LMD, MEH,   Russia
   REM, VTM
   BMK: ДОБРОВЕН   EMS: ДОБРОВЕ́ЙН
   BMK: 1894   EMS: 1894

DOBROWOLSKI, Andrzej   Poland   1921
    BB65, IMD, LMD, MEH, PKW, X64, X65, X66, X67, X68

DOBRZAŃSKI, Tadeusz   Poland   1916
    PKW, X66, X67

DODGE, Charles   USA   1942
    ASUC, BB71, X65, X66, X67

DODGSON, Stephen   Great Britain   1924
    X67

*DOEBLER, Kurt   Germany   1896
    LMD, REM

*DOFLEIN, Erich   Germany   1900
    REM

DÖHL, Friedhelm   Germany   1936
    PAP

*DOHNÁNYI, Ernö   Hungary   1877 1960
    BB65, BB71, EMS, EVM, IMD, LMD, MEH, REM, WTM,
    X65, X67, X68
    Also: DOHNANYI, Ernst von
    EMS: ДОНАНЬИ

DOIRE, René   France   1879 1959
    BB65, BB71, LMD

DE KRUYF, Ton
    See: KRUYF, Ton de

*DOLIN, Samuel Joseph   Canada   1917
    CCM, CCM71, CVM, MCO, NLC, PC71, X68

*DOLLERIS, Ludvig   Denmark   1886 1962

DOLUKHANIAN, Aleksandr
    Pavlovich   USSR   1910 1968
    MEH
    MEH: DOLUCHAN

DOŁZHITZKI, Adam   Bulgaria   1886
    BMK
    BMK: ДОЛЖИЦКИ

*DOŁŻICKI, Adam   Bulgaria   1886 Poland
    BMK
    BMK: ДОЛЖИЦКИ

DOMANSKÝ, Hanuš   Czechoslovakia
ZE70/1, ZE70/2, ZE70/3

DOMAŽLICKÝ, František Czechoslovakia
MNP69/4, X67, X68

DOMBAEV, Grigorii
Savelievich   USSR   1905
EMS, PPU69/2, X65, X68
EMS: ДОМЬАЕВ

*DOMBROWSKI, Hans Maria Germany 1897
EVM, IMD, LMD, REM, X67, X68

DOMINCHEN, Klimenty
Yakovlevich   USSR   1907
EMS, PPU29/2
EMS: ДОМИНЧЕН

DOMSELAAR, Jacob van Netherlands 1890
EVM

DONAHUE, Robert   USA   1931
PCM, PC71, X68

DONALD, Oscar
See: BANKS, Don

*DONATI, Pino   Italy   1907
BB71, IMD, LMD, REM

*DONATO, Anthony   USA   1909
ASUC, AS66, BB71, CA15, LCI, LMD, PCM, PC71, X64, X65,
X66, X67, X68

DONATO, Vincenzo di
See: DI DONATO

*DONATONI, Franco   Italy   1927
BB65, BB71, CME, EL:3, IMD, LMD, MEH, REM, TSC, X65,
X66, X67, X68

DONÁTOVÁ, Narcisa   Czechoslovakia 1928
CCZ

DONCEANU, Felicia   Rumania   1931
RCL, X64, X66

*DONDERER, Georg   Germany   1906
X66

*DONIACH, Shula   Great Britain   1905   Russia
   WI69

*DONINGTON, Robert   Great Britain   1907
   BB71, DAS, REM, X64, X65, X66, X67, X68

DONNER, Henrik Otto   Finland   1913
   CME, LMD, VTM, X65, X66

DONOSTIA, Pater José
  Antonio de   Spain   1886   1957
   BB65, BB71, REM
   REM: 1956

*DONOVAN, Richard Frank   USA   1891   1970
   BB71, CA15, EVM, IMD, LMD, PCM, REM, X64, X65

DOPF, Richard   1921
   IMD

DOPLICHER, Virgilio   Italy   1884
   LMD, REM

*DOPPELBAUER, Josef
  Friedrich   Austria   1918
   IMD, IMD2, X68

DORAN, Matt   USA   1921
   BB65, BB71, DN70, PCM, PC71

*DORATI, Antal   Great Britain   1906   Hungary
   BB65, BB71, CME, EVM, LMD, MEH, REM, X64, X65, X66,
   X67, X68

DORDEVIĆ, Jovan   Yugoslavia   1929
   KMJ

DORNBY, Finn   Denmark
   DMTsp

DOROSHUK, Igor Fedorovich
   See: BELZA, Igor Fedorovich

DÖRR, Adam   1933
   IMD

DORSAM, Paul   USA
   CAP, PC71

*DØRUMSGAARD, Arne   Norway   1921
   LMD

DORWARD, David   Great Britain   Scotland
   X67, X68

*DOST, Walter   Germany   1874
   EVM

*DOSTAL, Nico   Austria   1895
   EVM, LMD, MEH, REM, X66, X68

*DOUBRAVA, Jaroslav   Czechoslovakia 1909 1960
   BB65, BB71, CCZ, CME, IMD, IMD2, LMD, MEH, MNP70/2,
   SML, X65

DOUBRAVSKÝ, Petr   Czechoslovakia 1925 Austria
   CCZ

DOUCET, Clément   1894
   IMD

*DOUÉ, Jean   France   1922
   ACM

*DOUGHERTY, Celius   USA   1902
   AS66, BB65, BB71, CA9, LMD, PCM, PC71, X64, X67, X68
   LMD: DOUGHERT<u>H</u>Y

*DOUGLAS, Clive Martin   Australia   1903
   EVM, WI69

*DOUGLAS, Richard Roy   Great Britain 1907
   WI69

DOUGLAS, William   Canada
   X68

DOUNAÏVSKI, I. O.
   See: DUNAYEVSKY, I. O.

DOWD, John Andrew   USA
   ASUC

*DOWNES, Ralph William   Great Britain 1904
   X64, X65, X66, X67, X68

DOWNEY, John   USA   1927
   LCI, X68

DOWNIE, John   Great Britain
   X67

DRAEGER, Walter   Germany   1888
   MEH, SML, X64, X65, X66

DRAGA, George   Rumania   1935
    RCL, X64, X65, X66

DRAGAN, Rafael Radu   Israel   1909   Rumania
    WWI

DRAGATAKIS, Dimitris   Greece   1914
    EL:1, EL:2, EL:3, EL:4, PAP
    EL:3: DRAGRATAKIS

*DRAGOI, Sabin Vasile   Rumania   1894   1968
    BB71, CME, EVM, LMD, MEH, RCL, REM, SML, X64, X65

DRĂGULESCU, Theodor   Rumania   1932
    RCL

DRANSMANN, Hansheinrich   1894
    IMD

DRÈGE-SCHIELOWA, Łucja   Poland   1893   1962
    PKW

DREJSL, Radim   Czechoslovakia   1923   1953
    CCZ, IMD2, MEH

DREMLIUGA, Nikolai
  Vaselievich   USSR   1917
    EMS
    EMS: ДРЕМЛЮГА

*DRESDEN, Sem   Netherlands   1881   1957
    BB65, BB71, CME, DDM, EVM, IMD, LMD, MEH, NED, REM,
    SML, X64, X65

*DRESSEL, Erwin   Germany   1909   1972
    EVM, IMD, LMD, REM

DRESSLER, Franz Xaver   Rumania   1898
    RCL, X65

DRESSLER, Rudolf   Germany
    X67

DREW, James   USA
    X68

DREYFUS, George   Australia   1928   Germany
    AMM, X67, X68

*DRIESCH, Kurt Wilhelm
  Caeser   Germany   1904
    EVM, LMD, REM, WWG, X64

*DRIESSLER, Johannes   Germany   1921
    BB65, BB71, CME, DDM, EVM, IMD, LMD, REM, SML, WWG,
    X64, X65, X68

DRING, Madeleine   1923
    IMD

DRISCHNER, Max   Germany   1891
    EVM

DŘÍZGA, Eduard   Czechoslovakia
    MNP69/4

DROBNER, Mieczysław   Poland   1912
    PKW

*DROZDOV, Anotoli Nikolaevich   USSR   1883   1950
    BB65, EMS, EVM, IMD
    EMS: ДРОЗДО́В

DRUCKMAN, Jacob   USA   1928
    ASUC, EL:3, PCM, PC71, X64, X68

DRUSKIN, Mikhail Semenovich   USSR   1905
    EMS, PPU69/2, X66, X68
    EMS: ДРУ́СКИН

DSEGELENOK, Alexandre
Mihailovich
    See: DZEGELENOK

DSERSHINSKI, I. I.
    See: DZERZHINSKY, I. I.

*DUBENSKY, Arkady   USA   1890   1966
    AS66, BB71, EVM, IMD, LMD, MLA29/4, REM, X66 Russia

DUBENSKY, Leo   USA   1914   Russia
    AS66

DUBINSKY, R.   USSR
    PPU69/4

DUBLANC, Emilio Antonio   Argentina   1911
    CA12, IMD, LMD

DUBOIS, Pierre-Max   France   1930
    BB71, CMF22, CMF39, DDM, X68

DU BOIS, Rob
    See: BOIS, Rob du

*DUCASSE, Roger Jean-Jules-
  Aimable   France   1873   1954
  DMF, EVM, REM

DUCHÁČ, Miloslav   Czechoslovakia 1924
  MEH

CUCHAŇ, Jan   Czechoslovakia 1927
  CCZ

DUCHARME, Guy   Canada
  KEY

*DUCHOW, Marvin   Canada   1914
  KEY, X68

DUCKWORTH, William E.   USA   1943
  AA73, ASUC, CAP, PC71

*DUCOMMUN, Samuel   Switzerland   1914
  SCHW, X65

DUFRÈNE, François   1930

*DUGEND, Enno   Germany   1915
  WWG

DUGGER, Edwin   USA
  ASUC

*DUHAMEL, Antoine   France   1925
  CME, EVM, LMD, REM

*DUKE, Henry   Great Britain 1920
  WI69

*DUKE, John Woods   USA   1899
  AA73, AS66, EVM, LMD, PCM, PC71, REM, WI69, X65,
  X67, X68

DUKE, Vernon
  See: DUKELSKY, Vladimir

*DUKELSKY, Vladimir   USA   1903   1969
  AS66, BB71, DDM, EVM, IMD, LMD, MLA26/4,   Russia
  PCM, PC71, REM, X64, X65, X67, X68
  Pseudonym: DUKE, Vernon

*DUMAS, Louis (II)   France   1877   1952
  DMF, LMD, REM

*DUMESNIL, Maurice   USA   1886 1967
 BB71, X64   France

*DUMIČIĆ, Petar   Yugoslavia 1901
 HCM, KMJ

*DUMITRESCU, Georghe Rumania   1914
 CME, EMS, LMD, RCL, REM, SML, X64, X65, X66, X68
 EMS: ДУМИТРЕ́СКУ

*DUMITRESCU, Ion   Rumania   1913
 CME, EMS, LMD, MEH, RCL, REM, SML, X64, X65, X66
 EMS: ДУМИТРЕСКУ

DUNAEVSKY, Zinoviy Iosifovich USSR   1908
 PPU

*DUNAYEVSKY, Isaak Osipovich USSR   1900 1955
 BB65, BB71, DDM, EMS, EVM, LMD, MEH, REM, SML,
 X65, X68
 DDM: DOUNAÏVSKI EVM: DUNAJEWSKI LMD: DUNAEVSKIJ
 MEH, REM and SML: DUNAJEWSKI
 EMS: ДУНАЕ́ВСКИЙ

*DUNCAN, Carlyle   Canada   1893 1964
 X65

DUNFORD, Benjamin   USA   1917
 PC71

*DUNKLEY, Ferdinand Luis USA   1869 1956
 AS66, EVM   Great Britain

*DUNLOP, Isobel Violet Skelton Great Britain 1901 Scotland
 WI69

DU PAGE, Florence   USA
 AS66

DU PAGE, Richard   USA   1908
 AS66

*DUPÉRIER, Jean Eugène Louis France   1886 Switzerland
 DDM, EVM, LMD, QQF, SCHW

DU PLESSIS, Hubert L.
 See: PLESSIS, Hubert L. du

*DUPONT, Jacques   France   1906
 CMF65/10, DDM, DMF, REM, X66, X68
 DDM: JACQUES-DUPONT

DUPRAT, Rogerio   Brazil   1932
    FBC, X64, X68

*DUPRÉ, Marcel Jean Jules   France   1886   1971
    BB71, CMF14, CMF39, DDM, DMF, EMS, EVM, IMD, LMD,
    MEH, MLA28, QQF, REM, SML, X64, X65, X66, X67, X68
    EMS: ДЮПРЕ

*DUPUIS, Albert   Belgium   1877   1967
    BB71, CBC, DDM, EVM, LMD, REM, X68

*DUREY, Louis Edmond   France   1888
    BB71, CMF8, CMF20, CMF39, DDM, DMF, EMS, EVM, IMD,
    LMD, MEH, REM, SML, VNM, X64
    EMS: ДЮРЕЙ

DURHAM, Lowell Marsden   USA   1917
    DAS

DURKÓ, Zsolt   Hungary   1934
    CHC, CME, MEH, X66, X67, X68, ZSZ

*DURME, Jef van   Belgium   1907   1965
    BB65, BB71, CBC, EVM, LMD, MLA22/4, REM, WI69, X65,
    X66
    CBC: VAN DURME

*DURRA, Hermann   Germany   1871   1954
    EVM

DURRANT, Frederick Thomas   Great Britain   1895
    WI69

*DURUFLÉ, Maurice   France   1902
    CMF29, DDM, DMF, EMS, EVM, IMD, LMD, QQF, REM,
    X64, X65, X66, X68
    EMS: ДЮРЮФЛЕ

DUSHKIN, Dorothy   USA   1903
    PCM

DUSHKY, Mihail Iliich   USSR   1913   1942
    EMS
    EMS: ДУШСКИЙ

DUSSOURD, Aimé   France   1896
    ACM

DUSTIN, William   USA   1920   1964
    X65

*DUTILLEUX, Henry Paul
Julien   France   1916
     BB65, BB71, CMF12, CMF20, CMF39, CME, DDM, DMF,
     EMS, EVM, IMD, IMD2, LMD, MEH, QQF, REM, SML,
     X64, X65, X66, X67, X68
     EMS: ДЮТИЙЕ

*DUVOSEL, Seraphien Lieven   Belgium   1877   1956
     BB71, EVM, LMD, REM

*DVARIONAS, Balis Dominiko   USSR   1904   Lithuania
     BB65, BB71, DDM, EMS, LMD, PPU, REM, SML   1972
     SML: DWARIONAS   EMS: ДВАРИОНАС

*DVOŘÁČEK, Jiří   Czechoslovakia   1928
     BB65, BB71, CCZ, MNP64/3, MNP70/1, MNP70/9,
     MNP71/3, MNP72/6, MNP72/7

DVORSKY, Michel
     See: HOFMANN, Josef

*DYSON, George   Great Britain   1883   1964
     BB65, BB71, EVM, REM, X64, X65, X67

DŽAMBAZOV, Aleksandar   Yugoslavia   1936
     KMJ

*DZEGELÉNOK, Aleksandr
Mihailovich   USSR   1891   1969
     BB71, EMS, EVM
     EDM: DSEGELNOK   EVM: DSEGELNOK   EMS: ДЗЕГЕЛЁНОК

*DZERZHINSKY, Ivan
Ivanovich   USSR   1909
     BB65, BB71, CME, EMS, EVM, LMD, MEH, PPU, PPU69/3,
     REM, SML, X65
     EMS: ДЗЕРЖИНСКИЙ   SML: DSERSHINSKI

*DZHANGIROV, Dzhangir
Shirgreshtoglu   USSR   1921
     EMS, PPU
     EMS: ДЖАНГИРОВ

DZIEWULSKI, Eugeniusz   Poland   1889
     PKW

DZIEWUSKA, Maria   Poland   1909
     IMD, PKW

EAGLES, Moneta Morrison   Australia   1924
     PCM, WI69

EAKIN, Charles Gillian   USA   circa 1928
   AA73, X67, X68

EARLS, Paul   USA
   AA73, ASUC, X68

*EASDALE, Brian   Great Britain   1909
   DDM, EVM, LMD, REM, X66

*EAST, John Michael   Union of   1929   Great Britain
   PCM, X65, X68   South Africa

EASTHAM, Clark   USA
   AA73, X66, X68

*EASTWOOD, Thomas Hugh   Great Britain   1922
   WI69, X67, X68

EATON, John Charles   USA   1935
   AS66, BB71, PCM, X64, X66, X67, X68

*EATON, Richard Stephen   Canada   1914   1968
   NLC, X68

EBBAGE, David Arthur   Great Britain   1942
   WI69

*EBEL, Arnold   Germany   1883   1963
   BB65, BB71, EVM, IMD, LMD, REM, SML

*EBEN, Petr   Czechoslovakia   1929
   BB65, BB71, CCZ, CME, IMD, IMD2, LMD, MNP64/3,
   MNP65/6, MNP70/1, MNP70/3, MNP72/6, SML, X64,
   X65, X66, X67, X68

*EBENSTEIN, Viktor   Austria   1888   1968
   X66, X68

*EBERT, Hans   Germany   1889   1952
   EVM, LMD, REM

EBNER, Hans   Switzerland   1902
   SCHW

ECCHER, Celestino   Italy   1892
   LMD, REM

ECHEVARRIA, Victorino   Spain   1900   1965
   DDM

*ECKARTZ, Hubert   Germany   1903
   WWG

*ECKERBERG, Axel Sixten
  Lennart   Sweden   1909
  EVM, FST, KSV, LMD, REM, SIM, SIMa, VTM, X64

*ECKHARDT-GRAMATTÉ, Sophie
  Carmen   Canada   1902   Russia
  BB65, BB71, CA10, CCM, CCM71, IMD, KEY, LMD, MCO,
  REM, WI69, X68
  Formerly: de FRIEDMANN-KOCHEVSKAIA

*ECKLEBE, Alexander   Germany   1904   Poland
  REM

EDEL, Benjamin   France   1877 1952
  ACM

*EDEL, Yitzhak   Israel   1896   Poland
  ACU, IMD2

EDER, Hans   Germany
  PAP

*EDER, Helmut   Austria   1916
  BB65, BB71, IMD, IMD2, LMD, MEH, X65, X67, X68

EDLUND, Hans   Sweden   1927
  CME, SIMa

*EDMUNDS, Christopher M.   Great Britain   1899
  IMD

*EDMUNDS, John   USA   1913
  AS66, PCM, PC71, X66, X67

*EDMUNDSON, Garth   USA   1900
  AS66, X64, X65, X66, X67, X68

*EDWARDS, Clara   USA   1887
  BB71

EDWARDS, George   USA   1943
  X68

EDWARDS, H. Neil   USA   1931
  DN70

EDWARDS, Ross   Australia circa 1938
  X67

*EECKHOUTE, Prosper van   Belgium   1904
  EVM

*EFFINGER, Cecil   USA   1914
   AA73, AS66, EVM, LMD, PCM, PC71, REM, X64, X65, X66,
   X67, X68

EFTIMESCU, Florin   Rumania   1919
   RCL, X64

*EGENER, Frederic Tristram   Canada   1886
   KEY

*EGERTON, Arthur Henry   Canada   1891
   NLC

EGG, Arthur Henry
   See: EGERTON, Arthur Henry

*EGGE, Klaus   Norway   1906
   BB71, CME, CNO, DDM, EMS, EVM, IMD, LMD, REM, VTM,
   X66, X68
   EMS: ЭГГЕ

*EGGEN, Arne   Norway   1881 1955
   BB71, CNO, EVM, LMD, REM, VTM

EGGEN, Erik   Norway   1877 1957
   BB71, DDM, EVM, LMD, REM

EGGLESTON, Anne   Canada   1934
   CCM, CVM, CVMa, MCO, NLCa

EGIAZARIAN, Grigory
   Egiazarovich   USSR   1908
   EMS
   EMS: ЕГИАЗАРЯН

*EGK, Werner   Germany   1901
   BB65, BB71, CME, DDM, EMS, EVM, IMD, IMD2, LMD, MEH,
   MZW, REM, SML, VNM, WI69, WTM, WWG, X64, X65, X66,
   X67, X68

EGMOND, Pieter van   Netherlands 1912
   EVM

EGOROV, Aleksandr
   Aleksandrovich   USSR   1887 1959
   EMS
   EMS: ЕГО́РОВ

*EHRENBERG, Karl Emil
   Theodor   Germany   1878 1962
   BB65, BB71, IMD, LMD, REM

EHRENSPERGER, Carlos   Switzerland   1911   Columbia
SCHW

*EHRLICH, Abel   Israel   1915   Germany
ACU, CME, IMD, IMD2, MM59, X65

EHRLICH, Jesse   1920
WAN

*EHRLING, Evert Sixten   Sweden   1924
BB71, CME, LMD, VTM, X64, X65, X68
LMD: 1918

*EHRSTRÖM, Otto Jarl Sigurd   Finland   1891
EVM, KKO, VTM

EICHENWALD, Philipp   Switzerland   1915
SCHW, X67, X68

*EICHHORN, Bernhard   Germany   1904
WI69

EICHHORN, Wermene Warlick   USA   1906
AS66

*EIDENS, Joseph   Germany   1896
EVM

EIGES, Iosif Romanovich   USSR   1887   1953
EMS
EMS: ЭЙГЕС

EIGES, Oleg Konstantinovich   USSR   1905
EMS
EMS: ЭЙГЕС

EIKHENVALD, Anton
Aleksandrovich   USSR   1875   1952
EMS
EMS: ЭЙХЕНВАЛЬД

*EIMERT, Herbert   Germany   1897   1972
CME, DDM, EVM, LMD, MEH, REM, SML, X64, X65, X66,
X67, X68

*EINARSSON, Sigfus   Iceland   1877   1939
REM, VTM

*EINEM, Gottfried von   Austria   1918   Switzerland
BB65, BB71, CME, DDM, EMS, EVM, IMD, IMD2, LMD, MEH,
PAP, REM, SML, VNM, WI69, WTM, X64, X65, X66, X67, X68
PAP: VON EINEM, G.
EMS: ЭЙНЕМ

*EISBRENNER, Werner   Germany   1908
  EVM, IMD, SML, WI69, WWG

*EISEMANN, Will   Switzerland   1906   Germany
  EVM, IMD, LMD, REM, SCHW, X66

EISIKOVITS, Max   Rumania   1908
  RCL, X68

*EISLER, Hans   Germany   1898   1962
  BB65, BB71, CME, DDM, EMS, EVM, IMD,   Austria
  IMD2, LMD, MEH, REM, SML, X64, X65, X66, X67, X68
  EMS: ЭЙСЛЕР

EISMA, Will   Netherlands   1929   Indonesia
  BB65, BB71, IMD, LMD, NED, X64, X66, X67, X68

*EITLER, Esteban   Chile   1913   1960
  BB65, BB71, IMD, LMD, REM   Austria

*EK, Fritz Gunnar Rudolf   Sweden   1900
  EVM, FST, KSV, LMD, REM, SIM, SIMa, SOW, STS

*EKIER, Jan   Poland   1913
  BB65, BB71, IMD, MEH, PKW, X66, X68

*EKLÖF, Einar   Sweden   1886   1954
  FST, KSV, SIM, SIMa, STS

*EKLUND, Hans O.   Sweden   1927
  BB71, FST, IMD2, KSV, LMD, SIM, SIMa, SMT, STS, SWE,
  VTM, X65, X66, X67, X68

*EL-DABH, Halim   Egypt   1921
  BB65, BB71, IMD, LMD, MEH, REM, X66

ELENESCU, Emanuel   Rumania   1911
  RCL

ELÍAS, Alfonso de   Mexico   1902
  LMD, REM

ELÍAS, Manuel Jorge de   Mexico   1939
  BB71, CA15, HET/3

ELIASSON, Anders   Sweden   circa 1940
  X68

ELIEZER, Bentzion Nisim   Bulgaria   1920
  BMK, X67
  BMK: ЕЛИЕЗЕР

*ELIZALDE, Frederico   Philippines   1907
   DDM, EVM, LMD, REM

*ELKUS, Albert Israel   USA   1884   1962
   BB65, BB71, EVM, LMD, PCM

ELKUS, Jonathan B.   USA   1931
   AA73, ASUC, AS66, PCM, PC71, X64, X65, X66, X67, X68

*ELLER, Heino Yanovich   USSR   1887   1970
   EMS, EVM, LMD, X65, X67   Estonia

ELLIOTT, Lloyd   USA   1941
   DN70

ELLIS, Merrill   USA   1916
   AA73, X65, X66, X67, X68

ELLSASSER, Richard William USA   1926
   AS66, X67, X68

ELLSTEIN, Abraham   USA   1907   1963
   AS66, MJM, PCM

*ELMAN, Mischa   USA   1891   1967
   AS66, EVM, X64, X66, X67, X68   Russia

ELMER, Cedric Nagel   USA   1939
   AS66

*ELMORE, Robert Hall   USA   1913   India
   AA73, AS66, PCM, PC71, X64, X66, X67, X68

ELMSLIE, Kenward   USA   1929
   AS66

*ELOKAS, Ossi Erkki Timo   Finland   1904
   COF, KKO

*ELOVAARA, Toivo   Finland   1907
   COF

ELOY, Jean-Claude   France   1938
   BB65, BB71, CME, DDM, IMD, X64, X65

ELSTON, Arnold   USA   1907   1971
   X68

ELTON, Antony   Great Britain   1935
   WI69

*ELWELL, Herbert   USA   1898
   AS66, EVM, LMD, PCM, PC71, REM

*EMBORG, Jens Laursøn   Denmark   1876   1957
   EVM, IMD, LMD

EMER, Michel   France   1906   Russia
   QQF, WI69

*EMERICH, Paul   USA   1895   Austria
   IMD, WI69

EMMERT, Frantisek   Czechoslovakia
   MNP73/1

*ENACOVICI, George   Rumania   1891   1965
   BB71, EVM, RCL, SML, X65

*ENESCO, Georges   Rumania   1881   1955
   BB65, BB71, CME, DDM, EMS, EVM, IMD, LMD, MEH, RCL,
   REM, SML, WTM, X64, X65, X66, X67, X68
   Correct spelling: ENESCU
   EMS: ЭНЕСКУ

*ENGEL, A. Lehman   USA   1910
   BB71, EVM, IMD, LMD, PCM, REM, WI69, X66, X68

ENGEL, Jehuda   Israel   1924   Austria
   ACU

*ENGELBRECHT, Richard   Germany   1907
   IMD, WWG

*ENGELMANN, Hans Ulrich   Germany   1921
   BB71, CME, EVM, IMD, IMD2, LMD, MEH, PAP, REM, SML,
   X64, X65, X66, X67, X68

*ENGELMANN, Johannes   Germany   1890   1945
   IMD

ENGELS, Adriaan   Netherlands   1906
   EVM

ENGELSMANN, Walter   1881   1952
   IMD

*ENGER, Elling   Norway   1905
   CNO

*ENGLÄNDER, Richard   Sweden   1889   1966
   REM, X66, X67, X68   Germany

ENGLERT, Giuseppe E.   France

ENGLERT, Giuseppe Giorgio   Italy   1927
    IMD, WI69, X65, X68

ENGLISH, George Selwyn   Australia   1912
    AMM

*ENGLISH, Granville   USA   1895   1968
    AS66, BB71
    AS66: 1900

*ENGLUND, Sven Einar   Finland   1916
    CME, COF, EVM, IMD, KKO, LMD, REM, VTM, X65, X66

ENKE, Vladimir Robertovich   USSR   1908
    EMS
    EMS: ЭНКЕ

ENRIQUEZ, Manuel   Mexico   1926
    BB71, CA15, HET27

*ENTELIS, Leonid Arnoldovich USSR   1903
    X64, X65

*ENTHOVEN, Emile   Netherlands 1903   1950
    EVM, LMD, REM

EPHRIKIAN, Angelo   Italy   1913
    LMD, REM

EPHROS, Gershon   USA   1890   Poland
    AS66, MJM, X68

*EPPERT, Carl   USA   1882   1961
    AS66, BB65, BB71, EVM

*EPPS, David Ronald   Great Britain 1934
    X67

EPSTEIN, David M.   USA   1930
    ASUC, AS66, BB71, PCM, PC71, X64, X65

EPSTEIN, Paul   USA
    ASUC

ERB, Donald   USA   1927
    ASUC, BB71, PC71, X66, X67, X68

*ERBSE, Heimo   Germany   1924
    BB65, BB71, CME, IMD, IMD2, LMD, MEH, REM, SML, WWG,
    X68

*ERDLEN, Hermann   Germany   1893   1972
   MLA29/4, WWG

*ERDMANN, Eduard Paul Ernst Germany   1896   1958
   BB65, BB71, DDM, EVM, IMD, LMD, REM,   Latvia
   SML, WWG, X68

ERDMANN, Gunter   Germany
   X67

*ERHARD, Karl   Germany   1928
   WWG

ERICKSON, Frank W.   USA   1923
   PCM, PC71, X67, X68
   PC71: 1917

ERICKSON, Robert   USA   1917
   BB71, EL:3, PCM, PC71, VTM, X66, X68

*ERIKSSON, Josef   Sweden   1872   1957
   EVM, FST, KSV, SIM, SIMa, STS, VTM

*ERIKSSON, Nils F.   Sweden   1902
   FST, KSV, SIM, SIMa, STS

*ERKIN, Ulvi Cemal   Turkey   1906
   EMS, EVM, IMD, LMD, REM, X65
   EMS: ЭРКИН

*ERLEBACH, Rupert Oswald   Great Britain 1894
   EVM, LMD, REM

*ERMATINGER, Erhart   Switzerland   1900   1966
   EVM, IMD, LMD, MLA23/4, REM, SCHW, X66

*ERNESAKS, Gustav
  Gustavovich   USSR   1908   Estonia
   BB71, DDM, EMS, LMD, MEH, PPU, PPU68/1, PPU70/1,
   SML, X64, X65, X68
   EMS: ЭРНЕСАКС

*ERÖD, Ivan   1936
   IMD, IMD2, MNG, X68

*ERPF, Hermann   Germany   1891   1969
   BB71, IMD, REM, X66, X67, X68

*ESCHER, Peter Alfred   Switzerland   1915
   SCHW

*ESCHER, Rudolf George   Netherlands   1912
    CME, DDM, EVM, IMD, NED, REM, X64, X65, X68

*ESCOBAR, Luis Antonio   Colombia   1925
    BB65, BB71, CA8, LMD

ESCOBAR BUDGE, Roberto   Chile   1926
    BB71, CA14

ESCOT, Pozzio   Peru   1931
    ASUC, CA17, X65, X66, X67

ESCOVADO, Robin   USA   1931
    PCM, PC71

ESHPAI, Andrey Yakovlevich   USSR   1925
    BB65, BB71, CME, EMS, LMD, MEH, PPU69/2, PPU70/1,
    SML, X64, X65, X66, X67, X68
    LMD and MEH: EŠPAJ   SML: ESCHPAI   EMS: ЭШПА́Й

*ESHPAI, Jacov Andreyevich   USSR   1890   1963
    BB65, IMD, LMD
    Volume I: ESPAY, Jacov   EMS: ЭШПА́Й

ESPARZA OTEO, Alfonso   Mexico   1897   1950
    MMX

ESPINA, Noni   USA   1921   Philippines
    DN70

*ESPINOSA, Guillermo   Colombia   1905
    LMD, REM, X65, X67, X68

*ESPLÁ y TRIAY, Oscar   Spain   1886
    BB65, BB71, DDM, EVM, LMD, MEH, REM, X64, X65,
    X67, X68
    DDM and EVM: 1889

*ESPOILE, Raúl Hugo   Argentina   1888   1958
    LMD, REM

ESPOSITO, Alessandro   Italy   1913
    LMD, REM

ESPOSITO, Arnaldo d'   Argentina   1907   1945
    X68

ESTABROOK, Dean M.   USA
    CAP

ESTÉVES, Antonio   Venezuela   1916
    BB71, CA14, REM

*ESTRADA, Carlos   Uruguay   1909   1970
    CA16, EMS, IMD, LMD, MLA28, REM
    EMS: ЭСТРАДА

ESTRELLA, Blanca   Venezuela

*ETHERINGTON, Charles
Leslie   Canada   1903
    X65, X67

*ETLER, Alvin Derald   USA   1913   1973
    BB65, BB71, IMD, LMD, PCM, PC71, REM, X65, X66,
    X67, X68

*ETTI, Karl   Austria   1912
    WI69, X64, X68

*ETTINGER, Max Markus Wolf   Germany   1874   1951
    EVM, IMD, LMD, REM   Poland

EULAMBIO, Michele   Italy   1881
    REM

EVANGELATOS, Antiochos
    See: EVANGHELATOS

*EVANGELISTI, Franco   Italy   1926
    BB65, BB71, CME, EL:1, IMD, LMD, MEH, MNG, PAP,
    X64, X65, X66, X68

*EVANGHELATOS, Antiochos   Greece   1903
    CME, DDM, LMD, PAP, REM, X64, X65
    DDM and LMD: 1904

*EVANS, Lindley   Australia   1895   Union of
    AMM, WI69   South Africa

*EVANS, Peter Angus   Great Britain   1929
    WI69, X64, X65, X66, X67

EVANS, Robert   Canada
    CCM71

*EVERSON, Cromwell   Union of   1928
    EVM   South Africa

*EVETT, Robert   USA   1922
    BB65, BB71, CA10, LMD, PCM, X64, X65, X66, X67, X68

*EVJE, Johan   Norway   1874   1962
    CNO

EVJU, Helge   Norway   circa 1940
   X68

EVLAHOV, Orest
   Aleksandrovich   USSR   1912
   EMS, X64
   EMS: ЕВЛА́ХОВ

*EVSEYEV, Sergey
   Vassilievitch   USSR   1894 1956
   BB65, BB71, EMS, EVM, LMD, REM
   EVM: EWSEJEW   EMS: EBCÉEB
   BB65: 1893

EZAKI, Kenjiro   Japan   1926
   IMD, IMD2, X65

EZRAHI, Yariv   Israel   1905
   ACU

*FABER, Joachim Richard   Germany   1913
   WWG

*FABINI, Eduardo   Uruguay   1882 1950
   EMS, EVM, LMD, MEH, REM
   EMS, EVM and MEH: 1883
   EMS: ФАБИ́НИ

FABRIZI, Geremia   USA   1880 Italy
   REM

*FAGAN, Gideon   Union of   1904
   EVM, LMD, REM   South Africa

*FAIRCLOUGH, George Herbert Canada   1869 1954
   EVM

*FAIRLIE, Margaret   USA   circa 1928
   X64

*FAITH, Percy   USA   1908 Canada
   EVM, X66

FAIZI, Dzaudat Khraisovich USSR   1910
   EMS, LMD
   LMD: FAJZI
   EMS: ФА́ЙЗИ

FALABELLA CORREA, Roberto Chile   1926
   REM, X65

*FALCINELLI, Rolande   France   1920
    EVM, LMD, REM, X64, X65

FALCK, Robert   USA
    PAP

FALTUS, Leos   Czechoslovakia
    MNP69/4

*FANO, Guido Alberto   Italy   1875 1961
    BB65, BB71, DDM, LMD, REM

*FANO, Michel   France   1929
    CME, IMD, X65

*FARA, Giulio   Italy ·   1880 1949
    REM

FARBERMAN, Harold   USA   1930
    AS66, IMD, PCM, PC71, X65, X66, X67, X68

FARELL, Edwin
    See: RIEGGER, Wallingford

FARIA, Manuel Ferreira   Italy   1916
    DDM

FARINA, Edoardo   Italy   1939
    DDM, LMD, REM, X65

*FARINA, Guido   Italy   1903
    DDM, IMD, LMD, REM

*FARINAS CANTERO, Carlos   Cuba   1934
    REM, WI69

*FARKAS, Ferenc   Hungary   1905
    BB65, BB71, CHC, CME, DDM, EMS, EVM, IMD, IMD2,
    LMD, MEH, REM, SML, WI69, X65, X66, X67, X68
    EMS: ФА́РКАШ

*FARMER, Henry George   Great Britain   1882 1965
    BB71, DDM, EVM, REM, X64, X66, X67, X68

*FARNON, Robert Joseph   Great Britain   1917 Canada
    MCO, X67

FARQUHAR, David Andross   New Zealand   1928
    WI69

*FARWELL, Arthur   USA   1872 1952
    AS66, DDM, EVM, LMD, PCM, REM

*FASANO, Renato   Italy   1902
    IMD, LMD, REM

FAST, Jonathan   USA
    X68

FÁTIOL, Tiberiu   Rumania   1935
    RCL

*FAUCHARD, Auguste Louis
  Joseph   France   1881   1957
    DDM

*FAVRE, Georges   France   1905
    IMD, LMD, QQF, REM, WI69, X67

FAYZULLIN, D. Kh.   USSR
    PPU70/2

*FECKER, Adolf Emil   Germany   1912
    IMD

*FÉDOROV, Vladimir
  Mikhailovich   France   1901   Russia
    REM, X66, X67, X68

*FEICHT, Hieronim   Poland   1894   1967
    BB71, REM, X65, X66, X67, X68

FEIGIN, Leonid Veniaminovich USSR   1923
    EMS
    EMS: ФЕЙГИН

*FEILITZSCH, Karl von   Germany   1901
    WWG

*FEINBERG, Samuil
  Evgenievich   USSR   1890   1962
    BB65, BB71, EMS, IMD, LMD, REM, SML, X66, X67, X68
    LMD: FEJNBERG
    EMS: ФЕЙНБЕРГ

*FEKETE, Zoltán   Hungary   1909
    BB65, BB71, IMD, LMD

FELCIANO, Richard   USA   1930
    PCM, PC71, X65

*FELD, Jindřich   Czechoslovakia 1925
    BB65, BB71, CCZ, IMD2, MEH, MNP64/3, MNP64/9,
    MNP65/6, MNP68/6, MNP72/2, MNP72/4, SML, X64,
    X65, X66, X67, X68

*FELDERHOF, Jan Reindert
   Adriaan   Netherlands   1907
   EVM, LMD, REM

*FELDMAN, Ludovic   Rumania   1893
   EMS, IMD, LMD, MEH, RCL, REM, SML, X65
   EMS: ФÉЛЬДМАН

*FELDMAN, Morton   USA   1926
   BB65, BB71, EL:2, EL:3, IMD2, LMD, PAP, PCM, PC71,
   X64, X65, X66, X67, X68
   PC71: FELDMAN, Merten in index
   EL:3: 1925

FELDSTEIN, Saul   USA   1940
   AS66, PC71, X67, X68

*FELIX, Václav   Czechoslovakia 1928
   CCZ, IMD, IMD2, MEH, MNP72/9, X64, X67, X68

*FELLEGARA, Vittorio   Italy   1927
   IMD, LMD, REM, X65, X66, X67, X68

*FELLOWES, Edmund Horace Great Britain 1870 1951
   X64, X68

FELTZMAN, Oskar Borisovich USSR   1921
   EMS, X66
   EMS: ФÉЛЬЦМАН

*FELUMB, Svend Christian   Denmark   1898
   BB71, VTM

FEMELIDI, Vladimir
   Aleksandrovich   USSR   1905 1931
   EMS
   EMS: ФЕМЕЛИ́ДИ

*FENBY, Eric William   Great Britain 1906
   EVM, X66, X67, X68

FENIGSTEIN, Victor   Switzerland   1924
   SCHWn

FENNELLY, Brian Leo   USA
   X67, X68

*FENNEY, William   Great Britain 1891
   EVM

*FERE, Vladimir Georgievich Russia   1902
   BB71, EMS, LMD, X66, X67, X68
   EMS: ФЕРÉ

*FEREMANS, Jan-Jozef
  Francisca Gaston   Belgium   1907
  EVM, WI69

*FERENCZY, Otto F.   Czechoslovakia   1921
  CCZ, EVM, IMD, MEH, MNP64/5, MNP65/2, MNP71/6, X65,
  X67, X68, ZE69/1, ZE70/1, ZE70/2, ZE71/1, ZE71/2,
  ZE71/3, ZE72/1

FERGUSON, Edwin Earle   USA   1910
  PMC, PC71

*FERGUSON, Howard   Great Britain   1908 Ulster
  DDM, EVM, IMD, LMD, REM, WI69, X64, X65, X66, X67,
  X68

*FERNANDES, Armando José   Portugal   1906
  DDM, EVM, LMD, REM, X65

FERNEYOUGH, Brian   Great Britain   circa
  X68   1943

*FERNSTRÖM, John Axel   Sweden   1897 1961
  EVM, FST, IMD2, KSV, LMD, REM, SIMa,   China
  SOW, STS, VTM
  VTM: 1957

*FERRARA, Franco   Italy   1911
  LMD, REM, X64

FERRARI, Giorgio   Italy   1925
  LMD, REM

*FERRARI, Luc   France   1929
  IMD, LMD, MEH, QQF, REM, X65, X66, X68
  IMD and REM: 1928

*FERRARI TRECATE, Luigi   Italy   1884 1964
  BB65, BB71, DDM, EVM, IMD, LMD, REM, X64

FERRAZANO, Anthony Joseph   USA   1937
  DN72

*FERRÉ, Léo   Monaco   1916
  DMF, EVM, MEH, REM

*FERRER, Rafael   Spain   1911
  REM

*FERRERO, Willy   Italy   1906 1954
  EVM, LMD, REM   USA

*FERRETTO, Andrea   Italy   1864   1942
  REM

FERRITTO, John   USA
  X68

*FERRO, Pietro   Italy   1903   1960
  LMD, REM

*FERROUD, Pierre-Octave   France   1900   1936
  DDM, EVM, IMD, LMD, REM

FETLER, Paul   USA   1920
  PCM, PC71, X64, X65, X68

FEUCHTWANGER, Peter   Germany   1934
  MM59, X64

*FÉVRIER, Henri   France   1875   1957
  BB65, BB71, DDM, DMF, REM

*FIALA, George   Canada   1922 USSR
  BB65, BB71, CA17, CCM, CCM71, CVMa, KEY, LMD, MCO,
  MCO68, MCO71, NLC, TFB, X67, X68

FIALA, Jaromir   Czechoslovakia 1892
  CCZ

*FIALA, Jiři Julius   Czechoslovakia 1892
  CCZ, MEH

FIALA, Petr   Czechoslovakia 1943
  MNP69/4, MNP72/9

*FICHER, Jacobo   Argentina   1896 Russia
  DDM, EVM, IMD, LMD, REM, X66

*FICKENSCHER, Arthur   USA   1871   1954
  EVM, LMD, REM

*FIEBIG, Kurt   Germany   1908
  DDM, EVM, IMD, LMD, REM, X67

*FIGHERA, Mario   Italy   1903
  REM

FIGUEREDO, Carlos   Venezuela   1909
  BB71, CA14, REM

*FILAS, Thomas J.   USA   1908
  X64, X68

*FILIASI, Lorenzo   Italy   1878 1963
 BB65, BB71, EVM, LMD, REM

*FILIPPENKO, Arkadi
 Dmitrievich   USSR   1912
 EMS, PPU69/2
 EMS: ФИЛИППЕНКО

*FILIPPI, Amadeo de USA   1900 Italy
 AS66, EVM
 Pseudonym: WESTON, Philip

*FILLEUL, Henry   France 1877 1959
 BB65, BB71, EVM, LMD

*FILLMORE, Henry USA   1881 1956
 X68

FINAROVSKY, Grigori
 Abramovich   USSR   1906
 EMS
 EMS: ФИНАРОВСКИЙ

*FINE, Irving Gifford USA   1914 1962
 AS66, BB65, BB71, CME, EVM, IMD, LMD, PCM, PC71,
 REM, WI69, X65, X66, X68

*FINE, Vivian   USA   1913
 AA73, IMD, LMD, REM, X65

FINK, Michael   USA   1939
 AS66, PCM, PC71

FINK, Robert   USA
 ASUC

FINKBEINER, Reinhold Germany 1929
 CME, IMD, IMD2, X67

*FINKE, Fidelio Fritz Germany 1891 1968
 BB71, DDM, EMS, EVM, IMD, LMD, MEH, Bohemia
 MLA25/4, REM, SML, X64, X65, X66, X67, X68
 EMS: ФИНКЕ

*FINLEY, Lorraine Noel USA   1899 Canada
 AS66, X64, X65, X66, X67, X68

*FINN, William J.   USA   1881 1961
 AS66

*FINNEY, Ross Lee   USA   1906
   AA73, ASUC, AS66, BB65, BB71, CA11, DAS, DN72, EVM,
   IMD, LMD, PCM, PC71, REM, WI69, X64, X65, X66, X67,
   X68

FINNISSY, Michael   Great Britain 1945
   X67, X68

*FINZI, Gerald   Great Britain 1901 1956
   DDM, EVM, IMD, LMD, REM, X66, X67

*FIRFOV, Živko   Yugoslavia   1906
   KMJ, REM

*FIRKUŠNÝ, Rudolf   Czechoslovakia 1912
   LMD, REM, SML, X64, X65, X67, X68

FIRPO, Emilio   Italy   1890
   LMD, REM

FISCHER, Edith Stenkraus   USA   circa 1920
   DN70

*FISCHER, Edwin   Switzerland   1886 1960
   BB65, BB71, DDM, EVM, IMD, LMD, REM, SCHW, SML,
   X65, X68

*FISCHER, Erich   Germany   1887
   EVM, LMD, REM, SCHW

*FISCHER, Ernest   Germany   1900
   MEH

FISCHER, Irwin   USA   1903
   AA73, LCI, X64, X65, X66, X67, X68

*FISCHER, Jan F.   Czechoslovakia 1921
   CCZ, IMD2, MEH, MNP64/4, MNP64/5, MNP66/5, MNP71/4,
   MNP72/7, SML, X64, X65, X66, X68

*FISCHER, Wilhelm   Austria   1886
   BB65, BB71, EVM, REM, X64

FISCHER-DIESKAU, Klaus   Germany   1921
   WI69, X67

FIŠER, Jan   Czechoslovakia 1896 1963
   CCZ

FIŠER, Lubor   Czechoslovakia 1925
   MNP64/5, MNP64/6

FIŠER, Luboš   Czechoslovakia   1935
    BB71, CCZ, COO, IMD2, MEH, MNP64/3, MNP66/4,
    MNP67/1, MNP67/6, MNP67/7, MNP69/3, MNP69/8,
    MNP70/1, X65, X66, X67, X68

FISER-KVETON, Jan   Czechoslovakia   1896   1963
    MEH

FISHER, Isidor   Rhodesia   1884
    WSA

FISHER, Stephen D.   USA   1940
    BB65, BB71, PCM, X67

FISHER, Truman R.   USA   1927
    CAP

*FITCH, Theodore F.   USA   1900
    AS66, X64, X65, X66, X67, X68

FITCH, Mrs. Theodore F.
    See: FINLEY, Lorraine Noel

*FITELBERG, Grzegorz   Poland   1879   1953
    DDM, EMS, LMD, PKW, REM, SML
    EMS: ФИ́ТЕЛЬБЕРГ

*FITELBERG, Jerzy   USA   1903   1951
    DDM, EVM, IMD, LMD, PKW, REM   Poland

*FIUME, Orazio   Italy   1908
    BB65, BB71, LMD, REM

FLAGELLO, Nicholas   USA   1928
    ASUC, AS66, BB71, PCM, PC71, WI69, X66, X67

*FLAMENT, Éduard   France   1880   1958
    BB65, BB71, DDM, DMF, EVM, LMD, REM

*FLANAGAN, William, Jr.   USA   1928   1969
    BB65, BB71, CA12, LMD, MLA26/4, PCM, X64, X65, X66,
    X67, X68
    BB65: 1926   PCM: 1923

FLEGL, Josef   Czechoslovakia   1881   1962
    CCZ

*FLEISCHER, Anton (Antal)   Hungary   1891
    LMD, REM

*FLEISCHER, Hans   Germany   1896
    EVM, LMD, REM, X64

*FLEISCHMANN, Aloys Georg   Ireland   1910   Monaco
   LMD, WI69, X68

*FLEITES, Virginia   Cuba   1916
   IMD

FLEM, Paul le
   See: LE FLEM, Paul

*FLEMING, Robert James
   Berkeley   Canada   1921
     BB65, BB71, CA12, CCM, CCM71, CVM, CVMa, IMD, KEY,
     LMD, MCO, MCO68, NLC, NLCa, TFB, X68

*FLETCHER, Grant   USA   1913
     AA73, AS66, BB71, DN70, DN72, LMD, PCM, REM, X64,
     X65, X66, X67, X68

*FLEURY, André   France   1903
   DMF, EVM, LMD, REM

*FLICK-FLOOD, Dora   USA   circa 1895
   WI69

FLIFLET BRAEIN, Edvard
   See: BRAEIN, Edvard Fliflet

*FLIPSE, Eduard   Netherlands   1896
   EVM, X65, X68

FLORES, Bernal   Costa Rica   1937
   BB71, CA15, X67

*FLORIS, Franco   Italy   1906
   REM

*FLOSMAN, Oldřich   Czechoslovakia 1925
     BB65, BB71, CCZ, IMD2, MEH, MNP72/4, MNP72/6, X64,
     X65, X67, X68

*FLOTHUIS, Marius M.
   Hendrikus   Netherlands   1914
     CME, DDM, EVM, IMD, LMD, MEH, NED, REM, X64, X65,
     X66, X67, X68

*FLOYD, Alfred Ernest   Great Britain 1877
   WI69

*FLOYD, Carlisle   USA   1926
     AA73, AS66, BB65, BB71, LMD, OCM, PCM, PC71, REM,
     WTM, X64, X65, X66, X67, X68

FLOYD, Monte Keene   USA   1941
   DN70, DN72

*FLURY, Richard   Switzerland 1896 1967
   BB71, EVM, MLA24/4, REM, SCHW, X64, X68

FLYARKOVSKY, Aleksandr
  Georgievich   USSR   1931
   EMS, PPU69/2, X64, X65, X68
   EMS: ФЛЯРКОВСКИЙ

*FOCH, Dirk   USA   1886 1973
   REM   Java
   Formerly: FOCK

FOCKE, Free   Chile   1910 Netherlands
   REM

*FOERSTER, Josef Bohuslav Czechoslovakia 1859 1951
   BB65, BB71, DDM, EMS, IMD, MEH, REM, SML
   EMS: ФЁРСТЕР

*FOGELL, Martin Maurice Great Britain 1929 Scotland
   WI69

*FOGG, Charles William Eric Great Britain 1903 1939
   LMD, REM

*FOLDES, Andor   Great Britain 1913 Hungary
   REM, WI69, WWS, X64, X67, X68

FOLEY, Daniel   USA   1952
   BS70

FOLEY, Davis   1945
   WAN

*FOLPRECHT, Zdeněk   Czechoslovakia 1900 1961
   CCZ, EVM, IMD, IMD2, LMD, MEH, REM, X65, X67, X68

*FONGAARD, Björn   Norway   1919
   BB71, VTM, X68

*FONSECA, Julio   Costa Rica 1885 1950
   LMD, REM

FONT y de ANTA, Manuel Spain   1895
   EVM

*FONTYN, Jacqueline   Belgium   1930
   CBC, DDM, X65, X68

*FORBES, Watson   Great Britain 1909 Scotland
 WI69, X64

*FORDELL, Erik Fritiof Finland   1917
 COF

*FOREST, Jean Kurt   Germany 1909
 EMS, MEH, SML, X64, X65, X66, X67
 EMS: ФÓРЕСТ

FOREST-DIVONNE, Pierre de la
 See: LA FOREST DIVONNE, Pierre

*FORNEROD, Alöys   Switzerland 1890 1965
 BB65, BB71, DDM, EVM, LMD, MLA22/4, REM, SCHW,
 X64, X65

*FORREST, Hamilton   USA   1901 1964
 X64

*FORRESTER, Leon   Great Britain 1903
 WI69

*FORSMAN, John Väinö Denmark 1924 Finland
 IMD

FORST, Rudolf   USA   1900 1973
 EVM, PCM

FÖRSTER, Josef Bohuslav Czechoslovakia 1859 1951
 EMV, LMD

*FORSTER, Karl   Germany 1904 1963
 LMD, X64

FORSTER, Kurt   1935
 IMD

FORSTER, Paul   Switzerland 1915
 SCHW

FORTIER, Marc   Canada
 CCM71, MCO71

FÖRTIG, Peter   Germany
 PAP

FORTNER, Jack   USA
 ASUC

*FORTNER, Wolfgang   Germany   1907
    BB65, BB71, CME, DDM, DMM, EL:1, EVM, IMD, IMD2,
    LMD, MEH, MZW, PAP, REM, SML, TSC, VNM, WI69,
    X64, X65, X66, X67, X68
    EMS: ФÓPTHEP

*FOSS, Hubert James   Great Britain   1899   1953
    EVM, LMD, REM

*FOSS, Lukas   USA   1922   Germany
    AS66, BB65, BB71, CME, DDM, EVM, IMD, IMD2, LMD,
    MEH, PCM, PC71, REM, SML, WTM, X64, X65, X66,
    X67, X68

*FOSTER, Anthony   Great Britain   1926
    WI69

*FOSTER, Arnold Wilfred
    Allen   Great Britain   1898   1963
    DDM, EVM, LMD, X64

FOSTER, Dorothy   USA
    CAP

*FOSTER, Fay   USA   1886   1960
    AS66, BB65, BB71, EVM

FOSTER, Sidney   USA   1917
    WI69, X65, X66

FOTEK, Jan   Poland   1928
    PKW, X68

FOTSCH, Willy   Switzerland   1923
    SCHW

*FOUGSTEDT, Nils-Eric   Finland   1910   1961
    CME, COF, EVM, LMD, REM, VTM, X65
    LMD: 1963

*FOURESTIER, Louis Félix
    André   France   1892
    DMF, EVM, LMD, QQF, REM, WI69

FOURET, Maurice   France   1888   1962
    BB65, BB71

FOWLER, Marje   USA   1917
    CAP

FOX, Frank   Germany   1908
    WWG

FOX, Frederick A. (Fred)   USA
    AA73, ASUC, X66, X67

FOX, George   Canada
    CVMa, KEY, MCO68, NLC, NLCa

FOX, John Victor   Great Britain   1929
    WI69

FRABOTTA, Frederic Peter   USA   1941
    DN70

FRACKENPOHL, Arthur   USA   1924
    AA73, AS66, PCM, PC71, X64, X65, X66, X67, X68

FRAENKEL, Wolfgang   USA   1897   Germany
    BB65, BB71, IMD, LMD

FRAGAPANE, Paolo   Italy   1910
    LMD

FRAGNY, Robert de
    See: PROTON de la CHAPELLE, Robert

FRAJT, Ludmila   Yugoslavia   1919
    KMJ

*FRANCAIX, Jean René Désiré   France   1912
    BB65, BB71, CMF15, CMF20, CMF39, DDM, DMF, EDM,
    EMS, EVM, IMD, LMD, MEH, QQF, REM, SML, WTM,
    X64, X65, X66, X67, X68
    EMS: ФРАНСЕ

*FRANCE, William Edward   Canada   1912
    CVM, KEY, NLC, NLCa

FRANCHETTI, Aldo   Italy   1882
    REM

*FRANCHETTI, Arnold   USA   1906   Italy
    X65, X66, X67

*FRANCI, Carlo   Italy   1927   Argentina
    LMD, REM

FRANCISCI, Ondrej   Czechoslovakia 1915   Hungary
    CCZ, MEH, ZE71/2, ZE71/3

FRANCL, Jaroslav   Czechoslovakia 1906
    CCZ

FRANCO, Clare J.   USA
  CAP

FRANCO, Enrique   Spain
  CME, X65, X67, X68

*FRANCO, Johan H. G.   USA   1908   Netherlands
  AA73, BB71, EVM, LMD, PCM, PC71, REM, WI69, X64, X65,
  X66, X67, X68

FRANCO MENDES, Hans   Netherlands 1890   1951
  EVM

*FRANCY, Paul   Belgium   1927
  WI69

FRANK, Andrew   USA   1952
  BS70

FRANK, Marcel Gustave   USA   1909   Austria
  AS66, PC71

*FRANK, Marco   Austria   1881   1961
  DDM, EVM, LMD, REM

*FRANKEL, Benjamin   Great Britain 1906 1973
  BB71, DDM, EVM, LMD, MEH, REM, WI69, X65, X66, X67

FRANKEN, Wim   1922
  IMD, X66

FRANKENBURGER, Paul
  See: BEN-HAIM, Paul

FRANZ, Sigfried   1913
  IMD

*FRANZÉN, Bengt K. W.   Sweden   1914
  KSV, X67, X68

FRANZSON, Björn   Iceland   1906
  VTM

*FRASER, Norman George   Great Britain 1904 Chile
  REM, WI69

*FRAZZI, Vito   Italy   1888
  DDM, EVM, IMD, LMD, REM

FRECCIA, Massimo   Italy   1906
  EVM, LMD, REM, X68

FREDRICH, Günter　　　　　　Germany　　　1927
　　SML, X67

FREDRICKSON, Thomas　　　　USA　　　　　1928
　　AS66, PCM, PC71, X64

*FREED, Arnold　　　　　　　USA　　　　　1926
　　PCM, PC71

*FREED, Isadore　　　　　　　USA　　　　　1900　1960
　　BB65, BB71, EVM, LMD, MJM, REM, WI69　　　Russia

FREED, Olov Martin
　　See: WIGGEN, Knut

*FREEDMAN, Harry　　　　　Canada　　　1922　Poland
　　BB65, CA8, CCM, CCM71, CVM, CVMa, IMD, KEY, LMD,
　　MCO, MCO68, MCO71, NLC, NLCa, TFB, X68

*FREEMAN, Harry Lawrence　USA　　　　　1869　1954
　　X64

*FREITAS, Frederico de　　　Portugal　　　1902
　　CME, EVM, LMD, REM, X65

*FREITAS BRANCO, Luíz de　Portugal　　　1890　1955
　　DDM, EVM, LMD, REM

FREITAS BRANCO, Pedro da
　　Costa de　　　　　　　　Portugal　　　1896
　　EVM, LMD, X64

FRENKEL, Daniil Grigorievich　USSR　　　1906
　　EMS
　　EMS: ФРЕ́НКЕЛЬ

*FRENKEL, Stefan　　　　　　USA　　　　　1902　Poland
　　X67

*FREŠO, Tibor　　　　　　　Czechoslovakia　1918
　　CCZ, EVM, LMD, MEH, REM, X68, ZE70/3

FREY, Georges　　　　　　　France　　　　1890
　　ACM

FRIBEC, Krešimir　　　　　　Yugoslavia　　1908
　　BB65, BB71, CME, EMS, HCM, IMD, IMD2, KMJ, MEH, X65,
　　X66, X67, X68
　　EMS: ФРИ́БЕЦ

*FRICKER, Peter Racine　　　Great Britain　1920
　　ASUC, BB65, BB71, BCI, CME, DDM, EVM, IMD, LMD, MEH,
　　MNP64/4, REM, SML, TSC, WI69, X64, X65, X67, X68

*FRICKHOEFFER, Otto   Germany   1892
   EVM

*FRID, Géza   Netherlands   1904 Hungary
   CME, DDM, EVM, IMD, LMD, NED, REM, X64, X65, X66,
   X67, X68

FRID, Grigori Samuilovich   USSR   1915
   EMS, X68
   EMS: ФРИД

FRIDLENDER, Aleksandr
   Grigorievich   USSR   1906
   EMS
   EMS: ФРИ́ДЛЕНЕР

FRIDMANN-KOCHESKAIA, Sophia-Carmen de
   See: ECKHARDT-GRAMATTE, Sophia-Carmen

FRIED, Alexej   Czechoslovakia 1922
   CCZ, MEH, X68

*FRIEDLAND, Martin   Germany   1881
   EVM

FRIEDLANDER, Ernst   Canada   1916 1966
   CCM   Austria

FRIEDMAN, Donald Ernest USA
   X67

FRIEDMAN, Ken   USA   1939
   BB71

FRIEDMAN, Richard   USA   1944
   BB71

FRIEDRICH, Carl   Germany
   X67, X68

*FRIEMANN, Witold   Poland   1889
   EVM, IMD, PKW, X67

*FRIML, Rudolf   USA   1879 1972
   AS66, BB65, BB71, EVM, LMD, MEH,   Bohemia
   MLA29/4, REM, X64, X65, X66, X67, X68
   REM: 1884

*FRISCHENSCHLAGER,
   Friedrich   Austria   1885
   EVM, REM

*FRISKIN, James USA 1886 1967
BB71, EVM, X67, X68 Great Britain

FRITSCH, Johannes G. Germany 1941
IMD, IMD2, LMD, X67, X68

*FROIDEBISE, Pierre Jean
Marie Belgium 1914 1962
BB65, BB71, CBC, CME, DDM, EVM, LMD, REM, X64

FROMM, Herbert USA 1905 Germany
AA73, AS66, IMD, X64, X65, X66, X67, X68

*FROMMEL, Gerhard Germany 1906
DDM, EVM, IMD, LMD, REM, WWG, X66, X67

*FROMM-MICHAELS, Ilse Germany 1888
EVM, LMD, WWG, X66

FROST, John Harvey Great Britain 1924
WI69

FROST, Mary
See: PLUMSTEAD, Mary

*FRÜH, Huldreich Georg Switzerland 1903 1945
IMD, LMD, REM, SCHW

*FRUMERIE, PerGunnar
Fredrik de Sweden 1908
BB71, DDM, EVM, FST, IMD, KSV, LMD, REM, SIM, SIMa,
SOW, STS, SWE, TJU, VTM, X67

*FRYER, George Herbert Great Britain 1877 1957
EVM

*FRYSINGER, J. Frank USA 1878 1954
EVM

*FUCHS, Arno Germany 1909
IMD, LMD, REM

*FUCHS, Carl Emil USA 1907 Hungary
AS66
AS66: FUCHS, Charles Emilio

*FUCHS, Teodoro Argentina 1908 Germany
LMD

FUCHS, Theodor Rumania 1873 1953
RCL

*FUENTES, Juan Bautista   Mexico   1869   1955
    MMX, REM

*FUGA, Sandro   Italy   1906
    IMD, REM

FUKUSHIMA, Kazuo   Japan   1930
    BB65, BB71, IMD, LMD, REM, X64, X66, X68
    REM: FUKU<u>SC</u>IMA

*FULCHER, Ellen Georgina Great Britain circa
    WI69   1885

*FULEIHAN, Anis   USA   1900   1970
    AS66, BB65, BB71, EVM, LMD, PCM,   Cyprus
    PC71, REM, X68

*FULLER, Donald Sanborn   USA   1919
    EVM, REM

FULLER, Wesley M.   USA
    ASUC

*FULTON, Robert Norman   Great Britain 1909
    EVM, WI69, X68

FUNK, Eric   USA   1949
    DN72

FUNK, Heinrich   Germany   1893
    IMD, SML, X66, X68

FURER, Arthur   Switzerland   1924
    LMD, REM, SCHW, X65

*FURLOTTI, Arnaldo   Italy   1880   1958
    LMD, REM

*FURRER, Walter   Switzerland   1902
    SCHW, X65

FÜRST, Jaromir Karel   Czechoslovakia 1895
    CCZ

*FÜRST, Paul Walter   Austria   1926
    IMD, IMD2, X65, X67

*FURTWÄNGLER, Wilhelm
  Gustav Heinrich Ernst Martin Germany   1886   1954
    ACM, DDM, EMS, EVM, IMD, LMD, REM, X64, X65, X66,
    X67, X68
    EMS: ФУ́РТВЕНГЛЕР

*FURUHJELM, Erik Gustaf Finland 1883
 COF, EVM, IMD, LMD, REM, VTM

*FUSCO, Giovanni Italy 1906 1968
 LMD, REM

*FUSELLA, Gaetano Italy 1876
 REM

*FUSSAN, Werner Germany 1912
 IMD, LMD, REM

*FÜSSL, Karl Heinz Austria 1924 Czecho-
 CME, IMD, IMD2, MNG, X65, X66, X67 slovakia

FUSTER, Miguel Angel Venezuela

FYLYPENKO, Arkadie
 See: FILIPPENKO, A. D.

*GAÁL, Jenö Hungary 1906
 CHC, LMD, X68

*GABAYE, Pierre France 1930
 QQF

*GABITCHVADZE, Rebaz
 Kondratzevich USSR 1913
 EMS, LMD, PPU, X68
 EMS: ГАБИЧВАДЗЕ

GABOLD, Ingolf Denmark 1942 Germany
 DMTsp, X67, X68

*GABRIEL, Gavino Italy 1881
 LMD, REM

GABRIEL, Wolfgang Austria
 X67, X68

*GABRIEL-MARIE, Jean France 1907 1970
 MLA27

GABUNIYA, Nodar
 Kalistratovich USSR 1932
 MEH, X68
 MEH: GABUNIJA

GABURO, Kenneth Louis USA 1927
 AS66, BB65, BB71, IMD, LCI, LMD, PCM, PC71, X66, X67,
 X68
 IMD and PCM: 1926

*GADDA, Giulio   Italy   1905
  REM
  REM: 1841-1905

*GADE, Jacob   Denmark   1879   1963
  BB65, BB71

*GADOMSKI, Henryk   Poland   1907   1941
  EVM

*GADZHIBEKOV, Sultan
  Ismailoglu   USSR   1919
  EMS, EVM, LMD, PPU, PPU69/2, PPU69/4, X64
  EMS: ГАДЖИБЕ́КОВ

GADZHIBEKOV, Zulfugar Abdul
  Hussein   USSR   1884   1950
  LMD

*GADZHIEV, Akhmed Dzhevdet
  Ismailoglu Ogly   USSR   1917
  EMS, LMD, PPU
  EMS: ГАДЖИ́ЕВ

GADZHIEV, Rauf Soltanogly   USSR   1922
  EMS, PPU, X64
  EMS: ГАДЖИ́ЕВ

*GAGIĆ, Bogdan   Yugoslavia   1931
  HCM, IMD, IMD2, KMJ, LMD

*GAGNEBIN, Henri   Switzerland   1886   1960
  BB71, DDM, EVM, IMD, LMD, MEH, REM,   Belgium
  SCHW, WI69, WWS, X64, X66, X67, X68

GAGNON, Alain   Canada
  CCM71, CVMa, KEY, MCO68, MCO71

GAIDAMAKA, Petr Danilovich   USSR   1907
  EMS
  EMS: ГАЙДАМА́КА

*GAIGEROVA, Varvara
  Andrianovna   USSR   1903   1944
  EMS, EVM, REM
  EMS: ГА́ЙГЕРОВА

*GAILHARD, André Charles
  Samson   France   1885
  DMF, EVM, LMD, REM

*GAILLARD, Marius-François   France   1900   1973
  DDM, DMF, EVM, LMD, REM

*GAILLARD, Paul-André   Switzerland   1922
   LMD, REM, SCHW, X65, X66, X67, X68

*GAITO, F. Carlo   Italy   1900
   CA12, REM

*GAJDOV, Stevan   Yugoslavia   1905
   KMJ, REM

*GÁL, Hans   Great Britain   1890   Austria
   DDM, EMS, EVM, IMD, LMD, REM, WWG, X64, X65, X66,
   X67, X68
   EMS: ГАЛЬ

GALAEV, Boris Aleksandrovich USSR   1889
   EMS, X68
   EMS: ГАЛÁЕВ

*GALAJIKIAN, Florence
   Grandland   USA   1900
   EVM, LCI, X66

*GALAN, Natalio   Cuba   1919
   WI69

*GALINDO-DIMAS, Blas   Mexico   1910
   BB65, BB71, CA11, EVM, HET20, IMD, LMD, MMX, REM,
   X66

GALINESCU, Gavriil   Rumania   1883   1960
   RCL

*GALKAUSKAS, Konstantine
   Mikhailovich   USSR   1875   1963
   EMS   Lithuania
   EMS: ГАЛКÁУСКАС

GALLAHER, Christopher S.   USA
   ASUC

GALLA-RINI, Anthony   USA   1904
   BB65, BB71

GALLICO, Claudio   Italy   1929
   LMD, REM, X64, X66, X67, X68

*GALLICO, Paolo   USA   1868   1955
   LMD, REM   Italy

leGALLIENNE, Dorian   Australia   1915   1963

*GALLIERA, Alceo   Italy   1910
   REM, X65

*GALLOIS-MONTBRUN,
Raymond   France   1918   Indo-China
    DMF, IMD, QQF, REM, X68

*GALLON, Jean Charles
Claude   France   1878   1959
    BB71, DDM, EVM, REM

*GALLON, Noël Jean Charles
André   France   1891   1966
    BB65, BB71, DDM, DMF, EVM, MLA24/4, REM

GALUN, Andrija   Yugoslavia   1945
    KMJ

*GALYNIN, German
Germanovich   USSR   1922   1966
    EMS, IMD, LMD, MEH, REM, SCD, SML, X65, X66
    EMS: ГАЛЫНИН

*GAMBA, Pierino   Italy   1937
    REM

GAMER, Carlton   USA
    ASUC

GANDINI, Gerardo   Argentina   1936
    X66

GANDOLFI, Gino   Italy   1887
    LMD, REM

*GANEVAL, Emilienne   France   1896
    REM
    REM: MACHABEY

GANGEMI, Charles D.   USA
    ASUC

*GANZ, Rudolph   USA   1877   1972
    AS66, BB71, EVM, LCI, MLA29/4, REM,   Switzerland
    SCHW, X64, X65, X66, X67, X68

*GARANT, Albert Antonio Serge   Canada   1929
    BB71, BCL, CCM, CCM71, CVM, CVMa, DDM, KEY, MCO71,
    TFB, X68
    BB71: 1928

*GARAY, Narciso   Panama   1876   1953
    LMD, REM

GARBELOTTO, Antonio   Italy   1906
    LMD, REM

*GARCÍA, Juan Francisco   Dominican   1892
    EVM, LMD, REM,   Republic
    X67, X68

GARCIA ABRIL, Antón   Spain
    CME, X65, X67
    CME: ABRIL, Anton Garcia

*GARCÍA ASCOT, Rosa   Spain   1906
    REM

*GARCÍA CATURLA, Alejandro   Cuba   1906   1940
    DDM, IMD, LMD, REM

GARCÍA LEOZ, Jesús   Spain   1904   1953
    DDM

*GARCÍA-MORILLO, Roberto   Argentina   1911
    CA8, IMD, LMD, REM, X66, X68

*GARDELLI, Lamberto   Sweden   1915   Italy
    X64, X66, X67, X68

*GARDINER, Henry Balfour   Great Britain   1877   1950
    IMD, LMD, REM, X67

GARDINER, John Ernest   Great Britain   1928
    WI69

*GARDNER, John Linton   Great Britain   1917
    EVM, LMD, REM, WI69, X65, X67, X68

*GARDNER, Samuel   USA   1891   Russia
    AS66, EVM, LMD, REM, WI69, X68

GÁRDONYI, Zoltán   Hungary   1906
    CHC, LMD, SML, X64, X65, X68

*GARGUILO, Terenzio   Italy   1903   1972
    IMD, LMD, REM, WI69, X68
    LMD and WI69: 1905

GARLICK, Antony   USA   1928
    PC71

GAROFALO, Carlo Giorgio   Italy   1886   1962
    LMD, REM

*GARRATT, Percival   Great Britain   1877   1953
    EVM

*GARRIDO, Pablo   Puerto Rico   1905   Chile
    BB65, BB71, CA9, EVM, LMD, REM

GARRIDO LECCA, Celso   Peru   1926
    BB65, BB71, X64, X67, X68

GARSHNEK, Anatoliy Ivanovich   USSR   1918
    PPU

*GARSON, Alfred   Great Britain   1927   Union of
    CVM, MCO71   South Africa

GARTMAN, Foma
   Aleksandrovich   USSR   1885   1956
    EMS, X65
    EMS: ГА́РТМАН

*GARTON, Graham   Great Britain   1929
    WI69

GARZTECKA, Irena   Poland   1913
    PKW, X64

*GASANOV, Gotfrid Alievich   USSR   1900
    EMS, X64, X65, X68
    EMS: ГАСА́НОВ

GASLINI, Giorgio   Italy   1929
    LMD, MNG, REM, X64, X65, X66

GASPARINI, Jole   Italy   1882
    LMD, REM

*GASSMANN, Alfred Leonz   Switzerland   1876   1962
    SCHW

GASTYNE, Serge de   USA   1930   France
    AS66

GASZNER, Moshe   Israel   1929   Hungary
    ACU

GATES, Crawford   USA   1921
    AS66, X64, X65, X66, X68

*GATTI, Carlo   Italy   1876   1965
    EVM, LMD, REM, X65, X66, X68

*GATTI, Guido Mario   Italy   1892
    EVM, REM, X67, X68

GAUK, Aleksandr Vasilievich   USSR   1893 1963
   EMS, SML
   EMS: ГА́УК

*GAUSS, Otto   Germany   1877 1970
   EVM, LMD, MLA27/4

GAUTHERAT, Mario   France   1902
   ACM

*GAVAZZENI, Gianandrea   Italy   1909
   EVM, IMD, LMD, REM, X65, X67, X68

GAVRILIN, Valery
   Aleksandrovich   USSR
   X68

GAWLAS, Jan   Poland   1901 1965
   PKW, X65

GAYDAMAKA, Petr Danilovich USSR   1907
   PPU, PPU69/2

*GAYFER, James McDonald   Canada   1916
   CCM, CCM71, CVM, CVMa, KEY, MCO68, NLCa

GAZOULEAS, Stephanos   Greece   1931
   CME, EL:1, EL:2, EL:3, PAP, X65

GEARHART, Livingston   USA   1916
   AS66

*GEBHARD, Hans   Germany   1897
   EVM, IMD, LMD, REM, X67

*GEBHARD, Heinrich   USA   1878 1963
   BB65, BB71, LMD, X64, X65   Germany

*GEBHARD, Ludwig   Germany   1907
   IMD, LMD, REM

*GEBHARD, Max   Germany   1896
   EVM, IMD, LMD, REM

*GEDDA, Giulio Cesare   Italy   1899 1970
   BB71, LMD, REM

GEDDES, John Maxwell   Great Britain 1941 Scotland
   WI69

GEDIKE, A. F.
   See: GOEDICKE, A. F.

GEDZHADZE, Irakly   USSR   1925
     BB71

*GEEHL, Henry Ernest   Great Britain   1881   1961
     EVM

*GEHRING, Carl   USA   1897
     EVM

*GEIERHAAS, Gustav   Germany   1888
     EVM, LMD, X68

*GEISER, Walther   Switzerland   1897
     CME, DDM, EVM, IMD, LMD, MEH, REM, SCHW, WWS,
     X64, X65, X67, X68

*GEISLER, Christian   Denmark   1869   1951
     IMD

*GEISSLER, Fritz   Germany   1921
     EMS, IMD, IMD2, MEH, SML, X64, X65, X66, X67, X68
     EMS: ГЕЙСЛЕР

GEISTHARDT, Hans-Joachim   Germany   1925
     SML

*GELBRUN, Artur   Israel   1913   Poland
     ACU, BB71, MM59, REM, WWI

GELINEAU, Joseph   France   1920
     BB71, X65, X66, X68

GELLMAN, Steven   Canada
     KEY, MCO71, X67

GENTILE, Stefano   Italy   1872
     REM

GENTILI, Alberto   Italy   1873   1954
     LMD

GENTILUCCI, Armando   Italy   1939
     LMD, X65, X66, X67

GENTILUCCI, Ottorino   Italy   1910
     IMD, LMD, REM

*GENZMER, Harald   Germany   1909
     BB71, CME, DDM, EVM, IMD, IMD2, LMD, MZW, PAP,
     REM, SML, VNM, X64, X66, X67, X68

GEOFFRAY, César   France   1901
     DDM

*GEORGE, Earl   USA   1924
    AS66, PCM

*GEORGE, Graham   Canada   1912   England
    CCM, KEY, MCO, MCO68, MCO71, NLC, X66

GEORGESCU, Constantin   Rumania   1895   1960
    RCL

GEORGESCU, Remus   Rumania   1932
    RCL

GEORGIADIS, Georges   Greece   1912
    BB65, BB71

GEORGIEV, Emil Elevterov   Bulgaria   1926
    BMK
    BMK: ГЕОРГИЕВ

*GERAEDTS, Heinrich Joseph
    Hubert   Netherlands   1892
    EVM, X67
    X67: GERAEDITS, Henri

*GERAEDTS, Jaap   Netherlands   1924
    EVM, IMD, NED, X65, X66, X67

*GERBER, René   Switzerland   1908
    IMD, LMD, REM, SCHW, WI69

GERELLI, Ennio   Italy   1907   1970
    BB71, LMD, REM

*GERGELY, Jean   Hungary   1911
    X68

*GERHARD, Fritz Christian   Germany   1911
    X67

*GERHARD, Roberto   Great Britain   1896   1970
    BB65, BB71, CME, DDM, EVM, LMD, MEH,   Spain
    MLA27/4, PAP, REM, WI69, X64, X65, X66, X67, X68

*GERHARDT, Carl   Germany   1900   1945
    IMD, LMD

*GERMANI, Fernando   Italy   1906
    REM, X66

GEROV, Naiden Evlogiev   Bulgaria   1916
    BMK, X65, X66, X68
    BMK: ГЕРОВ

GERRISH, John   USA   1910
    PCM

*GERSCHEFSKI, Peter Edwin   USA   1909
    BB71, IMD, PCM, X64, X65, X66, X67

GERSHFELD, David
    Grigorievich   USSR   1911
    BB65, BB71, EMS
    EMS: ГЕ́РШФЕЛЬД

GERSOV, Viktor Aleksandrovich
    See: ORANSKI, V. A.

*GERSTBERGER, Karl Theodor   Germany   1892   1955
    EVM, IMD, LMD, REM

GERSTEL, Osward   Israel   1923   Rumania
    ACU

*GERSTER, Ottmar   Germany   1897   1969
    BB71, CME, DDM, EMS, EVM, IMD, IMD2, LMD, MLA26/4,
    SML, X64, X65, X66, X67, X68
    EMS: ГЕ́РСТЕР

GERTHOFFERT, Léon   France   1922
    ACM

*GERVASIO, Raffaele   Italy   1910
    LMD, REM

*GESENSWAY, Louis   USA   1906   Latvia
    AS66, BB71, X64, X68

GESTERMANN, Eugène   France   1905
    ACM

GESZLER, György   Hungary   1913
    CHC

GETHEN, Felix   Australia   1916   England
    AMM

GEVIKSMAN, Vitaliy
    Artemevich   USSR   1924
    PPU

GHECIU, Diamandi   Rumania   1892
    RCL

GHEDIKE, A. F.
    See: GOEDICKE, A. F.

*GHEDINI, Giorgio Federico   Italy   1892   1965
    BB65, BB71, DDM, EMS, EVM, IMD, IMD2, LMD, MLA22/4,
    SML, X64, X65, X66, X67, X68
    EMS: ГЕДИНИ

GHENT, Emmanuel   USA   1925   Canada
    ASUC, BB65, BB71, LMD, PC71, X66, X67

*GHEORGHIU, Valentin   Rumania   1928
    RCL, SML

GHEORGHIU, Victor   Rumania   1888   1951
    EVM, RCL
    EVM: GEORGKIN, Victor
    EMV: 1890

GHEORGHIU, Virgil   Rumania   1905
    RCL

GHIDIONESCU, Grigore   Rumania   1901   1968
    RCL

GHIGA, Ion   Rumania   1895
    RCL

*GHIONE, Franco   Italy   1886   1964
    BB65, BB71, LMD, REM, X64

*GHISI, Federico   Italy   1901   China
    LMD, REM, X64, X65, X68

*GHISLANZONI, Alberto   Italy   1897
    EDM, LMD, REM

GIACCHINO, Carmelo   Italy   1892
    REM

GIACCHINO CUSENZA, Maria   Italy   1898
    REM

GIAMPIERI, Alamiro   Italy   1893   1963
    LMD, REM, X64

*GIANNEO, Luis   Argentina   1897
    IMD, LMD, REM, X64, X67

*GIANNINI, Vittorio   USA   1903   1966
    AS66, BB65, BB71, EVM, IMD, LMD, MLA23/4, PCM, REM,
    X64, X65, X66, X67, X68

GIANNINI, Walter   USA   1917
    IMD, X65, X67

GIARDA, Goffredo   Italy   1886
REM

*GIARDA, Luigi Stefano   Italy   1868   1953
EVM, LMD, REM

*GIBALIN, Boris Dmitrivich   USSR   1911
EMS
EMS: ГИБА́ЛИН

GIBBS, Alan   Great Britain
X64

*GIBBS, Cecil Armstrong   Great Britain 1889 1960
BB65, BB71, DDM, EVM, LMD, REM, X67

GIBBS, Michel Clement   Great Britain
X68

*GIDEON, Miriam   USA   1906
AA73, BB71, PCM, WI69, X65, X67, X68

*GIELEN, Michael Andreas   Argentina   1927
CME, IMD, LMD, MNG, REM, VTM, X66, X67, X68

*GIESEKING, Walter Wilhelm Germany   1895 1956
BB65, BB71, DDM, EMS, EVM, IMD, LMD,   France
REM, SML, X64, X65, X67
EMS: ГИЗЕКИНГ

GIESELER, Walter   1919
IMD2, X68

GIFFORD, Helen   Australia circa 1937
X67

GIJE, Paul le   Belgium   1883
EVM

*GILARDI, Gilardo   Argentina   1889 1963
BB71, CA12, EVM, LMD, REM, X68

GILBERT, Anthony John   Great Britain 1934
WI69, X64, X66, X67, X68

GILBOA, Jacob   Israel   1920 Czecho-
ACU, IMD2, X68   slovakia

*GILDER, Eric   Great Britain 1911
WI69

GILL, Milton   USA   1932   1968
    ASUC, PCM, X64, X65, X68

*GILLIS, Don   USA   1912
    AS66, LMD, PCM, PC71, REM, X64, X65, X67, X68

*GIL-MARCHEX, Henri   France   1894   1970
    BB71, DDM, EVM

GILMORE, Bernard Howard   USA   1937
    CAP, DN70, DN72, X66

GILS, Gust   Netherlands   1924

*GILSE, Jan van   Switzerland   1881   1944
    REM   Netherlands

GILTAY, Berend   Netherlands   1910
    NED, X68

GIMENEZ, Herminio   Paraguay   1905
    CA15

*GIMÉNEZ, Remberto   Paraguay   1889
    REM, X66

*GINASTERA, Alberto Evaristo Argentina   1916
    BB65, BB71, DDM, EMS, EVM, IMD, HET10, HET11, LMD,
    MEH, QLA, REM, WTM, X64, X65, X66, X67, X68
    EMS: ХИНАСТЕРА

*GINNEKEN, Jaap van   Netherlands   1913   1972
    EVM

GIORGI, Carlo Piero   Italy   1897   1967
    LMD, REM

GIOVANETTI, Egisto   Italy   1884
    REM

GIOVANNETTI, Gustavo   Italy   1880   1968
    MLA25/4, REM, X68

*GIPPS, Ruth   Great Britain   1921   1965
    LMD, WI69, X64, X65, X66, X67

*GIRNATIS, Walter   Germany   1894
    WI69, WWG

GIRÓN LANDELL, Adolfo   Mexico   1904
   MMX

GIUCCI, Carlos   Uruguay   1904   1958
   CA17

*GIURANNA, Elena Barbara   Italy   1902
   EVM, IMD, REM

GIVULESCU, Cornel   Rumania   1893   1969
   RCL

*GJERSTØM, Gunnar   Norway   1891   1951
   CNO

*GLANTZ, Leib   Israel   1904   1964
   ACU, MJM   Russia

*GLANVILLE-HICKS, Peggy   USA   1912   Australia
   BB65, BB71, CA13, EVM, LMD, OCM, REM, X68

GLASER, Victoria   USA   1918
   AS66, PCM

*GLASER, Werner Wolf   Sweden   1910   Germany
   FST, SIM, SIMa, SOW

GLASS, Paul Eugene   USA   1934
   AS66, X66

GLASS, Philip   USA   1937
   PCM, PC71

*GLASSER, Albert   USA   1916
   AS66

*GLASSER, Stanley   Union of   1926
   WI69, X67   South Africa

GLEAVES, Ian Beresford   Great Britain   1937
   WI69

GLEBOV, Yevgeniy
   Aleksandrovich   USSR   1929
   EMS, PPU, X64, X67
   EMS: ГЛЕБОВ

*GLENCK, Hermann von   Switzerland   1883
   EVM

GLICK, Srul Irving   Canada   1934
   CCM, CCM71, CVM, CVMa, KEY, LMD, MCO, MCO68,
   MCO71, X68

*GLIERE, Reinhold Moritzovich   USSR   1875 1956
    BB65, BB71, CME, DDM, EMS, EVM, IMD, LMD, MEH, REM,
    SCD, SML, WTM, X65, X68
    EMS: ГЛИЭР

*GLINSKI, Mateusz Matteo   Italy   1892   Poland
    LMD, REM, X64, X68

GLOBOKAR, Vinko   Yugoslavia   1934
    KMJ, MSC, X67, X68

GLODEANU, Liviu   Rumania   1938
    RCL, X64, X65, X66, X68

GLUH, Mihail Aleksandrovich   USSR   1907
    EMS
    EMS: ГЛУХ

GMEINDL, Walter   Austria   1890
    EVM

*GNATTALI, Radamés   Brazil   1906
    CA16, FBC, IMD, LMD, REM

GNAZZO, Anthony J.   USA   1936
    BB71, PAP, X68

*GNECCHI, Vittorio   Italy   1876 1954
    BB71, DDM, EVM, IMD, LMD, REM

*GNESSIN, Mikhail Fabinovich   USSR   1883 1957
    BB65, BB71, DDM, EMS, EVM, IMD, LMD, MEH, REM,
    X66, X68
    EMS: ГНЕСИН

GNIOT, Walerian Józef   Poland   1902
    PKW

GOBEC, Radovan   Yugoslavia   1909
    KMJ

*GOEB, Roger   USA   1914
    PCM, WI69, X64

*GOEDICKE, Alexander
    Fedorovich   USSR   1877 1957
    BB65, BB71, DDM, EMS, EVM, IMD, LMD ,REM
    IMD: GEDIKE   LMD: GHEDIKE
    EMS: ГЕДИКЕ

*GOEHLER, Georg Karl   Germany   1874 1954
    LMD, REM

*GOEHR, Alexander   Great Britain   1932 Germany
   BB65, BB71, BCI, CME, DDM, IMD, LMD, OCM, REM, TSC,
   X64, X65, X66, X67, X68

*GOEHR, Walter   Great Britain   1903 1960
   BB65, BB71, CME, DDM, EVM, LMD, MEH,   Germany
   REM, SML

GOETSCHIUS, Marjorie   USA   1915
   AS66

*GOEYENS, Fernando   Belgium   1892
   EVM

*GOEYVAERTS, Karel August   Belgium   1923
   CBC, DDM, EVM, IMD, LMD, REM, X64, X68

GOEYVAERTS-FALK
   See: GOEYVAERTS, Karel August

GOITRE, Roberto   Italy   1927
   LMD

GO-JEN   China

*GOKIELI, Ivan Rafaelovich   USSR   1899
   EMS, PPU
   EMS: ГОКИЕ́ЛИ

GOLABOVSKI, Sotir   Yugoslavia   1937
   KMJ

*GOLD, Ernest   USA   1921 Austria
   BB65, BB71, IMD, LMD, PCM, PC71, X64, X65, X67, X68
   Pseudonym: GOLDNER

*GOLDBERG, Theo   Canada   1921 Germany
   BB65, BB71, CCM71, IMD, MCO, X68

GOLDENBERG, William Leon   USA   1936
   AS66

*GOLDENVEISER, Alexander
   Borisovich   USSR   1875 1961
   BB65, BB71, EMS, MEH, SML
   EMS: ГОЛЬДЕНВЕ́ЙЗЕР

*GOLDMAN, Edwin Franko   USA   1878 1956
   AS66, EVM, LMD, PCM, REM, X66, X67

*GOLDMAN, Richard Franko   USA   1910
   AS66, BB71, DAS, LMD, PCM, REM, X65, X66, X67, X68

GOLDMANN, Friedrich   1941
    IMD, X65, X66, X67

GOLDNER, Ernest
    See: GOLD, Ernest

*GOLDSCHMIDT, Bertold   Great Britain   1903   Germany
    EVM, IMD, LMD, REM, X64

GOLDSMITH, Edward David
  Barnabas   Rhodesia   1930
    WI69

GOLDSWORTHY, William
  Arthur   USA   1878   England
    AS66, X67

*GOLEMINOV, Marin Petrov   Bulgaria   1908
    BB65, BB71, BMK, EMS, EVM, LMD, MEH, REM, SML,
    X66, X67, X68
    BMK: ГОЛЕМИНОВ   EMS: ГОЛЕМИНОВ

*GOLESTAN, Stan   France   1875   1956
    DDM, EVM, IMD, LMD, MEH, RCL,   Rumania
    REM, SML
    LMD: 1876

*GOLLER, Vinzenz   Austria   1873   1953
    EVM, X64, X67

*GOLOVÁNOV, Nikolai
  Semenovich   USSR   1891   1953
    EMS, EVM, MEH, X66, X68
    EMS: ГОЛОВА́НОВ

GOLTZ, Boris Grigorievich   USSR   1913   1942
    EMS, EVM
    EMS: ГОЛЬЦ

*GOLUBENZEV, Alexander
  Alexandrovich   USSR   1899
    EMS, PPU
    EMS: ГОЛУБЕ́НЦЕВ

*GOLUBEV, Evgeny Kirillovich   USSR   1910
    EMS, EVM, LMD, REM
    EMS: ГО́ЛУБЕВ

*GOLYSHEV, Efim   Germany   1895   1970
    BB71, EVM, LMD, MEH, MLA28   Russia

GOMBAU GUERRA, Gerardo CME, DDM, X65	Spain	1906	
*GÓMEZ CARRILLO, Manuel REM	Argentina	1883	
*GOMEZ y GARCIA, Domingo Julio EVM, REM	Spain	1886	
*GOMOLYAKA, Vadim Borisovich EMS, PPU EMS: ГОМОЛЯ́КА	USSR	1914	
GONCHIKSUMLA EMS EMS: ГОНЧИКСУ́МЛА	USSR	1905	
GONZALEZ, Jose Luis HET16	Mexico	1937	
*GONZALEZ INIGUEZ, Hilario EVM	Cuba	1920	
*GONZÁLEZ-ZULETA, Fabio BB65, BB71, LMD, REM	Colombia	1920	
*GOODCHILD, Arthur WI69	Great Britain	1899	
GOODE, Jack C. LCI, PC71, X65, X66, X67	USA	1921	
*GOODENOUGH, Forrest X67	USA	1918	
GOODMAN, Alfred Grant BB71, WI69 Formerly: GUTTMANN	USA	1920	Germany
GOODMAN, Joseph PCM, PC71, X65, X68	USA	1918	
GOODMAN, Saul AS66, PCM, PC71	USA		
GOODWIN, Sydney BS72	USA	1951	Japan
GOOSEN, Frederic X68	USA		

*GOOSENS, Eugene Aynesley   Great Britain   1893   1962
    AMM, BB65, BB71, CME, DDM, EMS, EVM, IMD, LMD,
    MEH, REM, SML
    EMS: ГУ́ССЕНС

GOOSSEN, Frederic   USA
    AA73, X67, X68

GORBULSKIS, Gorbulski
  Benjaminos Iokubo   USSR   1925   Lithuania
    EMS
    EMS: ГОРБУ́ЛЬСКИС

GORDELI, Otar Mihailovich   USSR   1928
    BB65, BB71, EMS, LMD
    EMS: ГОРДЕ́ЛИ

*GORDON, Gavin Muspratt   Great Britain   1901   1970
    BB71   Scotland

GORDON, Louis B.   USA
    ASUC

GORDON, Philip   USA   1894
    AS66, PCM, PC71, X64, X67

GORE, Gerald Wifring
    See: RIEGGER, Wallingford

GÓRECKI, Henryk Mikolaj   Poland   1933
    BB65, BB71, CME, DDM, EMS, IMD, IMD2, LMD, MEH,
    PKW, REM, X64, X65, X66, X67, X68
    EMS: ГУРЕ́ЦКИЙ

*GORIN, Igor   USA   1914   Russia
    X64

*GORINI, Gino   Italy   1914
    EVM, IMD, LMD, REM, X67

GORINI FALCO, Roberto   Italy   1924
    LMD, REM

*GÖRNER, Hans-Georg   Germany   1908
    EVM, LMD, SML, WWG, X67, X68

*GORTON, Thomas Arthur   USA   1910
    WI69

GOSLICH, Siegfried   Germany
    X68

*GOSTUŠKI, Dragutin   Yugoslavia   1923
  BB65, BB71, IMD, KMJ, LMD, REM, X66, X67

*GOTKOWSKY, Ida   France   1933
  WI69

*GOTOVAC, Jakov   Yugoslavia   1895
  BB65, BB71, CME, EMS, EVM, HCM, IMD, KMJ, LMD, MEH,
  REM, SML, X64, X65, X66, X67, X68
  EMS: ГО́ТОВАЦ

GÖTSCH, Georg   Germany   1895   1956
  LMD

GOTTLIEB, Jack S.   USA   1930
  AA73, AS66, BB65, BB71, CA9, DN72, LMD, PCM, PC71,
  X64, X65, X66, X67, X68

*GOUDOEVER, Henri Daniel
  van   Netherlands   1898
  EVM

GOULD, Elizabeth   USA   1904
  AS66, PCM, PC71

*GOULD, Glenn Herbert   Canada   1932
  BB65, BB71, CCM, KEY, LMD, WI69, X64, X66, X67, X68

*GOULD, Morton   USA   1913
  AA73, AS66, BB65, BB71, EVM, LMD, MEH, PCM, PC71,
  REM, WI69, WTM, X64, X65, X66, X67, X68

GOURY, Suzanne
  See: REMONDON, Suzanne

*GOW, David Godfrey   Great Britain   1924
  WI69, X64, X68

GOZENPUD, Matvei Akimovich   USSR   1903   1961
  EMS
  EMS: ГОЗЕНПУ́Д

*GRABERT, Martin   Germany   1868   1951
  EVM

*GRABNER, Hermann   Austria   1886   1969
  BB71, DDM, EVM, IMD, LMD, MLA26/4, REM, SML,
  X66, X67

GRABÓCZ, Miklós   Hungary   1927
  CHC

GRABOVSKY, Leonid   USSR   1935
  BB65, BB71, CME, X65, X67, X68

GRAÇA, Fernando Lopes   Portugal   1906
  CME, REM, X65

*GRAD, Gabriel   Israel   1890   1950
  ACU, EVM, LMD, REM   Lithuania

*GRADENWITZ, Peter Emanuel   Israel   1910   Germany
  ACU, BB71, DDM, LMD, REM, SML, WWI, X64, X65, X66,
  X67, X68

*GRADSTEIN, Alfred   Poland   1904   1954
  EMS, IMD, LMD, PKW, REM
  EMS: ГРА́ДШТЕЙН

*GRAEFFE, Didier   USA
  PCM

*GRAETZER, Guillermo   Argentina   1914   Austria
  BB71, IMD, LMD, REM

*GRAF, Erich   Austria   1906
  X64, X68

*GRÄFLINGER, Franz   Austria   1876   1962
  BB71

GRAGNANI, Emilio   Italy   1900
  REM

GRAHAM, Susan Christine   Great Britain   1941
  WI69
  Formerly: THOMAS

*GRAINGER, Percy Aldridge   USA   1882   1961
  AMM, AS66, BB65, BB71, DDM, EMS, EVM,   Australia
  LMD, REM, X64, X66, X67, X68
  EMS: ГРЕ́ЙНДЖЕР

*GRAM, Peder   Denmark   1881   1956
  EVM, IMD, LMD, REM, VTM

*GRAMATGES, Harold   Cuba   1918
  EVM, IMD, LMD, REM

GRANDERT, Jonny   Sweden   1939
  FST, VTM, X68

GRANDIS, Renato de
  See: DE GRANDIS, Renato

*GRANDJANY, Marcel USA   1891 France
 AS66, QQF, REM, X66, X67

GRANDJÉ, Rosa   Belgium 1907
 EVM

GRANELLI, Edoardo USSR   1883 Italy
 REM

*GRANT, Allan L.   USA   1892 1965
 AS66, X65

*GRANT, William Parks USA   1932
 AA73, PC71, X65, X67, X68

GRÄSBECK, Gottfrid Gustaf
 Unosson   Finland 1927
 KKO, X66

*GRASSE, Edwin   USA   1884 1954
 EVM

*GRATTON, J. J. Hector Canada 1900
 CCM, KEY, MCO

GRAVES, William   USA   1916
 AS66, IMD, PCM, PC71

*GRAY, Allan   Great Britain 1902 Poland
 EVM   1973
 Pseudonym of: ZMIGROD, Joseph

*GRAY, Cecil William Turpie Great Britain 1895 1951
 OCM, REM, X66

GRAYSON, Alan   USA   1930 England
 AS66

GRBEC, Ivan   Yugoslavia 1889 1966
 KMJ

GRECIANINOV, A. T.
 See: GRETCHANINOV, A. T.

G'RDEV, Atanas Genov Bulgaria 1896 1964
 BMK
 BMK: ГЪРДЕВ

GREEN, Bernard   USA   1908
 AS66, PCM

GREEN, George   1930
 WAN

*GREEN, Ray   USA   1909
    AA73, AS66, IMD, LMD, PCM, REM, X64, X66, X68
    PCM: 1908

GREEN, Robert L.   USA
    CAP

GREEN, Russell   Canada
    KEY, NLC, NLCa

GREENBERG, Lionel   Canada   1926
    CCM, KEY, MCO68, NLC

GREENE, Douglass M.   USA
    ASUC

*GREENWOOD, John Darnforth
    Herman   Great Britain   1889
    EVM, REM, WI69

GREFIENS, Vinicius   Rumania   1916
    RCL

*GREGOR, Čestmír   Czechoslovakia   1926
    BB65, BB71, CCZ, IMD2, MEH, X64, X67

GREGORC, Janez   Yugoslavia   1934
    KMJ

GREGORC, Janko   Yugoslavia   1905
    KMJ

GREGORC, Jurij   Yugoslavia   1916
    KMJ

*GREGORI, Nininha   Brazil   1925
    IMD

GREGSON, Edward   Great Britain   1945
    WI69

*GREISSLE, Felix   USA   1899   Austria
    X66

*GRENZ, Arthur   Germany   1909
    EVM, IMD

GREŠÁK, Jozef   Czechoslovakia   1907
    CCZ, MEH, X68, ZE70/3, ZE71/2, ZE71/3

*GRETCHANINOV, Alexander
  Tikhonovich   USA   1864   1956
    BB71, DDM, EMS, EVM, IMD, LMD, MEH,   Russia
    REM, SML, WTM, X64, X68
    EVM: GRETSJANINOW   LMD: GRECIANINOV
    MEH: GREČANINOV   REM: GRECIANINOV
    EMS: ГРЕЧАНИ́НОВ

GREY, De Sayles R.   USA   1930
    DN70

*GREY, Geoffrey David   Great Britain   1934
    X68

*GRGOŠEVIĆ, Zlatko   Yugoslavia   1900
    EVM, HCM, KMJ

*GRIEND, Koos van de   Netherlands   1905   1950
    EVM

GRIESBACH, Karl Rudi   Germany   1916
    EMS, MEH, SML, X64, X66, X67, X68
    EMS: ГРИ́СБАХ

*GRIFFIS, Elliot   USA   1893   1967
    AS66, BB65, BB71, EVM, LMD, PCM, X64, X66

GRIFFITH, Peter   1943
    WAN

*GRIFFITHS, Thomas Vernon Great Britain   1894
    WI69

GRIGORIAN, Grant Aramovič USSR   1919   1962
    EMS, MEH
    EMS: ГРИГОРЯ́Н

GRIGORIU, Theodor   Rumania   1926
    EMS, LMD, RCL, X64, X65, X66, X68
    EMS: ГРИГО́РИУ

GRIMALDI, Niccolo   Italy   1875
    REM

*GRIMM, Carl Hugo   USA   1890
    WI69

*GRIMM, Friedrich-Karl
  Enrico Cavallesco   Germany   1902
    IMD, LMD, REM, WI69

*GRIMM, Hans   Germany   1886
   EVM, IMD

GRIVA, Dimitri Kristov   Bulgaria   1914
   BMK
   BMK: ГРИВА

GRKOVIĆ, Branko   Yugoslavia 1920
   KMJ

GROEBMING, Adolf   Yugoslavia 1891
   KMJ

*GROFÉ, Ferde Ferdinand
   Rudolph von   USA   1892 1972
     AS66, BB65, BB71, EVM, LMD, MLA29/4, PCM, REM, WTM,
     X64, X68

GROMON, Francis   USA   1890 Hungary
   AS66

*GRØNDAHL, Launy   Denmark   1886 1960
   EVM, IMD, IMD2, LMD, VTM

*GROOT, Cornelius Wilhelmus
   de   Netherlands 1914
     EVM, LMD, REM

*GROSCH, Georg Oskar August Germany circa 1902
   X67

GROSCHKE, Heinz   Germany   1914
   WWG

GROSS, Bethuel G.   USA   1905
   AA73, AS66, X64, X65, X66, X67, X68

GROSS, Robert   USA
   ASUC

GROSSI, Pietro   Italy   1917
   IMD, LMD, REM, X66

GROSSKOPF, Erhard   1934
   EL:4, IMD2, X65

*GROSSMANN, Ferdinand   Austria   1887 1970
   BB71, MLA27/4, X67, X68

GROSSMAN, Saša (Alexander) Czechoslovakia 1907
   CCZ

*GROTHE, Franz   Germany   1908
    WWG

*GROVÉ, Stefans   USA   1922   Union of
    LMD, REM, X66   South Africa

*GROVEN, Eivind   Norway   1901
    CNO, EVM, LMD, REM, VTM

GROVERMANN, Carl Hans   Germany   1905
    EVM

GRUBER, Georg   1904
    IMD

*GRUBER, Ludwig   Austria   1874 1964
    X64

GRUDZIŃSI, Gzesław   Poland   1911
    PKW, X68

*GRUEN, John   USA
    X68

*GRUENBERG, Louis   USA   1884 1964
    AS66, BB65, EMS, EVM, IMD, LMD, PCM,   Russia
    PC71, REM, WTM, X65
    EMS: ГРЮНБЕРГ
    AS66: 1883

GRUENTHAL, Josef
    See: TAL, Joseph

*GRUNDMAN, Clare E.   USA   1913
    DN72, PCM

GRÜNAUER, Ingomar   1938
    IMD2

*GRÜNENWALD, Jean-Jacques France   1911
    CMF23, CMF40, DDM, DMF, EVM, REM, WI69, X65
    DMF: GRUNENWALD

*GRÜNER-HEGGE, Odd   Norway   1899
    CNO, EVM, WI69

*GRUNMACH, Ulrich   Germany   1891
    IMD

GRZADZIELÓWNA, Eleonora Poland   1921
    PKW

GRŽINIĆ, Vjekoslav   Yugoslavia   1932
   HGM, KMJ

GUACCERO, Domenico   Italy   1927
   IMD, LMD, REM, X65, X66, X67, X68

GUARINO, Carmine   Switzerland   1893 1965
   BB65, BB71, LMD, MLA22/4, REM   Italy

GUARINO, Mario   Italy   1900
   LMD, REM

*GUARINO, Piero   Italy   1919
   LMD, REM

GUARNIERI, Antonio   Italy   1880 1952
   LMD

*GUARNIERI, Mozart Camargo   Brazil   1907
   BB65, BB71, EMS, EVM, IMD, LMD, MEH, WTM, X64,
   X67, X68
   EMS: ГУАРНЬЕРИ

*GUASTAVINO, Carlos   Argentina   1914
   EVM, LMD, REM

GUBA, Vladimir   USSR   1938
   BB65, BB71

GUBARENKO, Vitaly   USSR
   X68

GUBAYDULINA, Sofiya   USSR
   X68

*GUBITOSI, Emilia   Italy   1887
   EVM, IMD, LMD, REM
   LMD: NAPOLITANO, Emilia
   EVM: 1889

*GUDENIAN, Haig   USA   1886 Armenia
   EVM

GUDIASHVILI, Nikolay
   Ivanovich   USSR   1913
   PPU

*GUDMUNDSEN-HOLMGREEN,
   Pelle   Denmark   1932
   CME, DMTsp, IMD2, VTM, X65, X66, X67, X68

*GUDMUNDSSON, Björgvin   Canada   1891 1961
   VTM   Iceland

GUDMUNDSSON, Thórarinn   Iceland   1896
  VTM

GUENTHER, Ralph R.   USA
  AA73, X68

*GUERRA-PEIXE, César   Brazil   1914
  IMD, LMD, QLA, REM

*GUERRINI, Guido   Italy   1890 1965
  BB65, BB71, CA16, DDM, EVM, IMD, LMD, MLA22/4, REM,
  X64, X65

*GUEST, Douglas Albert   Great Britain   1916
  LMD, X64, X66, X68

GUÉZEC, Jean-Pierre   France   1934 1971
  BB71, X66, X67, X68

GUGLIELMI, Luis
  See: LOUIGUY

*GUI, Vittorio   Italy   1885
  EMS, EVM, LMD, MEH, REM, WI69, X68
  EMS: ГУИ

*GUIDE, Richard Jules
  Joseph de   Belgium   1909 1962
  X66

*GUILLAUME, Eugène   Belgium   1882 1953
  BB75, BB71

GUINJOÀN, Juan   Spain
  X68

*GUION, David Wendel
  Fentross   USA   1895
  AS66, EVM, LMD, REM, X67

*GULBRANSON, Eilif   Norway   1897 1958
  CNO

*GULDA, Friedrich   Austria   1930
  BB65, BB71, IMD, LMD, REM, SML, WI69, X64, X65, X66,
  X67, X68

GULYÁS, László   Hungary   1928
  CHC

GUMP, Richard   USA   1906
  AS66

*GUNDRY, Inglis   Great Britain   1905
    LMD, REM, WI69, X65, X67, X68

*GUNSBOURG, Raoul   France   1859   1955
    EVM, LMD, REM   Rumania

GUNTHER, William   USA   1924   Germany
    AS66, X68
    Formerly: SPRECHER, William Gunther

*GURIDI, Jesús   Spain   1886   1961
    BB65, BB71, DDM, EVM, LMD, REM

*GURLITT, Manfred   Germany   1890   1972
    DDM, EMS, EVM, IMD, LMD, MLA29/4, REM, SML, X65,
    X67
    EMS: ГӰРЛИТТ

GUROV, Leonid Simonovich   USSR   1910
    EMS
    EMS: ГӰРОВ

GÜRSCHING, Albrecht   Germany   1934
    BB65, BB71, IMD2, PAP

GUSMINI, Vincenzo   Belgium   1896   Italy
    LMD, REM

GUTCHË, Gene   USA   1907   Germany
    AA73, BB65, BB71, CA15, PCM, PC71, X64, X65, X66, X67,
    X68
    Formerly: GUTSCHE, Romeo E.

GUTHRIE, John   New Zealand   1912
    WI69

GUTIERREZ DEL BARRIO,
    Alejandro   Argentina   1895   Spain
    REM

GUTIERREZ DEL BARRIO,
    Ramon   Argentina   1903   Spain
    REM

GUTIERREZ HERAS, Joaquin   Mexico   1927
    HET14

GUTSCHE, Romeo E.
    See: GUTCHË, Gene

*GÜTTLER, Hermann   Germany   1887
    EVM, LMD, REM

GUTTMANN, Alfred Grant
  See: GOODMAN, Alfred Grant

GUTTOVEGGIO, Joseph
  See: CRESTON, Paul

GUYONNET, Jacques   Switzerland   1933
  IMD2, MNG, SCHW, X65, X66, X67, X68

GUY-ROPARTZ, Joseph Marie
  See: ROPARTZ, Joseph Guy Marie

*GWILT, David William   Great Britain   1932   Scotland
  WI69, X67

GWYNN WILLIAMS, William Sidney
  See: WILLIAMS, William Sidney

GYRING, Elizabeth   USA
  X66, X67

GYULA, David
  See: DAVID, Gyula

HAACK, Bruce C.   USA   1932   Canada
  AS66

*HAACKE, Walter Juliu   Germany   1909
  EVM, X65, X66, X67, X68

*HAAGER, Max Ludwig
  Michael   Austria   1905
  IMD, REM, WI69

*HAAPALAINEN, Väinö Ilmari   Finland   1916
  COF
  COF: 1893-1945

*HAAPANEN, Toivo Elias   Finland   1889   1950
  EVM, LMD, REM, VTM

*HAARKLOU, Andreas Nikolai   Norway   1896
  CNO, DDM, EVM, LMD, REM

*HAAS, Joseph   Germany   1879   1960
  BB65, BB71, DDM, EMS, EVM, IMD, LMD, MEH, REM,
  SML, X65, X68
  EMS: XAC

*HAAS, Robert-Maria   Austria   1886   1960
  LMD, REM, SML

HAASE, Miloš   Czechoslovakia 1948
 MNP72/9

*HÁBA, Alois   Czechoslovakia 1893 1973
 BB65, BB71, CCZ, CIS, CME, DDM, EMS, EVM, IMD, IMD2,
 LMD, MEH, MLA29/4, MNP67/6, MNP69/2, NZW, REM,
 SML, X64, X65, X67, X68
 EMS: XAБA
 Confused with HABA, Karel MLA29/4: 1972

HÁBA, Emil   Czechoslovakia 1900
 LMD

*HÁBA, Karel   Czechoslovakia 1898 1972
 CCZ, CME, DDM, EVM, IMD2, LMD, MEH, MNP68/3, REM,
 X68

HABER, Louis   1915
 WAN

*HABERL, Ferdinand   Germany 1906
 X67

HABIĆ, Slobodan   Yugoslavia 1923
 KMJ

HABICHT, Günter   Germany 1916
 SML

HADAR, Josef   Israel   1926
 ACU

*HADDA, David Gerhart Great Britain 1923 Germany
 MM59

*HADJIDAKIS, Manos   Greece   1925
 MEH, REM, X67

*HADLEY, Patrick Arthur
 Sheldon   Great Britain 1899 1973
 EVM, LMD, REM, WI69

HADZHIEV, P. T.
 See: KADZHIEV, P. T.

HADZIDAKIS, Manos   Greece   1925
 BB65, BB71, CME, LMD, X65, X66, X68
 LMD: HADJIDAKIS

HAENNI, Charles   Switzerland 1867 1953
 LMD, SCHW

*HAENNI, Georges   Switzerland   1896
  LMD, SCHW

*HAENTJES, Werner   Germany   1923
  X66, X68

HAEYER, Frans d'   Belgium   1889
  EVM

*HAGEMAN, Richard   USA   1882   1966
  AS66, BB71, EVM, LMD, MLA23/4,   Netherlands
  REM, X66, X67

*HAGERUP BULL, Edvard   Norway   1922
  CME, CNO, DDM, IMD
  Sometimes listed: BULL, Edvard Hagerup

*HAGERUP BULL, Sverre   Norway   1892
  CNO, EVM
  Sometimes listed: BULL, Sverre Hagerup
  Pseudonym: HELLE, Finn

*HAHN, Gunnar   Sweden   1908
  SIM

*HAIEFF, Alexei   USA   1914   Russia
  AS66, BB65, BB71, LMD, ORC, PCM, REM, X64

*HAIGH, Morris   USA   1932
  PCM, PC71

*HAINES, Edmund Thomas   USA   1914
  AS66, PCM, X66, X67, X68

HAJÁK, Károly   Rumania   1886   Hungary
  RCL

*HAJDU, Mihály   Hungary   1909
  CHC, SML, X68

HÁJEK, Aleš   Czechoslovakia
  MNP69/4

*HAJEK, Egon   Austria   1888   1964

HÁJEK, Maxmillián   Czechoslovakia   1909
  CCZ, COO

HAJOS, Karl   USA   1889   1950
  EVM   Hungary

*HALAHAN, Guy Frederick
  Crosby   Great Britain   circa
  WI69   1925

*HALAŚZ, Kalman   Austria   1919   Hungary
  IMD, LMD, REM

*HALES, Hubert James   Great Britain   1902   1965
  BB71, EVM, MLA22/4, X65, X66, X67

*HALFFTER, Christobal   Spain   1930
  BB65, BB71, CME, DDM, EL:4, HET24, IMD, LMD, MEH,
  MNG, REM, TSC, X64, X65, X66, X67, X68

*HALFFTER ESCRICHE,
  Ernesto   Portugal   1905   Spain
  BB65, BB71, CME, DDM, EVM, IMD, LMD, MEH, REM,
  X65, X68

*HALFFTER ESCRICHE,
  Rodolfo   Mexico   1900   Spain
  CME, DDM, HET9, HET16, IMD, LMD, QLA, REM, X68

HALIASSAS, Jack   Greece   1921
  EL:4

*HALL, John Gerald   Great Britain   1905
  WI69

*HALL, Pauline Margrete   Norway   1890   1969
  BB71, CME, DNO, EVM, LMD, REM, VTM

*HALL, Richard   Great Britain   1903
  IMD, WI69, X64

HALLBERG, Björn Wilho   Norway   1938
  CNO, VTM

HALLDÓRSSON, Skúli   Iceland   1914
  VTM

HALLER, Hans Peter   1929
  IMD, X67

*HALLER, Hermann   Switzerland   1914
  EVM, LMD, REM, SCHW, X64, X66, X67

*HALLNÄS, Johan Hilding   Sweden   1903
  BB71, EVM, FST, IMD2, LMD, REM, SIM, SIMa, SOW, SWE,
  TJU, VTM, X64, X67

*HALSKI, Czeslaw Raymond   Great Britain   1908   Poland
     EVM, WI69

*HALSTEAD, Edgar   Great Britain   1885
     WI69

*HALVORSEN, Leif Fritjof   Norway   1887   1959
     BB71, EVM, LMD, REM

*HAMANN, Berhard   Germany   1909   1968
     IMD, X68

*HAMBOURG, Boris   Canada   1884   1954
     REM   Russia

HAMBOURG, Mark   Great Britain   1879   1960
     BB65, REM   Russia

*HAMBRAEUS, Bengt   Sweden   1928
     BB71, CME, DDM, DNS, FST, IMD, IMD2, LMD, MEH, REM,
     SIM, SIMa, SMT, SOW, STS, SWE, TJU, VTM, X64, X65,
     X66, X67, X68

*HAMERIK, Ebbe   Denmark   1898   1951
     BB65, BB71, DDM, EVM, IMD, REM, VTM
     DDM: HAMMERICH, Ebbe

*HAMILTON, Iain Ellis   Great Britain   1922   Scotland
     ASUC, BB65, BB71, BCI, CME, DN72, EVM, IMD, IMD2,
     LMD, OCM, PAP, REM, TSC, X64, X65, X66, X67, X68

HAMILTON, Tom   USA   1946
     CAP

HAMM, Charles Edward   USA   1925
     DAS, PCM, X65, X66, X67, X68

*HAMMERSCHLAG, János   Hungary   1885   1954
     EVM, LMD, REM, SML, X67   Bohemia

HAMMOND, Don   1917
     WAN

*HAMMOND, Richard   USA   1896   Great
     EVM, LMD, REM   Britain

HAMMOND, Tom   Great Britain
     WI69

HAMPE, Charlotte   1910
     IMD

HAMPTON, Calvin　　　　　USA　　　　　1938
　　X67, X68

HANÁK, Mirko　　　　　　Czechoslovakia　1891
　　CCZ

HAND, Colin　　　　　　　USA　　　　　1929
　　WI69, X67

HANELL, Robert　　　　　Germany　　　1925
　　SML, X65, X67, X68

*HANNA, James R.　　　　USA　　　　　1922
　　X64, X65, X66, X67, X68

*HANNENHEIM, Norbert
　　Hann von　　　　　　　Austria　　　1898
　　EVM

HANNIG, Petr　　　　　　Czechoslovakia　1946
　　MNP69/4, MNP72/9

*HANNIKAINEN, Toivo Ilmari　Finland　　1892　1955
　　COF, EVM, LMD, MEH, REM, VTM

*HANNIKAINEN, Vainö Aatos　Finland　　1900　1960
　　COF, LMD, REM

HANOUSEK, Karel　　　　Czechoslovakia　1902
　　CCZ

HANOUSEK, Vladimír　　　Czechoslovakia　1907
　　CCZ, IMD2, X68

HANSEN, Ted　　　　　　USA　　　　　1935
　　CAP

*HANSON, Howard Harold　　USA　　　　1896
　　AS66, BB65, BB71, DAS, DDM, EMS, EVM, LMD, PCM,
　　PC71, REM, WI69, WTM, X64, X65, X66, X67, X68
　　EMS: ХАНСОН

HANSON, Raymond　　　　Australia
　　AMM

HANSON, Sten　　　　　　Sweden　　　1936
　　X68

*HANSSEN, Daniel　　　　Norway　　　1895
　　CNO

*HANSSEN, Johannes　　　Norway　　　1874　1967
　　CNO, X64

*HANUŠ, Jan   Czechoslovakia 1915
    CME, CCZ, IMD, IMD2, LMD, MEH, MNP65/4, MNP65/5,
    MNP65/6, MNP65/7, MNP70/1, MNP71/3, REM, SML,
    X64, X65, X68

*HAQUINIUS, Johan Algot   Sweden   1886 1966
    FST, IMD, KSV, MLA23/4, SIM, SIMa, STS, VTM, X66

HARADA, Higo   USA   1927
    ASUC, PCM

HARAŠTA, Milan   Czechoslovakia 1919 1946
    CCZ, CME, X65, X67

HARBISON, Denis   Great Britain
    X68

HARBISON, John   USA   1938
    ASUC, BB71, X66

HARBURGER, Walter   Monaco   1888 Germany
    EVM, REM

*HARCOURT, Marguerite
    Béclard d'   France   1884 1964
    BB71, X65

*HARDER, Knud   Denmark   1885 1967
    IMD, X67

HARDER, Paul O.   USA
    AA73, X66, X67, X68

HARDIE, Gary   USA   1948
    BS72

HARDIN, Burton E.   USA
    CAP, X65

HARDING, Gunnar   Sweden   1940

HARKNESS, Joan   USA   1945
    BS70

HARKNESS, Rebekah West   USA   1915
    AS66, X67
    Also: DEAN, Mrs. B. H.

*HÄRKÖNEN, Leo   Finland   1904
    COF

HARLAN, Charles L.   USA   1920
    CAP

*HARLINE, Leigh   USA   1907   1969
    BB71

*HARLING, William Franke   USA   1887   1958
    BB65, BB71, EVM, LMD, REM, X64   Great Britain

*HARMAN, Carter   USA   1918
    X68

*HARMAT, Artur   Hungary   1885   1962
    CHC, EVM

HARPER, Edward James   Great Britain   1941
    WI69

HARREX, Patrick   Great Britain   circa
    X68   1945

HARRIES, David John   Great Britain   1933
    WI69

*HARRINGTON, W. Clark   USA   1905
    AS66

*HARRIS, Albert   USA   1911
    AA73, PC71

HARRIS, Arthur   USA   1927
    PCM

HARRIS, Donald   USA   1931
    X68

*HARRIS, Neil Foster   Canada   1925
    X68

HARRIS, Roger W.   USA   1940
    CAP, X64

*HARRIS, Roy Leroy Elsworth   USA   1898
    BB65, BB71, CME, DDM, EMS, EVM, IMD, LMD, MEH,
    PCM, PC71, REM, WTM, X65, X66, X68
    EMS: ХÁРРИС

*HARRIS, William Henry   Great Britain   1883   1973
    EVM, WI69

HARRISON, David F.   USA
    ASUC

*HARRISON, Francis Llewellyn   Canada   1905   Ireland
    DDM, X64, X65, X66, X68

*HARRISON, Julius Allan
  Greenway   Great Britain   1885   1963
  BB65, BB71, DDM, EVM, LMD, REM

*HARRISON, Lou   USA   1917
  BB65, BB71, CA8, DDM, EVM, IMD, IMD2, LMD, OCM, PCM,
  PC71, REM, WI69, X65, X66, X67, X68

*HARRISON, Pamela   Great Britain   1915
  WI69

*HARSÁNYI, Tibor   France   1898   1954
  DDM, EVM, IMD, LMD, REM, X67   Hungary

*HART, Frederic Patton   USA   1898
  EVM

HART, Fritz   Australia   1925
  AMM

HARTER, Harry H.   USA
  X68

*HARTIG, Heinz Friedrich Germany   1907   1969
  IMD, MLA26/4, X65, X67, X68

HARTLEY, Walter Sinclair USA   1927
  AA73, AS66, PCM, PC71, X64, X65, X66, X67, X68

*HARTMANN, Arthur Martinus USA   1881   1956
  AS66, X64   Hungary

*HARTMAN, Karl Amadeus   Germany   1905   1963
  BB65, BB71, CME, DDM, DMM, EMS, EVM, IMD, IMD2,
  LMD, MEH, MZW, OCM, REM, SML, VNM, X64, X65,
  X66, X67, X68
  EMS: XÁPTMAH

*HARTMANN, Thomas
  Alexandrovich de   France   1886   1956
  EMV, LMD, REM   Russia

HARTULARY-DARCLÉE, Ion   Rumania   1886   1969
  RCL   France

HARTWELL, Hugh   Canada
  CCM71, CVMa, KEY, NLCa

HARTZELL, Eugene   1932
  IMD2

HARVEY, Jonathan Dean   Great Britain 1939
  WI69, X67, X68

*HASENÖEHRL, Franz   Austria   1885
 WI69, X66

HASHAGEN, Klaus   Germany   1926
 EL:2, PAP
 PAP: 1924

HASLAM, Herbert   USA   1928
 PCM, PC71

*HASQUENOPH, Pierre   France   1922
 CMF11, CMF20, CMF40, DDM, IMD, IMD2, LMD, QQF, X64,
 X68

*HASSE, Karl   Germany   1883 1960
 BB65, BB71, EVM, LMD, REM, X64

*HASSELAAR, Frans   Netherlands 1885 1950
 EVM

HASSELL, Jon   USA   1937
 BB71

HASSENBERG, Kurt   Germany
 CME

HASTINGS, Ross   USA   1915
 AS66

HATRÍK, Juraj   Czechoslovakia 1941
 MEH, X66, X67, X68, ZE70/1, ZE70/2, ZE70/3, ZE71/1,
 ZE71/2, ZE71/3

HATTWIG, Martin   Germany   1920
 SML

*HATZE, Josip   Yugoslavia 1879 1959
 BB65, BB71, HCM, KMJ, LMD, X67

*HAUBENSTOCK-RAMATI,
 Roman   Israel   1919 Poland
 BB65, BB71, CME, IMD, IMD2, LMD, MEH, MM59, MNG,
 MZW, REM, SML, WI69, X64, X65, X66, X67, X68

HAUBER, Robert   Yugoslavia 1931
 KMJ

*HAUBIEL, Charles   USA   1892
 AA73, AS66, BB65, BB71, EVM, LMD, PCM, PC71, WI69,
 X64, X65, X66, X68

*HAUDEBERT, Lucien   France   1877   1963
    BB65, BB71, DDM, DMF, EVM, LMD, REM

*HAUER, Josef Matthias   Austria   1883   1959
    BB65, BB71, CME, DDM, EMS, EVM, IMD, IMD2, LMD,
    MEH, MZW, PAP, REM, SML, TSC, X65, X66, X67, X68
    EMS: ХАУЭР

*HAUFRECHT, Herbert   USA   1909
    EVM, PCM, PC71, X66
    EVM: HAUFREUCHT

*HAUG, Gustav   Switzerland   1871   1956
    ACM, EVM, LMD, SCHW   Germany

*HAUG, Hans   Switzerland   1900   1967
    BB71, CME, DDM, EVM, LMD, MLA24/4, REM, SCHW, WWS,
    X65, X67, X68

HAUGLAND, Archie Oscar   USA
    AA73, X66, X67, X68

HAUK, Günter   Germany   1932
    SML, X68

HAUSDÖRFER, Friedrich   Netherlands   1916
    EVM

HAUSKA, Hans   Germany   1901   1965
    SML

*HAUSSERMANN, John   USA   1909   Philippines
    X67

*HAVELKA, Svatopluk   Czechoslovakia   1925
    BB65, CCZ, CME, IMD2, MEH, MNP65/2, MNP66/1,
    MNP67/6, MNP72/4, SML, X64, X65, X66, X68

*HAVEMANN, Gustav   Germany   1882   1960

HAWES, Jack Richards   Great Britain   1916
    WI69

HAWKINS, John   Canada
    CCM71, CVMa, KEY, MCO71, X64, X65, X68

HAWLÍK, Vladimír   1911
    IMD2

HAWORTH, Frank   Canada   1905   England
    CCM, CCM71, CVM, KEY, MCO, MCO71, NLC, X68

*HAWTHORNE-BAKER, Allan   Great Britain   circa
    WI69   1910

*HAY, Edward Norman   Great Britain   1889   1943
    LMD, REM   Ireland

*HAY, Frederick Charles   Switzerland   1888
    EVM

*HAYDON, Claude M.   New Zealand   1884   Australia
    EVM

*HAYDON, Glen   USA   1896   1966
    LMD, REM, X65, X67

HAZON, Roberto   Italy   1930
    DDM, LMD, REM, X65, X67

*HEAD, Michael Dewar   Great Britain   1900
    DDM, EVM, X65, X67

*HEADINGTON, Christopher
    John Magenis   Great Britain   1930
    BB65, BB71, WI69, X64, X66, X68

HEALEY, Derek Edward   Great Britain   1936
    WI69

HEARNE, John Michael   Great Britain   1937
    WI69

HECHTEL, Herbert   Germany   1937
    X68

*HEDAR, Josef   Sweden   1894   1960
    KSV, STS, X68

*HEDGES, Anthony John   Great Britain   1931
    WI69, X67, X68

*HEDWALL, Lennart   Sweden   1932
    FST, IMD, KSV, SIM, SIMa, SOW, STI, SWE, TJU, VTM,
    X64, X67, X68

HEER, Emil   Switzerland   1926
    SCHW, X67

HEGDAHL, Magne   Norway   circa
    X68   1940

*HEGER, Robert   Germany   1886
    ACM, EVM, IMD, LMD, REM, X65, X66, X67, X68

HEGGE, Odd Grüner
    See: GRÜNER-HEGGE, Odd

HEICKING, Wolfram   Germany   1927
    SML

*HEIDE, Harald   Norway   1876   1955
    CNO, EVM, VTM
    EVM: 1896

*HEIDEN, Bernhard   USA   1910   Germany
    ASUC, BB65, BB71, LMD, PCM, PC71, X64, X65, X66

*HEIDER, Werner   Germany   1930
    BB65, BB71, IMD, IMD2, LMD, PAP, X64, X65, X66, X67,
    X68

HEIDSIECK, Bernard   France   1928

HEIFETZ, Vladimir   USA   1893   Russia
    AS66

*HEILLER, Anton   Austria   1923
    CME, DDM, EVM, IMD, IMD2, LMD, MEH, MNG, REM,
    WI69, X64, X65, X66, X67, X68

HEILMAN, William Clifford   USA   1887
    PCM

*HEILMANN, Harald   Germany   1924
    X65, X67

*HEILNER, Irwin   USA   1908
    IMD, PC71

HEININEN, Paavo   Finland   1938
    CME, VTM, X65, X66, X67
    CME: HEINNINEN

HEINLEIN, Federico   Argentina   1912   Germany
    REM, X68

HEINRICH, Hanoch
    See: JACOBY, Hanoch

*HEISS, Hermann   Germany   1897   1966
    DDM, EVM, IMD, IMD2, LMD, MLA23/4, REM, SML, WWG,
    X64, X65, X67

HEISS, John C.   USA
    ASUC

*HELA, Martti Mikael   Finland   1890
  COF

*HELFER, Walter   USA   1896 1959
  AS66, BB65, BB71, EVM, IMD, LMD

*HELFMAN, Max   USA   1901 1963
  AS66, BB65, BB71   Poland

*HELFRITZ, Hans   Chile   1902 Germany
  EVM, LMD, REM

*HELGASON, Hallgrímur Iceland   1914
  LMD, REM, VTM

*HELLDÉN, Daniel   Sweden   1917
  FST, SIMa, STS

HELLE, Finn
  See: HAGERUP BULL, Sverre

*HELLER, Hans Ewald   USA   1894 1966
  BB71   Austria

*HELLER, James Gutheim USA   1892
  EVM, PCM

HELLERMAN, William   USA
  ASUC, X67

HELLIER, Harry Clifford Belgium   1905
  WI69

*HELLMAN, Ivar   Sweden   1891
  FST, KSV, SIM, SIMa

*HELM, Everett Burton   USA   1913
  BB71, DDM, IMD, LMD, PCM, PC71, REM, SML, X64, X65,
  X66, X67, X68

HELMS, Hans G.   Germany   1932
  BB65, BB71, X64, X65, X66, X67

HELPS, Robert   USA   1928
  BB71, PC71, X65, X66, X68

*HELY-HUTCHINSON,
  Christian Victor   Great Britain 1901 1947
  LMD, REM, X68   Union of
                                   South Africa

*HEMEL, Oscar van   Netherlands   1892   Belgium
    BB65, BB71, CME, DDM, EVM, IMD, IMD2, LMD, NED, REM,
    X64, X65, X68

HEMMER, Eugene   USA   1929
    AA73, AS66, PCM, PC71, X65, X66, X67, X68

*HEMMERLING, Carlo   Switzerland   1903   1967
    LMD, MLA24/4, WWS, X67, X68

HÉMON, Sedje   Netherlands
    EL:1

HEMPEL, Rolf   Germany   1932
    X68

*HEMSI, Alberto   Egypt   1898   Turkey
    IMD, LMD, REM

HENDERSON, Robert   USA
    X67

HENDL, Walter   USA   1917
    BB71, PCM, X64, X65, X66, X67

*HENDRIKS, Francis Milton   USA   1883
    AS66

HENGARTNER, Max   Switzerland   1898   1958
    SCHW

*HENGEVELD, Gerard   Netherlands   1910
    X67

*HENKEMANS, Hans   Netherlands   1913
    CME, DDM, EVM, IMD, LMD, NED, REM, WI69, X64, X65,
    X67, X68

HENKING, Bernhard   Switzerland   1897
    SCHW, X67

*HENNEBERG, Carl Albert
    Theodor   Sweden   1901
    FST, EVM, KSV, LMD, REM, SIM, SIMa, STS, TJU, X67

HENNING, Erwin Arthur   USA   1910
    BB65, BB71, PCM, LMD

HENNING, Roslyn Brogue
    See: BROGUE, Roslyn

*HENRICH, Hermann   Germany   1891
   EVM

*HENRY, Harold   USA   1884 1956
   BB65, BB71

HENRY, Joseph   USA
   CAP

*HENRY, Leigh Vaughn   Great Britain 1889 1958
   BB65, BB71, EVM, LMD, REM, X68

HENRY, Otto W.   USA
   ASUC

*HENRY, Pierre   France   1927
   CME, EVM, LMD, QQF, REM, X64, X66, X67, X68

*HENS, Charles   Belgium   1898 1967
   EVM, X68

*HENSEL, Richard   USA   1926
   CAP, PC71

*HENZE, Hans Werner   Germany   1926
   BB65, BB71, CME, DDM, DMM, EMS, EVM, IMD, IMD2,
   LMD, MEH, MZW, PAP, REM, TSC, VNM, WTM, X64,
   X65, X66, X67, X68
   EMS: ХЕНЦЕ

HEPPENER, Robert   Netherlands 1925
   NED, X67, X68

HERA, Willi   Germany   1903
   SML

*HERBAGE, Julian Livingston Great Britain 1904
   WI69, X67

*HERBERIGS, Robert   Belgium   1886
   CBC, DDM, EVM, IMD, LMD, REM, WI69

HERBST, Kurt   1883
   IMD

*HERCIGONJA, Nikola   Yugoslavia 1911
   BB65, BB71, KMJ, LMD, MEH, X66

HERDER, Ronald   USA   1931
   X68

HÉRICARD, Jeanne   France
   X68

HERMAN, Vasile   Rumania   1929
    RCL, X65, X68

*HERMANN, Paul   Germany   1904
    IMD

HERMANSON, Åke   Sweden   1923
    CME, DNS, FST, IMD, IMD2, PKW, SIM, SIMa, SOW, STI,
    STS, VTM, X68

HERNANDEZ, Hermilio   Mexico   1931
    HET18

*HERNANDEZ GONZALO,
    Gisela   Cuba   1912
    IMD, LMD, REM

HERNÁNDEZ-LÓPEZ, Rhazes   Venezuela   1918
    BB71, CA14, LMD, REM

*HERNÁNDEZ MONCADA,
    Eduardo   Mexico   1899
    HET15, IMD, LMD, QLA, REM

*HERNRIED, Robert Franz
    Richard   USA   1883   1951
    DDM, LMD, REM   Austria

HEROLD, Rudolf   1893
    IMD, X68

HERRERA, Humberto   USA   1900   Guatemala
    AS66

*HERRERA de la FUENTA,
    Luis   Mexico   1916
    LMD, X67

*HERMANN, Bernard   USA   1911
    EVM, LMD, PCM, REM, WI69, X67

*HERRMANN, Hugo   Germany   1896   1967
    BB71, DDM, EVM, IMD, LMD, MLA24/4, REM, SML, X65,
    X66, X67, X68

HERMANY, Petr   Germany
    MNP66/4

*HERSCHMANN, Heinz   Great Britain   1924   Austria
    WI69, X67, X68

HERTL, František   Czechoslovakia   1906
    CCZ, IMD2, HEM, X66

*HERTOG, Johannes den Netherlands 1904
 EVM

HERVIG, Richard USA
 ASUC

HESPOS, Hans Joachim Germany 1938
 X67, X68

*HESS, Ernst Switzerland 1912 1968
 LMD, MLA25/4, REM, SCHW, X67, X68

*HESS, Willy Switzerland 1906
 IMD, LMD, REM, SCHW, X64, X65, X66, X67, X68

*HESSELBERG, Eyvind Norway 1898
 CNO

*HESSENBERG, Kurt Germany 1908
 EVM, IMD, LMD, REM, SML, WWG, X68

HÉTU, Jacques Canada 1938
 CCM, CCM71, DDM, KEY, MCO, MCO68, MCO71, X67, X68

HEUKEROTH, J. Richard Netherlands 1885 1960
 EVM

HEUSSENSTAMM, George USA 1926
 DN70, DN72, PC71, X68

*HEWITT-JONES, David
Anthony Great Britain 1926
 WI69, X67, X68

HEYKENDAEL, Henri Hubert
Willem Mathieu Netherlands 1906
 EVM

*HEYL, Manfred Germany 1908
 IMD

*HEYMANN, Werner Richard USA 1896 1961
 BB71, EVM, LMD, REM

HIBBARD, William Alden USA
 ASUC, X65, X66, X67

*HICKMANN, Hans Robert
Hermann Germany 1908 1968
 BB71, REM, X64, X65, X66, X67, X68

HIDALGO CODORNIU, Juan Spain 1927
 CME, DDM, IMD, X65, X66, X68

*HIDAS, Frigyes Hungary 1928
 CHC, X66, X68

HIEBNER, Armand Switzerland 1898
 SCHW

HIGGINS, Richard C. USA 1938 Great Britain
 BB71

*HIJMAN, Julius USA 1901 Netherlands
 EVM, X66

*HILBER, Johann Baptist Switzerland 1891
 LMD, WWS

HILDENBRAND, Siegfried Switzerland 1917
 SCHW

*HILL, Alfred Francis Australia 1870 1960
 AMM, BB65, BB71, DDM, EMS, EVM, LMD, REM
 EMS: ХИЛЛ

*HILL, Edward Burlingame USA 1872 1960
 AS66, BB65, BB71, DDM, EMS, EVM, IMD, LMD, PCM, REM
 EMS: ХИЛЛ

HILL, Jackson USA
 ASUC

*HILL, Lewis Eugene Canada 1909
 MCO

HILLER, Felix Ferdinand Germany 1882
 LMD

HILLER, Lejaren A., Jr. USA 1924
 ASUC, AS66, IMD, IMD2, LMD, MEH, X64, X66, X67, X68

HILLERT, Richard Walter USA 1923
 DN72

*HINDEMITH, Paul Germany 1895 1963
 BB65, BB71, CME, DDM, EMS, EVM, IMD, IMD2, LMD,
 MEH, MZW, PAP, REM, SML, TCM, VNM, WTM, X64,
 X65, X66, X67, X68
 EMS: ХИНДЕМИТ

HINDEMITH, Rudolf 1900
 IMD

HINDERMANN, Walter F. Switzerland 1931
 SCHW, X67

HIND O'MALLEY, Pamela   Great Britain   1923
WI69

HINSTEIN, Gustav
See: SCHLEMM, Gustav Adolf

*HIPMAN, Silvester   Czechoslovakia   1893
CCZ, DDM

*HIRAO, Kishio   Japan   1907   1953
BB65, BB71

HIRNER, Teodor   Czechoslovakia   1910
CCZ, MEH, ZE70/3

HIRSCH, Hans Ludwig   1937
IMD2

*HIRSCHLER, Ziga   Yugoslavia   1894
EVM

HIRSCHMANN, Henri   France   1872
DMF, LMD

*HIRSHBERG, Yehoosh   Israel   1938
MM59

HIVELY, Wells   1902   1969
WAN

*HJELMBORG, Bjørn   Denmark   1911
VTM, X64, X68

HJÖRLEIFSSON, Siguringi
Eiríkur   Iceland   1902
VTM

*HJORT-ALBERTSEN, Per   Norway   1919
CNO

HLAVÁČ, Miroslav   Czechoslovakia   1923
CCZ, MNP71/3, MNP71/3, X66

*HLOBIL, Emil   Czechoslovakia   1901
CCZ, DDM, EVM, IMD, IMD2, LMD, MEH, MNP64/3,
MNP68/7, MNP71/8, REM, SML, X64, X68

*HLOUSCHEK, Theodor   Germany   1923   Czecho-
SML, X66, X68   slovakia

HO, Edward Suz-Nang   China   1939
WI69

HOAG, Charles Kelso   USA
    AA73, X66, X68

HOCH, Moshe   Israel   1918   Poland
    ACU

HOCHEL, Stanislav   Czechoslovakia   1950
    MNP72/9

*HOCHSTETTER, Armin
   Casper   Austria   1899
   WI69

*HODDINOTT, Alun   Great Britain   1929   Wales
    BB71, DDM, LMD, OCM, REM, WI69, X64, X65, X66, X67,
    X68

*HODEIR, André   France   1921
    BB71, CME, LMD, QQF, REM, X64, X65, X66, X67, X68

HODELL, Åke   Sweden   1919

HODKINSON, Sydney Phillip   Canada   1934
    ASUC, BB71, BCL, CCM71, CVMa, MCO71, PCM, PC71,
    X66, X67, X68

HODZA-EJTANOV, Leon
   See: KHODZHA-EINATOV, Leon

*HØEBERG, Georg   Denmark   1872   1950
    EVM

HOELLER, Karl
   See: HÖLLER, Karl

*HOÉRÉE, Arthur Charles
   Ernest   France   1897   Belgium
    DDM, DMF, EVM, LMD, REM

*HOESSLIN, Franz von   Germany   1885   1946
    REM

*HÖFER, Franz   France   1880   1953
    EVM, LMC, REM

*HOFER, Maria   Austria   1894
    IMD, X64

*HOFFDING, Niels Finn   Denmark   1899
    DDM, DMTsp, EVM, IMD, IMD2, LMD, REM, VTM, X64, X67

*HOFFMAN, Richard   USA   1925   Austria
    ASUC, BB65, BB71, IMD, LMD, MNG, X66

HOFFMAN, Theodore   USA
    ASUC

HOFFMANN, Adolf G.   USA   1890
    AS66

*HOFFMANN, Emil Adolf   Switzerland   1879   1963
    LMD, SCHW

HOFMAN, Shlomo   Israel   1909   Poland
    ACU, BB65, BB71, LMD, WWI, X64, X68

HOFMAN, Srdan   Yugoslavia   1944
    KMJ

*HOFMANN, Hermann Johannes   Switzerland   1894   1968
    MLA25/4, SCHW

*HOFMANN, Josef Casimir   USA   1876   1957
    EMS, EVM, LMD, REM, X66, X68   Poland
    Pseudonym: DVORSKY, Michel
    EMS: ГОФМАН

HOFMANN, Wolfgang   1922
    IMD2, X68

*HOFMEIER, Andreas   Germany   1872   1963

HOGG, Merle E.   USA
    CAP, PCM, PC71

*HÖGNER, Friedrich   Germany   1897
    EVM, IMD, X64, X67

*HOHENSEE, Wolfgang   Germany   1927
    SML, X64, X65, X66, X67, X68

*HOIBY, Lee   USA   1926
    AS66, BB65, BB71, LMD, PCM, PC71, REM, X64, X65, X67,
    X68

HOINIC, Mircea   Rumania   1910
    RCL

*HØJBY NIELSEN, Tage   Denmark   1918
    VTM

*HOLBROOKE, Joseph Charles   Great Britain   1878   1958
    BB65, BB71, DDM, EVM, LMD, REM, SML, X65, X66, X68
    Also: Josef

HOLD, Trevor James   Great Britain
   WI69, X66

*HOLDE, Artur   USA   1885   1962
   BB65, BB71, X67, X68   Germany

*HOLDEN, David Justin   USA   1911
   EVM, PCM, REM
   PCM: 1912

HOLDHEIM, Theodor   Israel   1923   Germany
   ACU, IMD2

*HOLENIA, Hanns   Austria   1890
   LMD, REM

*HOLEWA, Hans   Sweden   1905   Austria
   BB71, CME, FST, IMD2, SIMa, STI, STS, SWE, TJU, VTM,
   X65, X66, X67

*HOLLAND, Dulcie Sybil   Great Britain   1913   Australia
   AMM, WI69

HOLLANDER, Lorin   1944
   X68

HOLLANDER, Ralph   USA   1916
   AS66, X68

*HÖLLER, Karl   Germany   1907
   CME, DDM, EVM, IMD, IMD2, LMD, REM, WWG, X64, X67,
   X68

HOLLIGER, Heinz   Switzerland   1939
   BB65, BB71, CME, DDM, IMD, IMD2, LMD, NZW, SCHW,
   X64, X65, X66, X67, X68

*HOLLINGSWORTH, Stanley USA   1924
   PCM

HOLLOWAY, Elizabeth   USA
   ASUC

HOLLOWAY, Robin   Great Britain
   X67, X68

HOLM, Mogens Winkel   Denmark   1936
   DMTsp, VTM, X68

*HOLM, Peder   Denmark   1926
   VTM, X66

HOLMAN, Willis Leonard (Bill)   USA   1927
    PCM, X68

*HOLMBOE, Vagn   Denmark   1909
    BB65, BB71, CME, DDM, DMTsp, DNS, EVM, IMD, LMD,
    REM, VTM, WI69, X64, X65, X68

HOLMES, Markwood   USA
    AA73, CAP, X66, X67, X68

HOLMES, Paul   USA   1923
    PCM

HOLMQVIST, Evald   Sweden   1868 1954
    FST, SIM, SIMa

*HOLOUBEK, Ladislav   Czechoslovakia 1913
    CCZ, EVM, MEH, MNP66/3, MNP67/9, REM, X65, X66, X67,
    X68, ZE69/3, ZE70/2, ZE70/3, ZE71/3, ZE72/1

*HOLST, Imogen Clare   Great Britain   1907
    EVM, LMD, REM, X64, X65, X66, X67, X68

HOLUB, Josef   Czechoslovakia 1902
    CCZ

*HOLZMANN, Rodolfo   Peru   1910 Germany
    EVM, IMD, REM

*HOMER, Sidney   USA   1864 1953
    AS66

HOMOLA, Bernhard   Switzerland 1894
    SCHW

HOMS, Joaquim   Spain   1906
    BB71, CME, IMD, X66

*HONEGGER, Arthur   France   1892 1955
    BB65, BB71, CME, DDM, DMF, EMS, EMV,   Switzerland
    IMD, IMD2, LMD, MEH, MZW, PAP, REM, SCHW, SML,
    TCM, VNM, WTM, X64, X65, X66, X67, X68
    EMS: ОНЕГГЕР

HOOD, Boyde W.   1939
    WAN

HOOD, Mantle H.   USA   1918
    BB65, BB71, DAS, X64, X65, X66, X68

HOOF, Jef van   Belgium   1886 1959
    BB65, BB71, CBC, EVM, IMD, LMD, REM
    CBC: VAN HOOF

HOOGHE, Clément d'   Belgium   1899   1951
   EVM

HOPKINS, Antony   Great Britain   1921
   DDM, EVM, LMD, REM, WI69, X64, X65, X66, X67, X68
   Formerly: REYNOLDS

HOPKINS, Bill   USA   1943
   MNG, WI69, X66, X68

HORCEAG, Savel   Rumania   1898
   RCL

*HORENSTEIN, Jascha   USA   1899   Russia
   LMD, REM, X64, X65, X66, X67, X68
   REM: 1898

*HORKÝ, Karel   Czechoslovakia 1909
   BB71, CCZ, EVM, LMD, MNP69/9, MNP71/3, REM, X66

*HOROVITZ, Joseph   Great Britain   1926   Austria
   WI69, X64, X65, X66, X68

*HORST, Anthon van der   Netherlands   1899   1965
   BB71, DDM, EVM, IMD, LMD, NED, REM, X64, X67

HORST, John L.   USA
   ASUC

HORTON, Austin Asadata
   Dafora   USA   1890   1965
   BB65, BB71, LMD   Nigeria

*HORUSITZKY, Zoltán   Hungary   1903
   CHC, SML, X66, X68

HORVAT, Stanko   Yugoslavia   1930
   HCM, IND2, KMJ, X67

HORVÁTH, Ivan   Czechoslovakia 1935
   MEH

*HORVATH, Josef Maria   Germany   1931   Hungary
   IMD, X67, X68

HORVIT, Michael M.   USA
   ASUC

HOSALLA, Hans Dieter   Germany   1919
   SML

*HOSKINS, William Barnes USA
   ASUC, X66, X68

HOSMER, James B.   USA   1911
   PCM, X64

HOUDY, Pierick   France   1929
   QQF

HOVDESVEN, E. A.   USA   1893
   AS66

*HOVHANESS, Alan Scott   USA   1911
   BB65, BB71, CA11, DDM, DN72, EMS, EVM, IMD, LMD,
   MEH, OCM, PCM, PC71, REM, WTM, X64, X65, X66,
   X67, X68
   EMS: XÓBAHECC   EVM: HOVANESS

*HOVLAND, Egil   Norway   1924
   CME, CNO, DNS, IMD2, VTM, X65, X66

HOWARD, Bertrand   USA
   AA73, X67

HOWARD, Dean C.   USA   1919
   ASUC, LCI, PC71, X68

*HOWARD, John Tasker   USA   1890   1964
   AS66, BB65, BB71, EVM, LMD, OCM, PCM, REM, X64, X65,
   X66, X67

HOWARTH, Elgar   Great Britain   1935
   WI69

HOWE, Hubert S., Jr.   USA
   ASUC

*HOWE, Mary Alberta Bruce   USA   1882   1964
   AS66, BB65, BB71, EVM, IMD, LMD, PCM, X64, X65
   Also: HOWE, Mrs. Walter

*HOWELL, Dorothy   Great Britain   1898
   EVM, LMD, REM, WI69, X68

*HOWELLS, Herbert Norman   Great Britain   1892
   BB65, BB71, DDM, EVM, LMD, REM, WI69, X64, X66, X67

HOYER, Karl   1891
   IMD

HRADIL, František   Czechoslovakia   1898
   CCZ, X64

HRBÁČEK, Alois   Czechoslovakia   1947
   MNP72/9

HRISANIDE, Alexandru Dumitru Rumania 1936
  BB65, BB71, IMD2, LMD, RCL, X65, X67, X68

HRISIK, Taki Yugoslavia 1920
  KMJ

*HRISTIĆ, Stevan Yugoslavia 1885 1958
  BB65, CME, DDM, EVM, IMD, KMJ, LMD, MEH, REM, SML,
  X66, X67, X68

HRISTIĆ, Zoran Yugoslavia 1938
  KMJ

*HRUBY, Viktor Austria 1894
  X64

HRUŠKA, Jaromir Ludvik Czechoslovakia 1910
  CCZ, IMD2

HRUŠOVSKÝ, Ivan Czechoslovakia 1927
  CCZ, MEH, X64, X65, X66, X67, X68, ZE70/1, ZE70/2,
  ZE70/3, ZE71/1, ZE71/2, ZE71/3

HUAN TZU China 1903 1938
  EMS
  EMS: ХУ́АН ЦЗЫ

HUBBELL, Frank Allen USA 1907
  AS66, BB65, BB71

*HUBEAU, Jean France 1917
  DDM, DMF, EVM, IMD, LMD, QQF, REM

*HUBER, Eugen Switzerland 1909 Hungary
  SCHW

*HUBER, Klaus Switzerland 1924
  BB65, BB71, CME, DDM, IMD, IMD2, LMD, MEH, MNG,
  REM, SCHW, WWS, X64, X65, X66, X67, X68

HUBER, Nicolaus A. Germany 1939
  PAP

HUBER, Paul Switzerland 1918
  PAP, SCHW

HUBER, Walter Simon Switzerland 1898
  SCHW

*HUBER-ANDERACH, Theodor Germany 1885
  EVM, LMD

*HUBICKI, Lovel Katharine
  Margaret Olive   Great Britain   circa
  WI69   1905

HÜBSCHMAN, Werner   Germany   1901
  IMD, MEH, SML

HUDEC, Jiri   Czechoslovakia 1923
  CCZ, MEH

HUDSON, Frederick   Great Britain   1913   Germany
  WI69, X64, X67

HUDY, Wolfgang   Germany   1928
  SML, X66

HUEBER, Kurt Anton   Austria   1928
  X65

HUFF, Jay   USA
  ASUC, CAP, X65

HUFSCHMIDT, Wolfgang   Germany   1934
  IMD2, X66, X67, X68

HUGGLER, John   USA   1928
  X68

*HUGHES, Arwel   Great Britain   1909   Wales
  EVM, LMD, REM, X64, X66

*HUGHES, Dom Anselm   Great Britain   1889
  REM, WI69

*HUGHES, Gervase Alfred
  Booth   Great Britain   1905
  X64, X65, X67, X68

HUGHES, Kent   USA   1928
  CAP, PC71

*HUGHES, Patrick Cairns
  ("Spike")   Great Britain   1908
  DDM, LMD, WI69, REM, X66, X68

HUGHES, Phil   USA   1942
  PAP

*HUGHES, Robert Watson Australia   1912   Scotland
  AMM, WI69

*HUGON, Georges   France   1904
  DDM, DMF, LMD, QQF, REM

*HUÍZAR, Garcia de la Cadena
  Candelario   Mexico   1883
    DDM, EVM, LMD, MMX, REM
    DDM, EVM and REM: 1888

HŮLA, Zdeněk   Czechoslovakia 1901
    CCZ, MEH, MNP72/9

*HULBERT, Hugh Reginald   Great Britain 1884
    WI69

*HULLEBROECK, Emiel   Belgium   1878 1965
    EVM, X65

*HULSE, Camil van   Belgium   1897
    EVM

*HULTBERG, Sven   Sweden   1912
    SIMa

HULTSTRAND, O. Titus G   Sweden   1893 1963
    FST

HUMEL, Gerald   USA   1931
    IMD2, LMD, X66, X67, X68

*HUMMEL, Bertold   Germany   1925
    X64, X65

*HUMPERT, Hans   Germany   1901 1943
    REM

HUMPERT, Hans Ulrich   Germany   1940
    PAP

HUNCKLER, Victor   France   1922
    ACM

HUNGAR, Paul   1887
    IMD

HUNGER, Hans-Helmut   Germany   1920
    SML, X68

HUNKINS, Eusebia Simpson USA   1902
    AS66, PC71

HUNT, C. Warren   Canada   1924 USA
    CCM, CVM, MCO

*HUNT, Donald Frederick   Great Britain 1930
    X68

HUNT, Jerry   USA   1943
    BB71, IMD2

*HUNT, Reginald Heber   Great Britain   1891
    X66, X67, X68

*HURFORD, Peter   Great Britain   1930
    WI69, X65, X66, X67, X68

*HURNÍK, Ilja   Czechoslovakia 1922
    CCZ, DDM, IMD, IMD2, LMD, MEH, MNP64/3, MNP64/5,
    MNP64/6, MNP65/2, MNP65/5, MNP65/6, MNP66/3,
    MNP68/1, MNP71/1, MNP71/6, MNP72/1, MNP72/6,
    MNP72/9, REM, SML, X64, X65, X68

*HURST, George   Canada   1926   Scotland
    X64

*HURUM, Alf Thorvald   Norway   1882
    BB71, CNO, LMD, REM, VTM

*HUSA, Karel   USA   1921   Czecho-
    AA73, ASUC, BB71, DDM, DN72, EVM,   slovakia
    IMD, LMD, MEH, WI69, X66, X67, X68

HUSE, Peter   Canada
    CCM71, CMV, KEY, NLC, X68

*HUSS, Henry Holden   USA   1862   1953
    EVM, LMD, REM

HUSTON, Thomas Scott   USA
    AA73, X66, X67, X68

*HUTCHENS, Frank   Australia   1892   1965
    AMM, X65, X66, X67   New Zealand

*HUTCHESON, Ernest   USA   1871   1951
    AMM, EVM, LMD, REM, X65   Australia

HUTCHESON, Jere Trent   USA

*HUTCHINGS, Arthur James
   Bramwell   Great Britain   1906
    X64, X65, X66, X67, X68

*HUTCHINGS, Charles   Great Britain   1910   1965
    X65

HUTCHINGS, Peter   Great Britain
    X64, X67

HUTCHINSON, Godfrey Michael
Langley   Great Britain   1936
WI69

HUTCHINSON, Warner   USA   1930
DN70, DN72, PC71

*HUYBRECHTS, Lode   Belgium   1911
EVM

*HUZELLA, Elek   Hungary   1915
CHC

HYBLER, Jindřich   Czechoslovakia   1891
CCZ

*HYDE, Miriam Beatrice
Edwards   Great Britain   1913   Australia
AMM, EVM, WI69

*HYE-KNUDSEN, Johan   Denmark   1896
EVM, IMD

HYMAN, Dick   USA   1927
PCM

IBANEZ, Carmen   Spain   1895
EMV

IBARRA GROTH, Federico   Mexico   1946
IIET26

IBERÉ de LEMOS, Arthur   1901
IMD

*IBERT, Jacques   France   1890   1962
BB65, BB71, DDM, DMF, EMS, EVM, IMD, LMD, MEH, REM,
SML, TCM, WI69, WTM, X68
EMS: ИБЕР

ICHIYANAGI, Toshi   Japan   1933
EL:2, IMD2, LMD, X64, X68

IDELSON, Jerry   Union of   Latvia
WSA   South Africa

*IFUKUBE, Akira   Japan   1914
IMD, LMD, REM

*IGLESIAS VILLOUD, Hector   Argentina   1913
IMD, X68

IJAC, Vasile   Rumania   1899
RCL

*IKENOUCHI, Tomojiro   Japan   1906
DDM, LMD, REM

*IKONEN, Lauri Ilmari   Finland   1888   1966
COF, EVM, KKO, LMD, REM, SML, VTM

*IKONOMOV, Boyan Georgiev   Bulgaria   1900   1973
BB65, BB71, BMK, EMS, EVM, LMD, MEH, X66, X67, X68
BMK and EMS: ИКОНОМОВ

ILIC, Borivoje   Yugoslavia   1918
KMJ

ILIĆ, Miodrag   Yugoslavia   1924
KMJ

ILIĆ, Vojislav   Yugoslavia   1912
KMJ

ILIEV, Iliya Kristov   Bulgaria   1912
BMK, X67
BMK: ИЛИЕВ

*ILIEV, Konstantin Nikolov   Bulgaria   1924
BB65, BB71, BMK, LMD, MEH, X64, X66, X68
BMK: ИЛИЕВ   MEH: ILJEV

*ILIFF, James   Great Britain   1923
WI69

ILIN, Igor Pavlovich   USSR   1909
EMS, PPU69/2
EMS: ИЛЬИН

ILIN, Sava   Rumania   1935
RCL

ILLERSBERG, Antonio   Italy   1882   1953
LMD

ILLÍN, Evžen   Czechoslovakia   1924
CCZ, IMD, IMD2

*IMBERT, Maurice François   France   1893
LMD, REM

*IMBRIE, Andrew Welsh   USA   1921
ASUC, BB65, BB71, CA12, EVM, LMD, OCM, PCM, PC71,
REM, X65, X66, X67, X68

INCERTI, Bruno   Switzerland   1910   Italy
   LMD, SCHW

*INCH, Herbert Reynolds   USA   1904
   EVM, LMD, PCM, REM, WI69

INDRA, Yuozas Stasevich   USSR   1918   1968
   EMS, X68   Lithuania
   EMS: ИНДРА

*INFANTE, Manuel   France   1883   1958
   BB65, BB71, LMD, REM   Spain

INGENBRAND, Josef   Germany   1905
   REM

*INGENHOVEN, Jan   Netherlands 1876 1951
   EVM, IMD, REM

*INGHELBRECHT, Désiré-
   Émile   France   1880 1965
   BB71, CMF10, CMF65/10, DDM, DMF, EMS, EVM, IMD,
   LMD, MLA22/4, REM, X64, X65, X66
   EMS: ЭНГЕЛЬБРЕХТ

INGHILLERI, Giovanni   Italy   1894 1959
   LMD

*INGMAN, Olavi   Finland   1903
   VTM

*INGRAM, Harold   Great Britain 1904
   WI69

IOANNIDIS, Yannis   Greece   1930
   BB65, BB71, CMD, EL:1, EL:2, EL:3, PAP, X65

IONESCU, Liviu   Rumania   1928
   RCL

IONESCU, Nelu Ioan   Rumania   1906
   RCL

IORDAN, Irina Nikolaevna USSR   1910
   EMS
   EMS: ИОРДАН

IORDANSKY, Mihail
   Vyacheslavovich   USSR   1901
   EMS
   EMS: ИОРДАНСКИЙ

IOSIFOV, Iosif Aleksandrev   Bulgaria   1911
    BMK
    BMK: ЙОСИФОВ

*IPPISCH, Franz   Guatemala   1883   1953
    LMD, REM   Austria

IPUCHE-RIVA, Pedro   Uruguay   1924
    BB71, CA12, LMD, X64, X66

*IRELAND, John Nicholson   Great Britain   1879   1962
    BB65, BB71, BCI, DDM, EMS, EVM, IMD, LMD, MEH, REM,
    SML, X64, X65, X66, X67, X68
    EMS: АЙРЛЕНД

*IRGENS JENSEN, Ludvig Paul   Norway   1894   1969
    DDM, CNO, LMD, REM, VTM
    DDM: JENSEN, L. I.   LMD: JENSEN, L. P. I.
    VTM: JENSEN, L. I.

*IRINO, Yoshiro   Japan   1921
    BB71, IMD, IMD2, LMD, REM, X65

*ISAACS, Edward Maurice   Great Britain   1881   1953
    EVM, LMD

*ISAMITT, Carlos   Chile   1887
    CA13, EVM, IMD, LMD, REM, X66
    EVM and LMD: 1885

*ISHII, Kan   Japan   1921
    BB71, LMD, X67

ISHII, Maki   Japan   1936
    BB71, IMD, IMD2, LMD

*ISLANDSMOEN, Sigurd   Norway   1881   1964
    CNO, EVM

ISMAGILOV, Zagir Garipovich   USSR   1917
    EMS, LMD, PPU69/2, X68
    EMS: ИСМАГИЛОВ

*ISOLFSSON, Páll   Iceland   1893
    REM, VTM, X65

ISOZ, Etienne   Switzerland   1905   Hungary
    DAS

ISRAEL, Itzhak   Israel   1913   Bulgaria
    ACU

*ISSERLIS, Julius   Great Britain   1888   1968
  BB71, EVM, X68   Russia
  EVM: 1889

ISTRATE, Mircea   Rumania   1929
  RCL, X64, X68

*IŠTVÁN, Miloslav   Czechoslovakia   1928
  BB65, BB71, CCZ, CME, IMD2, LMD, MEH, MNP64/5,
  MNP64/6, MNP65/6, MNP66/10, MNP67/6, MNP72/4,
  SML, X64, X66, X67, X68

*ITIBERÊ da CUNHA LUZ,
  Brasilio   Brazil   1896   1967
  CA16, FBC, IMD, LMD, REM

*ITURBI, Jose   Spain   1895
  EVM, LMD, REM, X65, X66, X67, X68

ITURRIZAGA, Luis   1926
  IMD

IUSCEANU, Victor   Rumania   1905
  RCL

IVANOV, Georgi   Bulgaria   1924
  BB65, BB71, BMK, LMD, X66, X67, X68
  BMK: ИВАНОВ

*IVANOV, Yanis Andreevich   USSR   1906
  DDM, EMS, LMD, PPU, PPU69/2, SML, X65, X66
  Also: IVANOVS, Janis Andreevich
  EMS: ИВАНОВ

IVANOVIĆ, Cvjetko   Yugoslavia   1929
  KMJ

*IVÁNOV-RADKÉVICH, Nikolai
  Pavlovich   USSR   1904   1962
  BB65, BB71, EMS, EVM, LMD, REM
  EMS: ИВАНОВ-РАДКЕВИЧ

*IVANOVSKI, Blagoja   Yugoslavia   1921
  KMJ, X67

*IVES, Charles Edward   USA   1874   1954
  BB65, BB71, DDM, EMS, EVM, IMD, IMD2, LMD, MEH,
  MZW, PCM, PC71, REM, SML, WTM, X64, X65, X66,
  X67, X68
  EMS: АЙВС

*IVEY, Jean Eichelberger   USA   1923
    AA73, ASUC, X64, X65, X66, X67, X68

IZQUIERDO, Jose Manuel   Spain   1890
    EVM

IŻYKOWSKI, Roman Jan   Poland   1912
    PKW

*JACHIMECKI, Zdzisław   Poland   1882   1953
    LMD, MEH, REM, SML, X64, X65

*JACHINO, Carlo   Italy   1887   1971
    DDM, EVM, LMD, MLA28/4, REM, WI69
    EVM: 1889

JACKSON, David   USA
    CAP

JACKSON, Hanley   USA   1939
    DN70

JACKSON, John   1929
    IMD

*JACOB, Gordon Percival
    Septimus   Great Britain   1895
    DDM, EVM, IMD, LMD, REM, WI69, X66, X68

*JACOB, Maxime Dom Clement   France   1906
    DDM, DMF, EVM, LMD, REM, X64

*JACOBI, Frederick   USA   1891   1952
    AS66, EVM, IMD, LMD, PCM, REM, X64, X65

*JACOBI, Wolfgang   Germany   1894
    EVM, IMD, LMD, SML, WWG, X67

*JACOBSEN, Ejnar   Denmark   1897   1970

*JACOBSON, Gabriel   Israel   1923   1948
    ACU, IMD, MM59   Germany
    Also: BEN-YAACOV, Gabriel

*JACOBSON, Maurice   Great Britain   1896
    EVM, LMD, REM, WI69

*JACOBY, Hanoch   Israel   1909   Germany
    ACU, IMD, LMD, MM59, REM, WWI
    Formerly: JACOBY, Heinrich

JACQUES, John Michael Great Britain 1944
WI69

JACQUES-DUPONT
See: DUPONT, Jacques

*JAECKEL, Robert Austria 1896
EVM

*JAEGGI, P. Oswald Switzerland 1913 1963
IMD, LMD, SCHW

JAHNKE, Zdzislaw Poland 1895 1972

JAKEŠEVIĆ, Gavro Yugoslavia 1911
KMJ

JAKUBENAS, Vladas USA 1904 Lithuania

*JALAS, Armas Jussi Veikko Finland 1908
LMD, X66
Formerly: BLOMSEDT

*JAMES, Dorothy USA 1901
ASUC, EVM, LMD

*JAMES, Philip USA 1890
AS66, EVM, LMD, PCM, PC71, REM, X67, X68

*JAMES, William Garnel Australia 1895
AMM, LMD, REM
REM: 1892

JAMIN, Paul France 1922
ACM

*JANÁČEK, Bedřich Sweden 1920 Czecho-
X66 slovakia

JANČYS, Vytautas USA 1923 Lithuania
REM

*JANEČEK, Karel Czechoslovakia 1903 Poland
CCZ, EVM, IMD, LMD, MEH, MNP64/3, MNP68/2, MNP68/6,
REM, SML, X64, X67, X68

JANES, Aladar Italy 1917
LMD, REM

*JANOVICKY, Karel Great Britain 1930 Czecho-
IMD, WI69 slovakia
Pseudonym: SIMSA, B.

JANSEN, Simon Cornelius   Netherlands   1911
  EVM

JANSON, Alfred   Norway   1937
  CNO, VTM, X66, X67, X68

*JANSSEN, Werner   USA   1899
  AS66, EVM, LMD, REM
  AS66 and LMD: 1900

JANSSENS, Honoré   Belgium   1902
  EVM

JAQUE, Rhené   Canada
  KEY

*JAQUES-DALCROZE, Émile   Switzerland   1865   1950
  DDM, EVM, IMD, LMD, REM, SCHW,   Austria
  X65, X66, X67, X68
  Pseudonym: JAQUES, Emile

JARDA, Tudor   Rumania   1922
  RCL, X65, X68

*JÁRDÁNYI, Pál   Hungary   1920   1966
  BB65, BB71, CHC, CME, DDM, EVM, IMD, MEH, REM, SML,
  WI69, X64, X65, X67, X68

*JARECKI, Tadeusz   USA   1889   1955
  BB65, BB71, DDM, EVM, LMD, REM   Poland

*JARNACH, Philipp   Germany   1892   France
  BB65, BB71, DDM, EMS, EVM, IMD, LMD, MEH, REM, SML
  EMS: ЯРНАХ

*JÄRNEFELT, Edvard Armas   Sweden   1869   1958
  BB65, BB71, COF, DDM, EMS, EVM,   Finland
  LMD, MEH, SML, VTM
  EMS: ЯРНЕФЕЛЬТ

*JAROCH, Jiří   Czechoslovakia 1920
  CCZ, IMD2, MEH, MNP67/1, MNP67/4, MNP72/6, SML,
  X65, X66

*JARRE, Maurice Alexis   France   1924
  BB65, BB71, DDM, DMF, EVM, LMD, QQF, REM, X66
  EVM: 1925   QQF: 1928

*JAUBERT, Maurice Jacques-
  Joseph-Eugene   France   1900   1940
  DDM, DMF, EVM, IMD, LMD, REM

JAYARAMA IYER, T. K.   India   1894
  WHI

JEANNERET, Albert   Switzerland   1886
  SCHW, X66

JELESCU, Paul   Rumania   1901
  MEH, RCL, SML

JELIČANIN, Milan   Yugoslavia   1935
  KMJ

*JELINEK, Hanns   Austria   1901 1969
  BB71, CME, DDM, IMD, IMD2, LMD, MEH, MLA26/4, PAP,
  REM, SML, TSC, X65, X66, X67, X68

JELÍNEK, Stanislav   Czechoslovakia
  MNP69/4

*JEMNITZ, Sándor   Hungary   1899 1963
  BB65, BB71, CHC, CME, DDM, EVM, IMD, LMD, MEH, REM,
  SML, X64
  DDM and REM: 1890

JENEY, Zoltán   Hungary   1943
  CHC, X65, X68

*JENKINS, Cyril   Great Britain   1885 Wales
  EVM
  EVM: 1889

JENKINS, Joseph Wilcox   USA
  AA73

JENKS, Alden Feriss   USA   1940
  BB71

JENNI, Donald   USA   1937
  AA73, LCI, X65, X66, X68

*JENNY, Albert   Switzerland   1912
  LMD, SCHW, REM

JENSEN, James A.   USA
  CAP

JENSEN, Ludvig Paul Irgens
  See: IRGENS JENSEN, Ludvig Paul

*JENTSCH, Walter   Germany   1900
  IMD

JENTZSCH, Wilfried   Germany
     X67, X68

*JEPPESEN, Knud Christian   Denmark   1892
     BB65, DDM, EVM, LMD, REM, SML, VTM, WI69, X64, X65,
     X66, X67, X68

*JEREA, Hilda   Rumania   1916
     LMD, MEH, RCL, REM, SML, X65, X66, X68

*JEREMIÁŠ, Otakar   Czechoslovakia   1892   1962
     BB65, CCZ, CME, DDM, EMS, EVM, IMD, IMD2, LMD, MEH,
     REM, SML, X64, X65
     EMS: ЕРЕМИАШ

*JERGER, Wilhelm Franz   Austria   1902
     EVM, IMD, LMD, X64, X65, X66, X67, X68

JERSEY, Barrie de   Australia
     AMM

*JERSILD, Jørgen   Denmark   1913
     CME, DMTsp, IMD, LMD, VTM, X65, X66, X67

*JESINGHAUS, Walter   Switzerland   1902   1966
     EVM, IMD, LMD, MLA23/4, SCHW

JESSON, Roy   USA   1926
     PCM, X68

JETER, Albert   USA   1947
     DN70

*JEVONS, Reginald Augustus   Great Britain   1901
     WI69, X68

JEŽ, Jakob   Yugoslavia   1928
     KMJ, MSC, X67

*JEŽEK, Jaroslav   Czechoslovakia   1906   1942
     CCZ, EVM, IMD, MEH, SML, X65, X66, X68

JIGANOV, N. G.
     See: ZHIGANOV, N. G.

*JIMÉNEZ-MABARAK, Carlos   Mexico   1916
     BB65, CA8, EVM, IMD, LMD, X65

*JINDŘICH, Jindřich   Czechoslovakia   1876   1967
     CCZ, EVM, MEH, X67

*JIRÁK, Karel Boleslav   USA   1891 1972
   BB65, CCZ, CME, DDM, EVM, IMD, IMD2,   Czecho-
   LCI, LMD, MEH, MLA29/4, MNP69/1,   slovakia
   MNP72/5, REM, X64, X66

JIRANEK, Alois   Czechoslovakia 1858 1950
   EMV, LMD

JIRÁSEK, Ivo   Czechoslovakia 1920
   CCZ, COO, MEH, MNP69/3, MNP72/4, MNP72/5, X64, X65,
   X68

*JIRKO, Ivan   Czechoslovakia 1926
   BB65, CCZ, IMD2, MEH, MNP64/3, MNP67/1, SML, X64,
   X65, X66, X67, X68

*JOACHIM, Otto   Canada   1910 Germany
   BB65, BCL, CA10, CCM, CCM71, IMD, IMD2, KEY, LMD,
   MCO, MCO71, NLC, TFB, X66, X68

JOBST, Anton   Yugoslavia   1894
   KMJ

*JOCHUM, Otto   Germany   1898
   EVM, IMD, LMD, REM, WI69, WWG, X68

JODÁL, Gábor   Rumania   1913
   RCL

*JOFFE, Solomon   Israel   1900 Poland
   ACU

JOHANNESEN, Grant   USA   1921
   PC71, X68

JOHANSEN, David Monrad
   See: MONRAD JOHANSEN, David

*JOHANSEN, Gunnar   USA   1906 Denmark
   X68

JOHANSEN, Svend Aaquist   Denmark
   DMTsp

*JOHANSON, Martin S.   Sweden   1892 1956
   FST, SIM, SIMa

*JOHANSON, Sven-Eric
   Emanuel   Sweden   1919
   DDM, FST, IMD, IMD2, KSV, LMD, SIM, SIMa, SOW, STS,
   SWE, TJU, VTM, X64, X67

*JOHANSSON, Bengt Viktor   Finland   1914
    COF, KKO, VTM, X66, X67

*JOHANSSON, Björn Emanuel   Sweden   1913
    FST, KSV, SIM, SIMa, STI, TJU, X64, X67
    STI: JOHAN<u>SO</u>N

*JOHNER, Dominicus Franz   Germany   1874   1955
    LMD

JOHNS, Donald Charles   USA   1926
    PC71, X65, X67

*JOHNSEN, Hallvard   Norway   1916   Germany
    CNO, EVM

JOHNSON, Bengt Emil   Sweden   1936
    CME, STS, VTM, X66, X68

JOHNSON, David   Great Britain
    X68

JOHNSON, Harold Victor   USA   1918
    AS66

JOHNSON, Henry P., Jr.   USA   1911
    DN70, X68

*JOHNSON, Horace   USA   1893   1964
    AS66, BB65, EVM, LMD, WI69, X64

*JOHNSON, Hunter   USA   1906
    AS66, LMD, PCM, PC71, REM, X64, X65, X66

JOHNSON, J. J. James Louis   USA   1924
    PCM, X65, X66, X68

JOHNSON, James Price   USA   1891   1955
    AS66, LMD

*JOHNSON, John Rosamond   USA   1873   1954
    AS66

*JOHNSON, Lockrem   USA   1924
    PCM, X65, X67, X68

JOHNSON, Robert Sherlaw
    See: SHERLAW-JOHNSON, Robert

JOHNSON, Roger   USA
    CAP

*JOHNSON, Thomas Arnold   Great Britain   1908
WI69

JOHNSSON, Bengt   Denmark
VTM, X65, X67, X68

*JOHNSTON, Albert Richard   Canada   1917 USA
CVM, MCO, MCO68

JOHNSTON, Benjamin Burwell USA   1926
ASUC, IMD2, LMD, PCM, X64, X67, X68

*JOHNSTONE, Maurice   Great Britain   1900
WI69

JOIO, Norman dello
See: DELLO JOIO, Norman

*JOKL, Georg   USA   1896 Austria
LMD

*JOKL, Otto   USA   1891 Austria
BB65, EVM, LMD

*JOLAS, Betsy   France   1926
IMD2, X66, X67, X68

*JOLIVET, André   France   1905
BB65, BB71, CME, CMF4, CMF20, CMF40, DDM, DMF, EMS,
EVM, IMD, IMD2, LMD, MEH, PAP, QQF, REM, SML, TCM,
TSC, X64, X65, X66, X67, X68
EMS: ЖОЛИВЕ́

JONÁK, Zdeněk   Czechoslovakia 1917
CCZ

*JONES, Charles   USA   1910 Canada
AS66, BB65, BB71, MCO, PCM, PC71, X65, X67, X68

JONES, Charles "Big"   1931
WAN

*JONES, Daniel Jenkyn   Great Britain 1912 Wales
BB65, BB71, IMD, LMD, MEH, REM, X64, X67, X68

JONES, David   Great Britain   1929
EL:3

JONES, George Thaddeus   USA   1917
ASUC, AS66, X64, X66, X67, X68

*JONES, Kelsey   Canada 1922 USA
 BB71, CA11, CCM, CCM71, CVM, IMD, KEY, LMD, MCO,
 MCO68, NLC, TFB, X68

*JONES, Kenneth Baden Great Britain 1915
 WI69, X68

*JONES, Kenneth Victor Great Britain 1924
 WI69, X68

*JONES, Lewis Ernest Beddoe Great Britain 1933
 WI69

JONES, Robert W.   USA   1932
 PC71

JONES, Trevor Alan   Australia 1932
 AMM, X67, X68

*JONES, Trevor Morgan Canada 1899
 CVM, MCO68, MCO71

*JONG, Marinus de   Belgium 1891
 EVM, LMD, X67

*JONGEN, Joseph   Belgium 1873 1953
 CBC, DDM, EMS, EVM, IMD, IMD2, LMD, REM
 EMS: ЙОНГЕН

*JONGEN, Léon   Belgium 1884 1969
 BB71, CBC, DDM, EMS, EVM, LMD, REM, VMB8/6
 EMS: ЙОНГЕН
 CBC and EMS: 1885

JÓNSSON, Halldór   Iceland 1873 1952
 VTM

JÓNSSON, Jón S.   Iceland 1933
 VTM

*JONSSON, Josef Petrus Sweden 1887 1969
 BB71, FST, KSV, LMD, REM, SIM, SIMa, STS, TJU, X67

*JÓNSSON, Thórarinn Iceland 1900
 VTM

*JORA, Mihail   Rumania 1891 1971
 CME, DDM, EMS, EVM, LMD, MEH, MLA28, RCL, REM,
 SML, X64, X65, X68
 EMS: ЖОРА

JORDA, Enrique   Spain   1911
 WI69

*JORDAN, Sverre   Norway   1889
    CNO, EVM, LMD, REM, VTM

JORGE, Gonzalez Avila
    See: AVILA JORGE, Gonzalez

*JØRGENSEN, Erik   Denmark   1912
    DMTsp, IMD2, VTM

JØRGENSEN, Henrik Colding
    See: COLDING JØRGENSEN, Henrik

JORIO, Argenzio   Italy   1923
    LMD, REM

JÖRNS, Helmuth   1911
    IMD

*JOSEPHS, Wilfred   Great Britain   1927
    WI69, X64, X65, X66, X67, X68

*JOSIF, Enriko   Yugoslavia   1924
    DDM, IMD, KMJ, REM, X65, X67

*JOSTEN, Werner Eric   USA   1885   1963
    AS66, BB65, BB71, EVM, IMD, LMD, REM   Germany

JOUARD, Paul E.   USA   1928
    AS66

*JOUBERT, John   Union of   1927
                                South Africa
    BB65, BB71, DDM, LMD, OCM, REM, WI69, X64, X65, X66,
    X67, X68

JOVANOVIĆ, Vladimir   Yugoslavia   1937
    KMJ

JUCHELKA, Miroslav   Czechoslovakia   1922
    CCZ, MEH

*JUDA, Jo   Netherlands   1909
    X65

JULEA, Nicolae   Rumania   1908
    RCL

JUNGER, Erwin   Rumania   1931
    RCL, X68

JUNGK, Klaus   Germany   1916
    WI69

*JUNKER, Richard   Germany   1900   1966
    X66, X68

JURADO, Nicasio   Mexico   1888
    MMX

JURDZIŃSKI, Kazimierz   Poland   1894   1960
    PKW

JURISALU, Heino Arturovich   USSR   1930   Estonia
    EMS
    EMS: ЮРИСАЛУ

JUROVSKIJ, V. M.
    See: YUROVSKY, V. M.

*JUROVSKÝ, Šimon   Czechoslovakia   1912   1963
    BB71, CCZ, EVM, LMD, MEH, MNP64/4, MNP64/5,
    MNP65/2, REM, SML, X64, ZE69/1, ZE69/3

JUROVSKY, Vladimir
    See: YUROVSKY, Vladimir

JUVANEC, Ferdo   Yugoslavia   1908
    KMJ

*JUZELIŪNAS, Julius
    Aleksandro   USSR   1916
    BB65, BB71, EMS, LMD   Lithuania
    EMS: ЮЗЕЛЮНАС

*KABALÉVSKY, Dmitri
    Borisovich   USSR   1904
    BB65, BB71, CME, DDM, EMS, EVM, IMD, IMD2, LMD,
    MEH, PPU, PPU68/2, PPU69/2, REM, SCD, SML, WTM,
    X64, X65, X66, X67, X68
    EMS: КАБАЛЕВСКИЙ

*KABELÁČ, Miloslav   Czechoslovakia   1908
    BB65, BB71, CCZ, DDM, EL:3, EMS, EVM, IMD, IMD2, LMD,
    MNP64/3, MNP64/4, MNP64/5, MNP65/3, MNP65/7,
    MNP67/6, MNP68/9, REM, SML, WI69, X64, X65, X66,
    X67, X68
    EMS: КАБЕЛАЧ

KÄCH, Hugo   Switzerland   1927
    SCHW

KACINKAS, Jeronimas   Lithuania   1907
    BB65, BB71, LMD, X64

*KADOSA, Pál   Hungary   1903
   BB65, BB71, CHC, CME, EMS, EVM, IMD, LMD, MEH, REM,
   SML, X64, X65, X66, X67, X68
   EMS: КАДОША

KAEGI, Werner   Switzerland   1926
   LMD, SCHW, SCHWs, X67, X68
   SCHWs and X68: KÄGI, Werner

*KAELIN, Pierre   Switzerland   1913
   DDM, SCHW, X65, X66, X68

*KAFENDA, Frico   Czechoslovakia 1883 1963
   CCZ, EVM, LMD, MEH

*KAGEL, Mauricio   Argentina   1931
   BB65, BB71, CME, DDM, DMM, EL:1, IMD, IMD2, LMD,
   MEH, MNG, MZW, PAP, REM, WI69, X64, X65, X66, X67,
   X68

KAGEN, Sergius   USA   1909 1964
   BB65, BB71, PCM, X64, X68   Russia

*KAHN, Erich Itor   USA   1905 1956
   BB71, IMD, LMD, REM, X66   Germany

*KAHN, Percival Benedict   Great Britain 1880 1966
   MLA23/4, X66

*KAHN, Robert   Great Britain 1865 1951
   EVM, IMD, LMD,   and Germany   Germany
   REM, X65

KAHOWEZ, Günter   Austria   1940
   BB65, BB71, IMD, IMD2, LMD, X66, X68

KAISER, Daniel   France   1938
   ACM

KAISER, Hermann Josef   1938
   IMD2, X68

*KALABIS, Viktor   Czechoslovakia 1923
   BB65, BB71, CCZ, CME, IMD, IMD2, LMD, MEH, MNP64/3,
   MNP64/5, MNP64/6, MNP65/6, MNP69/5, SML, X64, X65,
   X67, X68

KALAN, Pavle   Yugoslavia   1929
   KMJ

*KALAŠ, Julius   Czechoslovakia 1902
   CCZ, IMD, LMD, MEH, SML, X67
   Formerly: KASSAL, Luis

KALČIĆ, Josip   Yugoslavia   1912
   KMJ

*KÁLIK, Václav   Czechoslovakia 1891 1951
   CCZ, EVM, IMD2, LMD, MEH, REM

KALLAUSCH, Kurt   Germany   1926
   SML, X66, X67

*KALLSTENIUS, Edvin   Sweden   1881 1967
   EVM, FST, IMD, IMD2, KSV, LMD, REM, SIM, SIMa, SOW,
   STS, SWE, TJU, VTM, X67, X68

*KÁLMÁN, Emmerich Imre   USA   1882 1953
   AS66, BB71, DDM, EMS, EVM, LMD,   Hungary
   MEH, REM, SML, X65
   EMS: КА́ЛЬМАН

*KALMANOFF, Martin   USA   1920
   AS66, PCM, PC71, X66, X67, X68

KALMÁR, László   Hungary   1931
   CHC, X67, X68

*KALNINS, Alfreds Yanovich USSR   1879 1951
   BB71, EVM, LMD, REM   Latvia

*KALNINS, Janis (John)   Canada   1904 Latvia
   CCM71, LMD, MCO, MCO68, NLC, REM, X68

*KALOMIRIS, Manolis   Greece   1883 1962
   BB65, BB71, CME, DDM, EMS, EVM, LMD, MEH, REM, SML
   EMS: КАЛОМИ́РИС

*KAMIENSKI, Lucjan   Poland   1885
   EVM, LMD, REM

KAMIŃSKI, Marcin   Poland   1913
   PKW

*KAMINSKY, Dimitri
Romanovich   USSR   1907
   EMS, X64, X67
   EMS: КАМИ́НСКИЙ

*KAMINSKY, Joseph   Israel   1903 1972
   ACU, IMD, LMD, MLA29/4, MM59, REM, WWI Russia
   LMD: 1906

KAMMEIER, Hans   1902
   IMD

KAMMERER, Immanuel
  Johannes   Switzerland   1896
  X64

*KÄMPF, Karl   Germany   1874   1950
  EVM, IMD

*KANITZ, Ernst   USA   1894   Austria
  AA73, AS66, BB65, BB71, DN72, EVM, LMD, PCM, REM,
  X64, X65, X66, X67, X68

*KANKAROVICH, Anatoli
  Issaakovich   USSR   1885 1956
  EMS
  EMS: КАНКАРОВИЧ

*KANN, Hans   Japan   1927   Austria
  IMD, IMD2, X65, X66, X67

*KANNER, Jerome Herbert USA   1903
  AS66

KANTOR, Joseph   USA   1930
  DN70

KANTUŠER, Božidar   France   1921 Yugoslavia
  DDM

KAPLAN, Josip   Yugoslavia 1910
  KMJ

*KAPP, Arthur Iosifovich USSR   1878 1952
  DDM, EMS, EVM, LMD, REM   Estonia
  EMS: КАПП

*KAPP, Eugen Arturovich USSR   1908 Estonia
  EMS, LMD, MEH, MNP72/7, PPU, PPU68/4, PPU69/2,
  PPU70/1, REM, SML
  EMS: КАПП

KAPP, Richard   USA   1936
  PCM

*KAPP, Villem Hansovich USSR   1913 1964
  BB71, EMS, LMD, REM   Estonia
  EMS: КАПП

*KAPR, Jan   Czechoslovakia 1914
  CCZ, CME, EL:1, EMS, EVM, IMD, IMD2, LMD, MEH,
  MNP65/6, MNP67/6, MNP67/7, MNP69/3, MNP69/4,
  MNP69/8, MNP72/6, PAP, REM, SML, X64, X65, X66,
  X67, X68
  EMS: КАПР

*KAPRÁLOVÁ, Vitězslava   Czechoslovakia 1915 1940
  CCZ, CME, DDM, EVM, IMD, IMD2, REM, X65

*KARAEV, Kara Abulfazoglu
  Ogly   USSR   1918
  CME, DDM, EMS, EVM, LMD, MEH, PPU, PPU68/1,
  PPU68/4, PPU69/2, SCD, SML, X65, X66, X67, X68
  EVM and SML: KARAJEW   MEH: KARAJEV
  PPU68/4: KARAYEV
  EMS: КАРАЕВ

KARAI, Jószef   Hungary   1927
  CHC, X68

*KARAM, Frederick   Canada   1926
  KEY, MCO, NLC

KARAS, Rudolf   Czechoslovakia 1930 Rumania
  CCZ

*KARASTOYANOV, Asen Pavlov   Bulgaria   1893
  BMK, X68
  BMK: КАРАСТОЯНОВ

KARAZHOV, Dimitri Ivanov   Bulgaria   1902
  BMK
  BMK: КАРАДЖОВ

*KARDOŠ, Dezider   Czechoslovakia 1914
  CCZ, EMS, EVM, IMD, LMD, MEH, MNP65/5, REM, SML,
  WI69, X65, X66, X67, ZE69/1, ZE70/1, ZE70/2, ZE70/3,
  ZE71/2, ZE71/3
  EMS: КАРДОШ

KARDOS, István   Hungary   1891
  CHC

*KARETNIKOV, Nikolai
  Nicolaivich   USSR   1930
  EMS, MNG, PPU, X64
  EMS: КАРЕТНИКОВ

*KARJALAINEN, Ahti Eino   Finland   1907
  COF, KKO

*KARKOFF, Maurice Ingvar   Sweden   1927
  BB71, CME, FST, IMD, KSV, LMD, SIM, SIMa, SMT, SOW,
  STS, SWE, TJU, VTM, X64, X65, X67

KARKOSCHKA, Erhard   1923
  IMD2, X65, X67, X68

KARLAN, Josip   Yugoslavia   1910
    HCM

KARLIN, Frederick James   USA   1936
    AS66

KARLINS, M. William   USA
    ASUC, X68

*KARNITZKAIA, Nina
    Andreevna   USSR   1906
    EMS
    EMS: КАРНИЦКАЯ

*KARNOVICH, Yuri Larovich   USSR   1884   Lithuania
    EVM

KAROLYI, Pal   Hungary   1934
    CHC, X67, X68

KARSEMEIJER, Rudolf Gerhard
    Alexander   Netherlands   1908
    EVM

*KARYOTAKIS, Theodoros   Greece   1903
    CME, EVM, LMD, REM, X65
    REM: KARIOTAKIS

KASANDJEV, Vassil   Bulgaria   1934

*KASEMETS, Udo   Canada   1919   Estonia
    BB65, BB71, BCL, CA8, CCM71, CVM, CVMa, IMD, KEY,
    LMD, MCO, NLC, X64, X66, X67, X68

*KASKI, Heino Wilhelm Daniel   Finland   1885   1957
    COF, EVM

KAŠLÍK, Václav   Czechoslovakia   1891   1951
    MNP64/4

*KAŠLÍK, Václav   Czechoslovakia   1917
    CCZ, CME, LMD, MEH, MNP66/4, SML, X66, X67, X68

KASSAL, Luis
    See: KALAŠ, Julius

*KASSERN, Tadeusz Zygfryd   Poland   1904   1957
    EVM, LMD, PKW, REM, X67

*KASSIANOV, Alexander
    Alexandrovich   USSR   1891
    EMS
    EMS: КАСЬЯНОВ

*KASTLE, Leonard USA 1929
AS66, BB65, BB71, PCM, X67, X68

*KATTNIGG, Rudolf USA 1895 1955
EVM, IMD, REM, SML Austria

*KATWIJK, Paul Van Netherlands 1885
WI69

*KATZ, Erich Germany 1900
EVM, PCM, PC71, WWG, X65

KATZ, Fred USA 1919
AS66

*KATZ, Sigizmund Abramovich USSR 1908
EMS, EVM, PPU, X68
EMS: КАЦ

KATZER, George Germany
X65, X68

KATZMAN, Klara Abramovna USSR 1916
EMS
EMS: КАЦМАН

*KAUDER, Hugo USA 1888 1972
EVM, IMD, LMD, MLA29/4, X64 Austria

*KAUFFMANN, Leo Justinus Germany 1901 1944
DDM, EVM, IMD, REM, SML
EVM: 1901-1943

*KAUFMAN, Barbara Israel 1912 Hungary
MM59

KAUFMAN, Fredrick USA 1936
DN70

KAUFMAN, Leonid Sergyevich USSR 1907
EMS, X64, X67
EMS: КАУФМАН

*KAUFMANN, Armin Austria 1902 Rumania
EVM, LMD, REM, WI69

*KAUFMANN, Ludwig Germany 1907
WI69

KAUFMANN, Nico Switzerland 1916
WWS

*KAUFMANN, Walter   USA   1907   Czecho-
    BB71, DAS, LMD, MCO, PCM, REM, X65,   slovakia
    X66, X67, X68

KAVECKAS, Conradas Vlado
    See: KAVIATSKAS

*KAVIATSKAS, Conradas Vlado   USSR   1905   Lithuania
    EMS
    EMS: КАВЯЦКАС

KAY, Don   Australia   1933
    AMM

KAY, Hershy   USA   1919
    AS66, BB65, LMD, PCM, PC71, X68

KAY, Norman   Great Britain
    X66, X67, X68

*KAY, Ulysses Simpson   USA   1917
    AA73, BB65, BB71, EMS, EVM, IMD, LMD, PCM, REM,
    WI69, X64, X65, X66, X67, X68
    EMS: КЕЙ

*KAYDEN, Mildred   USA
    AS66

*KAYE-PERRY, Leonard   Great Britain   1905
    WI69

*KAYN, Roland   Germany   1933
    IMD, LMD, MEH, REM, X64, X65, X66, X67

*KAYSER, Leif   Denmark   1919
    IMD, LMD, REM, VTM

KAZ, Sigismund Abramovich   USSR   1908   Poland
    LMD

*KAZACSAY, Tibor   Hungary   1892
    CHC, LMD, X68

KAZANDZHIEV, Vasil Ivanov   Bulgaria   1934
    BB65, BB71, BMK, LMD, MEH, X64, X66, X67, X68
    BMK: КАЗАНДЖИЕВ

*KAZASOGLOU, Georgios   Greece   1910
    EVM, LMD, REM
    LMD: KASASSOGLU   REM: KASASSOGLU

KAZIĆ, Josip   Yugoslavia   1917
    KMJ

KAZLAEV, Murad
    Mahomedovich   USSR   1931
    EMS, PPU69/2, X64, X68
    EMS: КАЖЛАЕВ

*KAZURO, Stanislas   Poland   1882   1961
    EVM, LMD, PKW, REM

KCHRENNIKOW, T.
    See: KHRENNIKOV, T.

KEATS, Donald   USA   1929
    ASUC, AS66, BB65, BB71, LMD, PC71, X65

KECHLEY, Gerald R.   USA   1919
    AA73, CAP, PCM, PC71, X66, X67, X68

*KEE, Cor   Netherlands   1900
    EVM, LMD, X65

*KEE, Piet   Netherlands   1927
    BB65, BB71, EVM, LMD, X67

KEETBAAS, Dirk   Canada   1921   Netherlands
    CCM, MCO68

KEF, Kees   1894   1961
    EVM

KEHRER, Willy   Germany   1902
    EVM

*KEILMANN, Wilhelm   Germany   1908
    WWG

*KELDORFER, Robert   Austria   1901
    IMD, LMD, REM, X66, X68

*KELDORFER, Victor   Austria   1873   1959
    BB65, BB71, EVM, LMD, REM

*KELEMEN, Milko   Yugoslavia   1924
    BB65, BB71, CME, DDM, EMS, HCM, IMD, IMD2, KMJ, LMD,
    MEH, MNG, MZW, PAP, REM, SML, X64, X65, X66, X67, X68
    EMS: КЕЛЕМЕН

KELEN, Hugó   Hungary   1888   1956
    CHC, LMD

*KELKEL, Manfred   Germany   1929
   DDM, IMD, LMD, REM, X67

KELLAWAY, Roger   USA   1939
   X67

KELLENBACH, Peter   Netherlands 1914
   EVM

KELLER, Alfred   Switzerland 1907
   SCHW, X65

*KELLER, Hermann   Germany   1885 1967
   BB71, LMD, REM, X64, X65, X66, X67, X68

*KELLER, Homer   USA   circa 1917
   ASUC, PCM, PC71

*KELLER, Wilhelm   Austria   1920
   IMD, LMD, REM, X64, X65, X66, X67

*KELLERMANN, Hellmut   Germany   1891
   EVM, LMD

KELLY, Bryan   Great Britain 1934
   WI69, X64, X66, X67

*KELLY, J. Robert   USA   1916
   AA73, ASUC, BB71, CA13, LCI, PCM, PC71, X64, X65, X67,
   X68

*KELTERBORN, Rudolf   Switzerland 1931
   BB65, BB71, CME, DDM, IMD, IMD2, LMD, MEH, REM,
   SCHW, X64, X65, X66, X67, X68

KEMP, Walter   Canada   1938
   MCO, NLC, NLCa

*KEMPE, Harald   Sweden   1900
   SIM, SIMa

KEMPFF, George   Germany   1893
   LMD, REM, SML

*KEMPFF, Wilhelm   Germany   1895
   EMS, EVM, DDM, IMD, LMD, REM, SML, WI69, X64, X65,
   X66, X67, X68
   EMS: КЕМПФ

KENDAL, Sydney
   See: MASON, Gladys Amy

*KENDELL, Iain Philip Great Britain 1931
 WI69, X64, X65, X68
 WI69: KEND<u>A</u>LL

*KENEL, Aleksandr
Aleksandrovich USSR 1898 1970

*KENESSEY, Jenö Hungary 1906
 CHC, CME, REM

*KENINS, Talivaldis Canada 1919 Latvia
 BB65, BB71, CA8, CCM, CCM71, KEY, LMD, MCO, MCO68,
 MCO71, NLC, NLCa, X68

*KENNAN, Kent Wheeler USA 1913
 AS66, PCM, SML, WI69, X64, X66

*KENNAWAY, Lamont Great Britain
 WI69

KENNEDY, John Brodbin USA 1934
 PCM, PC71

*KENT, Ada Twohy
 (Mrs. W. G.) Canada 1888 USA
 CVM, NLC

*KENTNER, Louis Philip Great Britain 1905 Hungary
 EVM, LMD, REM, X64

KEREN, Zvi Israel 1917 USA
 ACU

*KERENYI, György Hungary 1902
 CME, LMD, X64, X65, X67, X68

*KERESSELIDZE, Archil
 Pavlovich USSR 1912
 EMS, EVM, PPU
 EMS: КЕРЕСЕЛИ́ДЗЕ

*KERR, Harrison USA 1897
 EVM, IMD, PCM, PC71, REM, WI69

*KERSTERS, Willem Belgium 1929
 X66

*KESNAR, Maurits USA 1900 1957
 AS66 Netherlands

KESS, Ludwig 1915
 IMD

KESSLER, Ralph   USA   1919
   AS66

KESSLER, Thomas   Germany   circa 1938
   X67, X68

KESSNER, Daniel   USA   1946
   BS70

KESTNER, Felicitas
   See: KUKUCK, Felicitas

*KETÈLBEY, Albert William   Great Britain 1875 1959
   BB71, EVM, LMD, MEH
   MEH: 1880

KETTERING, Eunice Lea   USA   1906
   AA73, PCM, X64, X65, X66, X67, X68

*KETTING, Otto   Netherlands   1935
   BB65, BB71, CME, IMD, LMD, NED, TSC, X64, X65, X66,
   X68

*KETTING, Piet   Netherlands   1905
   EVM, IMD, LMD, NED, REM, X65, X68

KEYES, Nelson   USA   1928
   PC71, X67

*KEYS, Ivor Christopher
   Banfield   Great Britain   1919
   WI69, X68

KHACHATURYAN, Karen
   Surenovich   USSR   1920
   BB71, EMS, LMD, MEH, PPU, PPU69/2, PPU71/4, X67, X68
   BB71: KHATCHATURIAN   LMD: KHAČATURJAN
   MEH: CHAČATURIAN
   EMS: ХАЧАТУРЯН

*KHADZHIEV, Parashkev
   Todorov   Bulgaria   1912
   BB65, BB71, BMK, EVM, LMD, REM, SML, X66, X67, X68
   BB65 and BB71: HADZHIEV   EVM: HADJIEFF
   SML: HADSCHIEFF   X68: Also HADJIEV separate listing
   BMK: ХАДЖИЕВ

KHADZHIEV, Todor
   Parazhkevov   Bulgaria   1881 1956
   BMK
   BMK: ХАДЖИЕВ

KHAIT, Yuli Abramovich   USSR   1897
    EMS
    EMS: ХАЙТ

KHAMIDI, Latif Abdulaevich   USSR   1906
    EMS, LMD, X65, X67
    EMS: ХАМИДИ

*KHATCHATURIAN, Aram Ilyich USSR   1903
    BB65, BB71, CME, DDM, EMS, EVM, IMD, LMD, MEH, PPU,
    PPU69/3, REM, SCD, SML, WTM, X64, X65, X66, X67, X68
    EVM: CHATSJATOERJAN   LMD: KHAČATURJAN
    MEH: CHAČATURIAN   SCD: KHACHATURIA
    SML: CHATSCHATURJAN   EMS: ХАЧАТУРЯН

KHATCHATURIAN, Karen
    See: KHACHATURYAN

KHATCHATURIAN, Nina Vladimorova
    See: MAKAROVA, N. V.

KHODIASHEV, Viktor
    Aleksandrovich   USSR   1917
    LMD

*KHODZHA-EINATOV, Leon
    Aleksandrovich   USSR   1904   1955
    EMS, MEH, REM, X65
    MEH: HODZA-EJTANOV
    EMS: ХОДЖА-ЭЙНАТОВ

KHOLMINOV, Aleksandr
    Nikolaevich   USSR   1925
    EMS, PPU69/4, PPU69/2, PPU70/3, X66, X67, X68
    EMS: ХОЛМИНОВ

*KHRÉNNIKOV, Tikhon
    Nikolayevich   USSR   1913
    BB65, BB71, CME, DDM, EMS, EVM, LMD, MEH, PPU69/2,
    REM, SCD, SML, X64, X65, X66, X67, X68
    EVM: KCHRENNIKOW   MEH: CHRENNIKOV
    SML: CHRENNIKOW   EMS: ХРЕННИКОВ

KHRISTIANSEN, Lev Lvovich   USSR   1910
    EMS, PPU69/2
    EMS: ХРИСТИАНСЕН

KHRISTOSKOV, Petr Khristov   Bulgaria   1917
    BMK, X67, X68
    BMK: ХРИСТОСКОВ

KHRISTOV, Dimitr Iordanov   Bulgaria   1933
    BMK, X64, X66, X67, X68
    BMK: ХРИСТОВ

KHRISTU, Jannis
    See: CHRISTOU, Yannis

KICKSTAT, Paul   1893
    IMD

KIEFER, Bruno   Brazil   1923   Germany
    FBC

KIEFFER, Detlef   France   1944   Poland
    ACM

*KIELAND, Olav   Norway   1901
    BB71, CNO, EVM, VTM

KIENZEL, Wilhelm   Austria
    CME

KIERMEIR, Kurt   1906
    IMD

*KIESEWETTER, Tomasz   Poland   1911
    PKW, X65

*KILADZE, Grigory
    Varfolomeyevich   USSR   1902   1962
    BB65, BB71, EMS, EVM, REM, SML
    EMS: КИЛÁДЗЕ

KILAR, Wojciech   Poland   1932
    BB65, BB71, CME, DDM, IMD, LMD, MEH, PKW, X64, X65,
    X66, X67, X68

*KILENYI, Edward, Sr.   USA   1884   1968
    BB71, EVM, X68
    EVM: 1881

*KILLMAYER, Wilhelm   Germany   1927
    BB71, CME, IMD2, LMD, MEH, PAP, REM, SML, X64, X65,
    X66, X67, X68

*KILPINEN, Yrjö Henrik   Finland   1892   1959
    BB65, BB71, COF, DDM, EMS, EVM, IMD, LMD, REM, SML,
    VTM, X66, X67, X68
    EMS: КИЛЬПИНЕН

KIM, Earl   USA   1920
    ASUC, BB71, PCM, X68

*KIMOVEČ, Franz   Yugoslavia   1878
    EVM

KING, Jeffrey Thomas   USA
    ASUC

KING, Reginald   Great Britain   1904
    EVM

KINGSFORD, Charles   USA   1907
    AS66

KINGSLEY, Gershon   USA   1922   Germany
    X66

KINNEY, Gordon James   USA   1905
    DAS

KIRÀLY, Ernö   Yugoslavia   1919
    KMJ

*KIRBY, Percival Robson   Great Britain   1887   Scotland
    LMD, X67, X68

KIRCHGÄSSER, Wilhelm
   Bernhard   Germany   1933
    MNG

*KIRCHNER, Leon   USA   1919
    ASUC, BB65, BB71, CME, DDM, DN72, IMD, LMD, OCM,
    PCM, PC71, REM, WTM, X64, X65, X66, X67, X68

KIRCULESCU, Nicolae   Rumania   1905
    EMS, MEH, RCL, SML
    EMS: КУРКУЛЕСКУ   SML: KIRKUKESCU

KIREYKO, Vitaliy Dmitrievich   USSR   1926
    EMS, PPU, X67, X68
    EMS: КИРЕЙКО

*KIRIGIN, Ivo   Yugoslavia   1914   1964
    BB65, BB71, HCM, IMD, KMJ, LMD, REM, X65, X67

KIRIUKOV, Leonti Petrovich   USSR   1895   1965
    EMS
    EMS: КИРЮКОВ

KIRK, Theron   USA   1919
    AS66, PCM, PC71, X64, X65, X67, X68

*KIRKOR, Georgi Vasilievich   USSR   1910
    EMS
    EMS: КИРКОР

KIRKPATRICK, John   USA   1905
   PC71, X66, X67, X68

KIRMSSE, Herbert   Germany   1924
   SML, X65

*KISIELEWSKI, Stefan   Poland   1911
   BB65, BB71, EVM, IMD, LMD, PKW, REM, X64, X65, X66,
   X67, X68

*KIYOSE, Yasuji   Japan   1900
   IMD, LMD

*KJELDAAS, Arnljot   Norway   1916
   CNO

*KJELDAAS, Gunnar   Norway   1890   1963
   CNO

*KJELLSBY, Erling   Norway   1901
   CNO, EVM, VTM

*KJELLSTRÖM, Sven   Sweden   1875   1950
   EVM
   EVM: 1951

*KLASS, Julius   Germany   1888
   EVM, IMD

*KLAFSKY, Anton Maria
   Rudolf   Austria   1877   1965
   BB71, X65

*KLAMI, Uuno Kalervo   Finland   1900   1961
   BB65, BB71, CME, COF, EMS, EVM, IMD, LMD, MEH, REM,
   VTM, X66
   EMS: КЛÁМИ

KLAUSS, Kenneth Blanchard   USA
   ASUC, CAP

KLAUSS, Noah   USA
   CAP, PC71

*KLEBANOV, Dmitri Lvovich   USSR   1907
   EMS, PPU, X66, X68
   EMS: КЛЕБÁНОВ

*KLEBE, Giselher Wolfgang   Germany   1925
   BB65, BB71, CME, DDM, EMS, EVM, IMD, IMD2, LMD, MEH,
   MZW, PAP, REM, SML, TSC, VNM, X64, X65, X66, X67, X68
   EMS: КЛĒБЕ

*KLECHNIOWSKA, Anna Maria   Poland   1888
   PKW

*KLECKI, Pawel
   See: KLETZKI, Paul

KLEE, Hermann   Rumania   1883   Germany
   RCL

*KLEFISCH, Walter   Germany   1910
   LMD

KLEGA, Miroslav   Czechoslovakia 1926
   CCZ, MEH, X68

*KLEIBER, Erich   Austria   1890   1956
   BB71, LMD, REM, X66, X68

*KLEIN, Bernhard Ernst Thilo   Germany   1897
   SML

*KLEIN, Fritz Heinrich   Germany   1892   Hungary
   LMD, X68

KLEIN, Günter   Germany   1921
   SML

*KLEIN, John   USA   1915
   AS66, PCM, PC71, X68

KLEIN, Lothar   USA   1932   Germany
   AS66, BB65, BB71, CA17, LMD, PCM, PC71, X64, X66, X67,
   X68

*KLEIN, Richard Rudolf   Germany   1921
   X64, X68

KLEINIG, Karl   Germany   1902
   SML, X67

KLEINMAN, Isidor I.   USA   1913
   AS66

*KLEINSINGER, George   USA   1914
   AS66, PCM, PC71

KLEMENTI, Artur   Yugoslavia 1909
   KMJ

*KLEMETTI, Heikki Valentin   Finland   1876   1953
   COF, EVM, LMD, VTM, X66

*KLEMPERER, Otto   Switzerland 1885 1973
 BB65, BB71, EVM, IMD, LMD, MEH, REM,   Germany
 SML, WWS, X64, X65, X66, X67

KLENITZKIS, Abel Ruvimovich USSR   1910 Lithuania
 EMS, LMD, X65
 LMD: KLENITSKIS
 EMS: КЛЕНИЦКИС

KLENZ, William   USA   1915
 DAS, LMC, REM, X64, X67, X68

KLEPPER, Anna Benzia   Israel   1927 Rumania
 ACU

*KLEPPER, Leon   Israel   1900 Rumania
 ACU, IMD, LMD, REM

KLEPPER, Walter Mihai   Rumania 1929
 RCL, X65, X68

*KLERK, Albert de   Netherlands 1917
 EVM, LMD, NED, X64, X65, X67

*KLERK, Joseph de   Netherlands 1885 1969
 EVM, LMD, VMB8/6, X65   Belgium

*KLETZKI, Paul   Switzerland 1900 1973
 EVM, IMD, LMD, REM, SCHWn, SML, WWS, Poland
 X64, X65, X66, X67, X68
 Also: KLECKI

KLEVEN, Arvid   Norway
 VTM

*KLIEN, Walter   Austria   1928
 X64, X68

KLÍMA, Alois   Czechoslovakia 1905
 CCZ

KLIMKO, Ronald J.   USA   1936
 CAP

KLINČIĆ, Željko   Yugoslavia 1912
 HCM, KMJ

KLINGER, Charles   Germany   1879
 ACM

*KLINGLER, Karl   Germany   1879
 EVM, IMD, LMD, REM
 REM: KLINGER

*KLINGSOR, Tristan   France   1874 1966
  DDM, X66

KLINTBERG, Bangt af   Sweden   1938

KLIUZNER, Boris Lazarevich   USSR   1909
  EMS
  EMS: КЛЮЗНЕР

KLIUCHAREV, Aleksandr
  Sergievich   USSR   1906
  EMS, LMD
  LMD: KĽJUČAREV
  EMS: КЛЮЧАРЁВ

KLOBUČAR, Andelko   Yugoslavia   1931
  HCM, KMJ

*KLOTZ, Hans   Germany   1900
  REM, X66, X67

KLOVA, Vitautas Iuliono   USSR   1926 Lithuania
  EMS
  EMS: КЛÓВА

KLUDAS, Erich   1912
  IMD

KLUG, Ernst   Switzerland   1905
  SCHW

KLUPÁK, Jaroslav   Czechoslovakia
  MNP64/4

KLUSÁK, Jan   Czechoslovakia 1934
  BB65, BB71, CCZ, IMD, IMD2, LMD, MEH, MNP64/3,
  MNP64/5, MNP64/6, MNP65/5, MNP66/2, MNP67/1,
  MNP72/5, SML, X64, X65, X67, X68

*KLUSSMANN, Ernst Gernot   Germany   1901
  EVM, IMD, LMD, X65, X67

*KNAB, Armin   Germany   1881 1951
  DDM, EVM, IMD, LMD, REM, SML

*KNAPP, Arne   Germany   1913 1960
  IMD, WWG   Poland

*KNEIP, Gustav   Germany   1905
  EVM, LMD, REM, WWG

KNESSL, Lothar   1927
 IMD, X67, X68

KNIGHT, Gerald Hocken Great Britain 1908
 X66

*KNIGHT, Morris   USA   1933
 PCM

*KNIPPER, Lev Konstantinovich USSR   1898
 BB65, BB71, EMS, EVM, IMD, LMD, MEH, PPU, PPU69/2,
 REM, SML, X64
 EMS: КНИ́ППЕР

*KNÖCHEL, Wilhelm   Germany 1881
 EVM

*KNORR, Ernst-Lothar von Germany 1896 1973
 EVM, IMD, SML

KNOSP, Erwin   France   1912
 ACM

KNOX, Charles   1929
 WAN

*KNUDSEN, Thorkild   Denmark 1925
 VTM, X64

KNUSSEN, Oliver   Great Britain 1953
 X68

*KOBECK, Paul Johannes Germany 1891
 X64

*KOBIAS, Baruch   Israel   1895 1964
 ACU, MM59   Bohemia
 Formerly: BERTHOLD

KÖBLER, Robert   Germany 1912
 SML, X65, X68

KOBLITZ, David   USA   1948
 BS70

*KOBUNE, Kojiro   Japan   1907
 IMD

KOC, Marcelo   Argentina 1918 Russia
 CA14, REM, X66

KOCH, Frederick   USA   1923
   AA73, AS66, DN70, PCM, PC71, X64, X65, X67, X68
   DN70: 1924

KOCH, Johannes Hermann
  Ernst   Germany   1918
   LMD, X67

KOCH, John   USA   1928
   PCM, PC71, X66

*KOCH, Karl   Austria   1887
   BB71, X67, X68

*KOCH, Sigurd Christian
  Erland von   Sweden   1910
   BB71, EVM, FST, IMD, KSV, LMD, REM, SIM, SIMa, SMT,
   SOW, STS, SWE, TJU, VTM, X67, X68

*KOCHAN, Günter   Germany   1930
   EMS, IMD2, LMD, MEH, REM, SML, X64, X65, X66, X67,
   X68
   EMS: КÓХАН

*KOCHUROV, Juri Vladimirovich USSR   1907 1952
   EMS, EVM, LMD, REM
   EMS: КОЧУРОВ   EVM: KOTSJOERÓW   Vol. I: KOTCHUROV

*KOCIÁN, Jaroslav   Czechoslovakia 1883 1950
   BB65, BB71, EVM, LMD, REM

*KOCK, Sven   Denmark   1894
   IMD

KOCSÁR, Miklós   Hungary   1933
   CHC, X68, ZSZ

KODALLI, Nevit   Turkey   1924
   IMD, LMD, REM, X65

*KODÁLY, Zoltán   Hungary   1882 1967
   BB65, BB71, CHC, CME, DDM, EMS, EVM, IMD, LMD, MEH,
   MLA24/4, REM, SML, TCM, WI69, WTM, X64, X65, X66,
   X67, X68
   EMS: КÓДАЙ

*KOEBERG, Frits Ehrhardt
  Adriaan   Netherlands   1876 1961
   BB65, BB71, EVM, LMD, REM

*KOECHLIN, Charles Louis
  Eugene   France   1867 1950
    BB65, BB71, DDM, DMF, EMS, EVM, IMD, LMD, MEH, REM,
    TSC, X64, X65, X66, X67, X68
    EMS: КЕКЛЁН

*KOELLREUTTER, Hans-
  Joachim   Brazil   1915 Germany
    DDM, EVM, FBC, IMD, IMD2, LMD, REM, TSC, X68

*KOENIG, Gottfried Michael   Germany   1926
    DMM, IMD, LMD, MEH, MNG, PAP, REM, X66, X67

KOENNECKE, Fritz   Germany   1876 USA
    REM

KOERBLER, Milivoj   Yugoslavia   1930
    HCM, KMJ, X66

KOERING, René   France   1940
    ACM, IMD, X65, X66, X67

*KOERPPEN, Alfred   Germany   1926
    IMD, LMD, WWG, X66, X67, X68

KOERT, Han van   Netherlands 1913
    NED

*KOETEV, Philip   Bulgaria   1903
    EVM

*KOETSIER, Jan   Netherlands 1911
    BB65, BB71, EVM, IMD, LMD, NED, REM, X68
    NED: 1910

*KOGAN, Grigori Mihailovich   USSR   1901
    EMS, X65, X67
    EMS: КОГАН

KOGAN, Lev Lazarevich   USSR   1927
    EMS, X68
    EMS: КОГАН

KÖGLER, Hermann   Germany   1885 Poland
    IMD, LMD, X68

*KOGOJ, Marij   Yugoslavia   1895 1956
    CME, EMS, IMD, KMJ, LMD, MSC, REM, X67, X68
    EMS: КОГОЙ
    EMS: 1859-1956

KOH, Bunya   1910
   IMD

KOHA, Jan Oskarovich   USSR   1929   Estonia
   EMS
   EMS: КОХА

KÖHLER, Siegfried   Germany   1927
   SML, X65, X66, X67, X68

KOHN, Karl   USA   1926   Austria
   ASUC, BB65, BB71, LMD, PCM, PC71, X64, X65, X66, X68

KOHOUT, Josef   Czechoslovakia 1895   1958
   CCZ

*KOHOUTEK, Ctirad   Czechoslovakia 1929
   BB65, BB71, CCZ, IMD2, LMD, MEH, MNP64/5, MNP64/6,
   MNP71/7, X64, X66, X67, X68

*KOHS, Ellis Bonoff   USA   1916
   AA73, BB65, BB71, CA15, LMD, PCM, PC71, REM, TSC,
   WI69, X64, X65, X66, X67, X68

KOKA, Evgeni Konstantinovich USSR   1893   1954
   EMS
   EMS: КОКА

*KÓKAI, Rezsö   Hungary   1906   1962
   CHC, CME, IMD, LMD, SML, X68

*KOKKONEN, Joonas   Finland   1921
   BB71, CME, COF, IMD2, KKO, LMD, VTM, X64, X65, X66,
   X67, X68

*KOLAR, Victor   USA   1888   1957
   EVM   Bohemia

KOLASIŃSKI, Jerzy   Poland   1906
   IMD, PKW

KOLBERG, Kåre   Norway   1936
   CNO, VTM

KOLESSA, Nikolai Filaretovich USSR   1904
   EMS, LMD, MEH, PPU, REM
   EMS: КОЛÉССА

KOLETIC, Matija   Yugoslavia

*KOLIADA, Nicolas Terentievich USSR   1907   1935
   EMS
   EMS: КОЛЯДÁ

KOLLERT, Jiří   Czechoslovakia   1943
    MNP72/9

KOLMAN, Peter   Czechoslovakia   1937
    CCZ, IMD, MEH, MNP67/1, MNP67/9, X64, X65, X67, X68
    ZE69/1, ZE69/3, ZE70/2, ZE70/3, ZE71/1, ZE71/2, ZE71/3

KOLMANOVSKY, Eduard
   Savelievich   USSR   1923
    EMS, X64
    EMS: КОЛМАНÓВСКИЙ

KOLODUB, Lev Nikolaevich   USSR   1930
    EMS, PPU69/2
    EMS: КОЛОДỲБ

KÖLZ, Ernst   Austria   1929
    IMD, X66

KOMADINA, Vojin   Yugoslavia   1933
    KMJ, X68

*KOMMA, Karl Michael   Germany   1913
    LMD, X64, X65, X66, X68

KOMOROUS, Rudolf   Czechoslovakia   1931
    IMD2, LMD, MEH, MNG, MNP69/4, X64, X67, X68

*KOMPANEETZ, Zinovi
   Lvovich   USSR   1902
    EMS
    EMS: КОМПАНÉЕЦ

KON, Józef   USSR

KONDOR, Lipot   Hungary   1902
    LMD

*KONDORSSY, Leslie   USA   1915   Czecho-
    AA73, BB65, BB71, X64, X65, X66, X67, X68   slovakia

*KONDRACKI, Michal   Poland   1902
    DDM, EMS, EVM, LMD, PKW, REM, X68
    EMS: КОНДРÁЦКИЙ

*KONDRATIEV, Sergei
   Alexandrovich   USSR   1896
    EMS, X67
    EMS: КОНДРÁТЬЕВ

*KONIETZNY, Heinrich   1910
    X64, X66

*KONJOVIČ, Petar   Yugoslavia   1883 1970
  BB71, DDM, EMS, EVM, IMD, KMJ, LMD, MEH, MLA27/4,
  REM, SML, WI69, X67, X68
  EMS: КОНЬОВИЧ

KONO, Kristo   Albania   1907
  BB65, BB71, LMD

KONOE, Hidemare
  See: KONOYE, Hidemaro

*KONOYE, Hidemaro   Japan   1898 1973
  LMD, X68

KONRAD, J.
  See: KONDRACKI, Michal

*KONRATH, Anton   Austria   1888
  EVM

KONSTANTINIDIS, Ghiannis Greece   1903
  REM

*KONT, Paul   Austria   1920
  IMD, IMD2, X65, X67, X68

*KONTA, Robert   Switzerland   1880 1953
  IMD, LMD   Austria

KONTIS, Alekos   Greece   1899 1965
  LMD

KONVALINKA, Karel   Czechoslovakia 1885
  CCZ, MEH

*KONVALINKA, Miloš   Czechoslovakia 1919
  CCZ

*KOOL, Jaap   France   1891 Netherlands
  EVM, IMD, LMD

*KOOLE, Arend   Netherlands   1908
  BB65, BB71, X64, X65

KOOP, Olivier   Netherlands   1885
  EVM

KOPELENT, Marek   Czechoslovakia 1932
  CCZ, IMD2, LMD, MEH, MNG, MNP66/6, MNP67/1, MNP67/9,
  MNP70/1, X64, X65, X66, X67, X68

KOPORC, Srećko   Yugoslavia   1900 1965
  KMJ, MSC

KOPP, Frederick   USA   1914
   PC71, X68

*KOPPEL, Herman David   Denmark   1908
   CME, DMTsp, EVM, IMD, LMD, REM, WI69, VTM, X65

KOPPEL, Thomas Herman   Denmark   1944
   VTM, X66, X68

*KOPSCH, Julius   Germany   1887   1970
   LMD, MLA27/4, X65, X66, X67

*KORCHMAREV, Klimenty
   Arkadyevich   USSR   1899   1958
   BB65, BB71, EMS, EVM
   BB65 and BB71: KORTCHMAREV
   EMS: КОРЧМАРЁВ

*KORDA, Viktor   Austria   1900
   X66, X67, X68

KOŘÍNEK, Miloslav   Czechoslovakia   1925
   CCZ, COO, MEH, X68, ZE69/3, ZE70/3, ZE71/3
   CCZ: Miloš

KORN, Peter Jona   USA   1922   Germany
   AS66, BB65, BB71, LMD, PCM, PC71, X67, X68

*KORN, Richard Kaye   USA   1908
   WI69, X64, X67

*KORNAUTH, Egon   Austria   1891   1959
   BB65, BB71, DDM, EVM, IMD, LMD,   Bohemia
   MEH, REM

*KORNGOLD, Erich Wolfgang   USA   1897   1957
   AS66, BB65, BB71, CME, DDM, EMS, EVM,   Austria
   IMD, LMD, MEH, REM, SML, X64, X68
   EMS: КОРНГОЛЬД

KORTE, František   Czechoslovakia   1895   1962
   LMD

KORTE, Karl   USA   1928
   AA73, ASUC, AS66, DN70, PCM, PC71, X64, X66, X68

*KORTE, Oldřich František   Czechoslovakia   1926
   BB65, BB71, CCZ, IMD2, HEM, X64, X66

*KÖRVER, Boris Voldemarovich   USSR   1917   Estonia
   EMS
   EMS: КЫРВЕР

*KÓSA, György   Hungary   1897
    CHC, EVM, IMD, LMD, MEH, REM, SML, WI69, X64, X66,
    X67, X68

KOSAKOFF, Reuven   USA   1898
    AS66, BB65, BB71, LMD

*KOS-ANATOLSKY, Anatoli
    Iosifovich   USSR   1909
    EMS, LMD, PPU, PPU69/2
    EMS: КОС-АНАТОЛСКИЙ

*KOSMA, Joseph   France   1905   1969
    BB71, DDM, EVM, IMD, LMD, MEH, MLA26/4,   Hungary
    REM, SML, X64

*KOSTAKOWSKY, Jacobo   Mexico   1893   1953
    EVM, MMX   Russia

KOŠŤÁL, Arnošt   Czechoslovakia   1920
    CCZ, MNP72/9

KOŠŤÁL, Erno   Czechoslovakia   1889   1957
    CCZ

KOSTECK, Gregory   USA
    ASUC

KOSTIĆ, Dušan   Yugoslavia   1925
    BB65, BB71, KMJ, LMD, X67

KOSTIĆ, Vojislav   Yugoslavia   1931
    BB71, KMJ, X67

KOSZEWSKI, Andrzej   Poland   1922
    LMD, PKW, X66, X67

KOTCHUROV, Jury V.
    See: KOCHUROV, Juri V.

KOTIK, Petr   Czechoslovakia   1942
    IMD2, MNG, X64, X67

*KOTÓNSKI, Wlodzimierz   Poland   1925
    BB65, BB71, CME, IMD, IMD2, LMD, MEH, PKW, REM,
    X64, X65, X66, X67, X68

KÖTSCHAU, Joachim   1905
    IMD

KOTSJOERÓW, J. W.
    See: KOCHUROV, J. W.

KOUGHELL, Arkadie USA 1898 Russia
AS66, BB65, BB71, LMD

KOUJAMIAROV, K. K.
See: KUZHAMYAROV, K. K.

KOUNADIS, Arghyris Greece 1924 Turkey
BB65, BB71, CME, EL:1, IMD, IMD2, PAP, X65, X68

KOUNTZ, Richard USA 1896 1950
EVM

KOUROUPOS, George Greece 1942
EL:4

KOUSSEVITZKY, Fabien
See: SEVITZKY, Fabien

*KOUSSEVITZKY, Serge
Aleksandrovich USA 1874 1951
DDM, EMS, EVM, LMD, MEH, REM, Russia
X64, X66, X67, X68
MEH: KUSEVICKIJ REM: KUSSEVITZKI EMS: КУСЕВИЦКИЙ

*KOUTZEN, Boris USA 1901 1966
AS66, BB71, EVM, MLA23/4, PCM, PC71, Russia
X64, X65, X66, X67

KOVAC, Roland Austria 1927
WI69

KOVÁCH, András Switzerland 1915 Hungary
WWS, X65, X67, X68

*KOVÁL, Maryan Victorovich USSR 1907 1971
BB71, EMS, EVM, LMD, MEH, PPU69/3, REM, SML, X64,
X66, X67, X68
SML: KOWAL
EMS: КОВÁЛЬ

KOVAŘÍČEK, František Czechoslovakia 1924
CCZ, IMD2, MEH, MNP64/3

KOVÁTS, Barna 1920
IMD, IMD2

*KOVNER, Iosif Naoumovich USSR 1895 1959
EMS
EMS: КÓВНЕР

KOWALSKI, Július   Czechoslovakia   1904
   CCZ, COO, MEH, MNP64/4, MNP64/5, X64, X68, ZE69/3,
   ZE70/1, ZE70/2, ZE70/3, ZE71/1, ZE71/2, ZE71/3, ZE72/1,
   ZE72/2

*KOX, Hans   Netherlands   1930
   BB65, BB71, CME, DDM, EVM, IMD, LMD, NED, REM, X64,
   X65, X66, X67, X68

KOYAMA, Kiyoshige   Japan   1914
   BB71, X65

KOZAK, Yevgeniy Teodorovich   USSR   1907
   EMS, PPU
   EMS: КÓЗАК

KOŽELUHA, Lubomír   Czechoslovakia 1918
   CCZ

KOZEVNIKOV, Boris Tihonovich USSR   1906
   EMS, X67
   EMS: КОЖÉВНИКОВ

*KOZINA, Marjan   Yugoslavia   1907   1965
   EVM, IMD, KMJ, LMD, MEH, MNP71/3, REM, X66, X67, X68

KOZINSKY, David B.   USA   1917
   AS66, PCM

*KOZITSKY, Filip Emelyanovich USSR   1893   1960
   EMS
   EMS: КОЗѾЦКИЙ

*KOZLOVSKY, Alexei
Fedorovich   USSR   1905
   EMS, LMD, X65
   EMS: КОЗЛÓВСКИЙ

KOZMA, Géza   Rumania   1902
   RCL

KOZMA, Matei   Rumania   1929
   RCL

KRAEHENBUEHL, David   USA   1923
   PCM, PC71, X64, X67

*KRAFT, Karl Joseph   Germany   1903
   IMD, LMD

*KRAFT, Leo   USA   1922
   ASUC, PC71, X65, X68

KRAFT, Walter Wilhelm
   Johann   Germany   1905
   EVM, IMD, LMD, X66, X68

KRAFT, William   USA   1923
   AS66, BB65, BB71, DN70, IMD2, LMD, PC71

*KRAMER, Arthur Walter   USA   1890   1969
   AS66, BB71, EVM, LMD, MLA26/4, REM

KRAMER, Louis Herman   USA   1926
   DN72

*KRAMER-JOHANSEN, Jolly   Norway   1902   1968
   X68

KRANCE, John P., Jr.   USA   1935
   AS66, X65

KRAPF, Gerhard   USA   1924   Germany
   BB65, BB71, PCM, X64, X65, X67, X68

KRASA, Hans   Czechoslovakia 1899
   EVM

*KRASEV, Mikhail Ivanovich   USSR   1897   1954
   EMS
   EMS: КРАСЕВ

KRATOCHVÍL, Jiří   Czechoslovakia 1924
   CCZ, MNP72/9, X67, X68

KRAUS, George   Great Britain 1912   Austria
   WI69

KRATOCHWIL, Heinz   Austria
   X68

*KRAUSS, Clemens Heinrich   Austria   1893   1954
   EVM, IMD, REM, X64, X65, X66, X68

KRAUZE, Zygmunt   Poland   1938
   X68

*KREAL, Ernst   Austria   1891
   WI69

*KREBS, Helmut   Germany   1913
   WWG

*KREIN, Alexander Abramovich USSR   1883   1951
   BB65, BB71, DDM, EMS, EVM, IMD, LMD, MEH, REM, X65, X66
   LMD: KREJN   MEH: KREJN   EMS: КРЕЙН

*KREIN, Grigory Abramovich   USSR   1879   1955
  BB65, BB71, DDM, EMS, LMD, REM
  LMD: KREJN
  EMS: КРЕЙН
  EVM: 1880

*KREIN, Julian Grigorievich   USSR   1913
  DDM, EMS, EVM, IMD, LMD, REM, X65, X68
  LMD: KREJN
  EMS: КРЕЙН

*KREIS, Otto   Switzerland   1890   1966
  EVM, LMD, MLA23/4, SCHW, X66

KREIS, Robert   USA
  X68

*KREISLER, Fritz   USA   1875   1962
  AS66, BB65, BB71, EMS, IMD, LMD, MEH, REM, SML, X64,
  X68
  Pseudonym: PUGNANI
  EMS: КРЕЙСЛЕР

*KREITNER, Gueorgui
  Gustavovich   USSR   1903   1958
  EMS
  EMS: КРЕЙТНЕР

*KREJČÍ, Iša Frantisek   Czechoslovakia 1904   1968
  BB71, CCZ, CME, DDM, EVM, IMD, IMD2, LMD, MEH,
  MNP65/2, MNP66/6, REM, SML, X64, X65, X67, X68

*KREJČÍ, Miroslav   Czechoslovakia 1891   1964
  CCZ, EVM, IMD, IMD2, LMD, MEH, REM, X65, X67

*KREK, Uroš   Yugoslavia   1922
  KMJ, LMD, MEH, REM, X67

*KREMENLIEV, Boris Angelov   USA   1911   Bulgaria
  DAS, DN70, EVM, X65, X68

KREMLEV, Yuli Anatolievich   USSR   1908
  BB71, EMS, X68
  EMS: КРЕМЛЁВ

KRENEDIĆ, Kazimir   Yugoslavia   1896   1956
  KMJ

*KŘENEK, Ernst   USA   1900   Austria
  ASUC, BB65, BB71, CME, DDM, EMS, EVM, IMD, IMD2,
  LMD, MEH, MZW, PAP, REM, SCHWs, SML, TCM, TSC,
  VNM, WI69, WTM, X64, X65, X66, X67, X68
  EMS: КШРЕНЕК

*KRENZ, Jan   Poland   1926
  CME, IMD, LMD, MEH, PKW, REM, SML, WI69, X64, X65,
  X66, X67

*KRENTZLIN, Richard   Germany   1864 1956
  LMD

*KRESÁNEK, Jozef   Czechoslovakia 1913
  CCZ, LMD, MEH, REM, SML, X64, X65, X67, X68, ZE69/1

KRETTLY, Grégoire
  See: CALVI, Gérard

*KREUDER, Peter Paul   Germany   1905
  MEH, SML, WWS

*KREUTZ, Arthur   USA   1906
  AS66, PCM, X66, X67

*KREUTZER, Leonid   Germany   1884 1953
  LMD   Russia

*KŘIČKA, Jaroslav   Czechoslovakia 1882 1969
  BB71, CCZ, CME, DDM, EVM, IMD, IMD2, LMD, MEH,
  MNP69/3, REM, SML, X65, X67

KRIEG, Hans   Netherlands   1899
  EVM

KRIEGER, Armando   Argentina   1940
  BB65, BB71, LMD, X64, X67, X68

*KRIEGER, Edino   Brazil   1928
  BB65, BB71, CA13, FBC, LMD, QLA, X65, X68

*KRIPS, Henry Joseph   Australia   1914 Austria
  BB71, LMD, X67, X68

KRISTICH, Stevan   USSR   1885 1958
  EMS
  EMS: ХРИ́СТИЧ

KRISTINSSON, Sigursveinn
  David   Iceland   1911
  VTM

KRISTOFFERSEN, Frithjof   Norway   1894
  EVM

*KRIUKOV, Nikolai
  Nikolaievitch   USSR   1908
  EVM, LMD, REM
  EVM: KRJUKOW   LMD: KRJUKOV

*KRUIKOV, Vladimir
Nikilaievitch USSR 1902 1960
EMS, EVM, LMD, REM
EVM: KRJUKOW LMD: KRJUKOV
EMS: КРЮКОВ

*KŘIVINKA, Gustav Czechoslovakia 1928
BB65, BB71, CCZ, IMD2, LMD, MEH, MNP65/6, SML, X64,
X65

KRIVONOSOV, Vladimir
Mihailovich USSR 1904 1941
EMS
EMS: КРИВОНОСОВ

KRIWET, Ferdinand Germany 1942
EL:1, PAP, X67

KŘÍŽEK, Zdeněk Czechoslovakia 1927
CCZ, IMD2, X64

KRNIC, Boris Yugoslavia 1900
HCM, KMJ

*KROEGER, Karl USA 1932
BB65, BB71, PCM, PC71, X64, X65, X66, X68

KROEPFL, Francisco Argentina

*KROHN, Felix Julius Theofil Finland 1898
COF, EVM, LMD, REM

*KROHN, Ilmari Henrik
Reinhold Finland 1867 1960
BB65, BB71, COF, EVM, LMD, REM, VTM

KROL, Bernhard 1920
IMD, IMD2, X66

*KROLL, Erwin Germany 1886
EVM, LMD, REM, WWG, X67, X68

KRÖLL, Georg 1934
IMD, X68

KROLL, William USA 1901
AS66, IMD, PCM, X68

KROMBHOLC, Jaroslav Czechoslovakia 1918
CCZ, MEH, SML, X64, X66, X67, X68

KROMBOLC, Karlo Yugoslavia 1905 Hungary
BB71, KMJ

*KROMOLICKI, Józef   Germany   1882   1961
    BB71, EVM, LMD   Poland

*KRONSTEINER, Joseph   Austria   1910
    X66, ·X68

KROSHNER, Mihail Efimovich USSR   1900   1942
    EMS
    EMS: КРОШНЕР

*KRSTIČ, Petar   Yugoslavia   1877   1957
    BB65, BB71, EVM, KMJ, LMD, REM

KRUL, Eli   USA   1926   Poland
    BB65, BB71, PCM

KRÜTZFELD, Werner   1928
    IMD

KRUYF, Ton de   Netherlands   1937
    BB65, BB71, IMD2, LMD, NED, PAP, TSC, X65, X66, X67
    PAP: DE KRUYF, Ton   TSC: DE KRUYF, Ton

KRZEMIENSKI, Witold   Poland   1909
    PKW

*KUBELIK, Jeronym Rafael   Great Britain   1914   Czecho-
    BB65, BB71, DDM, EVM, IMD, LMD, MEH,   slovakia
    REM, SML, WI69, WWS, X64, X65, X66, X67, X68

*KUBIK, Gail Thompson   USA   1914
    AS66, BB71, EVM, IMD, LMD, PCM, PC71, REM, WI69, X64,
    X65, X66, X67, X68

*KUBÍN, Rudolf   Czechoslovakia   1909   1973
    CCZ, CME, EVM, IMD, IMD2, LMD, MEH, REM, SML, X65

KUBIZEK, Augustin   Austria   1918
    IMD, IMD2, X65, X66, X67, X68

KUČERA, Václav   Czechoslovakia   1929
    CCZ, MEH, MNP64/3, MNP64/5, MNP64/6, MNP64/9,
    MNP65/2, MNP70/1, MNP71/8, X64, X65, X66, X67, X68

KUDO, E. Takeo   USA
    CAP

*KUHN, Max   Switzerland   1896
    LMD, SCHW, X65, X68

KUHNERT, Rolf   Germany   1932
    PAP, X68

KUILER, Kor   Netherlands 1877 1951
 EVM

*KUKUCK, Felicitas Kestner Germany 1914
 IMD, LMD, WWG

KULJERIĆ, Igor   Yugoslavia 1938
 HCM, X67

KULM, Walter Müller von Switzerland 1899
 CME

KULIEV, Tofik Alekper Ogli USSR   1917
 EMS, PPU69/2
 EMS: КУЛЙЕВ

*KUMMER, Hans   Germany 1880
 X64

KUMOK, Jorge   Argentina
 X68

KUNAD, Rainer   Germany 1936
 SML, X65, X66, X67, X68

KUNADIS, Arghyris   Greece   1924
 LMD, REM
 LMD: KOUNADIS

KUNC, Ayme   France   1877 1958
 REM

*KUNC, Božidar   Yugoslavia 1903 1964
 BB65, BB71, HCM, IMD, KMJ, LMD, REM, X67

*KUNC, Jan   Czechoslovakia 1883
 CCZ, CME, EVM, LMD, MEH, REM, X65, X68

KUNERT, Kurt   Germany 1911
 SML, X65, X68

*KÜNNEKE, Eduard   Germany 1885 1953
 IMD, IMD2, LMD, SML

KUNST, Jos   Netherlands 1936
 X67, X68

KUNTARIĆ, Ljubo   Yugoslavia 1925
 HCM, KMJ

*KUNZ, Alfred   Canada   1929
 CCM, CVM, KEY, MCO68, MCO71, NLC, NLCa, X68

*KUNZ, Ernst   Switzerland   1891
   LMD, REM, SCHW, X64, X67

KUOSMA, Kauko Einari   Finland   1926
   KKO

*KUPFERMAN, Meyer   USA   1926
   AS66, BB65, BB71, LMD, PCM, PC71, X64, X65, X66, X67,
   X68

KUPKA, Karel   Czechoslovakia   1927
   CCZ, COO, IMD2, MEH, MNP64/3

KUPKOVIČ, Ladislav   Czechoslovakia   1936
   CCZ, IMD2, LMD, MEH, MNG, MNP70/5, X64, X65, X66,
   X67, X68, ZE69/3, ZE70/1, ZE70/2

KURI-ALDANA, Mario   Mexico   1931
   HET17

KURKA, Robert Frank   USA   1921   1957
   BB65, BB71, LMD, MEH, PCM, X64, X67, X68

KURTÁG, György   Hungary   1926   Rumania
   BB65, BB71, CHC, CME, IMD, IMD2, LMD, MEH, MNG, SML,
   X66, X67, X68, ZSZ

*KURTH, Burton Lowell   Canada   1890   USA
   NLC

KURTZ, Eugène   France   1923   USA
   DDM

*KURZ, Siegfried   Germany   1930
   IMD, IMD2, SML

*KURZBACH, Paul   Germany   1902
   EMS, EVM, LMD, MEH, REM, SML, X65, X66, X67, X68
   EMS: КУРЦБАХ

*KUSCHE, Ludwig Helmuth
   Walter   Germany   1901
   WWG, X64, X65, X67, X68

*KUSHNAREV, Christofor
   Stepanovich   USSR   1890   1960
   EMS, LMD, SML
   SML: KUSCHNARJOW
   EMS: КУШНАРЁВ

*KUSTERER, Arthur   Germany   1898   1967
   EVM, LMD, MLA24/25/4, X68

*KUTEV, Filip   Bulgaria   1903
    BB65, BB71, BMK, EMS, LMD, MEH, SML, X64, X65, X68
    BMK and EMS: КУТЕВ

*KUUSISTO, Taneli   Finland   1905
    COF, KKO, LMD, REM, VTM

KUYPER, Elisabeth   Netherlands   1877   1953
    EVM

*KUZHAMYAROV, Kuddus
    Khodzhamyarovich   USSR   1918
    DDM, EMS, MEH, PPU69/2, SML, X64, X68
    DDM: KOUJAMIAROV   MEH: KUŽAMIAROV
    SML: KUSHAMJAROW   EMS: КУЖАМЬЯРОВ

KUZMANOVIĆ, Milorad   Yugoslavia   1932
    KMJ

*KVANDAL, Johan   Norway   1919
    CNO, VTM

*KVAPIL, Jaroslav   Czechoslovakia 1892   1958
    BB65, BB71, CCZ, CME, EMS, EVM, IMD, LMD, MEH, REM,
    X65
    EMS: КВА́ПИЛ

KVĚCH, Otomar   Czechoslovakia 1950
    MNP72/9

KVERNADZE, Aleksandr
    Aleksandrovich   USSR   1928
    BB65, BB71, EMS, LMD, PPU, SML
    SML: KWERNADSE
    EMS: КВЕРНА́ДЗЕ

KYNASTON, Trent   USA
    CAP, PC71

*KYRVER, Boris Voldemarovich   USSR   1917
    PPU, PPU69/2, PPU70/1

LAABAN, Ilmar   Sweden   1921   Estonia
    VTM, X68

*LABEY, Marcel   France   1875   1968
    BB71, DDM, DMF, LMD, REM

LABEY, Charlotte Sohy   France   1887   1955
    DDM, LMD, REM
    Also: SOHY-LABEY, Charlotte
    DDM: 1887-1956

*LABROCA, Mario   Italy   1896   1973
   DDM, EVM, IMD, LMD, REM, SML, X64, X65

*LABUNSKI, Felix Roderyk   USA   1892   Poland
   AA73, AS66, BB65, BB71, EVM, LMD, REM, X64, X65, X66,
   X67, X68

*LABUNSKI, Wiktor   USA   1895   Poland
   EVM, LMD, REM, WI69, X64, X68

*LA CASINIÈRE, Yves de   France   1897
   EVM, LMD
   EVM: CASINIERE, Yves de la

LACERDA, Osvaldo   Brazil   1927
   FBC

*LACH, Robert   Austria   1874   1958
   BB65, BB71, EVM, LMD, REM, SML, X68

LACHENMANN, Helmut   Germany   1935
   IMD, IMD2, LMD, PAP, X64, X67, X68

LACHMAN, Heinz   Netherlands   1906
   EVM

*LACHMAN, Wacław   Poland   1882   1963
   LMD, PKW

LACHOWSKA, Stefania   Poland   1898
   PKW

LACK, Henri   France   1927
   ACM

LACKNER, Stephan   1910
   IMD

LA COUR, Niels
   See: COUR, Niels la

LADERMAN, Ezra   USA   1924
   AS66, BB71, LMD, PCM, PC71, X64, X65, X67, X68

LADIPO, Duro   Nigeria
   X65

*LADSCHECK, Max Leopold
   Henry   Germany   1889
   X64

*LAFARGE, Guy Pierre-Marie   France   1904
   QQF, WI69

*LA FORGE, Frank   USA   1879   1953
    AS66, EVM

LAFORTUNE, Lucien   Canada
    KEY

LAGIDZE, Pevaz Ilyich   USSR   1921
    EMS
    EMS: ЛАГИ́ДЗЕ

*LA GYE, Paul   Belgium   1883   1965
    LMD, REM, X65

*LAHMER, Reuel   USA   1912   Canada
    AS66, EVM, LMD, PCM, REM, X67

*LAHUSEN, Christian   Germany   1886   Argentina
    EVM, IMD, LMD, REM, WWG

*LAITINEN, Arvo   Finland   1893
    COF, VTM

LAJOVIC, Aleksander   Yugoslavia   1920   Czecho-
    KMJ, MSC   slovakia

*LAJOVIĆ, Anton   Yugoslavia   1878   1960
    EMS, EVM, IMD, KMJ, LMD, REM, SML, X67
    EMS: ЛАЙОВИЦ

*LAJTHA, László   Hungary   1892   1963
    BB65, BB71, CME, DDM, EVM, IMD, LMD, REM, SML,
    X64, X65, X67, X68

LAKE, Ian Thomson   Great Britain   1935
    WI69, X64, X65, X66, X67, X68

*LAKNER, Yehoshua   Israel   1924   Czecho-
    CME, IMD, MM59, WWI, X65   slovakia

*LAKS, Szymon   Poland   1901
    LMD, PKW, REM, X65

*LAMBERT, Constant   Great Britain   1905   1951
    DDM, EVM, LMD, REM, X65, X66, X67, X68

*LAMBERT, Marius   France   1868   1954
    LMD

*LAMBOTTE, Lucien   Luxemburg   1888   Belgium
    EVM

LAMBRO, Phillip   USA   1935
    AS66, PCM, X67

*LA MONTAINE, John   USA   1920
    AS66, BB65, BB71, CA9, LMD, PCM, PC71, X64, X65, X66,
    X67, X68

*LAMOTE de GRIGNON y RIBAS,
    Ricardo   Spain   1899   1962
    BB65, BB71, EVM, LMD, REM

*LAMONTHE, Ludovic   Haiti   1882
    REM

*LAMPART, Karl   Germany   1900
    WWG

*LAMPE, Walther   Germany   1872   1964
    BB65, BB71, EVM, LMD, X64, X66

LAMPERSBERG, Gerhard   Austria   1928
    IMD, MNG, X66, X67, X68

*LAMY, Fernand   France   1881   1966
    DDM, LMD

*LANCEN, Serge Jean   France   1922
    BB71, IMD, WI69
    Pseudonym: DERIVES, Jean

LANCIEN, Noël Daniel   France   1934
    QQF

*LANDAU, Siegfried   USA   1921   Germany
    AS66, BB71, X64, X68

*LANDMANN, Arno   Germany   1887
    IMD

LANDON, Howard Chandler
    Robbins   Austria   1926   USA
    BB71, REM, X64, X65, X66, X67, X68

*LANDOWSKA, Wanda   USA   1879   1959
    BB65, BB71, DDM, EMS, EVM, LMD, MEH,   Poland
    REM, SML, X64, X65, X66, X67, X68
    EMS: ЛАНДОВСКА
    BB65, EMS and EVM: 1877

*LANDOWSKI, Marcel François
    Paul   France   1915
    BB65, BB71, CME, CMF9, CMF20, CMF40, DDM, DMF, EVM,
    LMD, QQF, REM, X65, X66, X67, X68

*LANDRÉ, Guillaume Louis
  Frédéric   Netherlands   1905 1968
    BB65, BB71, CME, DDM, EVM, IMD, LMD, MEH, MLA26/4,
    NED, REM, X64, X65, X66, X67, X68

*LANE, Eastwood   USA   1879 1951
    AS66, BB71

LANE, Richard B.   USA   1933
    AS66, PCM, PC71

*LANG, Craig Sellar   Great Britain 1891 1971
    WI69   New Zealand

*LANG, Hans   Germany   1897 1968
    EVM, IMD, LMD, MLA25/4

LANG, Hermann   Switzerland   1883
    SCHW, X68

LANG, Ivana   Yugoslavia   1912
    HCM, IMD, KMJ

*LÁNG, István   Hungary   1933
    CHC, CME, MEH, X64, X65, X66, X67, X68, ZSZ

LANG, Margaret Ruthven USA   1867 1972
    BB71, EVM, LMD, MLA29/4, X68

*LANG, Max   Switzerland   1917
    SCHW, X66, X68

LANG, Philip J.   USA   1911
    PCM, X66

*LANG, Walter   Switzerland   1896 1966
    BB71, DDM, EVM, IMD, LMD, MLA23/4, REM, SCHW,
    X64, X66

LANGE, Arthur   USA   1889 1960
    AS66, BB71
    AS66: 1956

LANGELLA, Franco   Italy   1902
    LMD, REM

LANGENDOEN, Jacobus C. USA   1890 Netherlands
    AS66

*LANGENUS, Gustave   USA   1883 1957
    AS66   Belgium

*LANGGAARD, Rued Immanuel   Denmark   1893   1952
    DMTsp, EVM, IMD, LMD, REM, VTM, X68

*LANGLAIS, Jean-François   France   1907
    DDM, DMF, EVM, LMD, QQF, REM, WI69, X64, X65, X66,
    X67, X68

LANGLEY, Bernard Peter
   Francis   Union of   1929   Great Britain
   WI69   South Africa

LANGLEY, James   Great Britain   1927
   WI69

LANGLOIS, Théo   Belgium   1909
   EVM

LANGREE, Alain   France   1927
   ACM

*LANGSTROTH, Ivan Shed   USA   1887
   AS66, EVM, LMD, MLA28/4, REM, WI69, X64

*LANNOY, Robert   France   1915
   QQF

LANSKY, Paul   USA
   X68

*LANTIER, Pierre Luis
   César François   France   1910
   DMF, EVM, LMD, QQF, REM

LANZA, Alcides   Argentina   1929
   QLA, X66, X68

*LAPIERRE, Joseph-Eugène   Canada   1899
   MCO68

LAPINSKAS, Darius   1934
   IMD

LAPORTE, André   Belgium   1931
   LMD, X67

*LAPP, Horace   Canada   1904
   CVM, KEY, NLC

*LA PRADE, Ernest M.   USA   1889   1969
   BB71, LMD, MLA26/4

*LA PRESLE, Jacques Paul
  Gabriel Sauville de   France   1888   1969
  BB71, DDM, DMF, EVM, LMD

*LAQUAI, Reinhold Raoul   Switzerland   1894   1957
  BB71, EVM, LMD, REM, SCHW   Italy

LARA, Nelly Mele   Venezuela

LARA BAREIRO, Carlos   Paraguay   1914
  BB71

*LARCHET, John Francis   Ireland   1885
  EVM

*LARMANJAT, Jacques   France   1878   1952
  DDM, DMF, IMD, LMD

*LA ROSA PARODI, Armando   Italy   1904
  IMD, LMD, REM

*LA ROTELLA, Pasquale   Italy   1880   1963
  BB71, LMD, REM

*LARSSON, Lars-Erik Vilner   Sweden   1908
  DDM, EVM, FST, IMD, KSV, LMD, MEH, REM, SIM, SIMa,
  SML, SMT, SOW, STS, SWE, TJU, VTM, WI69, X67

*LASKA, Josef Julius   Austria   1886   1965
  X65, X68

LASKE, Otto Ernst   USA
  ASUC

LASKER, Henry   USA   1908
  AS66

LASKINE, Lily   France   1893
  CMF22

LASRY, Jacques   France   1918   Algiers
  REM, X65

*LÁSZLÓ, Alexander   USA   1895   Hungary
  AS66, EVM, LMD, REM

*LATHAM, William Peters   USA   1917
  AS66, PCM, PC71, X64, X65, X66, X67, X68

LATIMER, James H.   USA   1934
  AS66

*LATTUADA, Felice   Italy   1882   1962
   BB65, BB71, DDM, EVM, LMD, REM
   EVM: 1880

*LAUBER, Josef   Switzerland 1864   1952
   BB71, DDM, EVM, IMD, LMD, REM, SCHW

*LAUFER, Beatrice   USA   1923
   AS66, X66, X68

LAUFER, Edward C.   Canada
   MCO68, MCO71, X67, X68

*LAUFER, Robin   France   1909   1966
   X66   Poland

*LAUNIS, Armas Emanuel Finland   1884   1959
   COF, EVM, LMD, REM, VTM
   Formerly: LINDBERG

*LAURENCE, Frederick   Great Britain 1884
   EVM, LMD, REM

*LAURICELLA, Remo   Great Britain 1912
   WI69

*LAURICELLA, Sergio   Italy   1921
   EL:1, LMD, REM

LAURO, Antonio   Venezuela   1917
   BB65, BB71, CA14, LMD

LAURUSHAS, Vitautas Antano USSR   1930   Lithuania
   EMS, PPU69/2, X68
   EMS: ЛА́УРУШАС

*LAVAGNE, André   France   1913
   DDM, DMF, EVM, LMD, QQF, REM, X68

*LAVAGNINO, Angelo Francesco Italy   1909
   IMD, LMD, REM

LAVALLE GARCIA, Armando Mexico   1924
   BB71

*LAVATER, Hans   Switzerland 1885   1969
   EVM, IMD, LMD, MLA26/4, SCHW

*LAVIN, Carlos   Chile   1883   1962
   EVM, LMD, X67

*LA VIOLETTE, Wesley USA 1894
 AS66, LMD, PCM, PC71, REM, WI69, X68

LAVISTA, Mario Mexico 1943
 HET21

LAVISTA, Raúl Mexico 1913
 BB71, MMX

*LAVOTTA, Rezsö Hungary 1876 1962
 LMD

*LAVRY, Marc Israel 1903 1967
 ACU, BB71, CME, DDM, EMS, EVM, IMD, Lithuania
 LMD, MLA24/4, MM59, REM, X68
 EMS: ЛА́ВРИ

LAWSON, Gordon Balfour Grant Great Britain 1931
 WI69

*LAWTON, Sidney Maurice Great Britain 1924
 WI69

LAYA, José Clemente Venezuela 1913
 CA14

*LAYTON, Billy Jim USA 1924
 ASUC, AS66, BB65, BB71, CA9, LMD, PCM, PC71, X64, X65,
 X66, X67

*LAYTON, Robert Great Britain 1930
 LMD, X65, X66, X67, X68

LAYZER, Arthur USA
 ASUC

LAZARE-LEVY
 See: LEVY, Lazare

LAZAREV, Eduard Leonidovich USSR 1935
 EMS, X64, X68
 EMS: ЛАЗАРЕВ

LAZAROF, Henri USA 1932 Bulgaria
 ASUC, BB65, BB71, LMD, MM59, PCM, PC71, X64, X66,
 X67, X68

*LAZARUS, Daniel France 1898
 DDM, DMF, EVM, LMD, REM

LEACH, John Great Britain 1931
 WI69

LEBEDA, Miroslav   Czechoslovakia
   MNP69/4, X68

LEBIČ, Lotjze   Yugoslavia   1934
   KMJ, MSC, X67, X68

*LE BOUCHER, Maurice
   Georges Eugène   France   1882
   DMF, LMD, REM

*LECHNER, Konrad   Germany   1911
   IMD, IMD2, LMD, PAP, X64, X66, X68

LECHTHALER, Josef   Austria
   X67

*LECUNA, Juan Vincente   Venezuela   1899   1954
   BB65, BB71, CA14, EVM, LMD
   BB65: 1898   LMD: 1964

*LECUONA, Ernesto   Cuba   1896   1963
   BB65, BB71, EVM, LMD, MEH, X64

LEDENEV, Roman Semenovich   USSR   1930
   EMS, X65, X68
   EMS: ЛЕДЕНЁВ

*LEDERER, Joseph Anton   Germany   1877
   LMD

*LEDWINKA, Franz   Austria   1883
   EVM

*LEE, Dai-Keong   USA   1915
   AS66, LMD, PC71, REM

LEE, Ernest Markham   USA   1874   1956
   EVM, LMD   Great Britain

*LEE, Noël   USA   1924
   IMD, PCM, X64, X66, X68

LEE, Norman   USA
   CAP

LEEDY, Douglas   USA   1938
   BB71, X68

LEES, Benjamin   USA   1924   China
   AS66, BB65, BB71, CA12, LMD, PCM, PC71, X64, X65, X66,
   X67, X68

LEESON, Cecil   USA   circa 1911
   PC71

LEEUW, Reinbert de   Netherlands   1938
   NED

*LEEUW, Ton de   Netherlands   1926
   BB65, BB71, CME, DDM, EL:2, EVM, IMD, LMD, MEH, NED,
   REM, TSC, X64, X66, X67, X68
   EVM: LEEUW, Antonius Wilhelm Andrianus de
   TSC: DE LEEUW, Ton   EL:2: 1924

LE FANU, Elizabeth
   See: MACONCHY, Elizabeth

LE FANU, Nicola   Great Britain   1947
   BB71

*LEFELD, Jerzy Albert   Poland   1898
   PKW

*LEFÈVERE, Kamiel   USA   1888   Belgium
   AS66, LMD, X66

*LEFKOFF, Gerald   USA   1936
   X68

*LE FLEM, Paul Marie Achille
   Auguste   France   1881
   CMF/13, CMF/20, CMF/40, DDM, DMF, EVM, LMD, MEH,
   QQF, REM
   EVM: FLEM, Paul le

*LE FLEMING, Christopher
   Kaye   Great Britain   1908
   LMD, X64, X66, X67

*LEFTWICH, Vernon   USA   1881   Great Britain
   AS66, BB65, BB71, LMD

*LE GALLIENNE, Dorian   Australia   1916   1963
   AMM, X67

*LEGINSKA, Ethel   USA   1886   1970
   BB71, EVM, LMD, REM   Great Britain
   Formerly: LIGGINS, E.

*LEGLEY, Victor   Belgium   1915   France
   CBC, CME, DDM, EVM, IMD, LMD, MEH, REM, WI69,
   X67, X68

LEGRADY, Thomas T.   Canada   1920   Hungary
   CCM, CCM71, NLC, NLCa

*LEGUERNEY, Jacques France   1906
 DMF, EVM, LMD

LEHMANN, Hans Ulrich Switzerland 1937
 BB65, BB71, IMD, IMD2, LMD, SCHW, X65, X66, X67, X68

LEHMANN, Ulrich   Switzerland 1928
 SCHW, WWS

*LEHNER, Franz Xaver Germany   1904
 WWG, X66, X67

LEIB, Nachmann   Rumania   1905
 RCL

*LEIBOWITZ, René   France   1913 1972
 BB65, BB71, CME, DDM, EMS, EVM, IMD, Poland
 LMD, MEH, MLA29/4, QQF, REM, SML, TSC,
 WI69, X64, X66, X67, X68
 EMS: ЛЕЙБОВИЦ

*LEICHTENTRITT, Hugo USA   1874 1951
 LMD, REM   Poland

*LEICHTLING, Alan   USA   1947
 PC71

*LEIDZÉN, Erik   USA   1894 Sweden
 AS66, X66

*LEIFS, Jón Thorleifsson Iceland   1899 1968
 DDM, EVM, IMD, LMD, REM, SML, VTM, X64

*LEIGH, Walter   Great Britain 1905 1942
 BB71, IMD, LMD, REM, X68

*LEIGHTON, Kenneth   Great Britain 1929
 BB71, IMD, LMD, REM, WI69, X64, X66, X67, X68

*LEINERT, Friedrich Otto Germany   1908
 IMD, LMD

LEITERMEYER, Fritz   Austria
 X65, X66, X67

*LEIVISKÄ, Helvi Lemmikki Finland   1902
 COF, EVM, KKO

LEKBERG, Sven   USA   1899
 PCM, PC71

LEKKA-SAKKALI, Alexandra Greece   1927
 PAP

LEKOVSKI, Aleksandar   Yugoslavia   1933
    KMJ

*LELEU, Jeanne   France   1898
    DDM, DMF, EVM, LMD, QQF, REM, X64

*LEMACHER, Heinrich   Germany   1891   1966
    BB71, EVM, IMD, LMD, MLA23/4, REM, WWG, X64, X66,
    X67, X68

*LEMAN, Albert Semyonovitch   USSR   1915
    LMD, PPU, X65, X66, X68

LEMBA, Artur Gustavovich   USSR   1885   1963
    EMS, EVM   Estonia
    EMS: ЛЕМБА

LENDVAY, Kamilló   Hungary   1928
    CHC, MEH, X67, X68, ZSZ

*LENG, Haygus Alfonso   Chile   1884
    EVM, LMD, REM, X65

*LENSKY, Alexander
    Stepanovich   USSR   1910
    EMS, X66
    EMS: ЛЕНСКИЙ

LENTZ, Daniel K.   USA   1942
    X68

*LENZEWSKI, Gustav   Germany   1896
    X66

*LEON, Argeliers   Cuba   1914
    X66, X68

LEONARDI, Leonid   USA   1901   1967
    AS66, X67   Russia

LEOTSAKOS, George   Greece   1935
    CME, EL:1, PAP, X65

*LEOZ, Jesús García   Spain   1904   1953
    LMD, REM

*LEPIN, Anatoli Yakovlevich   USSR   1907
    X68

*LEPLIN, Emanuel   USA   1917   1972
    BB65, BB71, LMD, MLA29/4, X66

*LEPPARD, Raymond   Great Britain   1927
  X64, X66, X67, X68

*LERCHE, Nils   Finland   1905
  COF

LERESCU, Emil   Rumania   1921
  RCL

LERICH, Rudolf   1903
  IMD

LERMAN, Richard   USA   1944
  PAP

*LE ROUX, Maurice   France   1923
  BB65, BB71, CME, DDM, DMF, EVM, LMD, QQF, REM,
  X65, X68

*LERPERGER, Kurt   Austria   1921
  X64

LESEMANN, Frederick   USA
  ASUC

LESJAK, Borut   Yugoslavia   1931
  KMJ

*LESKOVIC, Bogomir   Yugoslavia   1909   Austria
  IMD, KMJ, LMD, MSC, REM
  LMD and REM: LESCOVIC

*LESSARD, John Ayres   USA   1920
  LMD, PCM, REM, WI69

LESSARD, John Ayres   USA   1920
  EVM, PC71

LESSER, Wolfgang   Germany   1923
  LMD, SML, X64, X66, X68

*LESTER, Thomas William   Great Britain   1889   1956
  EVM

*LESUR, Daniel Jean Yves   France   1908
  BB71, DMF, EVM, MEH, REM, X66, X67

*LETELIER LLONA, Alfonso   Chile   1912
  EVM, IMD, LMD, REM, X67, X68

LETŇAN, Julius   Czechoslovakia   1914
  CCZ, MEH, X67, ZE70/1

*LETONDAL, Arthur John
   Auguste   Canada   1869   1956
   KEY

*LEUKAUF, Robert   Austria   1902
   WI69

*LEVA, Enrico de   Italy   1867   1955
   EVM

LEVAN, Louis   USA   1906   Russia
   AS66

*LEVANT, Oscar   USA   1906   1972
   AS66, EVM, LMD, MEH, MLA29/4, REM, X65, X66

LEVASHOV, Valentin
   Sergievich   USSR   1915
   EMS, X64
   EMS: ЛЕВАШÓВ

LEVI, Natalia Nikolaevna   USSR   1901
   EMS
   EMS: ЛЕВИ́

*LEVI, Philip Augustus John Great Britain 1899   1967
   X67

LEVI, Vito   Italy   1899
   REM, X66, X67

LEVI, Zhul Efraim   Bulgaria   1930
   BMK, X67
   BMK: ЛЕВИ

*LEVIDIS, Dimitri   France   1886   1951
   CME, DDM, EVM, LMD, REM, X65   Greece

LEVINA, Zara Aleksandrovna USSR   1906
   EMS, SML, X66
   EMS: ЛЕ́ВИНА

*LEVINE, Philip   Great Britain
   WI69

LEVINSON, Gerald   USA   1951
   BS70

LEVITCH, Leon   USA   1927   Yugoslavia
   DN70

LEVITE, Miriam   Israel   1892   Russia
   ACU
   Also: RESNIKOFF-LEVITE, Miriam

*LEVITIN, Yuri Abramovitch   USSR   1912
   EMS, LMD, PPU, X64, X65, X66
   EMS: ЛЕВИ́ТИН

LEVY, Bertram J. (Burt)   USA   1936
   BB71, X68

LEVY, Edward I.   USA
   ASUC, X68

LEVY, Ellis   USA   1887
   BB65, BB71, LMD

*LÉVY, Ernst   USA   1895   Switzerland
   BB65, BB71, EVM, LMD, PCM, REM, SCHW, X66, X68

LEVY, Frank   USA   1930   France
   BB71, PC71

LEVY, Jules   Bulgaria

*LÉVY, Lazare   France   1882   1964
   BB65, BB71, DMF, EVM, LMD, X65   Belgium
   Also: LAZARE-LEVY

LEVY, Marvin David   USA   1932
   AS66, BB65, BB71, LMD, PCM, X64, X65, X66, X67, X68
   LMD: LEVY, Martin

*LÉVY, Michel-Maurice   France   1883   1965
   BB65, BB71, DDM, DMF, EVM, LMD, MLA22/4, REM, X65

LÉVY, Roland Alexis Manuel
   See: ROLAND-MANUEL, Alexis

LEWIN, David   USA
   X67, X68

LEWIN, Frank   1925
   X67, X68

*LEWIS, Anthony Carey   Great Britain   1915   Bermuda
   LMD, WI69, X64, X66, X68

*LEWIS, Haydn Francis   Great Britain   1910
   WI69

LEWIS, H. Merrills   USA   1908
   EVM

LEWIS, Jeffrey   Great Britain   1942   Wales
   WI69, X67

LEWIS, John Leo   USA   1911
   AS66, PCM

LEWIS, Joseph Perley   USA   1928
   DN70

LEWIS, Leon   USA   1890
   AS66

LEWIS, Malcolm   1925
   WAN

LEWIS, Peter   USA
   X66

LEWIS, Richard   USA
   X66

LEWIS, Robert Hall   USA   1926
   ASUC, PC71, X65, X66, X67

*LEWKOWITCH, Bernhard   Denmark   1927
   CME, DMTsp, DNS, LMD, VTM, X65, X68

LEWY, Ron   Israel

*LEY, Henry George   Great Britain   1887   1962
   EVM, LMD, X65, X68

*LEY, Salvador   Guatemala   1907
   BB65, BB71, CA12, LMD

*LEYGRAF, Hans   Sweden   1920
   CME, EVM, LMD, MEH, SIMa, VTM, X64, X68

*LHOTKA, Fran   Yugoslavia   1883   1962
   BB71, DDM, EMS, EVM, HCM, IMD, KMJ,   Bohemia
   LMD, MEH, REM, SML, X67
   EMS: ЛОТКА

*LHOTKA-KALINSKI, Ivo   Yugoslavia   1913
   DDM, EMS, HCM, IMD, KMJ, LMD, MEH, REM, SML, X65,
   X67, X68
   EMS: ЛОТКА-КАЛИНСКИЙ

LIADOVA, Ludmila Aleksievna   USSR   1925
  EMS
  EMS: ЛЯДОВА

*LIATOSHINSKY, Boris
  Nikolayevitch   USSR   1895 1968
  BB71, DDM, EMS, EVM, MLA25/4, PPU, REM, SML, X65,
  X68
  EVM: LJATOSJINSKI   MLA25/4 and PPU: LYATOSHINSKY
  SML: LJATSCHINSKI
  EMS: ЛЯТОШИНСКИЙ

LIBEROVICI, Sergio   Italy   1930
  REM

LIBIKH, Oto Emil   Bulgaria   1912 1960
  BMK
  BMK: ЛИБИХ

*LICHEY, Reinhold   Germany   1879 1957
  BB71, EVM, IMD
  EVM: 1880

LICHTENSTEIN, Tsvi
  See: SNUNIT, Tsvi

LICHTER, Charles   USA   1910
  PCM

*LIDHOLM, Ingvar Natanael   Sweden   1921
  BB65, BB71, CME, DDM, DNS, FST, IMD, IMD2, KSV, LMD,
  MEH, MNG, REM, SIM, SIMa, SMT, SOW, STS, SWE, TJU,
  VTM, X64, X65, X66, X67, X68

*LIDL, Václav   Czechoslovakia 1922
  BB65, BB71, CCZ, MNP72/9, X67

*LIE, Harald   Norway   1902 1942
  CNO, VTM

*LIEBERMANN, Rolf   Switzerland 1910
  BB65, BB71, CME, DDM, EVM, IMD, LMD, MEH, OCM, REM,
  SCHW, SML, WTM, WWS, VNM, X64, X65, X66, X67, X68

*LIEBERSON, Goddard   USA   1911 Great Britain
  AS66, BB71, EVM, PCM, X64, X65, X66, X68

*LIEDBECK, Sixten   Sweden   1916
  SIM

LIEPIŅŠ, Anotoli Jakovlovich USSR   1907
  EMS
  EMS: ЛЕПИН

*LIER, Bertus van   Netherlands   1906   1972
   CME, DDM, EVM, IMD, LMD, MLA29/4, NED, REM, X64,
   X65, X67
   MLA29/4: VAN LIER, Bertus

LIES, Carl Otto   Netherlands   1869   1955
   EVM

*LIEURANCE, Thurlow   USA   1878   1963
   AS66, BB65, BB71, EVM, LMD, X64

*LIGETI, György   Hungary   1923
   BB65, BB71, CME, DDM, DMM, IMD, IMD2, LMD, MEH, MNG,
   MZW, REM, SML, VTM, X64, X65, X66, X67, X68

LIGGINS, E.
   See: LEGINSKA, Ethel

*LILBURN, Douglas Gordon   New Zealand   1915
   DDM, IMD, MEH, X66, X67

*LILIEN, Ignace   Netherlands   1897   1964
   EVM, LMD, REM, X64, X65   Poland

*LILJA, Bernhard   Sweden   1895
   FST, KSV, SIM, SIMa

*LILJEFORS, Ingemar Kristian   Sweden   1906
   DDM, EVM, FST, IMD2, KSV, LMD, REM, SIM, SIMa, SOW,
   STS, SWE, TJU, VTM, X66, X67, X68

LILEHAUG, Leland A.   USA
   ASUC

LIMMER, Joachim   1938
   IMD

*LIMMERT, Erich   Germany   1909
   X64, X67, X68

LINDBERG, Armas
   See: LAUNIS, Armas Emanuel

*LINDBERG, Oskar Fredrik   Sweden   1887   1955
   EVM, FST, IMD, KSV, LMD, REM, SIM, SIMa, SOW, STS,
   VTM

*LINDE, Bo Anders Leif   Sweden   1933
   FST, KSV, SIM, SIMa, SOW, STI, SWE, TJU, VTM, X67

LINDE, Hans Martin   Switzerland   1930   Germany
   SCHW, X66, X67, X68

*LINDEDAL, Styrbjörn   Sweden   1904   Germany
  X64
  X64: LINDED<u>EHL</u>

LINDEMAN, Ben   USA
  ASUC

LINDEMAN, Osmo   Finland   1929
  COF, LMD, VTM

*LINDEMAN, Signe   Norway   1895
  CNO, LMD

*LINDEN, Dolf van der   Netherlands   1915
  EVM, LMD, X64
  Formerly: VAN LYNN

LINDENFELD, Harris   USA   1945
  DN72

LINDROTH, Ernst Fredrik
  See: LINKO, E. F.

*LINDROTH, Henry   Sweden   1910
  FST, KSV, SIMa, STS

*LINJAMA, Jaakko Armas   Finland   1909
  KKO
  Formerly: LINDEMAN

*LINK, Joachim-Dietrich   Germany   1925
  IMD, LMD, X66, X68

LINKE, Norbert   Germany   1933
  IMD2, X65, X68

*LINKO, Ernst Fredrik   Finland   1889   1960
  COF, EVM, LMD, VTM
  Formerly: LINDROTH until 1906

LINN, Robert   USA   1925
  AA73, AS66, DN72, PCM, X64, X66, X67

*LINNALA, Eero Leonard   Finland   1920
  KKO, LMD

*LINNALA, Eino Mauno
  Aleksanteri   Finland   1896
  COF, EVM, IMD, KKO, LMD, REM, VTM
  Formerly: BORGMAN until 1906

*LINSTEAD, George Fredrick Great Britain   1908   Scotland
  EVM, LMD, REM, WI69

*LINZ, Marta   Germany   1898   Hungary
    EVM, IMD, WWG

*LIONCOURT, Guy Henri
   Louis de   France   1885   1961
    BB65, BB71, DDM, DMF, EVM, LMD, REM

LIPAR, Peter   Yugoslavia   1912
    KMJ

*LIPATTI, Dinu   Switzerland   1917   1950
    BB65, BB71, CME, EMS, EVM, LMD, MEH,   Rumania
    RCL, REM, SCHW, SML, X64, X65, X66, X68
    EMS: ЛИПАТТИ

LIPKIN, Malcolm Leyland   Great Britain   1932
    BB65, BB71, LMD, WI69, X64, X66, X67

*LIPOVŠEK, Marijan   Yugoslavia   1910
    EMS, IMD, KMJ, LMD, REM, SML, X66, X67
    EMS: ЛИПОВШЕК

*LIPPOLIS, Italo   Italy   1910   1964
    LMD, REM

LIPSCOMB, Helen   USA   1921
    AS66, PCM, X67

LIPSKY, Alexander   USA   1901   Poland
    EVM

LÍŠKA, Zdeněk   Czechoslovakia   1922
    BB65, BB71, MEH

LISSAUER, Robert   USA   1917
    AS66

LIST, Kurt   USA   1913   1970
    BB71, X68   Austria

*LISTL, Paul   Germany   1890
    WWG

*LISTOV, Konstantin
   Jakovlevich   USSR   1900
    EMS, LMD, PPU69/3
    EMS: ЛИСТОВ

*LITAIZE, Gaston-Gilbert   France   1909
    DDM, DMF, EVM, LMD, X65, X66, X67, X68

*LITINSKY, Genrih Ilyich   USSR   1901
    BB71, EMS, EVM, LMD, REM, X65, X68
    EMS: ЛИТЙНСКИЙ

*LIUDKEVICH, Stanislav
    Filippovich   USSR   1879
    EMS, EVM, LMD, PPU, PPU70/1, REM, SML, X65
    EVM: LUDKEWYCZ   LMD: LJUDKEVIČ
    PPU and X65: LYUDKEVICH
    PPU70/1: LYUDKEVICH, Stanislav Vikent'yevich
    SML: LJUDKEWITSCH   EMS: ЛЮДКЕВИЧ

*LIVIABELLA, Lino   Italy   1902   1964
    BB71, DDM, EMS, IMD, LMD, REM, X64, X65
    EMS: ЛИВИАБЕ́ЛЛА

LIZZI, Amedeo   Italy   1919
    LMD

LIZZI, Michele (II)   Italy   1919
    LMD, REM, X64

LIZZI, Virgilio   Italy   1883
    LMD, REM

LLACER PLA, Francisco   Spain   1918
    DDM

*LLONGUERAS y BADÍA, Juan   Spain   1880   1953
    EVM, LMD, REM

*LLOYD, George   Great Britain   1913
    EVM, LMD, REM, X64

LLOYD, Gerald   USA   1938
    PC71, X67

LLOYD, Norman   USA   1909
    AS66, PCM, X64, X65, X67, X68

LOBACHEV, Girgori
    Grigorievich   USSR   1888   1953
    EMS, EVM
    EMS: ЛОБАЧЁВ

*LØBGER, Gregers Christian   Denmark   1888   1967
    X67

LOBKOVSKY, Abram
    Mihailovich   USSR   1912
    EMS
    EMS: ЛОБКО́ВСКИЙ

LOBO, Antsher   India   1905
   WHIad

*LOCKSPEISER, Edward   Great Britain   1905
   BB71, DDM, EVM, LMD, REM, X65, X66, X67, X68

LOCKWOOD, Anna Ferguson   New Zealand   1939
   BB71, WI69, X66

*LOCKWOOD, Normand   USA   1906
   AA73, EVM, LMD, PCM, PC71, REM, WI69, X64, X65, X67,
   X68

LOEHRER, Edwin   Switzerland   1906
   LMD

LOGAN, Wendell M.   USA   1940
   ASUC

*LOGAR, Mihovil   Yugoslavia   1902
   BB65, BB71, CME, EMS, IMD, KMJ, LMD, MEH, REM,
   X64, X65, X67, X68
   EMS: ЛОГАР

LOGOTHETIS, Anestis   Austria   1921   Greece
   BB65, BB71, CME, EL:1, EL:2, EL:3, EL:4, IMD, LMD, MNG,
   PAP, X65, X66, X67

LOHOFFER, Evelyn   USA   1921
   AS66

*LOHSE, Otto Fred   Germany   1908
   IMD, LMD, SML, X65, X66, X67, X68

LOKSHIN, Aleksandr Lazarevich USSR   1920
   EMS
   EMS: ЛОКШИН

LOMAN, Abraham Dirk, Jr.   Netherlands   1868   1954
   EVM

*LOMANI, Borys Grzegorz   Poland   1893
   LMD, PKW, REM

LOMBARDO, Carlo   Italy   1869   1959
   LMD, REM

LOMBARDO, Constantino   Italy   1882   1960
   LMD, REM

LOMBARDO, Mario   USA   1931
   AS66

LOMBARDO, Robert M.   USA   1932
    X67, X68

LONATI, Carlo   Italy   1890   1955
    LMD

*LONCQUE, Georges   Belgium   1900
    CBC, EVM, LMD

LONDON, Edwin   USA   1929
    ASUC

LONG, Edgar
    See: RIEGGER, Wallingford

*LONGAS, Federico   USA   1895   Spain
    EVM

*LONGO, Achille (II)   Italy   1900   1954
    EVM, IMD, LMD, REM

LONGOBARDI, Alfonso   Italy   1880   1964
    LMD, REM, X65

*LONQUE, Armand Josef   Belgium   1908
    LMD

*LOOMIS, Clarence   USA   1888   1965
    AS66, BB65, BB71, LMD

*LOOSER, Rolf   Switzerland   1920
    SCHW, WWS, X66, X67, X68

LOOTS, Joyce Mary Ann   Union of   1907
    WI69   South Africa

*LOPATNIKOFF, Nikolai
    Lvovich   USA   1903   Estonia
    AA73, ASUC, AS66, BB65, BB71, CA12, DDM, EVM, IMD,
    LMD, REM, SML, WI69, WTM, X64, X65, X66, X67, X68

*LOPES GRAÇA, Fernando   Portugal   1906
    DDM, EMS, EVM, LMD, X64, X65, X66, X68
    EMS: ЛÓПШИ ГРАСА

LOPEZ, Razhes Hernandez   Venezuela

*LOPEZ CHAVARRI, Eduardo   Spain   1875
    DDM, REM
    REM: CHARARRI, Lopez Eduardo
    DDM: 1871

LOPEZ DE LA ROSA, Horacio   Argentina
X68

LO PRESTI, Ronald PC71, X67	USA	1933	
LORÁND, István CHC	Hungary	1933	
LORA-TOTINO, Arrigo	Italy	1928	
LORD, David MNG, WI69, X67, X68	Great Britain	1944	
LORD, Philip John WI69, X64	Great Britain	1930	
LORENC, Antoni KMJ	Yugoslavia	1909	
LORENTZEN, Bent DMTsp, X67, X68	Denmark	1935	
*LORENZ, Ellen Jane AS66	USA	1907	

*LORIOD, Yvonne   France   1924
CME, EVM, LMD, REM, X65, X66, X68

LORRAIN, Denis BS72	Canada	1948	USA
LOSAVIO, Giovanni LMD	Italy	1872	1956
LOSONCZY, Andor LMD	Hungary	1932	

*LOTHAR, Friedrich Wilhelm   Germany   1885
ACM, IMD

*LOTHAR, Mark   Germany   1902
EVM, IMD, LMD, MEH, REM, SML, WWG, X68

LO TZUN-SHAN   China   1925
EMS
EMS: ЛО ЦЗУН-СЯНЬ

*LOUCHEUR, Raymond   France   1899
CMF6, CMF20, CMF40, DDM, DMF, EMS, LMD, QQF, REM,
X65
EMS: ЛУШЁР

LOUDOVA, Ivana   Czechoslovakia   1941
    MNP67/8, MNP72/9, X67, X68

*LOUËL, Jean Hippolyte Oscar   Belgium   1914
    CBC, DDM, EVM, LMD, REM

LOUGHLIN, George   Australia   1914   Great Britain
    AMM

*LOUIGUY, Louis Guglielmi   France   1916   Spain
    EVM
    Pseudonym: GUGLIELMI, Luis

*LOURIÉ, Arthur Vincent   USA   1892   1966
    BB65, BB71, EVM, LMD, MLA23/4, REM,   Russia
    X66, X67

LOVEC, Vladimir   Yugoslavia   1922
    KMJ, LMD, MSC

*LOVELOCK, William   Australia   1899   Great Britain
    AMM, WI69, X64, X65, X68

LOVINGWOOD, Penman, Sr.   USA   1895
    AS66

*LOWE, Jack W.   USA   1917
    WI69

LOWISOHN, Asher
    See: BENARI, Asher

*LÖWLEIN, Hans   Germany   1909
    IMD

LOWTZKY, Hermann   USSR   1871   1957
    BB65, BB71

LOY, Max   Germany   1913
    BB65, BB71, EVM

*LAULDI, Adriano   Italy   1885   1971
    BB65, BB71, DDM, EVM, IMD, LMC, MLA28, X65

*LUBAN, Issac Issacovitch   USSR   1906
    EMS
    EMS: ЛЮБАН

LUBIN, Ernest   USA   1916
    AS66, X65, X67, X68

LUBOSHUTZ, Pierre   USA   1891   1971
  AS66, BB71   Russia
  AS66: 1894

*LUBRICH, Fritz, Jr.   Germany   1888
  EVM, LMD

LUBRICH, Fritz, Sr.   Germany   1862   1952
  EVM

LUCAS, James   USA   1942
  DN72

*LUCAS, Leighton   Great Britain 1903
  EVM, LMD, REM, WI69, X68

*LUČIĆ, Franjo   Yugoslavia   1889
  HCM, IMD, KMJ, LMD, REM

LUCIER, Alvin   USA   1931
  BB71, BCL, EL:2, X68

ŁUCIUK, Juliusz   Poland   1927
  LMD, MEH, PKW, REM, X65, X67, X68

LUCKÝ, Štěpán   Czechoslovakia 1919
  CCZ, EVM, IMD, IMD2, LMD, MEH, MNP70/1, MNP70/9,
  MNP72/4, REM, WI69

*LUDEWIG, Wolfgang   Germany   1926
  X68

*LUDIG, Mikhkel Yakovlevich Argentina 1880   1958
  EMS, EVM   Estonia
  EMS: людиг

LUDKEWYCZ, S. F.
  See: LIUDKEVICH, S. F.

*LUDT, Finn   Norway   1918
  CNO, VTM

LUDVIG-PEČAR, Nada   Yugoslavia   1929
  KMJ

*LUDWIG, Franz   Germany   1889   1955
  EVM, IMD, LMD   Austria

LUDWIG, Joachim Carl Martin Germany   1934   Bohemia
  WI69

*LUENING, Otto   USA   1900
   AA73, ASUC, BB65, BB71, DDM, EVM, IMD, LMD, MEH,
   PCM, PC71, REM, X64, X65, X66, X67, X68

LUKÁŠ, Zdeněk   Czechoslovakia 1928
   MEH, MNP64/3, MNP69/4, MNP70/1, MNP70/3, MNP72/4,
   X64, X66, X68

LUKE, Ray E.   USA   1928
   PC71, X66, X68

*LUKIN, Philip Mironovich   USSR   1913
   EMS, PPU, PPU69/2, X68
   EMS: ЛУКИН

*LUMBY, Herbert Horace   Great Britain   1906
   WI69

LUMSDAINE, David Newton   Great Britain   1931   Australia
   WI69, X65

*LUND, Hanna   Denmark   1904
   X64

*LUND, Signe   Norway   1868   1950
   BB71, LMD

*LUNDBORG, Gösta   Sweden   1903   1966
   KSV, SIMa, X64

*LUNDE, Johann Backer   Norway   1874   1958
   LMD

LUNDE, Lawson   1935
   WAN

*LUNDÉN, Lennart Suneson   Sweden   1914   1966
   FST, KSV, MLA23/4, SIM, SIMa, STS, X67

*LUNDQVIST, Torbjörn   Sweden   1920
   BB71, FST, IMD2, KSV, SIM, SIMa, SOW, STI, STS, TJU,
   VTM, X67

LUNDSTEN, Ralph   Sweden   1936
   STS, X67, X68

*LUNDVIK, Hildor   Sweden   1885   1951
   FST, KSV, SIM, SIMa, STS

*LUNELLI, Renato   Italy   1895   1967
   LMD, REM, X64, X67, X68

LUNETTA, Stanley G.　　　　USA　　　　1937
　　BB71, IMD2, PCM, X67, X68

*LUNGHI, Fernand Lodovico　　Italy　　　1893
　　REM

LUNGU, Nicolae　　　　　　Rumania　　1900
　　RCL

*LUNVIK, Hildor　　　　　Sweden　　1885　1951
　　FST, KSV, SIM, SIMa, STS

*LUOLAJAN-MIKKOLA,
　Vilho Rafael　　　　　　Finland　　1911
　　COF, KKO

*LUPI, Roberto　　　　　　Italy　　　1908　1971
　　BB65, BB71, LMD, MLA28/4, REM, WI69

LUPU, Theodor　　　　　　Rumania　　1898　1962
　　RCL

*LUSTGARTEN, Egon　　　　Austria　　1887
　　EVM, LMD, REM

*LUSTIG, Moshe　　　　　　Israel　　1922　1958
　　ACU, MM59　　　　　　　　　　　Germany

LUTHI, Willy　　　　　　Switzerland　1901　Syria
　　SCHW

LÜTHI-WEGMANN, Elvira　　Switzerland　1896　Italy
　　SCHW, X67

*LUTOSŁAWSKI, Witold　　　Poland　　　1913
　　BB65, BB71, CME, DDM, EMS, EVM, IMD, IMD2, LMD, MEH,
　　MZW, OCM, PKW, REM, SML, WI69, WTM, X64, X65, X66,
　　X67, X68
　　EMS: ЛЮТОСЛА́ВСКИЙ

*LUTYENS, Elisabeth Agnes　　Great Britain　1906
　　BCI, CME, DDM, EVM, IMD, LMD, MEH, REM, TSC, WI69,
　　X64, X65, X66, X67, X68

LUŽEVIČ, Franjo　　　　　Yugoslavia　1903
　　KMJ

LUZZATTI, Arturo　　　　　Argentina　1875　1959
　　LMD, REM　　　　　　　　　　　Italy

LUZZATTO, Livio Moise　　　Italy　　　1897
　　REM, X66

LYATOSHINSKY, B. N.
See: LIATOSHINSKY, B. N.

LYBBERT, Donald   USA   1923
  BB65, BB71, PCM, PC71, TSC, X64, X67, X68

LYLLOFF, Bent   1930
  WAN

LYNN, George   USA   1915
  AS66, BB71, LMD, PCM, PC71, X64, X65, X66, X68

LYNN, Van
See: LINDEN, Dolf van der

LYON, David Norman   Great Britain 1938
  BB65, BB71, LMD, WI69, X64

LYUDKEVICH, S. F.
See: LIUDKEVICH, S. F.

*MAASALO, Armas Toivo
  Valdemar   Finland   1885 1960
  COF, EVM, LMD, REM
  Formerly: MASALIN

*MAASZ, Gerhard   Germany   1906
  EVM, IMD, LMD, REM, WI69, WWG, X65

MAAYANY, Ami-Hay   Israel   1936
  ACU, IMD, X68

MÁCAL, Zdeněk   Czechoslovakia 1936
  MNP68/9, X65, X68

MAČAVARIANI, A. D.
See: MACHAVARIANI, A. D.

MACCHI, Egisto   Italy   1928
  IMD, LMD, REM, X65, X66, X68

MAC COLL, Hugh F.   USA   1885 1953
  PCM

*MAC DERMID, James
  Gardiner   Canada   1875 1960
  BB71

MAC DONALD, James   USA
  CAP

*MAC DONALD, Malcolm Great Britain 1916
 WI69

MACERO, Teo Attilio Joseph USA   1925
 X66, X67, X68

*MACH, Constantin   Germany 1915
 LMD, X68

*MÁCHA, Otmar   Czechoslovakia 1922
 CCZ, IMD2, LMD, MEH, MNP65/6, MNP66/4, MNP70/1,
 MNP71/1, MNP72/1, MNP72/4, SML, X66, X67, X68

*MACHABEY, Armand France 1886 1966
 BB71, EVM, LMD, REM, X64, X66, X67, X68

MACHABEY, Emilienne
See: GANEVAL, Emilienne

MACHAN, Benjamin A. USA   1894 1966
 AS66

*MACHAVARIANI, Aleksei
 Davidovich   USSR   1913
 BB65, BB71, CME, DDM, EMS, LMD, MEH, PPU69/2, X65
 BB65, BB71, DDM and X65: MATCHAVARIANI
 LMD: MACAVARIANI MEH: MACAVARIANI
 EMS: МАЧАВАРИÁНИ

MACHE, François-Bernard France 1935
 CME, LMD, REM, X67

*MACHL, Tadeusz   Poland 1922
 BB65, BB71, IMD, LMD, PKW, X68

*MACIEJEWSKI, Roman USA   1910 Poland
 IMD, LMD, PKW, REM, X67

MAC ILWHAM, George Great Britian 1926 Scotland
 WI69

*MAC INNIS, Donald USA   1923
 AA73, ASUC, X65, X66, X67, X68

MAC KAY, Harper   USA
 AS66

*MACKEBEN, Theo   Germany 1897 1953
 EVM, LMD, REM, X67

MACKINLEY, Charles USA   1895
 EVM

*MACLEAN, Quentin Stuart
  Moravern   Canada   1896   1962
    BB65, EVM, LMD, MCO, NLC, REM   England

*MACMILLAN, Ernest
  Campbell   Canada   1893   1973
    BB71, CA11, CCM, CCM71, CVM, CVMa, EVM, KEY, LMD,
    MCO, MCO68, NLC, REM, TFB, WI69, X68

*MACNUTT, Walter Louis   Canada   1910
    CVM, KEY, NLC, NLCa

*MACONCHY, Elizabeth   Great Britain 1907
    BB65, BB71, DDM, EMS, EVM, LMD, MEH, REM, WI69,
    X64, X65, X66, X67, X68
    EMS: МЭКОНКИ

MACOUREK, Karel Harry   Czechoslovakia 1923
    CCZ, MEH, X68

MACUDZINSKI, Rudolf   Czechoslovakia 1907
    CCZ, MEH, X65, X66, X67, X68, ZE71/2, ZE72/1

MADATOV, Grigori Yakovlevich USSR   1898
    BB65, BB71

MADER, Clarence   USA   1904
    DN70

*MADERNA, Bruno   Italy   1920   1973
    BB65, BB71, CME, DDM, EVM, IMD, IMD2, LMD, MEH,
    MZW, OCM, REM, SML, WI69, X64, X65, X66, X67, X68

MADEY, Bogusław   Poland   1932
    PKW, X66

MADGE, Geoffrey D.   Australia
    X65

MADJERA, Gottfried   Germany   1905   Austria
    WI69

*MAEGAARD, Jan   Denmark   1926
    CME, DMTsp, IMD, IMD2, LMD, VTM, X64, X65, X66, X67,
    X68

MAEKELBERGHE, August R.   USA   1909   Belgium
    AS66, X65

MAELE, Gérard van   Belgium   1907
    ACM

MAERZENDORFER, Ernst   Austria   1921
    LMD, X65, X67

*MAES, Jef   Belgium   1905
    CBC, EVM, LMD, WI69

*MAGALOFF, Nikita   Switzerland   1912   Russia
    BB71, LMD, REM, SCHW, WWS, WI69, X65, X66, X67, X68

*MAGANINI, Quinto   USA   1897
    AS66, LMD, EVM, PCM, REM

MAGDALENIĆ, Miroslav   Yugoslavia   1906
    HCM, KMJ

MAGDIĆ, Josip   Yugoslavia   1937
    KMJ

MAGEAU, Sister Mary
    Magdalen   USA
    AA73

*MAGGIONI, Aurelio Antonio   Italy   1908
    BB71, LMD, REM

MAGHINI, Ruggero   Italy   1913
    LMD, REM

MAGIDENKO, Mihail
    Yakovlevich   USSR   1915
    EMS
    EMS: МАГИДЕ́НКО

MAGLIOCCO, Francesco   Italy   1880
    REM

MAGLIONI, Giovacchino   Italy   1891   1966
    LMD, REM, X66

MAGNANI, Luigi   Italy   1906
    LMD, X68

*MAGNE, Michel   France   1930
    IMD, LMD, QQF

MAGNUSON, Phillip   USA   1949
    BS70

MAHLER, Alma Marie   1879   1965
    IMD

MAHLER-KALKSTEIN, M. Israel
  See: AVIDOM, Menahem

MAHY, Pierre Belgium 1883
  EVM

*MAIBORODA, Georgi
  Illarionovich USSR 1913
  EMS, PPU, PPU69/2, REM, X65
  PPU and X65: MAYBORODA
  EMS: МАЙБОРОДА

*MAIBORODA, Platan
  Illarionovich USSR 1918
  EMS, LMD, PPU, REM
  LMD: MAJBORODA PPU: MAYBORODA EMS: МАЙБОРОДА

MAIGUASHCA, Mesias Ecuador
  X68

*MAILMAN, Martin USA 1932
  AA73, AS66, DN72, PCM, PC71, X67, X68

*MAINARDI, Enrico Italy 1897 1967
  IMD, LMD, REM, WI69, X66, X67, X68

*MAINE, Basil Stephen Great Britain 1894
  LMD

MAINKA, Jürgen Germany 1925
  SML

MAIONE, Rino Italy 1920
  LMD, REM

MAIUSUMI, Tosciro Japan 1929
  REM

*MAIZEL, Boris Sergeivich USSR 1907
  EMS
  EMS: МАЙЗЕЛЬ

MAIZTEGUI, Isidro B. 1905
  IMD

MAJER, Milan Yugoslavia 1895 1967
  HCM, KMJ, X67

*MAJEWSKI, Hans-Martin Germany 1911
  WWG

MAJOR, Douglas D.   Canada   1914   England
     MCO, MCO68, NLC

*MAJOR, Ervin   Hungary   1901   1967
     BB71, EVM, REM, SML, X68

MAKAROV, Evgenyi Petrovich   USSR   1912
     EMS, X68
     EMS: **МАКА́РОВ**

MAKAROV, Valentin Aleksievich   USSR   1908   1952
     EMS
     EMS: **МАКА́РОВ**

*MAKÁROVA, Nina Vladimirovna USSR   1908
     EMS, EVM, LMD, REM
     LMD: KHAČATURJAN
     EMS: **МАКА́РОВА**

*MAKAROV-RAKITIN, Constantin
     Dmitrievich   USSR   1912   1941
     EMS
     EMS: **МАКАРОВ-РАКИ́ТИН**

MA KE   China   1918
     EMS
     EMS: **МА КЭ**

MAKEDONSKI, Kiril   Yugoslavia   1925
     BB71

*MAKLAKIEWICZ, Jan Adam   Poland   1899   1954
     CME, DDM, EMS, EVM, IMD, LMD, MEH, PKW, REM, SML,
     X65
     EMS: **МАКЛЯКЕ́ВИЧ**

*MAKSIMOV, Stepan
     Maksimovich   USSR   1892   1951
     EMS, X67, X68
     EMS: **МАКСИ́МОВ**

MAKSIMOVIĆ, Rajko   Yugoslavia   1935
     BB71, KMJ, X67

MALATESTA, Luigi   Italy   1900
     LMD, REM

*MAŁAWSKI, Artur   Poland   1904   1957
     BB71, CME, DDM, EMS, IMD, LMD, MEH, PKW, REM, SML,
     X65, X68
     EMS: **МАЛЯВСКИЙ**

*MALCOLM, George John Great Britain 1917
 X64, X66, X68

*MALDYBAEV, Abdylas USSR 1906
 EMS, PPU, PPU69/2, X66
 EMS: **МАЛДЫБАЕВ**

*MALEC, Ivo Yugoslavia 1925
 CME, DDM, HCM, IMD, IMD2, KMJ, REM, X66, X67, X68

*MALEINGREAU, Paul de Belgium 1887 1956
 BB65, BB71, EVM, REM France
 Formerly: MALENGREAU

MÁLEK, Jan Czechoslovakia
 MNP69/4

MALEK, Viktor Czechoslovakia 1922
 BB71

*MALER, Wilhelm Germany 1902
 DDM, EVM, IMD, REM, SML, X64, X66, X68

*MALHERBE, Edmund Henry
 Paul France 1870 1963
 BB65, BB71, EVM, LMD, SML

MALIGE, Fred Germany 1895
 IMD, IMD2, LMD, SML, X65

*MALIPIERO, Gian Francesco Italy 1882 1973
 BB65, BB71, DDM, EMS, EVM, IMD, IMD2, LMD, MEH, MZW,
 REM, SML, TCM, VNM, WTM, X64, X65, X66, X67, X68
 EMS: **МАЛИПЬЕРО**

*MALIPIERO, Riccardo Italy 1914
 EL:1, IMD, LMD, REM, WI69, X64, X65, X66

*MALKO, Nikolay Andreyvich USA 1883 1961
 BB65, BB71, EVM, LMD, REM, X66, X68 Russia
 EVM: 1888

MALLANDER, Jan Olov Finland 1947

MALMFORS, Åke Sweden 1918 1951
 STS

MALMSTRÖM, Gunnar Sweden 1892 1961
 SIM, SIMa

MALOVEC, Jozef Czechoslovakia 1933
 CCZ, MEH, X65, X67, X68, ZE69/2, ZE69/3, ZE70/2,
 ZE70/3, ZE71/2, ZE71/3

MAMANGAKIS, Nikos   Greece   1929
    BB65, BB71, CME, EL:1, EL:2, EL:3, EL:4, IMD, LMD, PAP,
    X65, X67, X68

MAMISSACHVILI, Nodar   USSR
    X67

MAMIYA, Michio   Japan   1919
    IMD2, LMD, MEH, X67

MAMLOK, Ursula   USA
    ASUC

*MANA-ZUCCA, Ki-Lu   USA   1887
    AA73, AS66, BB65, BB71, LMD, WI69, X64, X65, X67
    AS66: 1894

MANDELBAUM, Joel   USA
    ASUC

MANDELLI, Alfredo   Italy   1927
    LMD

MANDELLI, Emanuele   Italy   1891
    REM

*MANDER, Francesco   Italy   1915
    LMD, WI69

*MANDIĆ, Josef   Yugoslavia   1883   1959
    BB65, BB71, EVM, LMD, REM

*MANÉN, Juan de   Spain   1883
    DDM, EMS, EVM, IMD, LMD, REM
    EMS: МАНЕН

*MANENTI, Luigi   Italy   1899
    LMD, REM
    REM: 1898

*MANEVICH, Aleksandr
   Mendelevich   USSR   1908
    EMS, PPU
    EMS: МАНЕВИЧ

MANGOIANU, Stefan   Rumania   1922
    RCL

MANGS, Runar   Sweden   1928
    SIM, SIMa, SWE

*MANICKE, Dietrich   Germany   1923
    REM, X66, X68

MANINI, Alfredo   Italy   1880
  REM

MANN, John David   USA   1954
  DN70

MANN, Leslie   Canada   1923
  CCM, CCM71, CVM, KEY, MCO, MCO68, MCO71

MANN, Robert W.   Italy   1925   USA
  IMD, REM

*MANNES, Leopold Damrosch   USA   1899   1964
  BB71, EVM, LMD, REM, X64

MANNEY, Charles Fonteyn   USA   1872   1951
  AS66

*MANNING, Kathleen Lockhart   USA   1890   1951
  AS66, LMD

*MANNING, Richard   USA   1914   1954
  AS66   Great Britain

*MANNINO, France   Italy   1924
  BB71, LMD, REM, XI69, X67

MANNINO, Vincenzo   Italy   1913
  LMD

MANOLOV, Khristo Emanuilov   Bulgaria   1900   1953
  BMK
  BMK: МАНОЛОВ

MANOLOV, Zdravko Khristo   Bulgaria   1925
  BMK, X67, X68
  BMK: МАНОЛОВ

MANOR, Friedl   Israel   1915   Germany
  ACU

*MANSFIELD, Purcell James   Great Britain   1889   1968
  BB71, LMD

MANSON, Eddy Lawrence   USA   1919
  AS66

*MANTIA, Aldo   Italy   1903
  LMD

MANTICA, Francesco   Italy   1875   1970
  EVM, LMD, REM

MANUEL, Alexis Roland
  See: ROLAND-MANUEL, Alexis

*MANZIARLY, Marcelle de   France   1900 Russia
  EVM, X65

*MANZONI, Giacomo   Italy   1932
  BB65, BB71, IMD, IMD2, REM, X64, X65, X67

MARAGNO, Virtú   Argentina   1928
  BB65, BB71, CA8, LMD

MARAIS, Josef   USA   1905 Union of
  AS66, X65   South Africa

MARBE, Myriam   Rumania   1931
  RCL, X65, X68

MARCACCI, Francesco   Italy   1885
  REM

MARCEL, Luc-André   France   1919
  CMF37, CMF40, DDM, EVM, LMD, X66

*MARCELLI, Nino   USA   1890 1967
  AS66, BB71, X67, X68   Chile

MARCHETTI, Walter   1931
  IMD

MARCILLY, Paul   France   1890
  EVM

*MARCKHL, Erich   Austria   1902
  LMD, WI69, X64, X65, X66, X67, X68

MARCO, Guy A.   USA   1927
  LCI, X65

MARCO, Tomás   Spain   circa 1942
  HET21, X67, X68

MARCZEWSKI, Aleksander   Poland   1911
  PKW

*MARECZEK, Fritz   Germany   1910 Bohemia
  WWG

*MAREK, Czeslaw Jozef   Switzerland 1891 Poland
  EVM, LMD, REM, SCHW

*MARESCOTTI, André-François   Switzerland   1902
    CME, DDM, IMD, LMD, REM, SCHW, WWS, X65, X67, X68

*MARGARITIS, Loris   Greece   1895   1953
    BB71, LMD, REM

*MARGOLA, Franco   Italy   1908
    EVM, IMD, LMD, REM

MARGOLIS, Jerome N.   USA
    ASUC

MARI, Pierrette   France   1929
    CCH, X68

*MARIĆ, Ljubica   Yugoslavia   1909
    BB65, BB71, CME, DDM, EMS, IMD, IMD2, KMJ, LMD, MEH,
    SML, X65, X67
    EMS: МАРИЧ

MARIE, Jean-Etienne   France   1917
    CMF32, CMF40

MARINKOVIĆ, Illija   Yugoslavia   1916   Hungary
    KMJ

MARINOV, Ivan Marinov   Bulgaria   1928
    BB65, BB71, BMK, X68
    BMK: МАРИНОВ

*MARINUZZI, Gino   Italy   1920   USA
    LMD, REM, X67

*MARION, Jacques   France   1903
    QQF

*MARIOTTI, Mario   Italy   1899   France
    LMD, REM

*MARISCAL, Juan Léon   Mexico   1899   1972
    EVM, HET27, MMX

MARKEN, Bob van   Netherlands   1915
    EVM

*MARKÉVITCH, Igor   Switzerland   1912   Russia
    DDM, EMS, EVM, IMD, LMD, MEH, QQF, REM, SCHW, SML,
    WWG, X64, X65, X66, X67, X68
    EMS: МАРКЕВИЧ

MARKIEWICZÓWNA, Władysława Poland   1900
    PKW

MARKOS, Albert   Rumania   1914
   RCL

MARKOVIĆ, Adalbert   Yugoslavia   1929
   HCM, KMJ

MARKOVIĆ, Vilim   Yugoslavia   1902
   HCM, KMJ

MARKOVIĆ, Zvonimir   Yugoslavia   1925
   HCM, KMJ

*MARKOWSKI, Andrzej   Poland   1924
   LMD, MEH, PKW, REM, X68
   Formerly: ANDRZEJEWSKI, Marek

*MAROS, Rudolf   Hungary   1917
   BB65, BB71, CHC, CME, EVM, IMD2, LMD, MEH, REM, SML,
   X64, X66, X67, X68

MARŠÁLEK, František   Czechoslovakia
   MNP69/4

MARSH, Charles Howard   USA   1885   1956
   AS66

*MARSH-EDWARDS, Michael
   Richard   Great Britain 1928
   WI69

MARSHALL, Jack   USA   1921
   PCM, X66

*MARSICK, Armand Louis-
   Joseph   Belgium   1877   1959
   BB65, BB71, CME, EVM, LMD, REM

MARTA, Eduardo   Mexico
   X68

*MARTELLI, Carlo   Great Britain 1935
   WI69

*MARTELLI, Henri   France   1899   Corsica
   CMF21, CMF40, DDM, DMF, EVM, LMD, QQF, REM
   DDM, EVM and QQF: 1895

*MARTENS, Ib   Denmark   1918
   IMD

MARTIN, David L.   Canada   1926
   CCM, KEY, MCO, MCO71

*MARTÍN, Edgardo   Cuba   1915
    DDM, LMD, REM

MARTIN, Émile   France   1914
    LMD, X68

*MARTIN, Frank   Switzerland   1890
    BB65, BB71, CME, DDM, EMS, EVM, IMD, IMD2, LMD, MEH,
    PAP, REM, SCHW, SML, TSC, WI69, WTM, WWS, X64, X65,
    X66, X67, X68
    EMS: МАРТЕН

MARTIN, Paul A.   USA
    ASUC

MARTIN, Vernon   USA   1929
    AS66

MARTINČEK, Dušan   Czechoslovakia 1936
    CCZ, MEH, X67, X68, ZE69/3, ZE70/1, ZE70/2, ZE70/3,
    ZE71/1, ZE71/2, ZE71/3

*MARTINET, Jean-Louis   France   1912
    CME, DDM, DMF, EVM, IMD, LMD, MEH, REM, X65
    MEH: 1914

*MARTINI, Gian Mario   Italy   1923
    REM

MARTINI, Renzo   Italy   1897
    IMD, LMD, REM

MARTINO, Donald James   USA   1931
    ASUC, BB65, BB71, LMD, PCM, PC71, TSC, X64, X65, X66,
    X67, X68

*MARTINON, Jean   France   1910
    BB65, BB71, CMF26, CMF40, DDM, DMF, EVM, IMD, IMD2,
    LMD, MEH, OCM, QQF, REM, WI69, X64, X65, X66, X67,
    X68

*MARTINŮ, Bohuslav   USA   1890   1959
    BB65, BB71, CCZ, CIS, CME, DDM, EMS,   Czecho-
    EVM, IMD, IMD2, LMD, MEH, MNP70/2,   slovakia
    MNP71/8, REM, SML, TCM, WTM, X64,
    X65, X66, X67, X68
    EMS: МАРТИНУ

MARTIRANO, Salvatore   USA   1927
   ASUC, BB71, IMD, LMD, PCM, PC71, X64, X65, X66, X67,
   X68

*MARTTINEN, Tauno Olavi   Finland   1912
   COF, KKO, LMD, REM, VTM, X66

*MARVIA, Kurt Einari   Finland   1915
   COF, KKO, X66

*MARX, Joseph   Austria   1882 1964
   BB65, BB71, CME, DDM, EMS, EVM, IMD, LMD, MEH, REM,
   SML, X64, X65, X67
   EMS: МАРКС

*MARX, Karl   Germany   1897
   DDM, EMS, EVM, IMD, LMD, REM, SML, WWG, X64, X66,
   X67, X68
   EMS: МАРКС

MASANETZ, Guido   Germany   1914
   LMD

MASCAGNI, Andrea   Italy   1917
   LMD, REM

MASELLI, Gianfranco   Italy   1929
   LMD, REM

*MASETTI, Enzo   Italy   1893 1961
   EVM, IMD, LMD, REM

MA SI TZUN   China   1912
   EMS
   EMS: МА СЫ-ЦУН

MASLANKA, David   USA
   ASUC

*MÁSLO, Jindrich   Czechoslovakia 1875 1964
   CCZ

*MASON, Daniel Gregory   USA   1873 1953
   AS66, DDM, EVM, LMD, PCM, PC71, REM, X68

*MASON, Gladys Amy   Great Britain   1899
   WI69
   Pseudonym: KENDAL, Sydney

*MASSALITINOV, Konstantin
   Iraklevich   USSR   1905
   EMS, PPU, PPU69/2, X65, X68
   EMS: МАССАЛИТИНОВ

*MASSANA, Antonio   Spain   1890
    LMD, REM

*MASSARANI, Renzo   Italy   1898
    LMD, REM

*MASSÉUS, Jan   Netherlands   1913
    EVM, IMD, NED, X66

*MASSIAS, Gérard   France   1933
    DDM

MASSIMO, Leone   Italy   1896
    LMD, REM

*MASSIS, Amable   France   1893
    DMF, LMD, QQF

MASSON, Gérard   France   1936
    BB71, LMD, X67, X68

*MASSON, Paul-Marie   France   1882   1954
    LMD, REM

*MAŠTALÍŘ, Jaroslav   Czechoslovakia   1906
    CCZ, EVM, LMD, WI69

*MATA, Julio   Costa Rica   1899
    REM

MATCHAVARIANI, Alexey
    Davidovitch
    See: MACHAVARIANI, Aleksei Davidovich

*MATĚJ, Jožka   Czechoslovakia   1922
    CCZ, IMD2, MEH, MNP65/6, MNP67/8, MNP69/7, MNP70/5,
    MNP72/2, MNP72/4, X64, X65, X68

MATEO, Mario   Spain   1889
    EVM

*MATETIĆ-RONJGOV, Ivan   Yugoslavia   1880   1960
    HCM, IMD, KMJ, LMD, REM, X67

MATHER, Bruce   Canada   1939
    BB71, CA13, CCM, CCM71, CVM, KEY, LMD, MCO, MCO68,
    MCO71, NLC, X65, X68

*MATHEY, Paul   Switzerland   1909
    SCHW

MATHIAS, William James   Great Britain   1934   Wales
    WI69, X64, X65, X66, X67, X68

*MATHIEU, André René   Canada   1929   1968
    X68

*MATHIEU, Rodolphe   Canada   1896
    CCM, CVM, KEY, MCO, MCO68

*MATIČIČ, Janez   Yugoslavia   1926
    BB65, BB71, CME, IMD, KMJ, LMD, REM, X67

MATOUŠEK, Lukáš   Czechoslovakia   1943
    MNP69/4, MNP72/9

MATSAVARIANI, A.
    See: MACHAVARIANI

MATSUDAIRA, Yoriaki   Japan   1931
    IMD, LMD, X65, X67

*MATSUDAÏRA, Yoritsune   Japan   1907
    DDM, IMD, IMD2, LMD, MEH, REM, X65, X67, X68

MATSUMURA, Teizo   Japan   1929
    IMD2, X67

MATSUSHITA, Shin-Ichi   Japan   1922
    BB71, IMD2, LMD, MNG, REM, X65

MATTER, René   France   1921
    ACM

MATTFELD, Julius   USA   1893   1968
    BB71, LMD, X64, X65, X66, X67, X68

MATTHES, René   Switzerland   1897   1967
    LMD, MLA24/4, REM, SCHW, X65, X67

*MATTHE, Wilhelm   Germany   1889
    EVM

*MATTHEWS, Denis   Great Britain   1919
    X64, X65, X67, X68

*MATTHEWS, Harvey Alexander   USA   1879   Great Britain
    AS66, BB71, X67
    AS66: MATTHEWS, Harry Alexander

MATTHEWS, Holon   USA   1904
    AS66, PCM, X66

MATTHEWS, William   USA   1950
    BS72

MATTHUS, Siegfried   Germany   1934
    LMD, SML, X64, X65, X67, X68

MATTILA, Edward C.   USA
    AA73, ASUC, CAP, X66, X67

*MATTON, Roger   Canada   1929
    DDM, KEY, MCO, MCO68, MCO71, TFB, X68

MATURANO, Eduardo   Chile   1920
    QLA

MATUSOW, Harvey   USA   1926

*MATVEYEV, Mikhail
    Aleksandrovich   USSR   1912
    LMD, PPU69/2

*MATYS, Jiří   Czechoslovakia 1927
    BB65, BB71, CCZ, LMD, MEH, X67

MATZ, Arnold   1904
    IMD

*MATZ, Rudolf   Yugoslavia   1901
    EVM, HCM, IMD, KMJ, LMD, X64, X67, X68

*MAUERSBERGER, Rudolf   Germany   1889   1971
    BB71, EMS, IMD, LMD, MLA28/4, SML, X64, X67, X68
    EMS: МАУЭРСБЕРГЕР

*MAURICE-JACQUET, H.   USA   1886   1954
    AS66   France

MAURICK, Ludwig   1898
    IMD

MAURY, Lowndes   USA   1911
    AS66, BB65, BB71, LMD, PCM, PC71, X64, X65, X67, X68

MAV, Lojze   Yugoslavia   1898
    KMJ

*MAW, Nicholas   Great Britain 1935
    BB65, BB71, CME, LMD, OCM, WI69, X64, X65, X66, X67,
    X68

*MAWET, Emile   France   1884
    ACM, EVM

MAXFIELD, Richard Vance   USA   1927
    BB71, IMD, X68

MAXWELL DAVIES, Peter
   See: DAVIES, Peter Maxwell

MAYBORODA, H.
   See: MAIBORODA, G. I.

MAYER, John Henry   Great Britain   1930   India
   WI69, X66

MAYER, Lise Maria   Austria   1894
   EVM

MAYER, William R.   USA   1925
   AA73, AS66, BB65, BB71, DN72, LMD, PCM, PC71, X64,
   X65, X66, X67, X68

MAYOR, Charles   Switzerland   1876   1950
   SCHW

MAYR, Hanns   1906
   IMD

*MAYUZUMI, Toshiro   Japan   1929
   BB65, BB71, DDM, IMD, IMD2, LMD, MEH, X64, X65, X66,
   X67, X68

*MAZAEV, Arkadi Nikolaevich   USSR   1909
   EMS, PPU
   EMS: МАЗАЕВ

*MAZELLIER, Jules   France   1879   1959
   DMF, EVM

MAZZACURATI, Benedetto   Italy   1898
   LMD

*MAZZOLENI, Ettore   Canada   1905   1968
   BB71, EVM, LMD, X68   Switzerland

MAZZOTTA, Bruno   Italy   1921
   LMD, REM

MC BETH, W. Francis   USA   1933
   PC71

*MC BRIDE, Robert Guyn   USA   1911
   CA9, EVM, LMD, PCM, REM

MC CABE, John   Great Britain   1939
   BB71, WI69, X64, X65, X66, X67, X68

MC CARTY, Frank Lee   USA   1941
   CAP, DN72

*MC CAULEY, William
  Alexander   Canada   1917
    CCM, CCM71, CVMa, MCO, MCO68, NLC, NLCa, PCM, X68

MC CURDY, John H.
  See: RIEGGER, Wallingford

MC DANIEL, William J.   USA   1918
  CAP, DN70, DN72

MC DONALD, Boyd   Canada
  KEY

*MC DONALD, Harl   USA   1899   1955
  AS66, EVM, LMD, PCM, REM

MC DOWELL, John Herbert   USA   1926
  BB71

MC GRATH, Joseph John   USA   1889   1968
  X68

MC GRAW, Cameron   USA   1919
  AS66, X64, X65, X66, X67, X68

MCHVEDLIDZE, Chalva
  Mihailovich
  See: MSHVELIDZE

*MC INTYRE, Margaret   Canada   England
  MCO

*MC INTYRE, Paul Poirier   Canada   1931
  CCM, CCM71, CVM, CVMa, MCO, MCO71, NLC, X65

MC KAY, Francis Howard   USA   1901
  AS66

*MC KAY, George Frederick   USA   1899   1970
  AS66, BB71, CAP, DN70, EVM, PCM, PC71, X64, X65, X66,
  X67, X68

MC KAY, Neil   USA   1924   Canada
  AA73, AS66, CAP, MCO, PCM

MC KIE, Duncan   Australia   1904   China
  AMM

MC KIE, William Neil   Australia   1901
  EVM, X68

*MC KINLEY, Carl Keister   USA   1895   1966
  BB71, LMD, REM, X66

MC LEAN, Barton   USA
  ASUC

MC MULLIN, Robert W.   Canada   1921 USA
  MCO, MCO68

MC NEIL, J. Charles   USA   1902
  AS66

*MCNULTY, Daniel Aloysius Ireland   1920
  WI69

MC PEEK, Benjamin D.   Canada   1934
  CCM, CVM, KEY

*MC PHEE, Colin   USA   1901 1964
  BB71, DDM, EVM, LMD, PCM, REM, X64,   Canada
  X66, X67, X68

MEAD, Edward G.   USA   1892
  AS66

MEAD, George   USA   1902
  AS66, X67, X68

MEALE, Richard Graham   Australia   1932
  AMM, X65, X66, X67

MECHEM, Kirke L.   USA   1925
  PCM, PC71, X65, X66, X67

MEDICI, Mario   Italy   1913
  REM

*MEDICUS, Waldo   Italy   1896
  REM

MEDIN, Nino   Italy   1904 1969
  LMD

MEDINS, Yakov Gregorievich USSR   1885 1971
  EMS, LMD   Latvia
  LMD: MEDINS, Jekabs
  EMS: МЕДЫНЬ

*MEDINŠ, Janis Ivan
  Gregorievich   USSR   1890 1966
  BB71, EMS, EVM, REM   Latvia
  EMS: МЕДЫНЬ

*MEDTNER, Nikolai Karlovich   USSR   1880 1951
  DDM, EMS, EVM, IMD, LMD, MEH, REM, SML, WTM,
  X65, X67
  MEH: METNER
  EMS: МЕТНЕР

*MEEK, Kenneth   Canada   1908 England
  CCM71, CVM, KEY, NLC

MEEROVICH, Ilya Mikhaylovich USSR   1906
  PPU

*MEESTER, Louis de   Belgium   1904
  DDM, EVM, LMD, REM

MÉFANO, Paul   France   1937
  BB71, LMD, QQF, X66, X67, X68

*MEHLER, Friedrich   Sweden   1896 Germany
  FST, IMD

*MEHLICH, Ernst   Brazil   1888 Germany
  EVM
  EVM: 1890

MEIER, Hermann   Switzerland   1906
  SCHW

MEIER, Jaroslav   Czechoslovakia 1923
  CCZ, MEH, X65, X68, ZE71/3

MEIER, Klaus
  See: CORNELL, Klaus

MEIJER, Bernard van den
  Sigtenhorst   Netherlands   1888 1953
  CME

*MEISEL, Will   Germany   1897 1967
  X64, X67

*MEISTER, Karl August   Germany   1903
  EVM, LMD, REM, X68

*MEITUS, Juli Sergeyevich   USSR   1903
  BB65, BB71, LMD, MEH, REM, X64, X66, X67
  LMD and MEH: MEJTUS
  EMS: МЕЙТУС

*MEJIA, Estanislao   Mexico   1882
  EVM

*MELACHRINO, George
   Miltiades   Great Britain   1909   1965
   X65, X67

*MELCHERS, Henrik Melcher   Sweden   1882   1961
   EVM, FST, KSV, LMD, REM, SIM, SIMa

*MELICHAR, Alois   Austria   1896
   BB71, EVM, IMD, LMD, REM, SML, WI69, WWG, X65, X66

MELIKOV, Arif Dzhangirovich   USSR   1933
   EMS, MEH, PPU, X65, X68
   EMS: МЕЛИКОВ

*MELITZ, Leo   Switzerland   1890
   EVM

*MELKIKH, Dmitri
   Mikheyevitch   USSR   1885   1943
   BB71

*MELLERS, Wilfred Howard   Great Britain   1914
   BB71, CME, DDM, LMD, OCM, REM, WI69, X65, X66, X68

MELLNÄS, Arne   Sweden   1933
   BB71, CME, FST, KSV, IMD, LMD, SIM, SIMa, SOW, STS,
   SWE, VTM, X65, X66, X67, X68
   CME and SWE: 1934

*MELNGAILIS, Emil
   Yakovlevich   USSR   1874   1954
   EMS, LMD, SML   Latvia
   EMS: МЕЛНГАЙЛИС

MELO GORIGOYTÍA, Héctor   1899
   IMD

*MENA, Luis Emilio   Dominican   1895   1965
   MLA22/4   Republic

*MENASCE, Jacques de   USA   1905   1960
   BB65, BB71, EVM, LMD, REM   Austria

*MENDELSOHN, Alfred   Rumania   1910   1966
   BB65, BB71, CME, EMS, LMD, MLA24/4, RCL, REM, SML,
   X64, X65, X66
   EMS: МЕНДЕЛЬСОН

*MENDELSOHN, Oscar   Australia   1896
   WI69
   Pseudonym: MILSEN, Oscar

MENDES, Roberto   Brazil

*MENDOZA, Vicente T.   Mexico   1894   1965
    EVM, IMD, QLA, X64, X65, X66

*MENGELBERG, Karel Willem
    Joseph   Netherlands   1902
    EVM, IMD, NED, X68

*MENGELBERG, Kurt Rudolf   Netherlands   1892   1959
    BB71, EVM, IMD, LMD, REM   Germany

MENGELBERG, Misja   Netherlands
    X67

*MENGES, Siegfried
    Frederick Herbert   Great Britain   1902   1972
    EVM, MLA29/4

MENKE, Emma   USA
    LCI

*MENNIN, Peter   USA   1923
    AS66, BB65, BB71, EVM, IMD, LMD, PCM, REM, WI69, WTM,
    X65, X66, X68
    Formerly: MENNINI

*MENNINI, Louis A.   USA   1920
    AS66, LMD, PCM, REM, X64

*MENOTTI, Gian-Carlo   USA   1911   Italy
    AS66, BB65, BB71, CME, DDM, EMS, EVM, IMD, IMD2,
    LMD, MEH, REM, SML, WI69, WTM, X64, X65, X66,
    X67, X68
    EMS: МЕНОТТИ

*MERCURE, Pierre   Canada   1927   1966
    BB65, BB71, CCM, CVM, CVMa, DDM, IMD, IMD2, LMD,
    MCO, MCO68, MLA23/4, NLC, TFB, X67

MERES, Corneliu   Rumania   1910
    RCL

*MERIKANTO, Aare   Finland   1893   1958
    BB65, BB71, COF, DDM, EMS, EVM, IMD, LMD, REM, VTM,
    X66
    EMS: МЕРИКАНТО

*MERILÄINEN, Usko Aatos   Finland   1930
    CME, COF, IMD2, KKO, LMD, VTM, X65, X66, X67

MERKU, Pavle   Italy   1927
    IMD2, KMJ, LMD, MSC, TSC, X67
    KMJ: 1929

MERMOUD, Robert   Switzerland   1912
    SCHW

*MERRICK, Frank   Great Britain   1886
    EVM, LMD, X65, X66, X67, X68

MERRILL, Lindsey   USA
    ASUC

*MERSSON, Boris   Switzerland   1921   Germany
    IMD, SCHW, X67

*MERZ, Viktor   Great Britain   1891   Germany
    EVM

MESHKO, Nina   USSR
    PPU69/4, X66

*MESSELL, Erik   Denmark   1891   1971

*MESSERVY, George Thomas Great Britain   circa
    WI69   1920

*MESSIAEN, Olivier Eugène
    Prosper Charles   France   1908
    BB65, BB71, CME, CMF5, CMF20, CMF40, DDM, DMF, DMM,
    EL:1, EMS, EVM, IMD, LMD, MEH, MZW, PAP, QQF, REM,
    SML, TCM, TSC, VNM, WI69, WTM, X64, X65, X66, X67,
    X68
    EMS: МЕССИАН

*MESSING, Roman   Israel   1911   Poland
    WWI

*MESSNER, Joseph   Austria   1893   1969
    BB71, EVM, LMD, REM, WI69, WWG, X67, X68

MESTRES QUADRENY, Jose
    Maria   Spain   1929
    CME, X67, X68

METDEPENNINGHEN, Gabriel Belgium   1877
    EVM

*MÉTÉHEN, Jacques   France   1903
    QQF

METIANU, Lucian   Rumania   1937
    RCL

METZLER, Friedrich   Germany   1910
    IMD, LMD, WI69

*MEULEMANS, Arthur
   Josephus Ludovicus   Belgium   1884   1966
     BB71, CBC, DDM, EVM, IMD, LMD, MLA23/4, REM, X64,
     X65, X66, X67

MEVER, Pieter Andriaan van   Netherlands   1899
   EVM

MEYER, Alexandre Henri   France   1896   1968
   ACM

*MEYER, Ernst Hermann   Germany   1905
     DDM, EMS, IMD, IMD2, LMD, MEH, REM, SML, WWG,
     X64, X65, X66, X67, X68
     EMS: МЕЙЕР

*MEYER, Gustav William   Germany   1887   1965
   X65

MEYER, Krzysztof   Poland   1943
   X68

*MEYER BREMEN, Alexander
   von   Germany   1930
   IMD

*MEYER-OLBERSLEBEN,
   Ernst Ludwig   Germany   1898
   LMD, WWG

*MEYEROWITZ, Jan   USA   1913   Germany
     BB65, BB71, LMD, OCM, PCM, REM, SML, X64, X65, X66,
     X67, X68

*MEYER-TORMIN, Wolfgang   Germany   1911
   IMD

MEYLINK, Cornelis Johannes   Netherlands   1894
   EVM

MEYTUS, Yuliy Sergeevich   USSR   1903
     EMS, PPU, PPU69/2, PPU69/4, X67
     EMS: МЕЙТУС

*MAISKOVSKY, Nikolay
   Yakovlevich   USSR   1881   1950
     BB65, BB71, CME, DDM, EMS, EVM, IMD, LMD, MEH, REM,
     SCD, SML, WTM, X64, X65, X66, X67, X68
     EVM: MJASKOWSKI   IMD: MJASKOWSKIJ
     LMD: MJASKOVSKIJ   SML: MJASKOWSKI
     EMS: МЯСКОВСКИЙ

*MICHAËL, Edward   France   1921
 IMD

MICHAELIDES, Peter S.   USA
 AA73, ASUC, X68

*MICHAELIDES, Solon   Greece   1905
 EVM

*MICHAELS, Jost   Germany   1922
 X68

MICHALSKY, Donal Ray   USA   1928
 PCM, PC71, X66

*MICHEELSEN, Hans Friedrich Germany   1902
 EVM, IMD, LMD, X64, X65, X67, X68

MICHELI, Umberto   1903
 IMD

MICHELOT, Maurice   France   1900

*MICHETTI, Vincenzo   Italy   1878 1956
 LMD, REM

MICHIELSENS, Hugo   Belgium   1903
 EVM

*MICHL, Artur   Austria   1897 1965
 EVM, LMD, MLA23/4, REM, X66

MICHROVSKY, Issachar
 See: MIRON, Issachar

MICU, Eugeniu   Rumania   1910
 RCL

*MIDDELEER, Jean de   Belgium   1908
 EVM

MIDDLETON, Robert E.   USA   1920
 AA73, ASUC, PCM, PC71, X64, X65, X66, X67, X68

*MIEG, Peter   Switzerland 1906
 BB65, BB71, CME, DDM, EVM, LMD, REM, SCHW, WI69,
 WWS, X64, X65, X66, X68

*MIERCZYŃSKI, Stanisław Poland   1894 1952
 LMD, X67

MIEREANU, Costin   Rumania   1943
 LMD, RCL, X67, X68

*MIERZEJEWSKI, Mieczyslaw   Poland   1905
   EVM

*MIES, Paul   Germany   1889
   EVM, X64, X65, X66, X67, X68

*MIESSNER, William Otto   USA   1880   1967
   EVM, X66, X67

*MIGGL, Erwin   Austria   1923
   X67

MIGNAN, Édouard-Charles-
   Octave   France   1884   1969
   BB71

*MIGNONE, Francisco   Brazil   1897
   DDM, EVM, IMD, LMD, REM, WTM, X67

*MIGOT, Georges Elbert   France   1891
   BB65, BB71, CMF19, CMF40, DDM, DMF, IMD, LMD, QQF,
   REM, WI69, X65, X66

MIHĂILESCU-TOSCANI,
   Dumitru   Rumania   1888   1962
   RCL

*MIHALOVICI, Marcel   France   1898   Rumania
   BB65, BB71, CMF15, CMF20, CMF40, DDM, DMF, EMS, EVM,
   IMD, IMD2, LMD, MEH, QQF, RCL, REM, SML, X65, X66,
   X68
   EMS: МИХА́ЙЛОВИЧ

*MIHALY, András   Hungary   1917
   BB65, BB71, CHC, CME, IMD, IMD2, LMD, MEH, REM, SML,
   X66, X67, X68

MIHELČIĆ, Slavko   Yugoslavia   1912
   KMJ

MIHULE, Jiří   Czechoslovakia   1907
   CCZ

MIKHAILIDIS, Solon   Cyprus   1905
   REM

MIKHAILOV, Nikolai
   Nikolaevich   USSR   1902
   EMS, PPU69/2, X66, X67
   EMS: МИХА́ЙЛОВ

*MIKKOLA, Viljo   Finland   1871   1960
   COF

MIKODA, Bořivoj   Czechoslovakia   1904
   CCZ, X64

MIKULA, Zdenko   Czechoslovakia   1916
   CCZ, MNP68/1, ZE69/3, ZE70/1, ZE70/3, ZE71/1, ZE71/2,
   ZE71/3

MILBURN, Ellsworth   USA
   AA73

MILCOVEANU, Dumitru   Rumania   1914
   RCL

MILENKOVIĆ, Jelna   Yugoslavia   1944
   KMJ

MILELLA, Dino   Italy   1907
   LMD

MILETIĆ, Miroslav   Yugoslavia   1925
   BB65, BB71, HCM, IMD, KMJ, LMD, X66

*MILFORD, Robin Humphrey   Great Britain   1903   1959
   BB65, BB71, DDM, EVM, IMD, LMD, REM, X64, X68

*MILHAUD, Darius   France   1892
   BB65, BB71, CME, CMF12, CMF20, CMF40, DDM, DMF,
   EL:1, EMS, EVM, IMD, IMD2, LMD, MEH, MZW, PAP,
   QQF, REM, SML, TCM, VNM, WI69, WTM, X64, X65,
   X66, X67, X68
   EMS: МИЙО

MILLER, Charles   USA   1899   Russia
   AS66

*MILLER, Douglas   Great Britain   1888
   WI69

MILLER, Edward Jay   USA   1930
   IMD, PC71, X65

MILLER, Jacques   USA   1900   Russia
   AS66, PCM

MILLER, Jesse   USA   1935
   PC71

MILLER, Lewis M.   USA
   AA73

*MILLS, Charles Borromeo   USA   1914
   EVM, LMD, REM

MILLS-COCKELL, John   Canada   1943
  BB71, BCL, MCO71

*MILMAN, Mark Vladimirovich USSR   1910
  EMS, LMD
  EMS: МИЛЬМАН

*MILNE, Helen C.   Great Britain   1897
  WI69

*MILNER, Anthony Francis
  Dominic   Great Britain   1925
  BB65, BB71, DDM, IMD, LMD, MNG, OCM, REM, WI69,
  X64, X65, X66, X67, X68

*MILNER, Mihail Arnoldovich USSR   1886   1953
  EMS, LMD
  EMS: МИЛЬНЕР

MILOJEVIĆ, Dorde   Yugoslavia   1921
  KMJ

MILORAVA, Shota Ermolaevich USSR   1925
  EMS
  EMS: МИЛОРА́ВА

*MILOŠEVIĆ, Predrag   Yugoslavia   1904
  IMD, KMJ, LMD, X65, X66, X68

*MILOŠEVIĆ, Vlado   Yugoslavia   1901
  KMJ, X66, X67, X68

MILSEN, Oscar
  See: MENDELSOHN, Oscar

*MILVEDEN, Ingmar   Sweden   1920
  FST, SIM, SIMa, X68

*MILYUTIN, Yuri Sergeevich   USSR   1903   1968
  EMS, LMD, PPU68/4, SML, X64, X68
  LMD: MILJUTIN   SML: MILJUTIN
  EMS: МИЛЮТИН

MIMAROGLU, Ilhan Kemaleddin Turkey   1926
  BB65, BB71, LMD, X66, X68

MINAMI, Hiroaki   Japan
  PAP

*MINDLIN, Abraham   Israel   1899   1961
  ACU   Russia

*MIRAMONTES, Arnulfo   Mexico   1882 1960
    EVM, MMX

MIRANTE, Thomas   USA   1931
    PC71, WI69

MIRK, Vasilij   Yugoslavia   1844 1962
    LMD, MSC

MIROGLIO, Francis   France   1924
    IMD, IMD2, LMD, MNG, X67, X68

*MIRON, Issachar   Israel   1920 Poland
    ACU, MM59, WWI, X68
    Formerly: MICHROVSKY

*MIRONOV, Nikolai Nazarovich   USSR   1870 1952
    EMS
    EMS: МИРОНОВ

*MIROUZE, Marcel   France   1906 1957
    DDM, DMF, IMD, LMD
    DMF: 1908-1956

MIRZOEV, M.   USSR

MIRZOYAN, Edvard
  Michailovich   USSR   1921
    BB65, BB71, CME, DDM, EMS, LMD, MEH, PPU69/2, SML,
    X64, X65, X67, X68
    SML: MIRSOJAN
    EMS: МИРЗОЯН

*MISRAKI, Paul   France   1908 Turkey
    EVM, QQF, WI69
    Formerly: MISRACHI

MISSAL, Joshua M.   USA
    AA73, X67, X68

MISTAK, Alvin Frank   USA   1930
    DN72

MISTERLY, Eugene   USA
    CAP

*MITCHEL, Lyndol   USA   1923 1964
    PCM, PC71

MITCHELL, Raymond Earle   USA   1895
    AS66

MITREA-CILARIANU, Mihai G.　Rumania　　1935
　LMD, RCL

*MITROPOULOS, Dimitri　　USA　　　1893　1961
　BB65, BB71, DDM, EL:1, EMS, EVM, LMD,　　Greece
　MEH, PAP, REM, SML, X67, X68
　EMS: МИТРОПУЛОС
　EMS: 1960

*MITSUKURI, Shukichi　　Japan　　1895
　DDM, IMD, LMD, REM
　DDM and LMD: MIT_UKURI

*MITTLER, Franz　　　USA　　　1893　1970
　BB71, EVM, IMD, X68　　　　　　Austria

*MIXA, Franz　　　Austria　　1902
　LMD, REM

*MIYAGI, Michio　　Japan　　1894　1956
　LMD

MIYOSHI, Akira　　Japan　　1933
　BB71, IMD2, LMD, X65

MIZELLE, Dary John　　USA　　1940
　BB71, X68

MLEJNEK, Vilém Prokop　　Czechoslovakia　1906
　CCZ

MŁODZIEJOWSKI, Jerzy　　Poland　　1909
　PKW, X64, X67

*MOBBS, Kenneth William　　Great Britain　1925
　X64, X65

MOCANU, Vasile　　Rumania　　1908
　RCL

MODR, Antonín　　Czechoslovakia　1898
　CCZ, X68

*MOERAN, Ernest John　　Great Britain　1894　1950
　DDM, EVM, LMD, REM, X64　　　　Ireland

*MOESCHINGER, Albert John　Switzerland　1897
　CME, DDM, EVM, IMD, IMD2, LMD, REM, SCHW, WI69,
　WWS, X65, X67, X68

*MOEVS, Robert W. USA 1921
  AA73, ASUC, BB65, BB71, LMD, PCM, PC71, X65, X66,
  X67, X68
  PCM and PC71: 1920

*MOFFAT, Alfred Edward Great Britain 1866 1950
  EVM, LMD, REM Scotland
  REM: 1868-1950

MOFFATT, Richard C. USA 1927
  AS66

*MOHAUPT, Richard Germany 1904 1957
  BB71, DDM, EMS, EVM, IMD, LMD, REM, SML, X66
  EMS: МОХАУПТ

*MOHLER, Philipp Heinrich Germany 1908
  DDM, EVM, IMD, LMD, REM, SML, WWG, X68

*MOHR, Wilhelm Germany 1904
  LMD, WWG, X64, X65, X66, X68

*MOISSE, Séverin Joseph Canada 1895 Belgium
  KEY

*MOJSISOVICS, Roderich,
  Edler von Mojsvar Austria 1877 1953
  EVM, IMD, LMD, REM

MOJZIS, Vojtech Czechoslovakia 1949
  MNP72/9

*MOKRANJAC, Vasilje Yugoslavia 1923
  BB71, KMJ, LMD, X66, X67, X68

MOKREJS, John USA 1875 1968
  BB65, BB71

*MOKROUSOV, Boris
  Andreevich USSR 1909 1968
  BB71, EMS, EVM, LMD, MEH, MLA25/4, PPU, SML, X68
  EMS: МОКРОУСОВ

*MOLCHANOV, Kiril
  Kladimirovich USSR 1922
  CME, EMS, LMD, MEH, REM, SML, X64, X65, X67, X68
  LMD and MEH: MOLČANOV REM: MOLCIANOV
  SML: MOLTSCHANOW
  EMS: МОЛЧАНОВ

MOLDOVAN, Mihai Rumania 1937
  RCL

MOLEIRO, Moisés   Venezuela   1905
  CA14

*MOLINA, Antonio J.   Philippines   1894
  X64

MØLLER, Peter   Denmark
  DMTsp

*MOLNÁR, Antal Jenö   Hungary   1890
  CHC, CME, DDM, EMS, EVM, LMD, REM, SML, X64, X68
  EMS: МОЛЬНАР

MOMPELLIO, Federico   Italy   1908
  IMD, REM, X67, X68

*MOMPOU, Federico   Spain   1893
  BB71, DDM, EVM, LMD, REM, WI69, X65

*MONCAYO, José Pablo   Mexico   1912   1958
  EVM, IMD, LMD, MMX

MONCHE, Rene   France   1898
  ACM

MONELLO, Spartaco Vindice USA   1909
  AS66, X64

MONFEUILLARD, René   France   1886   1958
  ACM

MONFRED, Avenir H. de   France   1903   Russia
  BB65, BB71, LMD

MONIER, Georges   Belgium   1892
  EVM

*MONNIKENDAM, Marius   Netherlands   1896
  DDM, EVM, LMD, NED, REM, X64, X66, X67

*MONRAD JOHANSEN, David   Norway   1888
  CNO, DDM, EVM, LMD, VTM
  DDM, EVM, LMD and VTM: JOHANSEN, David Monrad

MONS, Franz   Germany   1926

MONTANARI, Nunzio   Italy   1915
  LMD

*MONTANI, Giuseppe   Italy   1888
  LMD, REM

*MONTANI, Oreste   Italy   1900
    IMD, LMD, REM

*MONTANI, Pasquale   Italy   1885
    REM

*MONTANI, Pietro   Italy   1895   1967
    IMD, LMD, REM

*MONTECINO-MONTALVA,
    Alfonso   Chile   1924
    EVM, LMD, REM, X68

*MONTEMEZZI, Italo   Italy   1875   1952
    DDM, EMS, EVM, LMD, WTM, X64, X68
    EMS: МОНТЕМЕ́ЦЦИ

MONTÈS, Juan   Argentina   1902   Poland
    EVM

MONTIA, Emil   Rumania   1882   1965
    RCL, X65

MONTICO, Mario   Italy   1885   1959
    LMD

*MONTSALVATGE BASSOLS,
    Xavier   Spain   1912
    BB65, BB71, DDM, EVM, LMD, REM, X65

MOON, Charles L.   USA
    ASUC

*MOORE, Douglas Stuart   USA   1893   1969
    AS66, BB65, BB71, DDM, EVM, LMD, MLA26/4, PCM,
    PC71, REM, WI69, WTM, X64, X65, X66, X67, X68
    PC71: 1970

*MOORE, Ernest Alwyn   Canada   1899   England
    NLC, NLCa

*MOORE, Mary Carr   USA   1873   1957
    AS66

*MOORE, Timothy   Great Britain   1922
    WI69, X64

*MOORTEL, Arie van de   Belgium   1918
    EVM, WI69

*MORTGAT, Alfons J. I.   Belgium   1881
    WI69

MOPPER, Irving   USA   1914
 AS66

*MORALES, Ollalo Juan
 Magnus   Sweden 1874 1957
  BB65, BB71, EVM, FST, IMD, KSV, LMD, Spain
 SIM, SIMa

MORAN, Robert Leonard USA   1937
 BB71, IMD, MNG, PCM, X65, X68

*MORAWETZ, Oscar   Canada 1917 Czecho-
 BB65, BB71, CCM, CVM, CVMa, IMD, slovakia
 IMD2, KEY, LMD, MCO, MCO68,
 MCO71, NLC, NLCa, TFB, X68

*MORE, Margaret Elizabeth Great Britain 1903
 EVM

*MOREL, François d'Assise Canada 1926
 BB65, BB71, CCM, CCM71, DDM, IMD, KEY, LMD, MCO,
 MCO68, TFB, X68

MORENO, Gus   Mexico 1910 1950
 MMX

*MORENO, Segundo Luis Ecuador 1882
 LMD, REM

*MORENO GANS, José Spain   1897
 EVM, LMD

*MORENO TORROBA, Federico Spain   1891
 DDM, EVM, LMD, REM

*MOREUX, Serge   France 1900 1959
 EVM, LMD

MORGAN, David Sydney Great Britain 1932
 WI69, X68

MORGAN, Howard   Great Britain 1945
 WI69

MORGAN, Robert P.   USA
 ASUC

*MORGENROTH, Alfred Karl Germany 1900
 IMD

*MORGENSTERN, Sam USA
 PC71, X68

*MORILLO, Roberto García   Argentina   1911
   EVM

*MORITZ, Edvard   USA   1891   Germany
   EVM, LMD, PC71, WI69

*MOROI, Makoto   Japan   1930
   BB71, DDM, IMD, IMD2, LMD, MEH, REM, X65

*MOROI, Saburô   Japan   1903
   DDM, LMD, MEH, REM

MOROIANU, Bogdan   Rumania   1915
   LMD, RCL

*MOROSS, Jerome   USA   1913
   EVM, PCM, X64

*MOROZOV, Igor Vladimirovich USSR   1913
   EMS, EVM, PPU, X68
   EVM: MOROSOW
   EMS: МОРÓЗОВ

MOROZOV, Ioan   Rumania   1885   1965
   RCL

MORRICONE, Ennio   Italy   1928
   LMC, X65, X67

MORRIS, Franklin E.   1920
   WAN

*MORRIS, Harold Cecil   USA   1890   1964
   AS66, BB65, BB71, EVM, LMD, PCM, X64, X65

MORRIS, Haydn   Great Britain   1891   1965
   MLA23/4, X66, X67   Wales

MORRISON, Julia   USA
   AA73

*MORTARI, Virgilio   Italy   1902
   DDM, EL:1, EVM, IMD, LMD, X64

*MORTELMANS, Ivo Oscar   Belgium   1901
   EVM, LMD, REM

*MORTELMANS, Lodewijk   Belgium   1868   1952
   CME, DDM, EVM, LMD, REM, X67

*MORTENSEN, Finn   Norway   1922
   BB71, CME, CNO, DNS, LMD, VTM, X64, X65, X67

*MORTENSEN, Otto   Denmark   1907
    BB65, BB71, IMD, LMD, REM, VTM

MORTHENSON, Jan W.   Sweden   1940
    CME, DNS, FST, IMD, IMD2, LMD, PAP, SIM, SIMa,
    SOW, STS, SWE, VTM, X65, X66, X67, X68

MORÝ, Ján   Czechoslovakia   1892
    CCZ, MEH
    MEH: 1897

MORYL, Richard   USA
    AA73

MOSER, Camillo   Italy   1932
    LMD

*MOSER, Hans Joachim   Germany   1889   1967
    BB71, EMS, EVM, LMD, MEH, REM, SML, X64, X65, X66,
    X67
    EMS: МОЗЕР

*MOSER, Rudolf   Switzerland   1892   1960
    BB65, EVM, IMD, LMD, REM, SCHW, X64, X66

MOSHKOV, Boris Prokopievich   USSR   1903
    EMS
    EMS: МОШКОВ

MOSOLOV, Aleksandr
    Vasilievich   USSR   1900
    EMS, IMD, LMD, SML
    IMD and SML: MOSSOLOW
    EMS: МОСОЛОВ

*MOSS, Cyril   Canada   1891   England
    NLC

*MOSS, Lawrence Kenneth   USA   1927
    AA73, ASUC, BB65, BB71, DN70, LMD, PCM, PC71, X66,
    X67, X68

MOSSMAN, Ted   USA   1914
    AS66

MOSSO, Carlo   Italy   1931
    LMD

*MOSSOLOV, Alexander
    Vassilievich   USSR   1900
    DDM, EVM, MEH, REM
    MEH: MOSOLOV

MOSUSOVA, Nadežda   Yugoslavia   1928
    KMJ, X68

MOSZUMAŃSKA-NAZAR,
    Krystyna   Poland   1924
    IMD, PKW, X64, X65, X66, X67

*MOTTE, Diether de la   Germany   1928
    IMD, LMD, X64, X65, X66, X67, X68

*MOULAERT, Pierre   Belgium   1907   1967
    CBC, LMD, X66, X67

*MOULAERT, Raymond   Belgium   1875   1962
    BB65, BB71, CBC, DDM, EVM, IMD, LMD, REM

*MOULE-EVANS, David   Great Britain   1905
    WI69

MOUNSEY, Robert P.   USA   1952
    BS70

MOUSHEL, Georgii Aleksandrovich
    See: MUSHEL, Georgi Aleksandrovich

*MOYZES, Alexander   Czechoslovakia   1906
    CCZ, DDM, EMS, EVM, IMD, LMD, MEH, MNP66/6,
    MNP67/2, SML, X66, X68, ZE69/1, ZE69/3, ZE70/1,
    ZE70/2, ZE70/3, ZE71/1, ZE71/2, ZE71/3, ZE72/1
    EMS: МОЙЗЕС

MÓŽI, Aladar   Czechoslovakia   1923
    CCZ, X67

MROSZCZYK, Karol   Poland   1905
    PKW

*MSHVELIDZE, Shalva
    Mikhailovich   USSR   1904
    BB65, BB71, DDM, EMS, MEH, PPU, PPU69/2, SML, X64,
    X67, X68
    DDM: MCHVELIDZE   MEH: MŠVELIDZE   SML: MSCHWELIDSE
    EMS: МШВЕЛИДЗЕ

*MUCK, Karl   Germany   1893
    X65

*MUCZYNSKI, Robert   USA   1929
    AS66, BB65, BB71, CA9, PCM, PC71, X64, X67, X68

MUDDE, Willem   Netherlands   1909
    EVM

*MUELLER, Frederick USA 1921 Germany
    ASUC, DAS

MUELLER, Robert USA 1920
    LCI, X65

*MUEREN, Florentijn Jan
    Van der Belgium 1890 1966
    X67

MÜHE, Hansgeorg Germany 1929
    IMD, SML

*MÜHLHÖLZL, Friedrich Germany 1918
    WWG

*MUKHATOV, Velimuhamed USSR 1916
    EMS, LMD, PPU, PPU69/2, SML, X67
    SML: MUCHATOW
    EMS: МУХÁТОВ

*MUL, Jan Netherlands 1911
    DDM, EVM, IMD, LMD, NED, X64, X65, X66, X68

MULAZZI, Riccardo Italy 1915
    LMD, REM

*MULDER, Ernest Willem Netherlands 1898
    EVM

*MULÈ, Giuseppe Italy 1885 1951
    EVM, IMD, LMD

MULET, Henri France 1878 1967
    DDM, X68

*MULFINGER, George
    Leonidas USA 1900
    WI69

*MULGAN, Denis Mason Great Britain 1915 New Zealand
    WI69

*MÜLLER, Gottfried Germany 1914
    EVM, IMD

MULLER, Jean France 1894 1957
    ACM

*MÜLLER, Ludwig Germany 1879
    REM
    Formerly: WALDMÜLLER, Ludwig

MÜLLER, Ludwig Richard   Germany   1903   1967
    LMD, SML, X67

MÜLLER, Paul Zürich
    See: MÜLLER ZÜRICH, Paul

*MÜLLER, Sigfrid Walther   Germany   1905   1946
    IMD

*MÜLLER-HARTMANN, Robert   Great Britain   1884   1950
    EVM, LMD, REM   Germany

*MÜLLER-HERMANN, Johanna   Austria   1878
    IMD

*MÜLLER-KRAY, Hans   Germany   1908   1969
    LMD

*MÜLLER von KULM, Walter   Switzerland   1899   1967
    BB71, EVM, IMD, LMD, SCHW, WI69, X65, X66, X67, X68
    WI69: MULER von KULM, Walter

*MÜLLER-ZÜRICH, Paul   Switzerland   1898
    BB71, CME, DDM, EVM, IMD, LMD, SCHW, WWS, X64,
    X65, X66, X67, X68
    Frequently listed: MÜLLER, Paul Zürich

MULLINS, Hugh   USA
    CAP, PCM, X64

MUMMA, Gordon   USA   1935
    BB71, BCL, EL:2, X64, X67, X68

*MÜNCH, Hans   Switzerland   1893
    EVM, LMD, REM, SCHW, WWS, X66

MUNCH, Jean Sebastien   France   1893
    ACM

MUÑOZ, José Luis   Venezuela   1928
    CA14, X66

*MUÑOZ MOLLEDA, José   Spain   1905
    DDM, EVM, LMD, REM
    DDM: MUNOZ MOLLEDA, Manuel
    EVM: 1885

*MURADELI, Vano Irakly Ilich   USSR   1908   1970
    BB65, BB71, EMS, EVM, LMD, MEH, MLA27, PPU, PPU68/1,
    PPU69/1, PPU69/2, REM, SML, X64, X65, X66, X67, X68
    EMS: МУРАДÉЛИ

*MURAVLEV, Aleksei
  Alekseyevich   USSR   1924
    EMS, EVM, LMD, PPU
    EMS: МУРАЛЁВ

MURESIANU, Iuliu   Rumania   1900   1956
    LMD, RCL, X68

MURGATROYD, Vernon   Canada
    KEY

*MURGIER, Jacques   France   1912
    EVM, IMD, QQF, WI69

*MURRAY, Bain   USA   1926
    AA73, BB71, PCM, X64, X65, X66, X67, X68

*MURRAY, Lyn   USA   1909   Great Britain
    AS66, PCM, PC71, X64

*MURRILL, Herbert Henry
  John   Great Britain 1909 1952
    EVM, DDM, LMD

*MUSGRAVE, Thea   Great Britain 1928 Scotland
    BB65, BB71, CME, DDM, LMD, MEH, OCM, REM, X64, X65,
    X67, X68

*MUSHEL, Georgi
  Aleksandrovich   USSR   1909
    EMS, MEH, X67
    EMS: МУШЕЛЬ   MEH: MUŠEL   Vol. I: See: MOUSHEL

MUSOLINO, Angelo   USA   1923
    AS66

*MYCIELSKI, Zygmunt   Poland   1907
    BB65, BB71, CME, EMS, IMD, LMD, MEH, PKW, REM,
    WI69, X65, X66, X67, X68
    EMS: МЫЦЕЛЬСКИЙ

MYERS, Robert   USA   1930
    DN72, X68

*MYKLEGAARD, Åge   Norway   1904
    CNO

MYROW, Frederic E.   USA   1939
    AS66, PCM, X65, X66, X68
    PCM: 1940

*NABÓKOV, Nicolas   USA   1903   Russia
  BB65, BB71, DDM, EMS, EVM, IMD, LMD, REM, X65, X68
  EMS: НАБÓКОВ

NADELMANN, Leo   Switzerland   1913
  SCHW

*NADENENKO, Fedor
  Nikolaievich   USSR   1902
  LMD, X64

*NADEZHIN, Boris Borisovich USSR   1905
  EMS, LMD
  LMD: NADEZDIN
  EMS: НАДЁЖИН

*NADIROV, Ivan Nikitich   USSR   1907   1941
  EMS, EVM
  EMS: НАДИРОВ

*NAGAN, Zvi Herbert   Israel   1912   Germany
  ACU, MM59, X68
  Formerly: NEUGARTEN

*NAGINSKI, Charles   USA   1909   1940
  EVM   Egypt

*NAGLER, Franciscus
  Johannes   Germany   1873   1957
  EVM, LMD

*NAKHABIN, Vladimir
  Nikolayevich   USSR   1910
  EMS, EVM, LMD
  EVM: NACHIBIN
  EMS: НАХÁБИН

*NANCARROW, Conlon   USA   1912
  WAN

NANI, Paolo   Italy   1906   Malta

*NAPOLI, Jacopo   Italy   1911
  BB65, X64, X65

NAPOLITANO, Emilia
  See: GUBITOSI, Emilia

*NAPOLITANO, France
  Michele   Italy   1887   1960
  LMD

NAPRAVNIK, Karel   Yugoslavia   1882   1968
  KMJ   Slovakia

*NARDI, Nachum   Israel   1901   Russia
  ACU, EVM

*NARIMANIDZE, Nikolai
  Vasilievich   USSR   1905
  EMS, EVM, LMD
  EMS: НАРИМАНИДЗЕ

NASIDZE, Sulkhan Ivanovich   USSR   1927
  BB65, BB71, EMS
  EMS: НАСИДЗЕ

*NASTASIJEVIĆ, Svetomir   Yugoslavia   1902
  BB71, KMJ, LMD, X66, X67

*NAT, Yves Phillippe   France   1890   1956
  DDM, DMF, EVM, LMD

*NATALETTI, Giorgio   Italy   1907   1972
  LMD, REM

NATANSON, Tadeusz   Poland   1927
  PKW, X67

NATHAN, Robert   USA   1894
  AS66

*NATRA, Sergiu   Israel   1924   Rumania
  ACU, CME, IMD, X64, X65, X68

*NAUMANN, Siegfried Eugen   Sweden   1919
  DDM, FST, SIM, SIMa, SOW, STS, SWE, VTM, X66, X67

*NAYLOR, Bernard James   Great Britain   1907
  CCM71, CVMa, IMD, LMD, MCO68, NLC, NLCa, X64, X65,
  X66, X67, X68

NEBUŠKA, Otakar   Czechoslovakia 1875   1952
  EVM, LMD

*NECHAEV, Vasili Vasilievich   USSR   1895   1956
  EMS, EVM, LMD
  EVM: NETSJAJEW   Vol. I: NETCHAIEV
  EMS: НЕЧÁЕВ

NEDBAL, Karel   Czechoslovakia 1888   1964
  EVM, LMD, X64

*NEDBAL, Manfred Josef
Maria   Austria   1902
WI69

NEEF, Wilhelm   Germany   1916
LMD, SML, X64, X68

NEEMAN, Amitai   Israel   1926
ACU

NE ER   China   1912 1935
EMS
EMS: НЕ ЗР

*NEES, Staf Gustaaf Frans Belgium   1901 1965
EVM, X65, X66

*NEF, Albert   Switzerland 1882 1966
BB71, DDM, EVM, LMD, SCHW, WWG, X67

*NEGREA, Martian   Rumania   1893
BB65, BB71, CME, EMS, LMD, MEH, RCL, REM, SML, X64,
X65
EMS: НЕГРЯ

*NEGRETE WOOLCOCK,
Samuel   Chile   1893
EVM, IMD, LMD

*NEGRI, Gino   Italy   1919
DDM, LMD, REM

NEGULESCU, Claudiu   Rumania   1929
RCL

NEIDHARDT-CASTELBRUMNO,
Nino   Germany   1889 1950
EVM, LMD

NEIKRUG, Marc   Germany   1946 USA
X67

NEIMARK, Iosif Gustavovich USSR   1903
EMS
EMS: НЕЙМАРК

*NEJEDLÝ, Vit   Czechoslovakia 1912 1945
BB65, BB71, CCZ, EMS, IMD2, MEH, REM, SML
EMS: НЕЕДЛЫ

NELHYBEL, Vaclav   USA   1919 Czecho-
BB71, IMD, X66, X67, X68   slovakia

*NELLESEN, Herman Josef   Germany   1923
   LMD, X67

*NELLIUS, Georg   Germany   1891   1952
   EVM, LMD, REM

*NELSON, John Havelock   Great Britain   1917   Ulster
   WI69

NELSON, Oliver E.   USA   1932
   BB71, PCM, X64, X65, X66, X67

NELSON, Paul   USA   1929
   AS66, PCM, X64, X66

NELSON, Ronald J. (Ron)   USA   1929
   ASUC, AS66, DN72, PCM, PC71, X64, X65, X67, X68

*NĚMEČEK, Emil   Czechoslovakia   1902
   EVM, LMD

NEMESCU, Octavian   Rumania   1940
   RCL

NÉMETH-ŠAMORÍNSKY,
  Stefan   Czechoslovakia   1896
   CCZ, X66, X68, ZE69/3, ZE70/2, ZE71/1, ZE71/2, ZE71/3

*NEMIROFF, Isaac   USA   1912
   AA73, ASUC, AS66, PCM, PC71

*NENOV, Dimitri Stefanov   Bulgaria   1901   1953
   BMK, IMD, LMD, SML, X67
   BMK: НЕНОВ
   IMD, LMD and SML: 1902

*NÉRINI, Emile   France   1882   1967
   BB71, EVM, LMD

NERO, Paul   USA   1917   Germany
   AS66

NESSLER, Robert   1919
   IMD2, X67

NESTEROV, Arkadi
  Aleksandrovich   USSR   1918
   EMS, PPU69/2, X66, X68
   EMS: НЕСТЕРОВ

*NESTLER, Gerhard   Germany   1900
   X68

NESTYEV, Izrail Vladimirovich USSR   1911
     EMS, PPU69/2, X65, X67, X68
     EMS: НЕСТЬЕВ

NETSJAJEW, W. W.
     See: NECHAEV, V. V.

NEUGARTEN, Zvi
     See: NAGAN, Zvi Herbert

NEUGEBOREN, Henrik   1901   1959
     IMD

NEUHAUS, Max   Sweden   circa
     X64, X65, X66   1940

NEUMANN, Edgar   Germany
     X68

*NEUMANN, Friedrich Gustav
     Ernst   Austria   1915
     X65, X66

NEUMANN, Věroslav   Czechoslovakia 1931
     CCZ, BB71, IMD2, MEH, MNP65/6, MNP66/9, MNP67/1,
     MNP67/7, X68

*NEUMAEYER, Fritz   Germany   1900
     EVM, IMD, LMD, SML, WWG

*NEVITOV, Mikhail Invanovich   USSR   1887   1969
     EVM, X67
     EMV: NEWITOW

NEWCATER, Graham   Union of   1941
     WSA   South Africa

*NEWLIN, Dika   USA   1923
     AA73, DAS, IMD, LMD, X64, X65, X66, X67, X68

NEWMAN, Anthony   USA   1941
     X67, X68

NEWMAN, Kent   USA   1925
     PCM

NEWMAN, Max   USA   1914   Austria
     AS66

*NEWMAN, Sidney Thomas
     Mayow   Great Britain   1906
     LMD

*NEWMAN, William S.   USA   1912
   BB71, DAS, LMD, REM, X64, X65, X66, X67, X68

NEWSOM, Hugh Raymond   USA   1891
   BB71

*NEWSON, George John   Great Britain   circa
   IMD, WI69, X68   1930

*NEY, Günter   Germany   1927
   WWG

*NEZERITIS, Andreas   Greece   1897
   DDM, EVM, LMD, REM

NIAGA, Georgi Stepanovich   USSR   1922
   LMD, PPU69/2
   LMD: NJAGA

NIAGA, Stepan Timofeievic   USSR   1900   1951
   EMS, LMD, REM, SML
   LMD and SML: NJAGA
   EMS: НЯГА

*NIAZI, Tagui-Zade Zoulfougar
   Ogly   USSR   1912
   MEH
   MEH: NIJAZI

NIBELLE, Henri-Jules-Joseph France   1883   1967
   DDM, LMD, X68

NIBLOCK, James   USA   1917
   ASUC, AS66, PCM, X64, X65, X66, X67

*NICHOLAS, John Morgan   Great Britain   1895   1963

*NICHOLSON, Ralph Ward   Great Britain   1907
   WI69

*NICK, Edmund   Germany   1891   Bohemia
   IMD, LMD, SML, WWG, X64, X66

*NICKSON, Noel John   Australia   circa
   X67, X68   1915

NICOLOV, L. K.
   See: NIKOLOV, L. K.

NICULESCU, Stefan   Rumania   1927
   BB65, BB71, IMD2, LMD, MEH, RCL, X64, X65, X66, X68

*NIEDZIELSKI, Stanislas (II)   Poland   1905
   LMD, QQF

NIEHAUS, Manfred   Germany   1933
   PAP, X67, X68

NIËL, Matty   Netherlands
   NED

*NIELAND, Jan   Netherlands   1903   1963
   NED

*NIELSEN, Jørgen   Denmark   1912
   X66, X68

*NIELSEN, Ludvig   Norway   1906
   CNO, X67, X68

NIELSEN, Niels   Denmark
   DMTsp, X65, X68

*NIELSEN, Riccardo   Italy   1908
   EVM, IMD, LMD, REM

NIELSEN, Svend   Denmark   1937
   DNS, VTM

NIELSEN, Tage   Denmark   1929
   VTM, X67

NIELSEN, Tage Høljby
   See: HØJBY NIELSEN, Tage

*NIELSEN, Thorvald   Denmark   1891   1965
   IMD, X65

*NIEMAN, Alfred Abbe   Great Britain 1913
   WI69, X64, X66, X67

*NIEMANN, Walter   Germany   1876   1953
   EVM, IMD, LMD

*NIEMCZYK, Waclaw   Poland   1907
   EVM, WI69

*NIGG, Serge   France   1924
   BB65, BB71, CME, CMF13, CMF20, DDM, DMF, EMS, EVM,
   IMD, LMD, MEH, QQF, REM, SCHW, SML, TSC, X64, X65,
   X66, X67, X68
   EMS: НИГ

NIGGELING, Willi   1924
   IMD

*NIGGLI, Friedrich   Switzerland   1875   1959
   EVM, LMD, SCHW

NIJAZI, T. Z. O.
   See: NIAZI, T. Z. O.

NIJVEEN, Samuel   Netherlands   1912
   EVM

*NIKIPROWETZKY, Tolia   France   1916   Russia
   DDM, X64, X65, X68

*NIKOLAEV, Aleksei
  Aleksandrovich   USSR   1931
   CME, EMS, LMD, MEH, PPU69/2, SML, X64, X65, X66, X68
   EMS: НИКОЛАЕВ

*NIKOLAEVA, Tatyana Petrovna USSR   1924
   EMS, EVM, LMD, MEH, PPU, SML, X64, X68
   EMS: НИКОЛАЕВА

NIKOLESKI, Dimče   Yugoslavia   1943
   KMJ

*NIKOLOV, Lazar Kostov   Bulgaria   1922
   BB65, BB71, BMK, LMD, MEH, X64, X67, X68
   LMD: NICOLOV
   BMK: НИКОЛОВ

NIKOLOVSKI, Miajlo   Yugoslavia   1934
   KMJ

*NIKOLOVSKI, Vlastimir   Yugoslavia   1925
   EMS, KMJ, LMD, X66, X67, X68
   EMS: 1913
   EMS: НИКОЛОВСКИЙ

*NIKOLSKY, Yuri Sergeevich   USSR   1895   1962
   EMS
   EMS: НИКОЛЬСКИЙ

*NILIUS, Rudolf   Austria   1883   1962
   BB71, LMD

NILSON, Leo   Sweden   1939
   FST, STS, X67, X68

*NILSSON, Bo   Sweden   1937
   BB65, BB71, CME, DDM, DNS, FST, IMD, IMD2, LMD, MEH,
   MNG, MZW, REM, SIM, SIMa, SML, SOW, STS, SWE, TJU,
   VTM, X64, X65, X66, X67, X68

NILSSON, Torsten   Sweden   1920
    FST, SIMa, STS, SWE, VTM, X65

*NIMMONS, Phillip Rista   Canada   1923
    X66

*NIN-CULMELL, Joaquín
  Maria   USA   1908   Germany
    DDM, EVM, LMD, REM, WI69, X65, X67

NISSIMOV, Nissim   Israel   1909   1951
    ACU   Bulgaria

NIVERD, Raymond   France   1922
    QQF

*NIXON, Roger   USA   1921
    ASUC, BB71, PCM, PC71, X67

NIYAZI, Zulfugarovich   USSR   1912
    EMS
    EMS: НИЯЗИ

*NJAGA, Stepan Timofeievich Rumania   1900   1951
    EVM

NJIKOŠ, Julije   Yugoslavia 1924
    HCM

NJIRIĆ, Nikša   Yugoslavia 1927
    HCM, KMJ

NOACK, Friedrich   Germany   1890   1951
    LMD

NOACK-IHLENFELD, Paul   Germany   1902   1962
    SML

*NOBLE, Thomas Tertius   USA   1867   1953
    AS66, DDM, EVM, LMD, REM, X68   Great Britain

NOBRE, Marlos   Brazil   1939
    BB71, CA17, FBC, X68

*NOBUTOKI, Kiyoshi   Japan   1887
    LMD, REM

*NOETZEL, Hermann   Germany   1880   1951
    EVM, IMD, LMD

NOGUEIRA, Teodoro   Brazil   1928
    FBC

*NOLINSKY, Nikolai
  Mihailovich   USSR   1886   1966
    IMD, X66
    Pseudonym: SKRIABIN, Nikolai

*NONO, Luigi   Italy   1924
    BB65, BB71, CME, DDM, DMM, EMS, EVM, IMD, IMD2,
    LMD, MEH, MZW, OCM, REM, SML, VNM, X64, X65,
    X66, X67, X68
    EMS: HOHO

NONVEILLER, Harris   Yugoslavia   1941
    HCM

NOON, David   USA   1946
    BS70

NORBY, Erik   Denmark   1936
    VTM, X67

*NORDAL, Jón   Iceland   1926
    BB71, VTM

*NORDEN, Norris Lindsay   USA   1887   1956
    X67

NORDENSTROM, Gladys   1924
    IMD

*NORDGREN, H. Erik   Sweden   1913
    FST, LMD, SIM, SIMa

NORDGREN, Pehr Henrik   Finland   circa 1942
    X68

*NORDHEIM, Arne   Norway   1931
    BB71, CME, CNO, DNS, IMD, LMD, VTM, X64, X65, X66,
    X67, X68

*NORDIO, Cessare   Italy   1891
    LMD

*NORDOFF, Paul   USA   1909
    AS66, EVM, LMD, PCM, REM, WI69, X64, X65, X66, X67

*NØRGAARD, Helmer   Denmark   1923
    VTM, X64

*NØRGAARD, Per   Denmark   1932
    BB65, BB71, CME, DMTsp, DNS, IMD, LMD, VTM, X64, X65,
    X66, X67, X68

*NØRHOLM, Ib   Denmark   1923
    CME, DMTsp, LMD, VTM, X65, X66, X67

NORMET, Leopold Tarmovich   USSR   1922   Estonia
    EMS, X65, X66, X67
    EMS: HOPMET

*NORTH, Alex   USA   1910
    AS66, BB71, LMD, PCM

*NORTON, Spencer H.   USA   1909
    X64, X65, X66

*NOSOV, Georgi Nikiforovich   USSR   1911
    EMS, EVM
    EDM: NOSSOV
    EMS: HOCOB

NOSS, Luther   USA   1907
    DAS, PCM, X65, X66, X67, X68

NOTT, Douglas Duane   USA   1944
    DN70, PC71

NOTTARA, Constantin C.   Rumania   1890 1951
    EVM, LMD, RCL

NOVA, Jacqueline   Colombia

NOVÁČEK, Blahoslav Emanuel Czechoslovakia 1911
    CCZ, MEH
    MEH: NOVÁČEK, Sláva Eman

*NOVÁK, Jan   Czechoslovakia 1921
    CCZ, CME, IMD, IMD2, LMD, MEH, MNP66/8, X64, X66,
    X67

NOVÁK, Jiři F.   Czechoslovakia 1913
    CCZ

NOVAK, Ladislav   Czechoslovakia 1925

NOVÁK, Milan   Czechoslovakia 1927
    CCZ, MEH, MNP66/1, X68, ZE69/3, ZE70/1, ZE70/3,
    ZE71/2, ZE71/3

NÓVAK, Richard   Czechoslovakia 1931
    MEH

NOVÁK, Svatopluk   Czechoslovakia
    MNP69/4

*NOVIKOV, Anatoli
  Grigorevich   USSR   1896
    EMS, EVM, LMD, MEH, PPU, PPU69/2, PPU70/2, SML,
    X66, X68
    EMS: НОВИКОВ

NOVIKOV, Andrei Porfirievich USSR   1909
    EMS, PPU69/2
    EMS: НОВИКОВ

NOVOSAD, Lubomír   Czechoslovakia 1922
    CCZ

*NOWAK, Lionel   USA   1911
    LMD, PCM, REM, X64

*NOWAKOWSKI, Anton   Austria   1897
    X66

*NOWKA, Dieter   Germany   1924
    LMD, MEH, SML, X64, X66, X67, X68

*NOWOWIEJESKI, Hanns
  Thomas   Germany   1929
    IMD

*NUFFEL, Jules Joseph Paul
  Maria van   Belgium   1883   1953
    DDM, EVM, LMD, X64

*NUMMI, Seppo Antero
  Yrjönpoika   Finland   1932
    COF, KKO, LMD, REM, VTM, X66, X67

*NUSSIO, Otmar   Switzerland   1902   Italy
    IMD, LMD, MEH, REM, X64

*NUTEN, Piet   Belgium   1913
    EVM

NYMAN, Michael   Great Britain
    X68

*NYSTEDT, Knut   Norway   1915
    BB71, CNO, EVM, IMD, LMD, REM, VTM, X66

*NYSTRÖM, Gösta   Sweden   1890   1966
    BB71, CME, DDM, EVM, FST, IMD2, KSV, LMD, MEH,
    MLA23/4, REM, SIM, SIMa, SMT, SOW, STS, SWE, TJU,
    VTM, X65, X66, X67, X68

*NYVALL, Jacob   Sweden   1894
    KSV, SIMa

OAKES, Rodney   USA
    CAP

OATES, Ernest Henry   Great Britain   1891
    WI69

*OBORIN, Lev Nikolaevich   USSR   1907
    EMS, LMD, X64, X65, X66, X67, X68
    EMS: ОБОРИН

OBORNÝ, Václav   Czechoslovakia   1915
    CCZ

OBOUHOV, Nicolas
    See: OBUKHOV

*OBOUSSIER, Robert   Switzerland   1900   1957
    BB71, EVM, IMD, LMD, MEH, REM, SCHW,   Belgium
    SML, X68

*OBRADOVIĆ, Aleksandar   Yugoslavia   1927
    BB65, BB71, CME, EMS, KMJ, LMD, MEH, X65, X66, X67,
    X68
    EMS: ОБРАДОВИЧ

*OBRETENOV, Svetoslav   Bulgaria   1909   1955
    BB65, BB71, BMK, EMS, MEH, X64, X67
    BMK: ОБРЕТЕНОВ   EMS: ОБРЕТЕНОВ

O'BRIEN, Eugene   USA   1945
    BS70

O'BRIEN, John Tower   USA
    ASUC

OBROVSKÁ, Jana   Czechoslovakia   1930
    CCZ

*OBŪKHOV, Nikolaii   France   1892   1954
    EMS, EVM, LMD, MEH, REM   USSR
    EVM: OBOECHOW
    EMS: ОБУХОВ

*OČENÁŠ, Andrej   Czechoslovakia   1911
    CCZ, IMD, LMD, MEH, MNP65/6, MNP70/6, SML, X64, X65,
    X67, X68, ZE69/1, ZE70/2, ZE70/3, ZE71/1, ZE71/2

*O'CONNOR-MORRIS, Geoffrey   Ireland   1886   1964
    X64   Switzerland

ODĂGESCU, Irina   Rumania   1937
    RCL, X66, X68

*ODAK, Krsto   Yugoslavia   1888   1965
   DDM, EVM, HCM, IMD, KMJ, LMD, X65, X66, X67

*ODAKA, Hisatada   Japan   1911   1951
   EMS
   EMS: ОДА́КА

ODD, Conny
   See: ORTWEIN, Carlernst

ODSTRČIL, Karel   Czechoslovakia 1930
   MEH, MNP71/6, X67, X68

*OERTZEN, Rudolf von   Germany   1910
   LMD, REM, X64, X65, X67

OETIKER, August   Switzerland   1874   1963
   SCHW

*ÖFVERLUND, Albin   Finland   1883
   KKO

OGANESIAN, Edgar Sergeyevich   USSR   1930
   EMS, LMD, MEH, PPU69/2, X67
   MEH: OHANESJAN
   EMS: ОГАНЕСЯ́Н

OGAWA, Hiroocki   Japan   1925

OGDEN, Wilbur   USA   1921
   LCI

*OGDON, John Andrew Howard   Great Britain 1937
   BB71, CME, LMD, X64, X65, X66, X67, X68

*OGURA, Hiroshi Rō   Japan   1916
   LMD, X64

*OHANA, Maurice   Great Britain 1914   Spain
   BB65, BB71, CME, DDM, EL:3, EVM, LMD, REM, X65, X66,
   X67, X68
   REM: 1915

*O'HARA, Geoffrey   Canada   1882   1967
   BB71, EVM, X67

*OKKENHAUG, Paul   Norway   1908
   CNO

OLAH, Tiberiu   Rumania   1928
   BB65, BB71, CME, EMS, IMD2, LMD, MEH, RCL, X64, X65,
   X66, X67, X68
   EMS: О́ЛАХ

*OLDBERG, Arne   USA   1874   1962
     BB65, BB71, LMD

*OLDHAM, Arthur William   Great Britain   1926
     EVM, LMD, REM, WI69, X65

OLDS, Gerry   USA   1933
     BB65, BB71

*OLESOV, Yuri Viktorovich   USSR   1924
     LMD

OLIVARES, Carlos   Argentina   1890
     REM

OLIVEIRA, Jocy de   Brazil   1936
     BB71

OLIVER, Harold   USA
     ASUC

OLIVER, Richard   USA   1927
     DN72

OLIVEROS, Pauline   USA   1932
     BB71, EL:3, IMD, PC71, X64, X68

*OLIVIERO, Nino   Italy   1920
     X64

*d'OLLONE, (Max) Maximilien-
    Paul-Marie-Félix   France   1875   1959
     BB65, BB71, DDM, DMF, EVM, LMD

OLMSTEAD, Clarence   USA   1892
     AS66

OLOVNIKOV, Vladimir
    Vladimirovic̆   USSR   1919
     MEH

OLSEN, Loran   USA
     CAP

OLSEN, Paul Rovsing
    See: ROVSING OLSEN, Paul

*OLSEN, Sparre Carl Gustav   Norway   1903
     CNO, DDM, EVM, LMD, REM, VTM, X64

*OLSON, Daniel   Sweden   1898
     SIMa

OLSSON, Joel   Sweden   1882
  SIM

*OLSSON, Otto Emanuel   Sweden   1879   1964
  BB71, EVM, FST, KSV, LMD, SIM, SIMa, STS, TJU, X67

OLSSON, Phillip   USA   1923
  LCI, X66, X67, X68

ONITIU, Virgil   Rumania   1929
  RCL

O'PRESKA, John   USA   1945
  CAP

OPSOMER, Jaak   Belgium   1873   1952
  EVM

*ORANSKI, Viktor
  Aleksandrovich   USSR   1899   1953
  EMS
  Formerly: GERSHOV
  EMS: ОРАНСКИЙ

*ORBAN, Marcel   France   1884   1958
  DDM, REM   Belgium

*ØRBECK, Anne-Marie   Norway   1911
  CNO

*ORBELIAN, Constantin
  Agaparonovich   USSR   1928
  EMS, LMD, MEH
  EMS: ОРБЕЛЯН

*ORBÓN, Julián   Cuba   1925   Spain
  BB65, BB71, DDM, IMD, LMD, QLA, X68

*ORCHARD, William Arundel   Great Britain   1867   1961
  AMM, BB65, BB71

ORDZHONIKIDZE, Givi
  Shioevich   USSR   1917
  EMS, PPU69/2, X68
  EMS: ОРДЖОНИКИДЗЕ

*ORE, Harry Bruno Johannes   Hong Kong   1885   Russia
  WI69

*ORFF, Carl   Germany   1895
  BB65, BB71, CME, DDM, DMM, EL:1, EMS, EVM, IMD,
  IMD2, LMD, MEH, MZW, PAP, REM, SML, TCM, VNM,
  WTM, WWG, X64, X65, X66, X67, X68
  EMS: ОРФ

*ORGAD, Ben-Zion   Israel   1926   Germany
   ACU, CME, IMD2, MM59, X65, X68
   Formerly: BUSCHEL

*ORLANDO, Michele   Finland   1887   Italy
   LMD

*ORLANDO, Salvatore   Italy   1902
   LMD, REM

ORMICKI, Wlodzimierz   Poland   1905
   PKW

*ORNSTEIN, Leo   USA   1895   Russia
   EVM, LMD, REM

*ORR, Charles Wilfrid   Great Britain 1893
   OCM, X68

*ORR, Robin Robert Kemsley Great Britain 1909 Scotland
   BB65, BB71, LMD, OCM, REM, WI69, X65, X66, X67, X68

*ORREGO-SALAS, Juan
  Antonio   Chile   1919
   ASUC, BB65, BB71, DDM, EVM, LMD, QLA, REM, X64, X65,
   X66, X67

ORTAKOV, Dragoslav   Yugoslavia   1928
   KMJ

*ORTHEL, Léon   Netherlands 1905
   DDM, EVM, LMD, NED, REM, WI69, X65, X66

ORTON, Richard H.   Great Britain 1940
   X68

*ORTWEIN, Carlernst   Germany   1916
   SML, X67
   Pseudonym: ODD, Conny

ØRVAD, Timme   Denmark circa 1940
   X68

ORY, David   Israel

*OSBORNE, William Nathaniel Canada   1906
   X66, X67

OSBORNE, Willson   1906
   IMD

OSCHANITZKY, Richard Carol Rumania   1901
   RCL

OSGHIAN, Peter   Yugoslavia   1932
   BB65, BB71, KMJ, LMD, X65, X67

*OSIECK, Hans Hendrik Willem   Netherlands   1910
   EVM, LMD, NED, REM, X64, X65

*OSOKIN, Mihail Aleksievich   USSR   1903
   EMS
   Also: OSSOKIN
   EMS: ОСÓКИН

*OSTERC, Slavko   Yugoslavia   1895   1941
   CME, IMD, X66, X67, X68

*OSTHOFF, Helmuth   Germany   1896
   BB65, EVM, X65, X67, X68

OSTROVSKY, Arkadi Ilyich   USSR   1914
   EMS, SML, X64, X66, X67, X68
   EMS: ОСТРÓBCKИЙ

OTAKA, Hisatada   1911   1951
   IMD

*OTAÑO Y EGUINO, José
   Maria Nemesio   Spain   1880   1956
   BB65, BB71, EVM, LMD, REM

OTT, Joseph Henry   USA   1929
   LMD, PC71, REM, X66, X67, X68

*OTTE, Hans   Germany   1926
   IMD, LMD, MNG, REM, X65, X66, X67, X68

OTTEN, Ludwig   Netherlands   1924
   NED

*OTTERLOO, Willem Jan van   Netherlands   1907
   EVM, IMD, LMD, MEH, NED, REM, X65, X66

*OTTOSON, David   Sweden   1892
   SIM, SIMa

*OUBRADOUS, Fernand   France   1903
   LMD, QQF, REM

OUCHTERLONY, David   Canada
   KEY, NLC, NLCa

*OULIE, Einar   Norway   1890   1957
   CNO

*OVALLE, Jaime   Brazil   1894 1955
 CHB, IMD
 Full name: Jayme Rojas de Aragón y Ovalle
 CHB: Listed both 1954 and 1955.

OVANIN, Nikola Leonard USA   1911 Yugoslavia
 AS66, X68

*OVCHINIKOV, Evgueni
 Ivanovich   USSR   1903 1965
 MEH, X65
 MEH: OVČINNIKOV

*OVERHOFF, Kurt   Austria 1902
 EVM, LMD

*OVERTON, Hall   USA   1920 1972
 BB65, BB71, LMD, MLA29/4, PCM, X64, X66

OVEZOV, Dangatar   USSR   1911
 EMS, PPU
 EMS: ОВЕЗОВ

OVTCHINNIKOV, Viacheslav USSR
 X64

OWEN, Blythe   USA   1898
 AA73, ASUC, LCI, X64, X65, X66, X67, X68

OWEN, Harold   USA   1931
 PC71

OWEN, Richard   USA circa 1923
 X67, X68

OXLADE, John Stirling Great Britain 1946
 WI69

*OZOLIŅŠ, Janis Adol'fovich USSR   1908 Latvia
 EMS
 EMS: ОЗОЛИНЬ

*PAAP, Wouter   Netherlands 1908
 EVM, IMD, LMD, NED, REM, X64, X65, X66, X67, X68

*PABLO, Luis de   Spain   1930
 BB65, BB71, CME, DDM, IMD, IMD2, LMD, MEH, PAP, REM,
 TSC, X64, X65, X66, X67, X68
 BB65, BB71, PAP and TSC: DE PABLO, Luis

PACCAGNELLA, Ermenegildo Italy   1882
 LMD, REM, X65, X66, X68

*PACCAGNINI, Angelo   Italy   1930
    IMD, LMD, MNG, REM, X65, X66, X67

*PACHECO DE CESPEDES,
    Luis   Peru   1895
    EVM, REM

*PACHERNEGG, Alois   Austria   1892   1964
    EVM, LMD, SML, X64

PACHTCHENKO, A. F.
    See: PASHSCHENKO, A. F.

PACIORKIEWICZ, Tadeusz   Poland   1916
    PKW, X65, X66

PADDISON, Max   Great Britain   circa
    X68   1945

*PADE, Else Marie   Denmark   1924
    VTM, X65

PÁDIVÝ, Karol   Czechoslovakia   1908   1968
    MEH, X65

PADROS, Juame   Spain
    X67

PADWA, Vladimir   USA   1900   Russia
    AS66

PAFFRATH, Herbert   Germany   1913
    WWG

PAGLIA, Cesare (Gaianus)   Italy   1878   1957
    REM

*PAHISSA, Jaime   Spain   1880   1969
    DDM, EVM, LMD, REM

*PAHLEN, Kurt   Argentina   1907   Austria
    REM, X64, X66, X67, X68

*PAHOR, Karol   Yugoslavia   1896
    IMD, REM, X67

PAIK, Nam June   Korea   1932
    BB71, X68

PAKHMUTOVA, Aleksandra
    Nikolaevna   USSR   1929
    BB71, EMS, LMD, MEH, PPU69/2, SML, X64, X65, X68
    MEH: PACHMUTOVA   EMS: ПАХМУТОВА

PALACIO, Carlos   USSR   1911   Spain
   EMS, X66
   EMS: ПАЛА́СИО

PALADE, Constantin   Rumania   1915
   LMD, RCL

*PALADI, Radu   Rumania   circa 1927
   LMD, RCL

PALANGE, Louis Salvador   USA   1917
   AS66, BB71

*PALAU BOIX, Manuel   Spain   1893   1967
   BB71, DDM, LMD, REM

*PÁLENÍCEK, Josef   Czechoslovakia   1914   Yugoslavia
   CCZ, IMD, LMD, MEH, MNP68/7, REM, X64, X65, X66

*PALESTER, Roman   Poland   1907
   CME, DDM, EVM, IMD, LMD, REM, SML, X64, X65

PALIASHVILLI, Levan
   Petrovich   USSR   1895
   LMD

PALKOVSKÝ, Oldřich   Czechoslovakia   1907
   CCZ, X67

PALKOVSKÝ, Pavel   Czechoslovakia
   MNP69/4

*PALLANTIOS, Menelaos   Greece   1914
   EVM, LMD, REM

*PALMA, Athos   Argentina   1891   1951
   EVM, REM

*PALMER, Geoffrey Molyneux   Ireland   1882   Great Britain
   LMD, REM, X67, X68

*PALMER, John   Great Britain   1911
   WI69, X67

*PALMER, Robert Moffett   USA   1915
   EVM, LMD, PCM, REM, X64, X65, X68

*PALMGREN, Selim   Finland   1878   1951
   COF, DDM, EMS, EVM, IMD, LMD, MEH, REM, SML, VTM
   EMS: ПАЛМГРЕН

PALOMBO, Paul M.   USA
   AA73

*PALS, Leopold van der   Switzerland   1884   Russia
    SCHW

*PÁLSSON, Helgi   Iceland   1899   1964
    VTM

PAŁUBICKI, Konrad   Poland   1910
    PKW

*PANATERO, Mario   Italy   1919   1962
    IMD, LMD, REM

*PANDER, Oscar von   Germany   1883   1968
    EVM, IMD, LMD, MLA25/4, WWG, X68

PANDULA, Dusan   Czechoslovakia
    X67, X68

PANEL, Ludovic   France   1887   1952
    DDM

PANETTI, Joan   USA
    ASUC

*PANIZZA, Hector Ettore   Argentina   1875   1967
    BB71, EMS, EVM, LMD, MLA24/4, REM, X66, X68
    EMS: ПАНИСА

*PANNAIN, Guido   Italy   1891
    EMS, IMD, LMD, REM, X68
    EMS: ПАННАИН

PANNELL, Raymond   Canada
    X68

PANNI, Marcel   Italy
    CME

*PANOFF, Pater Assen   Bulgaria   1899   1953
    EVM

*PANUFNIK, Andrzej   Poland   1914
    BB65, BB71, CME, DDM, EVM, IMD, LMD, MEH, REM, SML,
    WI69, X64, X65, X66, X68

PANULA, Jorma Juhani   Finland   1930
    KKO, X67, X68

*PAPADOPOLOUS, Stamatios   France   1906   Greece
    EVM, REM

*PAPAIOANNOU, Yannis A.   Greece   1910
   BB65, BB71, EL:1, EL:2, EL:3, EL:4, EVM, IMD, LMD, PAP,
   REM, X65, X67
   EVM: 1909

*PAPANDOPULO, Boris   Yugoslavia   1906   Germany
   BB65, BB71, DDM, EMS, EVM, HCM, KMJ, LMD, MEH, REM,
   SML, X65, X67
   EMS: ПАПАНДÓПУЛО

*PAPINEAU-COUTURE, Jean   Canada   1916
   BB65, BB71, CCM, CCM71, CVM, CVMa, DDM, IMD, IMD2,
   KEY, LMD, MCO, MCO68, MCO71, MEH, NLC, NLCa, REM,
   TFB, X65, X66, X67, X68

PAPORISZ, Yoram   Israel   1940   Poland
   ACUad, IMD2, X68

PAPP, Lajos   Hungary   1935
   CHC, CME, X68, ZSZ

*PAPST, Eugen   Germany   1886   1956
   EVM

*PARAĆ, Ivo   Yugoslavia   1890   1954
   HCM, IMD, KMJ, LMD

PARANTAINEN, Martti Mathias   Finland   1903
   KKO

*PARAY, Paul M. A. Charles   France   1886
   DDM, DMF, EVM, LMD, REM, X65, X66, X68

PARCHMAN, Gene Louis   USA   1929
   AS66, PCM, X64

*PARÈS, Philippe   France   1901
   QQF, WI69

*PARIBENI, Giulio Cesare   Italy   1881   1964
   EVM, IMD, LMD, REM, X64

PARÍK, Ivan   Czechoslovakia 1936
   CCZ, IMD, MEH, X66, X68, ZE69/3, ZE70/1, ZE70/2,
   ZE70/3, ZE71/1, ZE71/2, ZE71/3

*PARK, Stephen   USA   1911
   AS66, X65, X66

*PARKER, David   Great Britain   1929
   X68

PARMEGIANI, Bernard   France   1927
    X68

*PARODI, Renato   Italy   1900
    LMD, REM

PARRIS, Herman M.   USA   1903   Russia
    AS66, BB71, PCM

*PARRIS, Robert   USA   1924
    BB65, BB71, CA10, LMD, PCM, PC71, X64, X66, X67

*PARRISH, Carl   USA   1904   1965
    BB71, LMD, REM, X64, X65, X66, X67, X68

*PARROTT, Horace Ian   Great Britain   1916
    DDM, EVM, LMD, REM, WI69, X64, X65, X66, X67, X68

*PARRY, William Stanley   Great Britain   1898
    WI69

PARSCH, Arnost   Czechoslovakia   1936
    MNP69/4, MNP70/5, MNP72/9

PARSI, Hector Campos   Puerto Rico

PÄRT, Arvo   USSR   1935   Estonia
    EMS, MEH, X67, X68
    EMS: ПЯРТ

*PARTCH, Harry   USA   1901
    BB65, BB71, IMD2, LMD, X64, X65, X66, X67, X68

*PARTOS, Oedoen   Israel   1907   Hungary
    ACU, CME, DDM, IMD, IMD2, LMD, MM59, REM, WWI,
    X64, X65, X67, X68
    ACU: 1909

PARTZKHALADZE, Aleksei
    Alekseevich   USSR   1897
    EMS
    EMS: ПАРЦХАЛАДЗЕ

PASATIERI, Thomas   USA   1945
    DN72, X68

*PASCAL, Claude René Georges   France   1921
    DDM, IMD, LMD, REM, QQF

*PAŠĆAN KOJAN, Svetolik   Yugoslavia   1892
    X66

PAŞCANU, Alexandru   Rumania   1920
   LMD, RCL

PASCARELLA, Enzo   USA   1901 Italy
   REM

PASCHILL, Iosif   Rumania   1877 1966
   RCL

*PASHCHENKO, Andrei
   Filipovich   USSR   1885
   DDM, EVM, LMD, MEH, REM, SML, X68
   DDM: PACHTCHENKO   EVM: PASJTSJENKO
   LMD and MEH: PAŠČENKO REM: PAŠČENKO
   SML: PASTSCHENKO
   EMS: ПÁШЕНКО
   EVM: 1883

PASKHALOV, Viacheslav
   Viktorovich   USSR   1873 1951
   EMS, LMD
   EMS: ПАСХÁЛОВ

*PASSANI, Émile Barthélemi   France   1905
   DDM, DMF, EVM, IMD, LMD, QQF, REM, WI69

PASSATIERI, Thomas   USA   1945
   X65

*PASTORE, Giuseppe Alfredo Italy   1915
   REM

*PASTURA, Francesco   Italy   1905 1968
   LMD, REM

*PASZTHORY, Casimir von   Austria   1886 1966
   IMD, X66   Hungary

PATA, Huért
   See: PATAKY, Hubert

PATACHICH, Iván   Hungary   1922
   CHC, LMD, X68

*PATÁKY, Hubert   Germany   1892 1953
   EVM, LMD   Belgium
   Pseudonym of PÀTA, Huért

PATIN, Jonel   Israel   1893 1961
   ACU   Rumania

PATLAENKO, Eduard
Nikolaevich   USSR   1936
X68

PÄTS, Riho Eduardovich   USSR   1899   Estonia
EMS
EMS: ПЯТС

PATTEN, James   Great Britain 1936
WI69

PATTERSON, Andy J.   USA
AA73, ASUC

PATTERSON, Paul Leslie Great Britain 1947
WI69, X67, X68

*PATTISON, Lee Marion   USA   1890 1966
BB71, EVM, MLA24/4, X67

PATWARDHAN, Vinayak
Rarayan   India   1898
WHI

*PAUEL, Heinz   Germany   1908
X66

*PAUER, Jiří   Czechoslovakia 1919
CCZ, CME, DDM, IMD, IMD2, LMD, MEH, MNP64/3,
MNP65/3, MNP65/7, MNP69/2, MNP70/4, MNP72/4,
MNP72/6, REM, SML, X64, X65, X66, X67, X68

PAUL, Alan   Great Britain 1905 1968
X68

*PAULMÜLLER, Alexander Germany   1914
X64

*PAULSON, Gustaf   Sweden   1898 1966
BB71, FST, KSV, LMD, MLA24/4, SIM, SIMa, VTM, X67

*PAUMGARTNER, Bernhard Austria   1887 1971
BB71, CME, DDM, EMS, EVM, REM, SML, WI69, X64, X66,
X67, X68
EMS: ПÁУМГАРТНЕР

*PAVLOV, Evgeni Pavlovich USSR   1894
EVM, X66, X67, X68

PAXTON, Glenn G., Jr.   USA   1921
AS66, X64

PAYMER, Marvin USA 1921
 AS66

PAYNE, Frank Lynn USA
 CAP

PAYNE, John USA 1941
 BB71

*PAZ, Juan Carlos Argentina 1897 1972
 DDM, EMS, EVM, IMD, MLA29/4, REM, TSC, X64, X66, X67
 EMS: ПAC

*PEACOCK, Kenneth Canada 1922
 CCM, CVM, KEY, MCO, X68

PEARL-MANN, Dora USA 1905 Russia
 AS66

PEARLE, George USA 1915
 CA15

*PEARS, James R. Canada 1881 England
 NLC

PEARSON, William Dean Great Britain 1905
 WI69, X68

PEDEMONTI, Guiseppe Italy 1910
 LMD, REM

*PEDERSEN, Axel Denmark 1897 1971

PEDERSEN, Gunnar Møller Sweden circa 1940
 X68

PEDERSEN, Jens Wilhelm Denmark 1939
 VTM, X66, X67

PEDERSEN, Paul Canada 1935
 CCM, MCO, MCO68, NLC

*PEDROLLO, Arrigo Italy 1878 1964
 BB65, BB71, EVM, IMD, LMD, REM, X65

PEDRON, Carlo Italy 1876 1958
 IMD, LMD, REM

*PEETERS, Emil Aloys
 Angelique Germany 1893 Belgium
 EVM, IMD, LMD, REM

*PEETERS, Flor   Belgium   1903
    CME, DDM, EVM, IMD, LMD, MEH, OCM, REM, WI69, X64,
    X65, X66, X67, X68

PEGRAM, Wayne Frank   USA   1939
    DN70

PEHKONEN, Elias   Great Britain circa
    X67, X68   1942

*PEIKO, Nikolai Ivanovich   USSR   1916
    EMS, EVM, LMD, MEH, PPU, PPU69/2, REM, SML, X65,
    X66, X68
    LMD and MEH: PEJKO   PPU, X65 and X68: PEYKO
    EMS: ПЕЙКО

*PEISIN, Abram Yakovlevich USSR   1894   1954
    EMS, LMD
    LMD: PEJSIN
    EMS: ПЕЙСИН

*PEIXE, Cesar Guerra   Brazil   1914
    FBC

PEIXINHO, Jorge Rosado   Portugal   1940
    CME, IMD, X67

PEK, Albert   Czechoslovakia 1893
    CCZ, LMD

*PELEMANS, Willem   Belgium   1901
    CBC, EVM, LMD, REM

PELIKÁN, Miroslav   Czechoslovakia 1922
    CCZ, IMD2

PELILLI, Lino Ennio   Italy   1892
    REM

*PELLEG, Frank   Israel   1910 1968
    ACU, MLA26/4, REM, WWI   Czecho-
                                    slovakia

*PELLEGRINI, Alfred   Germany   1892
    WWG

PELLEGRINO, Ronald   USA
    ASUC

*PELLETIER, Louis-Wilfrid Canada   1896
    BB65, BB71, DDM, X67, X68

*PEMBAUR, Josef, Jr.   Austria   1875   1950
   LMD, REM

PENBERTHY, James   Australia   1917
   AMM

PENDERECKI, Krzysztof   Poland   1933
   BB65, BB71, CME, DDM, DN70, EMS, IMD, IMD2, LMD,
   MEH, MZW, PAP, PKW, REM, X64, X65, X66, X67, X68
   EMS: ПЕНДЕРЕЦКИЙ

PENHERSKI, Zbigniew   Poland   1935
   PKW, X64

PENN, William A.   USA
   CAP

PENNARIO, Leonard   USA   1924
   AS66, X64, X66, X68

PENNISI, Francesco   Italy   1934
   LMD, X67

*PENTLAND, Barbara   Canada   1912
   BB65, BB71, CCM, CCM71, CVM, KEY, LMD, MCO, MCO68,
   MCO71, NLC, REM, TFB, TSC, X67, X68

*PENTTINEN, Toimi   Finland   1905
   COF

*PÉPIN, Jean Joseph Clermont   Canada   1926
   BB65, BB71, CCM, CCM71, CVM, DDM, IMD, KEY, LMD,
   MCO, MCO68, NLCa, TFB, X65, X67, X68

*PEPÖCK, August   Austria   1887   1967
   BB71, EVM, LMD, MLA24/4, X67, X68
   EVM: 1889

*PEPPING, Ernst   Germany   1901
   CME, DDM, EVM, IMD, IMD2, LMD, MEH, MZW, REM, SML,
   VNM, WWG, X64, X65, X66, X68

*PERAGALLO, Mario   Italy   1910
   BB65, DDM, EVM, IMD, LMD, MEH, REM, SML, X67, X68

*PERAK, Rudolf   Germany   1891   Austria
   WWG

*PERCEVAL, Julio   Argentina   1903   1963
   BB65, BB71, IMD, LMD   Belgium

PERERA, Ronald Christopher   USA   1941
   DN72

*PÉREZ CASAS, Bartolomeo   Spain   1873   1956
   DDM, EVM, LMD, REM

*PERGAMENT, Moses   Sweden   1893   Finland
   BB71, FST, KSV, LMD, REM, SIM, SIMa, SOW, STS, SWE,
   VTM, X68

PERGAMENT, Ruvim
  Samoilovich   USSR   1906   1965
   EMS, X65
   EMS: ПЕРГА́МЕНТ

PERGAMENT, Simon P.   1897
  Parmet   Finland   1897
   IMD2, LMD, X66

*PERIČIĆ, Vlastimir   Yugoslavia   1927
   BB65, BB71, EMS, IMD, KMJ, LMD, REM, X64, X66
   EMS: ПЕРИЧИЧ

PEŘINA, Hubert   Czechoslovakia 1890 1964
   CCZ, IMD2

*PERINELLO, Carlo   Italy   1877   1942
   REM

PERIŠIĆ, Ino   Yugoslavia   1920
   KMJ

PERKINS, Horace   Australia   1901
   AMM

PERKINS, John MacIvor   USA   1935
   ASUC, BB71, X65, X68

PERKINSON, Coleridge Taylor   USA
   X67

*PERKOWSKI, Piotr   Poland   1901
   CME, EMS, EVM, IMD, LMD, PKW, REM, X65, X67
   EMS, EVM, IMD and REM: 1902
   EMS: ПЕРКО́ВСКИЙ

PERL, Lothar   USA   1910   Germany
   AS66

*PERLE, George   USA   1915
   ASUC, AS66, BB71, DAS, IMD, LMD, PCM, TSC, WI69,
   X64, X65, X66, X67, X68

*PERLEA, Ionel   Rumania   1900   1970
   BB71, EVM, IMD, LMD, RCL, REM, X65

*PERNOO, Jacques Camille
  Henri   France   1921
  WI69

PERONI, Alessandro   Italy   1874 1964
  LMD, REM, X64

*PEROSI, Lorenzo   Italy   1872 1956
  BB71, DDM, EVM, LMD, MEH, REM, X67, X68

PEROSI, Marziano   Italy   1875 1959
  DDM, EVM, LMD, REM

PERPESSAS, Charilaos   Greece   1907
  LMD

*PERRACHIO, Luigi   Italy   1883 1966
  IMD, LMD, REM

*PERRAULT, Michel   Canada   1925
  CCM, CVM, IMD, MCO, MCO68, TFB, X68

PERRENOUD, Jean-Frédéric Switzerland 1912
  SCHW, X65

PERRIN, Jean-Charles   Switzerland 1920
  SCHW, WWS, X65, X66

PERRUCCI, Mario   Italy   1934
  LMD, X65

*PERRY, Julia   USA   1927
  PCM, PC71, WAN
  WAN: 1924

*PERSICHETTI, Vincent   USA   1915
  AS66, BB65, BB71, CA14, DDM, DN70, DN72, LMD, MEH,
  PCM, PC71, REM, WTM, X64, X65, X66, X67, X68

*PERSICO, Mario   Italy   1892
  IMD, REM, WI69

PERSKY, Stanley   USA
  ASUC

PERSON, Mats   Sweden   circa 1940
  X68

PESCETTO, Giuseppe   Italy   1928
  LMD, REM

PESCHKO, Johannes Sebastian Germany   1909
  WWG

*PESOLA, Väinö Johannes   Finland   1886   1966
   COF, KKO, LMD

*PESONEN, Olavi Samuel   Finland   1909
   COF, EVM, KKO, LMD, REM, VTM

*PETERKIN, George Norman   Great Britain 1886
   LMD, REM

*PETERSEN, Wilhelm   Germany   1890   1957
   EVM, IMD, LMD, REM

PETERSON, Wayne   USA   1927
   PC71

PETIN, Nikola   Yugoslavia   1920   USSR
   BB65, BB71, KMJ, LMD, X67

*PETIT, Pierre   France   1922
   CMF10, CMF20, DDM, DMF, EVM, IMD, LMD, QQF, REM,
   X65, X67

PETIT, Raymond   France   1893
   LMD, REM, X65

PETKOVIĆ, Dragiša   Yugoslavia   1922
   KMJ

PETRA-BASACOPOL, Carmen   Rumania   1926
   LMD, RCL, X65

PETRALIA, Tito   1896
   IMD

*PETRASSI, Goffredo   Italy   1904
   BB71, CME, DDM, EL:3, EMS, EVM, IMD, LMD, MEH, MZW,
   REM, SML, VNM, WI69, WTM, X64, X65, X66, X67, X68
   EMS: ПЕТРÁССИ

PETRI, Egon   Germany   1881   1962
   BB65, BB71, EVM, LMD, REM, X64

PETRI, Norbert   Rumania   1912
   LMD, RCL, X68

PETRIĆ, Ivo   Yugoslavia   1931
   IMD2, KMJ, LMD, MEH, MSC, X64, X65, X66, X67, X68

*PETRIDIS, Petro Jean   Greece   1892   Turkey
   CME, DDM, EVM, LMD, REM, X65

PETROV, Andrei Pavlovich   USSR   1930
    BB65, BB71, EMS, LMD, PPU69/2, REM, SCD, X65, X66,
    X67, X68
    EMS: ПЕТРОВ

PETROV, Ivan Vasilevich   USSR   1906
    PPU

PETROVÁ, Ivana   Czechoslovakia 1929
    MNP72/9

PETROVIĆ, Radomir   Yugoslavia   1923
    BB71, KMJ, LMD, X67

*PETROVICS, Emil   Hungary   1930 Yugoslavia
    BB65, BB71, CME, LMD, MEH, SML, X65, X66, X67, X68,
    ZSZ

PETRUSHKA, Shabtai Arieh   Israel   1903 Germany
    ACU, MM59, WWI

*PETRŽELKA, Vilém   Czechoslovakia 1889 1967
    BB71, CCZ, CME, EVM, IMD, IMD2, LMD, MEH, REM, SML,
    X64, X65, X67, X68

PETSCH, Kuno   Germany   1923 1967
    LMD, SML, X67, X68

PETTAN, Hubert   Yugoslavia   1912
    HCM, KMJ

*PETTERSSON, Allan Gustaf   Sweden   1911
    BB71, CME, FST, IMD2, LMD, REM, SIM, SIMa, SOW, STS,
    SWE, TJU, VTM, X67, X68

*PETYREK, Felix   Czechoslovakia 1892 1951
    DDM, EVM, IMD, LMD, REM

*PETZOLD, Rudolf   Germany   1908 Great Britain
    EVM, LMD, REM

*PETZOLDT, Richard   Germany   1907
    LMD, REM, X64, X65, X66, X67, X68

PEVI, Zul Efraim   Bulgaria   1930
    BMK

PEYKO, N. I.
    See: PEIKO, N. I.

PEXIDR, Karel   Czechoslovakia 1929
    MNP72/9

*PEYROT, Fernande   Switzerland   1888
    IMD, LMD, SCHW

*PFANNER, Adolf   Germany   1887
    WWG

PFAUTSCH, Lloyd   USA   1921
    PCM, PC71, X64, X65

PFEIFFER, Irena   Poland   1912
    PKW

PFIFFNER, Ernst   Switzerland   1922
    IMD, SCHW, WWS, X67

PFISTER, Hugo   Switzerland   1914   1969
    IMD2, LMD, SCHW, X65, X66, X67, X68

PHETTEPLACE, Jon   USA   1940

*PHILIP, Achille   France   1878   1959
    BB71, DDM, EVM, LMD, REM

*PHILIPP, Franz   Germany   1890   1972
    EVM, IMD, MLA29/4, REM

*PHILIPP, Isidor   France   1863   1958
    DDM, LMD, REM   Hungary

*PHILIPPOT, Michel   France   1925
    CMF25, IMD, LMD, QQF, X64, X65

PHILLIPS, Barre   1934
    WAN

*PHILLIPS, Burrill   USA   1907
    AA73, AS66, EVM, IMD, LCI, LMD, PCM, REM, WI69, X64,
    X65, X66, X67, X68

PHILLIPS, Charles Allen   USA   1940
    DN72

PHILLIPS, D. Valgene   USA
    CAP

PHILLIPS, Gordon   Great Britain   1908
    IMD, WI69

PHILLIPS, Linda   Australia
    AMM

PHILLIPS, Lois Elisabeth   Great Britain   1926
    WI69

*PHILLIPS, Montague Fawcett   Great Britain   1885   1969
   BB71, EVM, LMD

PHILLIPS, Peter   USA   1930
   X68

*PHILPOT, Stephen Rowland   Great Britain   1870   1950
   LMD

PIANTONI, Louis   Switzerland   1885   1958
   SCHW

PIART, Arvo   USSR   Estonia
   CME, X65

*PIASTRO, Josef Borissoff   USA   1890   Russia
   LMD, X64
   LMD: 1889

*PIATIGORSKY, Gregor   USA   1903   Russia
   BB71, EVM, X64, X65, X66, X67, X68

PIBERNIK, Zlatko   Yugoslavia   1926
   HCM, KMJ

PIBIK, Otto Emil   Bulgaria   1912   1960
   BMK

PICCAND, Jean   Switzerland   1904
   WWS, X65

*PICCHI, Luigi   Italy   1899   1970
   LMD, MLA27/4, REM, WI69

PICCHI, Silvano   Argentina   1922   Italy
   BB71

*PICCIOLI, Giuseppe   Italy   1905   1961
   IMD, LMD, REM

*PÍCHA, František   Czechoslovakia   1893   1964
   CCZ, EVM, IMD, IMD2, LMD, MEH, REM, X64

PICCHI, Silvano   Argentina   1922   Italy
   CA15

PIDOUX, Pierre   Switzerland   1905
   SCHW, X65, X66, X67, X68

*PIECHLER, Arthur   Germany   1896
   IMD, LMD

PIER, Georg   Austria
    X67, X68
    Formerly: PIRCKMAYER, Georg

*PIERNÉ, Paul   France   1874   1952
    EVM, LMD, REM

*PIERRONT, Noelie Marie
    Antoinette   France   1899
    X64, X65

PIETSCH, Edna Frida   USA
    AA73, X66, X67, X68

PIETSCH, Wolfgang   Germany
    X68

PIGGOTT, Patrick Edward
    Smardon   Great Britain
    X65

*PIKE, Eleanor B. Franklin   Great Britain
    WI69

*PIKET, Frederick   USA   1903   Turkey
    AS66, IMD, PCM

*PILATI, Mario   Italy   1903   1938
    EVM, LMD, REM

PILLIN, Boris   USA   1941
    DN70, PC71

*PILLNEY, Karl Hermann   Austria   1896
    LMD, X66

*PILSS, Karl   Austria   1902
    IMD

*PIMSLEUR, Solomon   USA   1900   1962
    BB65, BB71, CA13, LMD   France

PINCHARD, Max   France   1928
    DDM, X68

*PINEAU, Charles   France   1877   1958
    LMD, REM

*PINEDA-DUQUE, Roberto   Colombia   1910
    BB65, BB71, LMD, X65

*PINELLI, Carlo   Italy   1911
    LMD, REM

PINILLA, Enrique   Peru   1927
    CA11, LMD, X67

*PINKHAM, Daniel   USA   1923
    AA73, BB65, BB71, CA12, DN72, LMD, PCM, PC71, X64,
    X65, X66, X67, X68

PIÑOS, Alois   Czechoslovakia 1925
    CCZ, IMD2, MEH, MNP70/5, MNP72/1, X66, X68

PINTACUDA, Salvatore   Italy   1916
    REM, X67

PINTO, Alfredo A.   Argentina   1891   1968
    CA14, LMD

*PINTO, Octavio   Brazil   1890   1950
    X65

PINTO, Victor Macedo   Portugal
    CME

PINZON-URREA, Jesus   Colombia   1928
    CA17

*PIPKOV, Liubomir Panaiotiv Bulgaria   1904
    BB71, BMK, EMS, EVM, LMD, MEH, REM, SML, X64, X65,
    X66, X67, X68
    BMK: ПИПКОВ   EMS: ПИПКОВ

*PIRANI, Max Gabriel   Canada   1898   Australia
    LMD, WI69

PIRCKMAYER, Georg
    See: PIER, Georg

*PIRIOU, Adolphe   France   1878
    DMF, EVM

PIRNIK, Makso   Yugoslavia   1902
    KMJ

PIRONKOV, Simeon Angelov   Bulgaria   1927
    BB65, BB71, BMK, X67, X68
    BMK: ПИРОНКОВ

PIRUMOV, Aleksandr Ivanovich USSR   1930
    EMS
    EMS: ПИРУМОВ

*PISAROWITZ, Karl Maria   Germany   1901
  X66

*PISHNOV, Lev   USSR   1891
  EVM
  EVM: PYSJNOW

*PISK, Paul Amadeus   USA   1893   Austria
  AA73, ASUC, BB65, BB71, DAS, DDM, EVM, IMD, LMD,
  REM, WI69, X64, X65, X66, X67, X68

*PISTON, Walter Hamor   USA   1894
  BB65, BB71, CME, DDM, EMS, EVM, IMD, LMD, MEH,
  PCM, PC71, REM, WTM, X64, X65, X66, X68
  EMS: ПИСТОН

PISTOR, Carlfriedrich   Germany   1884
  LMD, SML, X64, X65

*PITFIELD, Thomas Baron   Great Britain 1903
  LMD, WI69, X66, X67, X68

*PITTALUGA, Gustavo   Spain   1906
  DDM, LMD, X64

*PIZZETTI, Ildebrando   Italy   1880
  BB65, BB71, DDM, EMS, EVM, IMD, LMD, MEH, MLA25/4,
  REM, VNM, WTM, X64, X65, X67, X68
  EMS: ПИЦЦЕТТИ

*PIZZINI, Carlo Alberto   Italy   1905
  LMD, REM

*PLACHETA, Hugo   Austria   1892
  IMD, X68

*PLAETNER, Jørgen   Denmark   1930
  VTM

PLAIN, Gerald   USA
  AA73

PLAMENAC, Dragan   USA   1895   Yugoslavia
  BB71, DAS, HCM, X64, X65, X68

PLANCHART, Alejandro   USA
  ASUC

PLANCHART, Alejandro
  Enrique   Venezuela
  X68

PLANICK, Annette Meyers   USA
    AA73, X66, X67, X68

*PLATEN, Horst   Germany   1884
    EVM

*PLATONOV, Nikolai Ivanovich USSR   1894   1967
    EMS, X64, X68
    EMS: ПЛАТОНОВ

*PLAVEC, Josef   Czechoslovakia 1905
    CCZ, EVM, LMD, MEH, REM, WI69, X65, X68

PLAZA-ALFONZA, Eduardo   Venezuela   1911
    CA14, LMD

*PLAZA-ALFONZA, Juan
  Bautista   Venezuela   1898   1965
    BB65, BB71, CA9, DDM, LMD, MLA22/4, X65, X66
    BB65 and BB71: 1964

*PLÉ-CAUSSADE, Simone   France   1897
    IMD

PLESKOW, Raoul   USA   1931
    ASUC, PC71, X66, X68

*PLESS, Hans   Austria   1884   1966
    X66

*PLESSIS, Hubert L. du   Union of   1922
    EVM, WSA   South Africa
    WSA: DU PLESSIS, H. L.

PLICHTA, Jan   Czechoslovakia 1898
    CCZ

PLONER, Josef Eduard   1894
    IMD

PLOTNICHENKO, Grigori
  Maksimovich   USSR   1918
    EMS, PPU69/2
    EMS: ПЛОТНИЧЕНКО

PLUISTER, Simon   Netherlands   1913
    EVM

PLUM, Abram M.   USA
    ASUC

*POCHON, Alfred   Switzerland   1878   1959
    AS66, BB65, BB71, LMD, REM, SCHW

399

*PODÉŠŤ, Ludvik Czechoslovakia 1921 1968
CCZ, IMD2, LMD, MEH, MNP64/3, SML, X64, X65

*PODEŠVA, Jaromir Czechoslovakia 1927
BB65, BB71, CCZ, IMD, IMD2, LMD, MEH, MNP64/3,
MNP72/4, SML, X64, X65, X66, X68

PODKOVIUROV, Petr Petrovich USSR 1910
EMS
EMS: ПОДКОВЫРОВ

POHL, Frederic Canada
CVM, MCO68, NLC

POIRIER, J. M. Canada 1919
MCO, MCO68

POKORNÝ, Antonín Czechoslovakia 1890
CCZ

*POKRASS, Daniil Yakovlevich USSR 1905 1954
EMS, LMD
EMS: ПОКРÁСС

*POKRASS, Dmitri Yakovlevich USSR 1899
EMS, LMD, MEH, PPU, PPU69/3, PPU70/2, PPU71/1, SML
EMS: ПОКРАСС

*POLDINI, Ede Hungary 1869 1957
EVM, IMD, LMD, REM

*POLIAKOV, Valeri Leonidovich
See: POLYAKOV, V. L.

POLIČ, Mirko Yugoslavia 1890 1951
LMD, MSC, X68

POLIFRONE, Jon J. USA 1937
AA73, PC71, X67, X68

*POLIGNAC, Armande de France 1876 1962
BB65, BB71, LMD

POLIN, Claire J. USA 1926
ASUC, DAS, DN70, PCM, PC71, X64, X65, X68
Married name: SCHAFF, Mrs. Merle S.

POLLAK, Frank
See: PELLEG, Frank

POLLOCK, Robert 1946
WAN

POLOLÁNÍK, Zdeněk   Czechoslovakia 1935
    CCZ, IMD2, MEH, MNP67/1, MNP69/4, X66, X67

POLONI, Gaetano   Italy   1893
    LMD, REM

*POLOVINKIN, Leonid
    Alexeievic   USSR   1894   1949
    REM

*POLTRONIERI, Alberto   Italy   1895
    REM

*POLYAKOV, Valeriy
    Leonidovich   USSR   1913   1970
    EMS, PPU, PPU70/2, X67, X68
    EMS: ПОЛЯКОВ   Vol. I: POLIAKOV

*PONC, Miroslav   Czechoslovakia 1902
    CCZ, CME, EVM, IMD, LMD, MEH, REM, X68

PONGRÁCZ, Zoltán   Hungary   1912
    CHC

*PONIRIDIS, Georgios   Greece   1892   Turkey
    BB65, BB71, CME, DDM, EL:1, EL:2, EL:4, LMD, PAP, REM,
    X65
    Also spelled: PONIRID_Y_, Georg_es_

PONIRIDY, George
    See: PONIRIDIS, Georgios

*PONOMARENKO, Nikolai
    Stepanovich   USSR   1893   1952
    EMS
    EMS: ПОНОМАРЕНКО

*PONS, Charles   France   1870   1957
    BB65, BB71, LMD

*PONSE, Luctor   Netherlands   1914   Switzerland
    EVM, IMD, NED
    EVM: 1911

*POOT, Marcel   Belgium   1901
    CBC, CME, DDM, EVM, IMD, LMD, REM, SML, X64

POP, Dariu   Rumania   1887   1965
    RCL

POPA, Aurel   Rumania   1917
    RCL, X67, X68

POPA, Mircea   Rumania   1915
LMD, RCL, X65

*POPATENKO, Tamara
Aleksandrovna   USSR   1912
EMS
EMS: ПОПАТЕ́НКО

*POPELKA, Joachim   Germany   1910   1965
WWG, X65

POPESCU, Stefan   Rumania   1884   1956
RCL

POPIEL, Stanislaw   Poland   1902
PKW

POPOV, Alexander   Bulgaria   1927
BB65, BB71, X68

*POPÓV, Gavriil Nikolayevich   USSR   1904   1972
BB71, CME, EMS, EVM, LMD, MEH, MLA29/4, PPU, REM,
SML, X64
EMS: ПОПОВ

POPOV, Todor Ivanov   Bulgaria   1921
BMK, MEH, X68
BMK: ПОПОВ

POPOVIĆ, Berislav   Yugoslavia   1931
KMJ

POPOVICI, Doru   Rumania   1932
BB65, BB71, EMS, LMD, RCL, X64, X65, X66, X67, X68
EMS: ПО́ПОВИЧ

POPOVICI, Timotei   Rumania   1870   1950
EMS
EMS: ПО́ПОВИЧ

POPOVICI, Vasile   Rumania   1900
EMS, RCL
EMS: ПО́ПОВИЧ

*PORADOWSKI, Stefan Bolesław   Poland   1902   1967
BB71, LMD, MLA24/4, PKW, REM, X64, X65, X67, X68

*PORENA, Boris   Italy   1927
IMD, IMD2, LMD, REM, X65, X67, X68

PORFEYTE, Andreas   Rumania   1927
LMD, RCL, X64, X65, X66, X68

*PORRINO, Ennio   Italy   1910   1959
    BB65, BB71, DDM, EVM, IMD, LMD, REM

*PORTE, Jacques   France   1910
    X68

*PORTER, Quincy   USA   1897   1966
    BB65, BB71, DDM, EVM, IMD, LMD, MLA23/4, PCM, PC71,
    REM, WTM, X64, X65, X66, X67, X68

PORTNOFF, Mischa   USA   1901   Germany
    AS66, LMD, X68

PORTNOFF, Wesley   USA   1910   Russia
    AS66

PORTUGAL, Marcus   Portugal
    CME

POSADA-AMADOR, Carlos   Colombia   1908
    CA8, IMD, LMD

*POSER, Hans   Germany   1917   1970
    IMD, LMD, MLA27/4, REM, X64

POSPÍŠIL, Juraj   Czechoslovakia 1931
    CCZ, MEH, X65, X66, X67, X68, ZE69/3, ZE70/1, ZE71/1,
    ZE71/2, ZE71/3, ZE72/1

*POST, Joseph   Australia   1906   1972
    X66

*POSTON, Elizabeth   Great Britain 1905
    EVM, LMD, WI69, X64, X67, X68

POSWIANSKY, B.
    See: BARDI, Benno

*POTIRON, Henri   France   1882
    LMD, REM, X64, X65, X68

*POTTER, Archibald James   Ireland   1918   Ulster
    WI69, X67

*POUEIGH, Jean Marie-
    Octave-Gerard   France   1876   1958
    BB65, BB71, DDM, DMF, EVM, LMD, REM
    Pseudonym: SÉRÉ, Octave

*POULENC, Francis   France   1899   1963
    BB65, BB71, CME, DDM, DMF, EMS, IMD, IMD2, LMD, MEH,
    REM, SML, TCM, VNM, WTM, X64, X65, X66, X67, X68
    EMS: ПУЛЕНК

POUPARD, Henri-Pierre
  See: SAUGUET, Henri

POUSHKOV, Venedikt Venediktovich
  See: PUSHKOV, Venedikt Venodiktovich

*POUSSEUR, Henri   Belgium   1929
  BB65, BB71, CBC, CME, DDM, DMM, IMD, IMD2, LMD,
  MEH, MNG, MZW, REM, SML, TSC, X64, X65, X66, X67,
  X68

*POUWELS, Jan   1898
  IMD

*POWELL, John   USA   1882 1963
  AS66, BB65, BB71, EVM, LMD, PCM, REM, X64

*POWELL, Laurence   USA   1899 Great Britain
  AA73, AS66, LMD, X64, X65, X66, X67, X68

*POWELL, Mel   USA   1923
  AS66, BB65, BB71, CA9, LMD, PCM, PC71, X64, X65, X66,
  X67, X68

POWELL, Morgan   USA   1938
  PCM, X68

*POYNTER, Arthur R.   Canada   1913
  CVM, CVMa, MCO68, MCO71, NLC, NLCa

*POZAJIĆ, Mladen   Yugoslavia   1905
  HCM, KMJ, LMD, X67

*POZDRO, John Walter   USA   1923
  AA73, BB65, BB71, LMD, PCM, X65, X66, X67

*POŹNIAK, Wlodzimierz   Poland   1904 1967
  LMD, PKW, REM, X64, X66, X67, X68

*POZZOLI, Ettore   Italy   1873 1957
  IMD, LMD, REM, X65

PRADELLA, Massimo   Italy   1924
  LMD, REM

PRÁŠIL, František   Czechoslovakia 1902
  MEH

*PRATELLA, Francesco Balilla Italy   1880 1955
  BB65, BB71, DDM, EVM, IMD, LMD, MEH, REM, X67

PREBANDA, Milan   Yugoslavia   1907
  KMJ

PŘECECHTĚL, Zbyněk Czechoslovakia 1916
 CCZ, MEH

PREGELJ, Ciril Yugoslavia 1887 1966
 KMJ

*PREGER, Leo France 1907 1965
 BB71

PREHN, Tom Sweden circa 1942
 X68

PREK, Stanko Yugoslavia 1915
 KMJ

*PREMRL, Stanko Yugoslavia 1880 1965
 IMD, KMJ, LMD, MSC

PREPREK, Stanislav Yugoslavia 1900
 KMJ

*PRESSER, William USA 1916
 AA73, DN72, PCM, PC71, X64, X65, X66, X67, X68

PRESTINI, Giuseppe Italy 1877 1955
 REM

*PRÊTRE, Georges France 1924
 BB71, LMD, QQF, X64, X65, X66, X68

PREUD'HOMME, Armand Belgium 1904
 EVM

PREVIN, André USA 1929 Germany
 AS66, BB71, LMD, PCM, WI69, X64, X65, X66, X67, X68

*PREVITALI, Fernando Italy 1907
 EVM, LMD, REM, WI69, X65, X66

PRÉVOST, André Canada 1934
 CCM, CCM71, CVM, CVMa, DDM, KEY, MCO68, MCO71, NLC,
 NLCa, X66, X67, X68

*PREY, Claude France 1925
 DDM, LMD, REM, X65, X67

*PRICE, Florence B. USA 1888 1953
 AS66

PRICE, John E. USA
 ASUC

*PRICE, Percival Frank   Canada   1901
    X64, X65, X68

PRICK VAN WELY, Max
    Arthur   Netherlands   1909
    EVM

PRICKMAYER, Georg
    See: PIER, Georg

PRIETO, María Teresa   Mexico   Spain
    QLA, X66, X67

PRIGOZHIN, Lyutsian
    Abramovich   USSR   1926
    CME, PPU, X68

PŘÍHODA, Váša   Czechoslovakia 1900 1960
    BB71, LMD

PRINČIČ, Vladimir   Yugoslavia   1888
    KMJ

PRINCIPE, Remy   Italy   1889
    LMD, REM

PRINGSHEIM, Heinz   Germany   1882
    LMD, REM, WWG

PRINGSHEIM, Klaus   Germany   1883 1972
    BB65, BB71, EVM, LMD, MEH, MLA29/4, REM

PRIOLO, Christopher E.   USA   1949
    CAP

PRISTER, Bruno   Yugoslavia   1909
    HCM, KMJ

*PRITCHARD, Arthur John   Great Britain   1908
    X64, X67

*PRITZKER, David Abramovich USSR   1902
    EMS
    EMS: ПРИЦКЕР

PROCTER, Leland   1914
    WAN

*PROCTER-GREGG, Humphrey   Great Britain   1895
    LMD, X65

*PROCTOR, Charles   Great Britain   1906
    EVM, WI69, X65, X66

PROCTOR, Gregory   USA
    ASUC

PRODROMIDÈS, Jean   France   1927
    QQF, X65

PROFETA, Laurentiu   Rumania   1925
    BB65, BB71, CME, LMD, RCL, X64, X65

PROFETA, Rubino   Italy   1910
    LMD, X64, X68

PRÖGER, Johannes   1917
    IMD, X66, X68

PROHASKA, Miljenko   Yugoslavia
    X67, X68

*PROKOFIEV, Serge
   Sergeevich   USSR   1891   1953
    BB65, BB71, CME, DDM, DMM, EMS, EVM, IMD, IMD2,
    LMD, MEH, MZW, PAP, REM, SCD, SML, TCM, VNM,
    WTM, X64, X65, X66, X67, X68
    EMS: ПРОКОФЬЕВ

*PROKOPIEV, Trajko   Yugoslavia   1909
    KMJ, REM, X67

PROŠEV, Toma   Yugoslavia   1931
    KMJ, X68

*PROSNAK, Jan   Poland   1904
    LMD, REM, X64, X65, X66, X68

PROSPERI, Carlo   Italy   1921
    IMD, LMD, REM, X65

PRÓSZYŃSKI, Stanislaw   Poland   1926
    PKW, X68

PROTON de la CHAPELLE,
   Robert   France   1894
    QQF, X65, X67
    Pseudonym of: FRAGNY, Robert de
    X67: FRAGNY, Robert de

*PROVAZNÍK, Anatol   Czechoslovakia   1887   1950
    CCZ, IMD, LMC

*PRÜMERS, Adolf   Germany   1877
  EVM

*PUETTER, Hugo   1913
  IMD

PUEYO, Salvador   Spain
  X67

PUGNANI
  See: KREISLER, Fritz

PUIG, Michel   France   1930

PUIG-ROGET, Henriette
  Marie Eulalie   France   1910
  LMD, QQF, REM

*PUJOL VILLARRUBI, Emilio   Spain   1886
  LMD, REM

PUKST, Grigori Konstantinovich   USSR   1900   1960
  EMS
  EMS: ПУКСТ

PULGAR VIDAL, Francisco   Peru   1929
  CA16

*PULVER, Lev Mihailovich   USSR   1883   1970
  EMS, X64
  EMS: ПУЛЬВЕР

PURDY, Winston   Canada   1941
  CCM, CVM, NLC

PURSER, John Whitley   Great Britain   1942   Scotland
  WI69, X67, X68

PURVIS, Richard   USA   1915
  PC71, X66, X67

*PUSHKOV, Venedikt
  Venodiktovich   USSR   1896
  EMS
  EMS: ПУШКОВ

PUTSCHE, Thomas   USA   1929
  X68

*PUYVELDE, Omer van   Belgium   1912
  EVM

PYLE, Francis Johnson   USA   1901
    AA73, ASUC, AS66, PC71, X64, X66, X67, X68

*PYLKKÄNEN, Tauno Kullervo   Finland   1918
    CME, COF, KKO, LMD, REM, VTM, X65, X66, X68

PYSJNOW, Lev
    See: PISHNOV, Lev

QUAGLIA, Mario   Italy   1901
    LMD

QUARANTA, Felice   Italy   1910
    LMD, REM, X65

QUARATINO, Pascual   Argentina   1904
    REM

*QUAYLE, Leo Gordon   Union of   1918
    LMD, REM   South Africa

*QUEROL GAVALDÁ, Miguel   Spain   1912
    DDM, LMD, REM, X65, X66, X68

QUEZADA K. , Armando   Mexico   1937
    MMX

QUILLING, Howard   USA   circa 1937
    DN72

*QUILTER, Roger   Great Britain   1877   1953
    EVM, LMD, REM

*QUINET, Fernand   Belgium   1898   1971
    CBC, DDM, EVM, IMD, LMD, MLA28/4, REM

*QUINET, Marcel   Belgium   1915
    CBC, CME, DDM, EVM, IMD, IMD2, LMD, REM

QUINN, J. Mark   USA   1936
    PCM

QUINTANA, Hetor   Mexico   1936
    CA15, HET18

QUINTERO, Abelardo   Chile

*QUINTIERI, Maurizio   Italy   1887
    LMD, REM
    LMD: 1884

QUIROGA, Manuel   Spain   1892   1961
    BB65, BB71, REM

*QUOIKA, Rudolf   Germany   1897   1972
    LMD, MLA29/4, REM, X66, X67, X68

*RAASTED, Niels Otto   Denmark   1888   1966
    EVM, IMD, LMD

RABE, Folke   Sweden   1935
    CME, DNS, FST, IMD, IMD2, SIMa, STI, STS, SWE, VTM,
    X65, X66, X67, X68

RABINOF, Sylvia   USA
    AS66, X68

*RABSCH, Edgar   Germany   1892   1964
    EVM, LMD, WWG, X64

*RACEK, Fritz   Austria   1911
    LMD, REM, X67

*RACHLEW, Anders   Norway   1882
    EVM, VTM

*RAČIÙNAS, Antanas Ionovich   USSR   1905   Lithuania
    EMS
    EMS: РАЧЮНАС   Vol. I: RATSHOUNAS

RACKLEY, Lawrence   USA   1932
    CAP, DN72

RACOVITZĂ-FLONDOR, Florica   Rumania   1897
    RCL

*RADAUER, Irmfried   Germany   1928
    IMD, X67

*RADENKOVIĆ, Milutin   Yugoslavia   1921
    BB65, BB71, IMD, KMJ, LMD, REM, X64, X67

*RADIĆ, Dusán   Yugoslavia   1929
    BB65, BB71, CME, DDM, IMD, KMJ, LMD, MEH, REM,
    X65, X67

RADICA, Ruben   Yugoslavia   1931
    BB65, BB71, CME, HCM, IMD2, KMJ, LMD, MEH, REM,
    X65, X67

RADOLE, Giuseppe   Italy   1921
    LMD, X68

*RADOUX-ROGER, Charles   Belgium   1877   1952
    EVM, LMD, REM

RADOVANOVIĆ, Vladan   Yugoslavia   1932
    BB65, BB71, KMJ, LMD, X64, X67, X68

RAFFMAN, Relly   USA
    ASUC

*RAFTER, Leonard   Great Britain   1911   1965
    X65, X67

RAGLAND, Robert Oliver   USA   1931
    AS66

*RAGNI, Guido   Italy   1899   1968
    LMD, REM

RAGO, Alexis   Venezuela   1930
    BB71, CA14

*RAICHEV, Alexander Ivanov   Bulgaria   1922
    BB65, BB71, BMK, EVM, LMD, MEH, X67, X68
    EVM: RAITCHEW   LMD: RAITŠJEV   MEH: RAJČEV
    BMK: РАЙЧЕВ

RAICHEV, Viktor Ivanov   Bulgaria   1920
    BMK, SML, X67, X68
    SML: RAITCHEV
    BMK: РАЙЧЕВ

*RAICHL, Miroslav   Czechoslovakia   1930
    BB65, BB71, CCZ, IMD2, LMD, MEH, MNP64/3, X64

*RAINIER, Priaulx   Great Britain   1903   Union of
    BB65, BB71, DDM, EVM, IMD, LMD, OCM,   South Africa
    REM, WI69, X64, X65, X67
    REM: Prialux

RAITHEL, Hugo   Germany   1932
    LMD, SML, X64

*RAJIČIĆ, Stanojlo   Yugoslavia   1910
    BB65, BB71, CME, EMS, EVM, IMD, KMJ, LMD, MEH, REM,
    SML, X64, X65, X66, X67
    EMS: РАЙЧИЧ

RAJNA, Thomas   Great Britain
    X67, X68

RAJTER, L'udovít   Czechoslovakia   1906
    CCZ, LMD, MEH, X66, X67, X68

RAKHMANKULOVA, Mariam
Mannalovna   USSR   1901
    EMS
    EMS: РАХМАНКУЛОВА

*RĀKOV, Nicolai Petrovich   USSR   1908
    EMS, EVM, LMD, MEH, PPU, REM, SML, X68
    EMS: РАКОВ

RALF, Richard   Germany   1897
    BB71

RAMAN, Gedert   USSR
    PPU68/3, PPU69/2, X65

*RAMETTE, Yves   France   1921
    EVM

*RAMIN, Günther   Germany   1898   1956
    DDM, EMS, EVM, LMD, MEH, REM, MEH
    EMS: РАМИН

RAMIREZ F., Filberto   Mexico   1920
    MMX

RAMM, Valentina Iosifovna   USSR   1888
    EMS
    EMS: РАММ

RAMOUS, Gianni   Italy   1930
    IMD, REM

*RAMOVŠ, Primož   Yugoslavia   1921
    BB65, BB71, CME, DDM, EMS, IMD, IMD2, KMJ, LMD, MEH,
    REM, TSC, X65, X66, X67, X68
    EMS: РАМОВШ

RAMPAL, Jean-Pierre   France   1922
    CMF19, QQF, X64, X65, X67

*RAMRATH, Konrad   Germany   1880
    WWG

*RAMSEY, Cyril Ernest   Great Britain   1904
    WI69

RAMSIER, Paul   USA   1927
    AS66, PCM

RANDALL, James K.   USA
    ASUC, X65, X66, X68

RANDS, Bernard Great Britain 1935
   BB65, BB71, IMD2, LMD, MNG, PAP, TSC, X66, X68

*RANKI, György Hungary 1907
   BB65, BB71, CHC, CME, EVM, IMD, LMD, MEH, REM, SML,
   WI69, X67, X68

*RANKL, Karl Franz Great Britain 1898 1968
   BB71, EVM, LMD, REM, WI69, X68 Austria

*RANSE, Marc de France 1881 1951
   DDM, LMD

*RANTA, Sulho Finland 1901 1960
   BB71, COF, DDM, EVM, IMD, LMD, REM, VTM

*RANTZÉN, Torsten Sweden 1889 1955
   KSV

*RÀPALGO, Ugo Italy 1914
   LMD, REM

*RAPHAEL, Günter Albert
   Rudolf Germany 1903 1960
   BB65, BB71, DDM, EVM, IMD, IMD2, MEH, REM, SML,
   WWG, X64, X67, X68

*RAPHLING, Samuel (Sam) USA 1910
   AA73, AS66, LMD, PCM, PC71, X66, X67, X68

RAPPAPORT, Moshe Israel 1903 Poland
   ACU

RAPTAKIS, Kleon USA 1905 Greece
   AS66

*RASBACH, Oscar USA 1888
   AS66, X68

*RASCH, Kurt Germany 1902
   EVM, LMD, REM

RASMUSSEN, Karl Aage Finland circa 1940
   X68

*RASSE, François Belgium 1873 1955
   DDM, EVM, LMD, MGG, REM

*RATHAUS, Karol USA 1895 1954
   AS66, EVM, IMD, LMD, MGG, PKW, Poland
   REM, X65

*RATHBURN, Eldon Davis   Canada   1916
    CA11, CCM, LMD, MCO, MCO68, MCO71, TFB

RATIU, Adrian   Rumania   1928
    LMD, RCL, X64, X65, X68

RATNER, Leonard Gilbert   USA   1916
    BB65, BB71, DAS, LMD, X64, X67

RATSHOUNAS, A. I.
    See: RAČIUNAS, A. I.

RATTALINO, Piero   Italy   1931
    REM, X64, X68

RATTENBACH, Augusto
    Benjamin   Argentina   1927
    BB71, CA12, LMD, X68

*RAU, Kurt Walter   Germany   1891
    EVM

RAUCH, František   Czechoslovakia   1910
    EVM, LMD, MEH, X64, X65, X66, X67

RAUCH, Joseph   1904
    IMD, X65

*RAUH, Adam   Germany   1909
    WWG

RAUKHVERGER, Mihail
    Rafailovich   USSR   1901
    EMS, LMD, X67, X68
    EMS: РАУХВЕ́РГЕР

*RAUTAVAARA, Eino Juhani   Finland   1928
    CME, COF, IMD, IMD2, KKO, LMD, MEH, MGG, REM, SML,
    VTM, X64, X65, X66, X67, X68

RAUTIO, Karl Erikovich   USSR   1889   1963
    EMS   Finland
    EMS: ПА́УТИО

*RAUTIO, Matti   Finland   1922
    COF, KKO, VTM, X68

*RAVASENGA, Carlo   Italy   1891   1964
    EVM, LMD, MGG, REM

RAVELLI, Alessandro   Italy   1880
    REM

*RAVELO, José de Jesús   Dominican   1876   1951
   REM   Republic

RAVI SHANKAR
   See: SHANKAR, Ravi

*RAVINA, Rabinovitz Menashe   Israel   1899   Russia
   WWI, X67

*RAVNIK, Janko   Yugoslavia   1891
   IMD, KMJ, LMD, MGG, REM, X67

*RAWLINSON, Harold   Great Britain   1891
   X64

*RAWSTHORNE, Alan   Great Britain   1905   1971
   BB65, BB71, CME, DDM, EVM, IMD, LMD, MEH, MGG,
   MLA28/4, REM, WI69, WTM, X64, X65, X66, X67, X68

RAXACH, Enrique   Spain   1932
   IMD, IMD2, LMD, X64, X66, X67, X68

*RAYBOULD, Robert Clarence   Great Britain   1886   1972
   MLA29/4, X65

*RAYMOND, Fred   Austria   1900   1954
   LMD, MGG

RAYMOND, Lewis   USA   1908   1965
   AS66, PCM, PC71

RAZZI, Fausto   Italy   1932
   BB71, MNP66/4, LMD, REM, X66, X67

*RAZZI, Giulio   Italy   1904
   IMD, LMD

REA, John   Canada
   CCM71, MCO71

*READ, Gardner   USA   1913
   AA73, AS66, BB65, BB71, CA8, DN72, EVM, LMD, PCM,
   PC71, REM, WI69, WTM, X64, X65, X66, X67

READ, H. Owen   USA
   ASUC

READ, John William   USA   1933
   DN72, X68

READ, Thomas L.   USA
   ASUC, CAP

*REAKS, Brian Harold James   Great Britain   1920
   X66, X68

*REBNER, Edward Wolfgang   Austria   1910
   IMD

RECHMENSKY, Nikolai
   Sergeevich   USSR   1897   1963
   EMS, X64, X68
   EMS: РЕЧМЕНСКИЙ

RECK, David   USA   1935
   IMD2, PCM, X65, X67, X68

RECK, Donald   USA
   X66

RECLI, Giulia   Italy   1890
   LMD, REM

RECUPITO, Marco Vinicio   Italy   1910
   LMD

*REDA, Siegfried   Germany   1916   1968
   DDM, EVM, IMD, IMD2, MGG, MLA26/4, REM, X64, X65,
   X66, X67, X68

*REDFERN, Philip Edwin   Great Britain   1908
   WI69

*REDLICH, Hans Ferdinand   Great Britain   1903   1968
   BB71, EVM, LMD, MGG, REM, X64, X65,   Austria
   X66, X67, X68

*REDMAN, Reginald   Great Britain   1892   1972
   IMD, LMD, MLA29/4, WI69

REED, Alfred   USA   1921
   AS66, PCM, PC71, X68

*REED, Herbert Owen   USA   1910
   AA73, AS66, LMD, PCM, PC71, REM, X64, X65, X66,
   X67, X68

*REED, William Leonard   Great Britain   1910
   DDM, EVM, LMD, REM, WI69, X66

REES, Howard   Great Britain
   X68

*REESEN, Emil   Denmark   1887   1964
   IMD

*REFICE, Licinio   Italy   1885 1954
  EVM, LMD, REM, X64

*REGAMEY, Constantin   Switzerland 1907 Russia
  BB65, BB71, CME, DDM, EVM, IMD, IMD2, LMD, MEH,
  MGG, PKW, REM, SCHW, WWS, X64, X65, X66, X67, X68

REGNER, Eric   USA
  ASUC

REGNER, Hermann   1928
  IMD2, X65, X66

*REHAN, Robert   Germany 1901
  IMD, X67, X68

*REHBERG, Walter   Switzerland 1900 1957
  EVM, LMD, MGG, SCHW

*REHMANN, Theodor Bernhard Germany 1895 1963
  MGG

ŘEHOŘ, Bohuslav   Czechoslovakia 1938
  MNP69/4, MNP72/9

REICH, Steve   USA   1936
  BB71, X68

*REICHEL, Bernard   Switzerland 1901
  DDM, EVM, LMD, MGG, REM, SCHW, WWS, X67, X68

*REIDARSON, Per   Norway 1879
  EVM, VTM

*REIDINGER, Friedrich Austria   1890
  X68

REIF, Paul   USA   1910 Czecho-
  AA73, AS66, BB65, BB71, LMD, PCM, PC71, slovakia
  X64, X65, X66, X67, X68

*REIMAN, Villem Madisovich USSR   1906 Estonia
  EMS, EVM, LMD, PPU, PPU70/1
  LMD: REJMAN   PPU: REYMAN
  EMS: РЕЙМАН

REIMANN, Aribert   Germany 1936
  BB71, IMD, IMD2, LMD, PAP, X64, X65, X66, X67, X68

REIMANN, Wolfgang   Germany 1887
  EVM, LMD, MGG, REM, X67

*REIN, Walter   Germany   1893   1955
    EVM, IMD, LMD, MGG

REINBERGER, Jiří   Czechoslovakia   1914
    CCZ, X65, X66, X67, X68

*REINER, Karel   Czechoslovakia   1910
    BB71, CCZ, CME, EVM, IMD, IMD2, LMD, MEH, MNP65/6,
    MNP65/7, MNP70/4, MNP72/4, REM, SML, WI69, X64, X65,
    X66, X68

*REINHARD, Kurt August
   Georg   Germany   1914
    REM, X64, X65, X68

REINHARDT, Bruno   Israel   1929   Rumania
    ACU

REINHART, Walther   Switzerland   1886
    LMD, SCHW

*REINHOLD, Otto   Germany   1899   1965
    EVM, IMD2, LMD, MEH, REM, SML, X64, X65, X67

*REINL, Franz Joseph   Germany   1903   Austria
    IMD

REISBERG, Horace   USA
    ASUC

*REISER, Alois   USA   1887   Bohemia
    AS66, EVM, LMD, REM

REISTRUP, James   USA
    AA73, X65, X66, X67, X68

REITER, Albert   Austria   1905
    IMD, X66, X68

REITER, Ernst (II)   Switzerland   1897
    LMD, SCHW

REITER, Hermann   Austria
    X68

*REIZENSTEIN, Franz
   Theodore   Great Britain   1911   1968
    BB65, BB71, EVM, LMD, MGG, MLA25/4,   Germany
    OCM, REM, WI69, X64, X65, X66, X67, X68

*REMACHA, Fernando   Spain   1898
    DDM, REM

REMENKOV, Stefan Nikolov   Bulgaria   1923
    BB65, BB71, BMK, MEH, X68
    BMK: РЕМЕНКОВ

*REMONDON, Suzanne   France   1884
    QQF, WI69
    Pseudonym: GOURY, Suzanne

*RENIÉ, Henriette   France   1875   1956
    DDM, LMD, MGG, REM

*RENNER, Willy   Germany   1883
    EVM

RENOSTO, Paolo   Italy   1935
    LMD, X68

*RENSHAW, Rosette   Canada   1920
    X68

*RENZI, Armando   Italy   1915
    LMD, REM, X64

RENZI, Luigi   Italy   1899
    LMD, REM

*RESCHOFSKY, Alex   Hungary   1887
    WI69

RESNIKOFF-LEVITE, Miriam
    See: LEVITE, Miriam

*RESPIGHI, Elsa   Italy   1894
    LMD, REM
    REM: RESPIGHI, Ottorino

*RÉTI, Rudolph   USA   1885   1957
    EVM, LMD, MGG, REM, X66, X67, X68   Serbia

*RETTICH, Wilhelm   Germany   1892
    LMD, REM, X67

*REUCHSEL, Maurice   France   1880   1968
    BB71, DDM, LMD, REM

*REUTER, Florizel von   USA   1890   USA
    LMD, REM

*REUTER, Fritz   Germany   1896   1963
    EVM, IMD, LMD, MGG, REM, SML, X64, X68
    IMD and REM: 1896-1962

*REUTTER, Hermann   Germany 1900
 BB71, CME, DDM, EMS, EVM, IMD, IMD2, LMD, MEH, MGG,
 REM, SML, WWG, X64, X65, X66, X67, X68
 EMS: РЕЙТЕР

*REVEL, Pierre   France 1901
 LMD, MGG, REM

*REVUTSKY, Lev Nikolayevich USSR 1889
 DDM, EMS, LMD, MEH, MGG, PPU, PPU68/1, PPU69/2,
 PPU69/3, REM, SML, X64
 MEH: REVUCKIJ SML: REWUZKI
 EMS: РЕВУЦКИЙ

*REXHÄUSER, Ferdinand Germany 1924
 WWG

*REY, Cemal Reschit   Turkey 1904
 DDM, EVM, REM, X65

REYMAN, V. M.
 See: REIMAN, V. M.

*REYNOLDS, Alfred Charles Great Britain 1884 1969
 WI69, X65

REYNOLDS, Roger   USA 1934
 BB65, BB71, DN72, EL:4, LMD, PCM, PC71, TSC, X65, X66,
 X67, X68

REYNOLDS, Verne   USA 1926
 BB71, LMD, PCM, PC71, WAN
 WAN: 1928

*ŘEZÁČ, Ivan   Czechoslovakia 1924
 CCZ, IMD2, LMD, MEH, MNP69/5, MNP72/4, MNP72/6, SML,
 X64, X65, X66

ŘEZNÍČIK, Petr   Czechoslovakia 1938
 MNP72/9

RHODES, Kenneth   USA
 X65

RHODES, Phillip   USA 1940
 ASUC, WAN, X68

RIAATS, Jan   USSR 1932
 CME, X66, X67, X68

*RIABOV, Aleksei
Pantelaymonvich   USSR   1899   1955
   EMS
   EMS: РЯБOB

*RIAUZOV, Serguei
Nikolayevich   USSR   1905
   EMS
   EMS: РЯУЗOB

RIBÁRI, Antal   Hungary   1924
   CHC, X68

*RIBAUPIERRE, Emile de   Switzerland   1887
   SCHW, WWS

RICCI-SIGNORINI, Antonio   Italy   1867   1965
   LMD

RICE, Thomas N.   USA
   AA73

RICHARDS, William
   See: RIEGGER, Wallingford

*RICHARDSON, Alan   Great Britain   1904   Scotland
   LMD, WI69

*RICHARDSON, Arnold   Great Britain   1914
   X66, X67

*RICHARDSON, William Henry   Great Britain   1883
   WI69

*RICHARTZ, Willi   Germany   1900   1972
   LMD, MGG, MLA29/4, SML, WWG

*RICHEPIN, Tiarko François
Denis   France   1884
   QQF

*RICHTER, Carl Arthur   Switzerland   1883   1957
   SCHW   Germany

RICHTER, Kurt Dietmar   Germany   1888
   LMD, SML, X65, X68

RICHTER, Marga   USA   1926
   AS66, PCM

RICHTER, Paul   Rumania   1875   1950
   RCL

*RICHTER-HAASER, Hans   Germany   1912
    LMD, REM, WI69, WWG, X64, X65, X66, X67, X68

*ŘÍDKÝ, Jaroslav   Czechoslovakia   1897   1956
    BB65, BB71, CCZ, CME, DDM, EVM, IMD, IMD2, LMD, MEH,
    MGG, MNP67/5, REM, SML, X64, X65, X67, X68

*RIDOUT, Alan Jones   Great Britain   1934
    WI69, X65, X66, X67
    WI69: Alan John

*RIDOUT, Godfrey   Canada   1918
    BB65, BB71, CA11, CVM, CVMa, IMD, KEY, LMD, MCO,
    MCO68, MCO71, NLC, NLCa, TFB, X68

*RIEDE, Erich   Germany   1903   Great Britain
    LMD, REM, X64, X65, X68

RIEDL, Josef Anton   Germany   1927
    EL:1, EL:3, LMD, MGG, PAP, REM, X67, X68
    EL:1, EL:3 and PAP: 1929

RIEDLBAUCH, Václav   Czechoslovakia   1947
    MNP69/4, MNP72/9

*RIEGGER, Wallingford
   Constantin   USA   1884   1961
    BB65, BB71, DDM, EMS, EVM, IMD, IMD2, LMD, MEH, MGG,
    PCM, PC71, REM, TSC, WTM, X64, X65, X66, X67, X68
    EMS: РИГГЕР

RIEHM, Rainer   Germany   1941
    PAP

RIEHM, Rolf   1937
    IMD2

RIEMANN, Ernst   Germany   1882   1953
    EVM

*RIESCO GREZ, Carlos   Chile   1925
    IMD, REM, X64

*RIETHMULLER, Heinrich   Germany   1921
    WWG

*RIETHMÜLLER, Helmut   Germany   1912   1966
    IMD, LMD, MGG, REM, SML, X66

*RIETI, Vittorio   Italy   1898   Egypt
    DDM, EMS, EVM, IMD, LMD, MGG, REM, X68
    EMS: РИЕ́ТИ

RIETZ, Johannes   1905
   IMD

*RIGACCI, Bruno   Italy   1921
   LMD, REM, X68

ŘÍHOVSKÝ, Vojtěch   Czechoslovakia 1871 1950
   LMD, MGG

*RIHTMAN, Cvjetko   Yugoslavia   1902
   EMS, KMJ, MGG
   EMS: РИХТМАН

*RIIS-MAGNUSSEN, Adolf   Denmark   1886 1950
   IMD, EVM
   EVM: 1883

*RIISAGER, Knudaage   Denmark   1897
   BB71, CME, DDM, DMTsp, EVM, IMD, LMD, MEH, MGG,
   REM, VTM, WI69, X65, X66, X67

RILEY, Dennis   USA   1943

RILEY, John   USA   1920
   BB65, BB71, PCM

RILEY, Terry   USA   1935
   BB71, X67, X68

RIMMER, Frederick   Great Britain
   X65

*RIMSKY-KORSAKOV, Georgy
  Mikhailovich   USSR   1901 1965
   EMS, EVM, LMD, REM, X66
   REM: RIMSKI-KORSAKOV, Nikolai
   EMS: РИМСКИЙ-КОРСАКОВ

RINEHART, John   USA
   ASUC

*RINGBOM, Nils-Erie   Finland   1907
   COF, KKO, LMD, MGG, SML, VTM, X66, X68

RINGEISEN, Joseph   Germany   1879 1952
   ACM

RINGGER, Rolf Urs   Switzerland   1935
   IMD, SCHW, X65, X66, X67, X68

RINGO, Henry James   USA   1926
   BB71, X68

RINGWALD, Roy   USA   1910
   PCM

*RISCHE, Quirin   Germany   1903
   IMD

RISINGER, Karel   Czechoslovakia   1920
   CCZ, COO, MEH, X64

*RISTIĆ, Milan   Yugoslavia   1908
   BB65, BB71, CME, EMS, IMD2, KMJ, LMD, MEH, MGG, REM,
   SML, X65, X66, X67
   EMS: РИСТИЧ

RIVARD, William H.   USA   1928
   ASUC, PC71

*RIVERTZ, Johannes Midelfart   Norway   1902
   CNO

*RIVIER, Jean   France   1896
   BB65, BB71, CME, CMF6, DMF20, DDM, DMF, EVM, IMD,
   LMD, MEH, MGG, QQF, REM, SML, X66, X68

*RIVÈRE, Jean-Claude   France   1924
   IMD2

*RIVIÈRE, Jean-Pierre   France   1929
   REM

RIVOLI, Gianfranco   Italy   1921
   LMD, REM, X65, X66

RIZZI, O. Bernardino   Italy   1891   1968
   LMD, REM, X68

ROBB, John Donald   USA   1892
   AA73, AS66, NLC, X64, X65, X66, X68

*ROBBIANI, Igino   Italy   1884   1966
   LMD, MLA23/4, REM

ROBBONE, Joseph   Italy   1916
   LMD, REM

*ROBERTS, Clifford   Great Britain   1889
   WI69

ROBERTS, Gertrud Kuenzel   USA   circa 1912
   AA73, X66, X67, X68

ROBERTS, Trevor   Great Britain

*ROBERTS, William Herbert
  Mervyn   Great Britain   1906   Wales
    EVM, LMD, MGG, REM, WI69

*ROBERTSON, Leroy Jasper   USA   1896   1971
    AS66, BB71, LMD, PCM, REM, WI69, X65, X67

*ROBINSON, Earl Hawley   USA   1910
    AS66, EMS, IMD, LMD, PC71, REM, X64, X67, X68
    EMS: РОБИНСОН

ROBINSON, Edward   USA   1905
    AS66

*ROBINSON, Stanford   Great Britain   1904
    EVM, LMD, X64, X66, X67

*ROCCA, Lodovico   Italy   1895
    DDM, EMS, EVM, IMD, LMD, MGG, REM, WI69
    EMS: РОКΚΑ

ROCCHI, R. Aldo   Italy   1921
    REM, X64, X65

*ROCHAT, Andrée   Italy   1900   Switzerland
    SCHW

*ROCHBERG, George   USA   1918
    AS66, BB65, BB71, CA10, DN72, IMD, IMD2, LMD, OCM,
    PCM, REM, TSC, X64, X65, X66, X67, X68

ROCHEFOUCAULD, Froncois-
  Marie de la   France   1920
    EVM

RODER, Milan   USA   1878   1956
    AS66   Slavonia

RODGERS, Richard   USA   1902
    CME, EVM, LMD, PCM, X64, X65, X66, X67, X68

*RODRIGO, Joaquín   Spain   1902
    DDM, EVM, IMD, LMD, MGG, REM, X67, X68

*RODRIGUEZ, Augusto   Puerto Rico   1904
    LMD

*RODRÍGUEZ, Esther   Cuba   1920
    LMD, REM

RODÜGIN, Evgenyi Pavlovich   USSR   1925
    EMS, X64
    EMS: ПОДЫГИН

ROE, Christopher John   Great Britain 1940
 WI69

*ROESELING, Kaspar   Germany 1894 1960
 LMD, MGG

*ROESGEN-CHAMPION,
 Marguerite Sara   France 1894 Switzerland
  DDM, EVM, LMD, REM
 Pseudonym of: DELYSSEE, Jean

*ROESKE, Frederik Jan   Netherlands 1868
 EVM

ROGAL-LEVITZKY, Dmitri
 Romanovich   USSR 1898 1962
  EMS, X66, X68
  EMS: ПОГАЛЬ-ЛЕВИЦКИЙ

*ROGALSKI, Theodor   Rumania 1901 1954
 BB65, BB71, CME, EMS, LMD, MEH, MGG, RCL, REM, SML,
 X64, X65
 EMS: РОГА́ЛЬСКИЙ

*ROGATIS, Pascual de   Argentina 1881 Italy
 CA12

*ROGER, Kurt George   USA 1895 1966
 CA15, MLA23/4, X64, X65, X66, X67   Austria

*ROGER-DUCASSE, Jean Jules
 Aimable   France 1873 1954
  BB65, BB71, EMS, IMD, LMD, MEH, MGG, REM
  EMS: РОЖЕ́-ДЮКА́С

ROGER HENRICHSEN, Børge   1916
 IMD2

*ROGERS, Bernard   USA 1893 1968
 AS66, BB71, CA10, EVM, IMD, LMD, MGG, MLA25/4, PCM,
 PC71, REM, X64, X67, X68

*ROGERS, Eddy   USA 1907 1964
 AS66, X64

ROGERS, John   USA
 ASUC

*ROGERS, William Keith   Canada 1921
 CCM, KEY, MCO, NLC

*ROGET, Henriette Puig   France 1910
 DDM, DMF, MGG, REM

ROGG, Lionel   Switzerland   1936
    SCHW, X65, X66, X67

ROGGERO, Giuseppe Paolo   Italy   1884
    REM

*ROGISTER, Jean   Belgium   1879   1964
    BB65, BB71, CME, LMD, MGG

*ROGOWSKI, Ludomir Michael   Poland   1881   1954
    DDM, EVM, LMD, MGG, PKW, REM

ROHE, Robert Kenneth   USA   1920
    AS66, X68

*ROHWER, Jens   Germany   1914
    DDM, EVM, IMD, LMD, MGG, X64, X65, X66, X68

*ROIHA, Eino Vilho Pietari   Finland   1904   1955
    EVM, LMD, MGG, SML, VTM

*ROIKJER, Kjell   Denmark   1901
    IMD

ROJEDESVENSKY, Vsevolod Petrovich
    See: ROZHDESTVENSKY

*ROLAND, Marc   Germany   1894
    WWG

*ROLAND-MANUEL, Alexis   France   1891   1966
    BB71, DDM, DMF, EMS, EVM, IMD, LMD, MGG, MLA23/4,
    REM, SML, X64, X65, X67, X68
    EVM: MANUEL, Roland Alexis
    Formerly: LÉVY, Roland Alexis Manuel
    EMS: РОЛАН-МАНЮЗЛЬ

*ROLDÁN, Amadeo   Cuba   1900   1939
    DDM, EMS, EVM, MGG, REM, SML
    EMS: РОЛЬДАН

*ROLLIN, Jean   France   1906
    BB71

*ROMAN, Elly   Rumania   1905
    RCL

*ROMANI, G.   Great Britain   1917
    WI69

ROMANI, Romano   USA   1881   1958
    REM   Italy

*ROMANOVSKY, Erich Maria   Austria   1929
    WI69, X66, X67, X68

ROMM, Roza Davidovna   USSR   1916
    EMS
    EMS: ПОММ

RONGA, Raffaele   Italy   1916
    LMD

*RONNEFELD, Peter   Denmark   1935   1965
    BB71, IMD2, LMD, MLA22/4, MNG, X65, X66, X67

RÖNTGEN, Johannes   Netherlands   1898
    EVM, LMD, X68

*ROOBENIAN, Amber   USA   1905
    AS66

*ROOPER, Jasper   Great Britain circa
    X67, X68   1905

*ROOS, Robert de   Netherlands   1907
    EVM, LMD, MGG, NED, REM, X65

*ROPARTZ, Joseph Guy Marie France   1864   1955
    ACM, CMF7, DDM, CMF, EMS, EVM, IMD, MEH, MGG, REM,
    X65, X68
    EMS: РОПАРЦ

ROPE, Arturi   Finland   1903
    KKO
    Formerly: ROBERTSSON

ROPEK, Jiří   Czechoslovakia
    MNP69/4, X65, X66, X68

ROPELEVSKI, Marjan   Yugoslavia   1911
    KMJ

*ROREM, Ned   USA   1923
    AA73, AS66, BB65, BB71, CA12, CN72, IMD, PCM, PC71,
    REM, X64, X65, X66, X67, X68

ROSA, Melchiorre   Italy   1884
    REM

*ROSATI, Giuseppe   Italy   1903   1962
    REM

*ROSE, Bernard William George Great Britain 1916
    LMD, WI69, X67
    LMD: 1915

ROSE, Griffith   1936
    IMD, X66

*ROSE, John Luke   Great Britain   1928
    WI69
    WI69: 1933

*ROSELIUS, Ludwig Wilhelm   Germany   1902
    EVM, IMD, LMD, REM, WWG

ROSEMONT, Walter Louis   USA   1895
    AS66

*ROSEN, Jerome   USA   1921
    BB65, BB71, PCM, PC71, X64, X66, X68

*ROSENBERG, Hilding
    Constantin   Sweden   1892 1962
    BB65, BB71, CME, DDM, EMS, EVM, FST, IMD, IMD2, KSV,
    LMD, MEH, MGG, REM, SIM, SIMa, SML, SMT, SOW, STS,
    SWE, TJU, VTM, X65, X66, X67, X68
    EMS: РУСЕНБЕРГ

*ROSENBERG, Kai   Denmark   1898
    IMD

ROSENBERG, Wolf   1915
    IMD, X65, X66, X68

*ROSENBERG-RUŽIĆ, Vjekoslav Yugoslavia   1870 1954
    EVM, HCM, KMJ, LMD, REM

*ROSENBLOOM, Sydney   Great Britain 1889 1967
    BB71, EVM, LMD, X68   Scotland

ROSENBOOM, David   USA   1947
    BB71, CAP

ROSENFELD, Gerhard   Germany   1931
    IMD2, SML, X65, X66, X67

ROSENMAN, Leonard   USA   1924
    AS66, BB71

*ROSENSTOCK, Joseph   USA   1895 Poland
    EVM, IMD, LMD, REM, X66

*ROSENTHAL, Manuel   France   1904
    CME, CMF21, DDM, DMF, EMS, EVM, MGG, QQF, REM,
    X64, X65
    EMS: РОЗЕНТА́ЛЬ

ROSINSKÝ, Jozef   Czechoslovakia 1897
   CCZ, MEH

*ROSLÁVETS, Nicolai
   Andreyevitch   USSR   1881   1930
   CME, EVM, MEH, MGG, REM

ROSOWSKY, Salomo   USA   1878   1962
   BB65, BB71, LMD   Latvia

*ROSS, Colin Archibald
   Campbell   Great Britain   1911   Wales
   WI69

*ROSS, George   Canada   1875   Scotland
   NLC

ROSS, Walter Beghtol   USA   1936
   DN70, DN72, X68

*ROUSSEAU, Norbert Oscar
   Claude   Belgium   1907
   CBC, DDM, EVM, LMD, MGG, REM

*ROSSELLINI, Renzo   Italy   1908
   BB65, BB71, DDM, EVM, IMD, LMD, MEH, MGG, REM, X66,
   X67, X68

ROSSI, Nino   1895
   IMD

ROSSI, Roberto   Italy   1877   1957
   IMD, REM

*RÖSSLER, Ernst Karl   Germany   1909
   IMD, LMD, MGG, X66

*ROSTAL, Max   Great Britain   1905   Austria
   LMD, X65, X68

ROSTROPOVIC, Mstislav
   Leopoldovich   USSR   1927
   BB71, EMS, LMD, PPU68/4, PPU71/2, REM, SML, X64, X65,
   X66, X67, X68
   EMS: РОСТРОПÓВИЧ

*ROTA, Nino   Italy   1911
   BB71, DDM, EVM, IMD, LMD, MGG, REM, X64, X66, X68

ROTAS, Nikiforos   1929
   IMD

*ROTERS, Ernst   Germany   1892
    EVM, LMD, REM, X67

ROTH, Daniel   France   1942
    ACM

*ROTHER, Artur Martin   Germany   1885
    LMD, X65

*ROTHER, P. Corbinian   Germany   1900
    X65, X66

*ROTHMULLER, Marko   Yugoslavia   1908
    LMD

*ROTHSCHILD, Fritz   USA   1891   Germany
    X65, X68

ROTONDI, Umberto   Italy   1937
    LMD

ROTSAERT, Julien Jozef
    Maurice   Belgium   1902
    LMD

RÖTSCHER, Konrad   1910
    IMD

*RÖTTGER, Heinz   Germany   1909
    IMD2, LMD, SML, X65, X66, X67, X68

ROUSE, Christopher   USA   1949
    BS72

ROUSSAKIS, Nicolas   USA   Greece
    ASUC, X67, X68

*ROUSSEAU, Marcel-Auguste-
    Louise   France   1882   1955
    BB71, DDM, DMF, LMD, REM
    DDM: SAMUEL-ROUSSEAU, Marcel

*RÖVENSTRUNCK, Bernard   Germany   1920
    IMD

ROVICS, Howard   USA
    X68

*ROVSING OLSEN, Poul   Denmark   1922
    BB65, BB71, CME, DMTsp, IMD, IMD2, LMD, VTM, X64,
    X65, X67, X68
    BB65, BB71, CME and X68: OLSEN, Paul Rovsing

ROWICKI, Witold   Poland   1914
    LMD, PKW, SML, X64, X67

ROWLAND, David   Great Britain
    X68

*ROWLEY, Alec   Great Britain   1892   1958
    DDM, EVM, IMD, LMD, MGG, REM

ROXBURGH, Edwin
    X67

ROXBURY, Ronald   USA
    CAP, X68

*ROY, Alphonse   Switzerland   1906
    LMD, REM, SCHW, X64

*ROY, Klaus George   USA   1924   Austria
    AA73, BB65, BB71, PCM, PC71, X64, X65, X66, X67

*ROYCE, Edward   USA   1886   1963
    BB65, BB71, PCM, X64

ROŽANC, Mihael   Yugoslavia   1885
    KMJ

ROZHDESTVENSKY, Vsevolod
    Petrovich   USSR   1918
    EMS, LMD, PPU
    Vol. I: ROJEDESVENSKY
    EMS: РОЖДЕСТВЕНСКИЙ

ROZMAN, Sarah   Israel   1911   Hungary
    ACU
    Formerly: DEBARO, Charlotte

ROZO-CONTRERAS, Jose   Colombia   1894
    LMD, REM

*RÓZSA, Miklós   USA   1907   Hungary
    BB71, CME, DDM, EVM, IMD, LMD, MEH, MGG, REM, WI69,
    X64, X67, X68

*RÓZYCKI, Ludomir   Poland   1884   1953
    DDM, EMS, EVM, IMD, LMD, MEH, PKW, REM, SML, X66
    EMS: РУЖИЦКИЙ

*RUBBRA, Edmund Duncan   Great Britain   1901
    BB71, BCI, CME, DDM, EVM, LMD, MGG, REM, WI69, X64,
    X65, X66, X67, X68

RUBENS, Hugo   USA   1905
   AS66

*RUBIN, Marcel   Austria   1905
   DDM, EMS, IMD2, LMD, MEH, MGG, REM, SML, X64, X65,
   X66, X68
   EMS: РУБИН

RUBIN, Vladimir Ilyich   USSR   1924
   EMS, X65, X68
   EMS: РУБИН

RUBIN DE CERVIN, Ernesto   Italy   1936
   LMD, REM

*RUBINO, Salvatore   Italy   1883
   REM

RUBINOV, Aleksandr
   Vaselievich   USSR   1906
   EMS
   EMS: РЫБНОВ

RUBINSTEIN, Artur   USA   1886   Poland
   DDM, EVM, LMD, REM, SML, X64, X66, X67, X68

*RUBINSTEIN, Beryl   USA   1898   1952
   LMD, PC71, REM
   PC71: RUBENSTEIN

*RUBSAMEN, Walter Howard USA   1911
   DAS, REM, X64, X65, X68

*RUBTZOV, Feodosi Antonovich USSR   1904
   EMS, X65, X66, X68
   EMS: РУБЦОВ

*RUCHT, Karl Kurt Magnus   Germany   1918
   WWG

*RUDHYAR, Dane   USA   1895   France
   DDM, EVM, LMD, REM
   Formerly: CHENNEVIÈRE, Daniel de

RUDIN, Andrew   USA   1939
   EL:4

*RUDNITSKY, Antin   USA   1902   Russia
   EVM, REM, X67

*RUDOLF, Bert   Austria   1905
   X68

*RUDOLF, Waldemar   Sweden   1882
    SIMa

RUDOLPH, Max   USA   1902   Germany
    LMD, REM, X65, X66, X67, X68

*RUDZINSKI, Witold   Poland   1913   Russia
    BB65, BB71, CME, DDM, EMS, LMD, MEH, MGG, PKW, REM,
    X64, X65, X66, X67, X68
    EMS: РУДЗИНЬСКИЙ

RUDZINSKI, Zbigniew   Poland   1935
    MEH, X65, X66, X67, X68

*RUEFF, Jeanine   France   1922
    DDM, EVM

*RUERA, Josep   Spain   1900
    EVM

*RUGGLES, Carl   USA   1876   1971
    BB65, BB71, EVM, IMD2, LMD, MGG, MLA28/4, PCM, REM,
    WTM, X66, X68

*RUMMEL, Walter Morse   Belgium   1887   1953
    EVM, LMD

*RUNBÄCK, Albert   Sweden   1894
    KSV, SIMa, STS

*RUNG-KELLER, Poul Sophus   Denmark   1879   1966
    LMD

*RUNNETT, Henry Brian   Great Britain   1935
    X67, X68

*RUNÓLFSSON, Karl Ottó   Iceland   1900
    VTM

RUNOV, Viktor Sergeevich   USSR   1907
    EMS
    EMS: РУНОВ

RUPNIK, Ivan   Yugoslavia   1911
    BB65, BB71, KMJ

RUSCONI, Gerardo   Italy   1922
    BB71

RUSH, Loren   USA   1935
    BB71

*RUSSELL, George Alexander USA 1880 1953
 AS66

*RUSSELL, William USA 1905
 PCM

*RUSSELL-SMITH, Geoffry
 Edwin Great Britain 1927
 WI69, X65, X66, X67

RUSSO, William Joseph (Bill) USA 1928
 AS66, BB65, BB71, LMD, X65, X66, X67, X68

*RUSSOTTO, Leo USA 1896
 AS66

*RUSTAMOV, Seid Ali Ogli USSR 1907
 EMS, PPU, PPU69/2
 EMS: РУСТАМОВ

RUSU, Liviu Rumania 1908
 RCL

RUTLAND, Harold Fred Great Britain 1900
 LMD, REM

RUTSCH, Fernand Germany 1918
 ACM

*RUYNEMAN, Daniël Netherlands 1886 1963
 BB65, BB71, CME, DDM, EVM, IMD, LMD, MGG, NED, PAP,
 REM, X64, X65

RUŽDJAK, Vladimir Yugoslavia 1922
 HCM, IMD, KMJ, LMD, X64, X68

RÛŽIČKA, Rudolf Czechoslovakia 1941
 MNP69/4, MNP70/5, MNP72/9, ZE70/2

RYDAL'CENKO, Vsevolod
 Petrovich USSR 1904
 LMD, X66

RYBÁŘ, Jaroslav Czechoslovakia 1942
 MNP69/4, MNP72/9

RYBICKI, Feliks Poland 1899
 PKW

*RYBRANT, Stig Alvar Sweden 1916
 FST, SIM, SIMa

*RYCHLÍK, Jan   Czechoslovakia   1916
    BB65, BB71, CCZ, CME, IMD, IMD2, LMD, MEH, MNP64/4,
    MNP64/5, MNP64/6, MNP66/6, REM, X64, X65, X66, X67

RYDMAN, Kari   Finland   1936
    BB71, LMD, VTM, X65, X66, X68

*RYELANDT, Joseph   Belgium   1870   1965
    BB65, BB71, CME, LMD, MGG, MLA22/4, REM, X65

*RYTEL, Piotr   Poland   1884
    EVM, LMD, MGG, PKW, REM, X65

RYTERBAND, Roman   USA   Poland 1914
    AS66

RYTTERKVIST, Hans   1926
    IMD, SIMa

RZAEV, Azer Guseinovich   USSR   1930
    EMS, X68
    EMS: РЗАЕВ

RZAEV, Gasan Guseinovich   USSR   1928
    EMS
    EMS: РЗАЕВ

RZAEVA, Agbadzi Ismail   USSR   1912
    EMS
    EMS: РЗАЕВА

RZEWSKI, Frederic   USA   1938
    BB71, X64, X66, X68

*SAAR, Hermann   Germany   1905
    WWG

*SAAR, Mart Mihailevich   USSR   1882   1963
    EMS, X64   Estonia
    EMS: CAAP

*SABANEYEV, Leonid
   Leonidovich   France   1881   Russia
    DDM, EVM, LMD, MGG, REM

*SABATA, Victor de   Italy   1892   1967
    BB71, EVM, MEH, MGG, OCM, X67, X68
    EMS, LMD, MEH and REM: DE SABATA
    EMS: ДЕ САБАТА

*SABATINI, Renzo Italy 1905
 LMD, REM, WI69

*SABEL, Hans Germany 1912
 IMD

SABININA, Marina Dimitrevna USSR 1917
 EMS, PPU69/2, X65, X66, X67, X68
 EMS: САБИНИНА

*SABRÁ, Wadí Lebanon 1876 1952
 EVM, LMD

SABZANOV, Yakub USSR
 X68

SACCO, John Charles USA 1905
 AS66

SACCO, P. Peter USA 1928
 DN70, X66, X67, X68

SACHS, Arie Erich Israel 1908
 ACUad, X68

*SACHS, Milan Yugoslavia 1884 1968
 KMJ, LMD, X68   Czecho-
    slovakia

SACHSE, Hans Wolfgang Germany 1899
 LMD, SML, X64, X67, X68

*SACHSSE, Hans Germany 1891 1960
 LMD, MGG, REM

SACKS, Stuart USA 1941
 BB65, BB71, X66

SADAI, Yizhak Israel 1935 Bulgaria
 ACU, CME, IMD2, X65, X68
 Formerly: SIDI, Yizhak

SADA'I, Yizhak Israel
 X68

*SADOVNIKOV, Viktor
 Ivanovich USSR 1886 1964
 X64

SAENZ, Pedro A. Argentina 1915
 BB71, CA12, LMD, X64, X68

*SAEVERUD, Harald Sigurd
  Johan   Norway   1897
    BB65, BB71, CME, CNO, DDM, EMS, EVM, IMD, LMD, MEH,
    MGG, REM, VTM, X66, X67
    EMS: СЕВЕРУД

SAEVERUD, Ketil   Norway   1939
    CNO

SAEYS, Eugène   Belgium   1887
    EVM

SAGAEV, Dimiter Konstaninov   Bulgaria   1915
    BB65, BB71, BMK, LMD, X67, X68
    BMK: САГАЕВ

SAIDASHEV, Salikh
  Zamaletdinovich   USSR   1900   1954
    EMS
    EMS: САЙДАШЕВ

SAIFIDDINOV, Sharofiddin
  Sanginovich   USSR   1929
    EMS, PPU69/2
    EMS: САЙФИДДИНОВ

*SAIKKOLA, Lauri   Finland   1906
    COF, EVM, KKO, LMD, MGG, REM, VTM

SAINT-GEORGES, Didia   Rumania   1888
    RCL

*SAINTON, Philip Prosper   Great Britain 1891   1968
    X68   France

*SAINT-REQUIER, Léon   France   1872   1964
    BB71, LMD, REM

*SAKAČ, Branimir   Yugoslavia   1918
    HCM, IMD, IMD2, KMJ, LMD, REM, TSC, X67, X68

SAKVA, Konstantin
  Konstantinovich   USSR   1912
    EMS, PPU69/2, X65, X67, X68
    EMS: САКВА

*SALAZAR, Adolfo   Mexico   1890   1958
    BB71, DDM, EMS, EVM, IMD, LMD,   Spain
    MGG, REM
    EMS: САЛАСАР

SALBERT, Dieter   Germany
    X68

SALGADO, Gustavo Enrique
    S. Torres   Ecuador   1905
    LMD, REM

SALGADO, José Francisco
    S. Ayala   Ecuador   1882
    LMD, REM

*SALGADO, Luis Humberto   Ecuador   1903
    LMD, REM

SALICH, Milan   Czechoslovakia   1927
    CCZ, MNP67/5, X66, X68

SALIMAN-VLADIMIROV, David
    Fedorovich   USSR   1903
    EMS
    EMS: САЛИМАН-ВЛАДИМИРОВ

*SALLINEN, Aulis   Finland   1935
    CME, COF, LMD, VTM, X65, X66

*SALMANOV, Vadim
    Nikolayevich   USSR   1912
    BB65, BB71, CME, EMS, IMD, LMD, MEH, REM, X64, X65,
    X67, X68
    EMS: САЛМАНОВ

SALMENHAARA, Erkki   Finland   1941
    CME, IMD2, KKO, LMD, VTM, X64, X65, X66, X67

*SALMHOFER, Franz   Austria   1900
    CME, DDM, EVM, IMD, LMD, MGG, REM, X65

*SALMON, Karel   Israel   1897   Germany
    ACU, CME, DDM, EVM, IMD, IMD2, LMD, MM59, REM,
    WWI, X68
    Formerly: SALOMON

SALOMON, Karel
    See: SALMON, Karel

SALOMON, Moses   Israel   1907   Rumania
    ACU

*SALOMON, Siegfried Naphtali   Denmark   1885   1962
    LMD, REM

*SALONEN, Sulo Nikolai   Finland   1899
    COF, KKO, LMD, VTM

*SALOP, Arnold   USA   1927 1967
 X64, X65, X68

SALTA, Menotti   USA   1893 Italy
 AS66

*SALTER, Lionel Paul Great Britain 1914
 EVM, LMD, WI69, X64, X65, X66, X67

SALVA, Tadeás   Czechoslovakia 1937
 X68, ZE69/2, ZE69/3, ZE70/1, ZE70/3, ZE71/1, ZE71/3

*SALVIUCCI, Giovanni Italy   1907 1937
 LMD, REM
 LMD: 1902-1957

SALVIUCCI, Paolo   Italy   1902 1957
 LMD, REM
 LMD: 1907-1937

*SALZEDO, Carlos   USA   1885 1961
 AS66, BB65, BB71, DDM, EMS, EVM, LMD, France
 PCM, REM
 EMS: САЛЬСЕ́ДО

*SALZEDO, Leonard Lopes Great Britain 1921
 WI69, X64, X65, X66, X67, X68

SALZMAN, Eric   USA   1933
 BB71, IMD, X65, X66, X67, X68

*SAMAZEUILH, Gustave Marie
 Victor Fernand   France 1877 1967
 BB71, CMF, DDM, DMF, EVM, IMD, LMD, MEH, MGG,
 MLA24/4, REM, X64, X65, X67, X68

SAMBAMURTHY, P.   India   1901
 WHI, X67

*SAMBURSKY, Daniel Israel   1909 Germany
 ACU, WWI

*SAMINSKY, Lazare Semenovich USA   1882 1959
 AS66, BB65, BB71, DDM, EMS, EVM, LMD, Russia
 REM, X66
 EMS: САМИНСКИЙ

*SAMMONS, Albert Edward Great Britain 1886 1957
 LMD

SAMSON, Joseph   France 1888 1957
 DDM, DMF, LMD, MGG

SAMUEL, Gerhard   Germany   1924
    BB71, X66, X67

SAMUEL, Harry Cecil   Great Britain 1927
    WI69

*SAMUEL, Lēopold   Belgium   1883
    EVM, LMD, MGG

*SAMUEL-ROUSSEAU, Marcel
    See: ROUSSEAU, Marcel

*SANCAN, Pièrre   France   1916 Morocco
    DDM, DMF, EVM, LMD, MGG, REM, X64, X66, X67

*SANCHEZ MÁLAGA, Carlos   Peru   1904
    EVM

*SANDBERG, Mordecai   USA   1897 Rumania
    REM   1973

SANDBERG, Steven   USA   1955
    BS70

*SANDBY, Herman   Denmark   1881 1965
    BB65, BB71, IMD, LMD, REM

SANDELEWSKI, Wiarosław,
    Józef   Italy   1913 Poland
    LMD, X64, X65, X67, X68

SANDER, Alexander   1940
    IMD

SANDER, Szarvas Peter   Great Britain 1933 Hungary
    WI69

SANDERS, Paul F.   Netherlands   1891
    EVM, LMD, REM

*SANDERS, Robert L.   USA   1906
    AS66, BB71, DDM, EVM, IMD, LMD, PCM, PC71, REM, X64,
    X65, X67, X68

*SANDI MENESES, Luis   Mexico   1905
    CA14, EVM, IMD, LMD, MGG, MMX, QLA, REM, X64, X67

*SANDLER, Oscar Aronovich   USSR   1910
    EMS, PPU71/1
    EMS: САНДЛЕР

*SANDLOFF, Peter   1924
    X68

*SANDOVAL, Andres   Venezuela   1924
    REM

*SANDOVAL, Miguel   USA   1903   1953
    AS66   Guatemala

SANDOZ, Maurice   Switzerland   1892   1958
    SCHW

*SANDVOLD, Arild Edvin   Norway   1895
    CNO, LMD

*SANGIORGI, Alfredo   Italy   1894   1962
    LMD, REM

*SANJUÁN, Pedro   USA   1886   Spain
    BB65, BB71, LMD, REM, X66
    LMD: SAN JUAN

SANKARASASTRI, Emani   India   1922
    WHI

*SANTA CRUZ WILSON,
    Domingo   Chile   1899
    BB65, BB71, DDM, EVM, LMD, MGG, QLA, REM, X64, X67
    MGG: SANTA CRUZ, Wilson Domingo

*SANTOLIQUIDO, Francesco   Italy   1883   1971
    DDM, EVM, LMD, MGG, MLA28/4, REM, WI69

*SANTORO, Cláudio   Brazil   1919
    BB65, BB71, CA9, DDM, EMS, EVM, FBC, IMD, LMD, MGG,
    REM, X65, X68
    EMS: САНТОРУ

*SANTÓRSOLA, Guido   Uruguay   1904   Italy
    CA8, EVM, IMD, MGG, REM

*SANTOS, José Manuel   Portugal   1924
    CME, MGG, REM

SANTUCCI, Pellegrino   Italy   1921
    LMD

SANUCCI, Frank   USA   Argentina

*SANZOGNO, Nino   Italy   1911
    LMD, OCM, REM, X65, X68

SAPERSTEIN, David   USA   1948
    BB71, X66

SAPIEYEVSKI, Jerzy   Poland   1945
    DN70, DN72

SAPONARO, Giacomo   Italy   1906
    LMD, REM

ŠAPORIN, Juri Alexandrovich
    See: SHAPORIN, Yuri A.

ŠAPOŠNIKOV, A. G.
    See: SHAPOSHNIKOV, A. G.

ŠAPOŠNIKOV, I. K.
    See: SHAPOSHNIKOV, I. K.

*SAPP, Allen Dwight   USA   1922
    ASUC, X64

SARACENI, Guidi Chigi   Italy   1879   1965

SARAI, Tibor   Hungary   1919
    BB65, BB71, CHC, CME, IMD, LMD, MEH, REM, SML, X68

SARAUER, Alois   Czechoslovakia   1901
    CCZ

SARCHIZOV, Sergiu   Rumania   1924
    LMD, RCL, X65, X66, X68

SARGENT, Paul   USA   1910
    AS66, PC71

*SARGENT, Malcolm   Great Britain   1895   1967
    BB71, EVM, LMD, MGG, REM, X64, X65, X66, X67, X68
    Also: SARGENT, Harold Malcolm Watts

SÁRI, József   Hungary   1935
    CHC

*SARIN, Marger Ottovich   USSR   1910   Latvia
    EVM, SML

*SÁRKÖZY, István   Hungary   1920
    CHC, IMD, X67, X68

*SARLY, Henri   Belgium   1884   1954
    BB71, EVM, LMD

*SARNETTE, Eric Antoine
    Joseph André   France   1898
    LMD, MGG, REM, X64

ŠÁROVÁ, Dagmar   1926
   IMD2

SARTORIO, Claudio   Brazil
   X68

SÁRY, László   Hungary   1940
   CHC

*SÁS (OCH ASSAL), Andrés   Peru   1900   France
   BB71, DDM, EMS, EVM, IMD, LMD, REM,   1967
   X67, X68
   EMS: САС ОРУАСАЛЬ

SATO, Keijiro   Japan   1927
   BB71

*ŠATRA, Antonín   Czechoslovakia 1901
   CCZ, IMD2, WI69

*SATYAN, Ashot Movsesovich   USSR   1906
   EMS
   EMS: САТЯН

*SAUCE, Angel   Venezuela   1911
   CA14, REM

ŠAUER, František   Czechoslovakia 1912   Austria
   CCZ

*SAUGUET, Henri   France   1901
   BB65, BB71, CME, CMF5, CMF20, DDM, DMF, EMS, EVM,
   IMD, LMD, MEH, MGG, QQF, REM, WI69, X64, X65, X66,
   X67, X68
   Formerly: POUPARD, Henri-Pierre
   EMS: СОГЕ

*SAUNDERS, Neil Nathaniel   Great Britain 1918
   WI69

SAUSSY, Tupper   USA
   X68

*SAUTER, Ernest   1928
   X67

SAVAGNONE, Giuseppe   Italy   1902
   EL:1, REM

SAVASTA, Antonio   Italy   1874   1959
   LMD

*SAVELYEV, Boris
  Vladimirovich   USSR   1896
  EMS
  EMS: САВЕ́ЛЬЕВ

*SAVERY, Carl Maria   Denmark   1897   Germany
  VTM

*SAVERY, Finn   Denmark   1933
  VTM, X65

SAVIN, Dragutin   Yugoslavia 1915
  HCM, KMJ, X68

SAVIN, Francisco   Mexico   1929
  HET25

SAVINIO, Alberto   Italy   1891   1952
  LMD
  Pseudonym of: CHIRICO, Andrea de

SAVINO, Domenico   USA   1882
  AS66

SAVNIK, Vinko   Yugoslavia 1921
  KMJ

SAXTON, Stanley   USA   1904
  AS66

*SAYGUN, Ahmed Adnan   Turkey   1907
  DDM, EMS, EVM, IMD, LMD, MEH, REM, X64, X65, X67,
  X68
  EMS: САЙГУН

SCAGLIA, Carlo Elia   Italy   1863   1965
  LMD

*SCALERO, Rosario   Italy   1870   1954
  LMD, MGG, REM

SCARLINO, Eriberto   Italy   1895   1962
  LMD, REM

*SCARMOLIN, Anthony Louis USA   1890   1969
  AS66, BB71, X66   Italy

SCARPINI, Pietro   Italy   1911
  LMD, X66

SCEBALIN, V. J.
  See: SHEBALIN, V. Y.

ŠČEDRINK, R. K.
   See: SHCHEDRIN, R. K.

ŠČEK, Breda   Yugoslavia   1893
   KMJ

ŠČEK, Ivan   Yugoslavia   1925
   KMJ

SCEKHTER, B. S.
   See: SHEKHTER, B. S.

*SCELSI, Giacinto   Italy   1905
   EL:1, EL:2, EVM, REM, X66

ŠČERBAČËV, V. V.
   See: SHCHERBACHEV, V. V.

SCHABBEL, Wilhelm   Germany   1904
   LMD, SML, X64, X66

*SCHAD, Walter   USA   1889 1966
   AS66

*SCHAEFER, Theodor   Czechoslovakia 1904
   BB65, BB71, CCZ, DDM, EVM, IMD, LMD, MGG, REM, X64
   LMD: SCHÄFER

*SCHAEFERS, Anton   Germany   1908
   IMD

*SCHAEFFER, Pierre   France   1910
   BB71, CME, CMF34, DDM, EMS, LMD, MEH, MGG, PAP,
   REM, X65, X66, X67
   LMD: SCHÄFFER
   EMS: ШЕФФЕР

SCHAEFFER, Theodor   Czechoslovakia 1903
   CME, MEH

*SCHAEUBLE, Hans-Joachim Switzerland 1906
   EVM, IMD, LMD, MGG, REM, SCHW, WI69, WWS, X67

*SCHÄFER, František   Czechoslovakia 1905
   CCZ, EVM, LMD

*SCHÄFER, Gerhart   Germany   1926
   X64

*SCHÄFER, Karl   Germany   1899
   IMD, IMD2, LMD, MGG, X64, X68

SCHAFER, R. Murray   Canada   1933
    BB71, BCL, CA10, CCM, CCM71, CVM, CVMa, LMD, MCO,
    MCO68, MCO71, NLC, NLCa, X66, X67, X68

SCHAFF, Mrs. Merle S.
    See: POLIN, Claire J.

SCHÄFFER, Bogusław   Poland   1929
    BB65, BB71, CME, DDM, EMS, IMD, IMD2, LMD, MEH, MGG,
    PKW, REM, TSC, X64, X65, X66, X67, X68
    EMS: ШЕФФЕР

SCHALLER, Paul   Switzerland   1913
    SCHW

SCHAPORIN, Juri A.
    See: SHAPORIN, Yuri A.

SCHAPOSCHNIKOW, A. G.
    See: SHAPOSHNIKOV, A. G.

SCHARF, Walter   USA
    AS66

*SCHARWENKA, Walter   Germany   1881
    EVM, LMD, REM

*SCHAT, Peter   Netherlands   1935
    BB65, BB71, CME, DDM, IMD, IMD2, LMD, MEH, NED, REM,
    TSC, X64, X65, X66, X67, X68

SCHATTMANN, Alfred   1876
    IMD

*SCHAUB, Hans Ferdinand   Germany   1880
    IMD

SCHEBALIN, W. J.
    See: SHEBALIN, V. Y.

*SCHEFFLER, Siegfried   Germany   1892
    EVM, IMD, REM

*SCHELB, Josef   Germany   1894
    IMD, LMD, MGG, REM, WWG, X65

SCHENSCHIN, A. A.
    See: SHENSHIN, A. A.

*SCHERCHEN, Hermann   Germany   1891   1966
    BB65, BB71, DDM, EMS, EVM, IMD, LMD, MGG, REM, SCHW,
    SML, X64, X65, X66, X67
    EMS: ШЕРХЕН

SCHERCHEN, Tona   Switzerland   1938
    IMD2, MNG, X67, X68

*SCHIBLER, Armin   Switzerland   1920
    BB65, CME, DDM, EVM, IMD, IMD2, LMD, MEH, MNG, REM,
    SCHW, TSC, WI69, WWS, X64, X65, X66, X68

*SCHICK, Philippine   Germany   1893   1970
    LMD, MGG, MLA27/4, REM, WWG, X64, X65, X66

SCHICKELE, Peter   USA   1935
    AS66, BB71, PCM, PC71, X64, X66, X67, X68

SCHIDLOWSKY GAETE, León   Chile   1931
    BB71, LMD, X66

SCHIEDERMAIR, Ludwig   Germany   1878   1957
    MGG

*SCHIFF, Helmut   Germany   1893   Austria
    X68

*SCHIFFMAN, Harold   USA   1928
    ASUC, X64, X65, X67, X68

SCHIFRIN, Lalo Boris   USA   1932   Argentina
    BB71, PC71, X65, X66, X67, X68

SCHILLING, Hans Ludwig   1927
    X64, X65, X68

*SCHILLING, Otto-Erich   Germany   1910   1967
    MLA24/4, WWG, X67, X68

SCHINDLER, Allen   1944
    WAN

*SCHINDLER, Gerhard   1921   1965
    X66

SCHINDLER, Walter   1909
    IMD, X65

*SCHINELLI, Achille   Italy   1882
    IMD, REM, WI69

SCHINHAN, Jan Philip   USA   1887   Austria
    DAS

*SCHIPA, Tito   Italy   1896   1965
    REM, X64, X65, X66, X67
    REM: 1889

SCHIRMER, Rudolph Edward   USA   1919
   X68

*SCHISKE, Karl Hubert Rudolf   Austria   1916   1969
   BB71, CME, DDM, EMS, EVM, IMD, IMD2,   Hungary
   LMD, MEH, MGG, MLA26/4, REM, WI69,
   X65, X66, X68
   EMS: ШИСКЕ

*SCHIUMA, Alfredo Luis   Argentina   1885   1963
   BB71, LMD, REM, X67

*SCHLEIN, Irving   USA   1905
   AS66, IMD, X66, X68

*SCHLEMM, Gustav Adolf   Germany   1902
   IMD, LMD, REM, WI69, WWG
   Formerly: HINSTEIN, Gustav

SCHLESINGER, Hanan   Israel   1893   Germany
   ACU, MM59

*SCHLIEPE, Ernst Heinrich   Germany   1893
   IMD

*SCHMALSTICH, Clemens   Germany   1880   1960
   EVM, LMD, REM

*SCHMID, Adolf   USA   1868   1958
   AS66, LMD   Austria

*SCHMID, Erich   Switzerland 1907
   EVM, LMD, MGG, REM, SCHW, WWS, X66, X67

*SCHMID, Heinrich Kaspar   Germany   1874   1953
   IMD, MGG, REM

*SCHMID, Waldemar   Germany   1881
   EVM

SCHMIDEK, Kurt   Austria   1919
   IMD2, X67, X68

SCHMIDT, Eberhard   Germany   1907
   LMD, SML, X64, X66, X67, X68

*SCHMIDT, Eric   Switzerland 1907
   SCHW

*SCHMIDT, Ole   Denmark   1928
   DNS, LMD, VTM, X64

*SCHMIDT, Werner Albert   1925
 IMD

SCHMIDT, William   USA   1926
 BB65, BB71, DN70, LMD, PCM, PC71

SCHMIDT-DUISBURG,
 Margarete   Germany 1906
 WWG

*SCHMIDT-GARRE, Helmut Germany 1907
 LMD, REM, WWG, X64, X65, X66, X67, X68

*SCHMIDT-ISSERSTEDT, Hans Germany 1900 1973
 BB71, EVM, LMD, MGG, REM, SML, X64, X65, X66, X67,
 X68

*SCHMIDTMANN, Friedrich Germany 1913
 WWG

SCHMIDT-WUNSTORF, Rudolf   1916
 IMD

*SCHMINKE, Oskar Eberhard USA   1881 1969
 BB71

*SCHMIT, Camille   Belgium 1908
 CBC, DDM, EVM, IMD, LMD, REM

*SCHMIT, Jean-Pierre   Luxembourg 1904
 W169

*SCHMITT, Florent   France 1870 1958
 CMF17, DDM, DMF, EMS, EVM, IMD, LMD, MEH, MGG,
 REM, WTM, X66, X68
 EMS: ШМИТТ

SCHMUTZ, Albert Daniel USA   1887
 AS66, PCM, PC71

*SCHNABEL, Alexander Maria Germany 1889 Latvia
 IMD

*SCHNABEL, Artur   Austria 1882 1951
 BB65, BB71, DDM, EMS, IMD, LMD, MEH, MGG, REM, SML,
 X64, X65, X68
 EMS: ШНАБЕЛЬ

*SCHNABEL, Karl Ulrich Germany 1909
 LMD, REM, X66, X68

SCHNEBEL, Dieter   Germany   1930
   EL:3, IMD, LMD, PAP, X64, X65, X66, X67

*SCHNEEWEIS, Jan   Czechoslovakia 1904
   CCZ, WI69

SCHNEIDER, Charles   Switzerland   1887 1956
   SCHWs

*SCHNEIDER, Hans   Austria   1906
   X68

*SCHNEIDER, Peter Otto   Switzerland   1901 Germany
   SCHW, X64, X67, X68

*SCHNEIDER, Simon   Germany   1886
   WWG

*SCHNEIDER, Willy   Germany   1907
   IMD, X67

*SCHNEIDERHAN, Walther   Austria   1901
   LMD, MGG, REM, WI69

*SCHNEIDER-TRNAVSKÝ,
Mikuláš   Czechoslovakia 1881 1958
   CCZ, LMD, MEH, MGG, REM, ZE71/2

*SCHNEIDT, Hanns-Martin Germany   1930
   X66

SCHNITKE, Alfred
   See: SHNITKE, Alfred

SCHNORRENBERG, Roberto Brazil   1929
   IMD

SCHOBER, Brian   USA   1951
   BS72

*SCHOECK, Othmar Gottfried Switzerland   1886 1957
   BB65, BB71, CME, DDM, EMS, EVM, IMD, LMD, MEH, MGG,
   REM, SCHW, SML, X65, X66, X67, X68
   EMS: ШЁК

*SCHOEMAKER, Maurice
Pierre   Belgium   1890 1964
   BB65, BB71, CBC, DDM, EVM, IMD, IMD2, LMD, MGG, REM

*SCHOENBERG, Arnold   Austria-USA   1874 1951
   AS66, BB71, CME, DDM, EL:1, EMS, EVM, IMD, IMD2, LMD,
   MEH, MGG, MZW, PAP, REM, SML, TCM, VNM, WTM, X64,
   X65, X66, X67, X68   EMS: ШЁНБЕРГ

SCHOENDLINGER, Anton   Germany   1919   Yugoslavia
    IMD, SML

*SCHOLLUM, Robert   Austria   1913
    BB65, BB71, CME, DDM, EMS, EVM, IMD, IMD2, LMD, MEH,
    MGG, REM, X64, X65, X66, X67
    EMS: ШОЛЛУМ

*SCHOLZ, Erwin Christian   Austria   1910
    LMD, MGG, X64, X65

*SCHÖNBACH, Dieter   1931
    BB65, BB71, IMD, IMD2, LMD, MEH, MNG, REM, X65, X67,
    X68
    MNG: SCHOENBACH

SCHÖNBERG, Stig Gustav   Sweden   1933
    FST, KSV, SIM, SIMa, SOW, STS, SWE, VTM

*SCHÖNHERR, Max   Austria   1903   Germany
    REM, X67, X68

SCHOOLEY, John Heilman   USA   1943
    DN70

SCHOOP, Paul   USA   1909   Switzerland
    AS66

SCHOSTAKOWITSCH, D. D.
    See: SHOSTAKOVICH, D. D.

*SCHOUWMAN, Hans   Netherlands   1902
    EVM, IMD, LMD, REM, X65, X67

SCHRAMM, Harold   USA   1935
    AS66, PCM, PC71, X64, X65, X66, X67, X68

SCHRAMM, Paul   Austria   1892
    EVM

SCHRATTENHOLZ, Leo   Germany   1872   1955
    LMD, MGG

*SCHREIBER, Frederick C.   USA   1895   Austria
    AS66, LMD, REM, X67

SCHREIBER, Josef   Czechoslovakia   1900
    CCZ

*SCHREITER, Heinz   1915
    IMD

SCHRODER, Friedrich   Switzerland   1910
    REM

SCHRÖDER, Hanning   Germany   1896
   LMD

*SCHROEDER, Hans Max
  Ludwig Wilhelm   Germany   1896
   WI69

SCHROEDER, Hermann   Germany   1904
   DDM, EVM, IMD, LMD, MGG, REM, WWG, X67, X68
   EVM: SCHRÖDER

SCHROEDER, William A.   USA   1888   1960
   AA73, AS66

*SCHRÖTER, Heinz   Germany   1907
   IMD, WWG, X67

SCHTSCHERBATSCHOW, W. W.
   See: SHCHERBACHEV, V. V.

SCHUBEL, Max   USA   1932
   X67, X68

*SCHULÉ, Bernard Emmanuel   Switzerland   1909
   LMD, REM, SCHW, WWS, X64

SCHÜLER, Johannes   Germany   1894   1966
   IMD, LMD, WWG, X64, X66, X67, X68

SCHÜLER, Karl   1894
   IMD

SCHÜLL, Norbert   1935
   IMD

*SCHULLER, Gunther   USA   1925
   BB65, BB71, CA10, CME, DN70, IMD, IMD2, LMD, MEH,
   MNG, OCM, PCM, PC71, REM, WTM, X64, X65, X66,
   X67, X68

*SCHULTHESS, Walter   Switzerland   1894   1971
   BB65, BB71, EVM, IMD, LMD, MGG, MLA28/4, REM, SCHW

*SCHULTZ, Svend Simon   Denmark   1913
   EVM, IMD, LMD, MGG, REM, VTM, X68

*SCHULTZE, Norbert   Germany   1911
   EVM, IMD, LMD, X65, X68

*SCHULZE-DESSAU, Fritz   Germany   1900
   SML

SCHUMAN, Ellis   USA   1931

*SCHUMAN, William Howard   USA   1910
    BB65, BB71, DDM, DN72, EMS, EVM, IMD, LMD, MGG, PCM,
    PC71, REM, WI69, WTM, X64, X65, X66, X67, X68
    EMS: ⅢУМЕН

*SCHUMANN, Georg Alfred   Germany   1866 1952
    EVM, IMD, LMD, MGG, X66

*SCHUMANN, Gerhard   Germany   1914
    IMD

*SCHURICHT, Karl   Germany   1880 1967
    BB71, EVM, LMD, MGG, REM, SML, X64, X65, X67, X68

SCHÜRMANN, Gerard   Great Britain 1928 Indonesia
    BB71, WI69, X67, X68

SCHUSTER, Giora   Israel   1915 Germany
    ACU

*SCHUURMAN, Frits Hans
  Erich   Netherlands 1898
    EVM, X66

SCHUYLER, Philippa Duke   USA
    AS66, X65, X66

SCHUYT, Nico   Netherlands 1922
    BB65, BB71, LMD, NED, X66, X67

SCHWAEN, Kurt   Germany   1909
    EMS, IMD, LMD, MEH, SML, X65, X66, X67, X68
    EMS: ⅢВЕН

SCHWANTNER, Joseph   USA   1943
    ASUC

SCHWARTZ, Elliott Shelling   USA   1936
    AA73, ASUC, DN72, PCM, PC71, X65, X67, X68

SCHWARTZ, Francis   USA   1940
    DN72

SCHWARTZ, Isaac   USSR   1923
    SCD

*SCHWARTZ, Paul   Austria   1907
    PCM, PC71, X67, X68

*SCHWARZ, Gerhard   Germany   1902
    IMD, MGG, X64, X66, X68

SCHWARZ, Ira Paul   USA   1922
    DN72

SCHWARZ, Lev A.
    See: SHVARTZ, Lev A.

SCHWARZ, Lubor   Czechoslovakia 1920
    CCZ

SCHWARZ, Maximilian   Germany   1899
    IMD, X65

*SCHWARZ-SCHILLING,
    Reinhard   Germany   1904
    IMD, LMD, MGG, REM, X65, X68

SCHWEITZER, Anton   Netherlands   1898
    EVM

*SCHWEIZER, Theodor   Switzerland   1916
    SCHW

*SCHWENN, Carljohan   Denmark   1905
    IMD

SCHWERTSIK, Kurt   Austria   1935
    CME, IMD2, MNG, X67

SCHWIERS, Adolf Gottfried Germany   1904
    LMD

SCIAMMARELLA, Valdo   Argentina   1924
    BB71, CA12, LMD

SCIANNI, Joseph   USA   1928
    AS66

SCIAPIRO, Michel   USA   1891   1956
    AS66   Russia

SCIAPORIN, Juri A.
    See: SHAPORIN, Yuri A.

SCIAPOŠNIKOV, A. G.
    See: SHAPOSHNIKOV, A. G.

SCIOSTAKOVIC, D. D.
    See: SHOSTAKOVICH, D. D.

SCLATER, James S.   USA
    CAP

SCOTSON, Walter
  See: RIEGGER, Wallingford

*SCOTT, Anthony Leonard
  Winstone   Great Britain   1911
    X68

*SCOTT, Charles Kennedy   Great Britain   1876   1965
    BB71, X65, X67

*SCOTT, Cyril Meir   Great Britain   1879   1971
    BB65, BB71, DDM, EMS, EVM, IMD, LMD, MEH, MGG,
    MLA28/4, REM, SML, WI69, X64, X66
    EMS: CKOTT

*SCOTT, Francis George   Great Britain   1880   1958
    BB71, EVM, LMD, MGG, REM

SCOTT, Stephen   USA
    ASUC, CAP

*SCOTT, Tom   USA   1912   1961
    BB65

*SCOTT-MADDOCKS, Daniel
  James Vincent   Great Britain   1932
    WI69

SCRIABINE, Marina   France   1911   Russia
    BB71

*SCUDERI, Gaspare   Italy   1889   1962
    IMD, LMD, REM

*SCULTHORPE, Peter Joshua Australia   1929
    AMM, BB71, WI69, X65, X66, X67

SEARCH, Frederick   USA   1899
    PCM

*SEARLE, Humphrey   Great Britain   1915
    BB65, BB71, BCI, CME, EVM, IMD, LMD, MEH, MGG, REM,
    TSC, WI69, X64, X65, X66, X67, X68

ŠEBALIN, V. J.
  See: SHEBALIN, V. Y.

*SEBASTIAN, Georg   France   1903   Hungary
    QQF, REM, X65, X67, X68

*SEBASTIAN, John   USA   circa 1915
    X66, X68

ŠECHTER, B. S.
See: SHEKHTER, B. S.

*SECUNDA, Sholom   USA   1894   Russia
AS66, WI69, X64, X67

SEDGWICK, Robert
See: RIEGGER, Wallingford

SEDLAČEK, Bohuslav   Czechoslovakia   1928
CCZ

SEDMIDUBSKÝ, Miloš   Czechoslovakia   1924
CCZ, COO, MEH, MNP65/6, X64

*SEEBOTH, Max   Germany   1904
IMD

*SEEGER, Charles Louis   USA   1886   Mexico
DAS, EVM, IMD, PCM, X64, X65, X66, X67, X68

SEEMANN, Helmut   1921
IMD

SEGAL, Charles   Union of   1929   Lithuania
WSA   South Africa

SEGALL, Bernardo   USA   1911   Brazil
AS66, X66

SEGALL, Manfred   USA   1904   Germany
WWG

SEGERSTAM, Leif   Finland   1944
LMD, VTM, X67

*SEGOND, Pierre   Switzerland   1913
SCHW, WWS, X67, X68

*SEHLBACH, Erich Oswald   Germany   1898
BB71, IMD, LMD, MGG, REM

*SEIBER, Matyás György   Great Britain   1905   1960
BB65, BB71, CME, DDM, EL:1, EVM, IMD,   Hungary
LMD, MEH, MGG, PAP, REM, X68

*SEIDEL, Jan   Czechoslovakia   1908
CCZ, EVM, IMD2, LMD, MEH, REM, SML, X65

SEIERØE-MORTENSEN, Anne   Denmark
DMTsp

ŠEKHTER, B. S.
   See: SHEKHTER, B. S.

SELETSKY, Harold   USA   1927
   PC71, X67

SELF, George   Great Britain
   X68

SELIG, Robert   1939
   WAN

SELLECK, John H.   USA
   ASUC

SELMER, Kathryn Lande   USA   1930
   AS66

SELTZER, Dov   Israel   1932   Rumania
   ACU

*SELVAGGI, Rito   Italy   1898
   LMD, REM

SEMEGEN, Daria   USA   1946   Germany
   CAP

SEMENOFF, Ivan   France   1917
   CMF65/10, X64

SEMINI, Carlo Florindo   Switzerland 1914
   LMD, REM, SCHW, X64

SEMMLER, Rudolf   Switzerland 1904
   SCHW

*SENDEREI, Samuil
   Zalmanovich   USSR   1905   1967
   EMS, X67
   EMS: СЕНДЕРЕЙ

*SENDREY, Albert Richard USA   1922
   AS66, BB71, LMD

*SENDREY, Alfred   USA   1884   Hungary
   BB71, EVM, LMD
   BB71: SZENDRIE, Aladar   EVM: SZENDRIE, Aladar
   Originally: SZENDREI

SENDT, Willy   1907   1952
   IMD

*SENFTER, Johanna   Germany   1880   1961

*SENN, Karl   Austria   1878   1964
    EVM, LMD, X64

*SENSTIUS, Kai   Denmark   1889   1966
    EVM, IMD, LMD, REM, X67

*SENTENAT   Cuba   1896
    WI69

SEPOS, Charles   USA   1950
    BS72

SÉRÉ, Octave
    See: POUEIGH, Jean

SEREBRIER, Jose   USA   1938   Uruguay
    BB65, BB71, X64, X65, X66, X67, X68

SERENDERO PROUST, David   Chile   1934
    BB71, CA15, X67

SERETTE, Francis   France   1926
    CMF65/10

*SERKIN, Rudolf   USA   1903   Austria
    LMD, MEH, REM, X64, X65, X66, X67, X68

*SERLY, Tibor   USA   1900   Hungary
    AS66, CME, EVM, LMD, REM, X64, X65, X66, X67, X68

*SEROCKI, Kazimierz   Poland   1922
    BB65, BB71, CME, DDM, EL:3, EMS, IMD, IMD2, LMD, MEH,
    MGG, MZW, PKW, REM, TSC, X64, X65, X66, X67, X68
    EMS: СЕРОЦКИЙ

*SESSIONS, Roger Huntington   USA   1896
    BB65, BB71, DDM, EMS, EVM, IMD, LMD, MEH, MGG, PCM,
    PC71, REM, SML, WI69, WTM, X64, X65, X66, X67, X68
    EMS: СЕШНС

ŠESTÁK, Zdeněk   Czechoslovakia   1925
    CCZ, X68

*SETER, Mordecai   Israel   1916   Russia
    ACU, CME, DDM, IMD, IMD2, LMD, MM59, REM, WWI,
    X64, X65, X66, X67
    MM59: SETTER
    Formerly: STAROMINSKY

SEVERIN, Petru   Rumania   1907   1970
    RCL

SEVITZKY, Fabien   USA   1891   1967
  AS66, BB71, LMD, X65, X66, X67   Russia
  Formerly: KOUSSEVITZKY
  AS66 and LMD: 1893

SEYFRIT, Michael   USA   1947
  BS70

*SEYMER, John William   Sweden   1890   1964
  FST, EVM, KSV, LMD, SIM, SIMa, STS, VTM

*SEYMOUR, John Laurence   USA   1893
  AS66

SFETSAS, Kyriakos   Greece   1945
  EL:4

*SGRIZZI, Luciano   Switzerland   1910   Italy
  LMD, REM, SCHW

SHACKFORD, Charles Reeve   USA   1918
  DAS

SHAFFER, Lloyd   USA   1901
  AS66

SHAHAN, Paul   USA   1923
  PCM

SHAKHIDI, Ziyadullo
  Mukadasovich   USSR   1914
  EMS, X64
  EMS: ШАХИДИ

SHALLENBERG, Robert   USA   1930
  ASUC

SHAMO, Igor Naumovich   USSR   1925
  EMS
  EMS: ШАМО

SHAND, David Austin   USA   1914
  DAS

SHANKAR, Ravi   India   1920
  BB65, BB71, EMS, MEH, WHI, WHIad, X64, X65, X66, X67,
  X68
  WHI: RAVI SHANKAR
  EMS: ШАНКАР

SHANTÜR, Grigori
  Aleksandrovich   USSR   1923
  EMS, X66
  EMS: ШАНТЫРЬ

*SHAPERO, Harold Samuel   USA   1920
   ASUC, AS66, DDM, EVM, LMD, PCM, PC71, REM, WI69, X68

*SHAPEY, Ralph   USA   1921
   AS66, BB71, EL:2, IMD, LMD, X64, X65, X66, X67, X68

*SHAPORIN, Yury Alexandrovich USSR   1887 1966
   BB65, BB71, CME, DDM, EMS, EVM, LMD, MEH, MGG,
   REM, SML, X64, X65, X66, X67, X68
   DDM: CHAPORINE   LMD and MEH: ŠAPORIN
   MGG and SML: SCHAPORIN   REM: SCIAPORIN
   X65: Additional listing under SJAPORINS
   EMS: ШAПOРИН

*SHAPOSHNIKOV, Adrian
  Grigorievich   USSR   1888 1967
   EMS, EVM, LMD, MGG, REM, SML, X67
   EVM: SJAPOSJNIKOW   LMD: ŠAPOŠNIKOV
   MGG and SML: SCHAPOSCHNIKOW   REM: SCIAPOŠNIKOV
   EMS: ШAПOШНИКOB

SHAPOSHINKOV, Ilya
  Kalustovich   USSR   1896 1953
   EMS, LMD
   LMD: ŠAPOŠNIKOV
   EMS: ШAПOШНИКOB

*SHAVERZASHVILI, Alexander
  Vasilievitch   USSR   1919
   EMS
   EMS: ШABEPЗAШBИЛИ

SHAVERZASHVILI, Tamara
  Antanovna   USSR   1891 1955
   EMS
   EMS: ШABEPЗAШBИЛИ

SHAW, Clifford   USA   1911
   AS66, PCM

*SHAW, Martin Edward Fallas   Great Britain 1875 1958
   BB65, BB71, LMD, MGG, PCM, X64, X65, X66

*SHCHEDRIN, Rodion
  Konstantinovich   USSR   1932
   BB65, BB71, CME, EMS, LMD, MEH, PPU69/2, PPU70/1,
   REM, SCD, SML, X64, X65, X66, X67, X68
   LMD, MEH and REM: ŠČEDRIN   SML: STSCHEDRIN
   X65: Additional listing under SJTJEDRIN
   EMS: ЩEДРИН

SHCHELOKOV, Vyacheslav
   Ivanovich   USSR   1904
    EMS
    EMS: ЩЁЛОКОВ

*SHCHERBACHEV, Vladimir
   Vladimirovich   USSR   1889   1952
    EMS, EVM, LMD, MGG, SML, X64   Poland
    EVM: SJTSERBATSJEW   LMD: ŠČERBAČĚV
    MGG: SCHTSCHERBATSCHOW   SML: STSCHERBATSCHOW
    EMS: ЩЕРБАЧЁВ

SHEBALIN, D.   USSR
    PPU69/4

*SHEBALIN, Vissarion
   Yakovlevich   USSR   1902   1963
    BB65, BB71, CME, EMS, EVM, IMD, LMD, MEH, MGG, OCM,
    REM, SCD, SML, X65, X66
    EVM: SJEBALIN   IMD, MGG and SML: SCHEBALIN
    LMD and MEH: ŠEBALIN   REM: SCEBALIN
    EMS: ШЕБАЛИН

SHEIBLER, Truvor Karlovich   USSR   1900   1960
    EMS
    EMS: ШЕЙБЛЕР

SHEINFELD, David   USA
    X67

SHEINKMAN, Mordechai   Israel   1926
    IMD, REM

SHEKERDZHIEV, Mikhail Kolev Bulgaria   1889   1957
    BMK
    BMK: ШЕКЕРДЖИЕВ

*SHEKHTER, Boris
   Semionovich   USSR   1900   1961
    BB65, BB71, EMS, EVM, LMD, MEH, REM
    EVM: SJECHTER   LMD: ŠEKHTER   MEH: ŠECHTER
    REM: SCEKHTER   EMS: ШЕХТЕР

SHELSTA, Scott   USA   1948
    DN70

*SHENSHIN, Alexander
   Alexeyevitch   USSR   1890
    IMD
    IMD: SCHENSCHIN

*SHEPHERD, Arthur USA 1880 1958
 AS66, EVM, LMD, MGG, PCM, REM

*SHER, Veniamin Iosifovich USSR 1900 1962
 EMS
 EMS: ШЕР

SHERA, Frank Henry Great Britain 1882 1956
 LMD

SHERIFF, Noam Israel 1935
 ACUad, CME, IMD2, MM59, X65, X68

SHERLAW-JOHNSON, Robert Great Britain 1932
 WI69, X64, X66, X67, X68
 WI69, X64 and X66: JOHNSON, Robert Sherlaw

*SHERMAN, Robert W. (Robb) USA 1921
 X65, X68

SHIBATA, Minao 1916
 IMD, X68

*SHIFRIN, Seymour J. USA 1926
 ASUC, BB65, BB71, DDM, IMD, IMD2, LMD, PCM, X64, X65,
 X66, X67

SHIGANOW, Nasib Gayasovich USSR 1911
 SML

*SHILAIEV, Nicolai Sergievitch USSR 1881
 EVM
 EVM: SJILAJEW

*SHILKRET, Nathaniel USA 1895
 AS66, LMD, REM

*SHIMIZU, Osamu Japan 1911
 BB65, BB71, LMD

SHINDO, Tak USA 1922
 AS66, BB65, BB71

SHINOHARA, Makoto Japan 1931
 EL:3, IMD, IMD2, X65, X68

*SHIRINSKY, Vasily Petrovich USSR 1901 1965
 BB65, BB71, EMS, EVM, LMD
 EVM: SJIRINSKI LMD: ŠIRINSKIJ
 EMS: ШИРИНСКИЙ

SHIRLEY, Donald Walbridge USA 1927 Jamaica
 WI69, X68

SHIRMA, Grigori Romanovich   USSR   1892
    EMS, PPU69/2, X67
    EMS: ШИРМА

*SHIRTCLIFF, James Stanley   Great Britain   1899
    WI69

*SHISHAKOV, Yuri Nikolayevich   USSR   1925
    EMS, X68
    EMS: ШИШАКОВ

*SHISHOV, Ivan Petrovich   USSR   1888
    EVM
    EVM: SJISJOW

*SHLONSKY, Verdina   Israel   1913   Russia
    ACU, WWI, X68

SHNITKE, Alfred   USSR   1934
    CME, EMS, MEH, MNG, X65, X66, X67, X68
    MEH: ŠNITKE   X65: SCHNITKE and SHNITKE
    EMS: ШНИТКЕ
    MEH: 1936

SHORT, Michael   Great Britain   1937   West Indies
    WI69, X68

*SHOSTAKOVICH, Dmitri
   Dmitrievich   USSR   1906
    BB65, BB71, CME, DDM, EMS, EVM, IMD, IMD2, LMD, MEH,
    MGG, MZW, PPU, PPU69/1, PPU69/2, PPU70/1, REM, SCD,
    SML, VNM, WI69, WTM, X64, X65, X66, X67, X68
    DDM: CHOSTAKOVITCH   EVM: SJOSTAKOWITSJ
    IMD, IMD2, MGG and SML: SCHOSTAKOWITSCH
    LMD and MEH: ŠOSTAKOVIČ   REM: SCIOSTAKOVIC
    EMS: ШОСТАКОВИЧ

*SHTOGARENKO, Andrei
   Yakovlevich   USSR   1902
    BB65, BB71, DDM, EMS, LMD, MEH, PPU, PPU69/2, X66,
    X67, X68
    DDM: CHTOGARENKO   LMD: ŠTOGARENKO
    MEH: ŠTOHARENKO
    EMS: ШТОГАРЕНКО

SHTREKHER, Lubov Lvovna   USSR   1888   1958
    EMS
    EMS: ШТРЕЙХЕР

SHUFFELL, Ovid Claypole   USA   1898

*SHULMAN, Alan   USA   1915
    AA73, AS66, BB65, BB71, PCM, X64, X68

SHUMAN, Davis   USA   1912
   PCM

SHUR, Yekutiel   Israel   1918   Latvia
   ACU

*SHURE, Ralph Deane   USA   1885
   AS66, X65, X68

SHUTENKO, Taisiya Ivanovna   USSR   1905
   EMS, X65
   EMS: ШУТЕНКО

*SHVARTZ, Lev Aleksandrovich   USSR   1898   1962
   EMS
   Vol. I: SCHWARZ
   EMS: ШВАРЦ

SHVEDOV, Dimitri Nicolaevich   USSR   1899
   EMS
   EMS: ШВЕ́ДОВ

*SHVEDOV, Konstantin
  Nicolaievich   USSR   1886
   EVM
   EVM: SJWEDOW

*SHVYADAS, Ionas Izidorovich   USSR   1908   1971
   EMS, MLA28/4, PPU, X68   Latvia
   Also spelled: ŠVEDAS
   EMS: ШВЯ́ДАС

SIALM, Duri   Switzerland   1891   1961
   SCHW

*SIBELIUS, Jean Julian
  Christian   Finland   1865   1957
   BB65, BB71, CME, COF, EMS, EVM, FST, IMD, LMD, MEH,
   MGG, REM, SML, VTM, WTM, X64, X65, X66, X67, X68
   Real first name: Johan
   EMS: СИБЕ́ЛИУС

SIBBING, Robert   USA   1928
   PC71

*SIBSON, Arthur Robert   Rhodesia   1906   Great Britain
   WI69

SÍČ, Jaroslav   Czechoslovakia
   MNP69/4

*SICCARDI, Honorio   Argentina   1897
   LMD, REM

*SICILIANI, Francesco Italy 1911
 LMD, REM, X68

*SICILIANOS, Georgos Greece 1922
 BB65, BB71, CME, EL:1, EL:2, EL:3, EL:4, IMD, LMD, PAP,
 X64, X65, X67

SIDI, Yizhak
 See: SADAI, Yizhak

SIEBER, Susanne Canada 1929 Germany
 CCM

SIEBERT, Wilhelm Dieter Germany 1931
 EL:2, X67, X68

SIEGEL, Arsene USA 1897 France
 AS66

*SIEGEL, Paul USA 1914
 AS66, X68

*SIEGL, Otto Austria 1896
 DDM, EVM, IMD, IMD2, LMD, MGG, REM, X66, X68

*SIEGMEISTER, Elie USA 1909
 AA73, AS66, BB65, BB71, EMS, IMD, LMD, PCM, PC71, REM,
 WI69, WTM, X64, X65, X66, X67, X68
 EMS: СИГМЕЙСТЕР

SIENNICKI, Edmund USA
 X68

*SIFONIA, Firmino Liberato Italy 1917 Switzerland
 LMD, REM

*SIGTENHORST-MEYER,
 Bernhard van den Netherlands 1888 1953
 EVM, IMD, LMD, REM

SIGURBJÖRNSSON, Thorkell Iceland 1938
 BB71, VTM

*SIKORSKI, Kazimierz Poland 1895 Switzerland
 CME, DDM, EMS, EVM, IMD, LMD, MEH, MGG, PKW, REM,
 SML, X65, X66, X67
 EMS: СИКОРСКИЙ

SIKORSKI, Tomasz Poland 1939
 LMD, MEH, PKW, X64, X65, X66, X68

SILÉSU, Lao Italy 1883 1953
 LMD

SILVA, Alfonse de   Peru   1903   1937
    CA13, EVM, REM

SILVA, Giulio   USA   1875   Italy
    LMD, REM

SILVA, Luigi   USA   1903   1961
    BB71, LMD   Italy

*SILVA, Oscar da   Portugal   1870   1958
    BB71, DDM, LMD

SILVERMAN, Stanley   USA   circa 1949
    X65, X68

*SILVESTER, Frederick Caton   Canada   1901   1966
    KEY, X66   England

*SILVESTRI, Constantin   Rumania   1913   1969
    BB71, IMD, LMD, MEH, MLA26/4, RCL, X64, X65, X66,
    X67, X68

*SILVESTRI, Renzo   Italy   1899
    IMD, LMD, REM, WI69

SILVERSTROV, Valentin   USSR   1937
    BB65, BB71, IMD2, LMD, MEH, PAP, X64, X66, X67, X68

ŠIMAI, Pavol   Czechoslovakia 1930
    CCZ, MEH, X64, X65, X67, X68, ZE69/3, ZE70/1, ZE70/2,
    ZE70/3

SIMANDL-PIÑOS, Alois
    See: PINOS, Alois

SIMIĆ, Borivoje   Yugoslavia   1920
    BB65, BB71, KMJ, LMD, X67

SIMIĆ, Darinka   Yugoslavia   1937
    KMJ

*SIMILÄ, Martti Iisakki   Finland   1898
    LMD

*SIMMONS, Homer   USA   1900
    AS66, LMD, X64, X65, X66, X67

SIMON, Emil   Rumania   1936
    RCL

SIMON, Hans Arno   Germany   1919
    WWG

SIMON, Josef   1881
    IMD

SIMON, Ladislav   Czechoslovakia
    MNP69/4

*SIMONDS, Bruce   USA   1895
    LMD, PCM, PC71, WI69

SIMONIS, George   Rumania   1885
    RCL, X64

*SIMONITI, Rado   Yugoslavia   1914
    KMJ, MSC

SIMONS, Netty   USA   1913
    X68

SIMONSEN, Fjeld   Denmark
    DMTsp

SIMONYAN, Nadezda Shogakat
    Simonovna   USSR   1922
        EMS
        EMS: СИМОНЯН

SIMOVICH, Roman Apollonovich   USSR   1901
        EMS
        EMS: СИМОВИЧ

*SIMPSON, Robert   Great Britain 1921
    BB71, LMD, REM, WI69, X64, X65, X66, X67, X68

*SIMS, Ezra   USA   1928
    BB71, X65, X66, X68

SIMSA, B.
    See: JANOVICKY, Karel

SINGER, George   Israel   1907   Czecho-
    ACU   slovakia

SINGER, Louis C.   USA   1912
    AS66, X66

SINISALO, Gelmer-Rainer
    Nesterovich   USSR   1920
        EMS, PPU69/2, X66
        EMS: СИНИСАЛО

SINK, Kuldar   1942
    X67, X68

*SIOHAN, Robert Lucien   France   1894
    DDM, EVM, LMD, MGG, REM, X65, X66, X67, X68

SIPILÄ, Eero   Finland   1918
    VTM

SIPPONEN, Urho Aatto   Finland   1915
    KKO

*SIQUEIRA, José de Lima   Brazil   1907
    CA16, EVM, FBC, IMD, LMD, REM

SIR, Niel   USA
    ASUC

ŠIRINSKIJ, V. P.
    See: SHIRINSKY, V. P.

*ŠIROLA, Božidar   Yugoslavia   1889   1956
    DDM, EVM, HCM, IMD, LMD, MEH, MGG, REM, X67

SIRULNIKOFF, Jack   Canada
    CCM71, CVMa, KEY, MCO68, MCO71

SITSKY, Larry   Australia circa 1937 China
    X67, X68

*ŠIVIC, Pavel   Yugoslavia   1908
    IMD, KMJ, LMD, MGG, REM, X66, X67, X68

SIXT, Paul   Germany   1908   1964
    LMD, REM, X64

SIXTA, Josef   Czechoslovakia 1940
    MEH, MNP66/4, MNP71/1, X68

SJAPORINS, Jurij A.
    See: SHAPORIN, Yuri A.

SJAPOSJNIKOW, A. G.
    See: SHAPOSHNIKOV, A. G.

SJEBALIN, W. J.
    See: SHEBALIN, V. Y.

SJECHTER, B. S.
    See: SHEKHTER, B. S.

SJILAJEW, N. S.
    See: SHILAIEV, N. S.

SJIRINSKI, W. P.
    See: SHIRINSKY, V. P.

SJOSTAKOWITSJ, D. D.
  See: SHOSTAKOVICH, D. D.

SJTJEDRIN, R. K.
  See: SHCHEDRIN, R. K.

SJTSERBATSJEW, W. W.
  See: SHCHERBACHEV, V. V.

*SKALKOTTAS, Nikos   Greece   1904   1949
  CME, DDM, EL:1, EL:2, EL:3, EL:4, EVM, IMD2, LMD, MEH,
  OCM, PAP, REM, SML, TSC, X65, X66, X67, X68

*SKALOVSKI, Todor   Yugoslavia   1909
  KMJ, LMD, REM, X67, X68

*ŠKERJANC, Lucijan Marija   Yugoslavia   1900   Austria
  DDM, EVM, IMD, KMJ, LMD, MEH, MSC, REM, SML, WI69,
  X64, X67

ŠKERL, Dane   Yugoslavia   1931
  KMJ, LMD, X67, X68

*SKLAVOS, Giorgios   Greece   1888   Rumania
  BB65, BB71, EVM, LMD, REM

SKLYAR, Ivan Mikhailovich   USSR   1906
  EMS
  EMS: СКЛЯР

*SKÖLD, Karl Yngve   Sweden   1899
  EVM, FST, IMD, KSV, LMD, REM, SIM, SIMa, SOW, X68

SKÖLD, Sven   Sweden   1899   1956
  FST, SIM, STI

*SKORULSKY, Mikhail
  Adamovich   USSR   1887   1950
  EMS
  EMS: СКОРУЛЬСКИЙ

*SKORZENY, Fritz   Austria   1900   1965
  IMD, LMD, MLA22/4, WI69, X65, X66

SKOULTAI, A. P.
  See: SKULTE, A. P.

SKRIABIN, Nikolai
  See: NOLINSKY, Nikolai Mihailovich

*SKROWACZEWSKI, Stanisław   USA   1923   Poland
  BB71, CME, IMD, LMD, MEH, MGG, PKW, REM, SML, WI69,
  X64, X65, X66, X67, X68

*SKULTE, Adolfs Petrovich   USSR   1909
    DDM, EMS, MEH, PPU
    DDM: SKOULTAI
    EMS: СКУЛТЭ

*ŠKVOR, Frantisek   Czechoslovakia   1898
    CCZ, IMD2, MEH, X68

ŠKVOR, Petr   Czechoslovakia
    MNP69/4

SLABÝ, Jan   Czechoslovakia   1904
    CCZ

SLADEK, Paul   USA   1896   Austria
    AA73, AS66, X64, X65, X66, X67, X68

*SLATES, Philip Marion   USA   1924
    X65, X66, X67

SLATEV-TSCHERKIN, Georgi
   Dimitrov
   See: ZLATEV-CHERKIN

*SLAVENSKI, Josip   Yugoslavia   1896   1955
    CME, DDM, EMS, EVM, HCM, IMD, IMD2, KMJ, LMD, MEH,
    MGG, REM, SML, X65, X66, X67, X68
    Formerly: ŠTOLCER
    EMS: СЛАВЕНСКИЙ

*SLAVICKÝ, Klement   Czechoslovakia   1910
    BB65, BB71, CCZ, EVM, IMD, IMD2, LMD, MEH, MGG,
    MNP65/7, MNP66/1, MNP67/5, MNP70/1, MNP70/9,
    MNP72/6, REM, SML, X65, X67, X68

ŠLIK, Miroslav   Czechoslovakia   1898
    CCZ, LMD

SLIMÁČEK, Jan   Czechoslovakia
    MNP69/4

SLIMÁČEK, Milan   Czechoslovakia
    MNP69/4

*SLONIMSKY, Nicolas   USA   1894   Russia
    AS66, BB65, BB71, CA15, EMS, EVM, LMD, MGG, REM,
    WI69, X64, X65, X66, X68
    EMS: СЛОНИМСКИЙ

SLONIMSKY, Sergey
   Michailovich   USSR   1932
    BB65, BB71, EMS, MEH, PPU69/2, X65, X66, X67, X68
    EMS: СЛОНИМСКИЙ

SŁOWIŃSKI, Właysław   Poland   1930
  PKW, X68

SLUKA, Luboš   Czechoslovakia 1928
  CCZ, IMD2

SMAJLOVIĆ, Avdo   Yugoslavia   1917
  KMJ

SMALLEY, Roger   Great Britain 1943
  BB71, CME, X64, X65, X66, X67, X68

*SMALLMAN, Frederick Basil
Rowley   Great Britain 1921
  WI69, X65, X67

SMATEK, Miloš   Czechoslovakia 1895
  CCZ, MEH

*SMETÁČEK, Václav   Czechoslovakia 1906
  CCZ, LMD, MEH, X66, X67, X68

SMETANA, Frantisek   Czechoslovakia 1914
  LMD, MEH, X64

SMIRNOV, Boris Fedorovich USSR   1912
  EMS, X67
  EMS: СМИРНОВ

SMIRNOVA, Galina
Konstantinovna   USSR   1910
  EMS
  EMS: СМИРНОВА

SMIT, Johannes   USA   1913
  CAP

*SMIT, Leo   Netherlands 1900 1944
  EVM

*SMIT, Leo   USA   1921
  AS66, EVM, LMD, PCM, PC71, REM, X64
  EVM: 1925

SMITH, Anita   USA   1922
  AS66

SMITH, Carlton Sprague USA   1905
  BB71, DAS, PCM, X67

*SMITH, Charles Thomas Great Britain 1887
  WI69

*SMITH, Edwin William   Great Britain   1914
   WI69, X65, X66

*SMITH, Hale   USA   1925
   PCM, PC71, X64, X66, X67

SMITH, John Shaffer, Jr.   USA   1913
   AS66, PCM

*SMITH, Joseph Leopold (Leo) Canada   1881 1952
   CCM, CVM, NLCa   Great Britain

*SMITH, Julia Frances   USA   1911
   AA73, AS66, DN72, PCM, PC71, X64, X65, X66, X68

SMITH, Laurence R.   USA
   ASUC

SMITH, Leland   USA   1925
   BB71, X66

SMITH, Melville   USA   1898
   PCM

*SMITH, Robert   Great Britain   1922
   WI69, X64

*SMITH, Ronald   Great Britain   1922
   WI69, X68

*SMITH, Russell   USA   1927
   PCM, X67

*SMITH, Warren Storey   USA   1885
   PCM, X64, X65

SMITH, William O.   USA   1926
   BB65, BB71, IMD, LMD, MNG, PCM, PC71, X64, X67, X68

*SMITH-BRINDLE, Reginald   Great Britain   1917
   IMD, LMD, REM, X64, X66, X67, X68

*SMOKVARSKI, Gligor   Yugoslavia   1914
   KMJ

SMUTNÝ, Jiří   Czechoslovakia 1932
   CCZ, COO, MNP64/3, MNP69/4, X68

ŠNITKE, A.
   See: SHNITKE, A.

SNÍŽKOVÁ-ŠKRHOVÁ, Jitka   Czechoslovakia 1924
   CCZ

SNORRASON, Áskell   Iceland   1888
   VTM

*SNUNIT, Zvi   Israel   1933   Germany
   MM59, X68
   Formerly: LICHTENSTEIN

SOBANSKI, Hans Joachim   1906
   IMD

*SOCOR, Matei   Rumania   1908
   BB65, BB71, EMS, LMD, MGG, RCL, REM, SML
   EMS: COKÓP

*SODDERLAND, Jan   Netherlands   1903
   NED

SÖDERHOLM, Vlademar   Sweden   1909
   FST, KSV, SIM, SIMa, STI, STS, SWE, VTM

SØDERLIND, Ragnar   Norway   1945
   CNO

*SODERLUND, Gustave Frederic USA   1881   Sweden
   LMD

*SÖDERLUNDH, Bror Axel
   (Lille Bror)   Sweden   1912   1957
   FST, KSV, SIM, SIMa, SOW, STS

SÖDERSTEN, Gunno   Sweden   1920
   FST

SODOMKA, Karel   Czechoslovakia
   MNP69/4

SOEGIJO, Paul Gutama   Indonesia   1934
   PAP

SÖHNER, Leo   1898
   IMD

SOHY-LABEY, Charlotte
   See: LABEY, Charlotte Sohy

ŞOIMA, Gheorghe   Rumania   1911
   RCL

*SOJO, Vincente Emilio   Venezuela   1887
   CA14, EVM

SOKHOR, Arnold Naumovich USSR   1924
   EMS, PPU69/2, X66, X67, X68   EMS: COXOP

*SOKOLA, Milos   Czechoslovakia 1913
    CCZ, IMD, IMD2, LMD, MEH, MNP72/4, REM, WI69

SOKOLOFF, Noel   USA   1923
    PCM

SOKORSKI, Jerzy   Poland   1916
    PKW

*SOLARES-ECHEVARRIA,
  Enrique   Guatemala   1910
    BB65, BB71, LMD

*SOLBERG, Leif   Norway   1914
    CNO

SOLER, Jose   Spain
    X67

SOLER, Josep   Spain   1935
    HET1, HET3, IMD

*SOLHEIM, Karsten   Norway   1869   1953
    CNO

*SOLITO de SOLIS, Aldo   USA   1905   Italy
    AS66

SOLLBERGER, Harvey   USA   1938
    ASUC, BB65, BB71, LMD, X64, X65, X66

SOLLIMA, Eliodoro   Italy   1926
    LMD, REM

SOLODUKHO, Yakov
  Semenovich   USSR   1911
    EMS, PPU69/2, X64, X65, X66, X68
    EMS: СОЛОДУХО

SOLOMON, Izler   USA   1910
    CME, LMD, X65

SOLOTAREV, V. A.
  See: ZOLOTAREV, V. A.

*SOLOVIEV-SEDOI, Vasili
  Pavlovich   USSR   1907
    DDM, EMS, EVM, LMD, MEH, MGG, PPU69/2, REM, SML,
    X64, X65, X67, X68
    LMD: SOLOV'ËV-SEDOJ   MEH: SOLOVIEV-SEDOJ
    MGG: SOLOWJOW-SEDOJ   SML: SOLOWJOW-SEDOI
    EMS: СОЛОВЬЁВ-СЕДОЙ

*SOŁTYS, Adam
Mietchislavovich   Poland   1890   1968
    BB71, EMS, LMD, PKW, REM
    EMS: СОЛТЫС

*SOMERS, Harry Stewart   Canada   1925
    BB65, BB71, BCL, CCM, CCM71, CVM, CVMa, IMD, KEY,
    LMD, MCO, MCO68, MCO71, NLC, NLCa, PCM, REM, TFB,
    X64, X65, X66, X67, X68

*SOMERS-COCKS, John   Great Britain   1907
    WI69

*SOMMA, Bonavetura   Italy   1893   1960
    REM

*SOMMER, Vladimír   Czechoslovakia   1921
    BB65, BB71, CCZ, CME, DDM, EMS, IMD, IMD2, LMD, MEH,
    MGG, MNP64/3, MNP64/4, MNP65/7, MNP71/2, REM, SML,
    X64, X65, X66, X67
    EMS: COMMEP

*SOMMERFELDT, Øistein   Norway   1919
    CNO

SOMMI-PICENARDI, Guido   Italy   1894
    REM

SOMOHANO, Arturo   USA   1910   Puerto Rico
    AS66

*SONNENBURG, Klaus   Germany   1927
    X67

SONNER, Rudolf   Germany   1894   1955
    LMD, REM

*SONNINEN, Ahti   Finland   1914
    CME, COF, EVM, KKO, LMD, REM, VTM, X66

*SØNSTEVOLD, Gunnar   Norway   1912
    CNO, VTM, X68

SØNSTEVOLD, Maj   Norway   1917   Sweden
    CNO

*SONZOGNO, Giulio Cesare   Italy   1906
    IMD, LMD, REM, WI69

SOPRONI, József   Hungary   1930
    CHC, IMD, X67, X68, ZSZ

*SORABJI, Kaikhosru Shapurji   Great Britain   1892
    BB71, DN70, EVM, LMD, MGG, REM, X66

*SÖRENSON, Torsten Napoleon   Sweden   1908
    FST, KSV, SIM, SIMa, STI, VTM

*SORESINA, Alberto   Italy   1911
    IMD, LMD, REM

*SORIANO, Alberto   Uruguay   1915   Argentina
    BB65, BB71, CA16, EMS, LMD, REM, X67
    EMS: СОРИАНО

*SORO BARRIGA, Enrique   Chile   1884   1954
    EVM, LMD, REM

*SOROKIN, Vladimir
    Constantinovich   USSR   1914
    EMS, X64
    EMS: СОРОКИН

*SOROZÁBAL, Pablo   Spain   1897
    EVM, LMD, MGG, REM, X68

SORRENTINO, Charles   USA   1906   Italy
    AS66

*SOSNOVTZEV, Boris
    Andreevich   USSR   1921
    EMS
    EMS: СОСНОВЦЕВ

ŠOSTAKOVIČ, D. D.
    See: SHOSTAKOVICH, D. D.

SOTNIKOV, Tikhon Ivanovich   USSR   1901
    EMS
    EMS: СОТНИКОВ

*SOUCHAY, Marc-André   Germany   1906
    LMD, REM, WWG

*SOUFFRIAU, Arsène   Belgium   1926
    WI69

SOUKUP, Vladimír   Czechoslovakia   1930
    CCZ, IMD2, MEH, MNP69/5, X64, X67, X68

*SOULAGE, Marcelle Fanny
    Henriette   France   1894   Peru
    DDM, DMF, LMD, QQF, WI69

SOULE, Emund F.　　　　　　USA　　　　　1915
　　DN72

*SOURIS, André　　　　　　Belgium　　　1899　1970
　　BB71, CBC, CME, DDM, IMD, LMD, MGG, REM, X64, X65,
　　X66, X67, X68

*SOUSA, Filipe de　　　　　Portugal　　　1927
　　LMD, REM, X64, X68

SOUSTER, Timothy Andrew
　　James　　　　　　　　　Great Britain　1943
　　BB71, WI69, X65, X66, X67, X68

SOUTHAM, Ann　　　　　　Canada
　　KEY, MCO68, X68

*SOUZA LIMA, João de　　　Brazil　　　　1898
　　EVM, LMD

SOWANDE, Fela　　　　　　Nigeria　　　　1905
　　BB65, BB71, X64, X66, X67, X68

*SOWERBY, Leo　　　　　　USA　　　　　1895　1968
　　AS66, BB65, BB71, EVM, IMD, LCI, LMD, MGG, MLA25/4,
　　PCM, PC71, REM, X64, X65, X66, X67, X68

*SPADAVEKKIA, Antonio
　　Emmanuelovich　　　　　USSR　　　　1907
　　CME, EMS, LMD, REM, SML, X65, X66, X67
　　EMS: СПАДАВЁККИА

*SPALDER, Frithjof　　　　Norway　　　　1896
　　CNO

*SPALDING, Albert　　　　USA　　　　　1888　1953
　　AS66, LMD, REM

*SPALDING, Eva Ruth　　　Great Britain
　　WI69

SPASOV, Georgi　　　　　Bulgaria　　　1891　1953
　　BMK, X67
　　BMK: СПАСОВ

SPASOV, Ivan　　　　　　Bulgaria　　　1934
　　LMD, X66, X68

SPĂTĂRELU, Vasile　　　　Rumania　　　1938
　　RCL

SPEARE-LUYTENS, Sally   USA
   CAP

SPEARS, Jared T.   USA   1936
   AA73, CAP, PC71

*SPEDDING, Frank Donald   Great Britain   1929
   WI69

*SPELMAN, Timothy Mather   USA   1891   1970
   BB71, LMD, REM

*SPENCER, Frank Woolley Sim   Great Britain   1911   Scotland
   WI69

*SPENCER, James Houston   USA   1895
   AS66

SPERRY, Don Ray   USA   1947
   DN72

*SPEZZAFERRI, Giovanni   Italy   1888   1963
   IMD, LMD, REM

*SPEZZAFERRI, Laszlò   Italy   1912
   LMD, REM, WI69

SPIALEK, Hans   USA   Austria
   AS66

*SPIER, Harry R.   USA   1888   1952
   AS66

*SPIERS, Pierre   France   1917
   QQF

SPIES, Claudio   USA   1925   Chile
   ASUC, AS66, CA15, PCM, PC71, X64, X65, X67

*SPIES, Leo   Germany   1899   1965
   EMS, LMD, MEH, MLA22/4, SML, X64, X65   Russia
   EMS: ШПИС

ŠPILER, Miroslav   Yugoslavia   1906
   HCM, KMJ, LMD, X67

SPILKA, Frantisek   Czechoslovakia   1877
   CCZ, EVM, LMD, MEH, MGG, REM

SPILLING, Robert   Germany   1907
   WWG

SPINDLE, Louise Cooper USA
 AS66

SPINELLI, Santo Italy 1902 1944
 REM

*SPINKS, Charles USA 1915
 IMD

*SPINNER, Leopold Great Britain 1906 Poland
 IMD

SPIREA, Andrei Rumania 1932
 ACU

*SPISAK, Michal France 1914 1965
 BB71, CME, DDM, EVM, IMD, LMD, MGG, Poland
 PKW, REM, SML, X64, X65, X66

SPIŠIAK FEST, Radovan Czechoslovakia 1900
 CCZ, MEH

SPITALNY, H. Leopold USA 1887 Russia
 AS66

*SPITTA, Heinrich Arnold
 Theodor Germany 1902 1972
 EVM, IMD, REM, X68

*SPITZMULLER HARMERSBACH,
 Alexander von Austria 1896 1962
 BB65, BB71, IMD, LMD, MGG, REM

ŠPOLJAR, Zlatko Yugoslavia 1892
 HCM, KMJ

ŠPOLJARIĆ, Vlado Yugoslavia 1926
 KMJ

SPRECHER, William Gunther
 See: GUNTHER, William

SPRING, Glenn USA
 CAP

*SPRINGER, Max Germany 1877 1954
 IMD, LMD, MGG

*SPRONGL, Norbert Austria 1892
 IMD, LMD, MGG, REM, WI69, X65, X67, X68

*SQUIRE, William Henry   Great Britain   1871
   BB65, BB71

ŠRÁMEK, Vladimír   Czechoslovakia 1923
   IMD2, LMD, MEH, MGG, X68

SRBULJ, Jovan   Yugoslavia   1893   1966
   KMJ

SREBOTNJAK, Alojz   Yugoslavia   1931
   BB65, BB71, CME, KMJ, LMD, MEH, MSC, REM, TSC, X67

*SRNKA, Jiří   Czechoslovakia 1907
   CCZ, IMD2, MEH, X67, X68

*ŠROM, Karel   Czechoslovakia 1904
   CCZ, EVM, IMD, IMD2, LMD, MEH, MNP69/7, REM

STACHOWIAK, Lechoslaw   Poland   1926
   PKW, X64, X68

STADLMAIR, Hans   Austria   1929
   IMD2

*STAEMPFLI, Edward   Switzerland   1908
   DDM, EVM, IMD, LMD, MGG, REM, SCHW, WWS, X67, X68

STAFFELLI, Attilio   Italy   1894   1957
   REM

STAFFORD, James E.   USA
   ASUC

STAHULJAK, Dubravko   Yugoslavia   1920
   HCM, KMJ, LMD

STAHULJAK, Juraj   Yugoslavia   1901
   HCM, KMJ, LMD

*STAHULJAK, Mladen   Yugoslavia   1914
   KMJ, LMD, REM, X67
   KMJ: STAHULJA<u>H</u>

*STAINOV, Petko Gruev   Bulgaria   1896
   BB65, BB71, BMK, LMD, MEH, MGG, REM, SML, X67, X68
   MEH, MGG and SML: STA<u>J</u>NOV
   BMK: **СТАЙНОВ**

STAJIĆ, Petar   Yugoslavia   1915
   KMJ

*STALLAERT, Alphonse   Netherlands   1920
   EVM

STALVEY, Dorrance   1930
  WAN

STAM, George   Netherlands   1905
  EVM

*STAM, Hendrikus Gerardus
  (Henk)   Netherlands   1922
  EVM, IMD

STANČEK, Ladislav   Czechoslovakia 1898
  CCZ, MEH

STANČIĆ, Svetislav   Yugoslavia   1895
  HCM, LMD, MGG

STANFORD, Patric   Great Britain
  WI69, X64, X68

*STANISLAV, Josef   Czechoslovakia 1897 1971
  CCZ, IMD, IMD2, MEH, MNP65/6, MNP66/10,   Germany
  MNP71/9, SML, X64, X65, X66, X67, X68

STANNARD, St/Bm Derek   Canada   1929 England
  CCM, MCO

*STARER, Robert   USA and Israel 1924
  AA73, AS66, BB65, BB71, IMD, LMD, MM59, PCM, PC71,
  REM, X64, X65, X66, X67, X68

STARK, Paul Rafael   Israel   1904 Serbia
  ACU

*STAROKADOMSKY, Mihail
  Leonidovich   USSR   1901 1954
  EMS, EVM, LMD, REM
  EMS: СТАРОКАДОМСКИЙ

STAROMINSKY, Mordecai
  See: SETER, Mordecai

*STASEVICH, Abram L'vovich USSR   1906
  X68

ŠŤASTNÝ, Vincenc   Czechoslovakia 1885
  CCZ

STAUFFER, Jacques-Eugene Germany   1948
  ACM

STEARNS, Peter Pindar   USA   1931
  ASUC, PCM, X65, X66

ŠTĚDROŇ, Miloš   Czechoslovakia   1942
   MNP69/4, MNP70/5, MNP71/6, MNP72/9, X65, X66, X67, X68

*ŠTĚDROŇ, Vladimír   Czechoslovakia   1900
   CCZ, EVM, IMD, LMC, REM

STEEL, Christopher Charles   Great Britain   1939
   WI69, X66, X67

STEELE, Helen   USA   1904
   AS66

*STEEN, Gert van der   Netherlands   1907
   NED

STEFANINI, Nikša   Yugoslavia   1905
   HCM

STEFANOV, Pavel Evstatiev   Bulgaria   1899   1961
   BMK
   BMK: СТЕФАНОВ

STEFÁNSSON, Fjölnir   Iceland   1930
   VTM

*STEFFEN, Wolfgang Johann
   Eberhard   Germany   1923
   IMD

STEFFENS, Walter   Germany   1934
   IMD2, X67, X68

*STEHMAN, Jacques   Belgium   1912
   CBC, DDM, EVM

STEIN, Herman   USA   1915
   DN72

*STEIN, Leon   USA   1910
   AA73, ASUC, EVM, LCI, LMD, PCM, PC71, REM, WI69,
   X64, X65, X66, X67, X68

STEIN, Leonard   USA
   ASUC

*STEIN, Max Martin   Germany   1911
   REM, WWF

STEINBAUER, Othmar   Austria   1895   1962
   BB65, BB71

STEINBERG, Zeev   Israel   1918   Germany
   ACUad

STEINER, George   USA   1900   1967
   AS66, X67   Hungary

STEINER, Gitta   USA   1932
   PC71, X68

*STEINER, Heinrich   Germany   1903
   WWG, X68

*STEINER, Max R.   USA   1888   1971
   AS66, MLA28/4   Austria

*STEINERT, Alexander Lang   USA   1900
   AS66, EVM, IMD, LMD, REM

STEINMAN, Vilém   Czechoslovakia   1880   1962
   CCZ

*STEKEL, Erik-Paul   France   1898   Austria
   DDM, MGG, QQF, WI69

*STEKKE, Léon   Belgium   1905
   EVM
   EMV: 1904

*STEKL, Konrad   Austria   1901   Yugoslavia
   MGG, WI69, X66

*STELZER, August   Austria   1900
   WI69

STENBERG, Jordan   USA   1947
   BB71

STEPANOV, Aleksey
   Arkhipovich   USSR   1913
   PPU, X64

*STEPANOV, Lev Borisovich   USSR   1908
   EMS, EVM, PPU
   EMS: СТЕПАНОВ

*STEPANYAN, Aro Levonovich   USSR   1897   1966
   EMS, EVM, LMD, MGG, REM, X67   Armenia
   EMS: СТЕПАНЯН

*STEPANYAN, Ruben
   Guerassimovich   USSR   1902   Armenia
   X66, X67

*STEPHANI, Hermann   Germany   1877   1960
   BB65, BB71, EVM, LMD, MGG, REM

*ŠTĚPKA, Karel Václav   Czechoslovakia   1908
   CCZ, WI69

STERN, Alfred   Switzerland   1901   1966
   SCHWs, X66   San Remo

STERN, Marcel   France   1909
   CMF65/10

STERN, Robert   USA   1934
   AA73, ASUC

*STERNBERG, Erich Walter   Israel   1891   Germany
   ACU, BB65, BB71, DDM, EVM, IMD, IMD2, LMD, MGG,
   MM59, REM, WWI, X68
   EVM and WWI: 1898

*STERNBERG, Hans   Germany   1910
   X67

STERNE, Colin Chase   USA   1921   Union of
   DAS, PCM, X64, X67   South Africa

*STERNEFELD, Daniel   Belgium   1905
   EVM, LMD, MGG, REM

STERNKLAR, Avraham   Israel   1930   Italy
   ACUad, X66, X67

STERNWALD, Jiří   Czechoslovakia   1910
   CCZ, MEH

STEUERMANN, Eduard   USA   1892   1964
   BB71, IMD, LMD, X65, X66, X67   Poland

*STEVENS, Bernard George   Great Britain   1916
   EVM, IMD, MGG, PCM, REM, WI69, X67, X68

*STEVENS, Halsey   USA   1908
   AA73, CA11, CN70, IMD, LMD, OCM, PCM, PC71, REM,
   WI69, X64, X65, X66, X67, X68

*STEVENS, James   Great Britain   1928
   WI69

*STEVENS, Paul James   Great Britain   1923
   EVM, LMD, REM

STEVENSON, Ronald   Union of   1928   Great Britain
   BB71, WI69, X64,   South Africa
   X65, X66, X67, X68

STEWART, Hascal Vaughan   USA
    CAP

STEWART, Robert J.   USA   1918
    ASUC, X67, X68

STIBILJ, Milan   Yugoslavia   1929
    BB65, BB71, CME, KMJ, LMD, MEH, MSC, X66, X67, X68

*STIEBER, Hans   Germany   1886
    EVM, IMD, LMD, REM, SML, X64, X66

STIEBLER, Ernst Albrecht   1934
    IMD2, X68

STIEL, Ludwig   Germany   1901   Austria
    WWG

*STIER, Alfred Friedrich   Germany   1880   1967
    IMD, LMD, X64, X65, X66, X67, X68

*STIERLIN, Kuno   Germany   1886
    LMD, REM

STIERLIN-VALLON, Henri   Switzerland   1887   1952
    EVM, LMD, MGG, SCHW

STILEC, Jiri   Rumania
    X65, X68

*STILL, Robert   Great Britain   1910
    BB71, X65

*STILL, William Grant   USA   1895
    AA73, AS66, BB65, BB71, DDM, EMS, EVM, LMD, MEH,
    MGG, PCM, REM, WI69, X64, X65, X66, X67, X68
    EMS: СТИЛЛ

STILLER, Andrew   USA   1946

STOCK, David F.   USA   1939
    BB71, X67

*STOCKHAUSEN, Karlheinz   Germany   1928
    BB65, BB71, DDM, DMM, EL:3, EMS, EVM, IMD, IMD2,
    LMD, MEH, MGG, MNG, MZW, OCM, PAP, REM, SML,
    TCM, TSC, VNM, WI69, WTM, X64, X65, X66, X67, X68
    EMS: ШТÓКХАУЗЕН

STOCKHOFF, Walter William   USA   1876   1968
    BB65, BB71, MLA25/4

STOCKMEIER, Wolfgang   Germany   1931
   MGG, X67, X68

*STÖGBAUER, Isidor   USA   1883 1966
   X67, X68   Germany

*STÖHR, Richard   USA   1874 1967
   BB71, IMD, LMD, MGG, REM, X68   Austria

ŠTOHARENKO, A. J.
   See: SHTOGARENKO, A. Y.

STOIA, Achim   Rumania   1910
   RCL, X68

STOIANOFF, A. A.
   See: STOYANOV, A. A.

STOIANOV, Vesselin
   See: STOYANOV, Vesselin

STOJANOFF, V. A.
   See: STOYANOV, V. A.

STOJANOV, A. A.
   See: STOYANOV, A. A.

STOJANOVIĆ, Josip   Yugoslavia   1909
   KMJ, X68

*STOJANOVIĆ, Petar Lazar   Yugoslavia   1877 1957
   EMS, EVM, KMJ, LMD, MGG, REM, SML   Hungary
   EMS: СТОЯНОВИЧ

STOJKOV, Stojan   Yugoslavia
   KMJ

STOKER, Richard   Great Britain   1938
   BB71, WI69, X64, X65, X66, X67, X68

STOKOWSKI, Leopold   USA   1887 Great Britain
   AS66, DDM, EVM, LMD, MGG, X64, X65, X66, X67, X68
   EMS: СТОКОВСКЛЙ
   DDM: 1882   EMS: 1882

ŠTOLCER, Josip
   See: SLAVENSKI, Josip

STOLL, Dennis Gray   Great Britain   1912
   WI69, X64, X65, X68

STOLL, Philip   USA   1956
   BS72

STOLTE, Siegfried　　　　　Germany　　　1925
　　SML

STOLTZE, Robert H.　　　　USA
　　ASUC

STOLZ, Leopold Jacob　　　Austria　　1866　1957
　　LMD

*STOLZ, Robert Elisabeth　　USA　　　1880　Austria
　　BB65, BB71, EVM, MEH, MGG, SML, X64, X66, X67, X68

STONE, Malcolm A.　　　　USA
　　CAP

*STONE, Robin Domnic
　　Alexander　　　　　　　Great Britain　1932
　　WI69

STORM, Ricardo　　　　　　Uruguay　　　1930
　　CA16

STOUCHEVSKI, J.
　　See: STUTCHEVSKY, J. Y.

STOUFFER, Paul M.　　　　USA　　　　1916
　　AS66

STOUT, Alan B.　　　　　　USA　　　　1932
　　AA73, BB71, PCM, PC71, X65, X66, X67, X68

*STOYANOV, Andrei Anastasov　Bulgaria　　　1890
　　BMK, EVM, LMD, SML, X66, X68
　　EVM: STOIANOFF　　　　　LMD: STOJANOV
　　BMK: СТОЯНОВ

*STOYANOV, Veselin
　　Anastasov　　　　　　　Bulgaria　　1902　1969
　　BB65, BB71, BMK, EMS, IMD, LMD, MEH, MGG, REM, SML,
　　X67, X68
　　IMD: STOJANOFF
　　LMD, MEH, MGG and SML: STOJANOV　Vol. I: STOIANOV
　　BMK: СТОЯНОВ　　　　　EMS: СТОЯНОВ

*STRAESSER, Hans Georg　Germany　　　1902
　　IMD

STRAESSER, Joep　　　　　Netherlands　1934
　　LMD, NED, X65, X66, X67, X68

STRAIGHT, Willard　　　　USA　　　　1930
　　AS66, PCM

STRANDBERG, Newton D.   USA
    ASUC

STRANDSJÖ, Göte   Sweden   1916
    KSV, SIMa

*STRANG, Gerald   USA   1908   Canada
    EVM, IMD, PCM, X65, X66, X67, X68

STRANGE, Allen   USA   1943
    CAP

*STRANNOLYUBSKY, Boris
   Mikhailovitch   USSR   1903
    REM

STRASSBURG, Robert   USA   1915
    AS66, BB71

*STRATEGIER, Herman   Netherlands   1912
    EVM, IMD, LMD, MGG, NED, REM, X68

*STRAUS, Oskar   Austria   1870   1954
    DDM, EVM, LMD, MGG, REM, X68

STRAUSS, John   USA   1920
    AS66

STRAUSS, Wolfgang   Germany   1927
    SML, X68

*STRAVINSKY, Igor Feodorovich USA   1882   1971
    AS66, BB65, BB71, CME, DDM, DN70,   Russia
    EL:3, EL:4, EMS, EVM, IMD, IMD2,
    LMD, MEH, MGG, MLA28/4, MZW, PAP, REM, SCHW,
    SML, VNM, WTM, X64, X65, X66, X67, X68
    EMS: СТРАВИНСКИЙ

*STRAVINSKY, Soulima   USA   1910   Switzerland
    IMD, LMD, REM

STREBOTNIAK, Alois   1931

*STRECKE, Gerhard Werner   Germany   1890
    EVM, IMD, LMD, MGG, WWG

STREET, Donald   Great Britain
    X67

*STRENS, Jules de   Belgium   1892
    EVM

STRESEMANN, Wolfgang   Germany   1904
    WWG

STRICKER, André   France   1931
    ACM

*STRICKLAND, Lily Teresa   USA   1887   1958
    AS66

*STRIEGLER, Kurt Emil   Germany   1886   1958
    LMD, MGG, REM

STRIETMAN, Willem Frederik   Netherlands   1918
    EVM

STRILKO, Anthony   USA   1931
    PCM, PC71, X64, X65

*STRIMER, Joseph   USA   1881   1962
    BB71   Russia

*STRINGFIELD, Lamar   USA   1897   1959
    AS66, BB71, LMD, PC71, REM

*STRINGHAM, Edwin John   USA   1890
    EVM, LMD, REM, WI69

STRIPP, Alan   Great Britain   1924
    WI69, X64, X68

*STRNIŠTĚ, Jiří   Czechoslovakia   1914
    CCZ

STROE, Aurel   Rumania   1932
    BB65, BB71, IMD2, LMD, MEH, RCL, X65, X68

STROHBACH, Siegfried   1929
    IMD

*STROM, Kurt Richard   Germany   1903
    IMD

*STROMENGER, Karel   Poland   1885
    X66

STRØMHOLM, Folke   Norway   1941
    CNO

STRUBE, Adolf   1894
    IMD

*STRUBE, Gustav　　　　　　USA　　　　　　1867　1953
　EVM, LMD, REM　　　　　　　　　　　　　　　　　Germany

STRUBIN, Philippe　　　　　France　　　　1894　1962
　ACM

STRUNK, Steven G.　　　　　USA
　ASUC

STRUTT, Clive　　　　　　　Great Britain
　X64

*STRÜVER, Paul　　　　　　Germany　　　　1896
　EVM

STSCHEDRIN, R. K.
　See: SHCHEDRIN, R. K.

STSCHERBATSCHOW, W. W.
　See: SHCHERBACHEV, V. V.

STUCKENSCHMIDT, Hans
　Heinz　　　　　　　　　　Germany　　　　　1901
　　ACM, BB71, DDM, MGG, REM, X64, X65, X66, X67, X68
　　ACM: STUCKENSCHMIDT, Jean Henri

*STUDER, Hans　　　　　　Switzerland　　1911
　EVM, LMD, MGG, REM, SCHW, WWS, X64, X65, X66, X67

STUDER, Otto　　　　　　　Switzerland　　1894
　SCHW

ŠTUHEC, Igor　　　　　　　Yugoslavia　　　1932
　KMJ, LMD, MSC, X67

STUPEL, Petr Isaev　　　　Bulgaria　　　　1923
　BMK, X66, X68
　BMK: СТУПЕЛ

*STÜRMER, Bruno　　　　　Germany　　　　1892　1958
　EVM, IMD, LMD, MGG, REM, WWG

*STURZENEGGER, Hans
　Richard　　　　　　　　　Switzerland　　1905
　　DDM, EVM, IMD, LMD, MGG, REM, SCHW, WWS, X64, X65,
　　X66

*STUTCHEVSKY, Joachim
　Yehoyachin　　　　　　　　Israel　　　　　1891　Russia
　　ACU, CME, DDM, EMS, IMD2, LMD, MGG, MM59, REM,
　　WWI, X64, X65, X66
　　ACU and MGG: STUTSCHEWSKY　　DDM: STOUCHEVSKI
　　LMD: STUCEVSKIJ　　REM: STUCEVSKI　　EMS: СТУЧÉВСКИЙ

STUVOLO, Alfeo   Italy

SUBOTNIK, Morton   USA   1933
  BB71, LMD, PCM, PC71, REM, X64, X65, X67, X68

*SUCHOŇ, Eugen   Czechoslovakia 1908
  BB65, BB71, CCZ, DDM, EMS, EVM, IMD, LMD, MEH, MGG,
  MNP64/3, MNP64/5, MNP65/2, MNP65/5, MNP67/9, MNP68/6,
  REM, SML, X64, X65, X66, X67, X68, ZE69/1, ZE70/1,
  ZE70/2, ZE70/3, ZE71/2, ZE72/1
  EMS: СУХОНЬ

*SUCHÝ, František   Czechoslovakia 1902
  CCZ, REM

*SUCHÝ, František Pražský Czechoslovakia 1891
  CCZ, LMD, REM

*SUCKLING, Norman Charles Great Britain 1904
  BB71, WI69

SUCOFF, Herbert   USA
  AA73

*SUDER, Joseph   Germany 1892
  EVM, MGG, WWG, X68

SUDERBURG, Robert Charles USA   1936
  DN72, X67

*SUESSE, Dana   USA   1911
  AS66

*SUFFERN, Carlos   Argentina 1905
  IMD

*SUGÁR, Rezsö   Hungary 1919
  BB65, BB71, CHC, CME, IMD, LMD, MEH, MGG, REM,
  SML, X68

*ŠULEK, Stjepan   Yugoslavia 1914
  BB65, BB71, CME, DDM, EMS, EVM, HCM, IMD, LMD,
  MGG, REM, SML, X65, X66, X67
  EMS: ШУЛЕК

SULLIVAN, Timothy   USA
  ASUC

SULYOK, Imre   Hungary 1912
  CHC

*SUMSION, Herbert Whitton Great Britain 1899
  X67

ŞUMSKI, Vadim   Rumania   1900   1956
   RCL

*SUNDBERG, John   Finland   1891
   X68

*SURDIN, Morris   Canada
   CCM71, CVM, MCO68, X68

*SURINACH, Carlos   USA   1915   Spain
   CA9, LMD, REM, X66, X67, X68

*SUSSKIND, Walter   Great Britain   1913   Bohemia
   BB65, BB71, LMD, X64, X66, X67, X68

*ŠUST, Jiří   Czechoslovakia   1919
   CCZ, IMD, MEH

*SUTER, Robert   Switzerland   1919
   BB65, BB71, CME, IMD, IMD2, LMD, MGG, REM, SCHW,
   X64, X65, X66, X67, X68

*SUTERMEISTER, Heinrich   Switzerland   1910
   BB65, BB71, CME, DDM, EMS, EVM, IMD, LMD, MEH, MGG,
   REM, SCHW, SML, WI69, WWS, X64, X65, X66, X67, X68
   EMS: ЗУТЕРМЕЙСТЕР

*SUTHERLAND, Margaret   Australia   1897
   AMM, MGG

*SUTTER, Jules Toussaint de   Belgium   1889
   EVM, LMD, REM

ŞUTZU, Rodica   Rumania   1913
   RCL

*ŠVARA, Danilo   Yugoslavia   1902
   CME, IMD, KMJ, LMD, MGG, MSC, REM, X64, X67

ŠVARC, Alfred   Yugoslavia   1907
   HCM, KMJ

SVATOŠ, Vladimír   Czechoslovakia   1928
   MNP69/4, MNP72/9

SVĚCENÝ, Ladislav   Czechoslovakia   1881
   CCZ

*SVECHNIKOV, Anatoli
  Grigor'evich   USSR   1908
   EMS
   EMS: СВЕ́ЧНИКОВ

ŠVEDAS, I. I.
See: SHVYADAS, I. I.

SVEINSSON, Atli Heimir   Iceland   1938
VTM

*SVENSSON, Sven Erik
Emanuel   Sweden   1899   1960
EVM, LMD, MGG, REM, SIM, SIMa

*SVETLANOV, Evgeny
Fedorovitch   USSR   1928
EMS, X65, X66, X67, X68
EMS: СВЕТЛАНОВ

*SVIRIDOV, Georgy Yuri
Vasilievich   USSR   1915
CME, DDM, EMS, EVM, LMD, MEH, PPU68/3, PPU69/1,
PPU69/2, PPU69/3, PPU71/1, REM, SCD, SML, X65, X66,
X67, X68
EVM and SML: SWIRIDOW
EMS: СВИРИДОВ

SVOBODA, Hanuš   Czechoslovakia   1876   1964
CCZ

*SVOBODA, Jiří   Czechoslovakia   1897
CCZ, WI69

SVOBODA, Tomáš   Czechoslovakia   1939   France
BB65, BB71, DN70, DN72, LMD, X67

*SWAIN, Freda Mary   Great Britain   1902
BB71, LMD, MGG, REM, WI69

SWALIN, Benjamin Franklin   USA   1901
DAS

*SWAN, Alfred Julius   USA   1890   1970
BB71, DAS, X67   Russia

SWANAY, John   USA
ASUC

SWANN, Jeffrey   USA   1951
CAP

*SWANSON, Howard   USA   1909
BB71, EVM, IMD, LMD, PCM, REM
LMD: 1919

*SWANSON, Walter Donald   Union of   1903   Great Britain
WSA   South Africa

SWICKARD, Ralph   USA
 AA73, X66, X67, X68

ŚWIDER, Józef   Poland 1930
 PKW

ŚWIERZYŃSKI, Adam   1914
 PKW, X64

*SWIERZYŃSKI, Michal Poland 1868 1957
 LMD, PKW

SWIFT, Richard G.   USA 1927
 AA73, ASUC, BB71, X65, X66, X67, X68

SWISHER, Gloria Wilson USA
 AA73

SWOLKIEN, Henryk   Poland 1910
 PKW, X65

*SYBERG, Franz Adolf Denmark 1904 1955
 DMTsp, EVM, VTM

*SYDEMAN, William   USA   1928
 BB65, BB71, EL:2, PCM, PC71, X64, X66, X67

SYGIETYŃSKI, Tadeusz Poland 1896 1955
 PKW

SÝKORA, Václav Jan Czechoslovakia 1918
 CCZ, X68

SYLVAIN, Jules   Sweden 1900
 Pseudonym of HANSSON, Stig Axel

*SYLVAN, Sixten   Sweden 1914
 SIM

SYMONDS, Norman A. Canada 1920
 BB71, CA11, CCM71, CVM, CVMa, MCO, MCO68, MCO71,
 NLC, TFB, X66, X67, X68

SYVERUD, Stephen Luther Canada 1938
 ASUC, DN70

*SZABELSKI, Bolesław Poland 1896
 BB65, BB71, CME, DDM, EMS, IMD, LMD, MEH, MGG, PKW,
 REM, SML, X65, X67, X68
 EMS: ШАБЕЛЬСКИЙ

SZABO, Csaba   Rumania 1936
 RCL

*SZABÓ, Ferenc   Hungary 1902 1969
 BB65, BB71, CHC, CME, EMS, IMD, LMD, MEH, MGG,
 MLA26/4, NZM, REM, SML, X65, X66, X67, X68
 EMS: САБО

*SZALONEK, Witold   Poland   1927
 BB65, BB71, CME, IMD, LMD, MEH, PKW, REM, X64, X65,
 X67, X68
 MEH: 1929

*SZAŁOWSKI, Antoni   Poland   1907
 CME, DDM, EVM, IMD, LMD, MGG, PKW, REM, X65

SZCZENIOWSKI, Boleslaw Canada 1898 Poland
 CCM, CVM, CVMa, KEY

*SZÉKELY, Endre   Hungary 1912
 CHC, IMD, LMD, MGG, REM, X64, X68

SZÉKELY, Erik   Switzerland 1927
 SCHW, X67

*SZÉKELY, Zoltán   Hungary 1903
 LMD, MGG, REM

*SZELÉNYI, Istvan   Hungary 1904
 CHC, EVM, IMD, LMD, MGG, REM, WI69, X64, X68

SZELEPCSÉNYI, Ján   Czechoslovakia
 ZE71/1

*SZELIGOWSKI, Tadeusz Poland 1896 1963
 BB71, CME, DDM, EMS, IMD, LMD, MEH, MGG, PKW, REM,
 SML, X64, X65, X67
 EMS: ШЕЛИГОВСКИЙ

*SZELL, George   USA   1897 1970
 BB71, EVM, IMD, LMD, MLA27/4, REM, Hungary
 SML, WI69, X64, X65, X66, X67, X68

SZELUTO, Apolinary   Poland 1884 1966
 PKW, X66

*SZENDREI, Aladár
 See: SENDREY, Alfred

SZENKAR, Eugen   Germany 1891 Hungary
 REM, SML, X66

*SZERVÁNSKY, Endre   Hungary 1911
 BB71, CHC, CME, DDM, EMS, EVM, IMD, LMD, MEH, MGG,
 REM, SML, WI69, X65, X66, X67, X68
 EMS: СЕРВАНСКИЙ   EVM: 1912

SZIRMAI, Albert   USA   1880   1967
    LMD, MGG, X67, X68   Hungary
    MGG: SIRMAY

*SZOKOLAY, Sándor   Hungary   1931
    CHC, CME, MEH, X65, X66, X67, X68, ZSZ

*SZÖLLÖSY, Andras   Hungary   1921
    CHC, CME, IMD, X67, X68

*SZÖNYI, Erzsébet   Hungary   1924
    CHC, MEH, X67, X68

*SZPILMAN, Wladislaw   Poland   1911
    X64

*SZULC, Bronislaw   Israel   1881   Poland
    EVM, REM

*SZULC, Jozef   Poland   1893
    LMD, REM

*SZULC, Josef Zygmunt   France   1875   1956
    EVM, LMD, REM   Poland

SZYMONOWICZ, Zbigniew   Poland   1922
    PKW, X68

TABACHNIK, Michel   Switzerland
    X65

TAFFS, Anthony   USA
    ASUC

TAGLIACOZZO, Riccardo   Italy   1878
    REM

*TAGLIAPIETRA, Gino   Italy   1887   1954
    EVM, LMD, MGG, REM, X66

*TAGLIAVINI, Luigi
    Ferdinando   Italy   1929
    LMD, MGG, REM, X64, X65, X66, X67, X68

*TAHOURDIN, Peter Richard   Great Britain   1928
    AMM, X68

*TAILLEFERRE, Germaine   France   1892
    DDM, DMF, EMS, EVM, IMD, LMD, MEH, MGG, QQF, REM,
    VNM, X64
    EMS: ТАЙФЕР

*TAJČEVIĆ, Marko   Yugoslavia   1900
    BB65, BB71, DDM, EMS, EVM, IMD, KMJ, LMD, MGG, REM, X67
    EMS: ТАЙЧЕВИЧ

*TAKÁCS, Jenö von   USA   1902   Hungary
    IMD, LMD, MGG, REM, X64, X68

TAKAHASHI, Yuji   Japan   1938
    X66, X67, X68

TAKATA, Saburo   1913
    WAN

TAKEMITSU, Toru   Japan   1930
    BB65, BB71, EL:2, IMD, IMD2, LMD, REM, X64, X65, X66, X67, X68
    IMD: 1931

*TAKTAKISHVILI, Otar
    Vasilevich   USSR   1924
    BB65, BB71, DDM, EMS, LMD, MEH, MGG, PPU69/2,
    PPU69/3, SCD, SML, X64, X65, X68
    EMS: ТАКТАКИШВИЛИ   MGG: 1927

*TAKTAKISHVILI, Shalva
    Mikhailovich   USSR   1900
    EMS, LMD, MGG, REM
    EMS: ТАКТАКИШВИЛИ

*TAL, Joseph   Israel   1910   Poland
    ACU, CME, DDM, IMD, IMD2, LMD, MGG, MM59, REM, TSC, X64, X65, X68
    Formerly: GRUENTHAL

TALIAFERRO, Lloyd   USA
    AA73, X65, X66, X68

*TALICH, Vaclav   Czechoslovakia   1883   1961
    BB65, BB71, EVM, X64, X65, X67, X68

*TALMA, Louise   USA   1906
    AS66, BB65, IMD, PCM, PC71, X64, X67, X68

TALMI, Yoav
    WAN

TAMAYO, Arturo   Spain   circa 1947
    X67, X68

TAMBERG, Eino Martinovich   USSR   1930   Estonia
    BB71, DDM, EMS, MEH, PPU69/2, SCD, X66, X68
    EMS: ТАМБЕРГ

*TANENBAUM, Elias   USA   1924
  X64

*TANGUAY, Georges-Emile   Canada   1893
  MCO

TANNER, Jerre E.   USA   1939
  CAP

TANNER, Paul   USA
  DN70, X68

*TANSMAN, Alexandre   France   1897   Poland
  CMF17, CMF20, DDM, EMS, EVM, IMD, LMD, MEH, MGG,
  PKW, QQF, REM, WI69, WTM, X64, X66, X67
  EMS: ТАНСМАН

*TARABA, Bohuslav   Czechoslovakia 1894
  CCZ, X65

TARANOV, Gleb Pavlovich   USSR   1904
  EMS, PPU, PPU69/2, X64
  EMS: ТАРАНОВ

TARANTINI, Leopoldo   Italy   1872
  REM

TĂRANU, Cornel   Rumania   1934
  LMD, RCL, X65, X66, X68

*TARDOS, Béla   Hungary   1910 1966
  BB65, BB71, CHC, CME, EVM, LMD, MGG, REM, SML, X67,
  X68

*TARP, Svend Erik   Denmark   1908
  DDM, EVM, IMD, IMD2, LMD, MGG, REM, VTM, WI69

*TARSKI, Alexander   Israel   1921   Poland
  ACU, WWI

*TATE, Phyllis Margaret
  Duncan   Great Britain 1911
  BB65, BB71, EVM, MGG, REM, WI69, X65, X66, X67

*TATTON, Jack Meredith   USA   1901   Great Britain
  AS66

TAUB, Bruce J.   USA   1948
  BS72

*TAUBERT, Karl Heinz   Germany   1912
  IMD

TAURIELLO, Antonio   Argentina 1931
 BB65, BB71, LMD, X66, X68

TAUSINGER, Jan   Czechoslovakia 1921
 CCZ, MEH, MNP64/3, MNP71/9, X64, X66

TAVARES, Mario   Brazil   1928
 CA16, FBC

TAVENER, John Kenneth Great Britain 1944
 BB71, X65, X66, X67, X68

TAYLOR, Clifford   USA
 ASUC, X67

*TAYLOR, Joseph Deems USA   1885 1966
 AS66, BB65, BB71, EVM, IMD, LMD, MLA23/4, MGG, PCM,
 REM, WTM, X64, X66, X67, X68

TAYLOR, Robert   USA   1932
 IMD, PAP, X66, X68

*TAYLOR, Vernon Husson USA   1911
 DAS

*TCHAIKOVSKY, Boris
 Alexandrovitch   USSR   1925
  BB71, EMS, LMD, PPU69/2, X65, X67, X68
  LMD: ČAJCOVSKIJ PPU69/2: <u>CH</u>AYKOVSK<u>IY</u>
  EMS: ЧАЙКОВСКИЙ

TCHAPLUGIN, Nikolai
 Petrovich   USSR   1905
  EMS
  EMS: ЧАПЛЫГИН

TCHEMBERDZI, Nikolai
 Karpowitsch   USSR   1903 1948
  EMS, EVM, MGG
  EVM: TSJEMBERDZJI MGG: TS<u>CH</u>EMBERD<u>SHI</u>
  EMS: ЧЕМБЕРДЖИ

TCHEREMUKHIN, Mikhail
 Mikhailovich   USSR   1900
  EMS
  EMS: ЧЕРЁМУХИН

*TCHEREPNIN, Alexander
 Nikolayevich   USA   1899 Russia
  BB65, BB71, DDM, EMS, EVM, IMD, IMD2, LCI, LMD, MGG,
  REM, SML, WI69, WTM, X64, X65, X66, X67, X68
  EVM: TSJEREPNIN   IMD and SML: TS<u>CH</u>EREPNIN
  LMD: <u>Č</u>EREPNIN REM: <u>C</u>EREPNIN EMS: ЧЕРЕПНИН

TCHEREPNIN, Ivan   USA   1943   France
    AS66, BB71, LMD, MGG
    LMD: ČEREPNIN   MGG: TSCHEREPNIN

TCHEREPNIN, Serge   USA   1941   France
    BB71, LMD, MGG
    LMD: ČEREPNIN   MGG: TSCHEREPNIN

TCHERNETZKY, Semen
    Aleksandrovich   USSR   1881   1950
    EMS
    EMS: ЧЕРНЕ́ЦКИЙ

TCHERNOV, Aleksandr
    Abramovich   USSR   1917   1971
    EMS
    EMS: ЧЕРНО́В

TCHERVINSKY, Nikolai
    Pavlovich   USSR   1925
    EMS
    EMS: ЧЕРВИ́НСКИЙ

TCHICHKOV, Yuri Mikhailovich   USSR   1929
    EMS
    EMS: ЧИЧКОВ

TCHIMAKADZE, Archil
    Ivanovich   USSR   1919
    EMS
    EMS: ЧИМАКА́ДЗЕ

*TCHISHKO, Oles Semenovich   USSR   1895
    EVM, MGG, REM
    Also see: CHISHKO   Vol. I: TCHISHKO
    EVM: TSJISKO   MGG: TSCHISCHKO   REM: CIŠKO

TCHISTYAKOV, Vladlen
    Pavlovich   USSR   1929
    EMS
    EMS: ЧИСТЯКОВ

TCHUGAEV, Aleksandr
    Georgievich   USSR   1924
    EMS
    Also see: CHUGAEV
    EMS: ЧУГА́ЕВ

TCHUGUNOV, Aleksandr
    Petrovich   USSR   1891   1964
    EMS
    EMS: ЧУГУНО́В

TCHULAKI, Mikhail Ivanovich　　USSR　　　　　1908
　　EMS, EVM, LMD, MGG
　　EVM: TSJOELAKI　　LMD: ČULAKI　　MGG: TSCHULAKI
　　Also see: CHULAKI
　　EMS: ЧУЛАКИ

TCIMPIDIS, George David　　USA　　　　　1938
　　WI69

*TEBALDINI, Giovanni　　Italy　　　　1864　1952
　　REM

TEDOLDI, Agide　　Italy　　　　1887　1962
　　REM

TEED, Roy　　Great Britain　1928
　　BB65, BB71, WI69, X67

*TELLO, Rafael J.　　Mexico　　　1872
　　REM

TEMKOV, Ilia Temkov　　Bulgaria　　1923
　　BMK, X68
　　BMK: ТЕМКОВ

*TEMPLETON, Alec Andrew　　USA　　　1910　1963
　　AS66, BB65, BB71, EVM, X64　　　　　Wales

*TENAGLIA, Raffaele
　　Guglielmo　　Italy　　　1884
　　LMD, REM

TENIDIS, Basilis　　Greece　　　1936
　　PAP

TEODOSSIU, Lucian　　Rumania　　1897
　　RCL

TERENTIEV, Boris
　　Mikhailovich　　USSR　　　1913
　　EMS, PPU69/2, X65, X68
　　EMS: ТЕРЕ́НТЬЕВ

TERÉNYI, Eduard　　Rumania　　1935
　　RCL, X68

TER-GEVONDIAN, Anushavan
　　Grigorievich　　USSR　　　1887　1961
　　EMS
　　EMS: ТЕР-ГЕВОНДЯ́Н

*TERHUNE, Anice   USA   1873   1964
   BB71
   Formerly: POTTER

TERNI, Clemente   Italy   1918
   LMD

TERRY, Frances   USA   1884
   PCM

TER-TATEVOSIAN, Dzon
  Gurnovich   USSR   1926
   EMS, MEH
   EMS: ТЕР-ТАТЕВОСЯН

TERTERIAN, Avet   USSR
   X67, X68

TERZAKIS, Dimitris   Greece   1938
   EL:1, EL:2, EL:3, EL:4, LMD, PAP

TĚŠÍK, Jan   Czechoslovakia 1922
   CCZ

TESSIER, Roger   France   1939
   BB71

*TESTI, Flavio   Italy   1923
   IMD, LMD, REM, X64, X66

*TEUSCHER, Hans   Germany   1907   1961
   IMD

*THALBEN-BALL, George
  Thomas   Australia   1896
   EVM, X67

*THÄRICHEN, Werner   Germany   1921
   IMD, X65, X67, X68

*THATCHER, Howard Rutledge USA   1878
   AS66, X68

THATE, Albert   1903
   IMD

*THEIL, Fritz   Germany   1886
   REM

*THEODORAKIS, Mikis   Greece   1925
   BB71, EMS, LMD, X67
   EMS: ТЕОДОРАКИС

*THERSTAPPEN, Hans Joachim   Germany   1905   1950
    LMD, MGG

THIEBAUT, Henri   Belgium   1865   1959
    LMD, MGG

THIELE, Siegfried   Germany
    X66, X67

THIEME, Ernst Maria
    Hermann   Germany   1924
    WI69

*THIEME, Karl   Germany   1909
    X64, X66, X67

*THIENEN, Marcel van   France   1922
    LMD, MGG, REM

*THIJSSE, Wilhelmus Hermanus Netherlands   1916
    EVM, NED, X65, X66, X68

*THILMAN, Johannes Paul   Germany   1906   1973
    IMD, IMD2, EMS, LMD, MEH, MGG, REM, SML, X64, X65,
    X66, X67, X68
    EMS: ТИЛЬМАН

*THIMAN, Eric Harding   Great Britain   1900
    LMD, MGG, REM, X65, X66, X67, X68

THIMMIG, Les   1943
    WAN

THIRIET, André   France   1906
    CMF7, CMF20, LMD, MGG

*THIRIET, Maurice Charles   France   1906   1972
    CMF, DDM, DMF, EVM, LMD, MGG, MLA29/4, QQF, REM, WI69

*THIRION, Louis Marie Joseph France   1879   1966
    DDM, EVM, LMD, MGG

THOMAS, Andrew   1939
    WAN

THOMAS, David Wynne
    See: WYNNE, David

*THOMAS, Edward Francis   Great Britain   1929   Scotland
    WI69, X68

*THOMAS, Juan Maria   Spain   1896
    IMD, MGG

*THOMAS, Kurt Georg Hugo Germany 1904 1973
 DDM, EVM, IMD, LMD, MGG, REM, WWG, X64, X65, X66,
 X67, X68

*THOMAS, Mansel Treharne Great Britain 1909 Wales
 EVM, MGG, X68

THOME, Joel USA
 X67

*THOMMESSEN, Reidar Norway 1889
 CNO, X64

*THOMPSON, Alan Dales Canada 1901 England
 NLC

*THOMPSON, Gordon Vincent Canada 1888 1965
 X65

*THOMPSON, Randall USA 1889 1969
 AS66, BB65, BB71, DDM, EMS, EVM, LMD, MEH, MGG, PCM,
 PC71, REM, WTM, X65, X67, X68
 AS66, EVM, LMD, MGG, REM: 1899
 EMS: ТОМРСОН

*THOMSEN, Geraldine Czechoslovakia 1917 England
 CCZ, WI69

THOMSON, Andrew Graham Great Britain 1944
 WI69

*THOMSON, Virgil USA 1896
 AS66, BB65, BB71, DDM, EMS, EVM, IMD, IMD2, LMD, MEH,
 MGG, PCM, PC71, REM, WI69, WTM, X64, X65, X66, X67,
 X68
 EMS: ТОМСОН

THOMSON, William Ennis USA 1927
 AS66, PCM, X66, X67, X68

*THÓRARINSSON, Jón Iceland 1917
 REM, VTM

THÓRARINSSON, Leifur   Iceland   1934
    VTM, X66

*THÓRDARSON, Sigurdur   Iceland   1895
    REM, VTM

THORNE, Francis Burritt   USA   1922
    AS66, BB71, X65, X68

*THORNE, Gordon   Great Britain   1912   1965
    X65, X67

*THORPE DAVIE, Cedric   Great Britain   1913
    EVM, LMD, MGG, REM, X67

THORSTEISON, Árni   Iceland   1870   1961
    VTM

*THYBO, Leif   Denmark   1922
    DMTsp, IMD2, LMD, REM, VTM, X64, X68

*THYRESTAM, Gunnar Olof   Sweden   1900
    FST, SIM, SIMa, STS, VTM

*TIBAY, Zoltan   Hungary   1910
    WI69

*TICCIATI, Niso   Great Britain   1924   1972
    IMD, WI69, X65, X66

TICHTCHENKO, B.
    See: TISHCHENKO, Boris

*TIESSEN, Heinz   Germany   1887   1971
    DDM, EVM, IMD, LMD, MLA28/4, REM, SML, WWG, X67, X68

*TIGGERS, Petrus Johannes
    (Piet)   Netherlands   1891
    EVM, LMD, REM, X68

*TIGRANIAN, Armen
  Tigranovich   USSR   1879 1950
    EMS, LMD, МЕН, REM   Armenia
    EMS: ТИГРАНЯН

*TIGRANIAN, Vartan Armenovic USSR   1906
    LMD, REM

TIGRANOV, Georgi
  Grigorievich   USSR   1908
    EMS, X67, X68
    EMS: ТИГРАНОВ

*TIJARDOVIĆ, Ivo   Yugoslavia   1895
    BB65, BB71, HCM, IMD, KMJ, LMD, X66, X67, X68

TIKHOMIROV, Georgi
  Vladimirovich   USSR   1913 1967
    EMS, X65, X67
    EMS: ТИХОМИРОВ

TIKKA, Kari   Finland   circa 1942
    X68

*TIKOTSKY, Evgeny Karlovich USSR   1893 1970
    BB71, EMS, EVM, LMD, MGG, PPU, REM, X64
    EVM: TIKHOTSI   MGG: TIKOZKI
    EMS: ТИКОЦКИЙ

TILICHEYEVA, Elena
  Nikolaevnia   USSR   1909
    EMS
    EMS: ТИЛИЧЕЕВА

TILLIS, Frederick C.   USA
    ASUC

TIMIS, Vasile   Rumania   1922
    RCL

TIMOFEYEV, Nikolai
  Andreevich   USSR   1906
    EMS
    EMS: ТИМОФЕЕВ

*TINEL, Emiel Jozef   Belgium   1885 1972
    WI69

*TINTORI, Giampiero   Italy   1921
    LMD, REM, X66, X67, X68

TIPLER, Brian Archer   Great Britain   1933
    WI69

*TIPPETT, Michael Kemp   Great Britain   1905
    BB65, BB71, BCI, CME, DDM, EVM, IMD, IMD2, LMD, MEH,
    MGG, REM, SML, WI69, WTM, X64, X65, X66, X67, X68

TIRCUIT, Heuwell Andrew   USA   1931
    BB71

TIRRO, Frank P.   USA   1935
    PCM, PC71, X66, X67, X68

*TISCHHAUSER, Franz   Switzerland   1921
    LMD, REM, SCHW, WWS

TISHCHENKO, Boris Ivanovich   USSR   1939
    BB65, BB71, CME, EMS, LMD, MEH, MNP66/4, X64, X65,
    X66, X67, X68
    LMD and MEH: TIŠČENKO
    EMS: ТИЩЕНКО

TISNÉ, Antoine   France   1932
    BB71, DDM, LMD, X67, X68
    X67: TISBE

TITONE, Antonino   1934
    IMD

*TITTEL, Ernst   Austria   1910
    CME, IMD, MGG, REM, X64, X65, X66, X67, X68

TJULIN, J. N.
    See: TYULIN, Y. N.

*TKALCIĆ, Juro   Yugoslavia   1877   1957
    HCM

*TOBIN, John   Great Britain   1891
    X64, X65, X66, X67, X68

*TOCCHI, Gian-Luca   Italy   1901
    EVM, REM, WI69

*TOCH, Ernst   USA   1887   1964
    AS66, BB65, BB71, DDM, EMS, IMD, IMD2,   Austria
    LMD, MEH, MGG, REM, TCM, WTM, X64, X65, X66, X68
    EMS: TOX

TODD, George B.   USA
    ASUC

TODOROVSKI, Ilija   Yugoslavia   1911
  KMJ

*TODUȚĂ, Sigismund   Rumania   1908
  BB65, CME, EMS, IMD, LMD, MEH, RCL, REM, X65, X68
  REM: TODUTZĂ
  EMS: ТОДУ́ЦЭ

*TOEBOSCH, Louis   Netherlands   1916
  BB65, BB71, DDM, EVM, NED, X65

TOFFOLETTI, Massimo   Italy   1913
  LMD, REM

*TOGNI, Camillo   Italy   1922
  CME, EVM, IMD, LMD, REM, X64, X65

TOGNI, Victor   Canada
  KEY

TOKUNAGA, Hidenori   Japan   1925
  TSC

TOLBA, Beniamin Savelievich USSR   1909
  EMS
  EMS: ТО́ЛЬБА

*TOLDRÁ, Eduardo   Spain   1895   1962
  BB65, BB71, DDM, LMD, MGG, REM

*TOLKOWSKY, Denise de Vries Belgium   1918   Great Britain
  EVM

*TOLONEN, Jouko Paavo
  Kalervo   Finland   1912
    COF, KKO

*TOLSTOI, Dmitri
  Alekseyevich   USSR   1923
  BB65, BB71, EMS, PPU, X64, X68
  EMS: ТОЛСТО́Й

TOMAN, Josef   Czechoslovakia 1894
  CCZ, X64

*TOMÁŠEK, Jaroslav   Czechoslovakia 1896
  CCZ, EMS, EVM, LMD, REM, X66
  EMS: ТОМАШЕК

*TOMASI, Henri-Frédien   France   1901   1971
  BB65, BB71, CME, DMF10, CMF20, DDM, DMF, EMS, EVM,

IMD, LMD, MEH, MGG, MLA28/4, REM, X64, X65, X66, X68
EMS: ТОМАЗИ

*TÓMASSON, Jonas   Iceland   1881
  VTM

TOMELLERI, Luciano   Italy   1913
  LMD, REM

TOMC, Matija   Yugoslavia 1899
  KMJ, MSC

*TOMILIN, Viktor
  Konstantinovich   USSR   1908   1941
  EMS
  EMS: ТОМИЛИН

*TOMLINSON, Ernest   Great Britain 1924
  WI69, X64, X67, X68

*TOMMASINI, Vincenzo Italy   1880 1950
  IMD, LMD, REM, WTM

TONELLI, Gian Luigi   Italy   1894 1963
  LMD, REM

TONELLI, Giulio   Italy   1908
  LMD, REM

*TONI, Alceo   Italy   1884 1969
  BB71, LMD, REM

TONI, G. Oliver   Brazil
  X68

*TOOTELL, George   Great Britain 1886 1969
  WI69

*TORADZE, David
  Aleksandrovich   USSR   1922
  EMS, LMD, MEH, MGG, PPU, REM
  EMS: ТОРАДЗЕ

TORCK, Léon   Belgium   1903 1969
  EVM

*TORJUSSEN, Trygve   Norway   1885
  CNO, EVM, LMD

*TORLIND, Tore   Sweden   1902
  SIMa

TORMIS, Velio Rikhovich   USSR   1930   Estonia
    EMS, MEH, X65, X67
    EMS: ТОРМИС

*TÖRNE, Bengt Axel von   Finland   1891   1967
    COF, KKO, LMD, MGG, MLA24/4, REM, VTM, X67, X68

TORNER, Eduardo Martinez   Great Britain   1888   1955
    LMD, REM   Spain

TORROBA, Federico Moreno   Spain   1891

TORTANI, Lino   1921
    IMD

*TORTELIER, Paul   France   1914
    LMD, MGG, REM, SML, WI69, X64, X65, X66, X67, X68

*TOSAR-ERRECART, Héctor   Uruguay   1923
    BB65, BB71, IMD, LMD, MGG, REM, X65, X66

*TOSATTI, Vieri   Italy   1920
    EVM, IMD, LMD, MGG, REM, X65, X67, X68

TOŠEVSKI, Stojče   Yugoslavia   1944
    KMJ

TOTZAUER, Josef   USA   1896   Austria
    WWG

TOUMA, Habib Hassan   Israel   1934
    ACU, CME, IMD, MM59, X65, X68

*TOURNIER, Marcel Lucien   France   1879   1951
    DDM, LMD, MGG, REM

TOWER, Joan   USA
    ASUC

*TOWNSEND, Douglas   USA   1921
    PCM, PC71, X64, X67

TOYAMA, Yuzo   Japan   1931
    BB71, MEH, X65, X66

*TOYE, John Francis   Great Britain   1883   1964
    BB65, BB71, LMD, MGG, OCM, REM, X64, X65, X67

TRACK, Gerhard   1934
    WAN

TRĂILESCU, Cornel   Rumania   1926
   RCL, X64

*TRAMBITSKY, Viktor
   Nilolayevitch   USSR   1895   1970
   BB65, BB71, EMS, MGG, X64
   EMS: ТРАМБИЦКИЙ

*TRANCHELL, Peter Andrew   Great Britain   1922   India
   EVM, LMD, MGG, REM, WI69

*TRANTOW, Herbert Otto Karl   Germany   1903
   EVM, IMD, LMD, REM, SML, WI69, X68

*TRAPP, Jacob   Germany   1895
   WWG

*TRAPP, Max   Germany   1887   1971
   DDM, EVM, IMD, LMD, MGG, MLA28/4, REM, SML, X68

*TRAUNFELLNER, Peter Carl   Austria   1930
   WI69

TRAVIS, Roy Elihu   USA   1922
   ASUC, X68

*TRBOJEVIĆ, Dušan   Yugoslavia   1925
   IMD, KMJ, LMD, REM, X67

TREBINSKY, Arkady   1897
   IMD

TREMAIN, Ronald   USA   1923   New Zealand
   WI69

*TREMBLAY, George Amédée   USA   1911   Canada
   X64, X65, X66, X67, X68

*TREMBLAY, Gilles Léonce   Canada   1932
   BB71, BCL, CCM71, CVMa, DDM, IMD, KEY, MCO68, X68

*TREXLER, Georg   Germany   1903
   IMD, LMD, MGG, SML, X64, X67, X68

TRIFUOVIĆ, Vitomir Voja   Yugoslavia   1916
   KMJ, X68

*TRILLAT, Ennemond   France   1890
   LMD, MGG, QQF

*TRIMBLE, Lester   USA   1923
   ASUC, BB71, CA10, LMD, PCM, PC71, X64, X65, X66, X67,
   X68

*TRINKAUS, George J.   USA   1878 1960
 AS66

TRIODIN, Petr Nikolaevich USSR   1887 1950
 EMS, LMD
 EMS: ТРИÓДИН

TROGAN, Roland   1933
 WAN

*TROJAN, Václav   Czechoslovakia 1907
 CCZ, CME, EVM, IMD, IMD2, LMD, MEH, MGG, MNP67/3,
 MNP72/5, REM, X65, X67

TROWBRIDGE, Luther   USA   1892
 PCM

*TROWELL, Arnold   Great Britain 1887 1966
 X66, X67   New Zealand

TROZNER, Jozef   Rumania   1904
 RCL

TRUDIĆ, Božidar   Yugoslavia 1911
 BB65, KMJ, LMD, X67

*TRUESDELL, Frederick
Donald   USA   1920
 X65, X66

*TRUNK, Richard   Germany   1879 1968
 IMD, LMD, MGG, MLA25/4, REM, WWG, X64, X68

*TRYTHALL, Harry Gilbert USA   1930
 AA73, ASUC, X66, X68

TSCHEREPNIN
 See: TCHEREPNIN

TSCHISCHKO, O. S.
 See: TCHISHKO, O. S.

TSCHULAKI, M. I.
 See: TCHULAKI, M. I.

TSFASMAN, Aleksandr
Naumovich   USSR   1906
 EMS, PPU, X66, X67
 EMS: ЦФÁСМАН

*TSINTSADZE, Sulkhan
Fedorovich   USSR   1925

CME, DDM, EMS, LMD, PPU, PPU69/2, PPU71/1, REM,
SML, X64, X67
CME: TZINDZADZE   SML: ZINZADSE   EMS: ЦИНЦА́ДЗЕ

TSJEREPNIN, A. N.
    See: TCHEREPNIN, A. N.

TSJISKO, O. S.
    See: TCHISHKO, O. S.

*TSOUYOPOULOS, Georgos S.   Greece   1930
    BB65, CME, EL:1, EL:2, LMD, PAP, X65

TSVETANOV, T. T.
    See: TZVETANOV, T. T.

*TUBIN, Eduard   Sweden   1905 Estonia
    EMS, FST, IMD2, LMD, REM, SIM, SIMa, SOW, STS, SWE, X67
    EMS: ТУ́БИН

*TULEBAEV, Mukan
    Tulebaevich   USSR   1913 1960
    EMS, MEH
    EMS: ТУЛЕБА́ЕВ

*TULIKOV, Serafim Sergeevich USSR   1914
    EMS, MEH, PPU, PPU69/2, PPU69/3, SML, X64, X66
    EMS: ТУ́ЛИКОВ

TULIN, Y. N.
    See: TYULIN, Y. N.

TULL, Fisher Aubrey   USA   1934
    AA73, X66, X67, X68

TUPKOV, Dimitr Kirilov   Bulgaria   1929
    BMK, X67
    BMK: ТЪПКОВ

*TURCHI, Guido   Italy   1916
    BB65, BB71, EL:1, EVM, IMD, LMD, MGG, REM

TURENKOV, Aleksei
    Evlampievich   USSR   1886 1958
    EMS, X64
    EMS: ТУРЕНКО́В

*TURESSON, Ander Gunnar   Sweden   1906
    X68

*TURNBULL, Percy Purvis   Great Britain 1902
    WI69

*TURNER, Charles   USA   1921
    PCM, X66

TURNER, Fred   Great Britain
    X64

*TURNER, Godfrey   USA   1913   1948
    IMD, PCM   Great Britair

*TURNER, Robert Comrie   Canada   1920
    BB65, BB71, CCM, CCM71, CVM, CVMa, IMD, KEY, LMD,
    MCO, MCO68, MCO71, MEH, NLC, REM, TFB, X66, X68

TUROK, Paul H.   1929
    CA16, X68

*TURSKI, Źbigniew   Poland   1908
    CME, DDM, EMS, LMD, MGG, PKW, REM, X65, X67, X68
    EMS: ТУРСКИЙ

*TURUNEN, Martti Johannes   Finland   1902
    COF, KKO, LMD, MGG, VTM

*TUSKIYA, Iona Iraklievich   USSR   1901   1963
    EMS, X64
    EMS: ТУ́СКИЯ

*TUTHILL, Burnet Corwin   USA   1888
    AA73, AS66, IMD, PCM, PC71, WI69, X64, X66, X67, X68

*TUUKKANEN, Kalervo   Finland   1909
    COF, EVM, KKO, LMD, MGG, REM, VTM

TUXEN-BANK, Carlos   Argentina
    X66, X67

*TVEITT, Geirr   Norway   1908
    CNO, DDM, LMD, MGG, REM, VTM, X65, X66, X68

*TWA, Andrew John   Canada   1919
    CCM, IMC, MCO, MCO68

TWARDOWSKI, Romuald   Poland   1930
    CME, MNP66/4, PKW, X64, X65, X66, X67, X68

TWEEDY, Donald   USA   1890
    PCM, X68

TYLŇÁK, Ivan   Czechoslovakia   1910
    CCZ

TYNSKY, Richard   1909
    IMD2, X68

*TYRER, Anderson   Great Britain   circa
    X68   1895

TYRWHITT-WILSON
    See: BERNERS, G. H. T. W.

*TYULIN, Yuri Nikloayevich   USSR   1893
    EMS, MGG, X67, X68
    MGG: TJULIN   Vol. I: TULIN
    EMS: ТЮЛИН

TZANKOV, Isnif Ivanov   Bulgaria   1911
    BMK
    BMK: ЦАНКОВ

TZINDZADZE, S. F.
    See: TSNTSADZE, S. F.

TZVETANOV, Tzvetan Tzvankov Bulgaria   1931
    BB65, BB71, BMK, X67
    X67: TSVETANOV
    BMK: ЦВЕТАНОВ

UBER, David Albert   USA   1921
    AS66, CAP, PC71, X65, X68

*UDDÉN, Åke O. S.   Sweden   1903
    FST, KSV, SIM, SIMa, STS

UDOW, Michael   USA   1949
    BS70

*UGARTE, Floro M.   Argentina   1884
    EVM, IMD, LMD, MGG, REM

*UHL, Alfred   Austria   1909
    CME, DDM, EMS, EVM, IMD, IMD2, LMD, MEH, REM, X64,
    X66, X67, X68
    EMS: УЛЬ

UHLÍŘ, Jan   Czechoslovakia 1894
    MEH, X64

*UHLMANN, Otto   Switzerland   1891
    SCHW, WWS, X67

*UKMAR, Vilko   Yugoslavia   1905
    EMS, IMD, KMJ, LMD, MSC, REM, X67
    EMS: УКМАР

*ULDALL, Hans   Germany   1903
    EVM, REM

ULEHLA, Ludmila   USA
    ASUC

*ULFRSTAD, Marius Moaritz   Norway   1890
    EVM, LMD, REM

ULLMAN, Bo   Sweden   1929
    SIM, SIMa

*ULLMANN, Viktor   Austria   1898   Czecho-
    EVM, LMD, REM   slovakia

*ULLRICH, Hermann   Austria   1888
    LMD, MGG, REM, X64, X65, X66, X68

ULLRICH, Josef   Czechoslovakia   1911
    CCZ

ULRICH, Boris   Yugoslavia   1931
    HCM

*UNGER, Hermann Gustav   Germany   1886   1958
    BB65, BB71, EVM, IMD, LMD, MGG, REM

*URACK, Otto   Germany   1884   1963
    X64

*URAY, Ernst Ludwig   Austria   1906
    EVM, IMD, IMD2, LMD, MGG, REM, WI69, X66, X67

URBAKH, Samuil Yulievich   USSR   1908   1969
    EMS, X68
    EMS: УРБАХ

URBAN, Štěpán   1913
    IMD

URBANEC, Bartolomej   Czechoslovakia   1918
    MEH, ZE71/2, ZE71/3

URBANNER, Erich   Austria   1936
    IMD, IMD2, TSC, X64, X66, X67, X68

*URIBE HOLGUÍN, Guillermo   Colombia   1880
    BB65, BB71, EMS, EVM, LMD, MGG, REM
    EMS: УРИБЕ ОЛЬГИН

URRETA, Alica   Mexico   1948
    HET24

*URRUTIA BLONDEL, Jorge   Chile   1905
   CA14, EVM, LMD, REM, X66, X67, X68

USAI, Remo   Brazil   1928
   FBC

*USMANBAŞ, Ilhan   Turkey   1921
   IMD, LMD, REM, X65

*USSACHEVSKY, Vladimir   USA   1911   Manchuria
   ASUC, CA9, LMD, MEH, MGG, REM, X65, X66, X68

USTVOLSKAYA, Galina
   Ivanovna   USSR   1919
   BB65, BB71, CME, EMS, MEH, PPU, X65, X66, X68
   EMS: УСТВОЛЬСКАЯ

VACEK, Karel Václav   Czechoslovakia   1908
   CCZ, MEH
   MEH: 1902

*VACEK, Miloš   Czechoslovakia   1928
   BB65, BB71, CCZ, LMD, MEH, MNP68/4, X64, X68

*VAČKÁŘ, Dalibor Cyril   Czechoslovakia   1906   Yugoslavia
   CCZ, EVM, IMD, IMD2, LMD, MGG, REM, SML, X65, X66,
   X67, X68
   EVM and REM: 1905

VAČKÁŘ, Václav   Czechoslovakia   1881   1954
   LMD, MGG

VAGNER, G. M.
   See: WAGNER, G. M.

*VAINBERG, Moysey
   Samuilovich   USSR   1919   Poland
   CME, EMS, LMD, MEH, PPU69/2, REM, X64, X66, X68
   MEH: VAINBERG
   EMS: ВАЙНБЕРГ

*VAINYUNAS, Stasys Andriaus   USSR   1909   Latvia
   EMS, LMD, MEH, MGG, PPU, SML
   LMD and MEH: VAJNJNAS   MGG: VAINŪNAS
   PPU: VAYNYUNAS   SML: WAINJUNAS   EMS: ВАЙНЮНАС

VALBE, Yoel   Israel   1900   Russia
   ACU

VALCARCEL, Edgar   Peru   1932
   CA17

*VALCARCEL, Teodoro   Peru   1900   1042
    EVM, IMD, MGG, REM
    EVM: 1900-1943

VALDAMBRINI, Francesco   1933
    IMD, IMD2

VÁLEK, Jiří   Czechoslovakia   1923
    CCZ, MNP72/9, X65, X67

*VALEN, Fartein   Norway   1887   1952
    BB65, BB71, CME, CNO, DDM, EVM, IMD, IMD2, LMD, MGG
    REM, TSC, VTM, X64, X65, X66, X68

*VALENCIA, Antonio María   Colombia   1902   1952
    REM, X64

VALENTINI, Giovanni, III   Italy   1888   1956
    LMD, REM

VALKARE, Gunnar   Sweden   circa 1940
    X68

*VALLERAND, Jean   Canada   1915
    CCM, CVM, MCO, MCO71, X67

*VALLS, Josep   Spain   1904
    EVM

VALLS GORINA, Manuel   Spain   1920
    CME, DDM, X66

VALOIS, Jean de   France   1886
    MGG

VAN APPLEDORN, Mary
Jeanne   USA   1927
    DN72

VÂNĂTORU, Sorin   Rumania   1912
    RCL

*VANBIANCHI, Arturo   Italy   1862   1942
    REM

*VANCEA, Zeno   Rumania   1900
    BB65, BB71, CME, EMS, LMD, MEH, MGG, RCL, REM, SML,
    X64, X65, X66, X67
    EMS: ВАНЧА

VAN DELDEN, Lex   Netherlands   1919
    BB65, BB71

VAN DER VELDEN, Renier
    See: van der VELDEN

*VANDELLE, Romuald   France   1895
    LMD

VAN DE MOORTEL, Arie
    See: MOORTEL, Arie van de

VANDERVALK, Bruce   USA   1935   Australia
    DN70

*VAN DE VATE, Nancy   USA   1931
    AA73, ASUC, PCM

VAN DIJK, Rudi   Canada
    CCM71, KEY, MCO68

VANDOR, Ivan   Italy   1932   Hungary
    CME, LMD, REM, X66

VAN HULSE, Camil   USA   1897   Belgium
    AS66, X66, X67, X68

VANIER, Jeannine   Canada   1929
    CCM

VAN LIER, Bertus
    See: LIER, Bertus van

VAN LYNN, Dolf
    See: LINDEN, Dolf D. G. van der

VAN OTTERLOO, Willem
    See: OTTERLOO, Willem van

VAN SAN, Hermann   1929
    IMD

*VAN VACTOR, David   USA   1906
    AA73, AS66, BB65, BB71, CA9, IMD, LMD, PCM, PC71,
    WI69, X64, X66, X67, X68
    IMD and LMD: VACTOR, David van

VARDI, Emmanuel   USA   1915
    PCM, X65, X66

*VARÈSE, Edgar   USA   1883   1965
    BB65, BB71, CME, DDM, DMF, EL:3,   France
    EMS, EVM, IMD, LMD, MEH, MGG, MLA22/4, MZW, PAP,
    REM, SML, WTM, X64, X65, X66, X67, X68
    EMS: BAPE3
    MEH: 1966   PAP: 1885

VARGA, Ovidiu   Rumania   1913
    BB65, BB71, CME, LMD, RCL, X65

VARGAS-WALLIS, Darwin
   Horacie   Chile   1925
    CA17

*VARNAI, Peter   Hungary   1922
    X65, X68

VAROTTI, Albino   Italy   1925
    LMD

*VARS, Henry   USA   1902   Poland
    AS66

*VARVOGLIS, Mario   Greece   1885   1967
    BB71, DDM, EMS, LMD, MGG, REM   Belgium
    EMS: ВАРВОГЛИС

VÁRY, Ferenc   Hungary   1928
    CHC

*VÁSÁRHELYI, Zoltán   Hungary   1900
    X67

*VASCONCELOS, Jorge Croner
   de Santana   Portugal   1910
    CME, MGG, X65

VASILESCU, Ion   Rumania   1903   1960
    LMD, RCL, SML, X65

*VASILIEV-BUGLAY, Dimitri
   Sepanovitch   USSR   1888   1956
    EMS, МЕН
    EMS: ВАСИЛЬЕВ-БУГЛАЙ

*VASQUEZ, José   Mexico   1895
    EVM

*VASS, Lajos   Hungary   1927
    CHC, X68

*VASSILENKO, Sergei
   Nikiforovich   USSR   1872   1956
    BB65, BB71, DDM, EMS, EVM, LMD, MEH, REM, SML
    EVM and SML: WASSILENKO   LMD and MEH: VASILENKO
    EMS: ВАСИЛЁНКО

VASSILIADIS, Stephanos   Greece   1933
    EL:4

*VASZY, Viktor   Hungary   1903
    LMD, MGG, X68

*VAUBOURGOIN, Jean-
Fernand   France   1880   1952
    DDM, DMF, LMD, MGG
    DDM: VAUBOURGOIN, Julien Fernand

*VAUBOURGOIN, Marc   France   1907
    DDM, DMF, LMD, MGG

VAUCLAIN, Constant   USA
    X65

VAUDA, Zlatan   Yugoslavia   1923
    IMD, KMJ

VAUGHAN, Clifford   USA   1893
    AS66, PC71

*VAUGHAN-WILLIAMS, Ralph   Great Britian   1872   1958
    BB65, BB71, CME, DDM, EMS, EVM, IMD, IMD2, LMD, MEH,
    MGG, REM, SML, TCM, WTM, X64, X65, X66, X67, X68
    EMS: ВОАН-УИЛЬЯИС

*VAURABOURG, Andrée   France   1894
    REM

VAVŘÍN, Petr   Czechoslovakia   1929
    MNP72/9

VAVRINECZ, Béla   Hungary   1925
    CHC

VAYNYUSAS, Stasis Andryaus
    See: VAINYUNAS, S. A.

VAZLIK, Miroslav   Czechoslovakia
    ZE70/3

VAZZANA, Anthony E.   USA   1922
    AA73, AS66, PC71, X65, X66

*VEALE, John   Great Britain   1922
    LMD, MGG, REM, WI69

*VÉCSEI, Desider Josef   USA   1882   1966
    BB71   Hungary

*VÉCSEY, Jenö   Hungary   1909   1966
    CHC, CME, LMD, MGG, X66, X67, X68

VEERHOFF, Carlos H.   Argentina   1926
   IMD, IMD2, REM, X66, X67, X68

*VEGA, Carlos   Argentina   1898 1966
   BB71, LMD, MGG, REM, X65, X66, X67, X68

*VEGA y PALACIO, Aurelio
de la   Cuba   1925
   ASUC, BB71, DDM, IMD, LMD, REM, X64, X65, X66

*VEIDL, Theodor   Czechoslovakia 1885 1946
   REM

VELASCO-LLANOS, Santiago   Colombia   1915
   BB71, CA13, LMD

*VELASCO-MAIDANA, José
María   Bolivia   1900
   CA11, EVM, LMD, MGG, REM
   EVM, MGG and REM: 1901

VELAZQUEZ, Higinio   Mexico   1926
   HET19

*VELDEN, Renier van der   Belgium   1910
   CBC, EVM, LMD, REM

VELEHORSCHI, Alexandru   Rumania   1918
   RCL

VELIKANOV, Vasily Vasilievich USSR   1898
   EMS
   EMS: ВЕЛИКА́НОВ

VELKE, Fritz   USA   1930
   PCM, PC71, X66, X68

*VELLÈRE, Lucie   Belgium   1896 1966

VELTE, Eugen Werner   Germany   1923
   PAP

*VENÉ, Ruggero   USA   1897 1961
   AS66, REM   Italy

*VENEZIANI, Vittore   Italy   1878 1958
   LMD, REM

*VEPRIK, Alexander Moisyevich USSR   1899 1958
   BB65, BB71, EMS, LMD, REM
   EMS: ВЕ́ПРИК

*VERBESSELT, August Frans   Belgium   1919
   LMD, WI69

VERCOE, Barry Lloyd   USA
   ASUC, X66, X68

*VEREMANS, Renaat   Belgium   1894   1969
   BB71, EVM, IMD, MLA26/4

*VERESS, Sándor   Switzerland   1907   Hungary
   CME, DDM, EVM, IMD, LMD, MGG, REM, SCHW, X65

*VERETTI, Antonio   Italy   1900
   DDM, EMS, EVM, IMD, LMD, REM, WI69, X66, X67
   EMS: ВЕРЕТТИ

VEREVKA, Grigory Gurievich   USSR   1895   1963
   BB65, BB71, EMS, X65
   EMS: ВЕРЁВКА
   BB65 and BB71: 1964

VERGANTI, Franco   Italy   1914
   REM

VERHAAR, Ary   Netherlands   1900
   NED

VERHEYDEN, Edward   Belgium   1878   1959
   BB65, BB71, EVM

*VERIKOVSKY, Mikhail
   Ivanovich   USSR   1896   1962
   EMS
   EMS: ВЕРИКОВСКИЙ

*VERMEULEN, Matthijs   Netherlands   1888   1967
   BB65, BB71, CME, DDM, EVM, IMD, LMD, MGG, NED, REM,
   X64, X65, X67, X68

*VERNEUIL, Raoul de   Peru   1899
   EVM, REM
   EVM and REM: 1901

*VERRALL, John W.   USA   1908
   LMD, PCM, PC71, REM, X64, X65, X66, X67, X68

*VERREES, Emiel-Constant   Belgium   1892
   EVM, WI69

VESCAN, Mauriciu   Rumania   1916
   RCL, X64

*VIANA, Frutuoso   Brazil   1896
   FBC, IMD, LMD, REM
   LMD and REM: VIAN<u>N</u>A

*VIBERT, Mathieu   Switzerland   1920
   REM, SCHW, WWS, X67

*VICTORY, Gerard   Ireland   1921
   LMD, WI69, X66

*VIDAKOVIĆ, Albe   Yugoslavia 1914   1964
   KMJ, LMD, REM

VIDAR, Jórunn   Iceland   1918
   VTM

*VIDERØ, Finn   Denmark   1906
   LMD, VTM, X64, X65, X66, X67

*VIDOŠIĆ, Tihomil   Yugoslavia 1902
   HCM, IMD, KMJ

VIEBIG, Ernst   Germany   1897
   EVM, REM

*VIERU, Anatol   Rumania   1926
   BB65, CME, EMS, IMD2, LMD, RCL, REM, X64, X65, X68
   EMS: ВИЕРУ

VIGNATI, Milos   Czechoslovakia 1897
   CCZ, LMD, MGG

VILEC, Michal   Czechoslovakia 1902
   CCZ, MEH, X67, X68, ZE69/3, ZE70/3, ZE71/1

VILINSKY, Nikolai Nikolaivich   USSR   1888   1956
   EMS
   EMS: ВИЛИНСКИЙ

*VILLALBA MUÑOZ, Alberto   Argentina   1879   Spain
   REM

*VILLA-LOBOS, Heitor   Brazil   1887   1959
   BB65, DDM, EMS, EVM, IMD, IMD2, LMD, MEH, MGG, PAP,
   QLA, REM, SML, WTM, X64, X65, X66, X67, X68
   EMS: ВИЛА ЛОЬОС

VILLALPANDO, Alberto   Bolivia
   HET22

*VIÑA MANTEOLA, Facundo
de la   Spain   1876   1952
REM

VINAVER, Chemjo   Israel   1900   Poland
WWI, X68

*VINCENT, John   USA   1902
AA73, AS66, BB65, CA8, LMD, MGG, PCM, PC71, REM, X64,
X65, X66, X67

*VINCZE, Imre   Hungary   1926   1969
CHC, X67, X68
X67: VIN<u>CE</u>

*VINTER, Gilbert   Great Britain 1909
X67

VINTILĂ, Ion   Rumania   1924
RCL

*VIOZZI, Giulio   Italy   1912
REM, X67

VIPLER, Vlatislav Antonín Czechoslovakia 1903
CCZ, MEH

VIRGILI, Lavinio   Italy   1902
REM

*VISKI, János   Hungary   1906   1961
BB65, CHC, CME, IMD, LMD, MEH, MGG, REM, SML
REM: 1960

VITALINI, Alberico   1921
WAN

*VITALIS, George   Greece   1895   1959
BB65

VITERNIK, Ludvig   Yugoslavia   1888
KMJ

VITOLINS, Janis   1886
IMD, X65

VITTORIA, Mario   France   1911
CMF65/10

VLACH, Luděk   Czechoslovakia
MNP69/4

VLACHOPOULOS, Yannis   Greece   1939
    EL:3, EL:4, PAP

*VLACH-VRUTICKÝ, Josef   Czechoslovakia   1897
    CCZ, REM, X66, X67

*VLÀD, Roman   Italy   1919   Rumania
    BB65, DDM, EMS, IMD, IMD2, LMD, MEH, MGG, MNG, REM,
    TSC, WI69, X65, X66, X67, X68
    EMS: ВЛАД

VLADIGEROV, Aleksandr   Bulgaria   1933
    LMD

*VLADIGEROV, Pantcho
    Kharalanov   Bulgaria   1899
    BB65, BMK, DDM, EMS, EVM, IMD, LMD, MEH, REM, SML,
    X64, X65, X67, X68
    EVM: WLADIGEROW   IMD: WLADIGEROFF
    BMK: ВЛАДИГЕРОВ   EMS: ВЛАДИГЕРОВ

VLADIMIROV, Vladimir   USSR   1925
    X68

VLĂDUTĂ, Ioan   Rumania   1875   1965
    RCL

VLAG, Harrend   Netherlands   1913
    EVM

VLAJIN, Milan   Yugoslavia   1912
    KMJ

*VLASOV, Vladimir
    Alexandrovich   USSR   1903
    EMS, LMD, MEH, PPU, X64, X65, X67
    EMS: ВЛАСОВ

*VLEUGELS, Hans   Germany   1899
    EVM

VLIJMEN, Jan Van   Netherlands   1935
    BB65, CME, DDM, IMD, LMD, NED, TSC, X65, X67, X68

*VOCHT, Lodewijk de   Belgium   1887
    EVM, MGG

VODAK, Josef   Czechoslovakia   1927
    CCZ

VODRÁŽKA, Karel   Czechoslovakia   1904
    CCZ

VOGEL, Ernst   Austria
   X67

*VOGEL, Jaroslav   Czechoslovakia   1894   1970
   CCZ, LMD, MEH, MGG, MNP65/2, MNP69/1, MNP71/6, REM,
   SML, WI69, X64, X65, X66, X68

*VOGEL, Wladimir Rudolfovich   Switzerland   1896   Russia
   BB65, CME, DDM, EVM, IMD, IMD2, LMD, MEH, MGG, MZW,
   REM, SCHW, TSC, WWS, X64, X65, X66, X67, X68

*VOGELSANG, Konrad
  Ferdinand   Germany   1928
   WWG

*VOGL, Adolf   Germany   1873   1961
   LMD, MGG, WWG

*VOGLER, Carl   Switzerland   1874   1951
   LMD, MGG, SCHW

*VOGT, Hans   Switzerland   1909
   SCHW, X65, X66

*VOGT, Hans   Germany   1911
   EVM, LMD, MGG, REM, X68

*VOHÁNKA, Rudolf   Czechoslovakia   1880   1963
   MGG

VOICULESCU, Dan   Rumania   1940
   RCL, X68

*VOLDAN, Bedřich   Czechoslovakia   1892
   LMD, REM

VOLEK, Jaroslav   Czechoslovakia   1923
   MGG, X64, X65, X66, X68

VOLKMANN, Karl Heinz   Germany   1919
   WI69

VOLKONSKY, Andrei
  Michailovich   USSR   1933   Switzerland
   BB65, CME, EMS, MEH, MNG, SCD, X67, X68
   EMS: ВОЛКОНСКИЙ

VOLKOV, Vyacheslav Ivanovich   USSR   1904
   EMS, X65
   EMS: ВОЛКОВ

VOLLENWEIDER, Hans   Switzerland   1918
   SCHW

VOLLRATH, Carl   USA

*VOLLY, Istvan   Hungary   1907
    X68

VOLOSHINOV, Viktor
   Vladimirovich   USSR   1905   1960
    BB65, BB71, EMS, LMD, REM, X64
    LMD: VOLOSINOV   REM: VOLOSCINOV
    EMS: ВОЛОШИНОВ

*VOMÁČKA, Boleslav   Czechoslovakia   1887   1965
    BB71, CCZ, CME, DDM, EMS, EVM, IMD, LMD, MEH,
    MNP65/5, REM, SML, X65, X66
    EMS: ВОМАЧКА

VON KOCH, Erland
   See: KOCH, Sigurd Christian Erland von

*VOORMOLEN, Alexander
   Nicolas   Netherlands   1895
    CME, IMD, LMD, NED, REM, X66

*VORLOVÁ, Sláva   Czechoslovakia   1894   1973
    CCZ, IMD, IMD2, LMD, REM, X64, X65

VOSS, Friedrich   Germany   1930
    CME, IMD

*VOSTŘÁK, Zbyněk   Czechoslovakia   1920
    CCZ, IMD2, LMD, MEH, MNG, MNP64/5, MNP64/6, MNP70/1,
    MNP72/4, X64, X65, X66, X67, X68, ZE70/2

*VÖTTERLE, Karl D.   Germany   1903
    X67, X68

*VOUILLEMIN, Sylvain   Belgium   1910
    EVM

*VRABEC, Ubald   Yugoslavia   1905
    KMJ, MSC

*VRÁNA, František   Czechoslovakia   1914
    CCZ, EVM, IMD, IMD2, LMD, REM, WI69

VRÁNA, Jan   Czechoslovakia
    MNP69/4

VRANKEN, Alphons   Netherlands   1879   1953
    EVM, LMD

*VRANKEN, Jaap   Netherlands   1897   1956
    EVM, LMD, NED, REM

*VREDENBURG, Max   Netherlands   1904   Belgium
  EVM, LMD, REM

VREE, Freddy de   Belgium   1939
  X66

VREMSAK, Samo   Yugoslavia   1930
  KMJ

*VRETBLAD, Patrik Viktor   Sweden   1876   1953
  EVM, FST, KSV, LMD, REM, SIM, SIMa

VRHOVSKI, Josip   Yugoslavia   1902
  KMJ

*VRIESLANDER, Otto   Switzerland   1880   1950
  LMD, REM   Germany

VRIES ROBBÉ, Willem de   Netherlands   1902
  EVM

*VUATAZ, Roger   Switzerland   1898
  BB65, BB71, CME, DDM, IMD, LMD, MEH, REM, SCHW,
  WWS, X64, X65, X67, X68

*VUČKOVIĆ, Vojislav   Yugoslavia   1910   1942
  BB65, BB71, EMS, EVM, LMD, REM, X68
  EMS: ВУЧКОВИЧ

*VUKDRAGOVIĆ, Mihajlo   Yugoslavia   1900
  BB65, BB71, CME, EMS, EVM, IMD, KMJ, LMD, MEH, REM,
  X65, X67, X68
  EMS: ВУКДРАГОВИЧ

*VYCPÁLEK, Ladislav   Czechoslovakia   1882   1969
  BB71, CCZ, CME, DDM, EVM, IMD, IMD2, LMD, MEH, REM,
  X65, X67

VYCPÁLEK, Vratislav   Czechoslovakia   1892   1962
  CCZ, MNP65/6, MNP67/4, MNP67/5

VYHNÁLEK, Ivo   Czechoslovakia   1930
  CCZ, COO, MEH

*VYSHNEGRADSKY, Ivan   France   1893   Russia
  REM

*VYVERMAN, Jules   Belgium   1900
  EVM

WADE, Walter   USA   1926
  PCM

*WAGENAAR, Bernard   USA   1894 1971
   AS66, BB71, EVM, LMD, MLA28/4,   Netherlands
   NED, PCM, REM, X66

WAGHALTER, Henryk   Poland   1869 1958
   PKW

WAGNER, Genrih Matusovich   USSR   1922 Poland
   EMS, LMD, PPU69/2, X67
   LMD and PPU69/2: VAGNER
   EMS: ВАГНЕР

*WAGNER, Joseph   Frederick   USA 1900
   AA73, AS66, BB65, BB71, CA12, LMD, PCM, PC71, REM,
   X64, X65, X67, X68

WAGNER, Lavern   USA
   LCI, X64, X67, X68

*WAGNER, Robert   Austria   1915
   LMD, REM, X66, X67, X68

WAGNER, Thomas   USA   1931
   AS66, PCM, X64

WAGNER, Werner S.   Argentina   1927 Germany
   CA15, QLA

*WAGNER-RÉGENY, Rudolf   Germany   1903 1969
   BB65, BB71, CME, DDM, EMS, EVM, IMD, LMD, MEH,
   MLA26/4, REM, SML, X64, X65, X66, X67, X68
   EMS: ВАГНЕР-РЕГЕНИ
   EMV: 1905

*WAHLBERG, Rune A.   Sweden   1910
   FST, KSV, SIM, SIMa

WAHREN, Karl Heinz   Germany   1933
   IMD2, X66, X67, X68

WAINJUNAS, S. A.
   See: VAINYUNAS, S. A.

WAINWRIGHT, David   Great Britain   circa
   X68   1945

WALACIŃSKI, Adam   Poland   1928
   PKW, X67, X68

WALBE, Joel   Israel   1898 Russia
   REM, X67

*WALD, Max   USA   1889 1954
 REM

WALDEN, Stanley   1932
 WAN

WALDMÜLLER, Ludwig
 See: MÜLLER, Ludwig

*WALDROP, Gid   USA   1919
 AA73, AS66, BB65, BB71, PCM, X64, X66, X68
 AS66: Gideon
 PCM: 1918

*WALDSTEIN, Wilhelm Austria   1897
 X64, X65, X66, X68

WALENTYOWICZ, Władysław Poland   1902
 PKW

WALKER, Arthur Dennis Great Britain 1932
 WI69, X64, X65, X67, X68

WALKER, Don   USA   1941

*WALKER, Ella May   Canada   1892 USA
 X67

*WALKER, George A.   USA   1922
 ASUC, PCM, X64, X65, X68

WALKER, James   Great Britain 1929
 WI69, X65

WALKER, James   USA   1937
 DN72

*WALKER, Nina   Great Britain circa
 X65   1927

WALKER, Richard   USA   1912
 PCM, PC71, X64

WALKER, Wayne A.   USA   1952
 BS72

WALSWORTH, Ivor   Great Britain 1909
 LMD, REM, WI69, X68

*WALTER, Arnold Maria Canada   1902 Austria
 BB65, BB71, CA11, CCM, KEY, MCO, TFB, X68

*WALTER, Bruno   USA   1876 1962
  BB65, BB71, DDM, EVM, IMD, LMD, X64, X65, X66, X67,
  X68

*WALTER, Fried Walter
 Schmidt   Germany   1907
  IMD, LMD, REM, X68

*WALTER, Karl Josef   Austria   1892
  X68

WALTERS, Derek   Great Britain
  X68

*WALTERS, Leslie   Great Britain 1902
  WI69

*WALTERSHAUSEN, Hermann
 Wolfgang Sartorius von Germany   1882 1954
  DDM, EVM, IMD, LMD, REM

*WALTHEW, Richard Henry Great Britain 1872 1951
  LMD, REM

*WALTON, William Turner Great Britain 1902
  BB71, BCI, CME, DDM, EMS, EVM, IMD, LMD, MEH, REM,
  TCM, WI69, WTM, X64, X65, X66, X67, X68
  EMS: УОЛТОН

*WALZEL, Leopold Matthias Austria   1902
  BB71, IMD, WI69, X68

*WAND, Günter   Germany   1912
  SML, WWG, X64, X68

*WANGENHEIM, Volker Germany   1928
  IMD, IMD2, X67, X68

*WARD, Robert E.   USA   1917
  BB65, BB71, CA9, EVM, IMD, LMD, PCM, PC71, REM, WTM,
  X64, X65, X66, X67, X68

WARD-STEINMAN, David USA   1936
  ASUC, PCM, PC71, X65, X66, X67, X68

*WARE, Harriet   USA   1877 1962
  AS66, BB65, BB71

WARFIELD, Gerald   USA
  ASUC

WARNER, Philip   USA   1901
  AS66, LCI

WARNER, Robert Austin   USA   1912
    DAS, X67, X68

*WARRACK, Guy Douglas
    Hamilton   Great Britain   1900   Scotland
    LMD, X64, X67

*WARREN, Elinor Remick   USA   1905
    AA73, AS66, BB65, PCM, PC71, WI69, X65, X66, X67, X68

WARREN, Raymond   Great Britain   1928
    BB65, BB71, LMD, WI69, X64, X65, X66, X67, X68

*WARTISCH, Otto Alexander
    Hermann   Germany   1893
    EVM, IMD

WASHBURN, Robert B.   USA   1928
    AA73, AS66, BB71, PCM, PC71, X65, X66, X67, X68

WASSILENKO, S. N.
    See: VASSILENKO, S. N.

WATERMAN, Adolf   Netherlands   1886
    EVM

*WATERS, Charles Frederick   Great Britain   1895
    WI69, X68

*WATSON, Robert Graham   Great Britain   1913
    WI69

WATSON, Walter Robert   USA   1933
    ASUC, PCM, PC71, X68

WATTS, John   1930
    WAN

*WATTS, Wintter   USA   1884   1962
    AS66, BB65, BB71

*WAXMAN, Franz   USA   1906   1967
    AS66, BB65, BB71, EVM, MLA24/4,   Germany
    X65, X67, X68

WAYDITCH, Gabriel   USA   1888   1969
    BB65, BB71, MLA26/4   Hungary
    Also: DÖNHOFF, Gabriel Wajditsch Verbovac von

*WAYENBERG, Daniel   Netherlands   1929
    X65, X66, X67

WEATHERS, Keith   USA   1943
 PC71

*WEATHERSEED, John Joseph Canada   1900 1965
 NLC, X65   England

*WEAVER, Powell   USA   1890 1951
 AS66, PCM

*WEBER, Alain   France   1930
 BB71, DDM, IMD, IMD2, LMD

*WEBER, Ben Brian   USA   1916
 AA73, BB65, BB71, CA9, EVM, IMD, IMD2, LMD, PCM,
 PC71, REM, TSC, WI69, X64, X65, X66, X67, X68

*WEBER, Heinrich   Germany   1901
 X65

WEBER, Sven Franklin Fridtjof Great Britain 1934 Denmark
 WI69

*WEDIG, Hans-Josef   Germany   1898
 WWG

WEED, Maurice J.   USA   1912
 ASUC, LCI, PCM, X65, X67, X68

WEEKS, John Ralph   Great Britain 1934
 WI69, X64

*WEGENER, Emmy Frensel Netherlands 1901
 NED

WEGENER, Siegfried Karl
 Hermann   Germany   1916
 WI69

*WEGENER-KOOPMAN, Bertha
 Frensel   Netherlands 1874 1953
 NED

WEHDING, Hans-Hendrik Germany   1915
 SML, X66, X68

*WEHLE, Gerhard Fürchtegott Germany   1884
 EVM, IMD, WWG, X65, X66

*WEIGEL, Eugene John   USA   1910
 PCM

WEIGL, Karl   USA
 X67, X68

WEIGL, Vally   USA   1899   Austria
    DDM, LMD, X66, X67

*WEILL, Kurt   USA   1900   1950
    AS66, DDM, EL:2, EMS, EVM, IMD, IMD2,   Germany
    LMD, MEH, MZW, REM, SML, WTM, X64,
    X65, X66, X67, X68
    EMS: ВЕЙЛЬ

WEINBERG, Henry   USA   1931
    ASUC, X68

*WEINBERG, Jacob   USA   1883   1956
    AS66, BB65, LMD, REM, X68   Russia
    REM: 1879-1956

WEINBERG, Moisei Samuilovich
    See: VAINBERG, Moisey Samuilovich

*WEINBERGER, Jaromir   USA   1896   1967
    AS66, BB65, BB71, DDM, EMS, EVM, IMD,   Bohemia
    LMD, MEH, MLA24/4, REM, SML, WTM, X67, X68
    EMS: ВЕЙНБЕРГЕР

*WEINER, Lazar   USA   1897   Russia
    AS66, REM, X68

*WEINER, Leo   Hungary   1885   1960
    BB65, BB71, CHC, DDM, EMS, IMD, LMD, MEH, REM, SML,
    X64, X65
    EMS: ВЕЙНЕР

WEINER, Stanley Milton   Belgium   1925   USA
    PCM, PC71, WI69

WEINER, Yehudi
    See: WYNER, Yehudi

*WEINZWEIG, John Jacob   Canada   1913
    BB65, BB71, CCM, CCM71, CVM, IMD, KEY, LMD, MCO,
    MCO68, MCO71, NLC, REM, TFB, TSC, X68

*WEIS, Carl Flemming   Denmark   1898
    CME, DMTsp, EVM, IMD, IMD2, LMD, REM, WI69, X64,
    X65, X68

*WEISGALL, Hugo David   USA   1912   Czecho-
    ASUC, AS66, BB71, LMD, PCM, PC71, REM,   slovakia
    WI69, X64, X65, X66, X67, X68

*WEISHAPPEL, Rudolf   Austria   1921
    X67, X68

*WEISMANN, Julius   Germany 1879 1950
 DDM, EVM, IMD, LMD, REM, SML, X67

*WEISMANN, Wilhelm   Germany 1900
 IMD, LMD, REM, SML, X64, X65, X68

*WEISS, Adolph Andreas USA   1891 1971
 BB65, BB71, REM, TSC

WEISS, Alfred   Germany 1867 1954
 ACM

WEISS, Manfred   Germany 1935
 SML, X65, X66, X67, X68

*WEISSENBÄCK, Franz Andreas Austria 1880 1960
 BB65, BB71, X68

*WEISSENSTEINER, Raimund Austria 1905
 LMD, WI69

WEISSHAUS, Imre
 See: ARMA, Paul

*WEISSMANN, John Schützer Great Britain 1910 Hungary
 LMD, X64, X66, X67, X68

WEISZ, Egon Max   Kenya   1909 Austria
 WI69

WELANDER, Svea   Sweden 1898
 KSV, SIMa

*WELANDER, Waldemar Sweden 1899
 FST, KSV, SIM, SIMa

*WELFFENS, Peter Michel Belgium 1924
 WI69

WELIN, Karl-Erik V.   Sweden 1934
 CME, DNS, FST, IMD, IMD2, LMD, SIMa, SMT, SOW, STI,
 STS, SWE, TJU, VTM, X65, X66, X67, X68

*WELLEJUS, Henning   Denmark 1919
 IMD

*WELLESZ, Egon Joseph Great Britain 1885 Austria
 BB65, BB71, CME, DDM, EMS, EVM, IMD, IMD2, LMD,
 MEH, REM, SML, WI69, X64, X65, X66, X67, X68
 EMS: ВЕЛЛЕС

*WELTER, Friedrich   Germany 1900
 EVM, X68

*WEMAN, Nils Henry   Sweden   1897
    SIMa, STS

WEN-CHUNG, Chou
    See: CHOU, Wen-Chung

WENDEL, Eugen   Rumania   1934
    RCL

WENDEL, Martin   Switzerland   1925
    IMD2, SCHW, WWS, X65

WENNEIS, Fritz   Germany   1889
    WWG

WENNERBERG-REUTER,
    Sara M. E.   Sweden   1875   1959
    FST, KSV, SIM, SIMa

*WENZEL, Eberhard   Germany   1896
    IMD, LMD, X64, X66, X67, X68

WEPRIK, Alexander   1899   1958
    IMD

*WERBA, Erik   Austria   1918
    LMD, WI69, X65, X66, X67, X68

WERDER, Felix   Australia   1922   Germany
    AMM, X66, X67

*WERDIN, Eberhard   Germany   1911
    IMD2, X68

WERLE, Lars Johan   Sweden   1926
    BB71, CME, DDM, DNS, FST, IMD2, LMD, SIM, SIMa, SMT,
    SOW, STI, STS, SWE, VTM, X64, X65, X66, X67, X68

*WERNER, Eric   USA   1901   Austria
    BB71, X64, X65, X66, X68

*WERNER, Fritz Eugen
    Heinrich   Germany   1898
    IMD, X64, X65

WERNER, Jean-Jacques   France   1935
    ACM, DDM, LMD

*WERNER, Theodor Georg
    Wilhelm   Germany   1874   1957
    BB65, LMD

WERNICK, Richard   USA   1934
   AS66, PC71, X64, X68

WERZLAU, Joachim   Germany   1913
   SML, X66, X67, X68

*WESSEL, Mark   USA   1894   1972
   REM

*WESTBROOK, Helen Searles   USA   1898   1967
   AS66, X67

*WESTERGAARD, Peter   USA   1931
   ASUC, IMD, PCM, PC71, X65, X67

*WESTERGAARD, Svend   Denmark   1922
   LMD, REM, VTM, X65, X66, X68

WESTERING, Paul Christaan
  van   Netherlands   1911
   EVM

WESTERMAN, Gerhart von   Germany   1894   1963
   EVM, IMD, LMD, REM, X64, X65, X66, X67
   EVM: 1884

WESTON, Philip
   See: FILIPPI, Amadeo de

*WESTRUP, Jack Allan   Great Britain   1904
   BB71, DDM, EVM, LMD, REM, X64, X65, X66, X67, X68

*WETTERBERG, Karl   Sweden   1894
   SIMa, X64

*WETZEL, Justus Hermann   Germany   1879
   BB71, EVM, IMD, LMD

*WEWELER, August   Germany   1868   1952
   LMD

WEYER, Jules   France   1878   1965
   ACM

*WEYRAUCH, Johannes Wilhem
  Robert   Germany   1897
   IMD

WHEAR, Paul William   USA   1925
   ASUC, BB65, BB71, PCM, PC71, X68

WHEELER, Joseph Hugh   Great Britain   1927
   WI69, X66, X68

*WHETTAM, Graham   Great Britain   1927
   WI69, X64, X65, X66, X68

*WHIPP, Ivy Mason   Great Britain   circa
   WI69   1920

*WHITE, Clarence Cameron   USA   1880   1960
   AS66, BB71, REM

WHITE, Donald H.   USA   1921
   X68

*WHITE, Herbert Dennis   Canada   1912
   NLC

WHITE, John   Great Britain
   X65

WHITE, John D.   USA   1931
   ASUC, AS66, PCM, PC71, X66, X68

WHITE, L. Keith   USA   1945
   DN72

WHITE, Michael   USA   1931
   AS66, BB71, CA9, X64

*WHITE, Paul Taylor   USA   1895
   AS66, BB65, PCM, REM, WI69, X64, X65, X66, X67, X68

*WHITEHEAD, Alfred Ernest   Canada   1887   England
   KEY, NLC, NLCa

*WHITHORNE, Emerson   USA   1884   1958
   AS66, IMD, LMD, PC71, REM
   Formerly: WHITTERN

WHITMAN, George   Great Britain   1917   Germany
   WI69, X65, X66, X67, X68

*WHITMER, Thomas Carl   USA   1873   1959
   BB65, BB71

WHITNEY, Maurice   USA   1909
   AS66, X65

*WHITNEY, Robert Sutton   USA   1904   Great Britain
   CME, X66, X68

WHITTAKER, Howard USA 1922
BB65, BB71, X64

WHITTENBERG, Charles USA 1927
ASUC, CA15, X68

WHITTERN, E.
See: WHITHORNE, Emerson

*WHITTINGTON, Dorsey USA 1899
WI69

*WHYTE, Ian Great Britain 1901 1960
EVM, LMD Scotland

WIBLÉ, Michel Switzerland 1923
SCHW

*WICK, Otto USA 1885 1957
AS66 Germany

WICKENS, Dennis John Great Britain 1926
WI69

*WIDÉEN, Ivar Sweden 1871 1951
KSV, FST, SIM, SIMa, STS

WIDMER, Ernst Switzerland 1927
IMD2, SCHW

*WIECHOWICZ, Stanisław Poland 1893 1963
BB71, CME, DDM, EMS, IMD, LMD, MEH, PKW, REM, SML,
X64, X65
EMS: ВЕХÓВИЧ

WIECZOREK, Jan Michał Poland 1904
PKW

WIEDERMANN, Bedrich Antonín Czechoslovakia 1883 1951
MEH

*WIELE, Aimée van der Belgium 1907
CME, EVM

*WIÉNER, Jean France 1896
DMF, EMS, EVM, IMD, LMD, REM
EMS: ВЬЕНÉР

WIENHORST, Richard USA 1920
PCM, PC71, X68

*WIENIAWSKI, Adam Tadeusz   Poland   1879   1950
   BB65, EVM, REM

WIERUSZOWSKI, Lili   Switzerland   1899   Germany
   SCHW

WIESE, Hans-Heinrich   1921
   IMD2

*WIESLANDER, Ingvar Axel
   Otto   Sweden   1917   1963
   FST, KSV, SIM, SIMa, STS, SWE, TJU, VTM

*WIETH-KNUDSEN, Knud
   Asbjørn   Denmark   1878   1962
   IMD

*WIGGEN, Knut   Norway   1927
   CME, VTM, X67, X68
   Pseudonym: FREED, Olov Martin

*WIGGLESWORTH, Frank   USA   1918
   LMD, PCM, REM

*WIJDEVELD, Wolfgang   Netherlands   1910
   EVM, IMD, NED, X64, X65, X66

WIJNGAARDEN, Johannes
   Hendrik van   Netherlands   1912
   EVM

*WIKANDER, David   Sweden   1884   1955
   FST, KSV, SIM, SIMa, STS

*WIKLUND, Adolf   Sweden   1879   1950
   EVM, FST, KSV, LMD, REM, SIM, SIMa, SOW, STS

WILBRANDT, Jürgen   Germany   1922
   SML, X67

*WILCKENS, Friedrich   Austria   1899
   IMD, LMD, REM

WILCOX, A. Gordon   USA

WILCOX, Joseph L.   USA
   ASUC

*WILDBERGER, Jacques   Switzerland   1922
   BB65, BB71, CME, IMD, IMD2, LMD, MEH, MZW, REM,
   X64, X65, X66, X67, X68

*WILDER, Alexander Lafayette
Chew (Alec)   USA   1907
   BB71, PCM, PC71, X66, X67

*WILDGANS, Friedrich   Austria   1913 1965
   BB71, EVM, IMD, IMD2, LMD, MEH, MLA22/4, REM, SML,
   X65, X66, X67, X68

WILDING-WHITE, Raymond   USA   1922
   X67, X68

WILDSHUT, Clara   Netherlands 1906 1950
   EVM

*WILKES, Josué Teófilo   Argentina   1883
   LMD, REM, X65

*WILKINSON, Arthur H.   Great Britain 1919 1968
   WI69, X68

*WILKINSON, Marc   Great Britain 1929 France
   IMD, MNG, WI69

*WILKINSON, Philip George Great Britain 1929
   WI69

*WIŁKOMIRSKI, Kazimierz   Poland   1900 Russia
   EMS, LMD, PKW, REM, X65, X66, X67, X68
   EMS: ВИЛКОМИ́РСКИЙ

WILL, Madeleine   France   1910
   ACM

*WILLAN, Healy   Canada   1880 1968
   BB71, CCM, CVM, CVMa, DDM, EVM,   Great Britain
   IMD, KEY, LMD, MCO, MCO68, NLC, NLCa,
   REM, TFB, X64, X65, X66, X67, X68

WILLEMS, Edgar   Switzerland 1890 Belgium
   SCHW, X65, X68

*WILLIAMS, Alan Robert   Great Britain 1910
   WI69
   Pseudonym: ALAN, Robert

*WILLIAMS, Alberto   Argentina   1862 1952
   DDM, EMS, EVM, IMD, LMD, REM, X68
   EMS: ВИ́ЛЬЯМС

*WILLIAMS, Christopher à
Becket   Great Britain 1890 1956
   EVM, LMD, REM

WILLIAMS, Clifton   USA   1923
    AA73

WILLIAMS, David McK.   USA   1887
    PCM

WILLIAMS, David Russell   USA
    ASUC

*WILLIAMS, Grace Mary   Great Britain   1906
    LMD, REM, X65, X66, X67, X68

WILLIAMS, Joan Frank   USA
    X67

WILLIAMS, John T.   USA   1932
    BB71, PCM

WILLIAMS, R. Vaughan
    See: VAUGHN WILLIAMS, Ralph

*WILLIAMS (GWYNN WILLIAMS),
    William Sidney Gwynn   Great Britain   1896   Italy
    WI69, X68

*WILLIAMSON, Malcolm
    Benjamin Graham
    Christopher   Great Britain   1931   Australia
    AMM, BB65, BB71, CME, DDM, REM, WI69, X65, X66,
    X67, X68

*WILLIS, Richard M.   USA   1929
    AA73, PCM, X65, X66, X67, X68

WILLMAN, Allan   USA   1909
    BB65, BB71

*WILLNER, Arthur   Great Britain   1881   1959
    BB65, BB71, EVM, IMD, LMD, REM   Bohemia

*WILLSON, Meredith   USA   1902
    AS66, BB71, WI69, X65, X66, X67, X68

*WILSON, Alfred   Canada   1901   Scotland
    WI69

*WILSON, Charles Mills   Canada   1931
    CCM71, CVMa, MCO68, MCO71, NLC, X68

WILSON, Donald Malcolm   USA
    X68

WILSON, Galen   USA   1926
     CAP

WILSON, George Balch   USA   1927
     ASUC, PCM, X67

WILSON, Mark Edwards   USA   1948
     BS72

WILSON, Olly Woodrow   USA   1937
     ASUC, X66, X68

WILSON, Richard   USA   1941
     ASUC, BB71, X66, X67

*WILSON, Robert James Barclay   Great Britain   circa
     WI69   1913

WILSON, Thomas Brendan   Great Britain   1927   USA
     WI69, X64, X67, X68

*WILTBERGER, Hans   Germany   1887
     ACM, X67
     ACM: WILTBERGER, <u>Jean</u>

*WIMBERGER, Gerhard   Austria   1923
     BB71, CME, EVM, IMD, IMD2, LMD, REM, WI69,
     X64, X65, X66, X67, X68

*WINDINGSTAD, Ole   Norway   1886   1959
     BB71

*WINDT, Herbert   Germany   1894   1965
     EVM, IMD, X65

*WINESANKER, Michael Max   USA   1913   Canada
     EVM, X66

WINHAM, Godfrey Charles   USA   Great Britain
     ASUC, X68

WINICK, Steven David   USA   1944
     DN70, DN72

WINKLER, Adalbert   Rumania   1930
     RCL

*WINKLER, Georg Carl   Germany   1902
     WWG

WINKLER, Georg Robert   Germany   1895   Russia
     WWG

WINKLER, Gerhard   Germany   1906
    EVM, REM, SML, WWG, X66

WINKLER, Peter K.   USA   1943
    BB71

WINSLOW, Richard K.   USA   1918
    PCM, X64

WINSOR, Philip   1938
    WAN

*WINSTANLEY, John Harold   Australia   1922
    WI69

*WINTER, Paul   Germany   1894   1970
    IMD, MLA27/4, X64, X67, X68

*WINTERS, Geoffrey Walter
  Horace   Great Britain   1928
    WI69, X68

*WIRÉN, Dag Ivar   Sweden   1905
    BB71, DDM, EVM, FST, IMD, KSV, LMD, MEH, REM, SIM,
    SIMa, SMT, SOW, STS, SWE, TJU, X64, X65, X67

WIRTH, Carl Anton   USA   1912
    AA73, AS66, X64

*WIRTH, Helmut Richard
  Adolf Friedrich-Karl   Germany   1912
    LMD, REM, WWG, X64, X67

WISCHER, Karl-Heinz   1907
    IMD

*WISHART, Peter Charles
  Arthur   Great Britain   1921
    IMD, WI69, X64, X65, X68

*WISŁOCKI, Stanisław   Poland   1921
    LMD, MEH, PKW, REM, X65, X67, X68

WISSE, Jan   Netherlands   1921
    EVM, IMD, NED, REM

*WISSMER, Pierre Alexandre   France   1915   Switzerland
    BB71, DDM, DMF27, EVM, IMD, QQF, LMD, REM, SCHW,
    WI69, WWS, X64, X65

WISZNIEWSKI, Zbigniew   Poland   1922
    IMD2, MEH, PKW, REM, X64, X65, X66, X67, X68

WITNI, Monica   USA   1928
   DN72

*WITTELSBACH, Rudolph   Switzerland   1902   1972
   EVM, IMD, LMD, MLA29/4, REM,   Turkey
   SCHW, WWS, X68

WITTINGER, Robert   Austria   1945
   IMD2, LMD, X68

WITTMER, Eberhard Ludwig   1905
   IMD, X65

WLADIGEROFF, P. K.
   See: VLADIGEROV, P. K.

*WOESTIJNE, David van de   Belgium   1915   England
   CBC, EVM, IMD, LMD, REM

*WOHL, Yehuda H.   Israel   1904
   MM59

*WOHLFAHRT, Frank   Germany   1894   1971
   EVM, LMD, MLA28/4, REM, WWG, X67, X68

*WOHLGEMUTH, Gerhard   Germany   1920
   EMS, IMD, IMD2, LMD, REM, SML, X66
   EMS: ВОЛЬГЕМУТ

*WOLF, Bodo   Germany   1888
   EVM, X64

WOLF, Jaroslav J.   Czechoslovakia   1932
   MNP72/9

WOLF, Robert Erich   USA   1915
   REM

WOLF, Stanley   USA   1924
   BB71

*WOLF, Winfried   Germany   1900
   X68

*WOLFE, Jacques   USA   1896   Rumania
   AS66, PCM

*WOLFF, Albert Louis   France   1884   1970
   BB71, CMF65/11, EVM, LMD, MLA27/4, REM, X64

*WOLFF, Christian   USA   1934   France
   BB65, BB71, CME, IMD, LMD, PCM, PC71, TSC,

X64, X65, X66, X68
PC71 and X65: WOLF<u>E</u>

*WOLFF, Hellmuth Christian   Germany   1906   Switzerland
    EVM, IMD, LMD, REM, SML, X65, X66, X68

WOLFF, Hugh M.   USA   1953   France
    BS70

WOLFF, Kurt von
    See: WOLFURT, Kurt von

*WOLFF, Werner   USA   1883   1961
    BB65, BB71, REM   Germany

*WOLFSOHN, Juliusz   Poland   1880   1944
    BB65, BB71, REM

*WOLFURT, Kurt von   Germany   1880   1957
    EVM, IMD, LMD, REM, SML   Latvia
    LMD: WOLFF, K.

*WOLPE, Stefan   USA   1902   1972
    ASUC, AS66, BB71as, CME, EVM, IMD, LMD,   Germany
    MLA29/4, REM, TSC, WI69, X64, X65, X66, X68

*WOLPERT, Franz Alfons   Germany   1917
    EVM, IMD, LMD, REM

WOLTERS, Gottfried   Germany   1910
    IMD, X67

*WOLTMANN, Frederick   USA   1908
    REM

*WOOD, Haydn   Great Britain   1882   1959
    BB65, BB71, EVM, LMD

WOOD, Hugh   Great Britain   1932
    BB65, BB71, IMD, MNG, X64, X65, X66, X68

*WOOD, Joseph   USA   1915
    AA73, BB65, BB71, X65

*WOOD, Ralph Walter   Great Britain   1902
    REM, WI69

*WOOD, Thomas   Great Britain   1892   1950
    EVM, LMD, REM, X68

WOOD, William   USA   1935
    MNP66/4, X66, X68

WOODBURY, Arthur N.   USA   1930
   BB71, X68

*WOODHAM, Ronald   Great Britain   1912
   X68

*WOOD-HILL, Mabel   USA   1870   1954
   AS66, EVM
   EVM: HILL, Mabel Wood
   AS66: 1891

WOOLDRIDGE, David Humphry
  Michael   Great Britain   1931
   BB71, WI69, X67
   BB71: 1927

WOOLF, Gregory   USA
   ASUC

*WOOLLEN, Russell   USA   1923
   IMD, PCM, PC71, X66, X67

*WORDSWORTH, William
  Brockelsby   Great Britain   1908
   BB65, BB71, EVM, LMD, REM, WI69, X64, X66, X67

WORK, Julian C.   USA   1910
   AS66, PCM

WORST, John   USA   1940
   CAP, DN72

WORTHING, R. D.   USA
   ASUC

*WOYTOWICZ, Bolesław   Poland   1899
   CME, DDM, EMS, EVM, IMD, LMD, MEH, PKW, REM, SML,
   TSC, X64, X65
   EMS: ВОЙТО́ВИЧ

*WRIGHT, Denis   Great Britain   1895   1967
   X64, X66, X67, X68

*WRIGHT, Kenneth Anthony   Great Britain   1899
   WI69, X67, X68

WROBEL, Feliks   Poland   1897   1954
   PKW

WUENSCH, Gerhard J.   Canada   1925
   CCM71, CVMa, KEY, MCO71, NLCa, PC71, X68

*WÜHRER, Friedrich   Austria   1900
    WI69, X64, X65, X67, X68

*WUNSCH, Hermann   Germany   1884   1954
    IMD, LMD, REM

*WUORINEN, Charles   USA   1938
    AA73, ASUC, BB65, BB71, DN72, IMD2, PCM, PC71, X64,
    X65, X66, X67, X68

*WURMSER, Leo Russell   Austria   1905   1967
    X64, X66, X67

WURTZLER, Astrid von   USA   1925   Hungary
    AS66

*WÜRZ, Anton   Germany   1903
    LMD, WWG, X67, X68
    WWG: WUERZ

*WÜRZ, Richard   Germany   1885   1965
    BB71, EVM, LMD

*WYK, Arnold van   Union of   1916
    IMD, LMD, REM, X68   South Africa
    Baptized: WYK, Arnoldus Christiaan Volk van

WYKES, Robert A.   USA   1926
    AA73, ASUC, AS66, BB65, BB71, LMD, X64, X65, X66, X67

WYLIE, Ruth Shaw   USA
    ASUC

WYNER, Yehudi   USA   1929   Canada
    ASUC, BB71, REM, X64, X67
    REM: Under father WEINER, Lazare
    Formerly: WEINER, Y.

WYNNE, David   Great Britain   1900   Wales
    LMD, REM, WI69, X66, X67, X68
    Pseudonym of: THOMAS, David Wynne

WYSCHNEGRADSKY, Ivan   1893
    IMD

WYTTENBACH, Jürg   Switzerland   1935
    BB65, BB71, IMD2, LMD, SCHW, X64, X65, X66, X67, X68

*XENAKIS, Yannis   France   1922   Rumania
    BB65, BB71, CME, DDM, DN70, EL:1, EL:2, EL:4, IMD,
    IMD2, LMD, MEH, PAP, QQF, REM, X64, X65, X66, X67, X68
    PAP: 1921

*XENOS, Alexandros   Greece   1912
   REM

YAKHIN, Rustem Mukhamet-
  Khazeyevich   USSR   1921
   EMS, PPU69/2, PPU71/4
   EMS: ЯХИН

*YAMADA, Košçaku   Japan   1886 1965
   BB71, DDM, EMS, EVM, LMD, MLA23/4, REM, X65, X66,
   REM: IAMADA
   EMS: ЯМАДА

YAMASH'TA, Stomu   Japan   1947

YAMPILOV, Baudorza
  Bazorovich   USSR   1916
   EMS, PPU69/2, X68
   EMS: ЯМПИЛОВ

YANNATOS, James   USA   1929
   PCM, X67

YANNAY, Yehuda   Rumania   1937
   IMD2, PAP

YARDEN, Elie S.   Israel   1923 USA
   ACU

*YARDUMIAN, Richard   USA   1917
   AS66, BB71, CA11, PCM, PC71, X65, X67, X68

YAROVINSKY, Boris Lvovich USSR   1922
   EMS
   EMS: ЯРОВИНСКИЙ

*YARULLIN, Farid
  Zagudoullovich   USSR   1914 1945
   EMS, EVM
   EVM: YAROELLIN
   EMS: ЯРУ́ЛЛИН

YARUSTOVSKY, Boris
  Mikhailovich   USSR   1911
   EMS, PPU69/2, X65, X66, X67, X68
   EMS: ЯРУСТОВСКИЙ

YASHIRO, Akio   Japan   1929
   BB71, IMD2, MEH

*YATES, Victor Henry   Great Britain 1915
   WI69

YATZEVICH, Yuri Mikhailovich   USSR   1901   1968
EMS, PPU69/4
EMS: ЯЦЕВИЧ
PPU69/4: 1969

YELLIN, Gleb   USA   1903   Russia
AS66

YELLIN, Victor   USA
ASUC

YOFFE, Shlomoh   Israel
MM59

YORK, Walter Wynn   USA   1914
DN70, X68

YOSHIFUMI, Mayeda   Finland   circa 1940

YOSHIOKA, Emmett   USA   1944
DN72

*YOUNG, Derek   Great Britain   1929
WI69

YOUNG, Douglas   Great Britain   1947
BB71

YOUNG, La Monte   USA   1935
BB65, BB71, IMD, X64, X65, X66, X67, X68

*YOUNG, Percy Marshall   Great Britain   1912
BB65, BB71, LMD, REM, WI69, X64, X65, X66, X67, X68

YOURISSALOU, K.   USSR   Estonia

YTTREHUS, Rolv   USA   1926
ASUC

YUASA, Joji   USA   1929
BB71

*YUDAKOV, Solomon
Aleksandrovich   USSR   1916
EMS, PPU, PPU69/2
EMS: ЮДАКОВ

YUDIN, Gavriil Yakovelevich   USSR   1905
EMS, X68
EMS: ЮДИН

*YUN, Isang   Korea   1917
BB71, DDM, IMD, IMD2, LMD, MEH, MZW, PAP, REM, X65,
X66, X67

*YUROSVKY, Vladimir
Mikhailovich   USSR   1915
    EMS, LMD, MEH, X68
    LMD: JUROVSKIJ   MEH: JUROVSKY
    EMS: ЮРОВСКИЙ

*YVAIN, Maurice   France   1891   1965
    BB71, CMF65/10, DDM, DMF, EVM, LMD, MLA22/4, X65,
    X66

YVOIRE, Claude
See: ZINSSTAG, Dolf

ZABRACK, Harold   USA   1929
    BB65, BB71, PC71, X67

ZACHARIAS, Helmut   Germany   1920
    WWG, WWS

*ZACHARIAS, Walter   Denmark   1909
    X67

ZACHER, Gerd   Germany
    X67

*ZÁDOR, Jenö   USA   1894   Hungary
    AA73, AS66, BB65, IMD, LMD, REM, WI69, WTM, X65, X68
    AS66 and IMD: ZADOR, Eugen   WTM: Eugene   X65: Egugene

*ZAFRED, Mario   Italy   1922
    BB65, DDM, EMS, EVM, IMD, LMD, MEH, REM, X64, X65,
    X68
    EMS: ДЗАФРЕД

ZAGORSKY, Vasily Georgievich   USSR   1926
    EMS, PPU69/2
    EMS: ЗАГОРСКИЙ

*ZAGWIJN, Henri   Netherlands   1878   1954
    BB65, BB71, DDM, EVM, IMD, LMD, REM

ZAHRADNÍK, Zdeněk   Czechoslovakia 1936
    CCZ, IMD2

ŹAK, Czesław   Poland   1895   1959
    PKW

ZAKARYAN, Karo Oganesovich   USSR   1895   1967
    EMS, X67
    EMS: ЗАКАРЯН

*ZAKHAROV, Vladimir
Grigorievich   USSR   1901   1956

EMS, MEH, X67, X68
MEH: ZACHAROV
EMS: ЗАХАРОВ

*ZALLINGER, Meinhard von   Germany   1897   Austria
X67

ZALLMAN, Arlene   USA
ASUC

ZAMACOIS, Joaquin   Spain   1894   Chile
DDM, LMC, REM

ZÁMEČNÍK, Evžen   Czechoslovakia   1939
MNP69/4, MNP72/9

*ZANABONI, Giuseppe   Italy   1926
LMD

ZANDER, Hans   Germany   1905
WI69

ZANETTI, Roberto   Italy   1938
LMD, X66

ZANGELMI, Piero Luigi   Italy   1927
LMD, REM

ZANINELLI, Luigi   USA   1932
PCM, PC71

ZANINOVIĆ, Aleksander   Yugoslavia   1934
KMJ

ZANON, Maffeo   Italy   1882   1968
LMD, REM

*ZANON, Sante   Italy   1899   1965
IMD, LMD, REM

ZARANEK, Stefania Anatolievna   USSR   1904
EMS
EMS: ЗАРАНЕК

*ZARATE, Eliodoro Ortiz de   Chile   1865   1953
EVM, LMD, REM

*ZARINŠ, Marger Ottovich   USSR   1910   Latvia
DDM, EMS, LMD, PPU, PPU69/2, X65, X66, X67
EMS: ЗАРИНЬ

ZARKOVSKIJ, E. E.
See: ZHARKOVSKY, E. E.

ZASLAVSKY, Semen Aronovich   USSR   1910
    EMS
    EMS: ЗАСЛÁВСКИЙ

ZATMAN, Andrew   1945
    WAN

ZBAR, Michel   France   1942
    BB71

*ZBINDEN, Julien-François   Switzerland   1917
    BB65, BB71, DDM, EVM, IMD, LMD, REM, SCHW, WWS,
    X64, X66, X67

*ŽEBRÈ, Demetrij   Yugoslavia   1912 1970
    EMS, KMJ, LMD
    EMS: ЖÉБРЕ

*ZECCHI, Adone   Italy   1904
    EVM, IMD, LMD, REM, X65, X66

ZECH, Carlferdinand   Germany   1928
    SML

ZECHLIN, Ruth   Germany   1926
    IMD, MEH, SML, X64, X65, X66, X67, X68

ZEHDEN, Hans   1912
    IMD

*ZEHELEIN, Alfred   Germany   1902
    WWG

*ZEHNDER, Max   Switzerland   1901 1972
    EVM, MLA29/4, LMD, REM, SCHW, WWS

*ZEIDMAN, Boris Isaacovich   USSR   1908
    EMS, X67
    X67: ZEYDMAN
    EMS: ЗÉЙДМАН

*ZEINALLY, Assaf   USSR   1909 1932
    EMS, EVM
    EMS: ЗÉЙНАЛЛЫ

*ZEISL, Eric   USA   1905 1959
    AS66, BB65, BB71, LMD, REM   Austria

*ZELENKA, Istvan   Hungary   1936
    BB65, BB71, IMD, IMD2, LMD, X66, X67

ŽELEZNÝ, Lubomir   Czechoslovakia 1925
    CCZ, IMD2, MEH

*ZELINKA, Jan Evangelista (II)   Czechoslovakia   1893
    CCZ, EVM, LMD, REM, WI69

ZELINKA, Otakar   Czechoslovakia   1876
    LMD

ZELJENKA, Ilja   Czechoslovakia   1932
    BB65, BB71, CCZ, IMD, IMD2, MEH, MNP64/5, MNP64/6,
    MNP67/1, MNP67/9, X64, X65, X66, X67, X68, ZE69/1,
    ZE69/2, ZE69/3, ZE70/1, ZE70/2, ZE70/3, ZE71/1, ZE71/2

ZELOBINSKI, Valeri   USSR   1913   1946
    REM

ZEMAN, Anton   Rumania   1937
    RCL

ZEMANOVSKÝ, Alfréd   Czechoslovakia
    ZE70/3, ZE71/2, ZE71/3

ZENDER, Hans   Germany   1936
    IMD, IMD2, LMD, PAP, X66, X67, X68

ZENTNER, Johannes   Switzerland   1903
    SCHW

*ŽGANEC, Vinko   Yugoslavia   1890
    HCM, REM, X64, X65, X68

ZHARKOVSKY, Evgeny
    Emmanuilovich   USSR   1906
    EMS, LMD, X67
    LMD: ŽARKOVSKIJ
    EMS: ЖАРКÓВСКИЙ

*ZHIGANOV, Nazib Gayazovich   USSR   1911
    DDM, EMS, LMD, MEH, PPU, PPU69/2, REM, X65, X66,
    X67, X68
    DDM: JIGANOV   LMD, MEH and REM: ZIGANOV
    EMS: ЖИГАНОВ

ZHINOVICH, Iosif Iosifovich   USSR   1907
    EMS
    EMS: ЖИНОВИЧ

ZHIRKOV, Mark Nikolaivich   USSR   1892   1951
    EMS
    EMS: ЖИРКÓВ

*ZHIVOTOV, Alexey
    Semionovich   USSR   1904   1964
    EMS, LMD, REM, X64
    LMD and REM: ŽIVOTOV   EMS: ЖИВОТОВ

ZHUBANOV, Ahmet Kuyanovich   USSR   1906   1968
    EMS, X68
    EMS: ЖУБАНОВ

ZHUBANOVA, Gaziza Ahmetovna USSR   1928
    EMS, PPU69/2, X65, X66, X68
    EMS: ЖУБАНОВА

*ZHUKOVSKY, Herman
    Leontievich   USSR   1913
    BB65, EMS, LMD, MEH, PPU, PPU69/2, REM, X64
    LMD: ŽUKOVSKIJ   MEH and REM: ZUKOVSKI
    EMS: ЖУКОВСКИЙ

*ZICH, Jaroslav   Czechoslovakia 1912
    CCZ, EVM, LMD, MEH, REM, X65, X68

*ZIEGLER, Benno   Germany   1891
    REM

ZIEMS, Harry   Germany   1907
    WI69

*ZIERITZ, Grete von   Germany   1899   Austria
    IMD, LMD, REM, WWG

ZIFFRIN, Marilyn J.   USA   1933
    AA73, ASUC, LCI, X65, X68

ŽIGON, Marko   Yugoslavia   1929
    KMJ

*ZIINO, Ottavio   Italy   1909
    LMD, REM, X68
    LMD: 1902

ZIKA, Pavel   Czechoslovakia 1926
    MEH

ZILINSKY, Arvid Yanovich   USSR   1905   Latvia
    EMS
    EMS: ЖИЛИНСКИЙ

*ZILLIG, Winfried   Germany   1905   1963
    BB65, BB71, CME, DDM, EVM, IMD, IMD2, LMD, MEH,
    REM, SML, X64, X65, X66, X67

*ZILLINGER, Erwin   Germany   1893
    X65, X68

ZIMARINO, Settimio   Italy   1885
    REM

*ZIMBALIST, Efrem
  Aleksandrovich   USA   1889   Russia
  AS66, BB71, EMS, EVM, LMD, MEH, REM, X65, X67
  EMS: ЦИМБАЛИСТ

*ZIMMER, Jan   Czechoslovakia 1926
  CCZ, IMD, LMD, MEH, X65, X68, ZE69/1, ZE69/3, ZE70/1,
  ZE70/3, ZE71/1, ZE71/2, ZE72/1

*ZIMMERMANN, Bernd Aloïs Germany   1918   1970
  BB65, BB71, DDM, EVM, IMD, IMD2, LMD, MEH, MLA27/4,
  MZW, PAP, REM, SML, TSC, X64, X65, X66, X67, X68

*ZIMMERMANN, Louis   Netherlands 1873   1954
  EVM, LMD, REM
  Sometimes spelled ZIMMERMAN

*ZIMMERMANN, Heinz Werner Germany   1930
  IMD2, LMD, PAP, REM, X64, X65, X66, X68

ZINDARS, Earl   USA   1927
  PCM, X66

ZINSSTAG, Dolf   Switzerland 1913
  SCHW
  Pseudonym of: VYOIRE, Claude

ZINTL, F. X.   1903
  IMD

ZINZADSE, S. F.
  See: TSINTSADZE, S. F.

*ZIPP, Friedrich Otto
  Gottfried   Germany   1914
  IMD, LMD, REM, X64, X65, X68

ZISKIN, Victor   USA   1937
  AS66

*ZÍTEK, Otakar   Czechoslovakia 1892   1955
  BB65, BB71, LMD, REM, X65

ZIV, Mihail Pavlovich USSR   1921
  EMS, X67, X68
  EMS: ЗИВ

*ŽIVKOVIĆ, Milenko   Yugoslavia   1901   1964
  BB65, BB71, IMD, LMD, REM, X65, X67
  REM: 1902

ŽIVKOVIĆ, Mirjana   Yugoslavia   1935
  KMJ, X65, X67

ZJIVOTOFF, Aleksei
See: ZHIVOTOV, A. S.

*ZLATEV-CHERKIN, Georgi
Dimitrov   Bulgaria   1905
BMK, X67, X68
BMK: ЗЛАТЕВ-ЧЕРКИН

*ZLATIĆ, Slavko   Yugoslavia   1910
EMS, HCM, IMD, LMD, KMJ, REM
EMS: ЗЛА́ТИЧ

*ZLATOV, Semen Vladimirovich USSR   1893 1970

ZMIGROD, Joseph
See: GRAY, Allan

*ZOELLNER, Richard   Germany   1896
LMD, REM
LMD: ZÖLLNER

ZOGRAFSKI, Tomislav   Yugoslavia   1934
KMJ, X68

*ZOLL, Paul   Germany   1907
IMD, X68

*ZOLOTAREV, Vassily
Andreyevich   USSR   1873 1964
BB65, BB71, EMS, LMD, MEH, REM, X64, X65
REM: SOLOTAREV
EMS: ЗОЛОТАРЁВ

ZOLTÁN, Aladár   Rumania   1929
RCL

ZONN, Paul   USA
ASUC, X68

*ZORAS, Leonidas   Greece   1905 1940
DDM, EVM, LMD, REM

ZORZI, Vittorio   Italy   1902
LMD, REM

ZORZOR, Stefan   Rumania   1932
RCL, X65, X66

ZOUHAR, Zdeněk   Czechoslovakia 1927
LMD

ZOULFOUGAROV, O.   USSR

ZRNO, Felix   Czechoslovakia 1890
  CCZ

ZUCCOLI, Gastone de   Italy   1887 1958
  REM

ZUCKERMANN, Augusta
  See: MANA-ZUCCA

ZUCKERT, León   Canada   1904 Russia
  CCM, CCM71, CVM, CVMa, KEY, MCO, MCO68, MCO71,
  NLC, X68

ZUCKMAYER, Eduard   Turkey   1890 Germany
  WWG

ZUKOVSKI, H. L.
  See: ZHUKOVSKY, H. L.

*ZUŁAWSKI, Wawrzyniec Jerzy Poland   1916 1957
  EVM, PKW, REM, X67

ŽUPANOVIĆ, Lovro   Yugoslavia   1925
  HCM, KMJ, X66, X67, X68

ZUPKO, Ramon   USA
  X67, X68

*ZVANKIN, Peter   Canada   1879 Russia
  MCO68

ZVEREV, Vasily Ivanovich   USSR   1904
  BB65, BB71, EMS
  EMS: ЗВЕРЕВ

ZWISSLER, Karl Maria   1900
  IMD, X68

*ZYKAN, Otto J. M.   Austria   1935
  BB65, BB71, IMD2, LMD, X66, X67, X68

VOLUME I CORRIGENDA
(omitted are the few instances of misalphabetizing
involving only one or two places)

page 5:   CHB should be HMB and should appear on page 8.

page 11: NDM was omitted:
  JACOBS, Arthur. A New Dictionary of Music. Harmondsworth,
  Middlesex, Penguin Books, Ltd., 1958. 416 pages.
  Short biographical entries. English text.

ADDISON, John.   Great Britain   1920
  EDM, GMM, MHHH, NDM, WIM
  (Omitted from page 18.)

BÅVEUDDE, Sven   Sweden   1896
  HHH
  (Omitted from page 38.)

BOSSI, Renzo   Italy   1883   1965
  GMM, HHH, MHHH
  (Omitted from page 55.)

BOURGUIGNON, Francis de (page 56) should be combined with:
  BOURGUINON, Francis Leon de (page 90)

BREITENBACK (page 58): should be BREITENBACH ...

BÜCHTGER (page 63): add source EDM

BUECHTGER (page 64): cancel this entry

BULL, Edvard Hagerup (page 64): add source VER

COMPOSTEL, Jacques   Canada   1904   1928
  CLA
  (Omitted from page 82.)

COSSETTO, Emil   Yugoslavia   1918
  YUG
  (Omitted from page 84.)

561

CVETKO, Dragotin   Yugoslavia   1911
    YUG
    (Omitted from page 86.)

DANIEL (page 89): should appear after DANEAU (page 88)

DELAQUERRIÈRE (page 92): should appear after DELANNOY
    (page 92)

DENY (page 93): should be DENNY

DEVREESE (page 95): first name should be Godefroid

DOLIN (page 97): cancel this entry

DOLLIN (page 97): add source CLA

DOULGALS, R. (page 99): should be DOUGLAS, R.

DUMIČIĆ, Peter   Yugoslavia   1901
    YUG
    (Omitted from page 101.)

EHRLING, Evert Sixten   Sweden   1924
    MHHH
    (Omitted from page 106.)

ESPAY (page 110): should be ESHPAI

FARELL (page 113): should appear after FARA (page 113)

FARRARI (page 116): should be FERRARI

FINE, Irving (page 118): middle name should be Gifford

FIRKOV (page 119): should be FIRFOV; should appear after
    FIORILLO (page 118)

FLETCHER (page 120): include source CA7

FONESCA (page 122): should be FONSECA

FUSELLA, Gaetano   Italy   1876
    EDM
    (Omitted from page 129.)

GABITCHVADZE (page 130): place of birth should be Soviet Georgia

GAICEROVA (page 130): should be GAIGEROVA

GARCÍA, J. (page 132): country should be Dominican Republic

GARRATT (page 133): should appear after GARGUILO (page 133)

GIBSON (page 137): should be GIBBON

GIL-MARCHEX (page 138): should appear after GILLIS

GOMEZ, Julio (page 142): cancel this entry; replace with following

GOMEZ y GARCIA, Domingo
Julio   Spain   1886
BBD, EDM, HHH
(Omitted from page 142.)

GOSTUŠKI (page 144): add source YUG

GOTOVAC (page 144): add source YUG

GROSSE (page 149): first name should be Erwin

HATZE, Josip   Yugoslavia   1879   1959
YUG
(Omitted from page 161.)

HELLINGER (page 164): should be HELLIGER

HERCIGONJA, Nikola   Yugoslavia   1911
YUG
(Omitted from page 166.)

HERMANN (page 168): should appear after HERMANN, Tona
(page 166)

HILDERBRAND (page 168): should be HILDEBRAND

HIRAI (page 169): first name should be Kozaburo

HØJBY NIELSEN, Tage   Denmark   1918
HHH, MHHH
HHH and MHHH: NIELSEN, Højby T.
(Omitted from page 172.)

HUGHES, Cervase (page 175): first name should be Gervase

JACOBI, F. (page 181): first name should be Frederick

HAEGGI (page 182): should be JAEGGI

JANDERA (p. 182): should appear just after JANÁČEK (p. 183)

JANDERA (p. 183): should appear just before JANEČEK (p. 183)

JARECKI (page 183): add source BBD

JORGEN (page 187): should be JONGEN

JOSIF (page 188): add source YUG

KHADZHIEV (page 197): add source EDM, MGGB; also add:
EDM: HADJIEV   MGGB: HADZHIEV

KIESLICH (page 197): date of death should be 1960

KJELLSTRÖM, Sven   Sweden   1875   1950
MHHH
(Omitted from page 199.)

KOBUNE (page 202): first name should be Kojire

KOCHUROV, Juri Vladimirovich
See: KOTCHUROV, Jury Vladimirovich.
(Omitted from page 202.)

KOTÓNSKI (page 207): add source VER 63

KOX (page 208): should appear after KOVNER (page 207)

LICHEY (page 227): add source KDK

LIGHT (page 227): should be LICHT

LIGHT, W. (page 227): should be LICHT

LIGHT, E. (page 227): should be LICHT; should appear after
LICHEY (page 227)

LIPOVŠEK (page 230): add source YUG

LOGAR (page 231): add source YUG

LONQUE (page 231): should be LONCQUE; should appear after
LOMANI (page 231)

LUKEWYCZ (page 234): should appear after LUENING

MORTENSEN, F. (page 261): EDM should be EMT

MÜHLHÖLZI (page 262): should be MÜHLHÖLZL

MUÑOZ MOLIEDA (page 264): should be MOLLEDA

NECHAYEV [also: NECHAEV] (page 267): should appear after
NEBOL'SIN (page 266); also add source EDM; also add
death date 1956

NIEMAN (page 267): should appear after NIELSEN (page 270)

NEJEDLÝ, Vit   Czechoslovakia   1912   1945
BBD
(Omitted from page 267.)

NIELAND, Jan   Netherlands   1903   1963
    EVM
    (Omitted from page 269.)

NIN-CULMELI (page 271): should be NIN-CULMELL

NJAGA (page 271): should appear after NIZOFF (page 271)

PAHOR (page 281): add source YUG

PAPANODOPULO (page 283): should be PAPANDOPULO; also add source YUG

PEYKO (page 290): combine entry with PEIKO (page 286); leave a cross reference

PIÉ-CAUSSADE (page 294): should be PLÉ-CAUSSADE

PRACHT (page 297): should appear after POZZOLI (page 298)

RANIER (page 302): should be RAINIER

RAUTAVAARA (page 304): add source GMM

RAVASENGA (page 305): add source GMM; also add death date 1964

ROSEN, Jerome   USA   1921
    BBD
    (Omitted from page 316.)

RUBSAMER (page 318): should be RUBSAMEN

SALZAR (page 322): should be SALAZAR; country should be Mexico

SCHEFFMANN (page 328): should appear after SCHEFFLER (page 328)

SHTOGARENKO (page 341): should appear after SHOSTAKOVICH (page 340)

SHVYADAS, Jonas Izidorovich   USSR   1908   Latvia
    SSR
    (Omitted from page 341.)

STANLEY (page 344): should be SLANEY

SPEAICHT, Joseph   Great Britain   1868
    GMM
    (Omitted from page 349.)

STCHEDRIN (page 352): should be SHCHEDRIN, Rodion Konstantino-vich; should appear after SHAW (page 339); leave a cross reference

STEVENS, James (page 354): cancel sources EDM and EDM--1923

STEVENS, Paul James (page 354): add source EDM

STONJANOV (page 355): should appear after STONE, R. (page 355)

SVENSSON (page 359): add source GMM

SVENTO (page 359): add source GMM

SZÉLENYI (page 361): add source GMM, HHH; also add: HHH: SEZELÉNYI, Etienne

TEBALDINI, Giovanni   Italy   1864   1952
BBD, GMM
(Omitted from page 364.)

TELLO (page 365): add source GMM

TÖRNE, Bengt von (page 370): cancel entry

TÖRNE (page 371): add source SMF

TRANCHELL (page 37): add source BBD

TRANSHELL (page 371): cancel this entry

TRUNK (page 373): add sources BBD, GMM, HHH; also add death date 1968

UKMAR (page 375): add source YUG

VENEZIANI (page 379): add source ITA

VERESS (3d entry, page 380): add source MHHH; (also should appear after VEREPUY)

VERESS (2d entry from bottom, page 380): cancel this entry

VOGL, Adolf   Germany   1873   1961
GMM
(Omitted from page 383.)

VORLOVÁ (page 383): add sources GMM, HHH, TKH

VRETBLAD (page 384): add sources GMM, HHH

WATERS (page 387): should appear after WATANABE (page 387)

WAXMAN (page 388): should appear after WAULIN (page 387)

WELANDER (page 390): first name should be Waldemar

WHITE (page 392): add source BBD

WHITE, Harold Robert GMM (Omitted from page 392.)	Ireland	1872
YUN, Isong VER 63 (Omitted from page 401.)	Korea	1917
YVAIN, Maurice BBD, GMM, HHH (Omitted from page 401.)	France	1891

ZAHN (page 402): should appear after ZAGWIJN (page 401)

ZHIVOTOV (page 403): add source HHH; also add HHH: ZJIVOTOFF

ZLATEV-CHERKIN, Georgi Dimitrov EDM EDM: SLATEV-TSCHERKIN (Omitted from page 405.)	Bulgaria	1905